Contributing writer: Tom Owens
Photography: Sam Griffith Studio, Inc.
Special thanks to: AU Sports Memorabilia, Skokie, Illinois

CONTENTS

INTRODUCTION

What's the difference between stocks, bonds, and baseball cards? In today's fast-paced hobby world, there isn't a big difference. All ages of collectors consider the value and investment potential of their cards long before they examine the photos or read the stats on the back. With the shrinking supply of older cards and the increasing cost of new issues, the actual value of baseball cards is increasingly important to study. Every day, some collector realizes that his nickel baseball card investment carries a current price tag of several dollars. Many adults who once speculated in stocks and bonds have switched instead to Score, Topps, and other companies for cardboard investment vehicles.

Skeptics may believe that the baseball card boom has been limited to 20- and 30-year-old products. Not so! Anyone wanting evidence of how cards can skyrocket in price need to look only at 1989. Upper Deck, a newly formed California company, defied the odds and produced an 800-card set to compete with the existing giants of the baseball card industry. Veteran hobbyists claimed that any set that went on sale for more than $30 couldn't be collectible. Those naysayers were silenced when the price of Upper Deck factory-collated sets topped $100 by Christmas.

Many similar surprises await card collectors in 1992 and beyond. That's why having a book like the *Official Baseball Card Price Guide* is so vital for survival in the hobby. This publication reviews all major card sets and offers values for selected cards that have been issued during the last 44 years, from 1948 Bowman through 1991 Upper Deck. Individual values are given for all major sets and for various series within a set.

In order to cover such a wealth of data, the first priority is to include the most notable cards of stars and rookies. Many cards of secondary players, of lesser interest to collectors and known as "commons," are also listed. This way readers will have the information they need the most. In all, more than 25,000 cards have been chosen.

Unlike other price guides, the *Official Baseball Card Price Guide* does more than simply list prices. Much more. Nearly 700 photos illustrate important cards from every set. And each list is preceded by an introduction to provide valuable background information about that specific set.

To help serve collectors better, "best buys" are designated in nearly every set. Denoted by a bullet (•), best buys are cards that are often available at bargain prices. More expensive best buys are key cards that could greatly increase in value over time. Overlooked rookies and Future Hall of Famers (including long-shot possibilities such as Dwight Evans and Sparky Anderson) are just two categories found in best buys. These selections, and prices of other sets, were established after thorough studies of previous card prices. Feedback from a number of card and hobby dealers helped to shape the price estimates that follow.

Do best buy suggestions help? Refer back to the first edition of the *Price Guide* and view the number of times cards for Jim Palmer and Joe Morgan were marked. Those who followed the tips before the pair were elected to the Hall of Fame could, in many cases, have tripled their money. Overlooked rookies, future Hall of Famers, and other forgotten stars are in this year's crop of best buys. Look them over and consider what future profits could develop for astute hobbyists.

The prices listed are estimated retail values. Hobbyists planning to sell their cards should expect dealers to pay anywhere from 50 to 60 percent of the prices given for star cards. Commons of poorer quality could be sold for about ten percent of these prices.

To make the most of the *Official Baseball Card Price Guide,* it's important to note that some names appear in italic type, and several abbreviations are used.

Names in *italics:* Rookie cards. A rookie card is defined as a card issued for the first appearance made by a player for any card company *during his rookie season.* When a player's name is printed in italic type, that card is considered to be a rookie card. However, a player who is shuttled between the majors and minors may not appear on a card for years. In that case he might not have a rookie card at all, though he would eventually have a First Card (FC) (see below). A rookie card may be part of a specially designated rookie issue shared by other players, or it may be an ordinary card.

In addition, fall extension sets like Fleer Update and Topps Traded have muddled the definition of rookie cards. Because they have not been sold individually through any sources outside of the hobby in the past, cards from fall-issued sets are not recognized by the *Official Baseball Card Price Guide* as genuine rookie cards. Topps and Donruss have sold complete sets of these late issues on a test basis through toy stores and by mail order. However, Upper Deck has been the only company through 1991 willing to include special updated cards mixed in individual packages with other standard-issue cards. When collectors have unlimited access to all the fall-issued cards (without being forced to buy separate packs for sets), then rookie card definitions can be reworked.

(DK): Diamond Kings. This refers to a yearly 26-card set of painted portraits of one player from each team—part of the Donruss sets since 1982.

(DP): Double-Printed cards. When Topps expanded its set size to more than 660 cards, uneven numbers neutralized the usual 132-card printing sheets. To compensate, the company printed certain cards twice on each sheet. The supply of some cards doubled as a result. When star cards were involved, this increase in supply lessened demand and lowered the value. Common cards of marginal players take drastic price drops when double-printing occurs.

(FC): First cards. This means that a listed card marks a player's *first appearance for a certain card company.* Sometimes a player's first card is *not* his rookie card. For example, the first card for Padres pitcher Andy Benes appeared in the 1990 Donruss set and identified him as a "Rated Rookie." However, it was not a true rookie card at all since he had appeared in several sets in 1989. Those 1989 appearances constitute his genuine rookie cards.

FS: Future Stars. A number of cards for promising young players carry this designation.

IA: In-Action cards. On several occasions Topps has produced both standard cards and action-photo cards of selected popular players.

(RR): "Rated Rookies." These are specially marked Donruss cards honoring promising newcomers.

Many set profiles also mention high-number and low-number cards. Before 1974, Topps issued cards throughout the summer in several series of approximately 110 cards each. Typically, the last 100-odd cards from a set are in shorter supply. This occurred because some retailers overstocked baseball cards early in the summer when demand was high. When the baseball season was winding down, the cards issued later in the season—those with higher numbers—were harder to find. Since fewer were sold in the past, fewer are available today. The result of this process is that such scarce high-numbered cards tend to be more valuable.

Condition, however, is even more important than supply and demand when determining card values. The prices listed in this guide are for cards in top condition—for all sets issued prior to 1980 that means Near Mint, and for all sets issued since 1980 that means Mint. Proper grading of your cards is of critical importance. The following guidelines will help you evaluate your cards.

Mint cards are perfect, well-centered cards showing absolutely no wear, fading, scratches, printing flaws, loss of luster, or other imperfections. True Mint cards prior to 1980 may command values that are 40 to 50 percent higher than the Near Mint price listed. But it would be a mistake to assume that cards found in factory-collated sets or freshly removed from wax packs will always be graded as Mint. Cards with printing flaws, uneven borders, or gum stains can be discounted by as much as 20 percent.

Near Mint cards are nearly perfect, with only a very minor flaw preventing a grade of full Mint. Such cards may be slightly off-center or have one imperfect corner. Near Mint cards issued since 1980 may be worth 70 to 80 percent of the Mint value listed.

Excellent cards may have lost some original surface gloss but will display very little wear, have no serious defects, and still have sharp corners. Excellent cards may be off-center, but will have no creases or stains from gum or wax. Cards in Excellent condition are generally worth approximately 40 to 60 percent of the Mint or Near Mint values listed.

Very Good cards will display some wear and have slightly rounded corners, minor creases, or stains. They will usually be valued at about 25 to 30 percent of the Mint or Near Mint values listed.

Good cards show a great amount of handling and perhaps even some abuse. They may have softened corners, major creases, and other defects, but all parts of the cards will still be intact, without being defaced by holes, tears, tape, or writing. This is generally the poorest condition that most collectors would even consider. Cards in Good condition are worth approximately 10 to 15 percent of the Mint or Near Mint values listed.

Fair and *Poor* cards show excessive wear or damage and are generally not considered collectible.

In addition to condition and scarcity, geographical demand influences card prices. While cards of well-known players from universally popular teams like the Dodgers or Yankees may command high prices nationwide, cards of other stars elicit different reactions from hobbyists.

As you read the *Official Baseball Card Price Guide,* keep in mind that it should be used only as a general aid in determining the value of baseball cards. Changes in methods of distribution by card companies and successes (or failures) by teams and players themselves can cause quick fluctuations in card values. The cards for emerging rookies like Scott Erickson or Chuck Knoblauch, for example, were cheap when the season began. But as they sparked the Twins through the pennant race, their cards gained value weekly.

Finally, this publication does not represent an offer by the publishers or any other party to buy or sell cards. Reputable hobby dealers remain the best source for collectors. And while every effort has been made to insure a high level of accuracy in the price estimates contained within this book, the publishers cannot assume any responsibility for errors that may occur.

Enjoy the *Official Baseball Card Price Guide,* but keep card price trends in perspective. While the cardboard stock used for these tiny creations has little intrinsic value, the loyalty and popularity generated by individual teams and players create the ever-changing worth of each individual card.

1948 BOWMAN

The Philadelphia-based Bowman Company entered the baseball card market in 1948 with this set of 48 cards. Featuring black-and-white photos of players on the front (with stadium backgrounds), and black printing on gray cardboard on the back, these 2⅛- by 2½-inch cards took Bowman to market dominance in a single year. The white-bordered cards were sold with a package of gum, one card per pack. A total of 12 cards were short-printed (numbers 7, 8, 13, 16, 20, 22, 24, 26, 28, 29, 30, and 34). With the exception of Phil Rizzuto, number 8, all short-prints are lesser-known players today. Eight Hall of Famers are included: Berra, Feller, Kiner, Mize, Musial, Schoendienst, Slaughter, and Spahn.

		NR MT
Complete set		**$3300.00**
Commons (1-36)		**16.00**
Commons (37-48)		**25.00**

1	Bob Elliott	$95.00
2	Ewell (The Whip) Blackwell	45.00
3	Ralph Kiner	140.00
4	Johnny Mize	90.00
5	Bob Feller	200.00
6	Larry (Yogi) Berra	450.00
7	Pete (Pistol Pete) Reiser	50.00
8	Phil (Scooter) Rizzuto	235.00
9	Walker Cooper	17.00
10	Buddy Rosar	16.00
12	Johnny Sain	50.00
13	Willard Marshall	32.00
14	Allie Reynolds	55.00
16	Jack Lohrke	32.00
17	Enos (Country) Slaughter	80.00
18	Warren Spahn	260.00
19	Tommy Henrich	25.00
20	Buddy Kerr	30.00
22	Floyd (Bill) Bevins	40.00
24	Emil (Dutch) Leonard	30.00
26	Frank Shea	40.00
28	Emil (The Antelope) Verban	30.00
29	Joe Page	40.00
30	"Whitey" Lockman	30.00

36 Stan Musial

34	Sheldon (Available) Jones	30.00
35	George (Snuffy) Stirnweiss	17.00
36	Stan Musial	750.00
38	Al "Red" Schoendienst	125.00
40	Marty Marion	60.00
41	Rex Barney	27.00
42	Ray Poat	25.00
43	Bruce Edwards	25.00
44	Johnny Wyrostek	25.00
45	Hank Sauer	25.00
46	Herman Wehmeier	25.00
47	Bobby Thomson	65.00
48	George "Dave" Koslo	60.00

1949 BOWMAN

Bowman's sophomore series of 240 cards for 1949 was one of the largest issues of that year. The 2⅛6- by 2½-inch cards feature colorized photo portraits with white borders on solid color backgrounds. The backs are cream-colored with red-and-blue printing. Rookie cards for Hall of Famers Robin Roberts and Duke Snider are included, and the great Satchel Paige makes a rare set appearance. An unusual error occurs on card number 240: It was supposed to show Babe Young, but somehow Bobby Young's photo was printed instead.

	NR MT
Complete set	**$15,000.00**
Commons (1-36)	**11.00**
Commons (37-73)	**13.00**
Commons (74-144)	**10.00**
Commons (145-240)	**60.00**

1	*Vernon Bickford*	$80.00
2	Carroll "Whitey" Lockman	17.00
3	Bob Porterfield	15.00
4	Jerry Priddy (no name on front)	13.00
4	Jerry Priddy (name on front)	35.00
5	Hank Sauer	15.00
6	Phil Cavarretta	21.00

226 Edwin "Duke" Snider

224 Leroy "Satchell" Paige

11	Lou Boudreau	60.00
14	*Curt Simmons*	25.00
15	Ned Garver	14.00
18	Bobby Thomson	22.00
19	*Bobby Brown*	50.00
20	Gene Hermanski	13.00
23	Bobby Doerr	75.00
24	Stan Musial	500.00
26	George Kell	60.00
27	Bob Feller	130.00
29	Ralph Kiner	75.00
32	Eddie Yost	13.00
33	Warren Spahn	165.00
35	*Vic Raschi*	40.00
36	Harold "Peewee" Reese	175.00
38	Emil "The Antelope" Verban	13.00

1949 Bowman

50 Jackie Robinson

40	George "Red" Munger ...	13.00
42	Walter "Hoot" Evers	13.00
44	Dave Philley	13.00
45	Wally Westlake	13.00
46	*Robin Roberts*	235.00
47	Johnny Sain..................	25.00
48	Willard Marshall.............	13.00
49	Frank Shea	15.00
50	Jackie Robinson	725.00
51	Herman Wehmeier	13.00
52	Johnny Schmitz	13.00
54	Marty "Slats" Marion	25.00
59	Jack "Lucky" Lohrke	13.00
60	Larry "Yogi" Berra	305.00
61	Rex Barney...................	16.00
62	Grady Hatton	13.00
63	Andy Pafko	16.00
64	Dom "The Little Professor" DiMaggio......	25.00
65	Enos "Country" Slaughter	75.00
66	Elmer Valo	13.00
67	Alvin Dark	25.00
70	Carl Furillo	50.00
78	Sam Zoldak (no name on front)	14.00
78	Sam Zoldak (name on front)	30.00
82	Joe Page	22.00
83	Bob Scheffing (no name on front)........	14.00
83	Bob Scheffing (name on front)	30.00
84	*Roy Campanella*..........	550.00
85	Johnny "Big John" Mize (no name on front)	75.00
85	Johnny "Big John" Mize (name on front)............	125.00
86	Johnny Pesky	14.00
88	Bill Salkeld (no name on front)	14.00
88	Bill Salkeld (name on front)	30.00
98	Phil Rizzuto (no name on front)	95.00
98	Phil Rizzuto (name on front)	200.00
100	*Gil Hodges*...................	215.00
110	*Early Wynn*	125.00
111	Al "Red" Schoendienst ..	72.00
114	Allie Reynolds................	30.00
145	Sylvester "Blix" Donnelly	60.00
146	Myron "Mike" McCormick	60.00
147	Elmer "Bert" Singleton ...	60.00
148	Bob Swift	60.00
149	Roy Partee	62.00
150	Alfred "Allie" Clark	60.00
151	Maurice "Mickey" Harris..............................	60.00
152	Clarence Maddern.........	60.00
153	Phil Masi.....................	60.00
154	Clint Hartung	60.00
155	Fermin "Mickey" Guerra	60.00
156	Al "Zeke" Zarilla	60.00
157	Walt Masterson	60.00
158	Harry "The Cat" Brecheen	65.00
159	Glen Moulder................	60.00
160	Jim Blackburn................	60.00
161	John "Jocko" Thompson	60.00
162	*Elwin "Preacher" Roe* ..	135.00
163	Clyde McCullough	60.00
164	Vic Wertz	65.00
165	George "Snuffy" Stirnweiss	65.00
166	Mike Tresh....................	60.00

167	Boris "Babe" Martin	60.00
168	Doyle Lade	60.00
169	Jeff Heath	60.00
170	Bill Rigney	65.00
171	Dick Fowler	60.00
172	Eddie Pellagrini	60.00
173	Eddie Stewart	60.00
174	Terry Moore	67.00
175	Luke Appling	135.00
176	Ken Raffensberger	60.00
177	Stan Lopata	62.00
178	Tommy Brown	60.00
179	Hugh Casey	62.00
180	Connie Berry	60.00
181	Gus Niarhos	60.00
182	Hal Peck	60.00
183	Lou Stringer	60.00
184	Bob Chipman	60.00

46 Robin Roberts

185	Pete Reiser	70.00
186	John "Buddy" Kerr	60.00
187	Phil Marchildon	60.00
188	Karl Drews	60.00
189	Earl Wooten	60.00
190	Jim Hearn	60.00
191	Joe Haynes	60.00
192	Harry Gumbert	60.00
193	Ken Trinkle	60.00
194	*Ralph Branca*	100.00
195	Eddie Bockman	60.00
196	Fred Hutchinson	75.00
197	Johnny Lindell	62.00
198	Steve Gromek	60.00
199	Cecil "Tex" Hughson	60.00
200	Jess Dobernic	60.00
201	Sibby Sisti	60.00
202	Larry Jansen	65.00
203	Barney McCosky	60.00
204	Bob Savage	60.00
205	Dick Sisler	60.00
206	Bruce Edwards	60.00
207	Johnny "Hippity" Hopp	60.00
208	Paul "Dizzy" Trout	65.00
209	Charlie "King Kong" Keller	95.00
210	Joe "Flash" Gordon	65.00
211	Dave "Boo" Ferriss	60.00
212	Ralph Hamner	60.00
213	Charles "Red" Barrett	60.00
214	*Richie Ashburn*	500.00
215	Kirby Higbe	60.00
216	Lynwood "Schoolboy" Rowe	60.00
217	Marino Pieretti	60.00
218	Dick Kryhoski	62.00
219	Virgil "Fire" Trucks	67.00
220	Johnny McCarthy	60.00
221	Bob Muncrief	60.00
222	Alex Kellner	60.00
223	Bob Hoffman	60.00
224	*Leroy "Satchell" Paige*	1100.00
225	*Gerry Coleman*	85.00
226	*Edwin "Duke" Snider*	925.00
227	Fritz Ostermueller	60.00
228	Jackie Mayo	60.00
229	*Ed Lopat*	130.00
230	Augie Galan	60.00
231	Earl Johnson	60.00
232	George McQuinn	50.00
233	*Larry Doby*	135.00
234	Truett "Rip" Sewell	65.00
235	Jim Russell	50.00
236	Fred Sanford	60.00
237	Monte Kennedy	50.00
238	Bob Lemon	230.00
239	Frank McCormick	60.00
240	Norman "Babe" Young (photo actually Bobby Young)	135.00

1950 BOWMAN

In its third year Bowman increased its set size to 252 cards. No double printing was necessary, since 36 cards of 2¹⁄₁₆ by 2½ inches fit on each printer's sheet, making an even series of seven sheets. Instead of using actual photographs, Bowman introduced paintings based on photographs, which have become well known. The backs have red-and-black print on a cream-colored background. Ted Williams made his Bowman debut, while Luke Appling made his farewell card appearance. Although no rookies of note are featured, Bowman started something big by featuring non-playing managers Leo Durocher, Frank Frisch, and Casey Stengel.

		NR MT
Complete set		$8550.00
Commons (1-72)		40.00
Commons (73-252)		15.00

1	Mel Parnell	$200.00
2	Vern Stephens	35.00
3	Dom DiMaggio	60.00
4	*Gus Zernial*	50.00
5	Bob Kuzava	40.00
6	Bob Feller	150.00
7	Jim Hegan	40.00
8	George Kell	80.00
9	Vic Wertz	40.00
10	Tommy Henrich	50.00
11	Phil Rizzuto	130.00

98 Ted Williams

22 Jackie Robinson

12	Joe Page	48.00
13	Ferris Fain	42.00
14	Alex Kellner	40.00
15	Al Kozar	40.00
16	*Roy Sievers*	50.00
17	Sid Hudson	40.00
18	Eddie Robinson	40.00
19	Warren Spahn	150.00
20	Bob Elliott	40.00
21	Harold Reese	165.00
22	Jackie Robinson	600.00
23	*Don Newcombe*	100.00
24	Johnny Schmitz	40.00
25	Hank Sauer	40.00
26	Grady Hatton	40.00
27	Herman Wehmeier	40.00
28	Bobby Thomson	57.00

29	Ed Stanky	42.00
30	Eddie Waitkus	40.00
31	Del Ennis	40.00
32	Robin Roberts	115.00
33	Ralph Kiner	110.00
34	Murry Dickson	40.00
35	Enos Slaughter	105.00
36	Eddie Kazak	40.00
37	Luke Appling	62.00
38	Bill Wight	40.00
39	Larry Doby	62.00
40	Bob Lemon	110.00
41	Walter "Hoot" Evers	40.00
42	Art Houtteman	40.00
43	Bobby Doerr	75.00
44	Joe Dobson	40.00
45	Al "Zeke" Zarilla	40.00
46	Larry "Yogi" Berra	350.00
47	Jerry Coleman	48.00
48	Leland "Lou" Brissie	40.00
49	Elmer Valo	40.00
50	Dick Kokos	40.00
51	Ned Garver	40.00
52	Sam Mele	40.00
53	Clyde Vollmer	40.00
54	Gil Coan	40.00
55	John "Buddy" Kerr	40.00
56	*Del Crandell*	48.00
57	Vernon Bickford	40.00
58	Carl Furillo	60.00
59	Ralph Branca	57.00
60	Andy Pafko	42.00
61	Bob Rush	40.00
62	Ted Kluszewski	55.00
63	Ewell Blackwell	42.00
64	Alvin Dark	50.00
65	Dave Koslo	40.00
66	Larry Jansen	42.00
67	Willie Jones	42.00
68	Curt Simmons	42.00
69	Wally Westlake	40.00
70	Bob Chesnes	40.00
71	Al Schoendienst	75.00
72	Howie Pollet	40.00
73	Willard Marshall	15.00
74	*Johnny Antonelli*	20.00
75	Roy Campanella	300.00
76	Rex Barney	17.00
77	Edwin "Duke" Snider	275.00

19 Warren Spahn

78	Mickey Owen	15.00
79	Johnny Vander Meer	17.00
80	Howard Fox	15.00
81	Ron Northey	15.00
82	Carroll Lockman	15.00
83	Sheldon Jones	15.00
84	Richie Ashburn	75.00
85	Ken Heintzelman	15.00
86	Stan Rojek	15.00
87	Bill Werle	15.00
88	Marty Marion	21.00
89	George Munger	15.00
90	Harry Brecheen	18.00
91	Cass Michaels	15.00
92	Hank Majeski	15.00
93	Gene Bearden	15.00
94	Lou Boudreau	45.00
95	Aaron Robinson	15.00
96	Virgil "Fire" Trucks	17.00
97	Maurice McDermott	15.00
98	Ted Williams	600.00
99	Billy Goodman	15.00
100	Vic Raschi	27.00
101	Bobby Brown	27.00
102	Billy Johnson	15.00
103	Eddie Joost	15.00
104	Sam Chapman	15.00
105	Bob Dillinger	15.00
106	Cliff Fannin	15.00
107	Sam Dente	15.00

77 Edwin "Duke" Snider

108	Rae Scarborough	15.00
109	Sid Gordon	15.00
110	Tommy Holmes	15.00
111	Walker Cooper	15.00
112	Gil Hodges	85.00
113	Gene Hermanski	15.00
114	Wayne Terwilliger	15.00
115	Roy Smalley	15.00
116	Virgil "Red" Stallcup	15.00
117	Bill Rigney	17.00
118	Clint Hartung	15.00
119	Dick Sisler	15.00
120	John Thompson	15.00
121	Andy Seminick	15.00
122	Johnny Hopp	15.00
123	Dino Restelli	15.00
124	Clyde McCullough	15.00
125	Del Rice	15.00
126	Al Brazle	15.00
127	Dave Philley	15.00
128	Phil Masi	15.00
129	Joe "Flash" Gordon	17.00
130	Dale Mitchell	15.00
131	Steve Gromek	15.00
132	James Vernon	17.00
133	Don Kolloway	15.00
134	Paul "Dizzy" Trout	17.00
135	Pat Mullin	15.00
136	Warren Rosar	15.00
137	Johnny Pesky	17.00
138	Allie Reynolds	28.00
139	Johnny Mize	65.00
140	Pete Suder	15.00
141	Joe Coleman	15.00
142	Sherman Lollar	17.00
143	Eddie Stewart	15.00
144	Al Evans	15.00
145	Jack Graham	15.00
146	Floyd Baker	15.00
147	Mike Garcia	18.00
148	Early Wynn	62.00
149	Bob Swift	15.00
150	George Vico	15.00
151	Fred Hutchinson	18.00
152	Ellis Kinder	15.00
153	Walt Masterson	15.00
154	Gus Niarhos	15.00
155	Frank "Spec" Shea	15.00
156	Fred Sanford	15.00
157	Mike Guerra	15.00
158	Paul Lehner	15.00
159	Joe Tipton	15.00
160	Mickey Harris	15.00
161	Sherry Robertson	15.00
162	Eddie Yost	15.00
164	Sibby Sisti	15.00
165	Bruce Edwards	15.00
166	Joe Hatten	15.00
167	Elwin Roe	27.00
172	Peanuts Lowery	15.00
180	Harry Walker	15.00
186	Ken Keltner	15.00
193	Harold "Pete" Reiser	15.00
194	Billy Cox	17.00
195	Phil Cavaretta	17.00
203	Danny Murtaugh	17.00

212	Gerry Priddy	15.00
215	Ed Lopat	25.00
216	Bob Porterfield	15.00
217	Casey Stengel	125.00
218	Cliff Mapes	15.00
219	*Hank Bauer*	50.00
220	Leo Durocher	50.00
222	Bobby Morgan	15.00
223	Jimmy Russell	15.00
224	Jack Banta	15.00
225	Eddie Sawyer	17.00
226	Jim Konstanty	25.00
229	Frank Frisch	40.00
232	*Al "Flip" Rosen*	40.00
233	Allie Clark	15.00
234	*Bobby Shantz*	20.00
246	*Walt Dropo*	25.00
248	Sam Jethroe	17.00
251	John Lester Moss	17.00
252	Billy DeMars	100.00

1951 BOWMAN

At 324 cards, Bowman's 1951 baseball card set was the most complete issue up to that time. In addition to making the set larger for 1951, Bowman made the individual cards larger. The 2⅛- by 3⅛ -inch size would be maintained for two years. Each card displays the player name in a horizontal black box. Card backs use red-and-blue printing on gray cardboard, but no statistics are provided. Few changes were made from the 1950 Bowman edition. In fact, some of the same color paintings of the players from the 1950 issue were used in an enlarged version for 1951. Bowman started a trend for the 1950s by issuing a card for each major league skipper. The rising value of the 1951 Bowman set comes largely from a high-number series that includes the prized rookie cards of Willie Mays and Mickey Mantle.

	NR MT
Complete set	**$18,000.00**
Commons (1-36)	**13.00**
Commons (37-252)	**10.00**
Commons (253-324)	**40.00**

1	*Ed "Whitey" Ford*	$1400.00
2	Larry "Yogi" Berra	475.00
3	Robin Roberts	75.00
4	Del Ennis	13.00
5	Dale Mitchell	13.00
6	Don Newcombe	35.00
7	Gil Hodges	75.00
8	Paul Lehner	13.00
9	Sam Chapman	13.00
10	Al "Red" Schoendienst	72.00
11	George "Red" Munger	13.00
12	Hank Majeski	13.00
13	Ed Stanky	16.00
14	Alvin Dark	25.00
15	Johnny Pesky	16.00
16	Maurice McDermott	13.00
17	Pete Castiglione	13.00
18	Gil Coan	13.00
19	Sid Gordon	13.00
20	Del Crandall	16.00
21	George "Snuffy" Stirnweiss	13.00
22	Hank Sauer	13.00
23	Walter "Hoot" Evers	13.00
24	Ewell Blackwell	16.00
25	Vic Raschi	25.00
26	Phil Rizzuto	90.00
27	Jim Konstanty	15.00
28	Eddie Waitkus	13.00
29	Allie Clark	13.00
30	Bob Feller	125.00

1 Ed "Whitey" Ford

86	Harry Brecheen	13.00
92	Vern "Junior" Stephens	12.00
100	Sherman Lollar	13.00
103	Andy Pafko	12.00
104	Virgil "Fire" Trucks	12.00
109	Allie Reynolds	25.00
110	• Bobby Brown	25.00
111	Curt Simmons	12.00
113	Bill "Swish" Nicholson	10.00
114	Sam Zoldak	10.00
115	Steve Gromek	10.00
117	Eddie Miksis	12.00
118	Preacher Roe	25.00
119	Eddie Joost	10.00
120	Joe Coleman	10.00
121	Gerry Staley	10.00
122	Joe Garagiola	150.00
123	Howie Judson	10.00
125	Bill Rigney	12.00
126	Bobby Thomson	25.00
127	*Sal Maglie*	40.00
129	Matt Batts	10.00
131	Cliff Chambers	10.00
132	Cass Michaels	10.00
133	Sam Dente	10.00
134	Warren Spahn	110.00
135	Walker Cooper	10.00
136	Ray Coleman	10.00
138	Phil Cavarretta	15.00
141	Fred Hutchinson	12.00
143	Ted Kluszewski	25.00
144	Herman Wehmeier	10.00
147	Ken Heintzelman	10.00
148	Granny Hamner	10.00
149	Emory "Bubba" Church	10.00
150	Mike Garcia	13.00
151	Larry Doby	25.00
152	Cal Abrams	12.00
153	Rex Barney	12.00
156	Del Rice	10.00
160	Phil Masi	10.00
161	Wes Westrum	12.00
165	Ted Williams	575.00
166	Stan Rojek	10.00
167	Murry Dickson	10.00
170	Sibby Sisti	10.00
171	Buddy Kerr	10.00
172	Ned Garver	10.00
174	Mickey Owen	10.00

31	Roy Campanella	300.00
32	Duke Snider	235.00
33	Bob Hooper	13.00
34	Marty Marion	25.00
35	Al Zarilla	13.00
36	Joe Dobson	13.00
37	Whitey Lockman	10.00
40	*Dave "Gus" Bell*	22.00
41	Eddie Yost	13.00
46	George Kell	50.00
49	Jerry Coleman	16.00
50	Johnny Mize	50.00
52	Dick Sisler	10.00
53	Bob Lemon	50.00
54	Ray Boone	12.00
55	Gene Hermanski	12.00
56	Ralph Branca	30.00
58	Enos Slaughter	50.00
62	Lou Boudreau	50.00
65	Mickey Vernon	13.00
67	Roy Sievers	13.00
73	Tommy Byrne	15.00
78	Early Wynn	50.00
80	Harold "Peewee" Reese	135.00
81	Carl Furillo	32.00

253 Mickey Mantle

175	Wayne Terwilliger	10.00
176	Vic Wertz	12.00
177	Charlie Keller	12.00
181	Casey Stengel	90.00
182	Tom Ferrick	15.00
183	Hank Bauer	25.00
186	Richie Ashburn	50.00
187	Al "Flip" Rosen	25.00
188	Roberto Avila	12.00
189	Erv Palica	11.00
190	Joe Hatten	11.00
195	Paul Richards	15.00
196	Bill Pierce	15.00
198	*Monte Irvin*	100.00
203	Vernon Law	17.00
207	Billy Southworth	10.00
217	Joe Page	16.00
218	Ed Lopat	25.00
219	*Gene Woodling*	30.00
223	Johnny Vander Meer	20.00
224	Billy Cox	16.00
225	Dan Bankhead	15.00
226	Jimmy Dykes	15.00
227	Bobby Schantz	15.00
228	Cloyd Boyer	10.00
232	Nelson Fox	100.00
233	• Leo Durocher	50.00
234	Clint Hartung	10.00
238	Pete Reiser	15.00
242	Sam Jethroe	15.00
243	John Antonelli	15.00
245	*John Berardino*	20.00
248	Johnny Klippstein	15.00
253	*Mickey Mantle*	4600.00
254	*Jackie Jensen*	120.00
255	Milo Candini	40.00
256	Ken Silvestri	40.00
257	Birdie Tebbetts	40.00
258	Luke Easter	48.00
259	Charlie Dressen	45.00
260	Carl Erskine	100.00
261	Wally Moses	40.00
262	Gus Zernial	40.00
263	Howie Pollett	40.00
264	Don Richmond	40.00
265	Steve Bilko	40.00
266	Harry Dorish	40.00
267	Ken Holcombe	40.00
268	Don Mueller	40.00
269	Ray Noble	40.00
270	Willard Nixon	40.00
271	Tommy Wright	40.00
272	Billy Meyer	40.00
273	Danny Murtaugh	45.00
274	George Metkovich	40.00
275	Bucky Harris	75.00
276	Frank Quinn	40.00
277	Roy Hartsfield	40.00
278	Norman Roy	40.00
279	Jim Delsing	40.00
280	Frank Overmire	40.00
281	Al Widmar	40.00
282	Frank Frisch	75.00
283	Walt Dubiel	40.00

305 Willie Mays

284	Gene Bearden	42.00
285	Johnny Lipon	40.00
286	Bob Usher	40.00
287	Jim Blackburn	40.00
288	Bobby Adams	40.00
289	Cliff Mapes	40.00
290	Bill Dickey	175.00
291	Tommy Henrich	80.00
292	Eddie Pellagrini	40.00
293	Ken Johnson	40.00
294	Jocko Thompson	40.00
295	Al Lopez	85.00
296	Bob Kennedy	40.00
297	Dave Philley	40.00
298	Joe Astroth	40.00
299	Clyde King	42.00
300	Hal Rice	40.00
301	Tommy Glaviano	40.00
302	Jim Busby	40.00
303	Marv Rotblatt	40.00
304	Allen Gettel	40.00
305	*Willie Mays*	1900.00
306	*Jim Piersall*	85.00
307	Walt Masterson	40.00
308	Ted Beard	40.00
309	Mel Queen	40.00
310	Erv Dusak	40.00
311	Mickey Harris	40.00
312	Gene Mauch	65.00
313	Ray Mueller	40.00
314	Johnny Sain	60.00
315	Zack Taylor	40.00

316	Duane Pillette	40.00
317	*Forrest Burgess*	70.00
318	Warren Hacker	40.00
319	Red Rolfe	40.00
320	Hal White	40.00
321	Earl Johnson	40.00
322	Luke Sewell	40.00
323	*Joe Adcock*	90.00
324	*Johnny Pramesa*	110.00

31 Roy Campanella

1951 TOPPS BLUE BACKS

In addition to the designations for series A and B on the card fronts, the only differences between the Topps Blue Back and Red Back sets are secondary border colors on the cards and scarcity in distribution. Both 52-card issues were sold at approximately the same time and packaged with two cards and a piece of candy for a penny. A large supply of Red Backs was discovered in a Philadelphia warehouse in the 1980s, but the Blue Backs are tougher to find. Fortunately, the cards were printed on heavy cardboard and are found in top condition today. Each round-cornered card measures 2 by 2⅝ inches.

	NR MT
Complete set	**$2150.00**
Commons	**26.00**

1	Eddie Yost	$45.00
3	Richie Ashburn	100.00
4	Del Ennis	28.00
5	Johnny Pesky	30.00
6	Albert (Red) Schoendienst	90.00
7	Gerald Staley	28.00
8	Dick Sisler	28.00
9	Johnny Sain	45.00
10	Joe Page	40.00
12	Sam Jethroe	28.00
13	James (Mickey) Vernon	25.00
15	Eddie Joost	28.00
16	Murry Dickson	28.00
17	Roy Smalley	28.00
18	Ned Garver	28.00
20	Ralph Branca	37.00
21	Billy Johnson	28.00
23	Paul (Dizzy) Trout	28.00
24	Sherman Lollar	28.00
25	Sam Mele	28.00
26	Chico Carrsquel	28.00
27	Andy Pafko	25.00
28	Harry (The Cat) Brecheen	28.00
29	Granville Hamner	28.00
30	Enos (Country) Slaughter	115.00
32	Bob Elliott	28.00

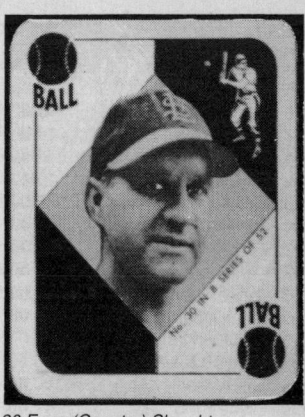

30 Enos (Country) Slaughter

34	Earl Torgeson	28.00
35	Tommy Byrne	28.00
36	Cliff Fannin	28.00
37	Bobby Doerr	100.00
39	Ed Lopat	40.00
40	Vic Wertz	35.00
41	Johnny Schmitz	28.00
43	Willie (Puddin' Head) Jones	30.00
45	*Bill Pierce*	40.00
48	Billy Cox	36.00
49	Henry (Hank) Sauer	30.00
50	Johnny Mize	120.00
52	Sam Chapman	33.00

1951 TOPPS RED BACKS

Although recognized as the first widespread baseball offering of the company, the 1951 Topps Red Backs set is one of the least appreciated of the early sets. The 52-card set was designed like a deck of playing cards, to be used in playing a basic baseball game, because Bowman, at that time, held an exclusive contract to produce bubble gum cards. In addition to a black-and-white player photo set in a baseball diamond in the card center, each round-cornered card features the player name, a short biography, and a number.

1 Larry (Yogi) Berra

		NR MT
Complete set		**$725.00**
Commons		**8.00**
1	Larry (Yogi) Berra	$75.00
3	Ferris Fain	8.00
4	Verne Stephens (Vern)	8.00
5	• Phil Rizzuto	24.00
6	Allie Reynolds	10.00
7	Howie Pollet	5.00
8	Early Wynn	25.00
9	Roy Sievers	6.00
10	Mel Parnell	6.00
12	Jim Hegan	5.00
13	Dale Mitchell	5.00
15	Ralph Kiner	25.00
16	Preacher Roe	8.00
17	*Dave Bell*	9.00
18	Gerry Coleman	8.00
20	Dominick DiMaggio	12.00
22	Bob Feller	25.00
23	*Ray Boone*	8.00
24	Hank Bauer	10.00
26	Luke Easter	8.00
29	Bob Kennedy	5.00
30	Warren Spahn	25.00
31	Gil Hodges	27.00
34	Grady Hatton	5.00
35	Al Rosen	10.00
36	Gus Zernial (Chicago in bio)	20.00
36	Gus Zernial (Philadelphia in bio)	12.00
37	Wes Westrum	6.00
38	Ed (Duke) Snider	67.00
39	Ted Kluszewski	12.00
40	Mike Garcia	8.00
41	Whitey Lockman	5.00
45	Andy Seminick	5.00
46	Billy Goodman	7.00
47	Tommy Glavino	6.00
48	Eddie Stanky	7.00
49	Al Zarilla	6.00
50	*Monte Irvin*	25.00
51	Eddie Robinson	5.00
52	Tommy Holmes (Boston in bio)	20.00
52	Tommy Holmes (Hartford in bio)	20.00

1952 BOWMAN

The 1952 Bowman set follows a format similar to the 1951 issue. Players on the card fronts are depicted in paintings made from photographs. Unlike 1951, however, each player name appears as a facsimile autograph on card fronts. Backs show black printing on gray cardboard but maintain the 1951 format of the player name and vital data along with a brief biography. Some cards advertise a mail-in offer, which provided a baseball cap for five wrappers and 50 cents. Despite the reduced number of cards (just 252, compared to 324 in 1951), the 1952 Bowman set has enjoyed non-stop popularity because of its simple design and striking paintings.

		NR MT
Complete set		**$8250.00**
Commons (1-36)		**12.00**
Commons (37-216)		**10.00**
Commons (217-252)		**21.00**

1	Larry "Yogi" Berra......	**$625.00**
2	Bobby Thomson	30.00
3	Fred Hutchinson	17.00
4	Robin Roberts	50.00
5	*Orestes Minoso*	62.00
6	Virgil "Red" Stallcup.......	12.00

218 Willie Mays

101Mickey Mantle

7	Mike Garcia	14.00
8	Harold "Pee Wee" Reese	150.00
9	Vern Stephens...............	12.00
10	Bob Hooper	12.00
11	Ralph Kiner...................	50.00
12	Max Surkont	12.00
13	Cliff Mapes	12.00
14	Cliff Chambers...............	12.00
15	Sam Mele	12.00
16	Omar Lown....................	12.00
17	Ed Lopat........................	25.00
18	Don Mueller....................	12.00

1952 Bowman

44 Roy Campanella

19	Bob Cain	12.00
20	Willie Jones	14.00
21	Nelson Fox	50.00
22	Willard Ramsell	12.00
23	Bob Lemon	45.00
24	Carl Furillo	22.00
25	Maurice McDermott	12.00
26	Eddie Joost	12.00
27	Joe Garagiola	65.00
28	Roy Hartsfield	12.00
29	Ned Garver	12.00
30	Al "Red" Schoendienst	55.00
31	Eddie Yost	12.00
32	Eddie Miksis	12.00
33	*Gil McDougald*	40.00
34	Al Dark	16.00
35	Gran Hamner	12.00
36	Cass Michaels	12.00
37	Vic Raschi	22.00
38	Whitey Lockman	10.00
39	Vic Wertz	12.00
40	Emory Church	10.00
41	Chico Carrasquel	10.00
43	Bob Feller	115.00
44	Roy Campanella	215.00
45	Johnny Pesky	12.00

48	Vern Bickford	10.00
49	Jim Hearn	10.00
50	Gerry Staley	10.00
51	Gil Coan	10.00
52	Phil Rizzuto	55.00
53	Richie Ashburn	45.00
54	Billy Pierce	22.00
56	Clyde King	12.00
58	Hank Majeski	10.00
59	Murray Dickson	10.00
60	Sid Gordon	10.00
61	Tommy Byrne	10.00
64	Roy Smalley	10.00
65	Hank Bauer	25.00
66	Sal Maglie	20.00
69	Joe Adcock	16.00
70	Carl Erskine	20.00
71	Vernon Law	13.00
73	Jerry Coleman	18.00
74	Wes Westrum	12.00
75	George Kell	40.00
76	Del Ennis	12.00
80	Gil Hodges	62.00
82	Gus Zernial	10.00
84	Sam Jethroe	10.00
85	• Marty Marion	14.00

116 Duke Snider

86	Cal Abrams	12.00
87	Mickey Vernon	12.00
93	Paul Richards	12.00
95	Luke Easter	12.00
96	Ralph Branca	18.00
98	Jimmy Dykes	12.00
100	Sibby Sisti	10.00
101	Mickey Mantle	1500.00
102	Peanuts Lowrey	10.00
104	Hal Jeffcoat	10.00
105	• Bobby Brown	18.00
107	Del Rice	10.00
109	Tom Morgan	14.00
110	Max Lanier	10.00
111	Walter "Hoot" Evers	10.00
112	Forrest "Smokey" Burgess	12.00
113	Al Zarilla	10.00
115	Larry Doby	20.00
116	Duke Snider	170.00
120	Chet Nichols	10.00
126	Phil Cavarretta	15.00
127	Dick Sisler	10.00
128	Don Newcombe	24.00
134	Al Brazle	10.00
139	Jerry Priddy	10.00
142	Early Wynn	45.00
145	Johnny Mize	50.00
146	• Leo Durocher	35.00
151	Al "Flip" Rosen	20.00
152	Billy Cox	12.00
154	Ferris Fain	12.00
156	Warren Spahn	85.00
158	Bucky Harris	30.00
159	Dutch Leonard	10.00
160	Eddie Stanky	12.00
161	Jackie Jensen	25.00
162	Monte Irvin	37.00
164	Connie Ryan	10.00
165	Saul Rogovin	10.00
166	Bobby Adams	10.00
167	Bob Avila	10.00
168	Preacher Roe	20.00
169	Walt Dropo	10.00
170	Joe Astroth	10.00
173	Gene Bearden	10.00
174	Mickey Grasso	10.00
175	Ransom Jackson	10.00
176	Harry Brecheen	12.00

8 Harold "Pee Wee" Reese

177	Gene Woodling	16.00
178	Dave Williams	10.00
179	Pete Suder	10.00
181	Joe Collins	15.00
184	Curt Simmons	12.00
188	Charlie Dressen	15.00
189	Jim Piersall	15.00
191	Bob Friend	15.00
196	Stan Musial	465.00
197	Charlie Silvera	13.00
198	Chuck Diering	10.00
199	Ted Gray	10.00
203	Steve Gromek	10.00
204	Andy Pafko	13.00
206	Elmer Valo	10.00
207	George Strickland	10.00
213	Monte Kennedy	10.00
214	Ray Boone	12.00
217	Casey Stengel	150.00
218	Willie Mays	825.00
219	Neil Berry	25.00
220	Russ Meyer	25.00
221	Lou Kretlow	25.00
222	Homer "Dixie" Howell	25.00
223	Harry Simpson	25.00
224	Johnny Schmitz	25.00

225	Del Wilber	25.00	239	Dale Mitchell	25.00
226	Alex Kellner	25.00	240	*Billy Loes*	32.00
227	Clyde Sukeforth	25.00	241	Mel Parnell	27.00
228	Bob Chipman	25.00	242	Everett Kell	25.00
229	Hank Arft	25.00	243	George "Red" Munger	25.00
230	Frank Shea	25.00	244	*Lew Burdette*	65.00
231	Dee Fondy	25.00	245	George Schmees	25.00
232	Enos Slaughter	75.00	246	Jerry Snyder	25.00
233	Bob Kuzava	25.00	247	John Pramesa	25.00
234	Fred Fitzsimmons	25.00	248	Bill Werle	25.00
235	Steve Souchock	25.00	249	Henry Thompson	25.00
236	Tommy Brown	25.00	250	Ivan Delock	25.00
237	Sherman Lollar	28.00	251	Jack Lohrke	31.00
238	Roy McMillan	27.00	252	Frank Crosetti	125.00

1952 TOPPS

By far the most valuable *set* of baseball cards of the post-World War II period, the marvelous 1952 Topps edition also contains the single most expensive *card* of that time: Number 311, showing the great Mickey Mantle, is currently valued at about $8500. Both in terms of size (2⅝ by 3¾ inches) and number of cards (407), the Topps set was the biggest baseball product of 1952. The cards offer colorized black-and-white photos along with the player name, facsimile autograph, and team logo on a movie marquee card front. The backs, for the first time, include both 1951 and lifetime statistics. The final series of cards (311-407) is extremely rare and commands premium prices. How popular is the 1952 Topps set? Even the reprinted edition, issued by Topps in 1983, has grown in price from $40 to as much as $200 today.

	NR MT
Complete set	**$41,000.00**
Commons (1-80)	**50.00**
Commons (81-250)	**20.00**
Commons (251-280)	**40.00**
Commons (281-300)	**45.00**
Commons (301-310)	**40.00**
Commons (311-407)	**150.00**

1	Andy Pafko	$1100.00
2	*James E. Runnells*	75.00
3	Hank Thompson	50.00
4	Don Lenhardt	50.00
5	Larry Jansen	55.00
6	Grady Hatton	50.00
7	Wayne Terwilliger	55.00
8	Fred Marsh	55.00
9	Bobby Hogue	60.00
10	Al Rosen	85.00
11	Phil Rizzuto	175.00
12	Monty Basgall	55.00
13	Johnny Wyrostek	55.00
14	Bob Elliott	50.00
15	Johnny Pesky	60.00
16	Gene Hermanski	55.00
17	Jim Hegan	55.00
18	Merrill Combs	50.00
19	Johnny Bucha	50.00
20	*Billy Loes*	150.00
21	Ferris Fain	60.00

22	Dom DiMaggio	**90.00**
23	Billy Goodman	**55.00**
24	Luke Easter	**60.00**
25	Johnny Groth	**55.00**
26	Monte Irvin	**100.00**
27	Sam Jethroe	**55.00**
28	Jerry Priddy	**50.00**
29	Ted Kluszewski	**80.00**
30	Mel Parnell	**60.00**
31	Gus Zernial	**60.00**
32	Eddie Robinson	**50.00**
33	Warren Spahn	**200.00**
34	Elmer Valo	**50.00**
35	Hank Sauer	**55.00**
36	Gil Hodges	**150.00**
37	Duke Snider	**275.00**
38	Wally Westlake	**50.00**
39	"Dizzy" Trout	**55.00**
40	Irv Noren	**50.00**
41	Bob Wellman	**50.00**
42	Lou Kretlow	**50.00**
43	Ray Scarborough	**50.00**
44	Con Dempsey	**50.00**
45	Eddie Joost	**50.00**
46	Gordon Goldsberry	**50.00**
47	Willie Jones	**55.00**
48	Joe Page (Johnny Sain bio)	**225.00**
48	Joe Page (correct bio)	**90.00**
49	Johnny Sain (Joe Page bio)	**225.00**
49	Johnny Sain (correct bio)	**90.00**
50	Marv Rickert	**50.00**
51	Jim Russell	**50.00**
52	Don Mueller	**50.00**
53	Chris Van Cuyk	**50.00**
54	Leo Kiely	**50.00**
55	Ray Boone	**60.00**
56	Tommy Glaviano	**55.00**
57	Ed Lopat	**75.00**
58	Bob Mahoney	**50.00**
59	Robin Roberts	**135.00**
60	Sid Hudson	**55.00**
61	"Tookie" Gilbert	**55.00**
62	Chuck Stobbs	**55.00**
63	Howie Pollet	**55.00**
64	Roy Sievers	**70.00**
65	Enos Slaughter	**135.00**

311 Mickey Mantle

66	"Preacher" Roe	**90.00**
67	Allie Reynolds	**95.00**
68	Cliff Chambers	**50.00**
69	Virgil Stallcup	**50.00**
70	Al Zarilla	**50.00**
71	Tom Upton	**50.00**
72	Karl Olson	**50.00**
73	William Werle	**50.00**
74	Andy Hansen	**50.00**
75	Wes Westrum	**55.00**
76	Eddie Stanky	**65.00**
77	Bob Kennedy	**50.00**
78	Ellis Kinder	**50.00**
79	Gerald Staley	**50.00**
80	Herman Wehmeier	**50.00**
81	Vernon Law	**25.00**
88	Bob Feller	**135.00**
91	Al Schoendienst	**65.00**
98	•Bill Pierce	**25.00**
99	Gene Woodling	**40.00**
106	Mickey Vernon	**25.00**
108	Jim Konstanty	**25.00**
117	Sherman Lollar	**25.00**
122	Jack Jensen	**60.00**
123	Eddie Yost	**25.00**
125	Bill Rigney	**25.00**
126	Fred Hutchinson	**25.00**

407 Ed Mathews

129	Johnny Mize	75.00
140	John Antonelli	25.00
162	Del Crandall	25.00
170	Gus Bell	25.00
175	*Billy Martin*	300.00
180	Charley Maxwell	25.00
189	Pete Reiser	25.00
191	Yogi Berra	360.00
195	*Orestes Minoso*	75.00
200	*Ralph Houk*	55.00
203	Curt Simmons	25.00
215	Hank Bauer	40.00
216	Richie Ashburn	60.00
219	Bobby Shantz	25.00
223	Del Ennis	25.00
226	Dave Philley	25.00
227	Joe Garagiola	65.00
229	Gene Bearden	25.00
232	Billy Cox	25.00
233	Bob Friend	25.00
235	Walt Dropo	25.00
237	Jerry Coleman	30.00
239	Rocky Bridges	25.00
243	Larry Doby	30.00
244	Vic Wertz	25.00
246	George Kell	50.00
247	Randy Gumpert	20.00
248	Frank Shea	20.00
249	Bobby Adams	20.00
250	Carl Erskine	50.00
251	Chico Carrasquel	40.00
252	Vern Bickford	40.00
253	*Johnny Berardino*	50.00
254	Joe Dobson	40.00
255	Clyde Vollmer	40.00
256	Pete Suder	40.00
257	Bobby Avila	40.00
258	Steve Gromek	40.00
259	Bob Addis	40.00
260	Pete Castiglione	40.00
261	Willie Mays	1200.00
262	Virgil Trucks	45.00
263	Harry Brecheen	45.00
264	Roy Hartsfield	40.00
265	Chuck Diering	40.00
266	Murry Dickson	40.00
267	Sid Gordon	40.00
268	Bob Lemon	150.00
269	Willard Nixon	40.00
270	Lou Brissie	40.00
271	Jim Delsing	40.00
272	Mike Garcia	45.00
273	Erv Palica	40.00
274	Ralph Branca	60.00
275	Pat Mullin	40.00
276	Jim Wilson	40.00
277	Early Wynn	150.00
278	Al Clark	40.00
279	Ed Stewart	40.00
280	Cloyd Boyer	40.00
281	Tommy Brown	45.00
282	Birdie Tebbetts	50.00
283	Phil Masi	45.00
284	Hank Arft	45.00
285	Cliff Fannin	45.00
286	Joe DeMaestri	45.00
287	Steve Bilko	45.00
288	Chet Nichols	45.00
289	Tommy Holmes	50.00
290	Joe Astroth	45.00
291	Gil Coan	45.00
292	Floyd Baker	45.00
293	Sibby Sisti	45.00
294	Walker Cooper	45.00
295	Phil Cavarretta	50.00
296	"Red" Rolfe	45.00

297	Andy Seminick	50.00
298	Bob Ross	45.00
299	Ray Murray	45.00
300	Barney McCosky	45.00
301	Bob Porterfield	40.00
302	Max Surkont	40.00
303	Harry Dorish	40.00
304	Sam Dente	40.00
305	Paul Richards	45.00
306	Lou Sleator	40.00
307	Frank Campos	40.00
308	Luis Aloma	40.00
309	Jim Busby	40.00
310	George Metkovich	40.00
311	Mickey Mantle	8500.00
312	Jackie Robinson	825.00
313	Bobby Thomson	175.00
314	Roy Campanella	1250.00
315	Leo Durocher	250.00
316	Davey Williams	150.00
317	Connie Marrero	150.00
318	Hal Gregg	150.00

261 Willie Mays

319	Al Walker	150.00
320	John Rutherford	150.00
321	*Joe Black*	200.00
322	Randy Jackson	150.00
323	Bubba Church	150.00
324	Warren Hacker	150.00
325	Bill Serena	150.00
326	George Shuba	150.00
327	Archie Wilson	150.00
328	Bob Borkowski	150.00
329	Ivan Delock	150.00
330	Turk Lown	150.00
331	Tom Morgan	155.00
332	Tony Bartirome	150.00
333	Pee Wee Reese	800.00
334	Wilmer Mizell	150.00
335	Ted Lepcio	150.00
336	Dave Koslo	150.00
337	Jim Hearn	150.00
338	Sal Yvars	150.00
339	Russ Meyer	150.00
340	Bob Hooper	150.00
341	Hal Jeffcoat	150.00
342	*Clem Labine*	200.00
343	Dick Gernert	150.00
344	Ewell Blackwell	155.00
345	Sam White	150.00

346	George Spencer	150.00
347	Joe Adcock	175.00
348	Bob Kelly	150.00
349	Bob Cain	150.00
350	Cal Abrams	155.00
351	Al Dark	180.00
352	Karl Drews	175.00
353	Bob Del Greco	150.00
354	Fred Hatfield	150.00
355	Bobby Morgan	150.00
356	Toby Atwell	150.00
357	Smoky Burgess	175.00
358	John Kucab	150.00
359	Dee Fondy	150.00
360	George Crowe	150.00
361	Bill Posedel	150.00
362	Ken Heintzelman	150.00
363	Dick Rozek	150.00
364	Clyde Sukeforth	150.00
365	"Cookie" Lavagetto	155.00
366	Dave Madison	150.00
367	Bob Thorpe	150.00
368	Ed Wright	150.00
369	*Dick Groat*	250.00
370	Billy Hoeft	150.00
371	Bob Hofrnan	150.00
372	*Gil McDougald*	250.00

373	Jim Turner	150.00	391	Ben Chapman (photo is Sam Chapman)	150.00
374	Al Benton	150.00	392	Hoyt Wilhelm	500.00
375	Jack Merson	150.00	393	Ebba St. Claire	150.00
376	Faye Throneberry	150.00	394	Billy Herman	200.00
377	Chuck Dressen	175.00	395	Jake Pitler	150.00
378	Les Fusselman	150.00	396	Dick Williams	175.00
379	Joe Rossi	150.00	397	Forrest Main	150.00
380	Clem Koshorek	150.00	398	Hal Rice	150.00
381	Milton Stock	150.00	399	Jim Fridley	150.00
382	Sam Jones	150.00	400	Bill Dickey	500.00
383	Del Wilber	150.00	401	Bob Schultz	150.00
384	Frank Crosetti	250.00	402	Earl Harrist	150.00
385	Herman Franks	150.00	403	Bill Miller	150.00
386	Eddie Yuhas	150.00	404	Dick Brodowski	150.00
387	Billy Meyer	150.00	405	Eddie Pellagrini	150.00
388	Bob Chipman	150.00	406	Joe Nuxhall	175.00
389	Ben Wade	150.00	407	Ed Mathews	2000.00
390	Glen Nelson	150.00			

1953 BOWMAN B&W

The 1953 Bowman black-and-white set was a separate issue from the Bowman color cards of the same year. The black-and-white cards came in a different wrapper and are numbered 1 through 64. In format, however, the sets are identical. Each one measures 2⅟ by 3¾ inches, with a full photo surrounded by a black line and a white border. Card backs show a bio, stats for 1952, and lifetime stats. A blank line to write in numbers for the current year was included; thankfully, few youngsters took advantage of the opportunity. As a result, nearly all cards found today are free of any writing.

		NR MT			
Complete set		**$2250.00**	10	Dick Sisler	25.00
Commons		**25.00**	11	Dick Gernert	25.00
			12	Randy Jackson	25.00
			15	Johnny Mize	125.00
			16	Stu Miller	25.00
1	Gus Bell	$80.00	17	Virgil Trucks	27.00
2	Willard Nixon	25.00	18	Billy Hoeft	25.00
3	Bill Rigney	28.00	20	Eddie Robinson	25.00
4	Pat Mullin	25.00	25	John Sain	50.00
5	Dee Fondy	25.00	26	Preacher Roe	50.00
7	Andy Seminick	25.00	27	Bob Lemon	100.00
8	Pete Suder	25.00	28	Hoyt Wilhelm	90.00

30	Walker Cooper	25.00
31	Gene Woodling	40.00
32	Rocky Bridges	25.00
33	Bob Kuzava	25.00
36	Jim Piersall	35.00
37	Hal Jeffcoat	25.00
39	Casey Stengel	300.00
40	Larry Jensen	25.00
42	Howie Judson	25.00
45	Irv Noren	25.00
46	Bucky Harris	50.00
50	Dutch Leonard	25.00
51	Lou Burdette	45.00
52	Ralph Branca	40.00
56	Roy Smalley	25.00
57	Andy Pafko	30.00
58	Jim Konstanty	27.00
59	Duane Pillette	25.00
60	Billy Cox	32.00
62	Keith Thomas	25.00
64	Andy Hansen	40.00

39 Casey Stengel

1953 BOWMAN COLOR

Many collectors consider Bowman's 1953 set of 160 cards—the first ever to make use of color photography (as opposed to colorized black-and-white photos)—to be the most beautiful ever created. The jump in technology was due to competition from Topps, which also encouraged Bowman to increase card size (2½ by 3¾ inches) and to include stats on the card backs (which are cream colored with red-and-black print). The splendid photographs are presented with a simple white border. Stan Musial made his farewell Bowman appearance in this set, while multiple player photos—a first in this century—include one card of Martin and Rizzuto; another of Mantle, Berra, and Bauer.

	NR MT
Complete set	**$12,100.00**
Commons (1-112)	**25.00**
Commons (113-128)	**35.00**
Commons (129-160)	**30.00**

1	Davey Williams	$105.00
2	Vic Wertz	27.00
3	Sam Jethroe	25.00
8	Al Rosen	50.00
9	Phil Rizzuto	90.00
10	Richie Ashburn	75.00

1953 Bowman Color

59 Mickey Mantle

11	Bobby Shantz	27.00
12	Carl Erskine	50.00
14	Billy Loes	27.00
16	Bob Friend	27.00
18	Nelson Fox	60.00
19	Al Dark	35.00
21	Joe Garagiola	70.00
24	Jackie Jensen	35.00
27	Vic Raschi	45.00
28	Forrest "Smoky" Burgess	27.00
30	Phil Cavarretta	27.00
31	Jimmy Dykes	27.00
32	Stan Musial	500.00
33	Harold "Peewee" Reese	300.00
36	Orestes Minoso	55.00
39	Paul Richards	27.00
40	Larry Doby	50.00
43	Mike Garcia	27.00
44	Hank Bauer, Yogi Berra, Mickey Mantle	400.00
46	Roy Campanella	300.00
48	Hank Sauer	25.00
49	Eddie Stanky	27.00
51	Monte Irvin	50.00
52	• Marty Marion	27.00

55	Leo Durocher	75.00
57	Lou Boudreau	50.00
59	Mickey Mantle	1300.00
60	Granny Hamner	25.00
61	George Kell	50.00
62	Ted Kluszewski	50.00
63	Gil McDougald	50.00
65	Robin Roberts	60.00
68	Allie Reynolds	50.00
69	Charlie Grimm	27.00
73	Billy Pierce	27.00
78	Carl Furillo	45.00
79	Ray Boone	27.00
80	Ralph Kiner	65.00
81	Enos Slaughter	70.00
84	Hank Bauer	50.00
85	Solly Hemus	25.00
90	Joe Nuxhall	27.00
92	Gil Hodges	100.00
93	Billy Martin, Phil Rizzuto	225.00
96	Sal Maglie	30.00
97	Eddie Mathews	100.00
99	Warren Spahn	135.00
101	Al "Red" Schoendienst	80.00
103	Del Ennis	25.00

153 Ed "Whitey" Ford

104	Luke Easter	25.00
106	Ken Raffensberger	25.00
107	Alex Kellner	25.00
111	Jim Dyck	25.00
113	Karl Drews	35.00
114	Bob Feller	280.00
115	Cloyd Boyer	35.00
116	Eddie Yost	35.00
117	Duke Snider	500.00
118	Billy Martin	300.00
119	Dale Mitchell	35.00
120	Marlin Stuart	35.00
121	Yogi Berra	500.00
122	Bill Serena	35.00
123	Johnny Lipon	35.00
124	Charlie Dressen	45.00
125	Fred Hatfield	35.00
126	Al Corwin	35.00
127	Dick Kryhoski	35.00
128	Whitey Lockman	35.00
129	Russ Meyer	35.00
130	Cass Michaels	30.00
131	Connie Ryan	30.00
132	Fred Hutchinson	35.00
133	Willie Jones	30.00
134	Johnny Pesky	35.00

32 Stan Musial

135	Bobby Morgan	30.00
136	Jim Brideweser	30.00
137	Sam Dente	30.00
138	Bubba Church	30.00
139	Pete Runnels	35.00
140	Alpha Brazle	30.00
141	Frank "Spec" Shea	30.00
142	Larry Miggins	30.00
143	Al Lopez	70.00
144	Warren Hacker	30.00
145	George Shuba	35.00
146	Early Wynn	135.00
148	Billy Goodman	30.00
149	Al Corwin	30.00
150	Carl Scheib	30.00
151	Joe Adcock	35.00
152	Clyde Vollmer	30.00
153	Ed "Whitey" Ford	525.00
154	Omar "Turk" Lown	30.00
155	Allie Clark	30.00
156	Max Surkont	30.00
157	Sherman Lollar	35.00
158	Howard Fox	30.00
159	Mickey Vernon (photo is Floyd Baker)	40.00
160	Cal Abrams	100.00

121 Yogi Berra

1953 TOPPS

Topps' second set was reduced to 274 cards because of disputes with Bowman over player contracts. Cards are numbered to 280, but due to last-minute legal considerations, six are missing (numbers 253, 261, 267, 268, 271, and 275). With no checklists to guide them, frustrated collectors pursued these non-existent cards in vain. Measuring 2⅝ by 3¾ inches, the fronts feature a color painting, a team logo, and a panel for player identification. Backs are red and black printed on gray cardboard, with the first of Topps' popular Dugout Quiz series. Although the Mick's card is the most expensive, Willie Mays' is scarcer, as is a mint Jackie Robinson. Numbers 221-280 command premium value if the player's personal stats in the upper red panel are listed in black instead of white.

	NR MT
Complete set	$12,500.00
Commons (1-165) single-print	25.00
Commons (1-165) double-print	20.00
Commons (166-220)	18.00
Commons (221-280) single-print	90.00
Commons (221-280) double-print	48.00

82 Mickey Mantle

1	Jackie Robinson	$700.00
2	Luke Easter	23.00
3	George Crowe	22.00
4	Ben Wade	22.00
5	Joe Dobson	23.00
6	Sam Jones	23.00
9	Joe Collins	30.00
10	Smoky Burgess	30.00
11	Sal Yvars	23.00
14	Clem Labine	24.00
15	Bobo Newsom	24.00
17	Billy Hitchcock	25.00
20	Hank Thompson	25.00
21	Billy Johnson	25.00
22	Howie Fox	25.00
24	Ferris Fain	25.00
25	Ray Boone	25.00
27	Roy Campanella	250.00
28	Eddie Pellagrini	25.00
29	Hal Jeffcoat	25.00
30	Willard Nixon	25.00
31	Ewell Blackwell	40.00
32	Clyde Vollmer	25.00
34	George Shuba	25.00
35	Irv Noren	25.00
37	Ed Mathews	100.00
39	Eddie Miksis	25.00
40	John Lipon	25.00
41	Enos Slaughter	75.00

43	Gil McDougald	35.00
44	Ellis Kinder	27.00
47	Bubba Church	20.00
50	Chuck Dressen	26.00
54	Bob Feller	100.00
57	Carl Scheib	25.00
58	George Metkovich	20.00
61	Early Wynn	85.00
62	Monte Irvin	35.00
64	Dave Philley	20.00
65	Earl Harrist	20.00
66	• Orestes Minoso	30.00
67	• Roy Sievers	21.00
68	Del Rice	20.00
69	Dick Brodowski	20.00
70	Ed Yuhas	20.00
71	Tony Bartirome	20.00
72	Fred Hutchinson	20.00
73	Eddie Robinson	20.00
74	Joe Rossi	20.00
75	Mike Garcia	20.00
76	Pee Wee Reese	150.00
77	John Mize	80.00
78	Al Schoendienst	50.00
79	Johnny Wyrostek	20.00
80	Jim Hegan	20.00
81	Joe Black	40.00
82	Mickey Mantle	2000.00

244 Willie Mays

83	Howie Pollet	20.00
85	Bobby Morgan	20.00
86	Billy Martin	115.00
87	Ed Lopat	35.00
96	Virgil Trucks	20.00
99	Dave Madison	19.00
100	Bill Miller	19.00
101	Ted Wilks	19.00
102	Connie Ryan	19.00
103	Joe Astroth	19.00
104	Yogi Berra	200.00
105	Joe Nuxhall	19.00
106	Johnny Antonelli	19.00
109	Alvin Dark	25.00
110	Herman Wehmeier	18.00
111	Hank Sauer	18.00
112	Ned Garver	18.00
113	Jerry Priddy	18.00
114	Phil Rizzuto	100.00
118	Gus Bell	19.00
119	John Sain	40.00
121	Walt Dropo	18.00
122	Elmer Valo	18.00
123	Tommy Byrne	18.00
124	Sibby Sisti	18.00
125	Dick Williams	23.00
126	Bill Connelly	19.00

Jackie Robinson

258 Jim Gilliam

154	Dick Groat	27.00
155	Dutch Leonard	20.00
156	Jim Rivera	19.00
157	Bob Addis	19.00
158	John Logan	20.00
159	Wayne Terwilliger	20.00
160	Bob Young	19.00
161	Vern Bickford	19.00
162	Ted Kluszewski	30.00
163	Fred Hatfield	19.00
164	Frank Shea	19.00
165	Billy Hoeft	20.00
167	Art Schult	19.00
169	Dizzy Trout	18.00
174	Billy Loes	19.00
183	Stu Miller	19.00
188	*Andy Carey*	20.00
191	Ralph Kiner	60.00
197	Del Crandall	21.00
207	Whitey Ford	150.00
210	Bob Cerv	20.00
214	Bill Bruton	18.00
215	Gene Conley	18.00
216	Jim Hughes	18.00
219	Pete Runnels (photo is Don Johnson)	18.00
220	Satchell Paige (Satchel)	400.00

127	Clint Courtney	19.00
128	Wilmer Mizell	21.00
129	Keith Thomas	19.00
130	Turk Lown	20.00
131	Harry Byrd	19.00
132	Tom Morgan	22.00
133	Gil Coan	19.00
134	Rube Walker	20.00
135	Al Rosen	30.00
136	Ken Heintzelman	20.00
137	John Rutherford	20.00
138	George Kell	90.00
139	Sammy White	19.00
140	Tommy Glaviano	19.00
141	Allie Reynolds	35.00
142	Vic Wertz	20.00
143	• Billy Pierce	23.00
144	Bob Schultz	19.00
145	Harry Dorish	19.00
146	Granville Hamner	20.00
147	Warren Spahn	115.00
148	Mickey Grasso	19.00
149	Dom DiMaggio	27.00
150	Harry Simpson	19.00
151	Hoyt Wilhelm	75.00
152	Bob Adams	19.00
153	Andy Seminick	20.00

263 John Podres

221	Bob Milliken	48.00	248	Gene Stephens	48.00
222	Vic Janowicz	48.00	249	Ed O'Brien	48.00
223	John O'Brien	48.00	250	Bob Wilson	48.00
224	Lou Sleater	48.00	251	Sid Hudson	48.00
225	Bobby Shantz	62.00	252	Henry Foiles	48.00
226	Ed Erautt	48.00	254	Preacher Roe	80.00
227	Morris Martin	48.00	255	Dixie Howell	48.00
228	Hal Newhouser	100.00	256	Les Peden	48.00
229	Rocky Krsnich	48.00	257	Bob Boyd	48.00
230	Johnny Lindell	48.00	258	*Jim Gilliam*	325.00
231	Solly Hemus	48.00	259	Roy McMillan	48.00
232	Dick Kokos	48.00	260	Sam Calderone	48.00
233	Al Aber	48.00	262	Bob Oldis	48.00
234	Ray Murray	48.00	263	*John Podres*	250.00
235	John Hetki	48.00	264	Gene Woodling	75.00
236	Harry Perkowski	48.00	265	Jackie Jensen	110.00
237	Clarence Podbielan	48.00	266	Bob Cain	48.00
238	Cal Hogue	48.00	269	Duane Pillette	48.00
239	Jim Delsing	48.00	270	Vern Stephens	48.00
240	Freddie Marsh	48.00	272	Bill Antonello	48.00
241	Al Sima	48.00	273	*Harvey Haddix*	125.00
242	Charlie Silvera	48.00	274	John Riddle	48.00
243	Carlos Bernier	48.00	276	Ken Raffensberger	48.00
244	Willie Mays	1500.00	277	Don Lund	48.00
245	Bill Norman	48.00	278	Willie Miranda	48.00
246	*Roy Face*	90.00	279	Joe Coleman	48.00
247	Mike Sandlock	48.00	280	Milt Bolling	350.00

1954 BOWMAN

Following the splendid 1953 set, Bowman's efforts in 1954 seem lackluster in comparison. The 224 cards (measuring 2½ by 3¾ inches) again use colorized photographs. A pastel rectangle at the bottom contains a facsimile autograph of each depicted player. The 1954 Bowman set is best known for having two number 66 cards: The common number 66 is of Jimmy Piersall; the scarce version is of Ted Williams, who appeared in a Topps set for the first time in 1954. It is believed that his contract with Topps prevented Bowman from using his image, and Williams' card was later pulled from circulation.

	NR MT			
		1	Phil Rizzuto	$150.00
Complete set	$4500.00	2	Jack Jensen	10.00
Commons (1-112)	7.00	4	Bob Hooper	7.00
Commons (113-224)	9.00	6	• Nelson Fox	15.00
		7	Walt Dropo	7.00

1954 Bowman

66 Ted Williams

8	James F. Busby	7.00
9	Dave Williams	7.00
10	Carl Daniel Erskine	10.00
11	Sid Gordon	7.00
12	Roy McMillan	7.00
14	Gerald Staley	7.00
15	Richie Ashburn	25.00
17	Tom Gorman	7.00
18	Walter "Hoot" Evers	7.00
19	Bobby Shantz	9.00
20	Artie Houtteman	7.00
21	Victor Wertz	8.00
22	Sam Mele	7.00
23	*Harvey Kuenn*	25.00
24	Bob Porterfield	7.00
25	Wes Westrum	7.00
26	Billy Cox	9.00
28	Jim Greengrass	7.00
29	Johnny Klippstein	7.00
30	Delbert Rice Jr.	7.00
31	"Smoky" Burgess	7.00
32	Del Crandall	8.00
33	Victor Raschi (with traded line)	25.00
35	Eddie Joost	7.00
36	George Strickland	7.00
37	Dick Kokos	7.00
38	• Orestes Minoso	12.00
39	Ned Garver	7.00
45	Ralph Kiner	40.00
50	George Kell	25.00
57	Hoyt Wilhelm	25.00
58	"Pee Wee" Reese	50.00
62	Enos Slaughter	32.00
64	Ed Mathews	50.00
65	Mickey Mantle	750.00
66	Ted Williams	3000.00
66	Jimmy Piersall	85.00
67	Carl Scheib	7.00
68	Bob Avila	7.00
72	Ed Yost	7.00
74	James Gilliam	10.00
75	Max Surkont	7.00
76	Joe Nuxhall	7.00
79	Curt Simmons	7.00
81	Jerry Coleman	8.00
82	Bill Goodman	8.00
84	• Larry Doby	8.00
89	Willie May (Mays)	350.00
90	Roy Campanella	160.00
91	Cal Abrams	7.00
93	Bill Serena	7.00
94	Solly Hemus	7.00
95	Robin Roberts	25.00
96	• Joe Adcock	8.00
97	Gil McDougald	12.00
99	Pete Suder	7.00
101	*Don James Larsen*	30.00
102	• Bill Pierce	7.00
103	Stephen Souchock	7.00
104	Frank Spec Shea	7.00
105	• Sal Maglie	9.00
106	"Clem" Labine	9.00
107	Paul E. LaPalme	7.00
108	Bobby Adams	7.00
109	Roy Smalley	7.00
110	Al Schoendienst	35.00
112	• Andy Pafko	7.00
113	Allie Reynolds	14.00
114	Willard Nixon	9.00
115	Don Bollweg	9.00
117	Dick Kryhoski	9.00
119	Fred Hatfield	9.00
121	Ray Katt	9.00
122	Carl Furillo	13.00

123	Toby Atwell	9.00
124	Gus Bell	10.00
127	Del Ennis	10.00
129	Hank Bauer	15.00
130	Milt Bolling	9.00
131	Joe Astroth	9.00
132	Bob Feller	75.00
134	Luis Aloma	9.00
135	Johnny Pesky	9.00
136	Clyde Vollmer	9.00
138	Gil Hodges	50.00
139	Preston Ward	9.00
140	Saul Rogovin	9.00
141	Joe Garagiola	40.00
142	Al Brazle	9.00
144	Ernie Johnson	9.00
145	Billy Martin	50.00
146	Dick Gernert	9.00
147	Joe DeMaestri	9.00
148	Dale Mitchell	9.00
149	Bob Young	9.00
151	Patrick J. Mullin	9.00
152	Mickey Vernon	10.00
153	Whitey Lockman	10.00
154	Don Newcombe	15.00
155	*Frank Thomas*	9.00
156	Everett Lamar Bridges	9.00
157	Omar Lown	9.00
158	Stu Miller	9.00
159	John Lindell	9.00
161	Yogi Berra	140.00
162	Ted Lepcio	9.00
163	Dave Philley (157 games with traded line)	9.00
163	Dave Philley (152 games w/o traded line)	25.00
164	Early "Gus" Wynn	35.00
165	Johnny Groth	9.00
170	Edwin D. Snider	150.00
174	Peter Paul Castiglione	9.00
177	Edward Ford	75.00
179	Morris Martin	9.00
180	Joe Tipton	9.00
182	Sherman Lollar	10.00
183	Matt Batts	9.00
184	Mickey Grasso	9.00
185	Daryl Spencer	9.00
186	Russell Meyer	9.00
187	Verne Law (Vern)	10.00

65 Mickey Mantle

190	Joe Presko	9.00
192	• Selva L. Burdette	15.00
193	Eddie Robinson	9.00
196	Bob Lemon	25.00
197	Lou Kretlow	9.00
198	Virgil Trucks	10.00
199	Steve Gromek	9.00
201	Bob Thomson	12.00
202	George Shuba	9.00
203	Vic Janowicz	9.00
204	Jack Collum	9.00
207	Stan Lopata	9.00
208	Johnny Antonelli	9.00
209	Gene Woodling (photo reversed)	12.00
210	Jimmy Piersall	12.00
212	Owen L. Friend	9.00
214	Ferris Fain	9.00
215	Johnny Bucha	9.00
216	Jerry Snyder	9.00
217	Henry Thompson	9.00
218	Preacher Roe	14.00
219	Hal Rice	9.00
222	Memo Luna	9.00
223	Steve Ridzik	9.00
224	William Bruton	30.00

1954 TOPPS

Topps came up with a number of innovations for its 250-card set in 1954, including the introduction of coach cards. This year marked Topps' first use of more than one player to a card and the first-ever instance of two distinct photographic images: These 2⅝- by 3¾-inch cards feature both a colorized portrait and a posed black-and-white photo on the front. The backs have green, red, and black printing on white cardboard. Ted Williams appears twice to honor his exclusive new contract with Topps. Rookies include Hank Aaron, Ernie Banks, Al Kaline, and Tommy Lasorda. This is Lasorda's only card appearance as a player.

		NR MT
Complete set		$7500.00
Commons (1-50)		15.00
Commons (51-75)		32.00
Commons (76-250)		15.00

128 Henry Aaron

1	Ted Williams	$600.00
2	Gus Zernial	17.00
3	Monte Irvin	35.00
5	Ed Lopat	25.00
7	Ted Kluszewski	25.00
9	Harvey Haddix	17.00
10	Jackie Robinson	250.00
12	Del Crandall	17.00
13	Billy Martin	85.00
14	Preacher Roe	60.00
15	Al Rosen	20.00
17	Phil Rizzuto	75.00
20	Warren Spahn	100.00
21	Bobby Shantz	17.00
25	*Harvey Kuenn*	30.00
30	Ed Mathews	75.00
32	Duke Snider	125.00
35	Junior Gilliam	30.00
36	Hoyt Wilhelm	45.00
37	Whitey Ford	100.00
43	Dick Groat	18.00
45	Richie Ashburn	30.00
50	Yogi Berra	235.00
51	Johnny Lindell	32.00
52	Vic Power	32.00
53	Jack Dittmer	32.00
54	Vern Stephens	32.00
55	Phil Cavarretta	35.00
56	Willie Miranda	32.00
57	Luis Aloma	32.00
58	Bob Wilson	32.00
59	Gene Conley	32.00
60	Frank Baumholtz	32.00
61	Bob Cain	32.00
62	Eddie Robinson	32.00
63	Johnny Pesky	35.00
64	Hank Thompson	32.00
65	Bob Swift	32.00
66	Ted Lepcio	32.00
67	Jim Willis	32.00
68	Sammy Calderone	32.00
69	Bud Podbielan	32.00

70	Larry Doby	40.00
71	Frank Smith	32.00
72	Preston Ward	32.00
73	Wayne Terwilliger	32.00
74	Bill Taylor	32.00
75	Fred Haney	32.00
77	Ray Boone	15.00
79	Andy Pakfo	15.00
80	Jackie Jensen	18.00
81	Dave Hoskins	15.00
82	Milt Bolling	15.00
83	Joe Collins	15.00
84	Dick Cole	15.00
85	*Bob Turley*	20.00
86	Billy Herman	20.00
87	Roy Face	17.00
88	Matt Batts	15.00
89	Howie Pollet	15.00
90	Willie Mays	360.00
91	Bob Oldis	15.00
92	Wally Westlake	15.00
93	Sid Hudson	15.00
94	*Ernie Banks*	650.00
95	Hal Rice	15.00
96	Charlie Silvera	15.00
97	Jerry Lane	15.00
98	Joe Black	15.00
100	Bob Keegan	15.00

250 Ted Williams

102	Gil Hodges	72.00
103	Jim Lemon	15.00
104	Mike Sandlock	15.00
105	Andy Carey	15.00
106	Dick Kokos	15.00
107	Duane Pillette	15.00
108	Thornton Kipper	15.00
109	Bill Bruton	15.00
110	Harry Dorish	15.00
112	Bill Renna	15.00
113	Bob Boyd	15.00
114	Dean Stone	15.00
115	"Rip" Repulski	15.00
117	Solly Hemus	15.00
119	Johnny Antonelli	15.00
120	Roy McMillan	15.00
121	Clem Labine	17.00
122	Johnny Logan	15.00
126	Ben Wade	15.00
127	Steve O'Neill	15.00
128	*Henry Aaron*	1250.00
129	Forrest Jacobs	15.00
130	Hank Bauer	30.00
131	Reno Bertoia	15.00
132	*Tom Lasorda*	185.00
133	Del Baker	15.00
134	Cal Hogue	15.00

201 Al Kaline

94 Ernie Banks

135	Joe Presko	15.00
136	Connie Ryan	15.00
137	*Wally Moon*	19.00
138	Bob Borkowski	15.00
139	Ed & Johnny O'Brien	20.00
140	Tom Wright	15.00
141	Joe Jay	15.00
142	Tom Poholsky	15.00
143	Rollie Hemsley	15.00
144	Bill Werle	12.00
145	Elmer Valo	12.00
149	Jim Robertson	12.00
151	Alex Grammas	12.00
153	"Rube" Walker	12.00
155	Bob Kennedy	12.00
158	"Peanuts" Lowrey	12.00
159	Dave Philley	12.00
162	Herman Wehmeier	12.00
166	Johnny Podres	25.00
170	Jim Rhodes	12.00
171	Leo Kiely	12.00
173	Jack Harshman	12.00
174	Tom Qualters	12.00
175	Frank Leja	14.00
177	Bob Milliken	12.00
180	Wes Westrum	13.00
182	Chuck Harmon	12.00
183	Earle Combs	20.00

184	Ed Bailey	15.00
185	Chuck Stobbs	15.00
187	"Heinie" Manush	30.00
191	Dick Schofield	15.00
192	"Cot" Deal	15.00
193	Johnny Hopp	15.00
194	Bill Sarni	15.00
195	Bill Consolo	15.00
196	Stan Jok	15.00
197	"Schoolboy" Rowe	15.00
198	Carl Sawatski	15.00
200	Larry Jansen	15.00
201	*Al Kaline*	650.00
205	Johnny Sain	25.00
209	Charlie Thompson	15.00
210	Bob Buhl	15.00
211	Don Hoak	15.00
213	John Fitzpatrick	15.00
215	Ed McGhee	15.00
216	Al Sima	15.00
217	Paul Schreiber	15.00
218	Fred Marsh	15.00
219	Chuck Kress	15.00
220	Ruben Gomez	15.00
221	Dick Brodowski	15.00
222	Bill Wilson	15.00
223	Joe Haynes	15.00
224	Dick Weik	15.00
225	Don Liddle	15.00
226	Jehosie Heard	15.00
227	Buster Mills	15.00
228	Gene Hermanski	15.00
229	Bob Talbot	15.00
230	Bob Kuzava	15.00
233	Augie Galan	15.00
234	Jerry Lynch	15.00
235	Vern Law	16.00
237	Mike Ryba	15.00
238	Al Aber	15.00
239	*Bill Skowron*	75.00
240	Sam Mele	15.00
241	Bob Miller	15.00
242	Curt Roberts	15.00
243	Ray Blades	15.00
245	Roy Sievers	15.00
246	Howie Fox	15.00
247	Eddie Mayo	15.00
248	Al Smith	15.00
250	Ted Williams	700.00

1955 BOWMAN

Both color and baseball were relatively new to television in 1955 when Bowman came out with its television set of cards, the last set issued by Bowman before the company was bought out by Topps. The front of each 2½- by 3¾-inch card features a color photo framed to look as if the player were on TV. The 320-card set has red-and-black printing on gray cardboard backs. In addition to the first umpire cards of the century, manager and coach cards were also released. Lots of superstars appear as well: Whitey Ford, Ralph Kiner, The Mick, and Pee Wee Reese.

		NR MT
Complete set		**$4750.00**
Commons (1-224)		**5.00**
Commons (225-320)		**14.00**

1	Hoyt Wilhelm	$90.00	15	Frank Sullivan	5.00
2	Al Dark	14.00	16	Jim Piersall	6.00
3	Joe Coleman	5.00	17	Del Ennis	5.00
4	Eddie Waitkus	5.00	18	Stan Lopata	5.00
5	Jim Robertson	5.00	19	Bobby Avila	5.00
6	Pete Suder	5.00	20	Al Smith	5.00
7	Gene Baker	5.00	21	Don Hoak	7.00
8	Warren Hacker	5.00	22	Roy Campanella	110.00
9	Gil McDougald	10.00	23	Al Kaline	125.00
10	Phil Rizzuto	40.00	24	Al Aber	5.00
11	Billy Bruton	5.00	25	Orestes "Minnie" Minoso	9.00
12	Andy Pafko	6.00	26	Virgil Trucks	6.00
13	Clyde Vollmer	5.00	27	Preston Ward	5.00
14	Gus Keriazakos	5.00	28	Dick Cole	5.00
			29	Al "Red" Schoendienst	35.00
			30	Bill Sarni	5.00
			31	Johnny Temple	5.00
			32	Wally Post	5.00
			33	• Nelson Fox	20.00
			34	Clint Courtney	5.00
			35	Bill Tuttle	5.00

202 Mickey Mantle

1955 Bowman

179 Hank Aaron

36	Wayne Belardi	5.00	64	Curt Simmons	6.00
37	Harold "Pee Wee" Reese	65.00	65	*Don Zimmer*	25.00
38	Early Wynn	22.00	66	George Shuba	6.00
39	Bob Darnell	5.00	67	Don Larsen	15.00
40	Vic Wertz	5.00	68	*Elston Howard*	40.00
41	Mel Clark	5.00	69	Bill Hunter	6.00
42	Bob Greenwood	5.00	70	• Lou Burdette	7.00
43	Bob Buhl	5.00	71	Dave Jolly	5.00
44	Danny O'Connell	5.00	72	Chet Nichols	5.00
45	Tom Umphlett	5.00	73	Eddie Yost	5.00
46	Mickey Vernon	6.00	74	Jerry Snyder	5.00
47	Sammy White	5.00	75	Brooks Lawrence	5.00
48	Milt Bolling (Frank Bolling on back)	6.00	76	Tom Poholsky	5.00
48	Milt Bolling (Milt Bolling on back)	15.00	77	Jim McDonald	5.00
			78	Gil Coan	5.00
49	Jim Greengrass	5.00	79	Willie Miranda	5.00
50	Hobie Landrith	5.00	80	Lou Limmer	5.00
51	Elvin Tappe	5.00	81	Bob Morgan	5.00
52	Hal Rice	5.00	82	Lee Walls	5.00
53	Alex Kellner	5.00	83	Max Surkont	5.00
54	Don Bollweg	5.00	84	George Freese	5.00
55	Cal Abrams	5.00	85	Cass Michaels	5.00
56	Billy Cox	5.00	86	Ted Gray	5.00
57	Bob Friend	6.00	87	Randy Jackson	5.00
58	Frank Thomas	5.00	88	Steve Bilko	5.00
59	Ed "Whitey" Ford	60.00	89	Lou Boudreau	22.00
60	Enos Slaughter	25.00	90	Art Ditmar	5.00
61	Paul LaPalme	5.00	91	Dick Marlowe	5.00
62	Royce Lint	5.00	92	George Zuverink	5.00
63	Irv Noren	6.00	93	Andy Seminick	5.00
			94	Hank Thompson	5.00
			95	Sal Maglie	10.00

97	John Podres	15.00
98	James "Junior" Gilliam	15.00
99	Jerry Coleman	7.00
100	Tom Morgan	8.00
101	Don Johnson (Braves' Ernie Johnson on front)	6.00
101	Don Johnson (Orioles' Don Johnson on front)	15.00
102	Bobby Thomson	8.00
103	Eddie Mathews	45.00
104	Bob Porterfield	5.00
105	Johnny Schmitz	5.00
106	Del Rice	5.00
107	Solly Hemus	5.00
108	Lou Kretlow	5.00
109	Vern Stephens	5.00
110	Bob Miller	5.00
111	Steve Ridzik	5.00
112	Gran Hamner	5.00
114	Vic Janowicz	5.00
115	Roger Bowman	5.00
117	Johnny Groth	5.00
118	Bobby Adams	5.00
130	Richie Ashburn	20.00
132	• Harvey Kueen (incorrect spelling on back)	7.00
132	Harvey Kuenn (correct spelling on back)	32.00
134	Bob Feller	75.00
143	Don Newcombe	8.00
157	Ernie Johnson (Braves' Ernie Johnson on front)	15.00
158	Gil Hodges	40.00
160	Bill Skowron	15.00
168	Larry "Yogi" Berra	85.00
169	Carl Furillo	15.00
170	Carl Erskine	9.00
171	Robin Roberts	25.00
179	Hank Aaron	235.00
184	Willie Mays	235.00
191	Bob Lemon	25.00
195	Erv Palica (traded line on back)	25.00
197	Ralph Kiner	35.00
201	Allie Reynolds	15.00
202	Mickey Mantle	410.00
204	*Frank Bolling* (Frank Bolling on back)	20.00
213	George Kell	25.00
225	Paul Richards	16.00
226	W.F. McKinley (umpire)	16.00
227	Frank Baumholtz	14.00
228	John M. Phillips	14.00
229	Jim Brosnan	16.00
230	Al Brazle	14.00
231	Jim Konstanty	18.00
232	Birdie Tebbetts	14.00
233	Bill Serena	14.00
234	Dick Bartell	14.00
235	J.A. Paparella (umpire)	16.00
236	Murray Dickson (Murry)	14.00
237	Johnny Wyrostek	14.00
238	Eddie Stanky	15.00
239	Edwin A. Rommel (umpire)	16.00

242 Ernie Banks

184 Willie Mays

240	Billy Loes	15.00
241	John Pesky	15.00
242	Ernie Banks	360.00
243	Gus Bell	15.00
244	Duane Pillette	14.00
245	Bill Miller	14.00
246	Hank Bauer	25.00
247	Dutch Leonard	14.00
248	Harry Dorish	14.00
249	Billy Gardner	14.00
250	Larry Napp (umpire)	16.00
251	Stan Jok	14.00
252	Roy Smalley	14.00
253	Jim Wilson	14.00
254	Bennett Flowers	14.00
255	Pete Runnels	15.00
256	Owen Friend	14.00
257	Tom Alston	14.00
258	John W. Stevens (umpire)	16.00
259	*Don Mossi*	15.00
260	Edwin H. Hurley (umpire)	16.00
261	Walt Moryn	15.00
262	Jim Lemon	15.00
263	Eddie Joost	14.00
264	Bill Henry	14.00
265	Albert J. Barlick (umpire)	85.00
266	Mike Fornieles	14.00
267	George "Jim" Honochick (umpire)	60.00
268	Roy Lee Hawes	14.00
269	Joe Amalfitano	14.00
270	Chico Fernandez	15.00
271	Bob Hooper	14.00
272	John Flaherty (umpire)	16.00
273	Emory "Bubba" Church	14.00
274	Jim Delsing	14.00
275	William T. Grieve (umpire)	16.00
276	Ivan Delock	14.00
277	Ed Runge (umpire)	16.00
278	*Charles Neal*	19.00
279	Hank Soar (umpire)	16.00
280	Clyde McCullough	14.00
281	Charles Berry (umpire)	16.00
282	Phil Cavarretta	16.00
283	Nestor Chylak (umpire)	16.00
284	William A. Jackowski (umpire)	16.00
285	Walt Dropo	16.00
286	Frank E. Secory (umpire)	16.00
288	Dick Smith	14.00
289	Arthur J. Gore (umpire)	16.00
291	Frank Dascoli (umpire)	16.00
292	Marv Blaylock	16.00
293	Thomas D. Gorman (umpire)	17.00
294	Wally Moses	15.00
295	E. Lee Ballanfant (umpire)	16.00
296	*Bill Virdon*	30.00
297	L.R. "Dusty" Boggess (umpire)	16.00

158 Gil Hodges

298	Charlie Grimm	**16.00**
299	Lonnie Warneke (umpire)	**16.00**
300	Tommy Byrne	**17.00**
301	William R. Engeln (umpire)	**16.00**
302	*Frank Malzone*	**17.00**
303	J.B. "Jocko" Conlan (umpire)	**95.00**
304	Harry Chiti	**14.00**
305	Frank Umont (umpire)	**16.00**
306	Bob Cerv	**17.00**
307	R.A. "Babe" Pinelli (umpire)	**16.00**
308	Al Lopez	**40.00**
309	Hal H. Dixon (umpire)	**16.00**
310	Ken Lehman	**15.00**
311	Lawrence J. Goetz (umpire)	**16.00**
313	A.J. Donatelli (umpire)	**17.00**
314	Dale Mitchell	**14.00**
315	Cal Hubbard (umpire)	**85.00**
316	Marion Fricano	**14.00**
317	Wm. R. Summers (umpire)	**16.00**
318	Sid Hudson	**14.00**
319	Albert B. Schroll	**14.00**
320	*George D. Susce, Jr.*	**70.00**

10 Phil Rizzuto

1955 TOPPS

Topps' first cards with a horizontal or landscape format again make use of a combination of portraits and full-figure photos. Both images on the 2⅝- by 3¾-inch fronts are colorized, with a horizontal bottom strip for player identification, a team logo in the upper right, and a facsimile autograph below. Unfortunately, many of the 206 portraits (Topps' smallest run ever) are reruns from the company's 1954 set. The backs feature red, black, and green printing on a white background. Rookies include Roberto Clemente, Harmon Killebrew, and Sandy Koufax.

		NR MT
Complete set		$5900.00
Commons (1-150)		7.00
Commons (151-160)		15.00
Commons (161-210)		23.00

1	"Dusty" Rhodes	$50.00
2	Ted Williams	400.00
3	Art Fowler	7.00
4	Al Kaline	175.00
5	Jim Gilliam	12.00
6	Stan Hack	7.00
7	Jim Hegan	7.00
9	Bob Miller	7.00
10	Bob Keegan	7.00
11	Ferris Fain	7.00
12	"Jake" Thies	7.00
14	Jim Finigan	7.00
16	Roy Sievers	8.00
18	Russ Kemmerer	7.00
19	Billy Herman	12.00

20	Andy Carey	9.00
21	Alex Grammas	7.00
22	Bill Skowron	15.00
24	• Hal Newhouser	8.00
25	Johnny Podres	20.00
26	Dick Groat	9.00
27	Billy Gardner	7.00
28	Ernie Banks	185.00
29	Herman Wehmeier	7.00
30	Vic Power	7.00
31	Warren Spahn	65.00
32	Ed McGhee	7.00
33	Tom Qualters	7.00
34	Wayne Terwilliger	7.00
35	Dave Jolly	7.00
36	Leo Kiely	7.00
37	*Joe Cunningham*	8.00
38	Bob Turley	12.00
39	Bill Glynn	7.00
40	Don Hoak	7.00
42	"Windy" McCall	7.00
43	Harvey Haddix	9.00

164 Roberto Clemente

123 "Sandy" Koufax

44	"Corky" Valentine	7.00	111	Bob Milliken	7.00
45	Hank Sauer	7.00	113	Harry Brecheen	8.00
46	Ted Kazanski	7.00	120	Ted Kluszewski	25.00
47	Hank Aaron	360.00	123	"Sandy" Koufax	800.00
48	Bob Kennedy	7.00	124	Harmon Killebrew	310.00
49	J.W. Porter	7.00	125	Ken Boyer	55.00
50	Jackie Robinson	240.00	126	Dick Hall	7.00
51	Jim Hughes	7.00	127	Dale Long	7.00
53	Bill Taylor	7.00	139	Steve Kraly	7.00
54	Lou Limmer	7.00	140	Mel Parnell	8.00
55	"Rip" Repulski	7.00	146	Dick Donovan	7.00
57	Billy O'Dell	7.00	151	"Red" Kress	15.00
58	Jim Rivera	7.00	152	Harry Agganis	80.00
59	Gair Allie	7.00	153	"Bud" Podbielan	15.00
61	"Spook" Jacobs	7.00	154	Willie Miranda	15.00
63	Joe Collins	7.00	155	Ed Mathews	100.00
64	Gus Triandos	7.00	156	Joe Black	20.00
65	Ray Boone	7.00	157	Bob Miller	15.00
67	Wally Moon	7.00	158	Tom Carroll	15.00
70	Al Rosen	15.00	159	Johnny Schmitz	15.00
75	Sandy Amoros	14.00	160	Ray Narleski	15.00
80	Bob Grim	8.00	161	Chuck Tanner	22.00
81	Gene Conley	7.00	162	Joe Coleman	23.00
84	Camilo Pascual	8.00	163	Faye Throneberry	23.00
85	Don Mossi	8.00	164	Roberto Clemente	1150.00
88	Bob Skinner	8.00	165	Don Johnson	22.00
90	Karl Spooner	9.00	166	Hank Bauer	33.00
92	Don Zimmer	22.00	167	Tom Cassagrande	23.00
99	Frank Leja	9.00	168	Duane Pillette	23.00
100	Monte Irvin	25.00	169	Bob Oldis	23.00
108	"Rube" Walker	7.00	170	Jim Pearce	23.00
109	Ed Lopat	12.00	171	Dick Brodowski	23.00
110	Gus Zernial	8.00	172	Frank Baumholtz	23.00

173	Bob Kline	23.00
174	Rudy Minarcin	23.00
175	Not Issued	
176	Norm Zauchin	23.00
177	Jim Robertson	23.00
178	Bobby Adams	23.00
179	Jim Bolger	23.00
180	Clem Labine	26.00
181	Roy McMillan	23.00
182	Humberto Robinson	23.00
183	Tony Jacobs	23.00
184	Harry Perkowski	23.00
185	Don Ferrarese	23.00
186	Not Issued	
187	Gil Hodges	160.00
188	Charlie Silvera	23.00
189	Phil Rizzuto	150.00
190	Gene Woodling	26.00
191	Ed Stanky	26.00
192	Jim Delsing	23.00
193	Johnny Sain	35.00
194	Willie Mays	515.00
195	Ed Roebuck	23.00
196	Gale Wade	23.00
197	Al Smith	23.00
198	Yogi Berra	225.00
199	Bert Hamric	23.00
200	Jack Jensen	50.00
201	Sherm Lollar	24.00
202	Jim Owens	23.00
203	Not Issued	
204	Frank Smith	23.00
205	Gene Freese	23.00
206	Pete Daley	23.00
207	Bill Consolo	23.00
208	Ray Moore	23.00
209	Not Issued	
210	Duke Snider	490.00

1956 TOPPS

Topps continued to improve upon its double-photo format by superimposing a colorized portrait over an action shot. A facsimile autograph is displayed on these horizontal 2⅝- by 3¾-inch cards, which have red, green, and black print on backs that are either white or gray. Three new types of cards were introduced in this 340-card set: teams, checklists, and league presidents. Of these, checklists are the most difficult to find today, although when issued they were thought of as disposable, of no value, and not tradable. Card backs feature humorous illustrations showing highlights from the player's career.

		NR MT
Complete set (without checklists)		**$6700.00**
Commons (1-100)		**7.00**
Commons (101-180)		**10.00**
Commons (181-260)		**15.00**
Commons (261-340)		**10.00**
1	William Harridge	$135.00
5	Ted Williams	275.00
8	*Walter Alston*	30.00
10	Warren Spahn	60.00
14	Ken Boyer	13.00
15	Ernie Banks	75.00
20	Al Kaline	75.00
25	Ted Kluszewski	13.00
30	Jackie Robinson	155.00
31	Hank Aaron	210.00
33	Roberto Clemente	300.00
35	Al Rosen	12.00
61	Bill Skowron	10.00
63	*Roger Craig*	20.00
79	Sandy Koufax	290.00
101	Roy Campanella	110.00
102	Jim Davis	10.00
103	Willie Miranda	10.00

135 Mickey Mantle

105 Al Smith	10.00	**141** Joe Frazier	10.00
106 Joe Astroth	10.00	**142** Gene Baker	10.00
107 Ed Mathews	37.00	**143** Jim Piersall	12.00
109 Enos Slaughter	25.00	**145** Gil Hodges	45.00
110 Yogi Berra	130.00	**146** Senators Team	12.00
111 Red Sox Team	12.00	**147** Earl Torgeson	10.00
112 Dee Fondy	10.00	**148** Alvin Dark	12.00
113 Phil Rizzuto	50.00	**149** "Dixie" Howell	10.00
115 Jackie Jensen	12.00	**150** "Duke" Snider	125.00
116 Eddie O'Brien	10.00	**151** "Spook" Jacobs	10.00
117 Virgil Trucks	11.00	**152** Billy Hoeft	10.00
118 "Nellie" Fox	20.00	**153** Frank Thomas	10.00
119 *Larry Jackson*	11.00	**155** Harvey Kuenn	12.00
120 Richie Ashburn	30.00	**156** Wes Westrum	10.00
121 Pirates Team	12.00	**157** Dick Brodowski	10.00
122 Willard Nixon	10.00	**158** Wally Post	10.00
123 Roy McMillan	10.00	**159** Clint Courtney	10.00
124 Don Kaiser	10.00	**160** Billy Pierce	12.00
125 "Minnie" Minoso	15.00	**161** Joe DeMaestri	10.00
127 Willie Jones	10.00	**162** "Gus" Bell	11.00
128 Eddie Yost	10.00	**163** Gene Woodling	11.00
129 "Jake" Martin	10.00	**164** Harmon Killebrew	115.00
130 Willie Mays	255.00	**165** "Red" Schoendienst	25.00
131 Bob Roselli	10.00	**166** Dodgers Team	200.00
132 Bobby Avila	10.00	**167** Harry Dorish	10.00
133 Ray Narleski	10.00	**168** Sammy White	10.00
134 Cardinals Team	12.00	**170** Bill Virdon	12.00
135 Mickey Mantle	800.00	**171** Jim Wilson	10.00
136 Johnny Logan	10.00	**172** *Frank Torre*	11.00
137 Al Silvera	10.00	**173** Johnny Podres	15.00
138 Johnny Antonelli	10.00	**174** Glen Gorbous	10.00
140 *Herb Score*	22.00	**175** Del Crandall	11.00

33 Roberto Clemente

176	Alex Kellner	10.00	208	Elston Howard	32.00
177	Hank Bauer	15.00	209	Max Surkont	15.00
178	Joe Black	11.00	210	Mike Garcia	16.00
179	Harry Chiti	10.00	211	Murry Dickson	15.00
180	Robin Roberts	25.00	212	Johnny Temple	15.00
181	Billy Martin	85.00	213	Tigers Team	18.00
182	Paul Minner	15.00	214	Bob Rush	15.00
183	Stan Lopata	15.00	215	Tommy Byrne	15.00
184	Don Bessent	15.00	216	Jerry Schoonmaker	15.00
185	Bill Bruton	15.00	217	Billy Klaus	15.00
186	Ron Jackson	15.00	218	Joe Nuxall (Nuxhall)	17.00
187	Early Wynn	35.00	219	• Lew Burdette	18.00
188	White Sox Team	17.00	220	Del Ennis	15.00
189	Ned Garver	15.00	221	Bob Friend	15.00
190	Carl Furillo	20.00	222	Dave Philley	15.00
191	Frank Lary	15.00	223	Randy Jackson	15.00
192	"Smoky" Burgess	15.00	224	"Bud" Podbielan	15.00
193	Wilmer Mizell	15.00	225	Gil McDougald	20.00
194	Monte Irvin	30.00	226	Giants Team	65.00
195	George Kell	30.00	227	Russ Meyer	15.00
196	Tom Poholsky	15.00	228	"Mickey" Vernon	16.00
197	Granny Hamner	15.00	229	Harry Brecheen	16.00
198	Ed Fitzgerald (Fitz Gerald)	15.00	230	"Chico" Carrasquel	16.00
199	Hank Thompson	15.00	231	Bob Hale	15.00
200	Bob Feller	95.00	232	"Toby" Atwell	15.00
201	"Rip" Repulski	15.00	233	Carl Erskine	20.00
202	Jim Hearn	15.00	234	"Pete" Runnels	16.00
203	Bill Tuttle	15.00	235	Don Newcombe	18.00
204	Art Swanson	15.00	236	Athletics Team	16.00
205	"Whitey" Lockman	15.00	237	Jose Valdivielso	15.00
206	Erv Palica	15.00	238	Walt Dropo	16.00
207	Jim Small	15.00	239	Harry Simpson	15.00
			240	"Whitey" Ford	100.00

79 Sandy Koufax

241	Don Mueller	16.00	280	Jim Gilliam	11.00
242	Hershell Freeman	15.00	281	Art Houtteman	10.00
243	Sherm Lollar	16.00	282	Warren Hacker	10.00
244	Bob Buhl	15.00	283	Hal Smith	10.00
245	Billy Goodman	15.00	284	Ike Delock	10.00
246	Tom Gorman	15.00	285	Eddie Miksis	10.00
247	Bill Sarni	15.00	288	Bob Cerv	12.00
248	Bob Porterfield	15.00	289	Hal Jeffcoat	10.00
249	Johnny Klippstein	15.00	290	Curt Simmons	11.00
250	Larry Doby	18.00	291	Frank Kellert	10.00
251	Yankees Team	225.00	292	*Luis Aparicio*	130.00
252	Vernon Law	17.00	293	Stu Miller	10.00
253	Irv Noren	15.00	294	Ernie Johnson	10.00
254	George Crowe	15.00	295	Clem Labine	12.00
255	Bob Lemon	25.00	296	Andy Seminick	10.00
256	Tom Hurd	15.00	297	Bob Skinner	10.00
257	Bobby Thomson	16.00	298	Johnny Schmitz	10.00
258	Art Ditmar	15.00	299	Charley Neal	11.00
259	Sam Jones	15.00	300	Vic Wertz	10.00
260	"Pee Wee" Reese	90.00	301	Marv Grissom	10.00
261	Bobby Shantz	11.00	302	Eddie Robinson	10.00
262	Howie Pollet	10.00	304	Frank Malzone	12.00
265	Sandy Consuegra	10.00	305	Brooks Lawrence	10.00
266	Don Ferrarese	10.00	306	Curt Roberts	10.00
268	Dale Mitchell	10.00	307	Hoyt Wilhelm	35.00
270	Billy Loes	11.00	308	"Chuck" Harmon	10.00
272	Danny O'Connell	10.00	309	*Don Blasingame*	12.00
273	Walker Cooper	10.00	310	Steve Gromek	10.00
274	Frank Baumholtz	10.00	312	Andy Pafko	11.00
275	Jim Greengrass	10.00	313	Gene Stephens	10.00
276	George Zuverink	10.00	314	Hobie Landrith	10.00
278	Chet Nichols	10.00	315	Milt Bolling	10.00
279	Johnny Groth	10.00	316	Jerry Coleman	11.00

317	Al Aber	10.00	**326**	Connie Johnson	10.00
318	Fred Hatfield	10.00	**327**	Bob Wiesler	10.00
319	Jack Crimian	10.00	**328**	Preston Ward	10.00
320	Joe Adcock	12.00	**329**	Lou Berberet	10.00
321	Jim Konstanty	12.00	**330**	Jim Busby	10.00
322	Karl Olson	10.00	**332**	Don Larsen	25.00
323	Willard Schmidt	10.00	**340**	Mickey McDermott	35.00
324	"Rocky" Bridges	10.00	**—**	Checklist 1/3	

1957 TOPPS

The Topps set was modernized in a number of ways for 1957. The cards were scaled down to a vertical 2½ by 3½ inches, the standard for today's sets. This edition also saw the first appearance of actual color photos in place of the colorized photos used earlier. While card fronts maintain simple designs, the backs are more sophisticated: Instead of giving statistics for only the previous season, complete year-by-year statistics for each player are now included. Hot rookies in this edition include Don Drysdale, Tony Kubek, and Brooks Robinson. Advanced collectors may want to pursue the four valuable checklist series cards, scarce survivors from 1957.

NR MT

Complete set (without checklists) $7250.00
Commons (1-264) 5.00
Commons (265-352) 15.00
Commons (353-407) 6.00

95 Mickey Mantle

1	Ted Williams	$450.00
2	Yogi Berra	150.00
3	Dale Long	5.00
4	Johnny Logan	5.00
5	Sal Maglie	8.00
6	Hector Lopez	5.00
7	Luis Aparicio	25.00
8	Don Mossi	5.00
9	Johnny Temple	5.00
10	Willie Mays	250.00
11	George Zuverink	5.00
12	• Dick Groat	7.00
13	Wally Burnette	5.00
14	Bob Nieman	5.00
15	Robin Roberts	20.00
16	Walt Moryn	5.00
18	*Don Drysdale*	200.00

19 Bob Wilson 5.00
20 Hank Aaron
(photo reversed) 250.00
21 Frank Sullivan.................. 5.00
22 Jerry Snyder (photo is
Ed Fitz Gerald) 5.00
23 Sherm Lollar 5.00
24 *Bill Mazeroski* 40.00
25 Whitey Ford 45.00
26 Bob Boyd......................... 5.00
27 Ted Kazanski................... 5.00
28 Gene Conley 5.00
29 *Whitey Herzog*.............. 21.00
30 Pee Wee Reese 50.00
31 Ron Northey 5.00
33 Jim Small......................... 5.00
34 Tom Sturdivant 5.00
35 *Frank Robinson* 300.00
36 Bob Grim 5.00
37 Frank Torre...................... 5.00
38 • Nellie Fox 15.00
39 Al Worthington................. 5.00
40 Early Wynn 18.00
41 Hal Smith......................... 5.00
42 Dee Fondy....................... 5.00
43 Connie Johnson 5.00
44 Joe DeMaestri 5.00
45 Carl Furillo...................... 9.00

1 Ted Williams

46 Bob Miller 5.00
47 Don Blasingame 5.00
48 Bill Bruton 5.00
49 Daryl Spencer................. 5.00
50 Herb Score 6.00
51 Clint Courtney.................. 5.00
53 Clem Labine 6.00
54 Elmer Valo....................... 5.00
55 Ernie Banks 75.00
56 Dave Sisler 5.00
57 Jim Lemon....................... 5.00
58 Ruben Gomez 5.00
59 Dick Williams 6.00
60 Billy Hoeft 5.00
61 Dusty Rhodes.................. 5.00
62 Billy Martin 42.00
63 Ike Delock....................... 5.00
64 Pete Runnels................... 6.00
65 Wally Moon..................... 5.00
66 Brooks Lawrence............. 5.00
67 Chico Carrasquel 5.00
69 Roy McMillan 5.00
70 Richie Ashburn 15.00
71 Murry Dickson 5.00
72 Bill Tuttle........................ 5.00
73 George Crowe 5.00
74 Vito Valentinetti 5.00

328 Brooks Robinson

10 Willie Mays

75	Jim Piersall	6.00
76	Bob Clemente	200.00
77	Paul Foytack	5.00
78	Vic Wertz	6.00
79	*Lindy McDaniel*	6.00
80	Gil Hodges	50.00
81	Herm Wehmeier	5.00
82	Elston Howard	10.00
83	Lou Skizas	5.00
84	Moe Drabowsky	5.00
85	Larry Doby	8.00
86	Bill Sarni	5.00
88	Harvey Kuenn	6.00
89	Roy Sievers	5.00
90	Warren Spahn	70.00
91	Mack Burk	5.00
92	Mickey Vernon	6.00
93	Hal Jeffcoat	5.00
94	Bobby Del Greco	5.00
95	Mickey Mantle	700.00
96	*Hank Aguirre*	6.00
97	Yankees Team	30.00
98	Al Dark	7.00
99	Bob Keegan	5.00
100	League Presidents (Warren Giles, William Harridge)	7.00

102	Ray Boone	5.00
103	Joe Nuxhall	6.00
104	Hank Foiles	5.00
105	Johnny Antonelli	5.00
106	Ray Moore	5.00
107	Jim Rivera	5.00
108	Tommy Byrne	5.00
109	Hank Thompson	5.00
110	Bill Virdon	6.00
113	Wilmer Mizell	5.00
114	Braves Team	10.00
115	Jim Gilliam	8.00
116	Mike Fornieles	5.00
117	Joe Adcock	6.00
118	Bob Porterfield	5.00
119	Stan Lopata	5.00
120	Bob Lemon	16.00
121	*Cletis Boyer*	13.00
122	Ken Boyer	8.00
123	Steve Ridzik	5.00
124	Dave Philley	5.00
125	Al Kaline	65.00
126	Bob Wiesler	5.00
127	Bob Buhl	5.00
129	Saul Rogovin	5.00
130	Don Newcombe	10.00
131	Milt Bolling	5.00
132	Art Ditmar	5.00
133	Del Crandall	6.00
134	Don Kaiser	5.00
135	Bill Skowron	12.00
136	Jim Hegan	5.00
137	Bob Rush	5.00
138	• Minnie Minoso	8.00
139	Lou Kretlow	5.00
140	Frank Thomas	5.00
141	Al Aber	5.00
142	Charley Thompson	5.00
143	Andy Pafko	6.00
144	Ray Narleski	5.00
146	Don Ferrarese	5.00
147	Al Walker	5.00
148	Don Mueller	5.00
149	Bob Kennedy	5.00
150	Bob Friend	6.00
151	Willie Miranda	5.00
152	Jack Harshman	5.00
153	Karl Olson	5.00
154	Red Schoendienst	20.00

155	Jim Bronsnan	5.00
156	Gus Triandos	5.00
157	Wally Post	5.00
158	Curt Simmons	6.00
160	Billy Pierce	6.00
161	Pirates Team	8.00
162	Jack Meyer	5.00
164	Tommy Carroll	5.00
165	Ted Kluszewski	18.00
166	Roy Face	6.00
167	Vic Power	5.00
168	Frank Lary	6.00
169	Herb Plews	5.00
170	Duke Snider	90.00
171	Red Sox Team	9.00
172	Gene Woodling	6.00
173	Roger Craig	8.00
174	Willie Jones	5.00
175	Don Larsen	7.00
176	Gene Baker	5.00
177	Eddie Yost	5.00
178	Don Bessent	5.00

18 Don Drysdale

180	Gus Bell	5.00	267	Danny Kravitz	15.00
181	Dick Donovan	5.00	268	Jackie Collum	15.00
182	Hobie Landrith	5.00	269	Bob Cerv	15.00
183	Cubs Team	8.00	270	Senators Team	25.00
184	*Tito Francona*	6.00	271	Danny O'Connell	15.00
185	Johnny Kucks	6.00	272	Bobby Shantz	25.00
187	Virgil Trucks	5.00	273	Jim Davis	15.00
188	Felix Mantilla	5.00	274	Don Hoak	17.00
189	Willard Nixon	5.00	275	Indians Team	25.00
190	Randy Jackson	5.00	276	Jim Pyburn	15.00
191	Joe Margoneri	5.00	277	Johnny Podres	60.00
192	Jerry Coleman	6.00	278	Fred Hatfield	15.00
193	Del Rice	5.00	279	Bob Thurman	15.00
194	Hal Brown	5.00	280	Alex Kellner	15.00
195	Bobby Avila	5.00	281	Gail Harris	15.00
196	Larry Jackson	5.00	282	Jack Dittmer	15.00
200	Gil McDougald	12.00	283	*Wes Covington*	18.00
203	Hoyt Wilhelm	18.00	284	Don Zimmer	20.00
210	Roy Campanella	80.00	285	Ned Garver	15.00
212	*Rocco Colavito*	75.00	286	*Bobby Richardson*	90.00
215	Enos Slaughter	20.00	287	Sam Jones	15.00
230	George Kell	18.00	288	Ted Lepcio	15.00
240	Hank Bauer	10.00	289	Jim Bolger	15.00
250	Ed Mathews	25.00	290	Andy Carey	18.00
252	Carl Erskine	10.00	291	Windy McCall	15.00
265	Harvey Haddix	20.00	292	Billy Klaus	15.00
266	Ken Kuhn	15.00	293	Ted Abernathy	15.00

1957 Topps

312 Tony Kubek

294	Rocky Bridges	**15.00**
295	Joe Collins	**18.00**
296	Johnny Klippstein	**15.00**
297	Jack Crimian	**15.00**
298	Irv Noren	**15.00**
299	Chuck Harmon	**15.00**
300	Mike Garcia	**18.00**
301	Sam Esposito	**15.00**
302	Sandy Koufax	**380.00**
303	Billy Goodman	**15.00**
304	Joe Cunningham	**18.00**
305	Chico Fernandez	**15.00**
306	Darrell Johnson	**17.00**
307	Jack Phillips	**15.00**
308	Dick Hall	**15.00**
309	Jim Busby	**15.00**
310	Max Surkont	**15.00**
311	Al Pilarcik	**15.00**
312	*Tony Kubek*	**125.00**
313	Mel Parnell	**17.00**
314	Ed Bouchee	**15.00**
315	Lou Berberet	**15.00**
316	Billy O'Dell	**15.00**
317	Giants Team	**40.00**
318	Mickey McDermott	**15.00**
319	Gino Cimoli	**16.00**
320	Neil Chrisley	**15.00**

321	Red Murff	**15.00**
322	Redlegs Team	**40.00**
323	Wes Westrum	**16.00**
324	Dodgers Team	**90.00**
325	Frank Bolling	**15.00**
326	Pedro Ramos	**15.00**
327	Jim Pendleton	**15.00**
328	*Brooks Robinson*	**365.00**
329	White Sox Team	**25.00**
330	Jim Wilson	**15.00**
331	Ray Katt	**15.00**
332	Bob Bowman	**15.00**
333	Ernie Johnson	**15.00**
334	Jerry Schoonmaker	**15.00**
335	Granny Hamner	**15.00**
336	*Haywood Sullivian*	**16.00**
337	Rene Valdes	**15.00**
338	*Jim Bunning*	**105.00**
339	Bob Speake	**15.00**
340	Bill Wight	**15.00**
341	Don Gross	**15.00**
342	Gene Mauch	**20.00**
343	Taylor Phillips	**15.00**
344	Paul LaPalme	**15.00**
345	Paul Smith	**15.00**
346	Dick Littlefield	**15.00**
347	Hal Naragon	**15.00**
348	Jim Hearn	**15.00**
349	Nelson King	**15.00**
350	Eddie Miksis	**15.00**
351	Dave Hillman	**15.00**
352	Ellis Kinder	**15.00**
356	Faye Throneberry	**5.00**
360	Johnny Groth	**5.00**
365	Ozzier Virgil	**5.00**
376	Don Elston	**5.00**
383	*Juan Pizarro*	**5.00**
385	Art Houtteman	**5.00**
390	Reno Bertoia	**5.00**
391	*Ralph Terry*	**8.00**
400	Dodgers' Sluggers (Campanella, Furillo, Hodges, Snider)	**175.00**
407	Yankees' Power Hitters (Berra, Mantle)	**350.00**
—	Checklist Series 1/2	**175.00**
—	Checklist Series 2/3	**175.00**
—	Checklist Series 3/4	**500.00**
—	Checklist Series 4/5	**750.00**

1958 TOPPS

Topps stretched its 1958 set to 494 cards, providing a vivid contrast to the mild-mannered issue of the previous year. The 2½- by 3½-inch vertical cards for 1958 show portraits or posed-action photos set against plain but brightly colored backgrounds. Team cards include set checklists on the card backs. Interestingly, 33 cards (dispersed randomly between numbers 2 and 108) are famous as yellow-letter variations. Either the player name or the team name on the card front is printed in yellow. This is indicated in the following list with (YP) or (YT), respectively, following the name. The more common style, with ordinary white printing, is marked (WP) or (WT). One of the most popular subsets in the 1958 edition consists of the 20 cards of All-Star players selected by *Sport* magazine (shown below with AS following the name). An additional All-Star card shows the two 1957 World Series managers, Fred Haney and Casey Stengel.

		NR MT
Complete set		**$4500.00**
Commons (1-110)		**6.00**
Commons (111-440)		**3.00**
Commons (441-494)		**2.00**

150 Mickey Mantle

No.	Player	Price
1	Ted Williams	$400.00
2	Bob Lemon (YT)	35.00
2	Bob Lemon (WT)	15.00
3	Alex Kellner	6.00
4	Hank Foiles	6.00
5	Willie Mays	155.00
6	George Zuverink	6.00
7	Dale Long	6.00
8	Eddie Kasko (YP)	15.00
8	Eddie Kasko (WP)	6.00
9	Hank Bauer	10.00
10	Lou Burdette	8.00
11	Jim Rivera (YT)	15.00
11	Jim Rivera (WT)	6.00
12	George Crowe	6.00
13	Billy Hoeft (YP)	15.00
13	Billy Hoeft (WP)	6.00
14	Rip Repulski	6.00
15	Jim Lemon	6.00
16	Charlie Neal	6.00
17	Felix Mantilla	6.00
18	Frank Sullivan	6.00
19	Giants Team/Checklist 1-88	11.00
20	Gil McDougald (YP)	25.00
20	Gil McDougald (WP)	10.00
21	Curt Barclay	6.00
22	Hal Naragon	6.00
23	Bill Tuttle (YP)	15.00
23	Bill Tuttle (WP)	6.00
24	Hobie Landrith (YP)	15.00
24	Hobie Landrith (WP)	6.00
25	Don Drysdale	40.00

1958 Topps

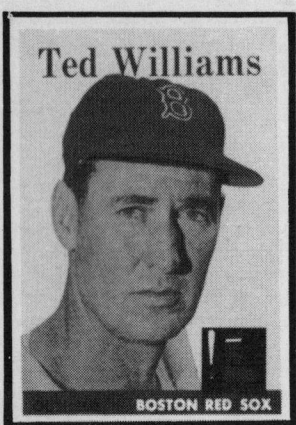

1 Ted Williams

27	Bud Freeman	6.00
28	Jim Busby	6.00
30	Hank Aaron (YP)	350.00
30	Hank Aaron (WP)	175.00
31	Tex Clevenger	6.00
32	J.W. Porter (YP)	15.00
32	J.W. Porter (WP)	6.00
33	Cal Neeman (YT)	15.00
33	Cal Neeman (WT)	6.00
34	Bob Thurman	6.00
35	Don Mossi (YT)	15.00
35	Don Mossi (WT)	6.00
36	Ted Kazanski	6.00
37	*Mike McCormick* (photo is Ray Monzant)	6.00
38	Dick Gernert	6.00
40	George Kell	12.00
41	Dave Hillman	6.00
42	*John Roseboro*	7.00
43	Sal Maglie	9.00
44	Senators Team/ Checklist 1-88	11.00
45	Dick Groat	7.00
46	Lou Sleater (WP)	6.00
47	*Roger Maris*	350.00
48	Chuck Harmon	6.00
49	Smoky Burgess	7.00
50	Billy Pierce (YT)	20.00
50	Billy Pierce (WT)	7.00
51	Del Rice	6.00
52	Bob Clemente (YT)	250.00
52	Bob Clemente (WT)	125.00
53	Morrie Martin (YP)	11.00
53	Morrie Martin (WP)	6.00
54	*Norm Siebern*	7.00
55	Chico Carrasquel	6.00
57	Tim Thompson (YP)	15.00
57	Tim Thompson (WP)	6.00
58	Art Schult (YT)	15.00
58	Art Schult (WT)	6.00
59	Dave Sisler	6.00
60	Del Ennis (YP)	15.00
60	Del Ennis (WP)	6.00
61	Darrell Johnson (YP)	15.00
61	Darrell Johnson (WP)	6.00
62	Joe DeMaestri	6.00
63	Joe Nuxhall	7.00
64	Joe Lonnett	6.00
65	Von McDaniel (YP)	15.00
65	Von McDaniel (WP)	6.00
66	Lee Walls	6.00
67	Joe Ginsberg	6.00
69	Wally Burnette	6.00
70	Al Kaline (WP)	75.00
70	Al Kaline (YP)	200.00
71	Dodgers Team/ Checklist 1-88	20.00
72	Bud Byerly	6.00
73	Pete Daley	6.00
74	• Roy Face	7.00
75	Gus Bell	6.00
76	Dick Farrell (YT)	15.00
76	Dick Farrell (WT)	6.00
77	Don Zimmer (YT)	15.00
77	Don Zimmer (WT)	6.00
78	Ernie Johnson (YP)	17.00
78	Ernie Johnson (WP)	6.00
79	Dick Williams (YT)	20.00
79	Dick Williams (WT)	7.00
80	Dick Drott	6.00
81	*Steve Boros* (YT)	17.00
81	*Steve Boros* (WT)	6.00
82	Ronnie Kline	6.00
83	Bob Hazle	6.00
84	Billy O'Dell	6.00
85	Luis Aparicio (YT)	50.00

85	Luis Aparicio (WT)	20.00
87	Johnny Kucks	7.00
88	Duke Snider	75.00
89	Billy Klaus	6.00
90	Robin Roberts	15.00
91	Chuck Tanner	7.00
02	Clint Courtney (YP)	15.00
92	Clint Courtney (WP)	6.00
93	Sandy Amoros	7.00
94	Bob Skinner	6.00
95	Frank Bolling	6.00
96	Joe Durham	6.00
97	Larry Jackson (YP)	15.00
97	Larry Jackson (WP)	6.00
98	Billy Hunter (YP)	15.00
98	Billy Hunter (WP)	6.00
99	Bobby Adams	6.00
100	Early Wynn (YT)	30.00
100	Early Wynn (WT)	15.00
101	Bobby Richardson (YP)	30.00
101	Bobby Richardson (WP)	10.00
102	George Strickland	6.00
103	Jerry Lynch	6.00
104	Jim Pendleton	6.00
105	Billy Gardner	6.00
106	Dick Schofield	6.00
107	Ossie Virgil	6.00
108	Jim Landis (YT)	15.00
108	Jim Landis (WT)	6.00
109	Herb Plews	6.00
110	Johnny Logan	6.00
112	Gus Zernial	3.00
113	Jerry Walker	3.00
114	Irv Noren	3.00
115	Jim Bunning	13.00
116	Dave Philley	3.00
117	Frank Torre	3.00
118	Harvey Haddix	3.00
119	Harry Chiti	3.00
120	Johnny Podres	5.00
121	Eddie Miksis	3.00
122	Walt Moryn	3.00
125	Al Dark	4.00
127	Tom Sturdivant	3.00
128	*Willie Kirkland*	3.00
129	Jim Derrington	3.00
130	Jackie Jensen	4.00
131	Bob Henrich	3.00
132	Vernon Law	4.00

47 Roger Maris

133	Russ Nixon	3.00
134	Phillies Team/ Checklist 89-176	10.00
135	Mike Drabowsky	3.00
137	Russ Kemmerer	3.00
138	Earl Torgeson	3.00
139	George Brunet	3.00
140	Wes Covington	3.50
142	Enos Slaughter	21.00
143	Billy Muffett	3.00
144	Bobby Morgan	3.00
145	Not Issued	
146	Dick Gray	3.00
147	*Don McMahon*	3.00
148	Billy Consolo	3.00
149	Tom Acker	3.00
150	Mickey Mantle	500.00
151	Buddy Pritchard	3.00
152	Johnny Antonelli	3.00
153	Les Moss	3.00
154	Harry Byrd	3.00
158	Indians Team/ Checklist 177-264	8.00
160	Don Hoak	3.00
161	Don Larsen	6.00
162	Gil Hodges	19.00
163	Jim Wilson	3.00

1958 Topps

343 Orlando Cepeda

164	Bob Taylor	3.00
165	Bob Nieman	3.00
166	Danny O'Connell	3.00
167	Frank Baumann	3.00
168	Joe Cunningham	4.00
169	Ralph Terry	4.00
170	Vic Wertz	3.50
171	Harry Anderson	3.00
172	Don Gross	3.00
173	Eddie Yost	3.00
174	A's Team/	
	Checklist 89-176	8.00
175	*Marv Throneberry*	9.00
176	Bob Buhl	3.00
177	Al Smith	3.00
178	Ted Kluszewski	5.00
179	Willy Miranda	3.00
180	Lindy McDaniel	3.00
181	Willie Jones	3.00
182	Joe Caffie	3.00
183	Dave Jolly	3.00
184	Elvin Tappe	3.00
185	Ray Boone	3.00
187	Sandy Koufax	135.00
188	Milt Bolling (photo	
	is Lou Berberet)	3.00
189	George Susce	3.00

190	Red Schoendienst	15.00
191	Art Ceccarelli	3.00
192	Milt Graff	3.00
193	*Jerry Lumpe*	5.00
194	Roger Craig	4.00
195	Whitey Lockman	3.00
196	Mike Garcia	3.00
197	Haywood Sullivan	3.00
198	Bill Virdon	3.50
199	Don Blasingame	3.00
200	Bob Keegan	3.00
201	Jim Bolger	3.00
202	*Woody Held*	3.00
203	Al Walker	3.00
204	Leo Kiely	3.00
205	Johnny Temple	3.00
206	Bob Shaw	3.00
207	Solly Hemus	3.00
208	Cal McLish	3.00
209	Bob Anderson	3.00
210	Wally Moon	3.00
211	Pete Burnside	3.00
212	Bubba Phillips	3.00
213	Red Wilson	3.00
214	Willard Schmidt	3.00
215	Jim Gilliam	5.00
216	Cardinals Team/	
	Checklist 177-264	7.00
217	Jack Harshman	3.00
218	Dick Rand	3.00
219	Camilo Pascual	3.25
220	Tom Brewer	3.00
221	Jerry Kindall	3.00
222	Bud Daley	3.00
223	Andy Pafko	3.50
224	Bob Grim	3.75
225	Billy Goodman	3.00
226	Bob Smith (photo is	
	Bobby Gene Smith)	3.00
227	Gene Stephens	3.00
228	Duke Maas	3.00
229	Frank Zupo	3.00
230	• Richie Ashburn	8.00
231	Lloyd Merritt	3.00
232	Reno Bertoia	3.00
233	Mickey Vernon	3.00
234	Carl Sawatski	3.00
235	Tom Gorman	3.00
236	Ed Fitz Gerald	3.00

237	Bill Wight	3.00
238	Bill Mazeroski	7.00
239	Chuck Stobbs	3.00
240	Moose Skowron	7.00
241	Dick Littlefield	3.00
242	Johnny Klippstein	3.00
243	Larry Raines	3.00
244	*Don Demeter*	3.00
245	*Frank Lary*	3.00
246	Yankees Team/ Checklist 177-264	30.00
247	Casey Wise	3.00
248	Herm Wehmeier	3.00
249	Ray Moore	3.00
250	Roy Sievers	3.00
251	Warren Hacker	3.00
252	Bob Trowbridge	3.00
253	Don Mueller	3.00
254	Alex Grammas	3.00
255	Bob Turley	6.00
256	White Sox Team/ Checklist 265-352	8.00

476 Stan Musial AS

257	Hal Smith	3.00
258	Carl Erskine	5.00
259	Al Pilarcik	3.00
260	Frank Malzone	3.00
261	Turk Lown	3.00
262	Johnny Groth	3.00
263	Eddie Bressoud	3.00
264	Jack Sanford	3.00
265	Pete Runnels	3.00
266	Connie Johnson	3.00
267	Sherm Lollar	3.00
268	Granny Hamner	3.00
269	Paul Smith	3.00
270	Warren Spahn	40.00
271	Billy Martin	10.00
272	Ray Crone	3.00
273	Hal Smith	3.00
274	Rocky Bridges	3.00
275	• Elston Howard	8.50
276	Bobby Avila	3.00
277	Virgil Trucks	3.00
278	Mack Burk	3.00
279	Bob Boyd	3.00
280	Jim Piersall	3.50
281	Sam Taylor	3.00
282	Paul Foytack	3.00
283	Ray Shearer	3.00

284	Ray Katt	3.00
285	Frank Robinson	65.00
286	Gino Cimoli	2.50
287	Sam Jones	2.50
288	Harmon Killebrew	55.00
296	*Ryne Duren*	10.00
304	• Tigers' Big Bats (Al Kaline, Harvey Kuenn)	8.00
307	Brooks Robinson	72.00
310	Ernie Banks	60.00
312	Red Sox Team/ Checklist 353-440	8.00
314	Dodgers' Boss and Power (Walt Alston, Duke Snider)	25.00
320	Whitey Ford	35.00
321	Sluggers' Supreme (Ted Kluszewski, Ted Williams)	20.00
324	Hoyt Wilhelm	15.00
340	Don Newcombe	7.00
343	*Orlando Cepeda*	62.00
351	Braves' Fence Busters (Hank Aaron, Joe Adcock, Del Crandall, Ed Mathews)	20.00
368	Rocky Colavito	10.00

370	Yogi Berra	80.00
375	Pee Wee Reese	50.00
377	Braves Team (numerical checklist)	60.00
386	Birdie's Young Sluggers (Ed Bailey, Frank Robinson, Birdie Tebbetts)	7.00
393	Tony Kubek	15.00
397	Tigers Team (numerical checklist)	60.00
400	• Nellie Fox	9.00
408	Orioles Team (numerical checklist)	60.00
417	Carl Furillo	6.00
418	World Series Batting Foes (Mickey Mantle, Hank Aaron)	100.00
420	*Vada Pinson*	20.00
428	Redlegs Team (numerical checklist)	50.00

436	Rival Fence Busters (Willie Mays, Duke Snider)	50.00
438	Whitey Herzog	4.00
440	Ed Mathews	30.00
450	Preston Ward	4.00
457	Milt Pappas	4.00
462	Gary Geiger	7.00
464	• *Curt Flood*	14.00
475	AS Managers (Fred Haney, Casey Stengel)	20.00
476	Stan Musial AS	33.00
479	Nellie Fox AS	8.00
480	Eddie Mathews AS	13.00
482	Ernie Banks AS	18.00
483	Luis Aparicio AS	11.00
484	Frank Robinson AS	17.00
485	Ted Williams AS	45.00
486	Willie Mays AS	35.00
487	Mickey Mantle AS	75.00
488	Hank Aaron AS	30.00
494	Warren Spahn AS	20.00

1959 TOPPS

Topps closed out the 1950s with a 572-card set, the largest of the decade, and added many specialty subsets to the regular player cards. Normal cards feature a nearly round color photo on a solid-color background outside the circle and a white outer border. A facsimile autograph appears across the photo. Card backs have year-by-year stats, a cartoon, and a short player biography. One specialty group is a ten-card subset highlighting events from the 1958 season. Other subsets include 31 Rookie Stars and 22 All-Star selections. Card number 550, titled Symbol of Courage, portrays Roy Campanella in his wheelchair following a near-fatal car accident.

	NR MT
Complete set	$4400.00
Commons (1-110)	4.00
Commons (111-506)	2.50
Commons (507-572)	10.00

1	Ford Frick	$60.00
2	Eddie Yost	5.00
3	Don McMahon	4.00

4	Albie Pearson	4.00
5	Dick Donovan	4.00
6	Alex Grammas	4.00
7	Al Pilarcik	4.00
8	Phillies Team/ Checklist 1-88	20.00
9	Paul Giel	4.00
10	Mickey Mantle	400.00
11	Billy Hunter	4.00
12	Vern Law	5.00

10 Mickey Mantle

514 Bob Gibson

1959 Topps

50 Willie Mays

63	Jim Hearn	4.00
64	Joe DeMaestri	4.00
65	Frank Torre	4.00
66	Joe Ginsberg	4.00
67	Brooks Lawrence	4.00
68	Dick Schofield	4.00
69	Giants Team/	
	Checklist 89-176	12.00
70	• Harvey Kuenn	5.00
71	Don Bessent	4.00
72	Bill Renna	4.00
73	Ron Jackson	4.00
74	Directing the Power	
	(Cookie Lavagetto,	
	Jim Lemon,	
	Roy Sievers)	4.50
75	Sam Jones	4.00
76	Bobby Richardson	15.00
77	John Goryl	4.00
78	Pedro Ramos	4.00
79	Harry Chiti	4.00
80	Minnie Minoso	5.00
81	Hal Jeffcoat	4.00
82	Bob Boyd	4.00
83	Bob Smith	4.00
84	Reno Bertoia	4.00
85	Harry Anderson	4.00

86	Bob Keegan	4.00
87	Danny O'Connell	4.00
88	Herb Score	4.50
89	Billy Gardner	4.00
90	Bill Skowron	9.00
91	Herb Moford	4.00
92	Dave Philley	4.00
93	Julio Becquer	4.00
94	White Sox Team/	
	Checklist 89-176	15.00
95	Carl Willey	4.00
96	Lou Berberet	4.00
97	Jerry Lynch	4.00
98	Arnie Portocarrero	4.00
99	Ted Kazanski	4.00
100	Bob Cerv	4.00
101	Alex Kellner	4.00
102	Felipe Alou	6.00
103	Billy Goodman	4.00
104	Del Rice	4.00
105	Lee Walls	4.00
106	Hal Woodeshick	4.00
107	Norm Larker	4.00
108	Zack Monroe	4.00
109	Bob Schmidt	4.00
110	George Witt	4.00
111	Redlegs Team/	
	Checklist 89-176	8.00

163 Sandy Koufax

115	Mickey Vernon	3.00
116	• Bob Allison	4.00
117	John Blanchard	3.00
118	John Buzhardt	2.50
119	John Callison	4.00
120	Chuck Coles	2.50
125	Ron Fairly	3.75
131	Deron Johnson	3.25
133	Bob Lillis	2.75
134	Jim McDaniel	2.50
135	Gene Oliver	2.50
136	Jim O'Toole	2.50
137	Dick Ricketts	2.50
138	John Romano	2.50
139	Ed Sadowski	2.50
140	Charlie Secrest	2.50
142	Dick Stigman	2.50
143	Willie Tasby	2.50
144	Jerry Walker	2.50
146	Jerry Zimmerman	2.50
147	Cubs' Clubbers (Ernie Banks, Dale Long, Walt Moryn)	9.00
148	Mike McCormick	2.50
149	• Jim Bunning	9.00
150	Stan Musial	130.00
151	Bob Malkmus	2.50
152	Johnny Klippstein	2.50

515 Harmon Killebrew

155	Enos Slaughter	15.00
156	• Ace Hurlers (Billy Pierce, Robin Roberts)	4.00
157	Felix Mantilla	2.50
158	Walt Dropo	2.50
159	Bob Shaw	2.50
160	Dick Groat	3.00
161	Frank Baumann	2.50
163	Sandy Koufax	130.00
164	Johnny Groth	2.50
165	Bill Bruton	2.50
166	• Destruction Crew (Rocky Colavito, Larry Doby, Minnie Minoso)	3.50
167	Duke Maas	3.00
169	Ted Abernathy	2.50
170	Gene Woodling	3.00
171	Willard Schmidt	2.50
172	A's Team/ Checklist 177-242	8.00
173	Bill Monbouquette	2.75
176	Preston Ward	2.50
177	Johnny Briggs	2.50
178	Ruben Amaro	2.50
179	Don Rudolph	2.50
180	Yogi Berra	63.00
181	Bob Porterfield	2.50

550 Roy Campanella

30 Nellie Fox

214	Marcelino Solis	2.50
216	Andre Rodgers	2.50
217	Carl Erskine	4.00
218	Roman Mejias	2.50
219	George Zuverink	2.50
220	Frank Malzone	2.50
221	Bob Bowman	2.50
222	Bobby Shantz	3.50
223	Cards Team/ Checklist 265-352	7.00
224	Claude Osteen	3.00
225	Johnny Logan	2.50
226	Art Ceccarelli	2.50
227	Hal Smith	2.50
228	Don Gross	2.50
229	Vic Power	2.50
230	Bill Fischer	2.50
231	Ellis Burton	2.50
232	Eddie Kasko	2.50
233	Paul Foytack	2.50
234	Chuck Tanner	3.00
237	• Run Preventers (Gil McDougald, Bobby Richardson, Bob Turley)	4.00
238	Gene Baker	2.50
239	Bob Trowbridge	2.50
240	Hank Bauer	7.50
241	Billy Muffett	2.50
243	Marv Grissom	2.50
244	Dick Gray	2.50
245	Ned Garver	2.50
246	J.W. Porter	2.50
247	Don Ferrarese	2.50
248	Red Sox Team/ Checklist 177-264	8.00
249	Bobby Adams	2.50
251	Cletis Boyer	4.50
252	Ray Boone	2.50
253	Seth Morehead	2.50
254	Zeke Bella	2.50
255	Del Ennis	2.75
256	Jerry Davie	2.50
257	Leon Wagner	3.00
259	Jim Pisoni	2.50
260	Early Wynn	15.00
261	Gene Stephens	2.50
262	• Hitters' Foes (Don Drysdale, Clem Labine, Johnny Podres)	8.00

183	Stu Miller	2.50
184	Harvey Haddix	2.75
185	Jim Busby	2.50
186	Mudcat Grant	2.50
187	Bubba Phillips	2.50
188	Juan Pizarro	2.50
190	Bill Virdon	3.00
191	Russ Kemmerer	2.50
192	Charley Beamon	2.50
194	Jim Brosnan	2.75
195	Rip Repulski	2.50
196	Billy Moran	2.50
197	Ray Semproch	2.50
198	Jim Davenport	2.50
199	Leo Kiely	2.50
200	• Warren Giles	2.75
202	Roger Maris	125.00
203	Ozzie Virgil	2.50
204	Casey Wise	2.50
205	Don Larsen	5.00
206	Carl Furillo	5.00
207	George Strickland	2.50
208	Willie Jones	2.50
211	Bob Blaylock	2.50
212	Fence Busters (Hank Aaron, Eddie Mathews)	50.00
213	Jim Rivera	2.50

263 Buddy Daley 2.50
264 Chico Carrasquel............. 2.50
267 John Romonosky............. 2.50
268 Tito Francona 2.50
269 Jack Meyer 2.50
270 Gil Hodges.................... 18.00
271 Orlando Pena 2.75
272 Jerry Lumpe 3.00
273 Joe Jay 2.50
274 Jerry Kindall.................... 2.50
275 Jack Sanford 2.50
277 Turk Lown 2.50
278 Chuck Essegian 2.50
279 Ernie Johnson 2.50
280 Frank Bolling 2.50
284 Steve Korcheck 2.50
285 Joe Cunningham 3.50
286 Dean Stone 2.50
287 Don Zimmer..................... 2.75
288 Dutch Dotterer 2.50
289 Johnny Kucks 2.75
290 Wes Covington 2.75
291 Pitching Partners (Camilo
      Pascual, Pedro Ramos) .. 2.75
292 Dick Williams 2.75
294 Hank Foiles 2.50
295 Billy Martin..................... 15.00
296 Ernie Broglio.................... 2.75
297 Jackie Brandt................... 2.50
298 Tex Clevenger 2.50
299 Billy Klaus........................ 2.50
300 Richie Ashburn 13.00
302 Don Mossi 2.50
303 Marty Keough 2.50
304 Cubs Team/
      Checklist 265-352............ 7.00
305 Curt Raydon 2.50
306 Jim Gilliam...................... 5.00
307 Curt Barclay..................... 2.50
308 Norm Siebern 3.00
309 Sal Maglie........................ 3.00
310 Luis Aparicio................. 15.00
311 Norm Zauchin.................. 2.50
312 Don Newcombe.............. 5.00
315 Joe Adcock...................... 3.00
316 Ralph Lumenti
      (with option statement) 2.50
316 Ralph Lumenti (w/o
      option statement).......... 80.00

360 Al Kaline

317 NL Hitting Kings (Richie
      Ashburn, Willie Mays).... 17.00
318 Rocky Bridges 2.50
320 Bob Skinner..................... 2.75
321 Bob Giallombardo
      (with option statement) 2.50
321 Bob Giallombardo (w/o
      option statement)........... 80.00
322 Harry Hanebrink (with
      trade statement) 2.50
322 Harry Hanebrink (w/o
      trade statement) 65.00
325 Ken Boyer........................ 5.00
326 Marv Throneberry............ 4.00
327 Gary Bell.......................... 2.75
329 Tigers Team/
      Checklist 353-429............ 8.00
336 Billy Loes (with trade
      statement) 2.50
336 Billy Loes (w/o trade
      statement) 65.00
338 *George Anderson*.......... 22.00
345 Gil McDougald................. 8.00
349 Hoyt Wilhelm 15.00
350 Ernie Banks................... 62.00
352 Robin Roberts 15.00
359 • *Bill White* 20.00

350 Ernie Banks

360	Al Kaline	50.00
362	Dolan Nichols (with option statement)	2.50
362	Dolan Nichols (w/o option statement)	80.00
380	Hank Aaron	100.00
383	Words of Wisdom (Don Larsen, Casey Stengel)	5.00
387	Don Drysdale	30.00
390	Orlando Cepeda	20.00
395	Elston Howard	7.00
397	Senators Team/ Checklist 430-495	7.00
408	• Keystone Combo (Luis Aparicio, Nellie Fox)	7.00
419	Braves Team/ Checklist 353-429	8.00
428	Buc Hill Aces (Roy Face, Bob Friend, Ron Kline, Vern Law)	3.50
430	Whitey Ford	30.00
435	Frank Robinson	40.00
439	Brooks Robinson	40.00
440	Lou Burdette	9.00
444	Ronnie Hansen	2.75
450	Ed Mathews	32.00
457	Dodgers Team/ Checklist 430-495	12.00

461	Mantle Hits 42nd Homer for Crown	30.00
462	Colavito's Great Catch Saves Game	3.00
463	Kaline Becomes Youngest Bat Champ	8.00
464	Mays' Catch Makes Series History	15.00
465	Sievers Sets Homer Mark	2.75
466	Pierce All-Star Starter	2.75
467	Aaron Clubs World Series Homer	12.00
468	Snider's Play Brings L.A. Victory	9.00
469	Hustler Banks Wins MVP Award	8.00
470	Musial Raps Out 3,000th Hit	12.00
476	Indians Team/ Checklist 496-572	7.00
478	Bob Clemente	95.00
480	Red Schoendienst	12.00
485	Ryne Duren	3.50
495	Johnny Podres	4.00
502	Al Dark	3.50
505	Tony Kubek	8.00
507	Bob Hale	10.00
508	Art Fowler	10.00
509	*Norm Cash*	30.00
510	Yankees Team/ Checklist 496-572	45.00
511	George Susce	10.00
512	George Altman	10.00
513	Tom Carroll	10.00
514	*Bob Gibson*	365.00
515	Harmon Killebrew	115.00
516	Mike Garcia	11.00
517	Joe Koppe	10.00
518	*Mike Cueller (Cuellar)*	15.00
519	Infield Power (Dick Gernert, Frank Malzone, Pete Runnels)	12.00
520	Don Elston	10.00
521	Gary Geiger	10.00
522	Gene Snyder	10.00
523	Harry Bright	10.00
524	Larry Osborne	10.00
525	Jim Coates	10.00

526	Bob Speake	10.00
527	Solly Hemus	10.00
528	Pirates Team/	
	Checklist 496-572	25.00
529	George Bamberger	11.00
530	Wally Moon	11.00
531	Ray Webster	10.00
532	Mark Freeman	10.00
533	Darrell Johnson	10.00
534	Faye Throneberry	10.00
535	Ruben Gomez	10.00
536	Dan Kravitz	10.00
537	Rudolfo Arias	10.00
538	Chick King	10.00
539	Gary Blaylock	10.00
540	Willy Miranda	10.00
541	Bob Thurman	10.00
542	*Jim Perry*	15.00
543	Corsair Outfield Trio	
	(Bob Clemente, Bob	
	Skinner, Bill Virdon)	35.00
544	Lee Tate	10.00
545	Tom Morgan	10.00
546	Al Schroll	10.00
547	Jim Baxes	10.00
548	Elmer Singleton	10.00
550	Roy Campanella	
	(Symbol of Courage)	125.00
551	Fred Haney AS	11.00
552	Casey Stengel AS	30.00
553	Orlando Cepeda AS	12.00
554	Bill Skowron AS	12.00
555	Bill Mazeroski AS	12.00
556	Nellie Fox AS	14.00
557	Ken Boyer AS	12.00
558	Frank Malzone AS	11.00
559	Ernie Banks AS	30.00
560	Luis Aparicio AS	20.00
561	Hank Aaron AS	125.00
562	Al Kaline AS	35.00
563	Willie Mays AS	125.00
564	Mickey Mantle AS	200.00
565	Wes Covington AS	11.00
566	Roy Sievers AS	11.00
567	Del Crandall AS	11.00
568	Gus Triandos AS	11.00
569	Bob Friend AS	11.00
570	Bob Turley AS	11.00
571	Warren Spahn AS	35.00
572	Billy Pierce AS	15.00

1960 TOPPS

In this 572-card set Topps revived the horizontal format used in 1955 and 1956. Color photos were used alongside smaller black-and-white photos on card fronts. The horizontal format and use of two photos, however, detract from the visual appeal of the cards. The backs, in contrast, are simpler than usual, with black-and-gold printing on gray or white cardboard. Card numbers 375-440 are slightly rarer in the white cardboard variety. For the first time, the 1960 set contained World Series highlight cards from the previous year. Hot cards include rookies Carl Yastrzemski, Willie McCovey, and Jim Kaat, along with superstars Bob Clemente, Mickey Mantle, and Roger Maris.

	NR MT
Complete set	**$3600.00**
Commons (1-286)	**1.50**
Commons (287-440)	**1.75**
Commons (441-506)	**3.50**
Commons (507-572)	**8.00**

1	Early Wynn	$35.00
2	Roman Mejias	2.00
3	Joe Adcock	2.25
5	Wally Moon	1.75
6	Lou Berberet	1.50
7	Master & Mentor (Willie	
	Mays, Bill Rigney)	9.00
9	Faye Throneberry	1.50

148 Carl Yastrzemski

10	Ernie Banks	35.00
11	Norm Siebern	1.75
12	Milt Pappas	1.75
13	Wally Post	1.50
14	Jim Grant	1.50
15	Pete Runnels	1.50
16	Ernie Broglio	1.50
17	Johnny Callison	1.75
18	Dodgers Team/ Checklist 1-88	10.00
19	Felix Mantilla	1.50
20	Roy Face	2.00
21	Dutch Dotterer	1.50
22	Rocky Bridges	1.50
25	Roy Sievers	3.50
26	Wayne Terwilliger	1.50
27	Dick Drott	1.50
28	Brooks Robinson	35.00
29	Clem Labine	1.75
30	Tito Francona	1.50
31	Sammy Esposito	1.50
32	Sophomore Stalwarts (Jim O'Toole, Vada Pinson)	3.50
33	Tom Morgan	2.25
34	George Anderson	2.50
35	Whitey Ford	20.00
36	Russ Nixon	1.50
37	Bill Bruton	1.75
38	Jerry Casale	1.50
40	Joe Cunningham	2.00
41	Barry Latman	1.50
42	Hobie Landrith	1.50
43	Senators Team/ Checklist 1-88	6.00
44	Bobby Locke	1.50
45	Roy McMillan	1.50
47	Don Zimmer	2.25
48	Hal Smith	1.50
50	Al Kaline	30.00
52	Dave Philley	1.50
53	Jackie Brandt	1.50
54	Mike Fornieles	1.50
55	• Bill Mazeroski	3.00
56	Steve Korcheck	1.50
57	Win Savers (Turk Lown, Gerry Staley)	1.75
58	Gino Cimoli	1.50
59	Juan Pizarro	1.50
60	Gus Triandos	1.50
61	Eddie Kasko	1.50
63	George Strickland	1.50
64	Jack Meyer	1.50
65	Elston Howard	6.00
67	Jose Pagan	1.75
70	Lou Burdette	3.25
71	Marty Keough	1.50
72	Tigers Team/ Checklist 89-176	8.00
73	Bob Gibson	40.00
74	Walt Moryn	1.50
75	Vic Power	1.50
77	Hank Foiles	1.50
78	Bob Grim	1.50
79	Walt Dropo	1.50

80	Johnny Antonelli	2.00	
82	Ruben Gomez	1.50	
83	Tony Kubek	4.50	
84	Hal Smith	1.50	
85	Frank Lary	1.75	
87	John Romonosky	1.50	
88	John Roseboro	1.75	
90	Bobby Avila	1.50	
91	Bennie Daniels	1.50	
92	• Whitey Herzog	3.25	
93	Art Schult	1.50	
94	Leo Kiely	1.50	
95	Frank Thomas	1.50	
96	Ralph Terry	2.50	
97	Ted Lepcio	1.50	
99	Lenny Green	1.50	
100	Nellie Fox	7.00	
101	Bob Miller	1.50	
109	Cletis Boyer	3.00	
111	Vic Wertz	1.75	
114	Ken Aspromonte	1.50	
115	Fork & Knuckler (Roy Face, Hoyt Wilhelm)	4.00	
119	*Chico Cardenas*	1.75	
125	Dick Ellsworth	1.75	
126	Chuck Estrada	1.75	
132	*Frank Howard*	10.00	
134	*Deron Johnson*	2.00	
136	*Jim Kaat*	25.00	
138	*Art Mahaffey*	1.75	
148	*Carl Yastrzemski*	350.00	
150	• Billy Pierce	2.25	

151	Giants Team/ Checklist 177-264	6.00	
153	Bobby Thomson	2.00	
159	Jim Piersall	2.00	
160	Rival All Stars (Ken Boyer, Mickey Mantle)	30.00	
164	Reds Team/ Checklist 89-176	7.00	
168	Alex Grammas	1.50	
169	Jake Striker	1.50	
170	Del Crandall	2.00	
171	Johnny Groth	1.50	
172	Willie Kirkland	1.50	
173	Billy Martin	8.00	
174	Indians Team/ Checklist 89-176	6.00	
176	Vada Pinson	3.25	
177	Johnny Kucks	1.50	
178	Woody Held	1.50	
181	Billy Loes	1.75	
183	Eli Grba	1.75	
188	Dick Williams	2.00	
190	Gene Woodling	1.75	
196	Andy Carey	2.00	
200	Willie Mays	105.00	
208	White Sox Team/ Checklist 177-264	6.00	
210	Harmon Killebrew	25.00	
212	Walt Alston	6.00	
213	Chuck Dressen	1.75	
216	Joe Gordon	1.75	
217	Charley Grimm	1.75	
219	Fred Hutchinson	1.75	

350 Mickey Mantle

316 Willie McCovey

221	Cookie Lavagetto	1.50
222	Al Lopez	5.00
223	Danny Murtaugh	1.75
224	Paul Richards	1.75
225	Bill Rigney	1.50
227	Casey Stengel	19.00
230	Mound Magicians (Bob Buhl. Lou Burdette. Warren Spahn)	6.00
235	Gus Bell	1.75
237	Elmer Valo	1.75
240	Luis Aparicio	10.00
241	Albie Pearson	1.50
242	Cards Team/ Checklist 265-352	6.00
245	Eddie Yost	1.75
247	Gil McDougald	4.50
249	*Earl Wilson*	1.75
250	Stan Musial	100.00
255	Jim Gilliam	3.25
258	Dick Groat	4.00
260	Power Plus (Rocky Colavito. Tito Francona)	3.00
262	Hank Bauer	2.00
264	Robin Roberts	13.00
270	Bob Turley	3.00
275	Curt Flood	3.00
279	Chuck Tanner	2.25
281	Ray Boone	1.75
282	Joe Nuxhall	1.75
283	John Blanchard	2.00
287	Felipe Alou	2.50
290	Jerry Lumpe	2.00
292	Dodger Backstops (Joe Pignatano. John Roseboro)	2.00
295	Gil Hodges	18.00
300	Hank Aaron	100.00
302	Phillies Team/ Checklist 353-429	7.00
305	Richie Ashburn	7.00
310	Frank Malzone	2.00
312	Charlie Lau	1.75
315	Bobby Shantz	3.00
316	*Willie McCovey*	150.00
320	Bob Allison	2.25
321	Ron Fairly	2.00
324	Jim Perry	2.50
326	Bob Clemente	80.00
330	Harvey Kuenn	2.75
332	Yankees Team/ Checklist 265-352	20.00
335	Red Schoendienst	10.00
340	Harvey Haddix	2.25
341	Carroll Hardy	1.75
343	Sandy Koufax	90.00
349	Moe Drabowsky	1.75
350	Mickey Mantle	325.00
351	Don Nottebart	1.75
352	Cincy Clouters (Gus Bell. Jerry Lynch. Frank Robinson)	5.00
353	Don Larsen	2.00
354	Bob Lillis	1.75

355	• Bill White	3.00
356	Joe Amalfitano	1.75
358	Joe DeMaestri	2.25
359	Buddy Gilbert	1.75
360	Herb Score	2.25
361	Bob Oldis	1.75
362	Russ Kemmerer	1.75
363	Gene Stephens	1.75
364	Paul Foytack	1.75
365	Minnie Minoso	3.00
366	*Dallas Green*	3.00
367	Bill Tuttle	1.75
368	Daryl Spencer	1.75
369	Billy Hoeft	1.75
370	Bill Skowron	6.00
371	Bud Byerly	1.75
373	Don Hoak	2.00
374	Bob Buhl	2.00
375	Dale Long	1.75
376	Johnny Briggs	1.75
377	Roger Maris	90.00
378	Stu Miller	1.75
379	Red Wilson	1.75
380	Bob Shaw	1.75
381	Braves Team/ Checklist 353-429	7.00
382	Ted Bowsfield	1.75
383	Leon Wagner	1.75
384	Don Cardwell	1.75
385	World Series Game 1 (Neal Steals Second)	3.50
386	World Series Game 2 (Neal Belts 2nd Homer)	3.50
387	World Series Game 3 (Furillo Breaks Up Game)	3.50
388	World Series Game 4 (Hodges' Winning Homer)	3.75
389	World Series Game 5 (Luis Swipes Base)	3.75
390	World Series Game 6 (Scrambling After Ball)	3.50
391	World Series Summary (The Champs Celebrate)	3.50
392	Tex Clevenger	1.75
393	Smoky Burgess	2.25
394	Norm Larker	1.75
395	Hoyt Wilhelm	15.00
396	Steve Bilko	1.75
397	Don Blasingame	1.75
398	Mike Cuellar	2.00
399	Young Hill Stars (Jack Fisher. Milt Pappas. Jerry Walker)	2.25
400	Rocky Colavito	5.00
401	Bob Duliba	1.75
402	Dick Stuart	2.00
403	Ed Sadowski	1.75
404	Bob Rush	1.75
405	Bobby Richardson	6.00
406	Billy Klaus	1.75
407	*Gary Peters* (color photo is J.C. Martin)	2.50
408	Carl Furillo	4.00
409	Ron Samford	1.75
410	Sam Jones	1.75

250 Stan Musial

300 Hank Aaron

411	Ed Bailey	1.75
412	Bob Anderson	1.75
413	A's Team/ Checklist 430-495	7.00
414	Don Williams	1.75
415	Bob Cerv	1.75
416	Humberto Robinson	1.75
417	Chuck Cottier	1.75
418	Don Mossi	1.75
419	George Crowe	1.75
420	Ed Mathews	30.00
421	Duke Maas	2.00
422	Johnny Powers	1.75
423	Ed Fitz Gerald	1.75
424	Pete Whisenant	1.75
425	Johnny Podres	1.75
426	Ron Jackson	1.75
427	Al Grunwald	1.75
428	Al Smith	1.75
429	• AL Kings (Nellie Fox, Harvey Kuenn)	2.25
430	Art Ditmar	1.75
431	Andre Rodgers	1.75
432	Chuck Stobbs	1.75
433	Irv Noren	1.75
434	Brooks Lawrence	1.75
435	Gene Freese	1.75
436	Marv Throneberry	2.00
437	Bob Friend	2.50
438	Jim Coker	1.75
439	Tom Brewer	1.75
440	Jim Lemon	1.75
442	Joe Pignatano	3.50
443	Charlie Maxwell	3.50
444	Jerry Kindall	3.50
445	Warren Spahn	30.00
446	Ellis Burton	3.50
447	Ray Moore	3.50
448	*Jim Gentile*	4.00
449	Jim Brosnan	3.75
450	• Orlando Cepeda	10.00
451	Curt Simmons	3.75
452	Ray Webster	3.50
453	Vern Law	4.00
454	Hal Woodeshick	3.50
455	Orioles Coaches (Harry Brecheen, Lum Harris, Eddie Robinson)	3.75
456	Red Sox Coaches (Del Baker, Billy Herman, Sal Maglie, Rudy York)	4.00
457	Cubs Coaches (Lou Klein, Charlie Root, Elvin Tappe)	3.75
458	White Sox Coaches (Ray Berres, Johnny Cooney, Tony Cuccinello, Don Gutteridge)	3.75
459	Reds Coaches (Cot Deal, Wally Moses, Reggie Otero)	3.75
460	Indians Coaches (Mel Harder, Red Kress, Bob Lemon, Jo-Jo White)	4.00

73 Bob Gibson

1960 Topps

565 Roger Maris AS

502	Jim Bunning	8.00
505	Ted Kluszewski	4.50
508	Billy Consolo	8.00
509	*Tommy Davis*	18.00
510	Jerry Staley	8.00
511	Ken Walters	8.00
512	Joe Gibbon	8.00
513	Cubs Team/ Checklist 496-572	22.00
514	*Steve Barber*	9.00
515	*Stan Lopata*	8.00
516	Marty Kutyna	8.00
518	*Tony Gonzalez*	8.50
519	Ed Roebuck	8.00
520	Don Buddin	8.00
521	Mike Lee	8.00
522	Ken Hunt	8.00
523	*Clay Dalrymple*	8.50
524	Bill Henry	8.00
525	Marv Breeding	8.00
526	Paul Giel	8.00
527	Jose Valdivielso	8.00
529	Norm Sherry	8.00
530	Mike McCormick	8.25
531	Sandy Amoros	8.00
532	Mike Garcia	8.75
533	Lu Clinton	8.00
534	Ken MacKenzie	8.00
535	Whitey Lockman	8.00
537	Red Sox Team/ Checklist 496-572	22.00
538	Frank Barnes	8.00
539	Gene Baker	8.00
540	Jerry Walker	8.00
541	Tony Curry	8.00
543	Elio Chacon	8.00
544	Bill Monbouquette	8.50
545	Carl Sawatski	8.00
546	Hank Aguirre	8.00
547	*Bob Aspromonte*	8.50
548	*Don Mincher*	9.00
549	John Buzhardt	8.00
550	Jim Landis	8.00
552	Walt Bond	8.00
553	Bill Skowron AS	16.00
554	Willie McCovey AS	50.00
555	Nellie Fox AS	20.00
556	Charlie Neal AS	14.00
557	Frank Malzone AS	14.00
558	Eddie Mathews AS	30.00
559	Luis Aparicio AS	23.00
560	Ernie Banks AS	40.00
561	Al Kaline AS	40.00
562	Joe Cunningham AS	14.00
563	Mickey Mantle AS	175.00
564	Willie Mays AS	90.00
565	Roger Maris AS	90.00
566	Hank Aaron AS	100.00
567	Sherm Lollar AS	14.00
568	Del Crandall AS	14.00
569	Camilo Pascual AS	9.00
570	Don Drysdale AS	30.00
571	Billy Pierce AS	14.00
572	Johnny Antonelli AS	20.00

1961 TOPPS

Topps returned to a vertical format in 1961 and issued a standard-sized edition of 589 cards. Two cards in the All-Star subset were never issued (numbers 587 and 588), but many of the released All-Star cards are currently among the most valuable in the set. On the whole, the set is simple, yet attractive. A large color photo is accented by a two-part horizontal rectangle below the photo for the player name, position, and team. Card backs again contain statistics by year and utilize black-and-green/gold printing on gray cardboard. The 1961 set features a unique 16-card subset honoring each MVP Award winner since 1951. Card numbers 523 through 589 are among the scarcest high numbers ever produced by Topps.

	NR MT
Complete set	$5300.00
Commons (1-370)	1.00
Commons (371-522)	1.50
Commons (523-589)	20.00

1	Dick Groat	$15.00
2	Roger Maris	200.00
5	Johnny Romano	1.00
6	Ed Roebuck	1.00
7	White Sox Team	2.50
8	Dick Williams	1.50
9	Bob Purkey	1.00

300 Mickey Mantle

589 Warren Spahn AS

10	Brooks Robinson	30.00
11	Curt Simmons	1.25
12	Moe Thacker	1.00
14	Don Mossi	1.25
15	Willie Kirkland	1.00
17	Checklist 1-88	5.00
19	Cletis Boyer	2.25
20	Robin Roberts	10.00
21	*Zorro Versalles (Zoilo)*	2.00
22	Clem Labine	1.25
23	Don Demeter	1.25
25	Red's Heavy Artillery (Gus Bell, Vada Pinson, Frank Robinson)	9.00

287 Carl Yastrzemski

28	Hector Lopez	1.25
29	Don Nottebart	1.00
30	Nellie Fox	6.00
32	Ray Sadecki	1.00
35	*Ron Santo*	32.00
40	Bob Turley	2.50
41	NL Batting Ldrs (Bob Clemente, Dick Groat, Norm Larker, Willie Mays)	4.00
42	AL Batting Ldrs (Minnie Minoso, Pete Runnels, Bill Skowron, Al Smith)	2.50
43	NL HR Ldrs (Hank Aaron, Ernie Banks, Ken Boyer, Eddie Mathews)	4.00
44	AL HR Ldrs (Rocky Colavito, Jim Lemon, Mickey Mantle, Roger Maris)	25.00
45	NL ERA Ldrs (Ernie Broglio, Don Drysdale, Bob Friend, Mike McCormick, Stan Williams)	3.25
46	AL ERA Ldrs (Frank Baumann, Hal Brown, Jim Bunning, Art Ditmar)	2.50
47	NL Pitching Ldrs (Ernie Broglio, Lou Burdette, Vern Law, Warren Spahn)	3.25
48	AL Pitching Ldrs (Bud Daley, Art Ditmar, Chuck Estrada, Frank Lary, Milt Pappas, Jim Perry)	2.50
49	NL SO Ldrs (Ernie Broglio, Don Drysdale, Sam Jones, Sandy Koufax)	4.00
50	AL SO Ldrs (Jim Bunning, Frank Lary, Pedro Ramos, Early Wynn)	3.00
51	Tigers Team	3.50
53	Russ Nixon	1.00
55	Jim Davenport	1.00
56	Russ Kemmerer	1.00
57	Marv Throneberry	2.00
58	Joe Schaffernoth	1.00
59	Jim Woods	1.00
60	Woodie Held	1.00
62	Al Pilarcik	1.00
63	Jim Kaat	9.00
65	Ted Kluszewski	4.00
68	Deron Johnson	1.50
69	Earl Wilson	1.00
70	Bill Virdon	2.00
71	Jerry Adair	1.00
74	Joe Pignatano	1.00
75	Lindy Shows Larry (Larry Jackson, Lindy McDaniel)	1.50
80	Harmon Killebrew	19.00
81	Tracy Stallard	1.00
82	Joe Christopher	1.00
86	Dodgers Team	3.50
88	Richie Ashburn	7.00
89	Billy Martin	7.00
90	Jerry Staley	1.00
91	Walt Moryn	1.00
92	Hal Naragon	1.00
93	Tony Gonzalez	1.00
94	Johnny Kucks	1.00
95	Norm Cash	3.50
98	Checklist 89-176 ("Checklist" in red on front)	7.00

98	Checklist 89-176 ("Checklist" in yellow, "98" in black on back)	5.00
98	Checklist 89-176 ("Checklist" in yellow, "98" in white on back)	7.00
100	Harvey Haddix	1.50
101	Bubba Phillips	1.00
102	Gene Stephens	1.00
103	Ruben Amaro	1.00
104	John Blanchard	1.25
106	Whitey Herzog	2.25
109	Johnny Podres	2.25
110	Vada Pinson	3.00
111	Jack Meyer	1.00
112	Chico Fernandez	1.00
114	Hobie Landrith	1.00
115	Johnny Antonelli	1.25
116	Joe DeMaestri	1.25
117	Dale Long	1.25
119	A's Big Armor (Hank Bauer, Jerry Lumpe, Norm Siebern)	1.50
120	Ed Mathews	20.00
122	Cubs Tea	2.50
124	J.C. Martin	1.00
125	Steve Barber	1.00
126	Dick Stuart	1.25
127	Ron Kline	1.00

150 Willie Mays

128	Rip Repulski	1.00
131	Paul Richards	1.25
132	Al Lopez	3.00
133	Ralph Houk	3.00
136	Walt Alston	4.00
141	*Billy Williams*	85.00
142	Luis Arroyo	1.50
147	Ed Rakow	1.00
149	Julian Javier	1.25
150	Willie Mays	105.00
159	Orioles Team	2.50
160	Whitey Ford	30.00
167	Giants Team	2.50
168	Tommy Davis	3.00
173	Beantown Bombers (Jackie Jensen, Frank Malzone, Vic Wertz)	2.00
180	Bobby Richardson	5.00
184	Steve Bilko	1.00
185	Herb Score	1.50
186	Elmer Valo	1.00
189	Checklist 177-264	5.00
200	Warren Spahn	25.00
205	Bill Pierce	1.75
207	Dodger Southpaws (Sandy Koufax, Johnny Podres)	15.00
211	Bob Gibson	32.00

417 Juan Marichal

415 Hank Aaron

213	*Bill Stafford*	2.00
215	Gus Bell	1.25
219	Gene Mauch	2.50
220	Al Dark	1.25
222	Jimmie Dykes	1.00
223	Bob Scheffing	1.00
224	Joe Gordon	1.25
225	Bill Rigney	1.00
226	Harry Lavagetto	1.00
227	Juan Pizzaro	1.00
228	Yankees Team	10.00
230	Don Hoak	1.25
232	• Bill White	1.50
238	Jim Gilliam	2.50
245	Joe Adcock	2.00
249	Reds Team	4.00
250	• Buc Hill Aces (Roy Face, Vern Law)	2.00
251	Bill Bruton	1.00
260	Don Drysdale	15.00
261	Charlie Lau	1.25
265	Tony Kubek	5.00
273	Checklist 265-352	5.00
275	Gene Woodling	1.25
280	Frank Howard	2.50
281	Frank Sullivan	1.00
282	Faye Throneberry	1.00
284	Dick Gernert	1.00

285	Sherm Lollar	1.25
287	Carl Yastrzemski	175.00
290	Stan Musial	80.00
295	Milt Pappas	1.25
297	Athletics Team	2.50
300	Mickey Mantle	300.00
306	World Series Game 1 (Virdon Saves Game)	3.50
307	World Series Game 2 (Mantle Slams 2 Homers)	20.00
308	World Series Game 3 (Richardson Is Hero)	4.00
309	World Series Game 4 (Cimoli Is Safe In Crucial Play)	3.00
310	World Series Game 5 (Face Saves the Day)	3.50
311	World Series Game 6 (Ford Pitches Second Shutout)	5.00
312	World Series Game 7 (Mazeroski's Homer Wins It!)	5.00
313	World Series Summary (The Winners Celebrate)	3.00
318	Danny O'Connell	1.00
319	Valmy Thomas	1.00
320	Lou Burdette	2.50
321	Marv Breeding	1.00
323	Sammy Esposito	1.00
324	Hank Aguirre	1.00
325	Wally Moon	1.25
327	*Matty Alou*	4.00
328	Jim O'Toole	1.00
329	Julio Becquer	1.00
330	Rocky Colavito	3.00
337	• Al's Aces (Al Lopez, Herb Score, Early Wynn)	4.00
340	Vic Wertz	1.25
344	Sandy Koufax	82.00
345	Jim Piersall	2.00
347	Cardinals Team	2.50
349	Danny McDevitt	1.25
350	Ernie Banks	30.00
355	Bob Allison	1.25
356	Ryne Duren	2.00
359	Dallas Green	1.25
360	Frank Robinson	30.00

361	Checklist 353-429 ("Topps Baseball" in black on front)	5.00
361	Checklist 353-429 ("Topps Baseball" in yellow on front)	6.00
365	Jerry Lumpe	1.25
369	Dave Philley	1.25
370	Roy Face	2.00
371	Bill Skowron	5.00
372	Bob Hendley	1.50
373	Red Sox Team	5.00
374	Paul Giel	1.50
375	Ken Boyer	5.00
376	Mike Roarke	1.50
377	Ruben Gomez	1.50
378	Wally Post	1.50
379	Bobby Shantz	2.50
380	• Minnie Minoso	3.00
381	Dave Wickersham	1.50
382	Frank Thomas	1.50
383	Frisco First Liners (Mike McCormick, Billy O'Dell, Jack Sanford)	2.00
384	Chuck Essegian	1.50
385	Jim Perry	2.50
386	Joe Hicks	1.50
387	Duke Maas	1.75

581 Frank Robinson AS

545 Hoyt Wilhelm

388	Bob Clemente	80.00
389	Ralph Terry	3.00
390	Del Crandall	2.25
391	Winston Brown	1.50
392	Reno Bertoia	1.50
393	Batter Bafflers (Don Cardwell, Glen Hobbie)	1.75
394	Ken Walters	1.50
395	Chuck Estrada	1.50
396	Bob Aspromonte	1.50
397	Hal Woodeshick	1.50
398	Hank Bauer	3.00
399	Cliff Cook	1.50
400	Vern Law	2.50
401	Babe Ruth Hits 60th Homer	15.00
402	Larsen Pitches Perfect Game	10.00
403	Brooklyn-Boston Play 26-Inning Tie	2.00
404	Hornsby Tops NL With .424 Average	3.50
405	Gehrig Benched After 2,130 Games	12.00
406	Mantle Blasts 565 Ft. HR	30.00
407	Jack Chesbro Wins 41st Game	2.50

141 Billy Williams

408	Mathewson Strikes Out 267 Batters	2.50
409	Johnson Hurls 3rd Shutout in 4 Days	3.50
410	Haddix Pitches 12 Perfect Innings	2.50
411	Tony Taylor	1.50
412	Larry Sherry	1.50
413	Eddie Yost	1.50
414	Dick Donovan	1.50
415	Hank Aaron	90.00
416	*Dick Howser*	7.00
417	*Juan Marichal*	115.00
418	Ed Bailey	1.50
419	Tom Borland	1.50
420	Ernie Broglio	1.50
421	Ty Cline	1.50
422	Bud Daley	1.50
423	Charlie Neal	1.50
424	Turk Lown	1.50
425	Yogi Berra	60.00
426	Not Issued	
427	Dick Ellsworth	1.50
428	Ray Barker	1.50
429	Al Kaline	40.00
430	Bill Mazeroski	10.00
431	Chuck Stobbs	1.50
432	Coot Veal	1.50
433	Art Mahaffey	1.50
434	Tom Brewer	1.50
435	Orlando Cepeda	8.00
436	*Jim Maloney*	2.50
437	Checklist 430-506	6.00
438	Curt Flood	2.50
439	*Phil Regan*	1.75
440	Luis Aparicio	12.00
441	Dick Bertell	1.50
442	Gordon Jones	1.50
443	Duke Snider	40.00
444	Joe Nuxhall	1.75
445	Frank Malzone	1.75
446	Bob "Hawk" Taylor	1.50
447	Harry Bright	1.50
448	Del Rice	1.50
449	*Bobby Bolin*	1.75
450	Jim Lemon	1.50
451	Power for Ernie (Ernie Broglio, Daryl Spencer, Bill White)	1.75
452	Bob Allen	1.50
453	Dick Schofield	1.50
454	Pumpsie Green	1.50
455	Early Wynn	15.00
456	Hal Bevan	1.50
457	Johnny James	1.50
458	Willie Tasby	1.50
459	Terry Fox	1.50
460	Gil Hodges	18.00
461	Smoky Burgess	2.50
462	Lou Klimchock	1.50
463	Braves Team (should be card 426)	4.00
463	Jack Fisher	1.75
464	*Leroy Thomas*	1.50
465	Roy McMillan	1.50
466	Ron Moeller	1.50
467	Indians Team	3.50
468	Johnny Callison	1.75
469	Ralph Lumenti	1.75
470	Roy Sievers	1.75
471	Phil Rizzuto MVP	12.00
472	Yogi Berra MVP	30.00
473	Bobby Shantz MVP	3.50
474	Al Rosen MVP	3.50
475	Mickey Mantle MVP	90.00
476	Jackie Jensen MVP	3.50

477 • Nellie Fox MVP 4.00
478 Roger Maris MVP 30.00
479 Jim Konstanty MVP 2.50
480 Roy Campanella MVP ... 25.00
481 Hank Sauer MVP............ 2.50
482 Willie Mays MVP 30.00
483 Don Newcombe MVP 3.50
484 Hank Aaron MVP............ 30.00
485 Ernie Banks MVP 20.00
486 Dick Groat MVP.............. 3.50
487 Gene Oliver 1.50
488 Joe McClain 1.50
489 Walt Dropo 1.75
490 Jim Bunning.................... 8.00
491 Phillies Team.................. 3.50
492 Ron Fairly 3.50
493 Don Zimmer.................... 2.00
494 Tom Cheney 1.50
495 Elston Howard 6.00
496 Ken MacKenzie 1.50
497 Willie Jones 1.50
498 Ray Herbert.................... 1.50
499 Chuck Schilling................ 1.50
500 Harvey Kuenn.................. 3.00
501 John DeMerit 1.50
502 Clarence Coleman........... 1.50
503 Tito Francona 1.50
504 Billy Consolo 1.75
505 Red Schoendienst 10.00
506 *Willie Davis*...................... 7.00
507 Pete Burnside.................. 1.50
508 Rocky Bridges 1.50
509 Camilo Carreon 1.50
510 Art Ditmar 2.00
511 Joe Morgan 1.50
512 Bob Will 1.50
513 Jim Brosnan 2.00
514 Jake Wood 1.50
515 Jackie Brandt.................. 1.50
516 Checklist 507-587........... 6.00
517 Willie McCovey.............. 60.00
518 Andy Carey..................... 1.50
519 Jim Pagliaroni................. 1.50
520 Joe Cunningham 1.75
521 Brother Battery
(Larry Sherry,
Norm Sherry).................. 2.00
522 Dick Farrell 1.50
523 Joe Gibbon 20.00

480 Roy Campanella

524 Johnny Logan................ 20.00
525 Ron Perranoski.............. 20.00
526 R.C. Stevens 20.00
527 Gene Leek 20.00
528 Pedro Ramos 20.00
529 Bob Roselli 20.00
530 Bobby Malkmus 20.00
531 Jim Coates 20.00
532 Bob Hale....................... 20.00
533 Jack Curtis 20.00
534 Eddie Kasko 20.00
535 Larry Jackson 20.00
536 Bill Tuttle.....................20.00
537 Bobby Locke.................. 20.00
538 Chuck Hiller 20.00
539 Johnny Klippstein 20.00
540 Jackie Jensen............... 30.00
541 Roland Sheldon 20.00
542 Twins Team................... 40.00
543 Roger Craig 35.00
544 George Thomas 20.00
545 Hoyt Wilhelm 60.00
546 Marty Kutyna 20.00
547 Leon Wagner................. 20.00
548 Ted Wills....................... 20.00
549 Hal R. Smith 20.00
550 Frank Baumann............. 20.00

551	George Altman	20.00	
552	Jim Archer	20.00	
553	Bill Fischer	20.00	
554	Pirates Team	35.00	
555	Sam Jones	20.00	
556	Ken R. Hunt	20.00	
557	Jose Valdivielso	20.00	
558	Don Ferrarese	20.00	
559	Jim Gentile	20.00	
560	Barry Latman	20.00	
561	Charley James	20.00	
562	Bill Monbouquette	20.00	
563	Bob Cerv	20.00	
564	Don Cardwell	20.00	
565	Felipe Alou	22.00	
566	Paul Richards AS	21.00	
567	Danny Murtaugh AS	20.00	
568	Bill Skowron AS	30.00	
569	Frank Herrera AS	18.00	

570	Nellie Fox AS	45.00
571	Bill Mazeroski AS	30.00
572	Brooks Robinson AS	85.00
573	Ken Boyer AS	30.00
574	Luis Aparicio AS	50.00
575	Ernie Banks AS	80.00
576	Roger Maris AS	100.00
577	Hank Aaron AS	135.00
578	Mickey Mantle AS	350.00
579	Willie Mays AS	135.00
580	Al Kaline AS	80.00
581	Frank Robinson AS	80.00
582	Earl Battey AS	20.00
583	Del Crandall AS	20.00
584	Jim Perry AS	25.00
585	Bob Friend AS	24.00
586	Whitey Ford AS	80.00
589	Warren Spahn AS	125.00

1962 TOPPS

Topps used a woodgrain border design in 1962 that resurfaced in 1987. At 598 cards, the 1962 set was larger than any previous edition. A ten-card subset highlighting the career of Babe Ruth is included, although the cards are surprisingly undervalued. One of the most notable features of the set is the first use of multiplayer photos for rookie cards, grouping four or five players together by position. Many challenges are posed for collectors of this set, with both a rare final series (cards 523-598) and several photo changes in later printings. All photo variations are found in cards 129-190.

	NR MT
Complete set	$4600.00
Commons (1-370)	1.50
Commons (371-522)	2.50
Commons (523-598)	12.00

1	Roger Maris	$250.00
2	Jim Brosnan	1.75
3	Pete Runnels	1.50
4	John DeMerit	2.00
5	Sandy Koufax	100.00
6	Marv Breeding	1.50

7	Frank Thomas	2.00
10	Bob Clemente	80.00
11	Tom Morgan	1.50
13	Dick Howser	1.75
14	•Bill White	2.00
17	Johnny Callison	1.75
18	Managers' Dream (Mickey Mantle, Willie Mays)	90.00
19	Ray Washburn	1.50
20	Rocky Colavito	3.00
21	Jim Kaat	4.00

22	Checklist 1-88 (numbers 33-88 on back)	6.00
22	Checklist 1-88 (numbers 121-176 on back)	5.00
24	Tigers Team	3.50
25	Ernie Banks	35.00
26	Chris Cannizzaro	2.00
28	Minnie Minoso	2.50
29	Casey Stengel	15.00
30	Ed Mathews	15.00
31	*Tom Tresh*	7.00
32	John Roseboro	1.75
33	Don Larsen	1.75
34	Johnny Temple	1.75
35	*Don Schwall*	1.75
36	Don Leppert	1.50
37	Tribe Hill Trio (Barry Latman. Jim Perry. Dick Stigman)	1.75
40	Orlando Cepeda	7.00
43	Dodgers Team	3.50
44	Don Taussig	1.50
45	Brooks Robinson	30.00
46	*Jack Baldschun*	1.50
47	Bob Will	1.50
48	Ralph Terry	2.50
50	Stan Musial	75.00
51	AL Batting Ldrs (Norm Cash. Elston Howard. Al Kaline. Jim Piersall)	3.00
52	NL Batting Ldrs (Ken Boyer. Bob Clemente. Wally Moon. Vada Pinson)	3.50
53	AL HR Ldrs (Jim Gentile. Harmon Killebrew. Mickey Mantle. Roger Maris)	20.00
54	NL HR Ldrs (Orlando Cepeda. Willie Mays. Frank Robinson)	3.50
55	AL ERA Ldrs (Dick Donovan. Don Mossi. Milt Pappas. Bill Stafford)	2.50
56	NL ERA Ldrs (Mike McCormick. Jim O'Toole. Curt Simmons. Warren Spahn)	3.00

200 Mickey Mantle

57	AL Win Ldrs (Steve Barber. Jim Bunning. Whitey Ford. Frank Lary)	3.00
58	NL Win Ldrs (Joe Jay. Jim O'Toole. Warren Spahn)	3.00
59	AL SO Ldrs (Jim Bunning. Whitey Ford. Camilo Pascual. Juan Pizarro)	3.00
60	NL SO Ldrs (Don Drysdale. Sandy Koufax. Jim O'Toole. Stan Williams)	3.50
61	Cardinals Team	2.50
63	*Tony Cloninger*	2.00
65	Bobby Richardson	6.00
66	Cuno Barragon (Barragan)	1.50
67	Harvey Haddix	1.75
70	Harmon Killebrew	15.00
72	Bob's Pupils (Steve Boros. Bob Scheffing. Jake Wood)	1.75
73	Nellie Fox	7.00
74	Bob Lillis	1.50
75	Milt Pappas	1.75

1 Roger Maris

78	Gene Green	1.50
79	Ed Hobaugh	1.50
80	• Vada Pinson	2.50
81	Jim Pagliaroni	1.50
84	Lenny Green	1.50
85	Gil Hodges	12.00
86	*Donn Clendenon*	1.75
87	Mike Roarke	1.50
88	Ralph Houk	2.50
89	Barney Schultz	1.50
90	Jim Piersall	2.00
93	John Blanchard	2.00
94	Jay Hook	2.00
95	Don Hoak	1.75
96	Eli Grba	1.50
97	Tito Francona	1.50
98	Checklist 89-176	4.00
99	*John Powell*	12.00
100	Warren Spahn	25.00
103	Don Blasingame	1.50
105	Don Mossi	1.50
108	Willie Davis	2.50
109	Bob Shaw	1.50
110	Bill Skowron	5.00
111	Dallas Green	1.75
112	Hank Foiles	1.50
113	White Sox Team	2.50

116	Herb Score	2.00
117	Gary Geiger	1.50
118	Julian Javier	1.75
121	Billy Hitchcock	1.50
123	Mike de la Hoz	1.50
125	Gene Woodling	1.75
126	Al Cicotte	1.50
127	Pride of the A's (Hank Bauer, Jerry Lumpe, Norm Siebern)	1.75
128	Art Fowler	1.50
129	Lee Walls (facing left)	8.00
129	Lee Walls (facing right)	1.50
130	Frank Bolling	1.50
131	*Pete Richert*	1.75
132	Angels Team (with inset photos)	10.00
132	Angels Team (w/o inset photos)	3.00
133	Felipe Alou	1.75
134	Billy Hoeft (green sky)	8.00
134	Billy Hoeft (blue sky)	1.50
135	Babe as a Boy	7.00
136	Babe Joins Yanks	7.00
137	Babe and Mgr. Huggins	7.00
138	The Famous Slugger	7.00
139	Hal Reniff (pitching)	35.00
139	Hal Reniff (portrait)	12.00
139	Babe Hits 60	7.00
140	Gehrig and Ruth	9.00
141	Twilight Years	7.00
142	Coaching for the Dodgers	7.00
143	Greatest Sports Hero	7.00
144	Farewell Speech	7.00
147	Bill Kunkel (pitching)	8.00
147	Bill Kunkel (portrait)	1.50
148	Wally Post	1.50
150	Al Kaline	25.00
151	Johnny Klippstein	1.50
152	Mickey Vernon	1.50
153	Pumpsie Green	1.50
157	Wes Covington	1.50
158	Braves Team	3.00
159	Hal Reniff	2.00
162	Sammy Drake	2.00
163	Hot Corner Guardians (Cletis Boyer, Billy Gardner)	3.00

167	*Tim McCarver*	20.00
168	Leo Posada	1.50
169	Bob Cerv	1.75
170	Ron Santo	7.00
171	Dave Sisler	1.50
173	Chico Fernandez	1.50
174	Carl Willey (with cap)	8.00
174	Carl Willey (w/o cap)	1.50
175	Frank Howard	3.00
176	Eddie Yost (batting)	8.00
176	Eddie Yost (portrait)	1.50
177	Bobby Shantz	1.75
180	Bob Allison	1.75
183	Roger Craig	3.00
184	Haywood Sullivan	1.50
185	Roland Sheldon	2.00
186	*Mack Jones*	1.50
190	Wally Moon (with cap)	9.00
190	Wally Moon (w/o cap)	1.75
192	Checklist 177-264	4.00
193	Eddie Kasko	1.50
194	*Dean Chance*	3.00
195	Joe Cunningham	1.50
199	*Gaylord Perry*	150.00
200	Mickey Mantle	450.00
208	Billy Martin	6.00
209	*Jim Fregosi*	5.00
213	Richie Ashburn	6.00
217	Walt Alston	4.00
218	*Joe Torre*	10.00
219	*Al Downing*	4.00
243	Robin Roberts	12.00
251	Yankees Team	8.00
288	Billy Williams	30.00
300	Willie Mays	150.00
310	Whitey Ford	25.00
312	Spahn Shows No-Hit Form	7.00
313	Maris Blasts 61st	17.00
315	Ford Tosses A Curve	6.00
316	Killebrew Sends One Into Orbit	5.00
317	Musial Plays 21st Season	15.00
318	The Switch-Hitter Connects (Mickey Mantle)	40.00
320	Hank Aaron	150.00
325	Luis Aparicio	15.00

425 Carl Yastrzemski

340	Don Drysdale	25.00
350	Frank Robinson	30.00
360	Yogi Berra	60.00
371	Earl Battey	2.75
372	Jack Curtis	2.50
373	Al Heist	2.50
374	Gene Mauch	2.75
375	Ron Fairly	3.00
376	Bud Daley	2.75
377	Johnny Orsino	2.50
378	Bennie Daniels	2.50
379	Chuck Essegian	2.50
380	• Lou Burdette	4.00
381	Chico Cardenas	2.50
382	Dick Williams	3.50
383	Ray Sadecki	2.50
384	Athletics Team	3.50
385	Early Wynn	17.00
386	Don Mincher	2.50
387	Lou Brock	185.00
388	Ryne Duren	2.75
389	Smoky Burgess	2.75
390	Orlando Cepeda AS	5.00
391	Bill Mazeroski AS	3.50
392	Ken Boyer AS	3.50
393	Roy McMillan AS	3.50
394	Hank Aaron AS	35.00

387 Lou Brock

395	Willie Mays AS	**30.00**
396	Frank Robinson AS	**18.00**
397	John Roseboro AS	**3.00**
398	Don Drysdale AS	**15.00**
399	Warren Spahn AS	**15.00**
400	Elston Howard	**7.00**
401	AL & NL Homer Kings (Orlando Cepeda, Roger Maris)	**20.00**
402	Gino Cimoli	**2.50**
403	Chet Nichols	**2.50**
404	Tim Harkness	**2.50**
405	Jim Perry	**3.00**
406	Bob Taylor	**2.50**
407	Hank Aguirre	**2.50**
408	Gus Bell	**3.00**
409	Pirates Team	**3.50**
410	Al Smith	**2.50**
411	Danny O'Connell	**2.50**
412	Charlie James	**2.50**
413	Matty Alou	**3.50**
414	Joe Gaines	**2.50**
415	Bill Virdon	**3.50**
416	Bob Scheffing	**2.50**
417	Joe Azcue	**2.50**
418	Andy Carey	**2.50**
419	Bob Bruce	**2.50**
420	Gus Triandos	**2.75**
421	Ken MacKenzie	**2.50**
422	Steve Bilko	**2.50**
423	Rival League Relief Aces (Roy Face, Hoyt Wilhelm)	**5.00**
424	Al McBean	**2.50**
425	Carl Yastrzemski	**200.00**
426	Bob Farley	**2.50**
427	Jake Wood	**2.50**
428	Joe Hicks	**2.50**
429	Bill O'Dell	**2.50**
430	Tony Kubek	**7.00**
431	*Bob Rodgers*	**3.00**
432	Jim Pendleton	**2.50**
433	Jim Archer	**2.50**
434	Clay Dalrymple	**2.50**
435	Larry Sherry	**2.50**
436	Felix Mantilla	**2.50**
437	Ray Moore	**2.50**
438	Dick Brown	**2.50**
439	Jerry Buchek	**2.50**
440	Joe Jay	**2.50**
441	Checklist 430-506	**5.00**
442	Wes Stock	**2.50**
444	Ted Wills	**2.50**
446	Don Elston	**2.50**
447	Willie Kirkland	**2.50**
448	Joe Gibbon	**2.50**
449	Jerry Adair	**2.50**
450	Jim O'Toole	**2.50**
451	*Jose Tartabull*	**2.75**
452	Earl Averill	**2.50**
453	Cal McLish	**2.50**
454	Floyd Robinson	**2.50**
455	Luis Arroyo	**2.75**
456	Joe Amalfitano	**2.50**
457	Lou Clinton	**2.50**
458	Bob Buhl ("M" on cap)	**2.50**
458	Bob Buhl (plain cap)	**50.00**
459	Ed Bailey	**2.50**
460	Jim Bunning	**9.00**
461	*Ken Hubbs*	**11.00**
462	Willie Tasby ("W" on cap)	**2.50**
462	Willie Tasby (plain cap)	**50.00**
463	Hank Bauer	**3.00**
464	*Al Jackson*	**3.50**
465	Reds Team	**4.00**
466	Norm Cash AS	**4.00**

467	Chuck Schilling AS	3.00
468	Brooks Robinson AS	18.00
469	Luis Aparicio AS	13.00
470	Al Kaline AS	15.00
471	Mickey Mantle AS	75.00
472	Rocky Colavito AS	8.00
473	Elston Howard AS	8.00
474	Frank Lary AS	5.00
475	Whitey Ford AS	14.00
476	Orioles Team	3.50
477	Andre Rodgers	2.50
478	Don Zimmer	3.50
479	*Joel Horlen*	2.75
480	Harvey Kuenn	3.50
481	Vic Wertz	2.75
482	Sam Mele	2.50
483	Don McMahon	2.50
484	Dick Schofield	2.50
485	Pedro Ramos	2.50
486	Jim Gilliam	4.00
487	Jerry Lynch	2.50
488	Hal Brown	2.50
489	Julio Gotay	2.50
490	Clete Boyer	3.75
491	Leon Wagner	2.50
492	Hal Smith	2.50
493	Danny McDevitt	2.50
494	Sammy White	2.50
495	Don Cardwell	2.50
496	Wayne Causey	2.50
497	Ed Bouchee	2.50
498	Jim Donohue	2.50
499	Zoilo Versalles	2.75
500	Duke Snider	40.00
501	Claude Osteen	2.75
502	Hector Lopez	2.50
503	Danny Murtaugh	2.75
504	Eddie Bressoud	2.50
505	Juan Marichal	30.00
506	Charlie Maxwell	2.50
507	Ernie Broglio	2.50
508	Gordy Coleman	2.50
509	*Dave Giusti*	2.75
510	Jim Lemon	2.50
511	Bubba Phillips	2.50
512	Mike Fornieles	2.50
513	Whitey Herzog	4.00
514	Sherm Lollar	2.75
515	Stan Williams	2.50

530 Bob Gibson

516	Checklist 507-598	8.00
517	Dave Wickersham	2.50
518	Lee Maye	2.50
519	Bob Johnson	2.50
520	Bob Friend	3.00
521	Jacke Davis	2.50
522	Lindy McDaniel	2.50
523	Russ Nixon	12.00
524	Howie Nunn	12.00
525	George Thomas	12.00
526	Hal Woodeshick	12.00
527	*Dick McAuliffe*	13.00
528	Turk Lown	12.00
529	John Schaive	12.00
530	Bob Gibson	180.00
531	Bobby G. Smith	12.00
532	Dick Stigman	12.00
533	Charley Lau	13.00
534	Tony Gonzalez	12.00
535	Ed Roebuck	12.00
536	Dick Gernert	12.00
537	Indians Team	14.00
538	Jack Sanford	12.00
539	Billy Moran	12.00
540	Jim Landis	12.00
541	Don Nottebart	12.00
542	Dave Philley	12.00

5 Sandy Koufax

543	Bob Allen	12.00
544	Willie McCovey	150.00
545	Hoyt Wilhelm	55.00
546	Moe Thacker	12.00
547	Don Ferrarese	12.00
548	Bobby Del Greco	12.00
549	Bill Rigney	12.00
550	Art Mahaffey	12.00
552	Cubs Team	14.00
553	Jim Coates	12.00
556	Al Spangler	12.00
557	Bob Anderson	12.00
559	Mike Higgins	12.00
560	Chuck Estrada	12.00
561	Gene Oliver	12.00
562	Bill Henry	12.00
563	Ken Aspromonte	12.00
564	Bob Grim	12.00
565	Jose Pagan	12.00
566	Marty Kutyna	12.00
568	Jim Golden	12.00
569	Ed Sadowski	12.00
570	Bill Stafford	12.00
571	Billy Klaus	12.00
572	Bob Miller	12.00
573	Johnny Logan	12.50
574	Dean Stone	12.00

575	Red Schoendienst	30.00
576	Russ Kemmerer	12.00
578	Jim Duffalo	12.00
579	Jim Schaffer	12.00
580	Bill Monbouquette	12.00
583	Larry Osborne	12.00
584	Twins Team	12.00
585	Glen Hobbie	12.00
586	Sammy Esposito	12.00
588	Birdie Tebbets	12.00
589	Bob Turley	18.00
590	Curt Flood	18.00
591	Rookie Parade Pitchers (Sam McDowell, Ron Mischwitz, Art Quirk, Dick Radatz, Ron Taylor)	45.00
592	Rookie Parade Pitchers (Bo Belinsky, Joe Bonikowski, Jim Bouton, Dan Pfister, Dave Stenhouse)	60.00
593	Rookie Parade Pitchers (Craig Anderson, Jack Hamilton, Jack Lamabe, Bob Moorhead, Bob Veale)	18.00
594	Rookie Parade Catchers (Doug Camilli, Doc Edwards, Don Pavletich, Ken Retzer, Bob Uecker)	110.00
595	Rookie Parade Infielders (Ed Charles, Marlin Coughtry, Bob Sadowski, Felix Torres)	18.00
596	Rookie Parade Infielders (Bernie Allen, Phil Linz, Joe Pepitone, Rich Rollins)	60.00
597	Rookie Parade Infielders (Rod Kanehl, Jim McKnight, Denis Menke, Amado Samuel)	18.00
598	Rookie Parade Outfielders (Howie Goss, Jim Hickman, Manny Jimenez, Al Luplow, Ed Olivares)	75.00

1963 FLEER

Nearly three decades after its quiet debut, the 1963 Fleer set is finally gaining recognition from the collecting world. In 1963, Fleer challenged Topps in the "confectionary" department by issuing its cards not with gum but with a cookie. Topps responded by hauling Fleer into court. No one knew whether or not the Philadelphia-based Fleer would have added to the 66-card issue in the absence of legal roadblocks. In any case, Fleer topped Topps by providing the first nationally distributed card of Maury Wills, the base-stealing star of the LA Dodgers. Wills, still upset that Topps had neglected him in his rookie days, seemed to enjoy sharing his fame with a rival company. Other stars in the set include Roberto Clemente, Bob Gibson, Sandy Koufax, Willie Mays, Brooks Robinson, Warren Spahn, and Carl Yastrzemski. However, the rarest cards in the set are for Joe Adcock, number 46, and an unnumbered checklist. The scarcity is supposedly due to short-printing of these two cards.

	NR MT
Complete set	**$965.00**
Commons	**4.00**

1	Steve Barber	$9.00
2	Ron Hansen	4.00
3	Milt Pappas	6.00
4	Brooks Robinson	40.00
5	Willie Mays	100.00

46 Joe Adcock

56 Roberto Clemente

6	Lou Clinton	4.00
7	Bill Monbouquette	4.00
8	Carl Yastrzemski	75.00
9	Ray Herbert	4.00
10	Jim Landis	4.00
11	Dick Donovan	4.00
12	Tito Francona	4.00
14	Frank Lary	4.00
15	Dick Howser	6.00

16	Jerry Lumpe	4.00		47	Roger Craig	7.00
17	Norm Siebern	4.00		49	Rod Kanehl	4.00
18	Don Lee	4.00		50	Ruben Amaro	4.00
19	Albie Pearson	5.00		51	John Callison	4.00
20	Bob Rodgers	4.00		52	Clay Dalrymple	4.00
21	Leon Wagner	4.00		53	Don Demeter	4.00
22	Jim Kaat	8.00		54	Art Mahaffey	4.00
23	Vic Power	6.00		55	"Smoky" Burgess	4.00
25	Bobby Richardson	9.00		56	Roberto Clemente	135.00
26	Ralph Terry	5.00		57	Elroy Face	6.00
29	Jimmy Piersall	5.00		58	Vernon Law	6.00
32	Ron Santo	8.00		59	Bill Mazeroski	8.00
34	Vada Pinson	8.00		60	Ken Boyer	8.00
40	Tommy Davis	5.00		61	Bob Gibson	40.00
41	Don Drysdale	35.00		62	Gene Oliver	4.00
42	Sandy Koufax	125.00		63	Bill White	8.00
43	*Maury Wills*	65.00		64	Orlando Cepeda	10.00
44	Frank Bolling	4.00		65	Jimmy Davenport	5.00
45	Warren Spahn	30.00		66	Billy O'Dell	7.00
46	Joe Adcock	125.00		—	Checklist 1-66	325.00

1963 TOPPS

This set of 576 cards is most remembered as the one in which Pete Rose made his premiere. His rookie card is far from glamorous: It is shared with three other players, and only their heads are shown, reduced to the size of postage stamps. Yet it is one of the most valuable cards of the decade. Aside from the rookie cards, the only specialty subsets in 1963 honor league leaders (the first 10 cards) and the 1962 World Series. The 1963 Topps set also features an ultrascarce series, from 447 to 506, which commands a premium.

	NR MT
Complete set	**$4400.00**
Commons 1-283	**.75**
Commons 284-446	**2.00**
Commons 447-506	**8.00**
Commons 507-576	**5.00**

1 NL Batting Ldrs (Hank Aaron, Tommy Davis, Stan Musial, Frank Robinson, Bill White) ... **$40.00**

2 AL Batting Ldrs (Chuck Hinton, Mickey Mantle, Floyd Robinson, Pete Runnels, Norm Siebern) .. 25.00

3 NL HR Ldrs (Hank Aaron, Ernie Banks, Orlando Cepeda, Willie Mays, Frank Robinson) 13.00

4 AL HR Ldrs (Norm Cash, Rocky Colavito, Jim Gentile, Harmon Killebrew, Roger Maris, Leon Wagner) 4.00

537 1963 Rookie Stars

200 Mickey Mantle

1963 Topps

553 1963 Rookie Stars

540 Bob Clemente

116 Jim Brosnan .... .90
118 Sherm Lollar .... .90
120 Roger Maris 50.00
121 Jim Hannan .... .75
123 Frank Howard 2.50
124 Dick Howser 1.50
125 Robin Roberts 6.00
126 Bob Uecker 30.00
128 Matty Alou .... .90
129 Gary Bell .... .75
130 Dick Groat 1.50
131 Senators Team 2.25
133 Gene Freese .... .75
134 Bob Scheffing .... .75
135 Richie Ashburn 5.00
136 Ike Delock .... .75
138 Pride of NL (Willie Mays,
     Stan Musial) 30.00
140 Frank Lary .... .90
141 *Manny Mota* 4.00
142 World Series Game 1
     (Yanks' Ford Wins
     Series Opener) 3.50
143 World Series Game 2
     (Sanford Flashes
     Shutout Magic) 2.25
144 World Series Game 3
     (Maris Sparks Yankee
     Rally) 5.00

390 Hank Aaron

145 World Series Game 4
     (Hiller Blasts Grand
     Slam) 2.25
146 World Series Game 5
     (Tresh's Homer Defeats
     Giants) 3.00
147 World Series Game 6
     (Pierce Stars In 3
     Hit Victory) 3.00
148 World Series Game 7
     (Yanks Celebrate As
     Terry Wins) 3.00
150 Johnny Podres 2.00
151 Pirates Team 2.25
154 Walt Alston 4.00
155 Bill Stafford 1.00
156 Roy McMillan .... .75
157 *Diego Segui* 1.00
158 1963 Rookie Stars
     (Rogelio Alvarez, *Tommy
     Harper,* Dave Roberts,
     Bob Saverine) 1.00
162 Twins Team 2.25
163 Don Larsen 1.00
165 Jim Kaat 5.00
166 Johnny Keane .... .75
167 Jim Fregosi 1.50

500 Harmon Killebrew

1963 Topps

120 Roger Maris

377 Orioles Team 3.50
378 Bill Henry 2.00
379 Bob Anderson 2.00
380 Ernie Banks 40.00
381 Frank Baumann 2.00
382 Ralph Houk 3.50
385 Art Mahaffey 2.00
386 1963 Rookie Stars
     (*John Bateman*, Larry
     Bearnarth, *Ed Kirkpatrick*,
     Garry Roggenburk) 2.25
387 Al McBean 2.00
388 Jim Davenport 2.00
389 Frank Sullivan 2.00
390 Hank Aaron 135.00
391 Bill Dailey 2.00
392 Tribe Thumpers
     (Tito Francona,
     Johnny Romano) 2.25
393 Ken MacKenzie 2.25
394 • Tim McCarver 4.00
395 Don MacMahon 2.00
396 Joe Koppe 2.00
397 Athletics Team 3.50
398 • Boog Powell 5.00
399 Dick Ellsworth 2.00
400 Frank Robinson 45.00
401 Jim Bouton 8.00
402 Mickey Vernon 2.25
403 Ron Perranoski 2.25
404 Bob Oldis 2.00
405 Floyd Robinson 2.00
406 Howie Koplitz 2.00
407 1976 Rookie Stars (Larry
     Elliot, Frank Kostro,
     Chico Ruiz, Dick
     Simpson) 2.00
408 Billy Gardner 2.00
409 Roy Face 2.50
410 Earl Battey 2.25
411 Jim Constable 2.00
412 Dodgers' Big Three (Don
     Drysdale, Sandy Koufax,
     Johnny Podres) 25.00
413 Jerry Walker 2.00
414 Ty Cline 2.00
415 Bob Gibson 30.00
416 Alex Grammas 2.00
417 Giants Team 3.50

360 Don Drysdale

420 Bobby Richardson 8.00
421 Tom Morgan 2.00
422 Fred Hutchinson 2.25
423 Ed Hobaugh 2.00
424 Charley Smith 2.00
425 Smoky Burgess 2.25
426 Barry Latman 2.00
427 Bernie Allen 2.00
428 Carl Boles 2.00
429 Lou Burdette 3.00
430 Norm Siebern 2.25
431 Checklist 430-506
     ("Checklist" in black
     on front) 7.00
432 Checklist 430-506
     ("Checklist" in white
     on front) 4.50
433 Denis Menke 2.25
434 Johnny Callison 2.50
435 Woody Held 2.00
436 Tim Harkness 2.00
437 Bill Bruton 2.00
438 Wes Stock 2.00
439 Don Zimmer 2.75
440 Juan Marichal 21.00
441 Lee Thomas 2.00
442 J.C. Hartman 2.00

126 Bob Uecker

515	Don Elston	5.00
517	Hal Woodeshick	5.00
518	Don Blasingame	5.00
519	Claude Raymond	5.00
520	Orlando Cepeda	20.00
521	Dan Pfister	5.00
523	Bill Kunkel	5.50
524	Cardinals Team	7.50
525	Nellie Fox	12.00
526	Dick Hall	5.00
527	Ed Sadowski	5.00
528	Carl Willey	5.00
529	Wes Covington	5.00
530	Don Mossi	5.00
531	Sam Mele	5.00
532	Steve Boros	5.00
533	Bobby Shantz	5.50
535	Jim Perry	5.50
536	Norm Larker	5.00
537	1963 Rookie Stars (Pedro Gonzalez, *Ken McMullen*, *Pete Rose*, *Al Weis*)	625.00
538	George Brunet	5.00
539	Wayne Causey	5.00
540	Bob Clemente	175.00
541	Ron Moeller	5.00
542	Lou Klimchock	5.00
543	Russ Snyder	5.00
544	1963 Rookie Stars (Duke Carmel, Bill Haas, Dick Phillips, *Rusty Staub*)	35.00
545	Jose Pagan	5.00
546	Hal Reniff	5.00
547	Gus Bell	5.50
548	Tom Satriano	5.00
549	1963 Rookie Stars (*Marcelino Lopez*, Pete Lovrich, Elmo Plaskett, Paul Ratliff)	5.50
550	Duke Snider	50.00
551	Billy Klaus	5.00
552	Tigers Team	5.50
553	1963 Rookie Stars (Brock Davis, Jim Gosger, John Herrnstein, *Willie Stargell*)	225.00

446 Whitey Ford

555	John Blanchard	5.50
556	Al Worthington	5.00
557	Cuno Barragan	5.00
558	1963 Rookie Stars (Bill Faul, *Ron Hunt*, Bob Lipski, Al Moran)	5.75
559	Danny Murtaugh	5.50
560	Ray Herbert	5.00
561	Mike de la Hoz	5.00
562	1963 Rookie Stars (Randy Cardinal, *Dave McNally*, Don Rowe, Ken Rowe)	14.00
563	Mike McCormick	5.50
564	George Banks	5.00
565	Larry Sherry	5.00
566	Cliff Cook	5.00
567	Jim Duffalo	5.00
568	Bob Sadowski	5.00
569	Luis Arroyo	5.00
570	Frank Bolling	5.00
571	Johnny Klippstein	5.00
572	Jack Spring	5.00
573	Coot Veal	5.00
574	Hal Kolstad	5.00
575	Don Cardwell	5.00
576	Johnny Temple	5.50

1964 TOPPS

A simple yet striking format highlights Topps' 1964 set of 587 cards. Close-up poses and a lack of clutter make the cards especially attractive. For the first time ever, Topps grouped rookies together by team, with two players per card. Richie Allen, Tommy John, Phil Niekro, and Lou Piniella are the most recognizable names found in the first-year cards, while Mickey Mantle and Pete Rose are the set's most valuable. One of the most unusual cards is an In Memoriam card for Chicago Cubs second baseman Ken Hubbs, who was killed in a plane crash.

	NR MT
Complete set	$2750.00
Commons (1-370)	.75
Commons (371-522)	1.00
Commons (523-587)	5.00

50 Mickey Mantle

1 NL ERA Ldrs (Dick Ellsworth, Bob Friend, Sandy Koufax) $10.00
2 AL ERA Ldrs (Camilo Pascual, Gary Peters, Juan Pizarro) 3.00
3 NL Pitching Ldrs (Sandy Koufax, Jim Maloney, Juan Marichal, Warren Spahn) 5.00
4 AL Pitching Ldrs (Jim Bouton, Whitey Ford, Camilo Pascual) 3.50
5 NL SO Ldrs (Don Drysdale, Sandy Koufax, Jim Maloney) 4.00
6 AL SO Ldrs (Jim Bunning, Camilo Pascual, Dick Stigman) 3.00
7 NL Batting Ldrs (Hank Aaron, Bob Clemente, Tommy Davis, Dick Groat) 5.00
8 AL Batting Ldrs (Al Kaline, Rich Rollins, Carl Yastrzemski) 5.00
9 NL HR Ldrs (Hank Aaron, Orlando Cepeda, Willie Mays, Willie McCovey) 5.00
10 AL HR Ldrs (Bob Allison, Harmon Killebrew, Dick Stuart)................................ 4.50
11 NL RBI Ldrs (Hank Aaron, Ken Boyer, Bill White) 4.00
12 AL RBI Ldrs (Al Kaline, Harmon Killebrew, Dick Stuart)............................... 4.00
13 Hoyt Wilhelm 8.00
14 Dodgers Rookies (Dick Nen, Nick Willhite).... .75
15 Zoilo Versalles................... .80
16 John Boozer .... .75
20 Bob Friend...................... 1.25

21	Yogi Berra	30.00
22	Jerry Adair	.75
23	Chris Zachary	.75
25	Bill Monbouquette	.75
26	Gino Cimoli	.75
27	Mets Team	3.50
28	Claude Osteen	1.00
29	Lou Brock	35.00
30	Ron Perranoski	.80
32	Dean Chance	1.25
33	Reds Rookies (Sammy Ellis, Mel Queen)	.80
34	Jim Perry	1.25
35	Ed Mathews	12.00
36	Hal Reniff	.75
37	Smoky Burgess	1.25
38	• *Jim Wynn*	2.00
39	Hank Aguirre	.75
40	Dick Groat	1.50
41	Friendly Foes (Willie McCovey, Leon Wagner)	3.00
42	Moe Drabowsky	.75
43	Roy Sievers	.90
44	Duke Carmel	.80
45	Milt Pappas	.90
46	Ed Brinkman	.80
47	Giants Rookies (*Jesus Alou*, Ron Herbel)	1.25
50	Mickey Mantle	210.00
54	Sam Mele	.75
55	Ernie Banks	20.00
58	Don Demeter	.75
59	Ernie Broglio	.75
60	Frank Malzone	.80
61	Angel Backstops (Bob Rodgers, Ed Sadowski)	.80
63	Johnny Orsino	.75
64	Ted Abernathy	.75
65	Felipe Alou	1.25
66	Eddie Fisher	.75
67	Tigers Team	3.50
68	Willie Davis	1.50
69	Clete Boyer	1.50
70	Joe Torre	2.50
72	Chico Cardenas	.75
73	*Jimmie Hall*	.80
76	Checklist 1-88	3.00
77	Jerry Walker	.75
79	Bob Heffner	.75

125 Pete Rose

80	Vada Pinson	2.50
81	All-Star Vets (Nellie Fox, Harmon Killebrew)	4.00
83	Gus Triandos	.75
85	Pete Ward	.80
86	Al Downing	1.50
87	Cardinals Team	4.00
88	John Roseboro	.80
89	Boog Powell	2.50
90	Earl Battey	.80
91	Bob Bailey	.80
92	Steve Ridzik	.75
93	Gary Geiger	.75
95	George Altman	.80
96	Bob Buhl	.80
97	Jim Fregosi	1.25
98	Bill Bruton	.80
100	Elston Howard	5.00
101	Walt Alston	3.00
102	Checklist 89-176	3.00
103	• Curt Flood	2.00
104	Art Mahaffey	.75
105	Woody Held	.75
106	Joe Nuxhall	.80
109	Rusty Staub	5.00
110	Albie Pearson	.75
111	Don Elston	.75

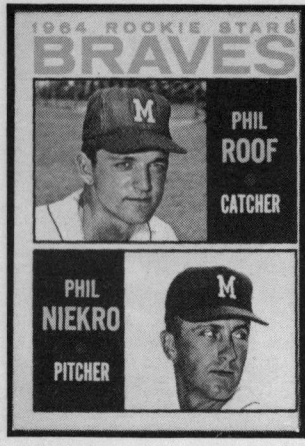

541 Braves Rookies

267	*Wilbur Wood*	1.50
274	Checklist 265-352	3.00
280	Juan Marichal	13.00
281	Yankees Rookies (Jake Gibbs, Tom Metcalf)	1.00
283	*Tommy McGraw*	.80
285	Robin Roberts	12.00
287	Red Sox Rookies (*Tony Conigliaro*, Bill Spanswick)	20.00
290	• Bob Allison	.90
293	Phillies Team	2.25
295	• Roger Craig	1.50
300	Hank Aaron	90.00
306	Giant Gunners (Orlando Cepeda, Willie Mays)	15.00
310	Jim Gilliam	3.00
318	Twins Team	2.25
320	Rocky Colavito	3.00
324	Casey Stengel	12.00
331	AL Bombers (Norm Cash, Al Kaline, Mickey Mantle, Roger Maris)	60.00
342	Willie Stargell	40.00
343	Senators Team	2.25
350	Willie McCovey	20.00
353	Wally Moon	.75
354	Dave Giusti	.75
355	Vic Power	.75
358	Ron Kline	.75
359	Jim Schaffer	.75
360	Joe Pepitone	.75
362	Checklist 353-429	3.00
363	Dick McAuliffe	.80
365	Cal McLish	.75
368	White Sox Rookies (Fritz Ackley, *Don Buford*)	.90
369	Jerry Zimmerman	.75
370	Hal Woodeshick	.75
371	Frank Howard	3.00
372	Howie Koplitz	1.00
373	Pirates Team	3.00
374	Bobby Bolin	1.00
375	Ron Santo	4.00
376	Dave Morehead	1.50
377	Bob Skinner	1.00
378	Braves Rookies (Jack Smith, *Woody Woodward*)	1.25

150 Willie Mays

379	Tony Gonzalez	1.00
380	Whitey Ford	25.00
381	Bob Taylor	1.00
382	Wes Stock	1.00
383	Bill Rigney	1.00
384	Ron Hansen	1.00
385	Curt Simmons	1.25
386	Lenny Green	1.00
387	Terry Fox	1.00
388	Athletics Rookies (John O'Donoghue, George Williams)	1.00
389	Jim Umbricht	1.00
390	Orlando Cepeda	6.00
391	Sam McDowell	1.25
392	Jim Pagliaroni	1.00
393	Casey Teaches (Ed Kranepool, Casey Stengel)	4.00
394	Bob Miller	1.00
395	Tom Tresh	3.00
396	Dennis Bennett	1.00
397	Chuck Cottier	1.00
398	Mets Rookies (Bill Haas, Dick Smith)	1.25
399	Jackie Brandt	1.00
400	Warren Spahn	25.00

300 Hank Aaron

401	Charlie Maxwell	1.00
402	Tom Sturdivant	1.00
403	Reds Team	3.50
404	Tony Martinez	1.00
405	Ken McBride	1.00
406	Al Spangler	1.00
407	Bill Freehan	3.00
408	Cubs Rookies (Fred Burdette, Jim Stewart)	1.00
409	Bill Fischer	1.00
410	Dick Stuart	1.25
411	Lee Walls	1.00
412	Ray Culp	1.00
413	Johnny Keane	1.00
414	Jack Sanford	1.00
415	Tony Kubek	5.00
416	Lee Maye	1.00
417	Don Cardwell	1.00
418	Orioles Rookies (*Darold Knowles*, Les Narum)	1.25
419	*Ken Harrelson*	4.00
420	Jim Maloney	1.25
421	Camilo Carreon	1.00
422	Jack Fisher	1.25
423	Topps in NL (Hank Aaron, Willie Mays)	80.00
424	Dick Bertell	1.00
425	Norm Cash	2.50
426	Bob Rodgers	1.25
428	Red Sox Rookies (Archie Skeen, Pete Smith)	1.00
429	Tim McCarver	3.00
430	Juan Pizarro	1.00
431	George Alusik	1.00
432	Reuben Amaro	1.00
433	Yankees Team	8.00
434	Don Nottebart	1.00
435	Vic Davalillo	1.00
436	Charlie Neal	1.00
437	Ed Bailey	1.00
438	Checklist 430-506	4.00
439	Harvey Haddix	1.25
440	Bob Clemente	80.00
441	Bob Duliba	1.00
442	Pumpsie Green	1.25
443	Chuck Dressen	1.25
444	Larry Jackson	1.00
445	Bill Skowron	2.50
446	Julian Javier	1.25
447	Ted Bowsfield	1.00
448	Cookie Rojas	1.25
449	Deron Johnson	1.00
450	Steve Barber	1.00
451	Joe Amalfitano	1.00
452	Giants Rookies (Gil Garrido, *Jim Hart*)	1.25
454	Tommie Aaron	1.25
455	Bernie Allen	1.00
456	Dodgers Rookies (*Wes Parker*, John Werhas)	4.00
457	Jesse Gonder	1.00
458	Ralph Terry	2.00
459	Red Sox Rookies (Pete Charton, Dalton Jones)	1.00
460	Bob Gibson	15.00
461	George Thomas	1.00
462	Birdie Tebbetts	1.00
464	Dallas Green	1.25
465	Mike Hershberger	1.00
466	Athletics Rookies (*Dick Green*, Aurelio Monteagudo)	1.25
467	Bob Aspromonte	1.00
468	Gaylord Perry	30.00
469	Cubs Rookies (Fred Norman, Sterling Slaughter)	1.00

470	Jim Bouton	3.00
471	*Gates Brown*	3.00
472	Vern Law	1.50
473	Orioles Team	3.00
474	Larry Sherry	1.00
475	Ed Charles	1.00
476	Braves Rookies (*Rico Carty,* Dick Kelley)	5.00
478	Dick Howser	2.00
479	Cardinals Rookies (Dave Bakenhaster, Johnny Lewis)	1.00
481	Chuck Schilling	1.00
482	Phillies Rookies (*Danny Cater,* John Briggs)	1.25
483	Fred Valentine	1.00
484	Bill Pleis	1.00
485	Tom Haller	1.25
486	Bob Kennedy	1.00
487	Mike McCormick	1.25
488	Yankees Rookies (Bob Meyer, Pete Mikkelsen)	1.50
489	Julio Navarro	1.00
490	Ron Fairly	1.50
491	Ed Rakow	1.00
492	Colts Rookies (Jim Beauchamp, Mike White)	1.00
493	Don Lee	1.00
494	Al Jackson	1.25
495	Bill Virdon	2.50
496	White Sox Team	3.00
497	Jeoff Long	1.00
498	Dave Stenhouse	1.00
499	Indians Rookies (Chico Salmon, Gordon Seyfried)	1.00
500	Camilo Pascual	1.25
501	Bob Veale	1.25
502	Angels Rookies (*Bobby Knoop,* Bob Lee)	1.25
503	Earl Wilson	1.00
504	Claude Raymond	1.00
505	Stan Williams	1.50
506	Bobby Bragan	1.00
507	John Edwards	1.00
508	Diego Segui	1.00
509	Pirates Rookies (*Gene Alley,* Orlando McFarlane)	1.25

543 Bob Uecker

510	Lindy McDaniel	1.00
511	Lou Jackson	1.00
512	Tigers Rookies (Willie Horton, Joe Sparma)	4.00
513	Don Larsen	1.25
514	Jim Hickman	1.25
515	Johnny Romano	1.00
516	Twins Rookies (Jerry Arrigo, Dwight Siebler)	1.00
517	Checklist 507-587	4.50
518	Carl Bouldin	1.00
522	Bobby Tiefenauer	1.00
523	Lou Burdette	7.00
524	Reds Rookies (Jim Dickson, Bobby Klaus)	5.00
527	Larry Bearnarth	5.00
528	Athletics Rookies (*Dave Duncan,* Tom Reynolds)	5.50
529	Al Dark	5.50
530	Leon Wagner	5.50
531	Dodgers Team	9.00
532	Twins Rookies (Bud Bloomfield, Joe Nossek)	5.00
533	Johnny Klippstein	5.00
534	Gus Bell	5.50
535	Phil Regan	5.00

331 AL Bombers

536	Mets Rookies (Larry Elliot, John Stephenson) ... 5.50	**561**	Phillies Rookies (Dave Bennett, *Rick Wise*) 6.00
537	Dan Osinski 5.00	**562**	Pedro Ramos 5.00
538	Minnie Minoso 7.00	**563**	Dal Maxvill 5.50
539	Roy Face 6.00	**564**	AL Rookies (Joe McCabe,
540	Luis Aparicio 16.00		Jerry McNertney) 5.00
541	Braves Rookies (*Phil Niekro*, Phil Roof) 150.00	**565**	Stu Miller 5.00
		566	Ed Kranepool.................. 6.00
542	Don Mincher 5.50	**567**	Jim Kaat 9.00
543	Bob Uecker 75.00	**568**	NL Rookies (Phil
544	Colts Rookies (Steve Hertz, Joe Hoerner) 5.00		Gagliano, Cap Peterson) ... 5.00
		569	Fred Newman 5.00
545	Max Alvis 5.50	**570**	Bill Mazeroski 8.00
546	Joe Christopher 5.25	**571**	Gene Conley 4.50
547	Gil Hodges....... .... 13.00	**572**	AL Rookies (Dick Egan,
548	NL Rookies (Wayne Schurr, Paul Speckenbach) 5.00		Dave Gray) 5.00
		573	Jim Duffalo 5.00
		574	Manny Jimenez 5.00
549	Joe Moeller...................... 5.00	**575**	Tony Cloninger 5.50
550	Ken Hubbs...................... 13.00	**576**	Mets Rookies (Jerry
551	Billy Hoeft 5.00		Hinsley, Bill Wakefield).... 5.50
552	Indians Rookies (Tom Kelley, *Sonny Siebert*)..... 5.50	**577**	Gordy Coleman 5.00
		578	Glen Hobbie 5.00
553	Jim Brewer 5.00	**579**	Red Sox Team 6.00
554	Hank Foiles 5.00	**580**	Johnny Podres 7.00
555	Lee Strange..................... 5.00	**581**	Yankees Rookies
556	Mets Rookies (Steve Dillon, Ron Locke) 5.50		(Pedro Gonzalez, Archie Moore) 6.00
		582	Rod Kanehl..................... 5.50
557	Leo Burke 5.00	**583**	Tito Francona 5.50
558	Don Schwall 5.00	**586**	Jim Piersall 7.00
559	Dick Phillips 5.00	**587**	Bennie Daniels 8.00

1965 TOPPS

Team logos returned to the front of the 1965 Topps set of 598 cards. Each 2½- by 3½-inch card also has a team pennant. Cartoons and year-by-year stats are the main elements of card backs. A number of first-class players have rookie cards in the 1965 set: The most valuable are for Steve Carlton, Jim Hunter, Joe Morgan, and Tony Perez. For the first time since 1957, no multiplayer feature cards are included except rookie and league-leader cards. An eight-card subset highlights the Cardinals World Series win over the Yankees. Noted baseball funnyman Bob Uecker (card number 519), a catcher who hit right-handed, tricked the photographer and posed as if a left-handed batter.

	NR MT
Complete set	**$3600.00**
Commons (1-198)	**.70**
Commons (199-446)	**.90**
Commons (447-552)	**1.25**
Commons (553-598)	**4.00**

350 Mickey Mantle

1 AL Batting Ldrs (Elston Howard, Tony Oliva, Brooks Robinson) $8.00
2 NL Batting Ldrs (Hank Aaron, Rico Carty, Bob Clemente.................. 5.00
3 AL HR Ldrs (Harmon Killebrew, Mickey Mantle, Boog Powell) 20.00
4 NL HR Ldrs (Johnny Callison, Orlando Cepeda, Jim Hart, Willie Mays, Billy Williams)........ 4.50
5 AL RBI Ldrs (Harmon Killebrew, Mickey Mantle, Brooks Robinson, Dick Stuart) .. 20.00
6 NL RBI Ldrs (Ken Boyer, Willie Mays, Ron Santo) .. 4.50
7 AL ERA Ldrs (Dean Chance, Joel Horlen)....... 2.50
8 NL ERA Ldrs (Don Drysdale, Sandy Koufax)... 4.50
9 AL Pitching Ldrs (Wally Bunker, Dean Chance, Gary Peters, Juan Pizarro, Dave Wickersham) 4.00
10 NL Pitching Ldrs (Larry Jackson, Juan Marichal, Ray Sadecki) 3.50
11 AL SO Ldrs (Dean Chance, Al Downing, Camilo Pascual) 2.50
12 NL SO Ldrs (Don Drysdale, Bob Gibson, Bob Veale)........................ 4.00
15 Robin Roberts 8.00
16 Houston Rookies (*Sonny Jackson, Joe Morgan*) 180.00
20 • Jim Bunning 4.00

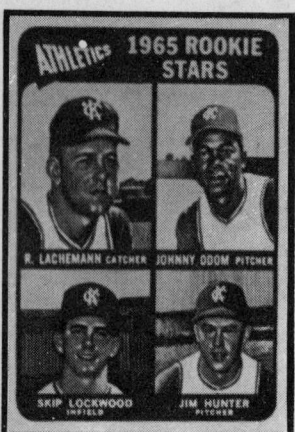

526 Athletics Rookies

206	Willie Horton	1.25
207	Pete Rose	150.00
208	• Tommy John	10.00
209	Pirates Team	2.50
210	Jim Fregosi	1.50
217	Walt Alston	3.50
218	Dick Schofield	.90
220	Billy Williams	11.00
224	Bob Chance	.90
225	Bob Belinsky	1.00
226	Yankees Rookies (Jake Gibbs, Elvio Jimenez)	1.25
227	Bobby Klaus	.90
230	Ray Sadecki	.90
231	Jerry Adair	.90
232	*Steve Blass*	1.00
233	Don Zimmer	1.50
234	White Sox Team	4.00
235	Chuck Hinton	.90
236	*Dennis McLain*	14.00
237	Bernie Allen	.90
239	Doc Edwards	1.00
242	George Brunet	.90
243	Reds Rookies (*Tommy Helms*, Ted Davidson)	1.00
244	Lindy McDaniel	.90
245	Joe Pepitone	3.00
247	Wally Moon	1.00
248	Gus Triandos	1.00
249	Dave McNally	1.25
250	Willie Mays	100.00
251	Billy Herman	2.00
252	Pete Richert	.90
253	Danny Cater	1.00
254	Roland Sheldon	1.25
255	Camilo Pascual	1.00
256	Tito Francona	1.00
257	• Jim Wynn	1.25
258	Larry Bearnarth	1.00
259	Tigers Rookies (*Jim Northrup*, Ray Oyler)	2.00
260	Don Drysdale	15.00
261	Duke Carmel	1.00
264	Bob Buhl	1.00
266	*Bert Campaneris*	4.00
267	Senators Team	2.50
268	Ken McBride	.90
269	Frank Bolling	.90
270	Milt Pappas	1.00

207 Pete Rose

273	Checklist 265-352	3.25
275	Dick Groat	1.75
276	Hoyt Wilhelm	10.00
277	Johnny Lewis	1.00
280	Dick Stuart	1.00
281	Bill Stafford	1.25
282	Giants Rookies (Dick Estelle, *Masanori Murakami*)	2.00
284	Nick Willhite	.90
285	Ron Hunt	1.00
286	Athletics Rookies (Jim Dickson, Aurelio Monteagudo)	.90
290	Wally Bunker	.90
291	Jerry Lynch	.90
292	Larry Yellen	.90
293	Angels Team	2.50
294	Tim McCarver	4.00
295	Dick Radatz	1.00
296	Tony Taylor	1.00
297	• Dave DeBusschere	3.50
298	Jim Stewart	.90
299	Jerry Zimmerman	.90
300	Sandy Koufax	100.00
301	Birdie Tebbetts	.90
302	Al Stanek	.90

16 Houston Rookies

303	Johnny Orsino	.90
304	Dave Stenhouse	.90
305	Rico Carty	1.50
306	Bubba Phillips	.90
308	Mets Rookies (Cleon Jones. Tom Parsons)	1.75
309	Steve Hamilton	1.25
310	Johnny Callison	1.50
312	Joe Nuxhall	1.25
314	Sterling Slaughter	.90
315	Frank Malzone	1.25
316	Reds Team	2.75
318	Matty Alou	1.00
319	Ken McMullen	.90
320	Bob Gibson	25.00
321	Rusty Staub	3.50
322	Rick Wise	1.00
323	Hank Bauer	1.00
325	Donn Clendenon	1.00
330	Whitey Ford	21.00
331	Dodgers Rookies (Al Ferrara. John Purdin)	1.00
335	Mickey Lolich	3.50
336	Woody Held	.90
337	Mike Cuellar	1.50
338	Phillies Team	2.50
339	Ryne Duren	1.00
340	• Tony Oliva	5.00
342	Bob Rodgers	1.00
343	Mike McCormick	1.00
344	Wes Parker	1.00
346	Bobby Bragan	1.00
347	Roy Face	1.50
350	Mickey Mantle	375.00
351	Jim Perry	1.25
352	Alex Johnson	1.00
353	Jerry Lumpe	1.00
355	Vada Pinson	2.50
358	Albie Pearson	.90
360	Orlando Cepeda	6.00
361	Checklist 353-429	3.25
363	Bob Johnson	.90
364	Galen Cisco	1.00
365	Jim Gentile	1.00
367	Leon Wagner	1.00
368	White Sox Rookies (Ken Berry. Joel Gibson)	1.00
369	Phil Linz	1.00
370	Tommy Davis	2.00
372	Clay Dalrymple	.90
373	Curt Simmons	1.00
374	Angels Rookies (Jose Cardenal. Dick Simpson)	1.00
377	Willie Stargell	25.00
379	Giants Team	2.50
380	Rocky Colavito	3.00
381	Al Jackson	1.00
383	Felipe Alou	1.00
384	Johnny Klippstein	.90
385	Carl Yastrzemski	90.00
387	Johnny Podres	2.00
388	John Blanchard	1.00
389	Don Larsen	1.25
390	Bill Freehan	1.50

477 Cardinals Rookies

300 Sandy Koufax

478	Wilbur Wood	1.25
479	Ken Harrelson	2.75
480	Joel Horlen	1.25
481	Indians Team	3.00
482	Bob Priddy	1.25
483	George Smith	1.25
484	Ron Perranoski	1.50
485	Nellie Fox	6.00
486	Angels Rookies (Tom Egan, Pat Rogan)	1.25
487	Woody Woodward	1.50
488	Ted Wills	1.25
489	Gene Mauch	1.50
490	Earl Battey	1.50
492	Gene Freese	1.25
493	Tigers Rookies (Bruce Brubaker, Bill Roman)	1.25
494	Jay Ritchie	1.25
495	Joe Christopher	1.25
496	Joe Cunningham	1.75
497	Giants Rookies (*Ken Henderson*, Jack Hiatt)	1.50
498	Gene Stephens	1.25
499	Stu Miller	1.25
500	Ed Mathews	30.00
501	Indians Rookies (Ralph Gagliano, Jim Rittwage)	1.25
503	Phil Gagliano	1.25
504	Jerry Grote	1.50
505	Ray Culp	1.25
506	Sam Mele	1.25
508	Checklist 507-598	4.00
509	Red Sox Rookies (Bob Guindon, Gerry Vezendy)	1.25
510	Ernie Banks	60.00
511	Ron Locke	1.50
512	Cap Peterson	1.50
513	Yankees Team	10.00
514	Joe Azcue	1.25
515	Vern Law	2.00
516	Al Weis	1.25
517	Angels Rookies (Paul Schaal, Jack Warner)	1.25
518	Ken Rowe	1.25
519	Bob Uecker	45.00
520	Tony Cloninger	1.50
523	Mike Brumley	4.00
524	Dave Giusti	4.00
525	Eddie Bressoud	4.00
526	Athletics Rookies (*Jim Hunter, Rene Lachemann, Skip Lockwood, Johnny Odom*)	160.00
527	Jeff Torborg	9.00
528	George Altman	4.00
529	Jerry Fosnow	4.00
530	Jim Maloney	4.50
531	Chuck Hiller	4.00
532	Hector Lopez	4.50
533	Mets Rookies (Jim Bethke, *Tug McGraw,* Dan Napolean, *Ron Swoboda*)	20.00
534	John Herrnstein	4.00
535	Jack Kralick	4.00
536	Andre Rodgers	4.00
537	Angels Rookies (Marcelino Lopez, *Rudy May,* Phil Roof)	5.00
538	Chuck Dressen	4.75
539	Herm Starrette	4.00
540	Lou Brock	50.00
541	White Sox Rookies (Greg Bollo, Bob Locker)	4.00
542	Lou Klimchock	4.00

545	Jesus Alou	4.75
546	Indians Rookies (Ray Barker, Bill Davis, Mike Hedlund, Floyd Weaver)	4.00
547	Jake Wood	4.00
548	Dick Stigman	4.00
549	Cubs Rookies (*Glenn Beckert,* Roberto Pena)	5.25
550	*Mel Stottlemyre*	15.00
551	Mets Team	12.00
552	Julio Gotay	4.00
553	Astros Rookies (Dan Coombs, Jack McClure, Gene Ratliff)	4.00
554	Chico Ruiz	4.00
555	Jack Baldschun	4.00
556	Red Schoendienst	11.00
557	Jose Santiago	4.00
558	Tommie Sisk	4.00
559	Ed Bailey	4.00
560	Boog Powell	9.00
561	•Dodgers Rookies (Dennis Daboll, *Mike Kekich, Jim Lefebvre,* Hector Valle)	8.00
562	Billy Moran	4.00
563	Julio Navarro	4.00
564	Mel Nelson	4.00
565	Ernie Broglio	4.00
566	Yankees Rookies (Gil Blanco, Art Lopez, Ross Moschitto)	5.00
567	Tommie Aaron	4.50
568	Ron Taylor	4.00
569	Gino Cimoli	4.00
570	Claude Osteen	4.50
571	Ossie Virgil	4.00
572	Orioles Team	6.00
573	Red Sox Rookies (*Jim Lonborg,* Gerry Moses, Mike Ryan, Bill Schlesinger)	10.00
574	Roy Sievers	4.50
575	Jose Pagan	4.00
576	Terry Fox	4.00
577	AL Rookies (Jim Buschhorn, Darold Knowles, Richie Scheinblum)	4.00

581 NL Rookies

578	Camilo Carreon	4.00
579	Dick Smith	4.00
580	Jimmie Hall	4.00
581	NL Rookies (Kevin Collins, *Tony Perez,* Dave Ricketts)	80.00
582	Bob Schmidt	4.00
583	Wes Covington	4.00
584	Harry Bright	4.00
585	Hank Fischer	4.00
586	Tommy McGraw	4.00
587	Joe Sparma	4.00
588	Lenny Green	4.00
589	Giants Rookies (Frank Linzy, Bob Schroeder)	4.00
590	Johnnie Wyatt	4.00
591	Bob Skinner	4.25
592	Frank Bork	4.00
593	Tigers Rookies (Jackie Moore, John Sullivan)	4.00
594	Joe Gaines	4.00
595	Don Lee	4.00
596	Don Landrum	4.00
597	Twins Rookies (Joe Nossek, Dick Reese, John Sevcik)	4.50
598	Al Downing	10.00

1966 TOPPS

Multiplayer cards reappeared in 1966, but no surprises were unveiled in this 598-card set. Well-known rookies who made their debuts in the 1966 Topps offering include Ferguson Jenkins, Bobby Murcer, Jim Palmer, George "Boomer" Scott, and Don Sutton. The set features two series that are tough to locate today: Cards numbering 447 to 522 are somewhat hard to find, while the high numbers from 523 through 598 constitute one of the scarcest series of the 1960s. Short supply and his election to the Hall of Fame explain the $335 value placed on Gaylord Perry's card, number 598.

		NR MT
Complete set		$4600.00
Commons (1-110)		.60
Commons (111-446)		.70
Commons (447-522)		4.50
Commons (523-598)		16.00

1	Willie Mays	$190.00
24	Don Kessinger	1.50
28	Phil Niekro	12.00
30	Pete Rose	60.00
36	Jim Hunter	25.00
50	Mickey Mantle	185.00

598 Gaylord Perry

62	Merritt Ranew (with sold statement)	.60
62	Merritt Ranew (w/o sold statement)	15.00
70	Carl Yastrzemski	60.00
72	Tony Perez	18.00
76	Red Schoendienst	3.00
90	Luis Aparicio	9.00
91	Bob Uecker (with trade statement)	15.00
91	Bob Uecker (w/o trade statement)	80.00
92	Yankees Team	4.00
99	Buc Belters (Donn Clendenon, Willie Stargell)	3.50
100	Sandy Koufax	100.00
101	Checklist 89-176 (115 is Spahn)	7.00
101	Checklist 89-176 (115 is Henry)	3.00
103	Dick Groat (with trade statement)	1.50
103	Dick Groat (w/o trade statement)	20.00
104	Alex Johnson (with trade statement)	.70
104	Alex Johnson (w/o trade statement)	15.00
110	Ernie Banks	25.00
111	Gary Peters	.80
112	Manny Mota	.90
113	Hank Aguirre	.70
116	Walt Alston	2.50
117	Jake Gibbs	1.00
118	Mike McCormick	.80
119	Art Shamsky	.70

120	Harmon Killebrew	15.00
122	Joe Gaines	.70
123	Pirates Rookies (Frank Bork, Jerry May)	.70
124	Tug McGraw	3.00
125	Lou Brock	20.00
126	*Jim Palmer*	250.00
128	Jim Landis	.70
129	Jack Kralick	.70
130	Joe Torre	2.25
131	Angels Team	2.25
132	Orlando Cepeda	3.50
134	Wes Parker	.85
135	Dave Morehead	.70
136	Woody Held	.70
137	Pat Corrales	1.00
138	Roger Repoz	1.00
139	Cubs Rookies (Byron Browne, Don Young)	.70
143	Jose Tartabull	.70
144	Don Schwall	.70
145	Bill Freehan	.90
146	George Altman	.70
147	Lum Harris	.70
148	Bob Johnson	.70
150	Rocky Colavito	3.00
151	Gary Wagner	.70

50 Mickey Mantle

152	Frank Malzone	.80
153	Rico Carty	1.50
154	Chuck Hiller	.80
155	Marcelino Lopez	.70
156	DP Combo (Hal Lanier, Dick Schofield)	1.00
157	Rene Lachemann	.80
158	Jim Brewer	.70
159	Chico Ruiz	.70
160	Whitey Ford	20.00
161	Jerry Lumpe	.70
162	Lee Maye	.70
163	Tito Francona	.80
164	White Sox Rookies (Tommie Agee, Marv Staehle)	.90
167	Boog Powell	3.00
170	Cookie Rojas	.70
171	Nick Willhite	.70
172	Mets Team	3.00
173	Al Spangler	.70
175	Bert Campaneris	1.50
176	Jim Davenport	.70
177	Hector Lopez	.90
178	Bob Tillman	.70
179	Cardinals Rookies (Dennis Aust, Bob Tolan)	.80

126 Jim Palmer

288 Dodgers Rookies

180	Vada Pinson	2.50
181	Al Worthington	.70
182	Jerry Lynch	.70
183	Checklist 177-264	2.50
184	Denis Menke	.75
185	Bob Buhl	.75
186	Ruben Amaro	.90
189	John Roseboro	.90
191	Darrell Sutherland	.70
192	Vic Power	.70
193	Dave McNally	1.00
194	Senators Team	2.25
195	Joe Morgan	40.00
197	Sonny Siebert	.80
198	*Mickey Stanley*	1.00
199	Chisox Clubbers (Floyd Robinson, Johnny Romano, Bill Skowron)	1.00
200	Ed Mathews	10.00
202	Clay Dalrymple	.70
203	Jose Santiago	.70
204	Cubs Team	2.25
205	Tom Tresh	2.00
209	Tigers Rookies (Fritz Fisher, *John Hiller*)	2.00
210	Bill Mazeroski	2.25
212	Ed Kranepool	1.00
213	Fred Newman	1.00
214	Tommy Harper	.80
215	NL Batting Ldrs (Hank Aaron, Bob Clemente, Willie Mays)	9.00

216	AL Batting Ldrs (Vic Davalillo, Tony Oliva, Carl Yastrzemski)	4.00
217	NL HR Ldrs (Willie Mays, Willie McCovey, Billy Williams)	6.00
218	AL HR Ldrs (Norm Cash, Tony Conigliaro, Willie Horton)	2.50
219	NL RBI Ldrs (Deron Johnson, Willie Mays, Frank Robinson)	4.00
220	AL RBI Ldrs (Rocky Colavito, Willie Horton, Tony Oliva)	2.50
221	NL ERA Ldrs (Sandy Koufax, Vern Law, Juan Marichal)	4.00
223	NL Pitching Ldrs (Tony Cloninger, Don Drysdale, Sandy Koufax)	4.00
224	AL Pitching Ldrs (Jim Grant, Jim Kaat, Mel Stottlemyre)	3.00
225	NL SO Ldrs (Bob Gibson, Sandy Koufax, Bob Veale)	4.00
226	AL SO Ldrs (Mickey Lolich, Sam McDowell, Denny McLain, Sonny Seibert)	2.50
229	Hank Bauer	.80

583 Tigers Team

100 Sandy Koufax

254 Fhillies Rookies

440	Deron Johnson	.75	
442	Orioles Rookies (Ed Barnowski, Eddie Watt)	.75	
444	Checklist 430-506	5.00	
445	• Jim Kaat	4.00	
446	Mack Jones	.70	
447	Dick Ellsworth (photo is Ken Hubbs)	4.50	
448	Eddie Stanky	4.75	
449	Joe Moeller	4.50	
450	Tony Oliva	7.00	
451	Barry Latman	4.50	
452	Joe Azcue	4.50	
453	Ron Kline	4.50	
454	Jerry Buchek	4.50	
455	Mickey Lolich	6.00	
456	Red Sox Rookies (Darrell Brandon, Joe Foy)	4.50	
457	Joe Gibbon	4.50	
458	Manny Jiminez (Jimenez)	4.50	
459	Bill McCool	4.50	
460	Curt Blefary	4.50	
461	Roy Face	5.50	
462	Bob Rodgers	4.50	
463	Phillies Team	6.00	
464	Larry Bearnarth	4.50	
465	Don Buford	4.50	
466	Ken Johnson	4.50	
467	Vic Roznovsky	4.50	
468	Johnny Podres	6.00	
469	Yankees Rookies (*Bobby Murcer*, Dooley Womack)	12.00	
470	Sam McDowell	5.00	
471	Bob Skinner	4.50	
474	Dick Schofield	4.50	
475	Dick Radatz	4.75	
476	Bobby Bragan	4.75	
477	Steve Barber	4.50	
478	Tony Gonzalez	4.50	
479	Jim Hannan	4.50	
480	Dick Stuart	4.75	
481	Bob Lee	4.50	
482	Cubs Rookies (John Boccabella, Dave Dowling)	4.50	
483	Joe Nuxhall	4.75	
484	Wes Covington	4.50	
486	Tommy John	16.00	
487	Al Ferrara	4.50	
489	Curt Simmons	4.75	
490	Bobby Richardson	13.00	
492	Athletics Team	6.00	
493	Johnny Klippstein	4.50	
494	Gordon Coleman	4.50	
495	Dick McAuliffe	4.75	
496	Lindy McDaniel	4.50	
497	Chris Cannizzaro	4.50	
498	Pirates Rookies (*Woody Fryman*, *Luke Walker*)	5.00	

1966 Topps

500 Hank Aaron

500	Hank Aaron	85.00
503	Steve Hamilton	4.50
504	Grady Hatton	4.50
505	Jose Cardenal	4.50
506	Bo Belinsky	4.50
508	*Steve Hargan*	4.75
509	Jake Wood	4.50
510	Hoyt Wilhelm	17.00
511	Giants Rookies (Bob Barton, *Tito Fuentes*)	4.75
512	Dick Stigman	4.50
513	Camilo Carreon	4.50
514	Hal Woodeshick	4.50
515	Frank Howard	6.00
517	Checklist 507-598	10.00
520	Jim Wynn	5.50
523	Bob Sadowski	16.00
524	Giants Rookies (Ollie Brown, Don Mason)	21.00
525	Gary Bell	16.00
526	Twins Team	51.00
527	Julio Navarro	16.00
528	Jesse Gonder	21.00
529	White Sox Rookies (*Lee Elia*, Dennis Higgins, Bill Voss)	19.00
530	Robin Roberts	35.00
531	Joe Cunningham	17.00
532	Aurelio Monteagudo	16.00
533	Jerry Adair	16.00
534	Mets Rookies (Dave Eilers, Rob Gardner)	19.00
535	Willie Davis	25.00
536	Dick Egan	16.00
537	Herman Franks	18.00
538	Bob Allen	16.00
539	Astros Rookies (Bill Heath, Carroll Sembera)	16.00
540	Denny McLain	45.00
541	Gene Oliver	16.00
542	George Smith	16.00
543	Roger Craig	24.00
544	Cardinals Rookies (Joe Hoerner, George Kernek, Jimmy Williams)	21.00
545	Dick Green	21.00
547	*Horace Clarke*	21.00
548	Gary Kroll	21.00
549	Senators Rookies (Al Closter, Casey Cox)	16.00
550	Willie McCovey	100.00
551	Bob Purkey	21.00
552	Birdie Tebbetts	18.00
553	Major League Rookies (Pat Garrett, Jackie Warner)	16.00
554	Jim Northrup	19.00
555	Ron Perranoski	19.00
556	Mel Queen	20.00
557	Felix Mantilla	16.00
558	Red Sox Rookies (Guido Grilli, Pete Magrini, *George Scott*)	20.00
559	Roberto Pena	16.00
560	Joel Horlen	16.00
561	Choo Choo Coleman	22.00
562	Russ Snyder	16.00
563	Twins Rookies (Pete Cimino, Cesar Tovar)	19.00
564	Bob Chance	16.00
565	Jimmy Piersall	31.00
566	Mike Cuellar	21.00
567	Dick Howser	24.00

568	Athletics Rookies (Paul Lindblad, Ron Stone)	16.00
569	Orlando McFarlane........	16.00
570	Art Mahaffey	20.00
571	Dave Roberts	16.00
572	Bob Priddy.....................	16.00
573	Derrell Griffith	16.00
574	Mets Rookies (Bill Hepler, Bill Murphy).......	19.00
575	Earl Wilson	16.00
576	Dave Nicholson	21.00
578	Chi Chi Olivo	16.00
579	Orioles Rookies (Frank Bertaina, Gene Brabender, Dave Johnson)	25.00
580	Billy Williams	85.00
581	Tony Martinez................	16.00
582	Garry Roggenburk.........	16.00

583	Tigers Team	100.00
584	Yankees Rookies (Frank Fernandez, *Fritz Peterson*)...............	19.00
586	Claude Raymond...........	16.00
587	Dick Bertell	16.00
588	Athletics Rookies (Chuck Dobson, Ken Suarez)..........................	16.00
590	Bill Skowron..................	31.00
591	NL Rookies (*Grant Jackson*, Bart Shirley) ...	21.00
592	Andre Rodgers	16.00
593	Doug Camilli	21.00
594	Chico Salmon	16.00
595	Larry Jackson	16.00
596	Astros Rookies (*Nate Colbert,* Greg Sims).......	19.00
597	John Sullivan	16.00
598	Gaylord Perry	335.00

1967 TOPPS

Scarcity and attractiveness make the 1967 Topps set one of the hottest collectibles of the 1960s. The 609 cards in the set made it the largest produced by Topps as of the time of issue. The standard-sized cards feature large color photos with facsimile autographs (except for Milt Pappas, number 254, which lacks an autograph). Card backs are the first ever from Topps to utilize a vertical format. The set is highlighted by a 12-card subset of 1966 league leaders and a five-card series honoring the previous World Series. An ultrarare final series, from 534 through 609, makes completing the set a real challenge since four key cards in the series (Tommy John, Brooks Robinson, and rookie cards of Rod Carew and Tom Seaver) together are valued at over $2000.

	NR MT
Complete set	**$5000.00**
Commons (1-110)	.60
Commons (111-370)	.70
Commons (371-457)	.80
Commons (458-533)	3.00
Commons (534-609)	6.00

1	The Champs (Hank Bauer, Brooks Robinson, Frank Robinson)..........	$17.00
5	Whitey Ford	16.00
10	Matty Alou	.80
12	Dodgers Rookies (Jimmy Campanis, Bill Singer)	.70

581 Mets Rookies

20	• Orlando Cepeda	5.00
25	Elston Howard	3.00
26	Bob Priddy (with trade statement)	.60
26	Bob Priddy (w/o trade statement)	8.00
30	Al Kaline	16.00
33	Athletics Rookies (*Sal Bando,* Randy Schwartz)	2.00
35	Rico Carty	1.00
39	Curt Simmons	.80
42	Mets Team	3.00
44	Joe Nuxhall	.80
45	Roger Maris	45.00
48	Bill Freehan	.80
49	Roy Face	1.25
50	Tony Oliva	2.50
55	Don Drysdale	12.00
59	Ralph Terry	.80
60	Luis Aparicio	5.00
62	Checklist 1-109 (Frank Robinson)	3.00
63	Cards' Clubbers (Lou Brock, Curt Flood)	5.00
66	Manny Mota	.80
70	Ron Santo	2.00
71	Camilo Pascual	.70
72	Tigers Rookies (George Korince, John Matchick)	.70
73	Rusty Staub	3.00
75	George Scott	1.00
78	Pat Corrales	1.00
81	Eddie Stanky	.70
85	Johnny Callison	.80
86	Mike McCormick (with trade statement)	.70
86	Mike McCormick (w/o trade statement)	9.00
88	Mickey Lolich	2.25
89	*Felix Millan*	.85
93	Yankees Rookies (*Stan Bahnsen,* Bobby Murcer)	2.50
94	Ron Fairly	.80
97	Mike Cuellar	.80
100	Frank Robinson	18.00
102	Phillies Team	6.00
103	Checklist 110-196 (Mickey Mantle)	8.00
105	Ken Boyer	2.00
109	Tribe Thumpers (Rocky Colavito, Leon Wagner)	1.50
123	Pirates Rookies (Jim Price, Luke Walker)	.70
125	Moe Drabowsky	.70
131	Yankees Team	4.00
140	Willie Stargell	20.00
143	Sox Sockers (Don Buford, Pete Ward)	.80
146	Steve Carlton	105.00
150	Mickey Mantle	200.00
151	World Series Game 1 (Moe Mows Down 11)	2.00

600 Brooks Robinson

569 AL Rookies

238	NL SO Ldrs (Jim Bunning, Sandy Koufax, Bob Veale) **4.00**	**264** Ron Swoboda .... **.80**	
		265 Lou Burdette **1.50**	
239	AL Batting Ldrs (Al Kaline, Tony Oliva, Frank Robinson) **4.00**	**266** Pitt Power (Donn Clendenon, Willie Stargell) **3.50**	
240	NL Batting Ldrs (Felipe Alou, Matty Alou, Rico Carty) **2.00**	**270** Zoilo Versalles .... **.80**	
		272 Cubs Rookies (Bill Connors, Dave Dowling) .... **.75**	
241	AL RBI Ldrs (Harmon Killebrew, Boog Powell, Frank Robinson) **3.50**	**278** Checklist 284-370 (Jim Kaat) **3.00**	
242	NL RBI Ldrs (Hank Aaron, Richie Allen, Bob Clemente) **5.00**	**280** Tony Conigliaro **3.00**	
		282 Johnny Odom .... **.80**	
		284 Johnny Podres **2.00**	
243	AL HR Ldrs (Harmon Killebrew, Boog Powell, Frank Robinson) **3.50**	**285** Lou Brock **15.00**	
		287 Mets Rookies (Greg Goossen, Bart Shirley) ...... **.80**	
244	NL HR Ldrs (Hank Aaron, Richie Allen, Willie Mays) .. **5.00**	**289** Tom Tresh **1.75**	
245	• Curt Flood **1.50**	**290** • Bill White **1.50**	
246	Jim Perry **1.00**	**294** Walt Alston **3.00**	
247	Jerry Lumpe .... **.80**	**295** Sam McDowell **1.00**	
248	Gene Mauch .... **.80**	**296** Glenn Beckert .... **.80**	
250	Hank Aaron **75.00**	**299** Norm Siebern .... **.80**	
253	Indians Rookies (Bill Davis, Gus Gil) .... **.70**	**300** • Jim Kaat **4.00**	
		302 Orioles Team **2.00**	
254	Milt Pappas .... **.80**	**306** *Bud Harrelson* **2.00**	
255	Frank Howard **2.50**	**308** Al Downing **1.25**	
260	Jim Lefevbre **1.00**	**309** Hurlers Beware (Richie Allen, Johnny Callison) **2.00**	
262	Athletics Team **2.00**	**310** Gary Peters .... **.80**	
		311 Ed Brinkman .... **.80**	

314	Red Sox Rookies (*Mike Andrews, Reggie Smith*)..	4.00
315	• Billy Williams	10.00
326	Bob Uecker	20.00
327	Angels Team	2.00
328	Clete Boyer	.90
329	Charlie Lau	.80
330	Claude Osteen	.80
332	Jesus Alou	.75
334	• Twin Terrors (Bob Allison, Harmon Killebrew)	3.50
335	Bob Veale	.80
337	Joe Morgan	21.00
340	Joe Pepitone	2.00
341	Giants Rookies (*Dick Dietz,* Billy Sorrell)	.80
344	Ossie Chavarria	.70
346	Jim Hickman	.80
347	Grady Hatton	.70
348	Tug McGraw	2.25
350	Joe Torre	2.00
351	Vern Law	1.25
354	Cubs Team	2.00
355	Carl Yastrzemski	90.00
357	Bill Skowron	1.50
358	Ruben Amaro	1.00
360	Leon Wagner	.80

146 Steve Carlton

609 Tommy John

361	Checklist 371-457 (Bob Clemente)	4.50
363	Dave Johnson	2.00
365	John Roseboro	.80
369	Jim Hunter	12.00
370	Tommy Davis	1.50
371	Jim Lonborg	2.00
372	Mike de la Hoz	.80
373	White Sox Rookies (Duane Josephson, Fred Klages)	.80
375	Jake Gibbs	.90
376	Don Lock	.80
377	Luis Tiant	2.25
378	Tigers Team	3.00
379	Jerry May	.80
380	Dean Chance	.90
381	Dick Schofield	.80
382	Dave McNally	1.00
383	Ken Henderson	.80
384	Cardinals Rookies (Jim Cosman, Dick Hughes)	.80
385	Jim Fregosi	1.25
386	Dick Selma	.85
387	Cap Peterson	.80
388	Arnold Earley	.80

570 Maury Wills

389	Al Dark	.90
390	Jim Wynn	1.00
391	Wilbur Wood	.90
392	Tommy Harper	.90
393	Jim Bouton	2.25
394	Jake Wood	.80
395	Chris Short	.90
396	Atlanta Aces (Tony Cloninger, Denis Menke)	1.00
397	Willie Smith	.80
398	Jeff Torborg	.90
399	Al Worthington	.80
400	Bob Clemente	75.00
401	Jim Coates	.80
402	Phillies Rookies (Grant Jackson, Billy Wilson)	.80
403	Dick Nen	.80
404	Nelson Briles	.90
405	Russ Snyder	.80
406	Lee Elia	.90
407	Reds Team	2.50
408	Jim Northrup	.90
409	Ray Sadecki	.80
411	Dick Howser	1.50
412	• Astros Rookies (Norm Miller, *Doug Rader*)	1.00

413	Jerry Grote	.90
417	Bob Bruce	.80
418	Sam Mele	.80
419	Don Kessinger	.90
420	Denny McLain	3.00
421	Dal Maxvill	.90
422	Hoyt Wilhelm	8.00
423	Fence Busters (Willie Mays, Willie McCovey)	14.00
424	Pedro Gonzalez	.80
425	Pete Mikkelsen	.80
426	Lou Clinton	.80
427	Ruben Gomez	.80
428	Dodgers Rookies (Tom Hutton, *Gene Michael*)	1.00
429	Gary Roggenburk	.80
430	Pete Rose	75.00
431	Ted Uhlaender	.80
433	Al Luplow	.80
434	Eddie Fisher	.85
435	Mack Jones	.80
436	Pete Ward	.80
437	Senators Team	2.25
441	Jim Davenport	.80
442	Yankees Rookies (*Bill Robinson,* Joe Verbanic)	2.50
443	Tito Francona	.90

200 Willie Mays

444	George Smith	.90
445	• Don Sutton	18.00
447	Bo Belinsky	1.00
448	Harry Walker	.90
450	Richie Allen	3.00
452	Ed Kranepool	1.00
453	Aurelio Monteagudo	.80
454	Checklist 458-533 (Juan Marichal)	4.50
455	Tommie Agee	.75
456	• Phil Niekro	8.00
458	Lee Thomas	3.00
459	Senators Rookies (*Dick Bosman*, Pete Craig)	4.00
460	Harmon Killebrew	55.00
461	Bob Miller	3.00
462	Bob Barton	3.00
463	Tribe Hill Aces (Sam McDowell, Sonny Siebert)	4.00
464	Dan Coombs	3.00
465	Willie Horton	4.00
466	Bobby Wine	3.00
467	Jim O'Toole	3.00
468	Ralph Houk	4.50
469	Len Gabrielson	3.00
470	Bob Shaw	3.00
471	Rene Lachemann	3.00
472	Pirates Rookies (John Gelnar, George Spriggs)	3.00
473	Jose Santiago	3.00
474	Bob Tolan	3.75
475	Jim Palmer	80.00
476	Tony Perez	75.00
477	Braves Team	4.75
478	Bob Humphreys	3.00
479	Gary Bell	3.00
480	Willie McCovey	25.00
481	Leo Durocher	5.00
482	Bill Monbouquette	3.25
483	Jim Landis	3.00
484	Jerry Adair	3.00
485	Tim McCarver	4.50
486	Twins Rookies (Rich Reese, Bill Whitby)	3.00
488	Gerry Arrigo	3.00
489	Doug Clemens	3.00
490	Tony Cloninger	3.75

400 Bob Clemente

491	Sam Bowens	3.00
492	Pirates Team	4.75
493	Phil Ortega	3.00
494	Bill Rigney	3.00
495	Fritz Peterson	3.75
496	Orlando McFarlane	3.00
497	Ron Campbell	3.00
498	Larry Dierker	3.75
499	Indians Rookies (George Culver, Jose Vidal)	3.00
500	Juan Marichal	18.00
501	Jerry Zimmerman	3.00
502	Derrell Griffith	3.00
503	Dodgers Team	5.00
504	Orlando Martinez	3.00
505	Tommy Helms	3.00
506	Smoky Burgess	3.00
507	Orioles Rookies (Ed Barnowski, Larry Haney)	3.00
508	Dick Hall	3.00
509	Jim King	3.00
510	Bill Mazeroski	4.50
511	Don Wert	3.00
512	Red Schoendienst	7.00
513	Marcelino Lopez	3.00

430 Pete Rose

515	Bert Campaneris	4.00
516	Giants Team	5.00
517	Fred Talbot	3.00
518	Denis Menke	3.00
519	Ted Davidson	3.00
520	Max Alvis	3.00
521	Bird Bombers (Curt Blefary, Boog Powell)	4.50
522	John Stephenson	3.00
523	Jim Merritt	3.00
524	Felix Mantilla	3.00
525	Ron Hunt	3.00
526	Tigers Rookies (*Pat Dobson,* George Korince)	3.75
527	Dennis Ribant	3.00
528	Rico Petrocelli	6.00
529	Gary Wagner	3.00
530	Felipe Alou	3.00
531	Checklist 534-609 (Brooks Robinson)	8.00
532	Jim Hicks	3.00
533	Jack Fisher	3.00
534	Hank Bauer	6.50
535	Donn Clendenon	6.50
536	Cubs Rookies (*Joe Niekro,* Paul Popovich)	30.00
538	J.C. Martin	6.00
539	Dick Egan	6.00
540	Norm Cash	30.00
541	Joe Gibbon	6.00
542	Athletics Rookies (*Rick Monday,* Tony Pierce)	13.00
543	Dan Schneider	6.00
544	Indians Team	10.00
545	Jim Grant	6.00
546	Woody Woodward	6.00
547	Red Sox Rookies (Russ Gibson, Bill Rohr)	6.00
548	Tony Gonzalez	6.00
549	Jack Sanford	8.00
550	Vada Pinson	7.00
551	Doug Camili	6.00
552	Ted Savage	6.00
553	Yankees Rookies (Mike Hegan, Thad Tillotson)	24.00
554	Andre Rodgers	6.00
555	Don Cardwell	6.00
556	Al Weis	6.00
557	Al Ferrara	8.00
558	Orioles Rookies (*Mark Belanger,* Bill Dillman)	35.00
559	Dick Tracewski	6.00
560	Jim Bunning	42.00
561	Sandy Alomar	6.00
562	Steve Blass	7.00
563	Joe Adcock	19.00
564	Astros Rookies (Alonzo Harris, Aaron Pointer)	6.00
565	Lew Krausse	6.00
566	Gary Geiger	6.00
567	Steve Hamilton	7.00
568	John Sullivan	6.00
569	AL Rookies (Hank Allen, *Rod Carew*)	500.00
570	Maury Wills	85.00
571	Larry Sherry	7.00
572	Don Demeter	7.00
573	White Sox Team	16.00
574	Jerry Buchek	7.00
575	*Dave Boswell*	7.00
576	NL Rookies (Norm Gigon, Ramon Hernandez)	19.00
577	Bill Short	6.00
578	John Boccabella	6.00

579	Bill Henry 6.00	**595**	Cookie Rojas 6.00
580	Rocky Colavito 70.00	**596**	Galen Cisco 6.00
581	Mets Rookies (Bill Denehy, *Tom Seaver*) 1300.00	**597**	Ted Abernathy 6.00
		598	White Sox Rookies (Ed Stroud, Walt Williams) 7.50
582	Jim Owens 6.00	**599**	Bob Duliba 6.00
583	Ray Barker 6.00	**600**	Brooks Robinson 235.00
584	Jim Piersall 19.00	**601**	Bill Bryan 6.00
585	Wally Bunker 6.00	**602**	Juan Pizarro 6.00
586	Manny Jimenez 6.00	**603**	Athletics Rookies (Tim Talton, Ramon Webster).. 6.00
587	NL Rookies (Don Shaw, Gary Sutherland) 16.00	**604**	Red Sox Team 90.00
588	Johnny Klippstein 6.00	**605**	Mike Shannon 8.00
589	Dave Ricketts 6.00	**606**	Ron Taylor........................ 6.00
590	Pete Richert...................... 6.00	**607**	Mickey Stanley 18.00
591	Ty Cline 6.00	**608**	Cubs Rookies (Rich Nye, John Upham) 7.00
592	NL Rookies (Jim Shellenback, Ron Willis) .. 7.00	**609**	Tommy John................. 125.00

1968 TOPPS

Collectors think of the 1968 Topps issue of 598 cards as the "burlap sack" issue. That's because the photos appear on backgrounds of brown mesh. Card backs are still in a vertical format, but the cartoon now appears at the bottom, with year-by-year statistics in the middle. An All-Star subseries returned in 1968 that featured 20 players chosen by *The Sporting News.* Topps continued the practice of placing a small mug shot of a star like Orlando Cepeda or Juan Marichal on the usually bland checklists. Rookie cards of Johnny Bench and Nolan Ryan are by far the most valuable in the set, while Roger Maris and Eddie Mathews made the last card appearances of their careers in 1968.

	NR MT
Complete set	**$2850.00**
Commons (1-533)	**.60**
Commons (534-598)	**1.00**

1	NL Batting Ldrs (Matty Alou, Bob Clemente, Tony Gonzalez) **$10.00**
2	AL Batting Ldrs (Al Kaline, Frank Robinson, Carl Yastrzemski) 4.00
3	NL RBI Ldrs (Hank Aaron, Orlando Cepeda, Bob Clemente) 4.00
4	AL RBI Ldrs (Harmon Killebrew, Frank Robinson, Carl Yastrzemski) 4.00
5	NL HR Ldrs (Hank Aaron, Willie McCovey, Ron Santo, Jim Wynn) 4.00
6	AL HR Ldrs (Frank Howard, Harmon Killebrew, Carl Yastrzemski) 4.00

177 Mets Rookies

51	Bob Locker	.60
52	Hawk Taylor	.60
53	Gene Alley	.65
54	Stan Williams	.60
55	Felipe Alou	1.00
56	Orioles Rookies (Dave Leonhard, Dave May)	.60
57	Dan Schneider	.60
58	Ed Mathews	8.00
59	Don Lock	.60
60	Ken Holtzman	1.00
61	Reggie Smith	1.50
62	Chuck Dobson	.60
65	John Roseboro	.75
66	Casey Cox (yellow team letters)	60.00
66	Casey Cox (white team letters)	.60
67	Checklist 1-109 (Jim Kaat)	3.00
69	Tom Tresh	1.75
71	Vern Fuller	.60
72	Tommy John	5.00
73	Jim Hart	.90
74	Milt Pappas	.75
75	Don Mincher	.80
76	Braves Rookies (Jim Britton, *Ron Reed*)	1.00

280 Mickey Mantle

77	*Don Wilson*	.90
78	Jim Northrup	.70
79	Ted Kubiak	.60
80	Rod Carew	115.00
82	Sam Bowens	.60
84	Bob Tolan	.70
85	Gaylord Perry	9.00
86	Willie Stargell	11.00
87	Dick Williams	1.00
88	Phil Regan	.60
89	Jake Gibbs	.80
90	Vada Pinson	2.00
92	Ed Kranepool	.80
93	Tony Cloninger	.80
96	Senators Rookies (Frank Coggins, Dick Nold)	.60
97	Tom Phoebus	.60
99	Rocky Colavito	2.25
100	Bob Gibson	10.00
101	Glenn Beckert	.90
102	Jose Cardenal	6.00
103	Don Sutton	6.00
105	Al Downing	1.00
107	Checklist 110-196 (Juan Marichal)	3.50

45 Tom Seaver

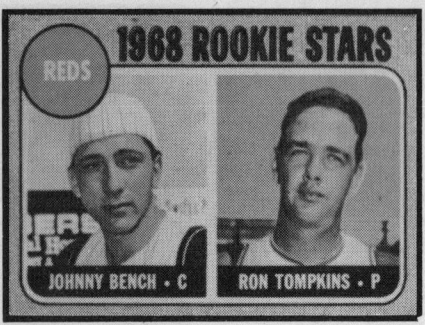

247 Reds Rookies

166	Claude Raymond	.60
167	Elston Howard	3.00
168	Dodgers Team	2.50
170	Jim Fregosi	1.00
175	Maury Wills	3.50
177	Mets Rookies (*Jerry Koosman, Nolan Ryan*)	1400.00
180	Curt Flood	1.50
190	• Bill White	1.00
192	Checklist 197-283 (Carl Yastrzemski)	5.00
195	Joe Pepitone	2.00
198	Roy Face	1.25
199	A's Rookies (Darrell Osteen, Roberto Rodriguez)	.60
200	Orlando Cepeda	4.00
201	Mike Marshall	1.75
205	Juan Marichal	8.00
208	Willie Davis	1.00
210	Gary Peters	.75
215	Jim Bunning	5.00
220	Harmon Killebrew	13.00
225	Richie Allen	2.25
228	Dodgers Rookies (Jack Billingham, Jim Fairey)	.80

50 Willie Mays

230	Pete Rose	50.00
233	George Scott	.90
235	Ron Santo	1.50
236	Tug McGraw	2.00
237	Alvin Dark	.90
240	Al Kaline	13.00
241	Felix Millan	.75
247	Reds Rookies (Johnny Bench, Ron Tompkins)	375.00
250	Carl Yastrzemski	35.00
257	Phil Niekro	5.00
280	Mickey Mantle	185.00
290	Willie McCovey	9.00
300	Rusty Staub	2.00
310	Luis Aparicio	5.00
321	• Leo Durocher	2.25
330	Roger Maris	30.00
334	Orioles Team	2.00
350	Hoyt Wilhelm	6.00
351	Bob Barton	.60
352	Jackie Hernandez	.60
354	Pete Richert	.60
355	Ernie Banks	15.00
356	Checklist 371-457 (Ken Holtzman)	2.50
357	Len Gabrielson	.60
358	Mike Epstein	.70

80 Rod Carew

110 Hank Aaron

360	Willie Horton	1.00
361	Harmon Killebrew AS	5.00
362	Orlando Cepeda AS	2.75
363	Rod Carew AS	10.00
364	Joe Morgan AS	4.00
365	Brooks Robinson AS	6.00
366	Ron Santo AS	2.00
367	Jim Fregosi AS	1.00
368	Gene Alley AS	1.00
369	Carl Yastrzemski AS	12.00
370	Hank Aaron AS	12.00
371	Tony Oliva AS	2.00
372	Lou Brock AS	7.00
373	Frank Robinson AS	7.00
374	Bob Clemente AS	15.00
375	Bill Freehan AS	1.00
376	Tim McCarver AS	1.50
377	Joe Horlen AS	1.00
378	Bob Gibson AS	5.00
379	Gary Peters AS	1.00
380	Ken Holtzman AS	1.00
381	Boog Powell	2.50
382	Ramon Hernandez	.60
383	Steve Whitaker	.65
384	Reds Rookies (Bill Henry, *Hal McRae*)	9.00
385	Jim Hunter	10.00

386	Greg Goossen	.70
387	Joe Foy	.60
388	Ray Washburn	.60
389	• Jay Johnstone	.90
390	Bill Mazeroski	1.75
391	Bob Priddy	.60
392	Grady Hatton	.60
393	Jim Perry	1.00
394	Tommie Aaron	.90
395	Camilo Pascual	.80
396	Bobby Wine	.60
397	Vic Davalillo	.65
400	Mike McCormick	.75
401	Mets Team	4.50
402	Mike Hegan	1.00
403	John Buzhardt	.60
404	Floyd Robinson	.60
405	Tommy Helms	.70
406	Dick Ellsworth	.60
408	Steve Carlton	51.00
409	Orioles Rookies (Frank Peters, Ron Stone)	.60
410	• Ferguson Jenkins	3.50
412	Clay Carroll	.70
413	Tommy McCraw	.60
414	Mickey Lolich	2.75
415	Johnny Callison	1.00

150 Bob Clemente

416	Bill Rigney	.60
417	Willie Crawford	.60
419	Jack Hiatt	.60
420	Cesar Tovar	.65
421	Ron Taylor	.60
422	Rene Lachemann	.60
424	White Sox Team	2.00
425	Jim Maloney	.70
426	Hank Allen	.60
429	Tommie Sisk	.60
430	Rico Petrocelli	.90
431	Dooley Womack	.65
432	Indians Rookies (Bill Davis, Jose Vidal)	.60
433	Bob Rodgers	.85
434	Ricardo Joseph	.60
435	Ron Perranoski	.70
436	Hal Lanier	.75
437	Don Cardwell	.60
438	Lee Thomas	.60
440	Claude Osteen	.95
441	Alex Johnson	.60
444	Jack Fisher	.60
445	Mike Shannon	.70
446	Ron Kline	.60
447	Tigers Rookies (George Korince, Fred Lasher)	.60

575 Jim Palmer

449	Gene Oliver	.60
450	Jim Kaat	4.00
451	Al Spangler	.60
452	Jesus Alou	.70
453	Sammy Ellis	.60
454	Checklist 458-533 (Frank Robinson)	4.00
455	Rico Carty	1.00
456	John O'Donoghue	.60
457	• Jim Lefevbre	.70
458	Lew Krausse	.60
460	Jim Lonborg	1.00
461	Chuck Hiller	.60
463	Jimmie Schaffer	.60
464	Don McMahon	.60
465	Tommie Agee	.90
467	Dick Howser	1.50
468	Larry Sherry	.60
470	Bill Freehan	1.00
471	Orlando Pena	.60
472	Walt Alston	2.50
473	Al Worthington	.60
474	Paul Schaal	.60
475	Joe Niekro	2.25
476	Woody Woodward	.70
477	Phillies Team	2.00
478	Dave McNally	1.00

520 Lou Brock

355 Ernie Banks

562	Jim Bouton	2.50
563	Ed Charles.......................	1.25
564	Eddie Stanky	1.25
565	Larry Dierker....................	1.00
566	Ken Harrelson	2.00
567	Clay Dalrymple	1.00
568	Willie Smith.....................	1.00
569	NL Rookies (Ivan Murrell, Les Rohr)............	1.25
570	Rick Reichardt	1.00
571	Tony LaRussa	1.75
572	Don Bosch.......................	1.25
573	Joe Coleman	1.25
574	Reds Team	3.00
575	Jim Palmer	50.00
576	Dave Adlesh	1.00
577	Fred Talbot......................	1.25
578	Orlando Martinez.............	1.00
579	NL Rookies (*Larry Hisle, Mike Lum*).......................	2.00

580	Bob Bailey	1.00
581	Garry Roggenburk...........	1.00
582	Jerry Grote	1.25
583	Gates Brown....................	1.25
584	Larry Shepard..................	1.00
585	Wilbur Wood....................	1.25
586	Jim Pagliaroni.................	1.00
587	Roger Repoz	1.00
588	Dick Schofield.................	1.00
589	Twins Rookies (Ron Clark, Moe Ogier)	1.00
590	Tommy Harper	1.25
591	Dick Nen..........................	1.00
592	John Bateman	1.00
593	Lee Stange	1.00
594	Phil Linz..........................	1.25
595	Phil Ortega	1.00
596	Charlie Smith...................	1.00
597	Bill McCool	1.00
598	Jerry May........................	2.00

1969 TOPPS

Topps reached another record in terms of quantity with the release of its 664-card 1969 set. No team cards are included, however, and multiplayer feature cards appear for the last time. Other subsets include league stat leaders, World Series cards, a *Sporting News* All-Star group, and rookie cards for Rollie Fingers, Reggie Jackson, Graig Nettles, and others. The 2½- by 3½-inch cards feature color photos on the front with the player name and position in a circle in the upper corner, printed in a variety of color combinations. Cards with white letters occur in the range of 440 through 511. They are scarce, expensive, and not included in the full set price. Card backs, now in a horizontal format, feature lifetime stats, a brief bio, and a cartoon.

	NR MT
Complete set	$2075.00
Commons (1-218)	.40
Commons (219-327)	.90
Commons (328-512)	.40
Commons (513-664)	.70

1	AL Batting Ldrs (Danny Cater, Tony Oliva, Carl Yastrzemski)	$7.00
2	NL Batting Ldrs (Felipe Alou, Matty Alou, Pete Rose)	4.00
3	AL RBI Ldrs (Ken Harrelson, Frank Howard, Jim Northrup)	2.00

500 Mickey Mantle

4	NL RBI Ldrs (Willie McCovey, Ron Santo, Billy Williams)	**3.50**
5	AL HR Ldrs (Ken Harrelson, Willie Horton, Frank Howard)	**2.00**
6	NL HR Ldrs (Richie Allen, Ernie Banks, Willie McCovey)	**3.50**
7	AL ERA Ldrs (Sam McDowell, Dave McNally, Luis Tiant)	**2.00**
8	NL ERA Ldrs (Bobby Bolin, Bob Gibson, Bob Veale)	**3.00**
9	AL Pitching Ldrs (Denny McLain, Dave McNally, Mel Stottlemyre, Luis Tiant)	**2.00**
10	NL Pitching Ldrs (Bob Gibson, Fergie Jenkins, Juan Marichal)	**3.50**
11	AL SO Ldrs (Sam McDowell, Denny McLain, Luis Tiant)	**2.00**
12	NL SO Ldrs (Bob Gibson, Fergie Jenkins, Bill Singer)	**3.00**
13	Mickey Stanley	.50
14	Al McBean	.40
15	Boog Powell	**2.50**
17	Mike Marshall	**1.25**
18	Dick Schofield	.40
19	Ken Suarez	.40
20	Ernie Banks	**12.00**
21	Jose Santiago	.40
22	Jesus Alou	.50
23	Lew Krausse	.40
24	Walt Alston	**3.00**
25	Roy White	**1.00**
26	Clay Carroll	.50
28	Mike Ryan	.40
29	Dave Morehead	.40
30	Bob Allison	**1.00**
31	Mets Rookies (Gary Gentry, Amos Otis)	**1.50**
34	Gary Peters	.50
35	• Joe Morgan	**12.00**
36	Luke Walker	.40
38	Zoilo Versalles	.50
40	Mayo Smith	.40
42	Tommy Harper	**1.00**

260 Reggie Jackson

43	Joe Niekro	1.25
44	Danny Cater	.40
45	Maury Wills	2.50
46	Fritz Peterson	.80
47	Paul Popovich (with helmet logo)	4.00
47	Paul Popovich (w/o helmet logo)	.40
49	Royals Rookies (Steve Jones, Eliseo Rodriquez) ("Rodriquez" on front)	6.00
49	Royals Rookies (Steve Jones, Eliseo Rodriguez) ("Rodriguez" on front)	.40
50	Bob Clemente	36.00
51	Woody Fryman	.50
54	Cisco Carlos	.40
55	Jerry Grote	1.00
57	Checklist 1-109 (Denny McLain)	3.00
59	• Jay Johnstone	.70
60	Nelson Briles	.45
62	Chico Salmon	.40
63	Jim Hickman	.50
64	Bill Monbouquette	.50
65	Willie Davis	1.00
66	Orioles Rookies (Mike Adamson, *Merv Rettenmund*)	.70
69	Steve Hamilton	.50
70	Tommy Helms	.50
71	Steve Whitaker	.40
73	Johnny Briggs	.40
74	Preston Gomez	.40
75	Luis Aparicio	5.00
76	Norm Miller	.40
77	Ron Perranoski (with "LA" on cap)	4.50
77	Ron Perranoski (w/o "LA" on cap)	.40
79	Milt Pappas	.70
80	Norm Cash	1.75
82	Pirates Rookies (*Rich Hebner, Al Oliver*)	10.00
83	Mike Ferraro	.75
85	Lou Brock	12.00
86	Pete Richert	.40
87	Horace Clarke	.55
90	Jerry Koosman	2.50

533 Nolan Ryan

91	Al Dark	.75
92	Jack Billingham	.50
94	Hank Aguirre	.40
95	Johnny Bench	150.00
97	Buddy Bradford	.40
98	Dave Giusti	.40
99	Twins Rookies (Danny Morris, *Graig Nettles*) (with black loop above "Twins")	20.00
99	Twins Rookies (Danny Morris, *Graig Nettles*) (w/o black loop above "Twins")	12.00
100	Hank Aaron	50.00
103	Roger Repoz	.40
104	Steve Blass	.50
105	Rick Monday	.85
106	Jim Hannan	.40
107	Checklist 110-218 (Bob Gibson) (161 is Jim Purdin)	3.00
107	Checklist 110-218 (Bob Gibson) (161 is John Purdin)	6.00
109	Jim Lonborg	.90

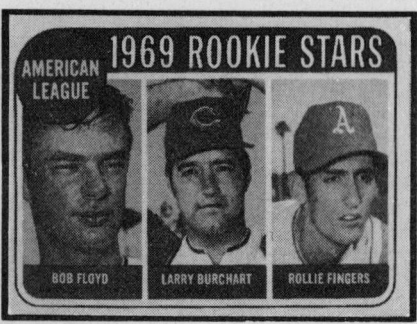

597 AL Rookies

110	Mike Shannon	.60
111	Johnny Morris	.70
112	J.C. Martin	.70
114	Yankees Rookies (Alan Closter, John Cumberland)	.70
118	Stan Williams	.40
119	Doug Rader	.50
120	Pete Rose	35.00
122	Ron Fairly	.80
123	Wilbur Wood	.75
125	Ray Sadecki	.40
127	Kevin Collins	.50
128	Tommie Aaron	.70
129	Bill McCool	.40
130	Carl Yastrzemski	30.00
131	Chris Cannizzaro	.40
132	Dave Baldwin	.40
133	Johnny Callison	1.00
135	Tommy Davis	1.50
136	Cards Rookies (Steve Huntz, Mike Torrez)	.50
140	•Jim Lefevbre	.50
142	Woody Woodward	.50
144	Bob Hendley	.60
145	Max Alvis	.50
146	Jim Perry	1.00
147	• Leo Durocher	2.25
150	Denny McLain	3.00
151	Clay Dalrymple (Phillies)	7.00
151	Clay Dalrymple (Orioles)	.40
153	Ed Brinkman	.50
156	Astros Rookies (Hal Gilson, Leon McFadden)	.40
157	Bob Rodgers	.70
160	Vada Pinson	2.00
162	World Series Game 1 (Gibson Fans 17; Sets New Record)	3.50
163	World Series Game 2 (Tiger Homers Deck the Cards)	2.50
164	World Series Game 3 (McCarver's Homer Puts St. Louis Ahead)	2.50
165	World Series Game 4 (Brock's Leadoff Homer Starts Cards' Romp)	3.50
166	World Series Game 5 (Kaline's Key Hit Sparks Tigers Rally)	3.50
167	World Series Game 6 (Tiger 10-Run Inning Ties Mark)	2.50
168	World Series Game 7 (Lolich Series Hero, Outduels Gibson)	2.75
169	World Series Summary (Tigers Celebrate Their Victory)	2.50
170	Frank Howard	2.00
175	• Jim Bunning	4.00
190	Willie Mays	50.00
200	Bob Gibson	12.00

480 Tom Seaver

100 Hank Aaron

255 Steve Carlton

383	Casey Cox	.40
385	Orlando Cepeda	3.50
388	Tom McCraw	.40
390	Bill Freehan	.75
393	Gene Brabender	.40
394	• Pilots Rookies (Lou Piniella, Marv Staehle)	3.00
400	Don Drysdale	8.00
410	Al Kaline	10.00
411	Larry Dierker	.50
412	Checklist 426-512 (Mickey Mantle)	7.00
413	Roland Sheldon	.80
414	Duke Sims	.40
416	Willie McCovey AS	4.00
417	Ken Harrelson AS	1.00
418	Tommy Helms AS	.70
419	Rod Carew AS	6.00
420	Ron Santo AS	1.00
421	Brooks Robinson AS	4.00
422	Don Kessinger AS	.70
423	Bert Campaneris AS	.80
424	Pete Rose AS	12.00
425	Carl Yastrzemski AS	12.00
426	• Curt Flood AS	1.00
427	Tony Oliva AS	1.50
428	Lou Brock AS	3.50
429	Willie Horton AS	.75
430	Johnny Bench AS	10.00
431	Bill Freehan AS	.70
432	Bob Gibson AS	3.50
433	Denny McLain AS	1.50
434	Jerry Koosman AS	1.00
435	Sam McDowell AS	.80
436	Gene Alley	.70
439	White Sox Rookies (Ed Herrmann, Dan Lazar)	.40
440	Willie McCovey (last name in white)	90.00
440	Willie McCovey (last name in yellow)	20.00
441	Dennis Higgins (last name in white)	10.00
441	Dennis Higgins (last name in yellow)	.40
444	Joe Moeller (last name in white)	10.00
444	Joe Moeller (last name in yellow)	.40
446	Claude Raymond	.40
447	Ralph Houk (last name in white)	15.00

130 Carl Yastremski

447 Ralph Houk (last
 name in yellow) 1.50
448 Bob Tolan .... .50
450 Billy Williams 6.00
451 Rich Rollins
 (first name in white) 10.00
451 Rich Rollins
 (first name in yellow) .... .80
452 Al Ferrera
 (first name in white) 10.00
452 Al Ferrera
 (first name in yellow) .... .40
453 Mike Cuellar .... .80
454 Phillies Rookies (Larry
 Colton, *Don Money*)
 (names in white) 10.00
454 Phillies Rookies (Larry
 Colton, *Don Money*)
 (names in yellow) .... .80
456 Bud Harrelson 1.00
460 Joe Torre 1.75
461 Mike Epstein
 (last name in white) 10.00
461 Mike Epstein
 (last name in yellow).......... .50
462 Red Schoendienst 1.50

573 Jim Palmer

464 Dave Marshall
 (last name in white) 10.00
464 Dave Marshall
 (last name in yellow).......... .40
468 Pirates Rookies
 (Bruce Dal Canton,
 Bob Robertson)
 (names in white) 10.00
468 Pirates Rookies
 (Bruce Dal Canton,
 Bob Robertson)
 (names in yellow) .... .40
470 Mel Stottlemyre
 (last name in white) 15.00
470 Mel Stottlemyre
 (last name in yellow)........ 1.50
471 Ted Savage
 (last name in white) 10.00
471 Ted Savage
 (last name in yellow).......... .40
473 Jose Arcia
 (first name in white) 10.00
475 Tim McCarver 1.50
476 Red Sox Rookies (*Ken
 Brett,* Gerry Moses)
 (names in white) 10.00

630 Bobby Bonds

250 Frank Robinson

476	Red Sox Rookies (*Ken Brett,* Gerry Moses) (names in yellow)	.50
478	Don Buford	.60
480	Tom Seaver	100.00
481	*Bill Melton*	.80
482	Jim Gosger (first name in yellow)	.40
483	Ted Abernathy	.40
484	Joe Gordon	.50
485	Gaylord Perry (last name in white)	75.00
485	Gaylord Perry (last name in yellow)	10.00
486	Paul Casanova (last name in white)	10.00
486	Paul Casanova (last name in yellow)	.40
489	Clete Boyer	.90
490	Matty Alou	1.00
491	Twins Rookies (Jerry Crider, George Mitterwald) (names in white)	10.00
491	Twins Rookies (Jerry Crider, George Mitterwald) (names in yellow)	.40

492	Tony Cloninger	.50
493	Wes Parker (last name in white)	10.00
493	Wes Parker (last name in yellow)	.70
495	Bert Campaneris	1.25
497	Julian Javier	.50
498	Juan Pizarro	.45
500	Mickey Mantle (last name in white)	500.00
500	Mickey Mantle (last name in yellow)	200.00
501	Tony Gonzalez (first name in white)	10.00
501	Tony Gonzales (first name in yellow)	.40
504	Checklist 513-588 (Brooks Robinson)	4.00
505	Bobby Bolin (last name in white)	10.00
505	Bobby Bolin (last name in yellow)	.40
506	Paul Blair	.50
507	Cookie Rojas	.40
508	Moe Drabowsky	.40
509	Manny Sanguillen	.50
510	Rod Carew	40.00

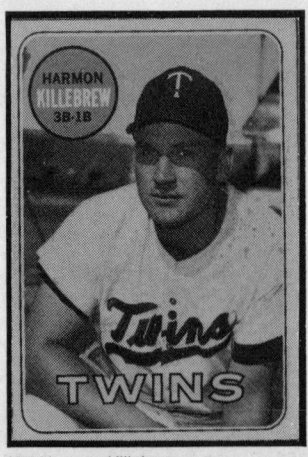

375 Harmon Killebrew

511 Diego Segui
(first name in white) **10.00**
511 Diego Segui
(first name in yellow) .... .80
512 Cleon Jones .... .80
513 Camilo Pascual .... .80
514 Mike Lum........................... .70
515 Dick Green .... .70
516 Earl Weaver 3.50
517 Mike McCormick............... .80
518 Fred Whitfield .... .70
519 Yankees Rookies (Len
Boehmer, Gerry Kenney).. **1.00**
520 Bob Veale .... .80
521 George Thomas .... .70
523 Bob Chance...................... .70
524 Expos Rookies (Jose
Laboy, Floyd Wicker)......... .70
525 Earl Wilson .... .70
526 Hector Torres .... .70
527 Al Lopez 3.00
528 Claude Osteen .... .90
529 Ed Kirkpatrick .... .70
530 Cesar Tovar...................... .70
531 Dick Farrell .... .70
532 Bird Hill Aces (Mike
Cuellar, Jim Hardin, Dave
McNally, Tom Phoebus).. **1.50**
533 Nolan Ryan................. **380.00**
534 Jerry McNertney .... .70
535 Phil Regan......................... .70
536 Padres Rookies (Danny
Breeden, *Dave Roberts*).... .80
537 Mike Paul........................... .70
538 Charlie Smith.................... .70
539 Ted Shows How (Mike
Epstein, Ted Williams)..... **3.25**
540 • Curt Flood 1.50
541 Joe Verbanic .... .90
542 Bob Aspromonte................ .70
543 Fred Newman..................... .70
544 Tigers Rookies (Mike
Kilkenny, Ron Woods)........ .70
545 Willie Stargell................ **10.00**
546 Jim Nash .... .70
547 Billy Martin........................ 3.25
548 Bob Locker .... .70
549 Ron Brand .... .70
550 Brooks Robinson **12.00**

545 Willie Stargell

551 Wayne Granger .... .70
552 Dodgers Rookies (*Ted
Sizemore, Bill Sudakis*) ..... .85
553 Ron Davis.......................... .70
554 Frank Bertaina................... .70
555 Jim Hart .... .80
556 A's Stars (Sal Bando,
Bert Campaneris,
Danny Cater) **1.50**
557 Frank Fernandez 1.00
558 *Tom Burgmeier*................... .85
559 Cards Rookies
(Joe Hague,
Jim Hicks)......................... .70
560 Luis Tiant 1.50
561 Ron Clark .... .70
562 *Bob Watson*...................... 1.00
563 Marty Pattin....................... .90
564 Gil Hodges......................... 6.00
565 Hoyt Wilhelm 6.00
566 Ron Hansen .... .70
567 Pirates Rookies
(Elvio Jimenez,
Jim Shellenback) .... .70
568 Cecil Upshaw .... .70
569 Billy Harris .... .70
570 Ron Santo 2.00
571 Cap Peterson .... .70

50 Bob Clemente

572	• Giants Heroes (Juan Marichal, Willie McCovey)	**7.00**
573	Jim Palmer	**25.00**
574	George Scott	.90
575	Bill Singer	.90
576	Phillies Rookies (Ron Stone, Bill Wilson)	.70
577	Mike Hegan	**1.00**
578	Don Bosch	.70
579	*Dave Nelson*	.80
580	Jim Northrup	.80
581	Gary Nolan	.70
582	Checklist 589-664 (Tony Oliva)	**3.00**
583	*Clyde Wright*	.80
585	Ron Swoboda	.80
586	Tim Cullen	.70
587	*Joe Rudi*	**2.00**
588	• Bill White	**1.00**
589	Joe Pepitone	**2.00**
590	Rico Carty	**1.00**
591	Mike Hedlund	.70
592	Padres Rookies (Rafael Robles, Al Santorini)	.70
593	Don Nottebart	.70
594	Dooley Womack	.70

595	Lee Maye	.70
596	Chuck Hartenstein	.70
597	AL Rookies (Larry Burchart, *Rollie Fingers,* Bob Floyd)	**95.00**
598	Ruben Amaro	.80
599	John Boozer	.70
600	• Tony Oliva	**2.25**
601	Tug McGraw	**2.00**
602	Cubs Rookies (Alec Distaso, Jim Qualls, Don Young)	.75
603	Joe Keough	.70
604	Bobby Etheridge	.70
605	Dick Ellsworth	.70
606	Gene Mauch	.90
607	Dick Bosman	.80
608	Dick Simpson	.70
609	Phil Gagliano	.70
610	Jim Hardin	.70
611	Braves Rookies (Bob Didier, Walt Hriniak, Gary Neibauer)	.70
612	Jack Aker	.70
613	Jim Beauchamp	.70
615	Len Gabrielson	.70
616	Don McMahon	.70
617	Jesse Gonder	.70
618	Ramon Webster	.70
619	Royals Rookies (Bill Butler, *Pat Kelly,* Juan Rios)	.80
620	Dean Chance	.80
621	Bill Voss	.70
622	Dan Osinski	.70
623	Hank Allen	.70
624	NL Rookies (Darrel Chaney, Duffy Dyer, Terry Harmon)	.80
625	Mack Jones	.70
626	Gene Michael	.70
627	George Stone	.70
628	Red Sox Rookies (*Bill Conigliaro,* Syd O'Brien, Fred Wenz)	.90
629	Jack Hamilton	.70
630	*Bobby Bonds*	**20.00**
631	John Kennedy	.70
632	Jon Warden	.70
633	Harry Walker	.80

634	Andy Etchebarren	.70
635	George Culver	.70
636	Woodie Held	.70
637	Padres Rookies (Jerry DaVanon, *Clay Kirby,* Frank Reberger)	.75
638	Ed Sprague	.70
639	Barry Moore	.70
640	Fergie Jenkins	10.00
641	NL Rookies (Bobby Darwin, Tommy Dean, John Miller)	.75
642	John Hiller	.80
643	Billy Cowan	.80
644	Chuck Hinton	.70
645	George Brunet	.70
646	Expos Rookies (Dan McGinn, *Carl Morton*)	.90
647	Dave Wickersham	.70
648	Bobby Wine	.70
649	Al Jackson	.80

650	• Ted Williams	10.00
651	Gus Gil	.90
653	• *Aurelio Rodriguez* (photo is team batboy Leonard Garcia)	1.50
654	White Sox Rookies (*Carlos May,* Rich Morales, Don Secrist)	.90
655	Mike Hershberger	.70
656	Dan Schneider	.70
657	Bobby Murcer	2.25
658	AL Rookies (Bill Burbach, Tom Hall, Jim Miles)	1.00
659	Johnny Podres	1.75
660	Reggie Smith	2.00
661	Jim Merritt	1.00
662	Royals Rookies (Dick Drago, Bob Oliver, George Spriggs)	.80
663	Dick Radatz	.90
664	Ron Hunt	2.00

1970 TOPPS

Team cards returned in 1970 with Topps' largest set to date of 720 cards. Card number 1 features a team photo of the new World Champion Mets, who make additional appearances in subsets highlighting the World Series and the first League Championship Series. Statistical leaders are grouped together, as are All-Star cards, which will not appear again until 1982. Backs of the 2½- by 3½-inch cards feature blue-and-yellow printing on white cardboard with yearly stats, brief bios, and a cartoon. Fronts show crisp color photos with team names in the upper corners and player names in script in the lower gray border. This set is a popular starting point for the modern collector.

	NR MT
Complete set	**$1750.00**
Commons (1-546)	.30
Commons (547-633)	.80
Commons (634-720)	2.00

1	World Champions (Mets Team)	$10.00

2	Diego Segui	.60
3	Darrel Chaney	.30
4	Tom Egan	.30
5	Wes Parker	.40
6	Grant Jackson	.30
7	Indians Rookies (Gary Boyd, Russ Nagelson)	.30
9	Checklist 1-132	2.50
10	Carl Yastrzemski	45.00

1970 Topps

712 Nolan Ryan

11	Nate Colbert	.30
12	John Hiller	.40
13	Jack Hiatt	.30
14	Hank Allen	.30
15	Larry Dierker	.40
17	Hoyt Wilhelm	5.00
21	Athletics Rookies (*Vida Blue, Gene Tenace*)	4.00
22	Ray Washburn	.30
23	Bill Robinson	.50
24	Dick Selma	.30
25	Cesar Tovar	.30
26	Tug McGraw	1.25
27	Chuck Hinton	.30
29	Sandy Alomar	.30
30	Matty Alou	.80
31	Marty Pattin	.50
32	Harry Walker	.40
33	Don Wert	.30
34	Willie Crawford	.30
36	Reds Rookies (Danny Breeden, *Bernie Carbo*)	.50
40	Rich Allen	1.50
45	Dave Johnson	1.00
50	Tommie Agee	.50
53	John Kennedy	.50
54	Jeff Torborg	.40
55	John Odom	.40
56	Phillies Rookies (Joe Lis, Scott Reid)	.30
57	Pat Kelly	.30
59	Dick Ellsworth	.30
60	• Jim Wynn	.60
61	NL Batting Ldrs (Bob Clemente, Cleon Jones, Pete Rose)	5.00
62	AL Batting Ldrs (Rod Carew, Tony Oliva, Reggie Smith)	3.00
63	NL RBI Ldrs (Willie McCovey, Tony Perez, Ron Santo)	3.00
64	AL RBI Ldrs (Reggie Jackson, Harmon Killebrew, Boog Powell)	2.50
65	NL HR Ldrs (Hank Aaron, Lee May, Willie McCovey)	3.00
66	AL HR Ldrs (Frank Howard, Reggie Jackson, Harmon Killebrew)	2.50
67	NL ERA Ldrs (Steve Carlton, Bob Gibson, Juan Marichal)	3.00

660 Johnny Bench

189 Yankees Rookies

68 AL ERA Ldrs (Dick
   Bosman, Mike Cuellar,
   Jim Palmer) **2.00**
69 NL Pitching Ldrs (Fergie
   Jenkins, Juan Marichal,
   Phil Niekro, Tom Seaver).. **2.50**
70 AL Pitching Ldrs (Dave
   Boswell, Mike Cuellar,
   Dennis McLain, Dave
   McNally, Jim Perry,
   Mel Stottlemyre) **2.50**
71 NL SO Ldrs (Bob Gibson,
   Fergie Jenkins, Bill
   Singer)............................. **2.50**
72 AL SO Ldrs (Mickey Lolich,
   Sam McDowell,
   Andy Messersmith).......... **2.00**
73 Wayne Granger................. .30
74 Angels Rookies (Greg
   Washburn, Wally Wolf)...... .30
75 Jim Kaat **2.50**
80 Don Kessinger.................. .40
82 Frank Fernandez .... .40
87 Steve Renko...................... .30
88 Pilots Rookies (Dick
   Baney, Miguel Fuentes) .... .50

90 Tim McCarver..................**1.00**
94 Fred Patek......................... .40
96 Cards Rookies (Leron
   Lee, *Jerry Reuss*) **2.00**
97 Joe Moeller....................... .30
98 Gates Brown...................... .30
99 Bobby Pfeil....................... .30
100 Mel Stottlemyre **1.00**
102 Joe Rudi .... .80
103 Frank Reberger .... .30
107 Bobby Etheridge................ .30
108 Tom Burgmeier.................. .30
109 Expos Rookies (Garry
    Jestadt, Carl Morton)......... .40
110 Bob Moose .... .30
111 Mike Hegan .... .50
112 Dave Nelson..................... .30
113 Jim Ray .... .30
114 Gene Michael .... .45
115 Alex Johnson.................... .40
116 • Sparky Lyle **1.00**
118 George Mitterwald............. .30
119 Chuck Taylor .... .30
120 Sal Bando......................... .80
121 Orioles Rookies (Fred
    Beene, *Terry Crowley*) ...... .90
124 Larry Jaster .... .30
125 Deron Johnson .... .30

300 Tom Seaver

10 Carl Yastrzemski

290 Rod Carew

700 Frank Robinson

203	Rudy May	.40
204	Len Gabrielson	.30
205	Bert Campaneris	.80
206	Clete Boyer	.85
207	Tigers Rookies (Norman McRae, Bob Reed)	.30
208	Fred Gladding	.30
210	Juan Marichal	8.00
211	• Ted Williams	7.00
212	Al Santorina	.30
213	Andy Etchebarren	.30
215	Reggie Smith	.65
216	Chuck Hartenstein	.30
217	Ron Hansen	.30
218	Ron Stone	.30
219	Jerry Kenney	.30
220	Steve Carlton	25.00
225	Lee May	.60
226	Ron Perranoski	.40
227	Astros Rookies (*John Mayberry*, Bob Watkins)	.30
228	Aurelio Rodriguez	.40
230	Brooks Robinson	10.00
240	Fergie Jenkins	7.50
242	Walter Alston	1.75
244	Checklist 264-372	2.75
248	Jesus Alou	.45

184	Ray Fosse	.45
185	Don Mincher	.50
188	Manny Sanguillen	.40
189	Yankees Rookies (*Thurman Munson*, Dave McDonald)	100.00
190	Joe Torre	1.25
193	Mike Wegener	.30
195	NL Playoff Game 1 (Seaver Wins Opener!)	3.00
196	NL Playoff Game 2 (Mets Show Muscle!)	1.75
197	NL Playoff Game 3 (Ryan Saves the Day!)	3.00
198	NL Playoffs Summary (We're Number One!)	2.00
199	AL Playoff Game 1 (Orioles Win A Squeaker!)	1.50
200	AL Playoff Game 2 (Powell Scores Winning Run!)	2.00
201	AL Playoff Game 3 (Birds Wrap it Up!)	1.50
202	AL Playoffs Summary (Sweep Twins in Three!)	1.50

220 Steve Carlton

1970 Topps

630 Ernie Banks

621 Braves Rookies

363	Tom Shopay	.30	458	Pete Rose AS 8.00
365	Zoilo Versalles	.40	459	Reggie Jackson AS 13.00
366	Barry Moore	.30	460	Matty Alou AS ..... .75
367	Mike Lum	.30	461	Carl Yastrzemski AS 8.00
368	Ed Herrmann	.30	462	Hank Aaron AS 8.00
370	Tommy Harper	.70	463	Frank Robinson AS 5.00
373	Roy White	1.00	464	Johnny Bench AS 10.00
375	Johnny Callison	.80	465	Bill Freehan AS ..... .50
380	Tony Perez	3.00	466	Juan Marichal AS 3.00
387	Orioles Team	1.50	467	Denny McLain AS ..... .80
394	Gil Hodges	4.00	468	Jerry Koosman AS ..... .60
403	Jim Bunning	3.25	469	Sam McDowell AS ..... .60
407	Bob Watson	.40	470	Willie Stargell 7.00
409	Bob Tolan	.40	471	Chris Zachary ..... .30
410	Boog Powell	2.00	472	Braves Team 1.25
411	Dodgers Team	1.50	473	Don Bryant ..... .50
416	Joe Verbanic	.40	475	Dick McAuliffe ..... .40
418	John Donaldson	.40	477	Orioles Rookies (Roger
420	Ken McMullen	.30		Freed, Al Severinsen) ..... .30
421	Pat Dobson	.40	479	Dick Woodson ..... .30
422	Royals Team	1.25	480	Glenn Beckert ..... .40
427	Fred Norman	.30	481	Jose Tartabull ..... .30
430	Andy Messersmith	.50	482	Tom Hilgendorf ..... .30
449	Jim Palmer	18.00	485	• Jay Johnstone ..... .50
450	Willie McCovey AS	3.50	486	Terry Harmon ..... .30
451	• Boog Powell AS	1.00	487	Cisco Carlos ..... .30
452	Felix Millan AS	.50	488	J.C. Martin ..... .30
453	Rod Carew AS	4.00	489	Eddie Kasko ..... .30
454	Ron Santo AS	1.00	490	Bill Singer ..... .40
455	Brooks Robinson AS	3.50	491	Graig Nettles 4.00
456	Don Kessinger AS	.50	492	Astros Rookies (Keith
457	Rico Petrocelli AS	.50		Lampard, Scipio Spinks) ... .30

459 Reggie Jackson AS

530 Bob Gibson

553	• Jim Lefebvre	.90
560	Gaylord Perry	7.00
565	Jim Hunter	7.00
580	Pete Rose	83.00
590	Mike Cuellar	.90
593	Cubs Team	1.75
595	Maury Wills	2.50
600	Willie Mays	50.00
601	Pete Richert	.80
602	Ted Savage	.80
603	Ray Oyler	.80
604	Clarence Gaston	.80
605	Rick Wise	.90
606	Chico Ruiz	.80
608	Pirates Team	1.75
609	*Buck Martinez*	.90
610	Jerry Koosman	1.25
611	Norm Cash	1.50
612	Jim Hickman	.90
613	Dave Baldwin	.90
614	Mike Shannon	.90
615	Mark Belanger	.90
620	Jim Perry	1.00
621	Braves Rookies (*Darrell Evans*, Rick Kester, Mike McQueen)	15.00
622	Don Sutton	4.50
623	Horace Clarke	.90
630	Ernie Banks	20.00
631	Athletics Team	1.75
634	Bud Harrelson	2.25
635	Bob Allison	2.25
636	Jim Stewart	1.75
637	Indians Team	3.00
638	Frank Bertaina	1.75
639	Dave Campbell	1.75
640	Al Kaline	35.00
641	Al McBean	1.75
642	Angels Rookies (Greg Garrett, Gordon Lund, Jarvis Tatum)	1.75
643	Jose Pagan	1.75
644	Gerry Nyman	1.75
645	Don Money	1.75
646	Jim Britton	1.75
647	Tom Matchick	1.75
648	Larry Haney	1.75
649	Jimmie Hall	1.75
650	Sam McDowell	2.50

502 Rollie Fingers

651	Jim Gosger	1.75
652	Rich Rollins	2.00
653	Moe Drabowsky	1.75
654	NL Rookies (Boots Day, *Oscar Gamble*, Angel Mangual)	2.50
655	John Roseboro	2.00
656	Jim Hardin	1.75
657	Padres Team	3.00
658	Ken Tatum	1.75
659	Pete Ward	2.00
660	Johnny Bench	150.00
661	Jerry Robertson	1.75
662	Frank Lucchesi	1.75
663	Tito Francona	2.00
664	Bob Robertson	1.75
665	Jim Lonborg	2.25
666	Adolfo Phillips	1.75
667	Bob Meyer	2.00
668	Bob Tillman	1.75
669	White Sox Rookies (Bart Johnson, Dan Lazar, Mickey Scott)	1.75
670	Ron Santo	3.00
671	Jim Campanis	1.75
672	Leon McFadden	1.75

449 Jim Palmer

673	Ted Uhlaender	1.75
674	Dave Leonhard	1.75
675	Jose Cardenal	2.00
676	Senators Team	3.00
677	Woodie Fryman	2.00
678	Dave Duncan	1.75
679	Ray Sadecki	1.75
680	Rico Petrocelli	2.00
681	Bob Garibaldi	1.75
682	Dalton Jones	1.75
683	Reds Rookies (Vern Geishert, Hal McRae, Wayne Simpson)	2.50
684	Jack Fisher	1.75
685	Tom Haller	2.00
686	Jackie Hernandez	1.75
687	Bob Priddy	1.75
688	Ted Kubiak	2.00
689	Frank Tepedino	2.00
690	Ron Fairly	2.00
691	Joe Grzenda	1.75
692	Duffy Dyer	1.75
693	Bob Johnson	1.75
694	Gary Ross	1.75
695	Bobby Knoop	1.75
696	Giants Team	3.00

697	Jim Hannan	1.75
698	Tom Tresh	2.25
699	Hank Aguirre	1.75
700	Frank Robinson	40.00
701	Jack Billingham	1.75
702	AL Rookies (Bob Johnson, Ron Klimkowski, Bill Zepp)	2.00
703	Lou Marone	1.75
704	Frank Baker	1.75
705	Tony Cloninger	2.00
706	John McNamara	2.25
707	Kevin Collins	1.75
708	Jose Santiago	1.75
709	Mike Fiore	1.75
710	Felix Millan	1.75
711	Ed Brinkman	2.00
712	Nolan Ryan	375.00
713	Pilots Team	12.00
714	Al Spangler	1.75
715	Mickey Lolich	5.00
716	Cards Rookies (Sam Campisi, *Reggie Cleveland*, Santiago Guzman)	2.00
719	Jim Roland	2.00
720	Rick Reichardt	4.00

230 Brooks Robinson

1971 TOPPS

Although Topps' 752-card set for 1971 makes a strong artistic statement, the black borders have proven difficult for collectors to maintain in mint condition. On the front, the team name appears in bold print across the top of the 2½- by 3½-inch cards, with the player name and position in smaller print just below. Facsimile autographs are superimposed at the bottom. Gray card backs with green-and-black printing were the first to feature player photos in a black-and-white inset. Brief player bios are rounded out with lifetime and 1970 stats, first pro and major league games, and abbreviated personal facts. Subsets include statistical leaders; league playoffs; World Series; and rookies, such as Dave Concepcion, Steve Garvey, and Ted Simmons.

		NR MT
Complete set		**$1850.00**
Commons (1-523)		**.35**
Commons (524-643)		**.80**
Commons (644-752)		**2.25**

341 Steve Garvey

1	World Champions (Orioles Team)	$7.00
2	Dock Ellis	.50
5	Thurman Munson	35.00
9	George Scott	.50
10	Claude Osteen	.50

513 Nolan Ryan

11	*Elliott Maddox*	.50
12	Johnny Callison	.60
13	White Sox Rookies (Charlie Brinkman, Dick Moloney)	.35
14	*Dave Concepcion*	8.00
16	*Ken Singleton*	1.75
20	Reggie Jackson	65.00
26	Bert Blyleven	65.00
27	Pirates Rookies (Fred Cambria, Gene Clines)	.35
30	Phil Niekro	3.25
35	Lou Piniella	1.25

1971 Topps

20 Reggie Jackson

26 Bert Blyleven

600 Willie Mays

160 Tom Seaver

5 Thurman Munson

55 Steve Carlton

640 Frank Robinson

1971 Topps

740 Luis Aparicio

384	Rollie Fingers	2.50
385	Maury Wills	1.25
386	Red Sox Team	1.50
388	Al Oliver	1.75
389	Ed Brinkman	.40
390	Glenn Beckert	.45
393	Merv Rettenmund	.40
394	Clay Carroll	.40
395	Roy White	.70
396	Dick Schofield	.35
397	Alvin Dark	.50
399	Jim French	.35
400	Hank Aaron	30.00
401	Tom Murphy	.35
402	Dodgers Team	1.50
403	Joe Coleman	.40
405	Leo Cardenas	.35
406	Ray Sadecki	.35
407	Joe Rudi	.60
409	Don Pavletich	.35
410	Ken Holtzman	.40
412	Jerry Johnson	.35
413	Pat Kelly	.35
414	Woodie Fryman	.40
415	Mike Hegan	.35
417	Dick Hall	.35
418	Adolfo Phillips	.35

419	Ron Hansen	.40
420	Jim Merritt	.35
421	John Stephenson	.35
422	Frank Bertaina	.35
425	Doug Rader	.35
426	Chris Cannizzaro	.35
427	Bernie Allen	.35
429	Chuck Hinton	.35
430	Wes Parker	.40
431	Tom Burgmeier	.35
433	Skip Lockwood	.35
434	Gary Sutherland	.35
435	Jose Cardenal	.40
436	Wilbur Wood	.50
437	Danny Murtaugh	.45
438	Mike McCormick	.50
439	Phillies Rookies (*Greg Luzinski*, Scott Reid)	2.00
440	Bert Campaneris	.75
441	Milt Pappas	.40
442	Angels Team	1.25
447	*Cesar Geronimo*	.60
448	Dave Roberts	.35
449	Brant Alyea	.35
450	Bob Gibson	10.00
452	John Boccabella	.35
453	Terry Crowley	.35
455	Don Kessinger	.40
456	Bob Meyer	.35
459	• Jim Lefebvre	.40
460	Fritz Peterson	.50
461	Jim Hart	.40
462	Senators Team	1.75
464	Aurelio Rodriguez	.40
465	Tim McCarver	.85
466	Ken Berry	.35
467	Al Santorini	.35
469	Bob Aspromonte	.35
470	Bob Oliver	.35
471	Tom Griffin	.35
472	Ken Rudolph	.35
475	Ron Perranoski	.35
476	Dal Maxvill	.40
477	Earl Weaver	1.00
478	Bernie Carbo	.40
480	Manny Sanguillen	.40
481	Daryl Patterson	.35
482	Padres Team	1.25
483	Gene Michael	.45

485	Ken McMullen	.35
488	Jerry Stephenson	.35
489	Luis Alvarado	.35
492	Ken Boswell	.35
493	Dave May	.35
494	Braves Rookies (Ralph Garr, Rick Kester)	.50
495	Felipe Alou	.65
496	Woody Woodward	.40
499	Checklist 524-643	2.50
500	Jim Perry	.60
501	Andy Etchebarren	.35
502	Cubs Team	1.25
503	Gates Brown	.40
504	Ken Wright	.35
505	Ollie Brown	.35
508	Roger Repoz	.35
510	Ken Harrelson	1.25
511	Chris Short	.40
513	Nolan Ryan	175.00
516	Ted Kubiak	.35
517	Charlie Fox	.35
520	Tommy John	3.00
522	Twins Team	1.25
523	John Odom	.40
524	Mickey Stanley	.90
525	Ernie Banks	18.00
526	Ray Jarvis	.80
527	Cleon Jones	.90
528	Wally Bunker	.80
529	NL Rookies (Bill Buckner, Enzo Hernandez, Marty Perez)	2.50
530	Carl Yastrzemski	43.00
531	Mike Torrez	.90
532	Bill Rigney	.80
533	Mike Ryan	.80
534	Luke Walker	.80
535	•Curt Flood	1.75
536	Claude Raymond	.80
537	Tom Egan	.80
538	Angel Bravo	.80
539	Larry Brown	.80
540	Larry Dierker	.80
541	Bob Burda	.80
542	Bob Miller	.80
543	Yankees Team	2.75
544	Vida Blue	2.50
545	Dick Dietz	.80

625 Lou Brock

546	John Matias	.80
547	Pat Dobson	.90
548	Don Mason	.80
549	Jim Brewer	.80
550	Harmon Killebrew	12.00
551	Frank Linzy	.80
552	Buddy Bradford	.80
553	Kevin Collins	.80
554	Lowell Palmer	.80
555	Walt Williams	.80
556	Jim McGlothlin	.80
557	Tom Satriano	.80
558	Hector Torres	.80
559	AL Rookies (Terry Cox, Bill Gogolewski, Gary Jones)	.90
560	Rusty Staub	2.25
561	Syd O'Brien	.80
562	Dave Giusti	.80
563	Giants Team	2.00
564	Al Fitzmorris	.80
565	Jim Wynn	1.00
566	Tim Cullen	.80
567	Walt Alston	2.50
568	Sal Campisi	.80
569	Ivan Murrell	.80
570	Jim Palmer	18.00

1971 Topps

300 Brooks Robinson

571	Ted Sizemore	.80
572	Jerry Kenney	.90
573	Ed Kranepool	1.00
574	Jim Bunning	4.00
575	Bill Freehan	1.00
576	Cubs Rookies (Brock Davis, Adrian Garrett, Garry Jestadt)	.80
577	Jim Lonborg	1.00
578	Ron Hunt	.90
579	Marty Pattin	.80
580	Tony Perez	4.00
581	Roger Nelson	.80
582	Dave Cash	.80
584	Indians Team	2.00
585	Willie Davis	2.25
586	Dick Woodson	.80
587	Sonny Jackson	.80
588	Tom Bradley	.80
589	Bob Barton	.80
590	Alex Johnson	.80
592	Randy Hundley	.80
593	Jack Aker	.80
594	• Cards Rookies (Bob Chlupsa, *Al Hrabosky*, Bob Stinson)	2.25
595	Dave Johnson	1.75
596	Mike Jorgensen	.80
597	Ken Suarez	.80
598	Rick Wise	.90
599	Norm Cash	2.00
600	Willie Mays	60.00
601	Ken Tatum	.80
602	Mary Martinez	.80
603	Pirates Team	3.00
604	John Gelnor	.80
605	Orlando Cepeda	3.50
606	Chuck Taylor	.80
607	Paul Ratliff	.80
608	Mike Wegener	.80
609	• Leo Durocher	2.25
610	Amos Otis	1.00
611	Tom Phoebus	.80
612	Indians Rookies (Lou Camilli, Ted Ford, Steve Mingori)	.80
613	Pedro Borbon	.90
614	Billy Cowan	.80
615	Mel Stottlemyre	1.75
616	Larry Hisle	.90
617	Clay Dalrymple	.80
618	Tug McGraw	2.25
619	Checklist 644-752	4.00
620	Frank Howard	2.25
621	Ron Bryant	.80
622	Joe Lahoud	.80
623	Pat Jarvis	.80
624	Athletics Team	2.00
625	Lou Brock	14.00
626	Freddie Patek	.90
627	Steve Hamilton	.80
628	John Bateman	.80
629	John Hiller	.90
630	Roberto Clemente	50.00
631	Eddie Fisher	.80
632	Darrel Chaney	.80
633	AL Rookies (Bobby Brooks, Pete Koegel, Scott Northey)	.80
634	Phil Regan	.80
635	Bobby Mercer	2.00
636	Denny Lemaster	.80
637	Dave Bristol	.80
638	Stan Williams	.80
639	Tom Haller	.80

450 Bob Gibson

640	Frank Robinson	23.00
641	Mets Team	3.50
642	Jim Roland	.80
643	Rick Reichardt	.80
644	Jim Stewart	2.25
645	Jim Maloney	2.50
646	Bobby Floyd	2.25
647	Juan Pizarro	2.25
648	Mets Rookies (Rich Folkers, Ted Martinez, *Jon Matlack*)	3.50
649	• Sparky Lyle	3.00
650	Rich Allen	8.00
651	Jerry Robertson	2.25
652	Braves Team	3.25
653	Russ Snyder	2.25
654	Don Shaw	2.25
655	Mike Epstein	2.50
656	Gerry Nyman	2.25
657	Jose Azcue	2.25
658	Paul Lindblad	2.25
659	Byron Browne	2.25
660	Ray Culp	2.25
661	Chuck Tanner	3.00
662	Mike Hedlund	2.25
663	Marv Staehle	2.25
664	Rookie Star Pitchers (Archie Reynolds, Bob Reynolds, Ken Reynolds)	2.25
665	Ron Swoboda	2.25
666	Gene Brabender	2.25
667	Pete Ward	2.25
668	Gary Neibauer	2.25
669	Ike Brown	2.25
670	Bill Hands	2.25
671	Bill Voss	2.25
672	Ed Crosby	2.25
673	Gerry Janeski	2.25
674	Expos Team	3.25
675	Dave Boswell	2.25
676	Tommie Reynolds	2.25
677	Jack DiLauro	2.25
678	George Thomas	2.25
679	Dan O'Riley	2.25
680	Don Mincher	2.25
681	Bill Butler	2.25
682	Terry Harmon	2.25
683	Bill Burbach	2.25
684	Curt Motton	2.25
685	Moe Drabowsky	2.25
686	Chico Ruiz	2.25
687	Ron Taylor	2.25
688	• Sparky Anderson	7.50
689	Frank Baker	2.25
690	Bob Moose	2.25
691	Bob Heise	2.25
692	AL Rookies (Hal Haydel, Rogelio Moret, Wayne Twitchell)	2.25
693	Jose Pena	2.25
694	Rick Renick	2.25
695	Joe Niekro	3.25
696	Jerry Morales	2.25
697	Rickey Clark	2.25
698	Brewers Team	3.25
699	Jim Britton	2.25
700	Boog Powell	7.00
701	Bob Garibaldi	2.25
702	Milt Ramirez	2.25
703	Mike Kekich	2.25
704	J.C. Martin	2.25
705	Dick Selma	2.25
706	Joe Foy	2.25
707	Fred Lasher	2.25
708	Russ Nagelson	2.25

709	Rookie Star Outfielders (*Dusty Baker, Tom Paciorek, Don Baylor*) ...	33.00
710	Sonny Siebert	2.25
711	Larry Stahl	2.25
712	Jose Martinez	2.25
713	Mike Marshall	2.75
714	Dick Williams	2.75
715	Horace Clarke	2.50
716	Dave Leonhard	2.25
717	Tommie Aaron	2.50
718	Billy Wynne	2.25
719	Jerry May	2.25
720	Matty Alou	2.75
721	John Morris	2.25
722	Astros Team	3.25
723	Vicente Romo	2.25
724	Tom Tischinski	2.25
725	Gary Gentry	2.25
726	Paul Popovich	2.25
728	NL Rookies (Keith Lampard, Wayne Redmond, Bernie Williams)	2.25
729	Dick Billings	2.25
730	Jim Rooker	2.25
731	Jim Qualls	2.25
732	Bob Reed	2.25
733	Lee Maye	2.25
734	Rob Gardner	2.25
735	Mike Shannon	2.50
737	Preston Gomez	2.25
738	Russ Gibson	2.25
739	Barry Lersch	2.25
740	Luis Aparicio	15.00
741	Skip Guinn	2.25
743	John O'Donoghue	2.25
744	Chuck Manuel	2.25
745	Sandy Alomar	2.25
746	Andy Kosco	2.25
747	NL Rookies (Balor Moore, Al Severinsen, Scipio Spinks)	2.25
748	John Purdin	2.25
749	Ken Szotkiewicz	2.25
750	Denny McLain	6.50
751	Al Weis	3.00
752	Dick Drago	3.00

1972 TOPPS

In 1972, Topps released a 787-card set, larger than any previous edition. Card fronts exhibit a wild design of various border colors, along with cartoonlike team headings. A number of subsets account for the increase of 35 cards over 1971. There is a seven-card series of traded players that includes Steve Carlton, Joe Morgan, and Frank Robinson. Eight cards show black-and-white boyhood photos, while thirty-four players are depicted both on standard and "in-action" cards (the latter indicated by "IA" on the card list). A high-number series (657-787) is hard to locate, and the rookie card of Carlton Fisk is currently the set's most valuable.

	NR MT
Complete set	**$1800.00**
Commons (1-394)	**.25**
Commons (395-525)	**.50**
Commons (526-656)	**.70**
Commons (657-787)	**2.25**

1	World Champtions (Pirates Team)	$5.00
4	Checklist 1-132	2.25
11	Bobby Valentine	.60
18	Juan Pizarro (green under "C" and "S")	3.50
21	Braves Team	.90

79 Red Sox Rookies

#		Price
29	Bill Bonham (green under "C" and "S")	**3.50**
30	Rico Petrocelli	**.50**
33	Billy Martin	**1.50**
34	Billy Martin IA	**.80**
37	Carl Yastrzemski	**18.00**
38	Carl Yastrzemski IA	**8.00**
41	Tommy Davis	**.60**
45	Glenn Beckert (green under "C" and "S")	**3.50**
49	Willie Mays	**25.00**
50	Willie Mays IA	**10.00**
51	Harmon Killebrew	**4.00**
52	•Harmon Killebrew IA	**2.00**
61	Cubs Rookies (Gene Hiser, *Burt Hooton*, Earl Stephenson)	**1.00**
65	Cesar Cedeno	**.80**
71	Angels Team	**.90**
72	Bruce Kison	**.80**
75	Bert Campaneris	**.60**
79	Red Sox Rookies (*Cecil Cooper, Carlton Fisk, Mike Garman*)	**150.00**
80	Tony Perez	**2.00**
85	NL Batting Ldrs (Glenn Beckert, Ralph Garr, Joe Torre)	**1.25**
86	AL Batting Ldrs (Bobby Murcer, Tony Oliva, Merv Rettenmund)	**1.25**
87	NL RBI Ldrs (Hank Aaron, Willie Stargell, Joe Torre)	**2.25**
88	AL RBI Ldrs (Harmon Killebrew, Frank Robinson, Reggie Smith)	**2.25**
89	NL HR Ldrs (Hank Aaron, Lee May, Willie Stargell)	**2.25**
90	AL HR Ldrs (Norm Cash, Reggie Jackson, Bill Melton)	**1.75**
91	NL ERA Ldrs (Dave Roberts, Tom Seaver, Don Wilson)	**1.75**
92	AL ERA Ldrs (Vida Blue, Jim Palmer, Wilbur Wood)	**1.50**
93	NL Pitching Ldrs (Steve Carlton, Al Downing, Fergie Jenkins, Tom Seaver)	**2.00**
94	AL Pitching Ldrs (Vida Blue, Mickey Lolich, Wilbur Wood)	**1.25**
95	NL SO Ldrs (Fergie Jenkins, Tom Seaver, Bill Stoneman)	**1.75**
96	AL SO Ldrs (Vida Blue, Joe Coleman, Mickey Lolich)	**1.25**

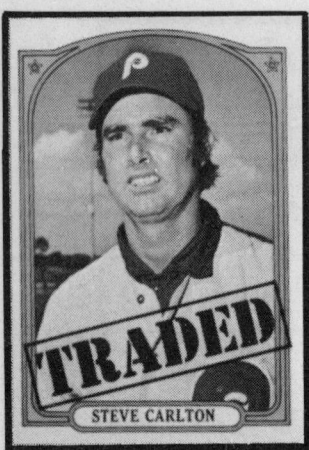

751 Steve Carlton Traded

49 Willie Mays

226	World Series Game 4	1.50
227	World Series Game 5	1.25
228	World Series Game 6	1.25
229	World Series Game 7	1.25
230	World Series Summary (Series Celebration)	1.25
233	• Jay Johnstone	.40
237	Yankees Team	1.25
240	Rich Allen	1.75
241	Rollie Fingers	2.50
250	Boog Powell	1.25
251	Checklist 264-394 (small print on front)	2.25
251	Checklist 264-394 (large print on front)	2.25
256	George Foster	1.50
259	Sparky Lyle	.70
262	Padres Team	.90
263	Felipe Alou	.50
264	Tommy John	2.00
267	Dave Concepcion	2.50
270	Jim Palmer	10.00
272	*Mickey Rivers*	1.00
276	Gene Mauch	.50
280	Willie McCovey	5.00
282	Astros Team	.90
285	Gaylord Perry	5.00
291	Hal McRae	.60

309 Roberto Clemente

299	Hank Aaron	24.00
300	Hank Aaron IA	12.00
303	Joe Pepitone	.50
309	Roberto Clemente	24.00
310	Roberto Clemente IA	12.00
313	Luis Aparicio	3.00
314	Luis Aparicio IA	1.50
316	Cardinals Rookies (*Jim Bibby*, Santiago Guzman, Jorge Roque)	.50
323	Earl Weaver	.80
325	Mel Stottlemyre	.80
327	*Steve Stone*	1.00
328	Red Sox Team	1.00
330	Jim Hunter	3.50
338	Bob Grich	.75
340	Roy White	.75
341	Boyhood Photo (Joe Torre)	.75
347	Boyhood Photo (Tom Seaver)	2.00
395	Matty Alou	.80
396	Paul Lindblad	.50
397	Phillies Team	.90
398	Larry Hisle	.60
399	Milt Wilcox	.60

435 Reggie Jackson

600 Al Kaline

425	Ken Singleton	.90
426	Ken Singleton IA	.60
427	Tito Fuentes	.50
428	Tito Fuentes IA	.50
429	Bob Robertson	.50
430	Bob Robertson IA	.50
431	Clarence Gaston	.50
432	Clarence Gaston IA	.50
433	Johnny Bench	25.00
434	Johnny Bench IA	10.00
435	Reggie Jackson	25.00
436	Reggie Jackson IA	13.00
437	Maury Wills	1.50
438	Maury Wills IA	.70
439	Billy Williams	3.50
440	Billy Williams IA	1.75
441	Thurman Munson	15.00
442	Thurman Munson IA	8.00
443	Ken Henderson	.50
444	Ken Henderson IA	.50
445	Tom Seaver	25.00
446	Tom Seaver IA	9.00
447	Willie Stargell	4.00
448	Willie Stargell IA	2.00
449	Bob Lemon	.90
450	Mickey Lolich	1.25
451	Tony LaRussa	1.00
452	Ed Herrmann	.50

400	Tony Oliva	1.50
401	Jim Nash	.50
402	Bobby Heise	.50
403	John Cumberland	.50
404	Jeff Torborg	.60
405	Ron Fairly	.75
406	*George Hendrick*	1.00
407	Chuck Taylor	.50
408	Jim Northrup	.60
409	Frank Baker	.60
410	Fergie Jenkins	4.00
411	Bob Montgomery	.50
412	Dick Kelley	.50
413	White Sox Rookies (Don Eddy, Dave Lemonds)	.50
414	Bob Miller	.50
415	Cookie Rojas	.50
416	Johnny Edwards	.50
417	Tom Hall	.50
418	Tom Shopay	.50
419	Jim Spencer	.50
420	Steve Carlton	18.00
421	Ellie Rodriguez	.50
423	Oscar Gamble	.60
424	Bill Gogolewski	.50

441 Thurman Munson

453 Barry Lersch .... .50
454 A's Team 2.00
455 Tommy Harper .... .60
456 Mark Belanger .... .60
457 Padres Rookies (Darcy
     Fast, Mike Ivie,
     Derrel Thomas) .... .60
458 Aurelio Monteagudo .... .50
459 Rick Renick .... .50
460 Al Downing .... .60
461 Tim Cullen .... .50
462 Rickey Clark .... .50
463 Bernie Carbo .... .50
464 Jim Roland .... .50
465 Gil Hodges....................... 3.00
466 Norm Miller .... .50
467 Steve Kline .... .50
468 Richie Scheinblum............. .50
469 Ron Herbel .... .50
470 Ray Fosse .... .50
471 Luke Walker .... .50
472 Phil Gagliano .... .50
473 Dan McGinn .... .50

550 *Brooks Robinson*

474 Orioles Rookies (Don
     Baylor, Roric Harrison,
     Johnny Oates) 3.50
475 Gary Nolan .... .50
476 Lee Richard .... .50
477 Tom Phoebus .... .50
478 Checklist 526-656............ 2.25
479 Don Shaw......................... .50
480 Lee May............................ .75
481 Billy Conigliaro.................. .50
482 Joe Hoerner...................... .50
483 Ken Suarez....................... .50
484 Lum Harris .... .50
485 Phil Regan........................ .50
486 John Lowenstein .... .50
487 Tigers Team 1.50
488 Mike Nagy .... .50
489 Expos Rookies (Terry
     Humphrey, Keith Lampard) .. .50
490 Dave McNally .... .75
491 Boyhood Photo
     (Lou Piniella) .... .85
492 Boyhood Photo
     (Mel Stottlemyre) .... .60
493 Boyhood Photo
     (Willie Horton)................... .60

495 Boyhood Photo
     (Bill Melton) .... .50
496 Boyhood Photo
     (Bud Harrelson) .... .65
497 Boyhood Photo
     (Jim Perry)........................ .60
498 Boyhood Photo
     (Brooks Robinson)........... 2.00
499 Vicente Romo.................... .50
500 Joe Torre 1.25
501 Pete Hamm .... .50
502 Jackie Hernandez.............. .50
503 Gary Peters .... .50
504 Ed Spiezio .... .50
505 Mike Marshall .... .70
506 Indians Rookies (Terry Ley,
     Jim Moyer, *Dick Tidrow*).... .80
507 Fred Gladding .... .50
508 Ellie Hendricks.................. .50
509 Don McMahon .... .50
510 • Ted Williams.................. 5.00
511 Tony Taylor .... .50
512 Paul Popovich .... .50
513 Lindy McDaniel .... .60
514 Ted Sizemore .... .50
515 Bert Blyleven 8.00

1972 Topps

474 Orioles Rookies

516	Oscar Brown	.50
517	Ken Brett	.60
518	Wayne Garrett	.50
519	Ted Abernathy	.50
520	Larry Bowa	1.25
521	Alan Foster	.50
522	Dodgers Team	1.25
523	Chuck Dobson	.50
524	Reds Rookies (Ed Armbrister, Mel Behney)	.50
525	Carlos May	.60
526	Bob Bailey	.70
527	Dave Leonhard	.70
528	Ron Stone	.70
529	Dave Nelson	.70
530	Don Sutton	3.50
531	Freddie Patek	1.25
532	Fred Kendall	.70
533	Ralph Houk	1.25
534	Jim Hickman	.80
535	Ed Brinkman	.80
536	Doug Rader	.70
537	Bob Locker	.70
538	Charlie Sands	.70
539	*Terry Forster*	1.25
540	Felix Millan	.70
541	Roger Repoz	.70
542	Jack Billingham	.70
543	Duane Josephson	.70
544	Ted Martinez	.70
545	Wayne Granger	.70
546	Joe Hague	.70
547	Indians Team	1.50
548	Frank Reberger	.70
549	Dave May	.70
550	Brooks Robinson	15.00
551	Ollie Brown	.70
552	Ollie Brown IA	.70
553	Wilbur Wood	.90
554	Wilbur Wood IA	.80
555	Ron Santo	1.50
556	Ron Santo IA	.80
557	John Odom	.70
558	John Odom IA	.70
559	Pete Rose	55.00
560	Pete Rose IA	25.00
561	Leo Cardenas	.70
562	Leo Cardenas IA	.70
563	Ray Sadecki	.70
564	Ray Sadecki IA	.70
565	Reggie Smith	.90
566	Reggie Smith IA	.80
567	Juan Marichal	6.00
568	Juan Marichal IA	3.00
569	Ed Kirkpatrick	.70
570	Ed Kirkpatrick IA	.70
571	Nate Colbert	.70
572	Nate Colbert IA	.70
573	Fritz Peterson	.75
574	Fritz Peterson IA	.75
575	Al Oliver	2.00
576	• Leo Durocher	1.25
577	Mike Paul	.70
578	Billy Grabarkewitz	.70

595 Nolan Ryan

695 Rod Carew

680	Dave Johnson	3.50
681	Bobby Pfeil	2.25
682	Mike McCormick	2.50
683	Steve Hovley	2.25
684	Hal Breeden	2.25
685	Joe Horlen	2.25
686	Steve Garvey	75.00
687	Del Unser	2.25
688	Cardinals Team	3.25
689	Eddie Fisher	2.25
690	Willie Montanez	2.50
691	Curt Blefary	2.25
692	Curt Blefary IA	2.25
693	Alan Gallagher	2.25
694	Alan Gallagher IA	2.25
695	Rod Carew	90.00
696	Rod Carew IA	37.00
697	Jerry Koosman	4.50
698	Jerry Koosman IA	2.50
699	Bobby Murcer	8.00
700	Bobby Murcer IA	3.00
701	Jose Pagan	2.25
702	Jose Pagan IA	2.25
703	Doug Griffin	2.25
704	Doug Griffin IA	2.25
705	Pat Corrales	2.50
706	Pat Corrales IA	2.25
707	Tim Foli	2.25
708	Tim Foli IA	2.25
709	Jim Kaat	8.00
710	Jim Kaat IA	5.25
711	Bobby Bonds	10.00
712	Bobby Bonds IA	6.00
713	Gene Michael	2.50
714	Gene Michael IA	2.50
715	Mike Epstein	2.50
716	Jesus Alou	2.50
717	Bruce Dal Canton	2.25
718	Del Rice	2.25
719	Cesar Geronimo	2.50
720	Sam McDowell	3.00
721	Eddie Leon	2.25
722	Bill Sudakis	2.25
723	Al Santorini	2.25
724	AL Rookies (John Curtis, Rich Hinton, Mickey Scott)	2.50
725	Dick McAuliffe	2.50
726	Dick Selma	2.25

655	Jerry Grote	.80
656	Rudy May	.80
657	Bobby Wine	2.25
658	Steve Dunning	2.25
659	Bob Aspromonte	2.25
660	Paul Blair	2.50
661	Bill Virdon	2.25
662	Stan Bahnsen	2.25
663	Fran Healy	2.25
664	Bobby Knoop	2.25
665	Chris Short	2.25
666	Hector Torres	2.25
667	Ray Newman	2.25
668	Rangers Team	3.25
669	Willie Crawford	2.25
670	Ken Holtzman	2.75
671	Donn Clendenon	2.50
672	Archie Reynolds	2.25
673	Dave Marshall	2.25
674	John Kennedy	2.25
675	Pat Jarvis	2.25
676	Danny Cater	2.25
677	Ivan Murrell	2.25
678	Steve Luebber	2.25
679	Astros Rookies (Bob Fenwick, Bob Stinson)	2.25

729	Bob Veale	2.50
730	Rick Monday	2.75
733	Jim Hart	2.50
734	Bob Burda	2.25
735	Diego Segui	2.25
736	Bill Russell	4.00
737	*Lenny Randle*	2.50
738	Jim Merritt	2.25
739	Don Mason	2.25
740	Rico Carty	4.00
744	*Jim Slaton*	2.50
745	Julian Javier	2.50
746	Lowell Palmer	2.25
747	Jim Stewart	2.25
749	Walter Alston	5.00
750	Willie Horton	2.75
751	Steve Carlton Traded	40.00
752	Joe Morgan Traded	32.00
753	Denny McLain Traded	8.00
754	Frank Robinson Traded	26.00
755	Jim Fregosi	2.75
756	Rick Wise Traded	2.75
757	Jose Cardenal Traded	2.50
759	Chris Cannizzaro	2.25
760	Bill Mazeroski	3.75
761	Major League Rookies (*Ron Cey, Ben Oglivie,* Bernie Williams)	15.00

445 Tom Seaver

762	Wayne Simpson	2.25
763	Ron Hansen	2.25
764	Dusty Baker	3.00
766	Steve Hamilton	2.25
768	Denny Doyle	2.25
769	Jack Aker	2.50
770	Jim Wynn	2.75
771	Giants Team	3.25
772	Ken Tatum	2.25
773	Ron Brand	2.25
774	Luis Alvarado	2.25
775	Jerry Reuss	3.50
776	Bill Voss	2.25
777	Hoyt Wilhelm	15.00
778	Twins Rookies (Vic Albury, *Rick Dempsey,* Jim Strickland)	3.25
779	Tony Cloninger	2.50
780	Dick Green	2.25
781	Jim McAndrew	2.25
782	Larry Stahl	2.25
783	Les Cain	2.25
784	Ken Aspromonte	2.25
785	Vic Davalillo	2.25
786	Chuck Brinkman	2.25
787	Ron Reed	5.00

711 Bobby Bonds

1973 TOPPS

Topps marked the end of an era with its 1973 edition: It was the last time a major set was issued piecemeal, one series at a time throughout the summer. Card fronts contain a small silhouetted figure depicting each player's position—an unusual design element. Card backs have a vertical format once again and retain the basic elements of cartoons, brief biographies, and year-by-year stats. The 660-card set is noted for odd-looking manager cards. These cards include tiny black-and-white portraits of team coaches along with pictures of each team skipper. They can be found with different backgrounds surrounding the photos of the coaches, although the variations have little difference in value. Without question the most popular card in the set is number 615, titled Rookie Third Basemen, which shows future Hall of Famer Mike Schmidt along with Ron Cey. It currently fetches prices of about $450.

		NR MT
Complete set		**$1250.00**
Commons (1-396)		**.25**
Commons (397-528)		**.40**
Commons (529-660)		**1.25**

220 Nolan Ryan

1	All Time HR Ldrs (Babe Ruth, Hank Aaron, Willie Mays)	$20.00
2	Rich Hebner	.30
3	Jim Lonborg	.30
5	Ed Brinkman	.30
7	Rangers Team	.90
10	Don Sutton	2.00
11	Chris Chambliss	.70
12	Padres Mgr./Coaches (Dave Garcia, Johnny Podres, Bob Skinner, Whitey Wietelmann, Don Zimmer)	.40
13	George Hendrick	.70
15	Ralph Garr	.30
23	Dave Kingman	1.25
25	Roy White	.40
26	Pirates Team	1.00
28	Hal McRae	.50
30	Tug McGraw	.60
31	*Buddy Bell*	4.00
35	Willie Davis	.50
40	Reggie Smith	.50
43	*Randy Moffitt*	.30
44	Rick Monday	.40
49	Twins Mgr./Coaches (Vern Morgan, Frank Quilici, Bob Rodgers, Ralph Rowe, Al Worthington)	.30
50	Roberto Clemente	25.00
54	Checklist 1-132	2.00
55	Jon Matlack	.40
59	*Steve Yeager*	.60
60	Ken Holtzman	.40

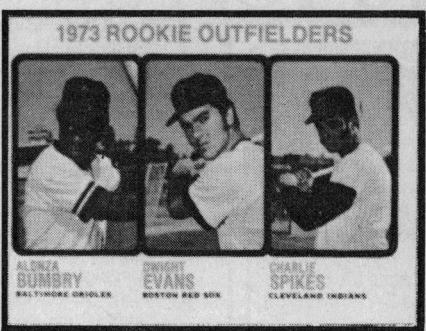

614 Rookie Outfielders

61	Batting Ldrs (Rod Carew, Billy Williams)	1.75
62	HR Ldrs (Dick Allen, Johnny Bench)	1.50
63	RBI Ldrs (Dick Allen, Johnny Bench)	1.50
64	SB Ldrs (Lou Brock, Bert Campaneris)	1.25
65	ERA Ldrs (Steve Carlton, Luis Tiant)	1.25
66	Victory Ldrs (Steve Carlton, Gaylord Perry, Wilbur Wood)	1.25
67	SO Ldrs (Steve Carlton, Nolan Ryan)	2.50
68	Leading Firemen (Clay Carroll, Sparky Lyle)	.80
70	Milt Pappas	.40
75	Vada Pinson	.80
80	Tony Oliva	1.50
81	Cubs Mgr./Coaches (Hank Aguirre, Ernie Banks, Larry Jansen, Whitey Lockman, Pete Reiser)	.55
84	Rollie Fingers	1.50
85	Ted Simmons	1.25
90	Brooks Robinson	5.00
91	Dodgers Team	1.00
100	Hank Aaron	22.00
108	Bill Russell	.40
109	Doyle Alexander	1.00
115	Ron Santo	.80
116	Yankees Mgr./Coaches (Jim Hegan, Ralph Houk, Elston Howard, Dick Howser, Jim Turner)	.75
118	John Mayberry	.40
119	Larry Bowa	.80
125	Ron Fairly	.40
127	Brewers Team	.90
130	Pete Rose	20.00
131	Red Sox Mgr./Coaches (Doug Camilli, Eddie Kasko, Don Lenhardt, Eddie Popowski, Lee Stange)	.40
136	Orioles Mgr./Coaches (George Bamberger, Jim Frey, Billy Hunter, George Staller, Earl Weaver)	.75
140	Lou Piniella	.80
142	Thurman Munson	9.00
145	Bobby Bonds	.70
148	*Dave Goltz*	.60
150	Wilbur Wood	.40
153	Al Hrabosky	.40
155	Sal Bando	.70
158	Astros Team	.90
160	Jim Palmer	9.00
165	Luis Aparicio	3.00
167	Steve Stone	.50
170	Harmon Killebrew	3.50

193 Carlton Fisk

613 Rookie Catchers

290	Cesar Cedeno	.40
292	Jose Cruz	.80
295	Bert Campaneris	.60
296	Reds Mgr./Coaches (Sparky Anderson, Alex Grammas, Ted Kluszewski, George Scherger, Larry Shepard)	.70
300	Steve Carlton	12.00
303	Nelson Briles	.25
305	Willie Mays	25.00
306	Tom Burgmeier	.25
310	Dick Allen	.80
316	Padres Team	.90
320	Lou Brock	4.00
322	*Garry Maddox*	.80
323	Tigers Mgr./Coaches (Art Fowler, Billy Martin, Joe Schultz, Charlie Silvera, Dick Tracewski)	1.00
325	Boog Powell	1.00
329	Ed Kranepool	.30
330	Rod Carew	18.00
332	*John Felske*	.30
333	Gene Clines	.25
338	Checklist 265-396	2.00
339	Dick Tidrow	.30
340	Nate Colbert	.30
341	Boyhood Photo (Jim Palmer)	1.50
342	Boyhood Photo (Sam McDowell)	.40
343	Boyhood Photo (Bobby Murcer)	.40
344	Boyhood Photo (Jim Hunter)	1.50
345	Boyhood Photo (Chris Speier)	.30
346	Boyhood Photo (Gaylord Perry)	1.50
347	Royals Team	.90
348	Rennie Stennett	.30
349	Dick McAuliffe	.30
350	Tom Seaver	20.00
352	*Don Stanhouse*	.40
353	Steve Brye	.30
355	Mike Marshall	.40
356	White Sox Mgr./Coaches (Joe Lonnett, Jim Maloney, Al Monchak, Johnny Sain, Chuck Tanner)	.50
357	Ross Grimsley	.30
360	Joe Rudi (photo is Gene Tenace)	.40
364	Rick Wise	.30
365	Rico Petrocelli	.30
367	Burt Hooton	.40
368	Bill Buckner	.75
369	Lerrin LaGrow	.25
370	Willie Stargell	4.00
372	Oscar Gamble	.30
373	Clyde Wright	.30
374	Darrell Evans	.75
375	Larry Dierker	.30

1 All Time HR Leaders

130 Pete Rose

330 Rod Carew

245 Carl Yastrzemski

174 Rich Gossage

478	SO Ldr (Walter Johnson) ..	**1.25**
479	Hal Lanier	.60
480	Juan Marichal	**3.50**
481	White Sox Team	**1.25**
482	• *Rick Reuschel*	**5.00**
483	Dal Maxvill	.45
484	Ernie McAnally	.40
485	Norm Cash	.85
486	Phillies Mgr./Coaches (Carroll Berringer, Billy DeMars, Danny Ozark, Ray Rippelmeyer, Bobby Wine)	.65
487	Bruce Dal Canton	.40
488	Dave Campbell	.40
489	Jeff Burroughs	.65
490	Claude Osteen	.65
492	Pedro Borbon	.45
493	Duffy Dyer	.40
494	Rich Morales	.40
495	Tommy Helms	.45
496	Ray Lamb	.40
497	Cardinals Mgr./Coaches (Vern Benson, George Kissell, Red Schoendienst, Barney Schultz)	.90

498	Graig Nettles	**2.50**
499	Bob Moose	.40
500	A's Team	**2.00**
501	Larry Gura	.50
502	Bobby Valentine	.65
503	• Phil Niekro	**3.00**
504	Earl Williams	.40
505	Bob Bailey	.40
506	Bart Johnson	.40
507	Darrel Chaney	.40
508	Gates Brown	.40
509	Jim Nash	.40
510	Amos Otis	.60
511	Sam McDowell	.65
512	Dalton Jones	.40
513	Dave Marshall	.40
514	Jerry Kenney	.40
515	Andy Messersmith	.50
516	Danny Walton	.40
517	Pirates Mgr./Coaches (Don Leppert, Bill Mazeroski, Dave Ricketts, Bill Virdon, Mel Wright)	.70
518	Bob Veale	.45
519	John Edwards	.40
520	Mel Stottlemyre	.65
521	Braves Team	**1.20**
522	Leo Cardenas	.40

142 Thurman Munson

THE ALL-TIME

BABE RUTH

2,209

474 RBI Leader

523	Wayne Granger	.40
524	Gene Tenace	.40
525	Jim Fregosi	.65
526	Ollie Brown	.40
527	Dan McGinn	.40
528	Paul Blair	.50
529	Milt May	1.25
530	Jim Kaat	3.25
531	Ron Woods	1.25
532	Steve Mingori	1.25
533	Larry Stahl	1.25
534	Dave Lemonds	1.25
535	John Callison	1.50
536	Phillies Team	2.50
537	Bill Slayback	1.25
538	Jim Hart	1.50
539	Tom Murphy	1.25
540	Cleon Jones	1.50
541	Bob Bolin	1.25
542	Pat Corrales	1.50
543	Alan Foster	1.25
544	Von Joshua	1.25
545	Orlando Cepeda	3.50
546	Jim York	1.25
547	Bobby Heise	1.25
548	Don Durham	1.25

549	Rangers Mgr./Coaches (Chuck Estrada, Whitey Herzog, Chuck Hiller, Jackie Moore)	2.00
550	Dave Johnson	3.00
551	Mike Kilkenny	1.25
552	J.C. Martin	1.25
553	Mickey Scott	1.25
554	Dave Concepcion	2.50
555	Bill Hands	1.25
556	Yankees Team	4.00
557	Bernie Williams	1.25
558	Jerry May	1.25
559	Barry Lersch	1.25
560	Frank Howard	2.25
561	Jim Geddes	1.25
562	Wayne Garrett	1.25
563	Larry Haney	1.25
564	Mike Thompson	1.25
565	Jim Hickman	1.50
567	Bob Fenwick	1.25
568	Ray Newman	1.25
569	Dodgèrs Mgr./Coaches (Red Adams, Walt Alston, Monty Basgall, Jim Gilliam, Tom Lasorda)	3.00
570	Bill Singer	1.50
571	Rusty Torres	1.50

ORLANDO CEPEDA
OAKLAND A'S   1st BASE

545 Orlando Cepeda

615 Rookie Third Basemen

573 Fred Beene...................... 1.25
574 Bob Didier........................ 1.25
575 Dock Ellis........................ 1.25
576 Expos Team 2.50
577 *Eric Soderholm*................ 1.50
578 Ken Wright....................... 1.25
579 Tom Grieve...................... 1.25
580 Joe Pepitone 2.00
581 Steve Kealey 1.25
582 Darrell Porter 1.75
583 Bill Greif.......................... 1.25
584 Chris Arnold.................... 1.25
585 Joe Niekro 2.00
586 Bill Sudakis..................... 1.50
587 Rich McKinney 1.25
588 Checklist 529-660.......... 10.00
589 Ken Forsch 1.25
590 Deron Johnson 1.25
591 Mike Hedlund 1.25
592 John Boccabella 1.25
593 Royals Mgr./Coaches
      (Galen Cisco, Harry
      Dunlop, Charlie Lau,
      Jack McKeon)................. 1.50
595 Don Gullett 1.50
596 Red Sox Team 2.75
597 Mickey Rivers 1.75
598 Phil Roof 1.25
600 Dave McNally 1.75
601 Rookie Catchers (George
      Pena, Sergio Robles,
      Rick Stelmaszek)............. 1.25

602 Rookie Pitchers (Mel
      Behney, Ralph Garcia,
      Doug Rau) 1.50
603 Rookie Third Basemen
      (Terry Hughes,
      Bill McNulty,
      Ken Reitz)...................... 1.50
605 Rookie First Basemen
      (Pat Bourque,
      Enos Cabell,
      Gonzalo Marquez).......... 1.75
606 Rookie Outfielders (*Gary
      Matthews*, Tom Paciorek,
      Jorge Roque)................. 2.25
607 Rookie Shortstops (Ray
      Busse, Pepe Frias,
      Mario Guerrero)............. 1.25
608 Rookie Pitchers (*Steve
      Busby*, Dick Colpaert,
      George Medich)............. 1.50
609 Rookie Second Basemen
      (Larvell Blanks, Pedro
      Garcia, *Dave Lopes*) 2.25
610 • Rookie Pitchers (Jimmy
      Freeman, Charlie Hough,
      Hank Webb) 1.75
611 Rookie Outfielders (Rich
      Coggins, Jim Wohlford,
      Richie Zisk).................. 1.50
612 Rookie Pitchers (Steve
      Lawson, Bob Reynolds,
      Brent Strom).................. 1.25

613 Rookie Catchers (*Bob Boone*, Mike Ivie, Skip Jutze).................... **35.00**
614 Rookie Outfielders (*Alonza Bumbry, Dwight Evans*, Charlie Spikes) .. **75.00**
615 Rookie Third Basemen (Ron Cey, Dave Hilton, *Mike Schmidt*)............. **450.00**
616 Rookie Pitchers (Norm Angelini, Steve Blateric, Mike Garman)................. **1.50**
617 Rich Chiles **1.25**
618 Andy Etchebarren............ **1.25**
619 Billy Wilson **1.25**
620 Tommy Harper **1.50**
621 Joe Ferguson **1.25**
622 Larry Hisle **1.50**
623 Steve Renko.................... **1.25**
624 Astros Mgr./Coaches (Leo Durocher, Preston Gomez, Grady Hatton, Hub Kittle, Jim Owens).... **2.25**
625 Angel Mangual **1.25**
627 Luis Alvarado.................. **1.25**
628 Jim Slaton....................... **1.25**
629 Indians Team................... **2.50**
630 Denny McLain **3.00**
631 Tom Matchick.................. **1.25**
632 Dick Selma...................... **1.25**
633 Ike Brown **1.25**
635 Gene Alley...................... **1.25**
636 Rick Clark....................... **1.25**
637 Norm Miller..................... **1.25**
638 Ken Reynolds.................. **1.25**
639 Willie Crawford **1.25**
640 Dick Bosman **1.35**
641 Reds Team...................... **2.75**
642 Jose Laboy...................... **1.25**
643 Al Fitzmorris **1.25**
644 Jack Heidemann.............. **1.25**
645 Bob Locker **1.25**
647 George Stone.................. **1.25**
648 Tom Egan........................ **1.25**
650 Felipe Alou **1.85**
651 Don Carrithers................ **1.25**
652 Ted Kubiak **1.25**
653 Joe Hoerner.................... **1.25**
654 Twins Team..................... **2.50**

213 Steve Garvey

655 Clay Kirby **1.25**
656 John Ellis **1.25**
657 Bob Johnson **1.25**
658 Elliott Maddox................. **1.50**
659 Jose Pagan **1.50**
660 Fred Scherman................ **2.50**

325 Boog Powell

1974 TOPPS

For the first time, instead of issuing cards by series—the traditional way—Topps issued all 660 cards at one time. That allowed collectors the chance to acquire any card number at any time instead of having to wait and piece together a collection made up of separate 132-card series throughout the summer. Because everyone guessed, falsely, that the San Diego Padres would be moved to Washington, D.C., Topps changed 15 Padres cards to read "Washington, Nat'l League." When the team stayed in San Diego, Topps quickly changed the cards, but not in time to prevent the release of many that contained the error. This was also the time that Hank Aaron was just two homers short of breaking Babe Ruth's career record, and Aaron is featured on the first six cards, which are reproductions of previous cards.

	NR MT
Complete set	$500.00
Commons	.20

283 Mike Schmidt

1	Hank Aaron	$30.00
2	Aaron Special 1954-57	3.00
3	Aaron Special 1958-61	3.00
4	Aaron Special 1962-65	3.00
5	Aaron Special 1966-69	3.00
6	Aaron Special 1970-73	3.00
7	Jim Hunter	3.00
9	Mickey Lolich	.60
10	Johnny Bench	15.00
11	Jim Bibby	.25
12	Dave May	.20
15	Joe Torre	.80
16	Orioles Team	.80
19	Gerry Moses	.25
20	Nolan Ryan	42.00
24	John Hiller	.25
25	Ken Singleton	.30
26	*Bill Campbell*	.40
27	George Scott	.30
28	Manny Sanguillen	.25
29	Phil Niekro	2.00
30	Bobby Bonds	.50
31	Astros Mgr./Coaches (Roger Craig, Preston Gomez, Grady Hatton, Hub Kittle, Bob Lillis)	.25
32	Johnny Grubb (Washington)	4.00
32	Johnny Grubb (San Diego)	.25
35	Gaylord Perry	2.50
36	Cardinals Team	2.25
37	Dave Sells	.20
38	Don Kessinger	.25
40	Jim Palmer	5.00
41	Bobby Floyd	.20
42	Claude Osteen	.30
43	• Jim Wynn	.30
44	Mel Stottlemyre	.40
45	Dave Johnson	.75
47	*Dick Ruthven*	.25
50	Rod Carew	10.00

456 Dave Winfield

400 Harmon Killebrew

20 Nolan Ryan

107	Alex Johnson	.20
108	Al Hrabosky	.30
109	Bob Grich	.40
110	Billy Williams	3.00
111	Clay Carroll	.25
112	Dave Lopes	.45
113	Dick Drago	.20
114	Angels Team	.80
115	Willie Horton	.30
116	Jerry Reuss	.30
117	Ron Blomberg	.25
118	Bill Lee	.25
119	Phillies Mgr./Coaches (Carroll Beringer, Bill DeMars, Danny Ozark, Ray Ripplemeyer, Bobby Wine)	.25
120	Wilbur Wood	.30
122	Jim Holt	.20
123	Nelson Briles	.20
125	Nate Colbert (Washington)	4.00
125	Nate Colbert (San Diego)	.30
126	Checklist 1-132	1.50
127	Tom Paciorek	.25
128	John Ellis	.20
129	Chris Speier	.25

130	Reggie Jackson	14.00
131	Bob Boone	1.50
132	Felix Millan	.25
133	*David Clyde*	.30
134	Denis Menke	.25
135	Roy White	.40
136	Rick Reuschel	.85
137	Al Bumbry	.25
138	Ed Brinkman	.25
139	Aurelio Monteagudo	.20
140	Darrell Evans	.60
141	Pat Bourque	.20
142	Pedro Garcia	.20
144	Dodgers Mgr./Coaches (Red Adams, Walter Alston, Monty Basgall, Jim Gilliam, Tom Lasorda)	1.50
145	Dock Ellis	.25
146	Ron Fairly	.30
147	Bart Johnson	.20
148	Dave Hilton (Washington)	4.00
148	Dave Hilton (San Diego)	.25
149	Mac Scarce	.20
150	John Mayberry	.30
151	Diego Segui	.20
152	Oscar Gamble	.30

252 Dave Parker

575 Steve Garvey

250 Willie McCovey

210	Bill Singer	.25
211	Cubs Team	.85
212	Rollie Fingers	2.50
215	Al Kaline	3.50
217	Tim Foli	.20
220	Don Sutton	2.00
221	White Sox Mgr./Coaches (Joe Lonnett, Jim Mahoney, Alex Monchak, Johnny Sain, Chuck Tanner)	.35
222	Ramon Hernandez	.20
223	Jeff Burroughs	.50
224	Roger Metzger	.20
225	Paul Splittorff	.25
226	Washington Nat'l. Team	7.00
226	Padres Team	1.00
229	Fritz Peterson	.30
230	Tony Perez	1.25
235	Dave McNally	.30
236	• Cardinals Mgr./Coaches (Vern Benson, George Kissell, Johnny Lewis, Red Schoendienst, Barney Schultz)	.30
237	Ken Brett	.25
238	Fran Healy	.20
239	Bill Russell	.30
240	Joe Coleman	.25
241	Glenn Beckert (Washington)	4.00
241	Glenn Beckert (San Diego)	.30
244	Carl Morton	.20
245	Cleon Jones	.25
246	A's Team	1.25
247	Rick Miller	.20
248	Tom Hall	.20
250	Willie McCovey (Washington)	25.00
250	Willie McCovey (San Diego)	4.00
251	Graig Nettles	1.50
252	*Dave Parker*	39.00
253	John Boccabella	.20
255	Larry Bowa	.40
257	Buddy Bell	1.25
259	Bob Reynolds	.20
260	Ted Simmons	.80
261	Jerry Bell	.20
263	Checklist 133-264	1.50
264	Joe Rudi	.40
265	Tug McGraw	.60
266	Jim Northrup	.25
267	Andy Messersmith	.30
270	Ron Santo	.50
271	Bill Hands	.20
273	Checklist 265-396	1.50
274	Fred Beene	.25
275	Ron Hunt	.25
278	Cookie Rojas	.20
279	Jim Crawford	.20
280	Carl Yastrzemski	12.00
281	Giants Team	.80
282	Doyle Alexander	.40
283	Mike Schmidt	115.00
284	Dave Duncan	.20
285	Reggie Smith	.40
286	Tony Muser	.20
287	Clay Kirby	.20
288	*Gorman Thomas*	1.00
289	Rick Auerbach	.20
290	Vida Blue	.60
291	Don Hahn	.20
292	Chuck Seelbach	.20
293	Milt May	.20
294	Steve Foucault	.20

598 Rookie Outfielders

1974 Topps

10 Johnny Bench

500	Lee May	.35
504	Joe Niekro	.40
505	Bill Buckner	.50
508	Expos Team	.80
511	Toby Harrah	.30
515	Willie Montanez	.25
517	Mike Hegan	.25
520	Tim McCarver	.60
522	J.R. Richard	.30
523	Cecil Cooper	1.50
529	Horace Clarke	.25
530	Mickey Stanley	.25
531	Expos Mgr./Coaches (Dave Bristol, Larry Doby, Gene Mauch, Cal McLish, Jerry Zimmerman)	.40
532	Skip Lockwood	.20
535	Bob Tolan	.25
536	Duffy Dyer	.20
537	Steve Mingori	.20
538	Cesar Tovar	.20
541	Indians Team	.80
542	Rich Gossage	2.00
543	Danny Cater	.20
544	Ron Schueler	.20
545	Billy Conigliaro	.20
546	Mike Corkins	.20
548	Sonny Siebert	.20
549	Mike Jorgensen	.20
550	Sam McDowell	.40
551	Von Joshua	.20
555	Woodie Fryman	.30
556	Dave Campbell	.25
558	Bill Fahey	.20
560	Mike Cuellar	.35
561	Ed Kranepool	.30
563	Hal McRae	.40
565	Milt Wilcox	.25
567	Red Sox Team	.90
568	Mike Torrez	.25
569	Rick Dempsey	.30
570	Ralph Garr	.30
575	Steve Garvey	15.00
578	Ralph Houk	.40
582	*Bucky Dent*	1.00
585	Merv Rettenmund	.25
587	*Larry Christensen*	.40
588	Hal Lanier	.40
593	Steve Yeager	.25

167 Luis Tiant

595	Steve Blass	.25
596	Rookie Pitchers (*Wayne Garland,* Fred Holdsworth, *Mark Littell,* Dick Pole)	.35
597	Rookie Shortstops (Dave Chalk, John Gamble, Pete Mackanin, *Manny Trillo*)	.80
598	Rookie Outfielders (Dave Augustine, *Ken Griffey,* Steve Ontiveros, Jim Tyrone)	20.00
599	Rookie Pitchers (Ron Diorio, Dave Freisleben, Frank Riccelli, Greg Shanahan) (Freisleben with Washington)	.80
599	Rookie Pitchers (Ron Diorio, Dave Freisleben, Frank Riccelli, Greg Shanahan) (Freisleben with San Diego— large print)	3.50
599	Rookie Pitchers (Ron Diorio, Dave Freisleben, Frank Riccelli, Greg Shanahan) (Freisleben with San Diego—small print)	6.00

1974 Topps

251 Graig Nettles

1975 TOPPS

Although all 660 cards in the 1975 Topps set were issued at once, collectors found that the first 132 cards (from the first of five printing sheets) were produced in a somewhat smaller quantity. Each card front uses three colors, two for the border and one for the bold team name at the top. A large subset of 24 cards features the American and National League MVPs since 1951, pictured in miniature versions of the Topps cards from their award-winning seasons. Rookie cards show four players, grouped by position. Famous rookies include George Brett, Gary Carter, Keith Hernandez, Fred Lynn, Jim Rice, and Robin Yount. Topps also test-marketed this set in a smaller format with cards measuring 2¼ by 3⅛ inches. This mini set is a rare commodity today.

228 George Brett

		NR MT
Complete set		**$800.00**
Commons (1-132)		**.30**
Commons (133-660)		**.20**
Complete Mini set		**1400.00**
Mini commons		**.45**

1	'74 Highlights (Hank Aaron)	$36.00
2	'74 Highlights (Lou Brock)	2.00
3	'74 Highlights (Bob Gibson)	1.75
4	'74 Highlights (Al Kaline)	1.75
5	'74 Highlights (Nolan Ryan)	6.00
6	'74 Highlights (Mike Marshall)	.40
7	'74 Highlights (Dick Bosman, Steve Busby, Nolan Ryan)	1.00
8	Rogelio Moret	.30
9	Frank Tepedino	.30
10	Willie Davis	.35
11	Bill Melton	.35
12	David Clyde	.35
13	Gene Locklear	.30
14	Milt Wilcox	.35
15	Jose Cardenal	.35
16	Frank Tanana	.40
17	Dave Concepcion	.60
18	Tigers Team (Ralph Houk)	.90
19	Jerry Koosman	.40
20	Thurman Munson	6.00
21	Rollie Fingers	4.00
22	Dave Cash	.30
23	Bill Russell	.35
24	Al Fitzmorris	.30
25	Lee May	.40
26	Dave McNally	.35
27	Ken Reitz	.30
28	Tom Murphy	.30
29	Dave Parker	15.00
30	Bert Blyleven	1.00
31	Dave Rader	.30

70 Mike Schmidt

58	Chuck Taylor	.30
59	Ken Henderson	.30
60	Fergie Jenkins	2.75
61	Dave Winfield	16.00
62	Fritz Peterson	.30
63	Steve Swisher	.30
64	Dave Chalk	.30
65	Don Gullett	.35
66	Willie Horton	.35
67	Tug McGraw	.50
68	Ron Blomberg	.35
69	John Odom	.35
70	Mike Schmidt	57.00
71	Charlie Hough	.35
72	Royals Team (Jack McKeon)	.80
73	J.R. Richard	.35
74	Mark Belanger	.35
75	Ted Simmons	.70
76	Ed Sprague	.30
77	Richie Zisk	.35
78	Ray Corbin	.30
79	Gary Matthews	.40
80	Carlton Fisk	11.00
81	Ron Reed	.35
82	Pat Kelly	.30
83	Jim Merritt	.30
84	Enzo Hernandez	.30
85	Bill Bonham	.30
86	Joe Lis	.30
87	George Foster	1.25
88	Tom Egan	.30
89	Jim Ray	.30
90	Rusty Staub	.60
91	Dick Green	.30
92	Cecil Upshaw	.35
93	Dave Lopes	.40
94	Jim Lonborg	.35
95	John Mayberry	.35
96	Mike Cosgrove	.30
97	Earl Williams	.30
98	Rich Folkers	.30
99	Mike Hegan	.30
100	Willie Stargell	2.50
101	Expos Team (Gene Mauch)	1.00
102	Joe Decker	.30
103	Rick Miller	.30
104	Bill Madlock	1.25

32	Reggie Cleveland	.30
33	Dusty Baker	.40
34	Steve Renko	.30
35	Ron Santo	.50
36	Joe Lovitto	.30
37	Dave Freisleben	.30
38	Buddy Bell	.80
39	Andy Thornton	.70
40	Bill Singer	.35
41	Cesar Geronimo	.35
42	Joe Coleman	.35
43	Cleon Jones	.35
44	Pat Dobson	.35
45	Joe Rudi	.40
46	Phillies Team (Danny Ozark)	.80
47	Tommy John	1.25
48	Freddie Patek	.30
49	Larry Dierker	.30
50	Brooks Robinson	5.00
51	*Bob Forsch*	.80
52	Darrell Porter	.35
53	Dave Giusti	.30
54	Eric Soderholm	.30
55	Bobby Bonds	.50
56	Rick Wise	.35
57	Dave Johnson	.80

105	Buzz Capra	.30
106	*Mike Hargrove*	.40
107	Jim Barr	.30
108	Tom Hall	.30
109	George Hendrick	.35
110	Wilbur Wood	.35
111	Wayne Garrett	.30
112	Larry Hardy	.30
113	Elliott Maddox	.30
114	Dick Lange	.30
115	Joe Ferguson	.30
116	Lerrin LaGrow	.30
117	Orioles Team (Earl Weaver)	1.00
118	Mike Anderson	.30
119	Tommy Helms	.30
120	Steve Busby (photo is Fran Healy)	.35
121	Bill North	.30
122	Al Hrabosky	.30
123	Johnny Briggs	.35
124	Jerry Reuss	.40
125	Ken Singleton	.40
126	Checklist 1-132	1.50
127	Glen Borgmann	.30
128	Bill Lee	.35
129	Rick Monday	.35
130	Phil Niekro	2.00
131	Toby Harrah	.35
132	Randy Moffitt	.30
133	Dan Driessen	.30
134	Charlie Spikes	.25
136	Jim Mason	.25
137	Terry Forster	.30
140	Steve Garvey	7.00
141	Mickey Stanley	.25
143	*Cliff Johnson*	.40
145	Ken Holtzman	.30
146	Padres Team (John McNamara)	.80
150	Bob Gibson	2.50
156	Dave Kingman	.90
158	Jerry Grote	.25
160	Graig Nettles	1.50
164	Mickey Rivers	.25
166	Woody Fryman	.25
170	Bert Campaneris	.40
172	Red Sox Team (Darrell Johnson)	1.25

1 Hank Aaron

173	Steve Rogers	.30
174	Bake McBride	.25
175	Don Money	.25
176	Burt Hooton	.20
180	Joe Morgan	3.00
183	Mel Stottlemyre	.40
185	Steve Carlton	8.00
189	1951—MVPs (Yogi Berra, Roy Campanella)	1.50
190	1952—MVPs (Hank Sauer, Bobby Shantz)	.40
191	1953—MVPs (Roy Campanella, Al Rosen)	.90
192	1954—MVPs (Yogi Berra, Willie Mays)	1.50
193	1955—MVPs (Yogi Berra, Roy Campanella)	1.50
194	1956—MVPs (Mickey Mantle, Don Newcombe)	6.00
195	1957—MVPs (Hank Aaron, Mickey Mantle)	7.00
196	1958—MVPs (Ernie Banks, Jackie Jensen)	.90
197	1959—MVPs (Ernie Banks, Nellie Fox)	.90
198	1960—MVPs (Dick Groat, Roger Maris)	1.25

29 Dave Parker

199 1961—MVPs (Roger
Maris, Frank Robinson) ... **1.50**
200 1962—MVPs (Mickey
Mantle, Maury Wills)......... **5.00**
201 1963—MVPs (Elston
Howard, Sandy Koufax) ... **1.50**
202 1964—MVPs (Ken Boyer,
Brooks Robinson)............. **1.25**
203 1965—MVPs (Willie
Mays, Zoilo Versalles) **1.25**
204 1966—MVPs (Bob
Clemente, Frank
Robinson)........................ **1.50**
205 1967—MVPs (Orlando
Cepeda, Carl
Yastrzemski) **1.25**
206 1968—MVPs (Bob
Gibson, Denny McLain)... **1.25**
207 1969—MVPs
(Harmon Killebrew,
Willie McCovey) **1.50**
208 1970—MVPs (Johnny
Bench, Boog Powell)........ **1.25**
209 1971—MVPs (Vida Blue,
Joe Torre)....................... **1.25**
210 1972—MVPs (Rich Allen,
Johnny Bench) **1.25**

211 1973—MVPs (Reggie
Jackson, Pete Rose) **4.00**
212 1974—MVPs (Jeff
Burroughs, Steve Garvey) ... **.90**
213 Oscar Gamble .... **.25**
215 Bobby Valentine .... **.30**
216 Giants Team
(Wes Westrum) .... **.30**
217 Lou Piniella....................... **.70**
220 Don Sutton **1.50**
221 Aurelio Rodriquez
(Rodriguez)...................... **.25**
223 *Robin Yount*................. **210.00**
225 Bob Grich .... **.40**
226 Bill Campbell .... **.25**
227 Bob Watson .... **.25**
228 *George Brett*................. **200.00**
230 • Jim Hunter..................... **2.00**
236 Angels Team
(Dick Williams).................. **.80**
240 Garry Maddox .... **.25**
241 Dick Tidrow....................... **.20**
242 Jay Johnstone .... **.25**
244 Bill Buckner **1.25**
245 • Mickey Lolich................... **.50**
246 • Cardinals Team
(Red Schoendienst)........... **.80**
247 Enos Cabell .... **.25**
248 Randy Jones .... **.25**
249 Danny Thompson .... **.25**
250 Ken Brett .... **.25**
253 Jesus Alou .... **.25**
254 Mike Torrez .... **.25**
255 Dwight Evans **6.00**
257 Checklist 133-264............ **1.50**
260 Johnny Bench................ **10.00**
263 Jim Perry .... **.40**
266 Sandy Alomar .... **.25**
268 Hal McRae.......................... **.40**
270 Ron Fairly .... **.30**
275 Paul Blair .... **.25**
276 White Sox Team
(Chuck Tanner) .... **.80**
280 Carl Yastrzemski **11.00**
284 Ken Griffey .... **.70**
290 Jon Matlack .... **.25**
291 Bill Sudakis .... **.25**
294 *Geoff Zahn* .... **.40**
295 • Vada Pinson.................... **.60**

299	Bucky Dent	.40
300	Reggie Jackson	15.00
302	*Rick Burleson*	.50
304	Pirates Team (Danny Murtaugh)	.85
306	Batting Ldrs (Rod Carew, Ralph Garr)	.80
307	HR Ldrs (Dick Allen, Mike Schmidt)	.90
308	RBI Ldrs (Johnny Bench, Jeff Burroughs)	.90
309	SB Ldrs (Lou Brock, Bill North)	.80
310	Victory Ldrs (Jim Hunter, Fergie Jenkins, Andy Messersmith, Phil Niekro)	.80
311	ERA Ldrs (Buzz Capra, Jim Hunter)	.50
312	SO Ldrs (Steve Carlton, Nolan Ryan)	1.75
313	Leading Firemen (Terry Forster, Mike Marshall)	.50
315	Don Kessinger	.25
320	Pete Rose	20.00
321	Rudy May	.25
324	Ed Kranepool	.30
325	Tony Oliva	.80
330	Mike Marshall	.30
331	Indians Team (Frank Robinson)	.90
334	*Greg Gross*	.30
335	Jim Palmer	7.00
339	Jim Fregosi	.40
340	Paul Splittorff	.25
344	Ben Oglivie	.30
345	Clay Carroll	.25
350	Bobby Murcer	.40
351	• Bob Boone	.40
356	Rico Petrocelli	.30
358	Al Bumbry	.25
360	George Scott	.30
361	Dodgers Team (Walter Alston)	1.00
370	Tom Seaver	12.00
375	Roy White	.40
380	Sal Bando	.40
382	Don Baylor	.60
384	Brewers Team (Del Crandall)	.75

370 Tom Seaver

385	Dock Ellis	.25
386	Checklist 265-396	1.50
388	Steve Stone	.30
390	Ron Cey	.40
392	Bruce Bochte	.40
395	Bud Harrelson	.25
397	Bill Freehan	.40
400	Dick Allen	.80
401	Mike Wallace	.25
402	Bob Tolan	.25
407	• *Herb Washington*	.30
410	Mike Cueller (Cuellar)	.40
414	Manny Mota	.30
415	John Hiller	.25
419	Dave Goltz	.25
420	Larry Bowa	.40
421	Mets Team (Yogi Berra)	1.00
422	Brian Downing	.30
426	George Medich	.25
429	*Jim Dwyer*	.30
430	• Luis Tiant	.50
437	*Al Cowens*	.40
439	Ed Brinkman	.25
440	Andy Messersmith	.30
443	Twins Team (Frank Quilici)	.80
444	Gene Garber	.25

622 Rookie Outfielders

260 Johnny Bench

622	Rookie Outfielders (Ed Armbrister, *Fred Lynn*, Tom Poquette, Terry Whitfield)	**12.00**	
623	Rookie Infielders (*Phil Garner, Keith Hernandez*, Bob Sheldon, Tom Veryzer)	**20.00**	
624	Rookie Pitchers (Doug Konieczny, *Gary Lavelle*, Jim Otten, Eddie Solomon)	.30	
625	Boog Powell	.75	
626	Larry Haney	.20	
628	*Ron LeFlore*	.80	
629	Joe Hoerner	.20	
630	Greg Luzinski	.75	
631	Lee Lacy	.25	
632	Morris Nettles	.20	
633	Paul Casanova	.20	
634	Cy Acosta	.20	
636	Charlie Moore	.20	
638	Cubs Team (Jim Marshall)	.80	
639	Steve Kline	.20	
640	Harmon Killebrew	4.00	
641	Jim Northrup	.25	
642	Mike Phillips	.20	
643	Brent Strom	.20	
645	Danny Cater	.20	
646	Checklist 529-660	1.50	
647	*Claudell Washington*	2.50	
648	Dave Pagan	.20	
649	Jack Heidemann	.20	
650	Dave May	.20	
651	John Morlan	.20	
652	Lindy McDaniel	.20	
653	Lee Richards	.20	
655	Rico Carty	.40	
656	Bill Plummer	.20	
658	Vic Harris	.20	
659	Bob Apodaca	.20	
660	Hank Aaron	30.00	

1976 TOPPS

Topps introduced a new design concept with its 1976 set, offering 660 cards which stress quality photos instead of gaudy borders. A large, clear photo appears on each card, complemented by just two color strips on the bottom that show the player name and team. Horizontal card backs have a simpler design and are easier to read than those of many earlier sets. One interesting subset in 1976 contains ten All-Time All-Stars selected by *The Sporting News*. Another shows five players (Buddy Bell, Bob Boone, Joe Coleman, Mike Hegan, and Roy Smalley) with their fathers, who were all major-leaguers themselves in their day. Later in the season Topps issued 43 "traded" cards which show players as members of the new teams to which they had been traded. This group of cards is not considered part of the major set, however, and sells, as a subset, for $10.00.

	NR MT
Complete set	**$525.00**
Commons	.15

1	'75 Record Breaker (Hank Aaron)	**$12.00**
2	'75 Record Breaker (Bobby Bonds)	.40
3	'75 Record Breaker (Mickey Lolich)	.35
4	'75 Record Breaker (Dave Lopes)	.35

19 George Brett

316 Robin Yount

98 Dennis Eckersley

330 Nolan Ryan

480 Mike Schmidt

550 Hank Aaron

385	Mickey Lolich	.40
390	Don Gullett	.20
392	Checklist 265-396	1.50
395	• Jim Wynn	.30
396	Bill Lee	.20
397	Tim Foli	.15
400	Rod Carew	7.00
405	Rollie Fingers	1.25
408	Charlie Spikes	.15
410	Ralph Garr	.20
411	Bill Singer	.20
412	Toby Harrah	.25
413	Pete Varney	.15
414	Wayne Garland	.15
415	• Vada Pinson	.50
416	Tommy John	1.25
418	Jose Morales	.15
419	Reggie Cleveland	.15
420	• Joe Morgan	5.00
421	A's Team	.80
424	Phil Roof	.15
425	Rennie Stennett	.15
426	Bob Forsch	.25
427	Kurt Bevacqua	.20
429	Fred Stanley	.20
430	Jose Cardenal	.20
431	Dick Ruthven	.20
432	Tom Veryzer	.15
433	Rick Waits	.15
434	Morris Nettles	.15
435	Phil Niekro	2.00
437	Terry Forster	.25
438	Doug DeCinces	.50
439	Rick Rhoden	.60
440	John Mayberry	.25
441	Gary Carter	15.00
442	Hank Webb	.15
443	Giants Team	.80
444	Gary Nolan	.15
445	Rico Petrocelli	.25
447	Gene Locklear	.15
449	Bob Robertson	.15
450	Jim Palmer	5.00
451	Buddy Bradford	.15
452	Tom Hausman	.15
453	Lou Piniella	.65
455	Dick Allen	.50
456	Joe Coleman	.20
457	Ed Crosby	.15

520 Willie McCovey

459	Jim Brewer	.15
460	Cesar Cedeno	.30
461	NL & AL Championships	.80
462	1975 World Series	.80
463	Steve Hargan	.15
465	Mike Marshall	.30
466	Bob Stinson	.15
467	Woodie Fryman	.20
468	Jesus Alou	.20
469	Rawly Eastwick	.20
470	Bobby Murcer	.35
472	Bob Davis	.15
473	Paul Blair	.25
475	Joe Rudi	.30
477	Indians Team (Frank Robinson)	.80
478	Lynn McGlothlen	.15
479	Bobby Mitchell	.15
480	Mike Schmidt	25.00
481	Rudy May	.25
483	Mickey Stanley	.20
484	Eric Raich	.15
485	Mike Hargrove	.20
486	Bruce Dal Canton	.15
487	Leron Lee	.15
488	Claude Osteen	.20
489	Skip Jutze	.15

346 Ty Cobb

490	Frank Tanana	.30
491	Terry Crowley	.15
493	Derrel Thomas	.15
495	Nate Colbert	.15
496	Juan Beniquez	.20
497	Joe McIntosh	.15
498	Glenn Borgmann	.15
500	Reggie Jackson	15.00
502	Tim McCarver	.50
503	Elliott Maddox	.15
504	Pirates Team (Danny Murtaugh)	.90
505	Mark Belanger	.20
506	George Mitterwald	.15
507	Ray Bare	.15
508	*Duane Kuiper*	.20
510	Amos Otis	.25
511	Jamie Easterly	.15
512	Ellie Rodriguez	.15
513	Bart Johnson	.15
514	Dan Driessen	.30
515	Steve Yeager	.15
517	John Milner	.15
518	*Doug Flynn*	.20
519	Steve Brye	.15
520	Willie McCovey	2.50
521	Jim Colborn	.15
522	Ted Sizemore	.20
524	Pete Falcone	.15
525	Billy Williams	2.25
526	Checklist 397-528	2.25
528	Dock Ellis	.20
529	Deron Johnson	.15
530	Don Sutton	1.50
531	Mets Team (Joe Frazier)	.90
532	Milt May	.15
533	Lee Richard	.15
534	Stan Bahnsen	.15
535	Dave Nelson	.15
536	Mike Thompson	.15
537	Tony Muser	.15
539	John Balaz	.15
540	Bill Freehan	.25
541	Steve Mingori	.15
542	Keith Hernandez	6.00
543	Wayne Twitchell	.15
544	Pepe Frias	.15
545	Sparky Lyle	.35
546	Dave Rosello	.15
547	Roric Harrison	.15
548	Manny Mota	.15
550	Hank Aaron	15.00
552	Terry Humphrey	.15
553	Randy Moffitt	.15
554	Ray Fosse	.15
556	Twins Team (Gene Mauch)	.80
557	Dan Spillner	.15
558	Clarence Gaston	.15
559	Clyde Wright	.15
560	Jorge Orta	.15
561	Tom Carroll	.15
562	Adrian Garrett	.15
564	Bubble Gum Blowing Champ (Kurt Bevacqua)	.30
565	Tug McGraw	.35
566	Ken McMullen	.15
567	George Stone	.15
568	Rob Andrews	.15
569	Nelson Briles	.15
570	George Hendrick	.20
571	Don DeMola	.15
572	Rich Coggins	.15
573	Bill Travers	.15
574	Don Kessinger	.20
575	• Dwight Evans	3.00

578 Ted Kubiak .... .15
579 Clay Kirby .... .15
580 Bert Campaneris .... .30
581 • Cardinals Team
    (Red Schoendienst)........... .80
582 Mike Kekich .... .15
583 Tommy Helms .... .15
584 Stan Wall .... .15
585 Joe Torre .... .50
589 Rookie Pitchers (Santo
    Alcala, *Mike Flanagan,*
    Joe Pactwa, Pablo
    Torrealba) 1.50
590 Rookie Outfielders (Henry
    Cruz, *Chet Lemon, Ellis
    Valentine,* Terry
    Whitfield) 1.00
591 Rookie Pitchers (Steve
    Grilli, Craig Mitchell, Jose
    Sosa, George Throop)....... .15
592 Rookie Infielders (Dave
    McKay, *Willie Randolph,
    Jerry Royster,* Roy
    Staiger)............................ 5.00
593 Rookie Pitchers (Larry
    Anderson, Ken Crosby,
    Mark Littell, *Butch Metzger*) ... .25
594 Rookie Catchers and
    Outfielders (Andy Merchant,
    Ed Ott, Royle Stillman,
    Jerry White) .... .20
595 Rookie Pitchers (Steve
    Barr, Art DeFillipis, Randy
    Lerch, Sid Monge) .... .15
596 Rookie Infielders (Lamar
    Johnson, *Johnny
    LeMaster,* Jerry Manuel,
    Craig Reynolds)................. .45
597 Rookie Pitchers (*Don
    Aase,* Jack Kucek, Frank
    LaCorte, Mike Pazik) .... .50
598 Rookie Outfielders (Hector
    Cruz, *Jamie Quirk,* Jerry
    Turner, Joe Wallis) .... .20
599 Rookie Pitchers
    (Rob Dressler, *Ron
    Guidry,* Bob McClure,
    Pat Zachry).................... 11.00
600 Tom Seaver.................... 8.00

341 Lou Gehrig

602 Doug Konieczny .... .15
603 Jim Holt .... .15
604 Joe Lovitto .... .15
605 Al Downing .... .20
606 Brewers Team
    (Alex Grammas) .... .80
607 Rich Hinton........................ .15
608 Vic Correll......................... .15
610 Greg Luzinski .... .45
611 Rick Folkers...................... .15
612 Joe Lahoud........................ .15
614 Fernando Arroyo .... .15
615 Mike Cubbage .... .15
616 Buck Martinez.................... .15
617 Darold Knowles .... .15
619 Bill Butler .... .15
620 Al Oliver........................... .70
621 Tom Hall .... .15
623 Bob Allietta .... .15
624 Tony Taylor .... .15
625 J.R. Richard....................... .25
626 Bob Sheldon...................... .15
628 John D'Acquisto .... .15
629 Sandy Alomar.................... .15
630 Chris Speier....................... .20
631 Braves Team (Dave
    Bristol)............................. .80

632	Rogelio Moret	.15	647	Ramon Hernandez .15
633	*John Stearns*	.30	648	Al Cowens .20
634	Larry Christenson	.15	649	Dave Roberts .15
635	Jim Fregosi	.25	650	Thurman Munson 7.00
636	Joe Decker	.15	651	John Odom .20
637	Bruce Bochte	.20	652	Ed Armbrister .15
638	Doyle Alexander	.30	653	*Mike Norris* .30
640	Bill Madlock	1.00	655	Mike Vail .15
641	Tom Paciorek	.20	656	White Sox Team
642	Dennis Blair	.15		(Chuck Tanner) .80
643	Checklist 529-660	1.50	657	*Roy Smalley* .40
645	Darrell Porter	.20	659	Ben Oglivie .25
646	John Lowenstein	.15	660	Dave Lopes .60

1977 TOPPS

The 1977 Topps set of 660 cards offered superior photos, but few major surprises in subject matter were introduced. An eight-card set of league leaders opens the 1977 issue, while a smaller set acknowledges the record-setting 1976 performances of George Brett, Minnie Minoso, Jose Morales, and Nolan Ryan. A unique four-card novelty series entitled Big League Brothers is a 1977 highlight. It features Paul and Rick Reuschel (wrongly identified on their card), George and Ken Brett, Bob and Ken Forsch, and Carlos and Lee May. The hottest cards are from the multi-player rookie card subset: Jack Clark, Andre Dawson, and Dale Murphy (identified as a catcher). The set also contains the last regular-issue card of Brooks Robinson.

		NR MT			
Complete set		$425.00	7	ERA Ldrs (John Denny, Mark Fidrych)	.30
Commons		.15	8	Leading Firemen (Bill Campbell, Rawly Eastwick)	.30
1	Batting Ldrs (George Brett, Bill Madlock)	$2.50	9	Doug Rader	.15
			10	Reggie Jackson	11.00
2	HR Ldrs (Graig Nettles, Mike Schmidt)	1.25	11	Rob Dressler	.15
			12	Larry Haney	.15
3	RBI Ldrs (George Foster, Lee May)	.50	15	Don Gullett	.20
			16	Bob Jones	.15
4	SB Ldrs (Dave Lopes, Bill North)	.30	17	Steve Stone	.25
			18	Indians Team (Frank Robinson)	.85
5	Victory Ldrs (Randy Jones, Jim Palmer)	.80	19	John D'Acquisto	.15
			20	Graig Nettles	.90
6	SO Ldrs (Nolan Ryan, Tom Seaver)	3.00	21	Ken Forsch	.20
			22	Bill Freehan	.25

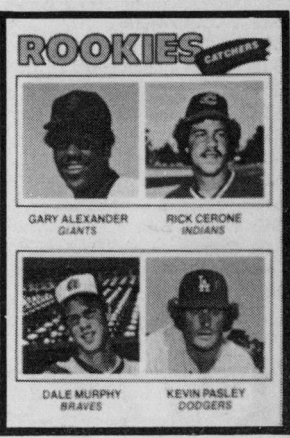

476 Rookie Catchers

473 Rookie Outfielders

488 Rookie Outfielders

650 Nolan Ryan

185	Sixto Lezcano	.20
188	Bob Tolan	.20
193	Larry Gura	.20
194	Gary Matthews	.25
195	Ed Figueroa	.20
198	Wilbur Wood	.20
199	Pepe Frias	.15
200	Frank Tanana	.30
201	Ed Kranepool	.25
206	Boog Powell	.50
208	Checklist 133-264	1.25
210	Fred Lynn	1.50
211	Giants Team (Joe Altobelli)	.70
213	Maximino Leon	.15
214	Darrell Porter	.20
215	Butch Metzger	.15
216	Doug DeCinces	.25
218	*John Wathan*	.60
219	Joe Coleman	.20
220	Chris Chambliss	.35
221	Bob Bailey	.15
222	Francisco Barrios	.15
224	Rusty Torres	.15
225	Bob Apodaca	.15
227	*Joe Sambito*	.25
228	Twins Team (Gene Mauch)	.80

580 George Brett

229	Don Kessinger	.20
230	Vida Blue	.40
231	Record Breaker (George Brett)	4.00
232	Record Breaker (Minnie Minoso)	.35
233	Record Breaker (Jose Morales)	.20
234	Record Breaker (Nolan Ryan)	7.00
235	Cecil Cooper	.65
236	Tom Buskey	.15
237	Gene Clines	.15
238	Tippy Martinez	.15
240	Ron LeFlore	.25
243	Ron Reed	.20
244	John Mayberry	.20
245	Rick Rhoden	.30
246	Mike Vail	.15
247	Chris Knapp	.15
249	Pete Redfern	.15
250	Bill Madlock	.40
251	Tony Muser	.15
252	Dale Murray	.15
253	John Hale	.15
254	Doyle Alexander	.30
255	George Scott	.20

120 Rod Carew

525 Dennis Eckersley

390 Dave Winfield

#	Player	Price
336	Denny Doyle	.15
339	Adrian Devine	.15
340	Hal McRae	.30
341	Joe Kerrigan	.15
342	Jerry Remy	.15
343	Ed Halicki	.15
344	Brian Downing	.25
345	Reggie Smith	.25
346	Bill Singer	.20
347	George Foster	1.25
348	Brent Strom	.15
349	Jim Holt	.15
350	Larry Dierker	.20
351	Jim Sundberg	.20
353	Stan Thomas	.15
354	Pirates Team (Chuck Tanner)	.80
355	Lou Brock	3.00
356	Checklist 265-396	1.25
357	• Tim McCarver	.50
358	Tom House	.15
359	Willie Randolph	.85
360	Rick Monday	.25
361	Eduardo Rodriguez	.15
362	Tommy Davis	.30
363	Dave Roberts	.15
364	Vic Correll	.15
365	Mike Torrez	.20
366	Ted Sizemore	.15
368	Mike Jorgensen	.15
369	Terry Humphrey	.15
370	John Montefusco	.20
371	Royals Team (Whitey Herzog)	.80
372	Rich Folkers	.15
373	Bert Campaneris	.30
374	• Kent Tekulve	.30
375	Larry Hisle	.20
376	Nino Espinosa	.15
378	Jim Umbarger	.15
379	Larry Cox	.15
380	Lee May	.25
381	Bob Forsch	.20
384	Darrel Chaney	.15
385	Dave LaRoche	.15
386	Manny Mota	.25
387	Yankees Team (Billy Martin)	1.25
389	Ken Kravec	.15
390	Dave Winfield	6.00
391	Dan Warthen	.15
392	Phil Roof	.15
393	John Lowenstein	.15
394	Bill Laxton	.15
395	Manny Trillo	.20
397	*Larry Herndon*	.40
398	Tom Burgmeier	.15
399	Bruce Boisclair	.15
400	Steve Garvey	5.00
401	Mickey Scott	.15
402	Tommy Helms	.15
403	Tom Grieve	.15
404	Eric Rasmussen	.15
405	Claudell Washington	.25
407	Dave Freisleben	.15
408	Cesar Tovar	.15
409	Pete Broberg	.15
410	Willie Montanez	.15
411	World Series Games 1 & 2	.70
412	World Series Games 3 & 4	.70
413	World Series Summary	1.00
414	Tommy Harper	.20
415	Jay Johnstone	.20
416	Chuck Hartenstein	.15
418	White Sox Team (Bob Lemon)	.80

170 Thurman Munson

491 Rookie Pitchers (Mike Dupree, *Denny Martinez*, Craig Mitchell, Bob Sykes)................................. 1.00
492 Rookie Outfielders (*Tony Armas, Steve Kemp,* Carlos Lopez, Gary Woods) 1.25
493 Rookie Pitchers (*Mike Krukow,* Jim Otten, Gary Wheelock, Mike Willis) ...... .70
494 Rookie Infielders (Juan Bernhardt, Mike Champion, *Jim Gantner, Bump Wills)*.. .50
495 Al Hrabosky .... .20
497 Clay Carroll........................ .20
498 Sal Bando........................... .25
500 Dave Kingman................... .60
503 Bill Lee................................ .20
504 Dodgers Team (Tom Lasorda)................. 1.00
505 Oscar Gamble .... .20
510 John Candelaria .... .80
517 *Pete Vuckovich*.................. .50
518 Cubs Team (Herman Franks) .... .70
520 Garry Maddox.................... .20
521 Bob Grich .... .25
523 • Rollie Fingers 2.50
525 Dennis Eckersley............. 7.00
526 Larry Parrish .... .35
530 Rick Reuschel .... .30
531 Lyman Bostock.................. .25
533 Mickey Stanley .... .20
534 Paul Splittorff .... .20
535 Cesar Geronimo .... .20
540 Bob Watson....................... .20
541 John Denny .... .20
543 Ron Blomberg .... .20
545 • Bob Boone .... .25
546 Orioles Team (Earl Weaver) .... .80
547 • Willie McCovey............. 3.00
548 *Joel Youngblood*................ .30
555 Dan Ford .... .20
560 Dave Concepcion .... .35
562 Checklist 529-660........... 1.25
564 Alan Ashby .... .20
565 Mickey Lolich..................... .50

270 Dave Parker

567 Enos Cabell .... .20
568 Carlos May .... .20
569 Jim Lonborg .... .20
570 Bobby Bonds .... .35
571 Darrell Evans..................... .40
574 Aurelio Rodriguez.............. .20
578 Bob Randall....................... .15
580 George Brett.................. 21.00
585 Rick Burleson .... .20
590 Buddy Bell .... .30
595 John Hiller .... .20
596 *Jerry Martin* .... .25
597 Mariners Mgr./Coaches (Don Bryant, Jim Busby, Darrell Johnson, Vada Pinson, Wes Stock) .... .25
598 • Sparky Lyle .... .35
600 • Jim Palmer 4.00
603 Willie Davis .... .25
610 Jose Cardenal .... .20
615 Phil Niekro 1.50
618 Pat Dobson........................ .20
620 Don Sutton 1.50
621 Tigers Team (Ralph Houk) .. .80
625 Ken Holtzman .... .25
626 Al Bumbry.......................... .20
629 Bobby Valentine .... .25

1978 TOPPS

The 1978 Topps set grew to 726 cards—the biggest since 1972. The simply designed cards use an extra-large photo and a minimal border. All Stars from 1977 are honored with a small red, white, and blue shield in the upper right-hand corner of their cards. Card backs contain a small box that features baseball situations such as a home run or ground out; this allows two people to play a simulated baseball game. Because Topps increased the set size, it needed to print 11 cards twice on each 132-card sheet. Although this increased the availability of those cards, prices for them have seen little fluctuation.

36 Eddie Murray

15	Tony Perez	.25
16	Roy White	.20
17	Mike Krukow	.20
18	Bob Grich	.25
19	Darrell Porter	.20
20	Pete Rose	3.50
21	Steve Kemp	.20
22	Charlie Hough	.25
25	Jon Matlack	.20
28	Ed Ott	.12
30	George Hendrick	.20
32	Garry Templeton	.25
34	Willie McCovey	2.00
35	• Sparky Lyle	.30
36	*Eddie Murray*	72.00
39	*Floyd Bannister*	1.00
40	Carl Yastrzemski	5.00
41	Burt Hooton	.20
44	Toby Harrah	.20
45	Mark Fidrych	.25
48	Don Baylor	.35
49	Ed Kranepool	.20
50	Rick Reuschel	.25
52	Jim Lonborg	.20
56	Randy Jones	.20
58	Bob Forsch	.20
60	Thurman Munson	2.50

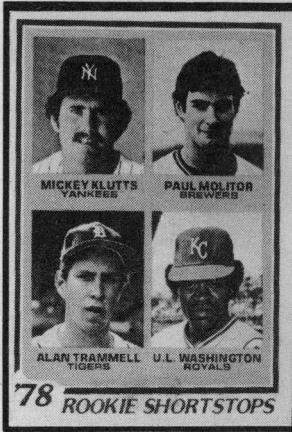

707 Rookie Shortstops

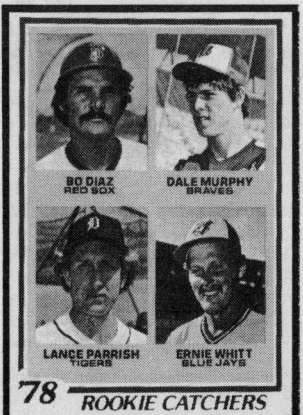

708 Rookie Catchers

62	Jim Barr	.20
65	Ken Singleton	.25
66	White Sox Team	.50
67	Claudell Washington	.25
70	Rich Gossage	.70
72	Andre Dawson	15.00
74	Checklist 1-121	.90
80	Ken Griffey	.25
82	Giants Team	.50
84	Kent Tekulve	.25
85	Ron Fairly	.20
89	Ken Clay	.15
90	Larry Bowa	.30
96	Orioles Team	.50
99	*Willie Hernandez*	.65
100	George Brett	5.00
109	Joe Torre	.30
110	Richie Zisk	.20
111	Mike Tyson	.12
112	Astros Team	.50
114	Paul Blair	.20
119	Denny Martinez	.25
120	Gary Carter	4.00
122	Dennis Eckersley	5.00
123	Manny Trillo	.20
124	*Dave Rozema*	.25
125	George Scott	.20

400 Nolan Ryan

173	Robin Yount	**10.00**
176	Milt May	.12
179	Dick Tidrow	.20
180	Dave Concepcion	.35
181	Ken Forsch	.20
183	Doug Bird	.12
184	Checklist 122-242	.90
185	Ellis Valentine	.25
186	*Bob Stanley*	.25
188	Al Bumbry	.20
189	Tom Lasorda	.25
190	John Candelaria	.25
192	Padres Team	.50
195	Larry Dierker	.20
200	Reggie Jackson	**7.00**
201	Batting Ldrs (Rod Carew, Dave Parker)	.80
202	HR Ldrs (George Foster, Jim Rice)	.25
203	RBI Ldrs (George Foster, Larry Hisle)	.25
205	Victory Ldrs (Steve Carlton, Dave Goltz, Dennis Leonard, Jim Palmer)	.65
206	SO Ldrs (Phil Niekro, Nolan Ryan)	.35
208	Leading Firemen (Bill Campbell, Rollie Fingers)	.35
211	• Earl Weaver	.20
214	Angels Team	.50
215	Darrell Evans	.35
221	Chris Speier	.15
230	Al Hrabosky	.20
232	Mickey Stanley	.20
235	• Tim McCarver	.35
238	Juan Beniquez	.20
239	Dyar Miller	.12
240	Gene Tenace	.20
241	Pete Vuckovich	.20
244	Expos Team	.20
245	Rick Burleson	.20
246	Dan Driessen	.20
250	Graig Nettles	.30
254	Dave Collins	.20
255	Jerry Reuss	.20
258	John Hiller	.20
259	Dodgers Team	.80
260	Bert Campaneris	.25
265	Sal Bando	.12

127	Chet Lemon	.20
128	Bill Russell	.20
130	Jeff Burroughs	.20
131	Bert Blyleven	.60
132	Enos Cabell	.20
134	*Steve Henderson*	.25
135	Ron Guidry	.90
140	Rollie Fingers	.75
141	Ruppert Jones	.20
142	John Montefusco	.20
143	Keith Hernandez	2.50
145	Rick Monday	.20
146	Doyle Alexander	.30
147	Lee Mazilli	.20
148	Andre Thornton	.25
150	Bobby Bonds	.35
152	*Ivan DeJesus*	.20
153	Steve Stone	.25
154	Cecil Cooper	.20
156	Andy Messersmith	.20
158	Joaquin Andujar	.25
159	Lou Piniella	.35
160	Jim Palmer	4.00
161	• Bob Boone	.25
168	Reggie Smith	.25
170	Lou Brock	2.00
172	Mike Hargrove	.20

360 Mike Schmidt

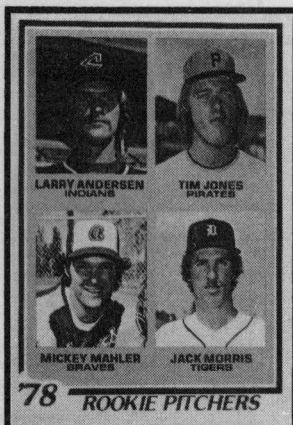

703 Rookie Pitchers

473	Bill Buckner	.30
474	Jim Slaton	.12
475	Gary Matthews	.20
479	Cardinals Team	.50
480	Ron LeFlore	.25
481	Jackson Todd	.12
482	Rick Miller	.12
483	Ken Macha	.12
485	Chris Chambliss	.30
486	John Curtis	.12
488	Dan Spillner	.12
489	Rudy Meoli	.12
490	Amos Otis	.20
491	Scott McGregor	.20
492	Jim Sundberg	.20
493	Steve Renko	.12
494	Chuck Tanner	.20
495	Dave Cash	.12
496	*Jim Clancy*	.30
498	Joe Sambito	.12
499	Mariners Team	.50
500	George Foster	.70
501	Dave Roberts	.12

580 Rod Carew

503	Ike Hampton	.12
504	Roger Freed	.12
505	Felix Millan	.12
508	Johnny Oates	.12
509	Brent Strom	.12
510	Willie Stargell	3.00
511	Frank Duffy	.12
512	Larry Herndon	.20
513	Barry Foote	.12
517	Andres Mora	.12
518	Tommy Boggs	.12
519	Brian Downing	.25
520	Larry Hisle	.20
521	Steve Staggs	.12
522	Dick Williams	.20
523	*Donnie Moore*	.25
524	Bernie Carbo	.12
526	Reds Team	.60
527	Vic Correll	.12
528	Rob Picciolo	.12
530	Dave Winfield	5.00
531	Tom Underwood	.12
532	Skip Jutze	.12
533	Sandy Alomar	.12
534	Wilbur Howard	.12
535	Checklist 485-605	.90

536	Roric Harrison	.12
537	Bruce Bochte	.20
538	Johnnie LeMaster	.12
539	Vic Davalillo	.12
540	Steve Carlton	4.00
543	Larry Harlow	.12
544	Len Randle	.12
545	Bill Campbell	.12
546	Ted Martinez	.12
547	John Scott	.12
549	Joe Kerrigan	.12
550	John Mayberry	.20
551	Braves Team	.50
552	Francisco Barrios	.12
553	*Terry Puhl*	.35
554	Joe Coleman	.20
555	Butch Wynegar	.20
556	Ed Armbrister	.12
559	Phil Mankowski	.12
560	Dave Parker	4.00
561	Charlie Williams	.12
563	Dave Rader	.12
564	Mick Kelleher	.12
565	Jerry Koosman	.25
566	Merv Rettenmund	.12
567	Dick Drago	.12

1978 Topps

270 Carlton Fisk

656	Dave Garcia	.12
657	Bombo Rivera	.12
658	Manny Sanguillen	.20
659	Rangers Team	.50
660	Jason Thompson	.20
661	Grant Jackson	.12
662	Paul Dade	.12
663	Paul Reuschel	.12
664	Fred Stanley	.15
665	Dennis Leonard	.25
666	Billy Smith	.12
667	Jeff Byrd	.12
668	Dusty Baker	.25
670	Jim Rice	3.50
672	Don Kessinger	.20
673	Steve Brye	.12
674	*Ray Knight*	1.00
675	Jay Johnstone	.20
677	Ed Herrmann	.20
680	Vida Blue	.30
682	Ken Brett	.20
684	Ralph Houk	.20
686	Gaylord Perry	2.00
687	*Julio Cruz*	.25
689	Indians Team	.50
690	Mickey Rivers	.25
691	Ross Grimsley	.20
692	Ken Reitz	.20
695	Dwight Evans	2.00
700	Johnny Bench	5.00

700 Johnny Bench

701	Rookie Pitchers (*Tom Hume*, Larry Landreth, *Steve McCatty*, Bruce Taylor)	.25
702	Rookie Catchers (Bill Nahorodny, Kevin Pasley, Rick Sweet, Don Werner)	.12
703	Rookie Pitchers (*Larry Andersen*, Tim Jones, Mickey Mahler, *Jack Morris*)	10.00
704	Rookie Second Basemen (*Garth Iorg*, Dave Oliver, Sam Perlozzo, *Lou Whitaker*)	13.00
705	Rookie Outfielders (*Dave Bergman*, Miguel Dilone, *Clint Hurdle*, Willie Norwood)	.25
706	Rookie First Basemen (Wayne Cage, Ted Cox, *Pat Putnam*, *Dave Revering*)	.20
707	Rookie Shortstops (Mickey Klutts, *Paul Molitor, Alan Trammell, U.L Washington*)	45.00
708	Rookie Catchers (*Bo Diaz*, Dale Murphy, *Lance Parrish*, Ernie Whitt)	27.00
709	Rookie Pitchers (Steve Burke, *Matt Keough*, Lance Rautzhan, Dan Schatzeder)	.25
710	Rookie Outfielders (Dell Alston, Rick Bosetti, *Mike Easler*, Keith Smith)	.50
712	Bobby Valentine	.25
715	Jim Kaat	.60
720	Fergie Jenkins	1.50
721	Billy Martin	2.00
724	Royals Team	.70
726	Wilbur Wood	.40

1979 TOPPS

Although Topps continued to supply collectors with attractive cards in 1979, few innovations were included in the 726-card set. For the first time, rookie prospect cards are arranged by team, with each card featuring three black-and-white photos of promising young players. Ozzie Smith led the rookie parade in 1979, and today his card is the most valuable of the entire set. Other rookies include Kevin Bass, Pedro Guerrero, Carney Lansford, Lonnie Smith, and Bob Welch. In early print runs Texas Rangers shortstop Bump Wills was mistakenly identified as a member of the Toronto Blue Jays, probably due to the letter "T" on his cap. Nevertheless, many collectors believe that the correct card is scarcer.

116 Ozzie Smith

		NR MT
Complete set		**$275.00**
Commons		**.12**
1	Batting Ldrs (Rod Carew, Dave Parker)	**$2.00**
2	HR Ldrs (George Foster, Jim Rice)	.50
3	RBI Ldrs (George Foster, Jim Rice)	.50
4	SB Ldrs (Ron LeFlore, Omar Moreno)	.25
5	Victory Ldrs (Ron Guidry, Gaylord Perry)	.50
6	SO Ldrs (J.R. Richard, Nolan Ryan)	.50
7	ERA Ldrs (Ron Guidry, Craig Swan)	.25
8	Leading Firemen (Rollie Fingers, Rich Gossage)	.40
10	Lee May	.20
15	Ross Grimsley	.20
16	Fred Stanley	.15
17	Donnie Moore	.20
20	Joe Morgan	.40
23	Terry Forster	.20
24	Paul Molitor	4.00
25	Steve Carlton	3.00
27	Dave Goltz	.20
30	Dave Winfield	3.00
35	Ed Figueroa	.20
39	Dale Murphy	8.00
40	Dennis Eckersley	2.00
41	Twins Team (Gene Mauch)	.50
45	Al Hrabosky	.20
50	Steve Garvey	1.25
55	Willie Stargell	2.00
58	Bob Randall	.15
60	Mickey Rivers	.20
61	Bo Diaz	.20
65	Mark Belanger	.20
66	Tigers Team (Les Moss)	.60
70	John Candelaria	.25
71	Brian Downing	.20
74	*Shane Rawley*	.70
80	Jason Thompson	.20
82	Mets Team (Joe Torre)	.60

115 Nolan Ryan

318 Bob Welch

640 Eddie Murray

610 Mike Schmidt

319	Wayne Garrett	.12
320	Carl Yastrzemski	2.50
321	Gaylord Perry	2.00
323	Lynn McGlothen	.12
325	Cecil Cooper	.40
326	Pedro Borbon	.12
327	Art Howe	.12
328	A's Team (Jack McKeon)	.50
329	Joe Coleman	.20
330	George Brett	10.00
331	Mickey Mahler	.12
333	Chet Lemon	.20
334	Craig Swan	.12
335	Chris Chambliss	.25
336	Bobby Thompson	.12
337	John Montague	.12
339	Ron Jackson	.12
340	Jim Palmer	5.00
341	*Willie Upshaw*	.40
342	Dave Roberts	.12
344	Jerry Royster	.12
345	Tug McGraw	.30
346	Bill Buckner	.30
347	Doug Rau	.12
348	Andre Dawson	8.00
349	Jim Wright	.12
350	Garry Templeton	.20
351	Wayne Nordhagen	.12
353	Checklist 243-363	.60
355	Lee Mazzilli	.20
356	Giants Team (Joe Altobelli)	.50
357	Jerry Augustine	.12
358	Alan Trammell	10.00
359	Dan Spillner	.12
360	Amos Otis	.20
361	Tom Dixon	.12
362	Mike Cubbage	.12
364	Gene Richards	.12
365	• Sparky Lyle	.30
366	Juan Bernhardt	.12
367	Dave Skaggs	.12
368	Don Aase	.20
369	Bump Wills (Blue Jays)	3.00
369	Bump Wills (Rangers)	3.50
370	Dave Kingman	.35
372	Lamar Johnson	.12
374	Ed Herrmann	.12
376	Gorman Thomas	.20
377	Paul Moskau	.12

330 George Brett

380	John Mayberry	.20
381	Astros Team (Bill Virdon)	.50
382	Jerry Martin	.12
383	Phil Garner	.20
384	Tommy Boggs	.12
386	Francisco Barrios	.12
387	Gary Thomasson	.12
388	Jack Billingham	.12
389	Joe Zdeb	.12
390	Rollie Fingers	3.00
391	Al Oliver	.50
392	Doug Ault	.12
393	Scott McGregor	.20
394	Randy Stein	.12
395	Dave Cash	.20
396	Bill Plummer	.12
398	Ivan DeJesus	.12
400	Jim Rice	2.50
401	Ray Knight	.25
402	Paul Hartzell	.12
403	Tim Foli	.12
404	White Sox Team (Don Kessinger)	.50
405	Butch Wynegar	.20
406	Joe Wallis	.12
407	Pete Vuckovich	.20

358 Alan Trammell

212 Carney Lansford

680 Carlton Fisk

567	Rich Hebner	.12
569	Bob Sykes	.12
570	Cesar Cedeno	.25
571	Darrell Porter	.20
572	Rod Gilbreath	.12
573	Jim Kern	.12
574	Claudell Washington	.20
575	Luis Tiant	.30
576	Mike Parrott	.12
577	Brewers Team (George Bamberger)	.50
578	Pete Broberg	.12
580	Ron Fairly	.20
581	Darold Knowles	.12
582	Paul Blair	.20
584	Jim Rooker	.12
585	Hal McRae	.35
586	*Bob Horner*	1.00
587	Ken Reitz	.12
590	J.R. Richard	.20
591	Mike Hargrove	.20
592	Mike Krukow	.20
593	Rick Dempsey	.15
594	Bob Shirley	.12
595	Phil Niekro	1.25
596	Jim Wohlford	.12
597	Bob Stanley	.20
598	Mark Wagner	.12
599	Jim Spencer	.20
600	George Foster	.60
601	Dave LaRoche	.12
602	Checklist 485-605	.60
605	Rick Monday	.12
606	Expos Team (Dick Williams)	.55
607	Omar Moreno	.12
608	Dave McKay	.12
609	Silvio Martinez	.12
610	Mike Schmidt	12.00
611	Jim Norris	.12
612	*Rick Honeycutt*	.30
613	Mike Edwards	.12
614	Willie Hernandez	.20
615	Ken Singleton	.20
616	Billy Almon	.12
617	Terry Puhl	.12
618	Jerry Remy	.12
619	*Ken Landreaux*	.20
620	Bert Campaneris	.25
621	Pat Zachry	.12
622	Dave Collins	.20
623	Bob McClure	.12
624	Larry Herndon	.20
625	Mark Fidrych	.25
626	Yankees Team (Bob Lemon)	.85
629	Gene Garber	.12
630	Bake McBride	.12
631	Jorge Orta	.12
632	Don Kirkwood	.12
633	Rob Wilfong	.12
634	Paul Lindblad	.12
635	Don Baylor	.50
636	Wayne Garland	.12
637	Bill Robinson	.12
638	Al Fitzmorris	.12
639	Manny Trillo	.20
640	Eddie Murray	14.00
641	*Bobby Castillo*	.12
642	Wilbur Howard	.12
643	Tom Hausman	.12
644	Manny Mota	.20
645	George Scott	.20
648	Lou Piniella	.35
649	John Curtis	.12
650	Pete Rose	4.00

651	Mike Caldwell	.12
652	Stan Papi	.12
653	Warren Brusstar	.12
654	Rick Miller	.12
655	Jerry Koosman	.30
656	Hosken Powell	.12
657	George Medich	.12
658	Taylor Duncan	.12
659	Mariners Team (Darrell Johnson)	.50
660	Ron LeFlore	.12
661	Bruce Kison	.12
662	Kevin Bell	.12
663	Mike Vail	.12
664	Doug Bird	.12
665	Lou Brock	1.50
666	Rich Dauer	.12
669	Checklist 606-726	.60
670	• Jim Hunter	.70

310 Thurman Munson

671	Joe Ferguson	.12
672	Ed Halicki	.12
673	Tom Hutton	.12
674	Dave Tomlin	.12
675	Tim McCarver	.30
676	Johnny Sutton	.12
677	Larry Parrish	.25
679	Derrel Thomas	.12
680	Carlton Fisk	3.00
681	*John Henry Johnson*	.12
684	Jamie Easterly	.12
685	Sixto Lezcano	.12
686	Ron Schueler	.12
687	Rennie Stennett	.12
688	Mike Willis	.12
689	Orioles Team (Earl Weaver)	.70
690	Buddy Bell	.12
691	Dock Ellis	.12
692	Mickey Stanley	.20
693	Dave Rader	.12
694	Burt Hooton	.20
695	Keith Hernandez	2.00
696	Andy Hassler	.12
697	Dave Bergman	.12
698	Bill Stein	.12
700	Reggie Jackson	3.00
701	Orioles Prospects (Mark Corey, John Flinn, *Sammy Stewart*)	.20
702	Red Sox Prospects (Joel Finch, Garry Hancock, Allen Ripley)	.12
703	Angels Prospects (Jim Anderson, Dave Frost, Bob Slater)	.12
704	White Sox Prospects (Ross Baumgarten, Mike Colbern, *Mike Squires*)	.20
705	Indians Prospects (*Alfredo Griffin,* Tim Norrid, Dave Oliver)	.70
706	Tigers Prospects (Dave Stegman, Dave Tobik, Kip Young)	.20
707	Royals Prospects (Randy Bass, Jim Gaudet, Randy McGilberry)	.15
708	Brewers Prospects (*Kevin Bass, Eddie Romero,* Ned Yost)	1.25
709	Twins Prospects (Sam Perlozzo, Rick Sofield, Kevin Stanfield)	.12
710	Yankees Prospects (Brian Doyle, *Mike Heath,* Dave Rajsich)	.35

1979 Topps

340 Jim Palmer

650 Pete Rose

1980 TOPPS

Topps began the new decade with another 726-card issue. The Topps logo, which diminishes the appeal of the 1979 set, was dropped from the front of the 2½- by 3½-inch cards. Another improvement in 1980 involves the Future Stars cards (indicated with "FS" on the following list). Top names include Jesse Orosco and Mike Scott of the Mets, Tom Herr of the Cardinals, Dan Quisenberry of the Royals, and Dickie Thon of the Astros. This subset is arranged by team, with three players to a card, and, unlike the preceding year, all the mug shots are in color. Some of the most important rookies in the main set were overlooked, however, including Rickey Henderson, Dave Stieb, and Rick Sutcliffe.

482 Rickey Henderson

		MINT
Complete set		**$325.00**
Commons		**.12**

1	1979 Highlights (Lou Brock, Carl Yastrzemski)	**$1.50**
2	1979 Highlights (Willie McCovey)	.80
3	1979 Highlights (Manny Mota)	.20
4	1979 Highlights (Pete Rose)	2.00
5	1979 Highlights (Garry Templeton)	.20
6	1979 Highlights (Del Unser)	.12
17	Bruce Sutter	.45
25	Lee Mazzilli	.20
30	Vida Blue	.30
31	Jay Johnstone	.20
35	Luis Tiant	.30
40	Carlton Fisk	.95
41	Rangers Team (Pat Corrales)	.50
42	*Dave Palmer*	.40
45	Frank White	.25
46	Rico Carty	.20
50	J.R. Richard	.20
53	Ben Oglivie	.20
55	Bill Madlock	.40
56	Bobby Valentine	.20
57	Pete Vuckovich	.15
60	Bucky Dent	.25
62	Mike Ivie	.12
63	Bob Stanley	.20
65	Al Bumbry	.15
66	Royals Team (Jim Frey)	.60
67	Doyle Alexander	.25
70	Gary Carter	2.50
73	Dave Collins	.20
75	Bill Russell	.20
77	*Dave Stieb*	12.00
80	Ron LeFlore	.20
82	Astros Team (Bill Virdon)	.50
83	*Steve Trout*	.30
85	Ted Simmons	.40
88	Ken Landreaux	.20
90	Manny Trillo	.20
91	Rick Dempsey	.15
92	Rick Rhoden	.20

580 Nolan Ryan

77 Dave Stieb

393 Ozzie Smith

389	Pete LaCock	.12
390	Fergie Jenkins	.75
391	Tony Armas	.15
392	Milt Wilcox	.12
393	Ozzie Smith	10.00
394	Reggie Cleveland	.12
395	Ellis Valentine	.12
398	Barry Foote	.12
399	Mike Proly	.12
400	George Foster	.50
401	Pete Falcone	.12
402	Merv Rettenmund	.12
403	Pete Redfern	.12
404	Orioles Team	
	(Earl Weaver)	.60
405	Dwight Evans	1.00
406	Paul Molitor	1.50
407	Tony Solaita	.12
408	Bill North	.12
409	Paul Splittorff	.20
410	Bobby Bonds	.25
411	Frank LaCorte	.12
412	Thad Bosley	.12
414	George Scott	.20
415	Bill Atkinson	.12
416	*Tom Brookens*	.35
417	Craig Chamberlain	.12

418	Roger Freed	.12
419	Vic Correll	.12
420	Butch Hobson	.12
424	Yankees Team	
	(Dick Howser)	.75
425	Mark Belanger	.20
428	Pat Zachry	.12
429	Duane Kuiper	.12
430	Larry Hisle	.12
431	Mike Krukow	.20
432	Willie Norwood	.12
434	Johnnie LeMaster	.12
435	Don Gullett	.20
436	Billy Almon	.12
437	Joe Niekro	.20
438	Dave Revering	.12
440	Don Sutton	1.00
441	Eric Soderholm	.12
442	Jorge Orta	.12
445	Mark Fidrych	.20
446	Duffy Dyer	.12
447	Nino Espinosa	.12
449	Doug Bair	.12
450	George Brett	8.00
451	Indians Team	
	(Dave Garcia)	.50
452	Steve Dillard	.12
454	Tom Donohue	.12
455	Mike Torrez	.20
456	Frank Taveras	.12
457	Bert Blyleven	.60
458	Billy Sample	.12
459	• Mickey Lolich	.12
460	Willie Randolph	.25
461	Dwayne Murphy	.12
462	Mike Sadek	.12
463	Jerry Royster	.12
465	Rick Monday	.20
466	Mike Squires	.12
467	Jesse Jefferson	.12
468	Aurelio Rodriguez	.20
469	Randy Niemann	.12
470	• Bob Boone	.30
471	Hosken Powell	.12
472	Willie Hernandez	.20
473	Bump Wills	.12
475	Cesar Geronimo	.12
477	Buck Martinez	.12
478	Gil Flores	.12

479	Expos Team (Dick Williams)	.50
480	Bob Watson	.20
481	Tom Paciorek	.12
482	*Rickey Henderson*	200.00
483	Bo Diaz	.15
484	Checklist 364-484	.50
485	Mickey Rivers	.20
486	Mike Tyson	.12
487	Wayne Nordhagen	.12
490	Lee May	.20
491	Steve Mura	.12
492	Todd Cruz	.12
493	Jerry Martin	.12
494	Craig Minetto	.12
495	Bake McBride	.12
496	Silvio Martinez	.12
497	Jim Mason	.12
498	Danny Darwin	.20
499	Giants Team (Dave Bristol)	.50
500	Tom Seaver	3.00

265 Robin Yount

501	Rennie Stennett	.12
502	Rich Wortham	.12
503	Mike Cubbage	.12
504	Gene Garber	.12
505	Bert Campaneris	.20
506	Tom Buskey	.12
507	Leon Roberts	.12
508	U.L. Washington	.12
509	Ed Glynn	.12
510	Ron Cey	.25
511	Eric Wilkins	.12
512	Jose Cardenal	.12
513	Tom Dixon	.12
514	Steve Ontiveros	.12
515	Mike Caldwell	.12
516	Hector Cruz	.12
517	Don Stanhouse	.12
518	Nelson Norman	.12
519	Steve Nicosia	.12
520	Steve Rogers	.20
521	Ken Brett	.12
522	Jim Morrison	.12
523	Ken Henderson	.12
524	Jim Wright	.12
525	Clint Hurdle	.12
526	Phillies Team (Dallas Green)	.70

527	Doug Rau	.12
528	Adrian Devine	.12
530	Jim Sundberg	.12
531	Eric Rasmussen	.12
532	Willie Horton	.20
533	Checklist 485-605	.50
534	Andre Thornton	.25
535	Bob Forsch	.20
536	Lee Lacy	.12
537	*Alex Trevino*	.20
538	Joe Strain	.12
539	Rudy May	.12
540	Pete Rose	4.50
541	Miguel Dilone	.12
542	Joe Coleman	.12
543	Pat Kelly	.12
544	*Rick Sutcliffe*	3.00
545	Jeff Burroughs	.20
546	Rick Langford	.12
547	John Wathan	.20
548	Dave Rajsich	.12
549	Larry Wolfe	.12
550	Ken Griffey	.50
551	Pirates Team (Chuck Tanner)	.50
552	Bill Nahorodny	.12
553	Dick Davis	.12

232 Alan Trammell

500 Tom Seaver

200 Jim Rice

1980 Topps

590 Jim Palmer

650 Joe Morgan

1981 DONRUSS

Following a favorable legal ruling in favor of Fleer, Donruss joined that company and Topps in the baseball card market in 1981 with a set of 605 cards. In the past, Donruss had marketed its bubble gum products only with card sets unrelated to sports. And from the looks of their initial offering, it is obvious that Donruss had little experience with baseball cards. To begin with, the set was printed on ultra-thin cardboard, which makes the cards more susceptible to damage. The color reproductions are of poor quality, and the set is filled with factual and photographic errors (38 of which were corrected). Few of the errors add significant value to the affected cards. Donruss did acknowledge the popularity of superstars George Brett, Steve Garvey, Reggie Jackson, Pete Rose, and Mike Schmidt, all of whom appear more than once in the set.

		MINT
Complete set		$55.00
Commons		.06

1	Ozzie Smith	$1.25
2	Rollie Fingers	.50
3	Rick Wise	.08
5	Alan Trammell	.60
6	Tom Brookens	.08
7	Duffy Dyer	.10
8	Mark Fidrych	.08
11	Mike Schmidt	2.50
12	Willie Stargell	.50
13	Tim Foli	.06
18	Joe Morgan	.55
22	Manny Trillo	.08
23	• *Dave Smith*	.45
25	Bump Wills	.06
26	John Ellis	.10
27	Jim Kern	.06
28	Richie Zisk	.08
29	John Mayberry	.08
32	Al Woods	.06
33	Steve Carlton	1.00
34	Lee Mazzilli	.06
37	Mike Scott	.85
44	Ron Reed	.08
49	Rod Carew	1.00
50	Bert Campaneris	.08
51	Tom Donahue (incorrect spelling)	1.00
51	Tom Donohue (correct spelling)	.10

RICKEY HENDERSON OUTFIELD

119 Rickey Henderson

52	Dave Frost	.06
54	Dan Ford	.06
55	Garry Maddox	.10
56	Steve Garvey	.75
57	Bill Russell	.08
58	Don Sutton	.35
59	Reggie Smith	.10
60	Rick Monday	.10
61	Ray Knight	.08
62	Johnny Bench	1.10
63	Mario Soto	.08
65	George Foster	.15

TIM RAINES SECOND BASE

538 Tim Raines

66	Jeff Burroughs	.08
67	Keith Hernandez	.35
68	Tom Herr	.35
69	Bob Forsch	.08
71	Bobby Bonds	.15
72	Rennie Stennett	.10
73	Joe Strain	.06
77	Gene Garber	.06
80	Ron Hassey	.06
82	*Joe Charboneau*	.15
83	Cecil Cooper	.10
84	Sal Bando	.10
85	Moose Haas	.06
87	Larry Hisle	.10
88	Luis Gomez	.06
89	Larry Parrish	.10
90	Gary Carter	.50
91	*Bill Gullickson*	.25
94	Carl Yastrzemski	1.10
96	Dennis Eckersley	.40
97	Tom Burgmeier	.10
99	Bob Horner	.10
100	George Brett	2.00
102	Dennis Leonard	.08
103	Renie Martin	.06
104	Amos Otis	.08
105	Graig Nettles	.15

107	Tommy John	.20
109	Lou Piniella	.15
111	Bobby Murcer	.10
112	Eddie Murray	1.50
113	Rick Dempsey	.08
114	Scott McGregor	.08
115	Ken Singleton	.10
119	Rickey Henderson	24.00
120	Mike Heath	.06
121	Dave Cash	.06
122	Randy Jones	.08
127	Jack Morris	.30
128	Dan Petry	.08
131	Pete Rose	1.50
132	Willie Stargell	.40
134	Jim Bibby	.06
135	Bert Blyleven	.25
136	Dave Parker	.40
140	J.R. Richard	.10
141	Ken Forsch	.06
142	Larry Bowa	.15
145	Buddy Bell	.12
146	Ferguson Jenkins	.35
148	John Grubb	.06
149	Alfredo Griffin	.08
151	*Paul Mirabella* (FC)	.10
152	Rick Bosetti	.06
156	*Jeff Reardon*	1.40
160	Lamarr Hoyt (LaMarr)	.20
162	Thad Bosley	.06
163	Julio Cruz	.06
164	Del Unser	.10
167	Shane Rawley	.08
168	Joe Simpson	.06
169	Rod Carew	1.00
170	Fred Patek	.06
171	Frank Tanana	.10
173	Chris Knapp	.06
174	Joe Rudi	.10
175	Greg Luzinski	.15
176	Steve Garvey	.75
178	Bob Welch	.50
179	Dusty Baker	.10
180	Rudy Law	.06
181	Dave Concepcion	.15
182	Johnny Bench	1.10
184	Ken Griffey	.20
187	Garry Templeton	.10
189	Pete Vukovich	.08

190	John Urrea	.06
192	Darrell Evans	.12
193	Milt May	.06
194	Bob Knepper	.08
196	Larry Herndon	.08
198	Andre Thornton	.08
201	Rick Waits	.06
202	Rick Manning	.06
203	Paul Molitor	.35
208	Bruce Benedict	.08
211	Bill Lee	.12
212	Andre Dawson	1.25
214	Carl Yastrzemski	1.10
215	Jerry Remy	.06
216	Mike Torrez	.08
218	Fred Lynn	.20
219	Chris Chambliss	.10
220	Willie Aikens	.08
221	John Wathan	.08
222	Dan Quisenberry	.35
223	Willie Wilson	.15
224	Clint Hurdle	.08
225	Bob Watson	.08
226	Jim Spencer	.06
227	Ron Guidry	.25
228	Reggie Jackson	1.50
229	Oscar Gamble	.08
231	Luis Tiant	.12
233	Dan Graham	.06
234	Mike Flanagan	.10
235	John Lowenstein	.06
237	Wayne Gross	.06
238	Rick Langford	.06
239	Tony Armas	.10
240	Bob Lacy (incorrect spelling)	1.00
240	Bob Lacey (correct spelling)	.10
241	Gene Tenace	.08
243	Gary Lucas	.08
246	Stan Papi	.06
247	Milt Wilcox	.06
249	Steve Kemp	.10
251	Pete Rose	1.25
252	Bill Madlock	.15
253	Dale Berra	.06
254	Kent Tekulve	.10
258	Art Howe	.06
259	Alan Ashby	.06

260 Nolan Ryan

260	Nolan Ryan	4.50
261	Vern Ruhle (photo is Ken Forsch)	1.25
261	Vern Ruhle (correct photo)	.10
262	Bob Boone	.10
263	Cesar Cedeno	.10
264	Jeff Leonard	.15
266	Jon Matlack	.08
269	Damaso Garcia	.10
273	Tug McGraw	.10
275	Pat Zachry	.06
276	Neil Allen	.08
279	*Britt Burns*	.10
280	*Rich Dotson*	.25
283	Ted Cox	.06
284	Sparky Lyle	.10
285	Larry Cox	.06
286	Floyd Bannister	.10
289	Bobby Grich	.10
290	Dickie Thon	.08
294	Rick Miller	.06
295	Lonnie Smith	.35
296	Ron Cey	.12
297	Steve Yeager	.06
299	Manny Mota	.10
300	Jay Johnstone	.10
301	Dan Driessen	.08

1981 Donruss

100 George Brett

323 Robin Yount

370	Sparky Anderson	.10
371	Pete Rose	1.25
374	John Candelaria	.06
376	Lee Lacy	.06
377	John Milner	.06
379	Luis Pujois (incorrect spelling)	1.00
379	Luis Pujols (correct spelling)	.10
380	Joe Niekro	.15
381	Joaquin Andujar	.10
382	*Keith Moreland*	.25
383	Jose Cruz	.12
384	Bill Virdon	.06
385	Jim Sundberg	.08
386	Doc Medich	.06
387	Al Oliver	.15
389	Bob Bailor	.06
390	Ernie Whitt	.08
392	Roy Howell	.06
393	*Bob Walk*	.30

PETE ROSE FIRST BASE

131 Pete Rose

399	Marvis Foley	.06
400	Steve Trout	.06
402	Tony Larussa (LaRussa)	.08
404	Bake McBride	.06
406	Rob Dressler	.06
408	Tom Paciorek	.06
409	Carney Lansford	.20
410	Brian Downing	.10
411	Don Aase	.06
412	Jim Barr	.06
413	Don Baylor	.10
414	Jim Fregosi	.08
415	Dallas Green	.08
416	Dave Lopes /	.10
417	Jerry Reuss	.10
418	Rick Sutcliffe	.25
420	Tommy LaSorda (Lasorda)	.15
421	*Charlie Leibrandt*	.30
422	Tom Seaver	1.10
423	Ron Oester	.06
425	Tom Seaver	1.10
426	Bobby Cox	.06
427	*Leon Durham*	.25
428	Terry Kennedy	.08
430	George Hendrick	.08
431	Red Schoendienst	.15
433	Vida Blue	.10
434	John Montefusco	.08
436	Dave Bristol	.06
437	Dale Murphy	1.25
439	Jorge Orta	.06
442	Dave Garcia	.06
443	Don Money	.06
444	Buck Martinez (photo backward)	1.00
444	Buck Martinez (photo correct)	.10
446	Ben Oglivie	.08
447	Jim Slaton	.06
448	Doyle Alexander	.10
451	Dave Palmer	.06
453	Dick Williams	.06
454	Rick Burleson	.08
456	Bob Stanley	.06
457	*John Tudor*	1.00
458	• Dwight Evans	.35
459	Glenn Hubbard	.08
461	Larry Gura	.08
462	Rich Gale	.06
463	Hal McRae	.10
464	Jim Frey	.06
465	Bucky Dent	.10
467	Ron Davis	.06
468	Reggie Jackson	1.50
469	Bobby Brown	.06

1981 Donruss

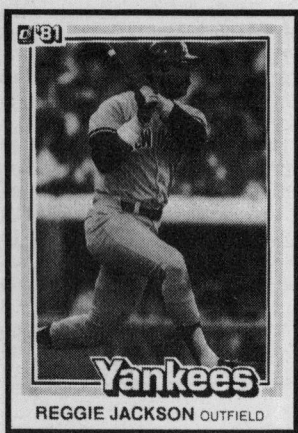

REGGIE JACKSON OUTFIELD

348 Reggie Jackson

470	*Mike Davis*	.25
471	Gaylord Perry	.35
472	Mark Belanger	.08
473	Jim Palmer	.75
474	Sammy Stewart	.06
475	Tim Stoddard	.06
476	Steve Stone	.08
477	Jeff Newman	.06
479	Bill Martin	.20
480	Mitchell Page	.06
481	Cy Young 1980 (Steve Carlton)	.40
482	Bill Buckner	.10
483	Ivan DeJesus	.10
484	Cliff Johnson	.06
485	Lenny Randle	.06
488	John Castino	.06
489	Ron Jackson	.06
490	Dave Roberts	.10
491	MVP (George Brett)	1.10
493	Rob Wilfong	.06
496	Mickey Rivers	.08
498	Mike Sadek	.06
501	Dave Roberts	.06
502	Steve Dillard	.06
503	Jim Essian	.06
505	Darrell Porter	.06
506	Joe Torre	.08
508	Bill Travers	.06
510	Bob McClure	.06
511	*Steve Howe*	.10
512	Dave Rader	.06
514	Kiko Garcia	.06
516	Willie Norwood	.10
517	Bo Diaz	.06
518	Juan Beniquez	.06
520	Jim Tracy	.06
521	Carlos Lezcano	.06
524	Ray Burris	.10
526	Mickey Hatcher	.08
527	John Goryl	.06
528	Dick Davis	.06
530	Sal Butera	.06
531	Jerry Koosman	.10
532	Jeff Zahn (Geoff)	.10
533	Dennis Martinez	.08
535	Steve Macko	.06
536	Jim Kaat	.15
537	Best Hitters (George Brett, Rod Carew)	1.75
538	Tim Raines	6.25
539	Keith Smith	.06
540	Ken Macha	.06
541	Burt Hooton	.08
543	Bill Stein	.06
545	Bob Pate	.06
548	Pete Redfern	.06
550	Al Hrabosky	.08
551	Dick Tidrow	.06
553	Dave Kingman	.20
554	Mike Vail	.10
555	Jerry Martin	.10
556	Jesus Figueroa	.10
559	Tim Blackwell	.06
560	• Bruce Sutter	.20
561	Rick Reuschel	.10
563	Bob Owchinko	.10
564	John Verhoeven	.06
565	Ken Landreaux	.06
566	Glen Adams (incorrect spelling)	1.00
566	Glenn Adams (correct spelling)	.10
567	Hosken Powell	.06
568	Dick Noles	.06
569	• *Danny Ainge*	.75

570	Bobby Mattick	.06	586	Bill Caudill	.06
571	Joe Lefebvre	.08	587	Doug Capilla	.06
572	Bobby Clark	.06	588	George Riley	.06
573	Dennis Lamp	.06	589	Willie Hernandez	.10
574	Randy Lerch	.06	590	MVP (Mike Schmidt)	1.30
575	Mookie Wilson	.60	591	Cy Young 1980	
576	Ron LeFlore	.08		(Steve Stone)	.08
577	Jim Dwyer	.06	592	Rick Sofield	.06
578	Bill Castro	.06	593	Bombo Rivera	.06
579	Greg Minton	.06	594	Gary Ward	.08
580	Mark Littell	.08	595	Dave Edwards	.10
581	Andy Hassler	.06	596	Mike Proly	.06
582	Dave Stieb	.85	597	Tommy Boggs	.06
583	Ken Oberkfell	.06	598	Gregg Gross	.06
584	Larry Bradford	.06	599	Elias Sosa	.06
585	Fred Stanley	.06	600	Pat Kelly	.06

1981 FLEER

A 1980 Pennsylvania court ruling allowed Fleer to break the virtual monopoly held by Topps and produce its own set of baseball cards. This legal victory permitted the Philadelphia company to make independent contracts with major league baseball and the Players Association—rights that had been held exclusively by Topps since 1964. The Fleer set of 660 cards is not first-rate, however, with photographic quality a notch below the standard established by Topps. It is also marred by 40 different errors, although the error cards were corrected in two subsequent press runs and aren't collected by most hobbyists, who stop with 660 cards. Graig Nettles' card, number 87, is the only notable exception. In early press runs his name appeared on the back as "Craig." The corrected version is far more common than the card with the error.

		MINT
Complete set		
(without variations)		**$55.00**
Commons		**.06**
1	Pete Rose	$1.75
2	Larry Bowa	.15
3	Manny Trillo	.08
4	Bob Boone	.10
5	Mike Schmidt (batting)	1.00
5	Mike Schmidt (portrait)	1.25
6	Steve Carlton ("Lefty" on front)	1.00
6	Steve Carlton ("Pitcher of the Year" on front, date "1066" on back)	.60
6	Steve Carlton ("Pitcher of the Year" on front, date "1966" on back)	2.00
7	Tug McGraw ("Game Saver" on front)	.50
7	Tug McGraw ("Pitcher" on front)	.12

1981 Fleer

351 Rickey Henderson

140 Fernand Valenzuela

88	Ron Guidry	.25
89	Rich Gossage	.20
91	• Gaylord Perry	.30
93	Bob Watson	.10
94	Bobby Murcer	.10
98	Oscar Gamble	.10
109	Willie Randolph	.10
110	Steve Garvey	.50
111	Reggie Smith	.10
112	Don Sutton	.30
113	Burt Hooton	.08
114	Davy Lopes (Davey) (with fingerlike mark on back)	1.00
114	Davy Lopes (Davey) (w/o mark on back)	.10
115	Dusty Baker	.10
116	Tom Lasorda	.10
117	Bill Russell	.10
119	Terry Forster	.06
120	Robert Welch ("Bob Welch" on back)	.20
120	Robert Welch ("Robert Welch" on back)	1.00
122	Rick Monday	.10
125	Rick Sutcliffe	.15
126	Ron Cey (with fingerlike mark on back)	1.00
126	Ron Cey (w/o mark on back)	.10
127	Dave Goltz	.10
128	Jay Johnstone	.08
130	Gary Weiss	.06
131	*Mike Scioscia*	.90
132	Vic Davalillo	.08
133	Doug Rau	.06
135	Mickey Hatcher	.08
136	*Steve Howe*	.08
139	Rudy Law	.06
140	*Fernand Valenzuela (Fernando)*	4.50
141	Manny Mota	.08
142	Gary Carter	.45
143	Steve Rogers	.08
145	Andre Dawson	.40
146	Larry Parrish	.10
150	*Bill Gullickson*	.15
154	Ron LeFlore	.08
155	Rodney Scott	.06

481 Kirk Gibson

157	Bill Lee	.08
159	Woodie Fryman	.08
160	Dave Palmer	.06
161	Jerry White	.06
165	*Charlie Lea*	.10
167	Ken Macha	.06
169	Jim Palmer	.40
171	Mike Flanagan	.10
172	Al Bumbry	.06
173	Doug DeCinces	.10
174	Scott McGregor	.08
175	Mark Belanger	.08
177	Rick Dempsey (with fingerlike mark on front)	1.00
177	Rick Dempsey (w/o mark on front)	.10
178	Earl Weaver	.10
180	Dennis Martinez	.08
183	Lee May	.08
184	Eddie Murray	1.50
185	Benny Ayala	.06
188	Ken Singleton	.10
189	Dan Graham	.06
192	Dave Ford	.06
195	Doug DeCinces	.10
196	Johnny Bench	.90
197	Dave Concepcion	.15

1981 Fleer

57 Nolan Ryan

650 Reggie Jackson

243 Dale Murphy

645 Triple Threat

6 Steve Carlton

427	Steve Braun	.06
428	Bob Davis	.06
429	Jerry Garvin	.06
430	Alfredo Griffin	.08
432	Vida Blue	.12
433	Jack Clark	.25
434	• Willie McCovey	.40
435	Mike Ivie	.06
436	Darrell Evans ("Darrel" on front)	.15
436	Darrell Evans ("Darrell" correct on front)	.75
437	Terry Whitfield	.06
438	Rennie Stennett	.06
439	John Montefusco	.08
440	Jim Wohlford	.06
441	Bill North	.06
442	Milt May	.06
443	Max Venable	.06
444	Ed Whitson	.06
445	*Al Holland*	.08
447	Bob Knepper	.06
448	Gary Lavelle	.06
449	Greg Minton	.06
450	Johnnie LeMaster	.06
451	Larry Herndon	.08
452	Rich Murray	.06
454	Allen Ripley	.06
455	Dennis Littlejohn	.06
456	Tom Griffin	.06
459	Steve Kemp	.08
460	Sparky Anderson	.10
461	Alan Trammell	.40
462	Mark Fidrych	.08
463	Lou Whitaker	.30
465	Milt Wilcox	.06
466	Champ Summers	.06
467	Lance Parrish	.35
468	Dan Petry	.08
469	Pat Underwood	.06
470	Rick Peters	.06
471	Al Cowens	.06
472	John Wockenfuss	.06
473	Tom Brookens	.08
474	Richie Hebner	.06
475	Jack Morris	.35
476	Jim Lentine	.06
477	Bruce Robbins	.06
478	Mark Wagner	.06

421 Lloyd Moseby

480	Stan Papi ("Pitcher" on front)	.15
480	Stan Papi ("Shortstop" on front)	.70
481	*Kirk Gibson*	4.00
482	Dan Schatzeder	.06
483	Amos Otis	.15
484	Dave Winfield	.50
485	Rollie Fingers	.35
486	Gene Richards	.06
487	Randy Jones	.08
488	Ozzie Smith	.40
489	Gene Tenace	.08
492	Dave Cash	.06
493	Tim Flannery (negative reversed, batting right)	.15
493	Tim Flannery (correct photo, batting left)	.70
494	Jerry Mumphrey	.06
495	Bob Shirley	.06
496	Steve Mura	.06
498	Broderick Perkins	.06
499	Barry Evans	.06
500	Chuck Baker	.06
501	*Luis Salazar*	.15
502	Gary Lucas	.08
503	Mike Armstrong	.06

485 Rollie Fingers

1981 TOPPS

The 1981 Topps set contains 726 cards, but because it was printed in six sheets of 132 cards each, 66 cards were printed twice. This happened because each sheet had one row of 11 cards that was printed a second time, making such cards twice as common as the others. Among the double-printed cards are those for Mike Schmidt and Rich Dotson. The 1981 set marks the last appearance of team cards with the manager's photo in the upper right. Once again, three Future Stars from each team share a card. At the time this set was released, and for the first time in years, Topps was facing major competition in the baseball card market.

	MINT
Complete set	**$105.00**
Commons	**.08**

#		
1	Batting Ldrs (George Brett, Bill Buckner)	$ .75
2	HR Ldrs (Reggie Jackson, Ben Oglivie, Mike Schmidt)	.40
3	RBI Ldrs (Cecil Cooper, Mike Schmidt)	.30
4	SB Ldrs (Rickey Henderson, Ron LeFlore)	.25
5	Victory Ldrs (Steve Carlton, Steve Stone)	.20
6	SO Ldrs (Len Barker, Steve Carlton)	.20
7	ERA Ldrs (Rudy May, Don Sutton)	.15
8	Leading Firemen (Rollie Fingers, Tom Hume, Dan Quisenberry)	.10
9	Pete LaCock	.08
10	Mike Flanagan	.10
11	Jim Wohlford	.08
12	Mark Clear	.08
13	*Joe Charboneau*	.15
14	*John Tudor*	1.25
15	Larry Parrish	.12
16	Ron Davis	.08
17	Cliff Johnson	.08
18	Glenn Adams	.08
19	Jim Clancy	.08
20	Jeff Burroughs	.10
21	Ron Oester	.08

261 Rickey Henderson

#		
23	Alex Trevino	.08
24	Don Stanhouse	.08
25	Sixto Lezcano	.08
26	U.L. Washington	.08
27	Champ Summers	.08
28	Enrique Romo	.08
29	Gene Tenace	.10
30	Jack Clark	.50
31	Checklist 1-121	.10
32	Ken Oberkfell	.08
34	Aurelio Rodriguez	.08
35	Mitchell Page	.08
36	Ed Farmer	.08
37	Gary Roenicke	.08

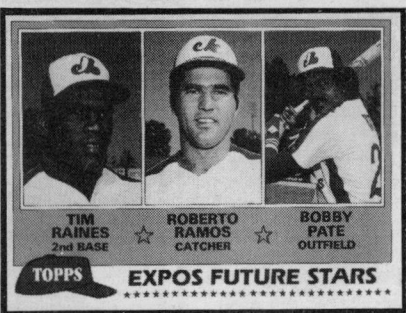

479 Expos Future Stars

38	Win Remmerswaal	.08
39	Tom Veryzer	.08
40	Tug McGraw	.20
41	Rangers FS (Bob Babcock, John Butcher, Jerry Don Gleaton)	.10
42	Jerry White	.08
43	Jose Morales	.08
45	Enos Cabell	.08
46	Rick Bosetti	.08
47	Ken Brett	.10
48	Dave Skaggs	.08
49	Bob Shirley	.08
50	Dave Lopes	.10
51	Bill Robinson	.08
52	Hector Cruz	.08
53	Kevin Saucier	.08
54	Ivan DeJesus	.08
55	Mike Norris	.08
56	Buck Martinez	.08
59	Dan Petry	.08
60	Willie Randolph	.10
61	Butch Wynegar	.08
62	Joe Pettini	.08
64	Brian Asselstine	.08
65	Scott McGregor	.10
67	Ken Kravec	.08
68	Matt Alexander	.08
69	Ed Halicki	.08
70	Al Oliver	.15
71	Hal Dues	.08
72	Barry Evans	.08
74	Mike Hargrove	.08
75	Reggie Smith	.15
76	Mario Mendoza	.08
77	Mike Barlow	.08
78	Steve Dillard	.08
79	Bruce Robbins	.08
80	Rusty Staub	.15
81	Dave Stapleton	.08
83	Mike Proly	.08
84	Johnnie LeMaster	.08
85	Mike Caldwell	.08
86	Wayne Gross	.08
87	Rick Camp	.08
88	Joe Lefebvre	.08
90	Bake McBride	.08
91	Tim Stoddard	.08
94	Harry Spilman	1.08
95	Jim Sundberg	.10
96	A's FS (Dave Beard, Ernie Camacho, Pat Dempsey)	.12
97	Chris Speier	.08
98	Clint Hurdle	.08
99	Eric Wilkins	.08
100	Rod Carew	2.00
101	Benny Ayala	.08
102	Dave Tobik	.08
103	Jerry Martin	.08
104	Terry Forster	.10
105	Jose Cruz	.15
106	Don Money	.08
107	Rich Wortham	.08

108	Bruce Benedict	.08
109	Mike Scott	.85
110	Carl Yastrzemski	2.00
111	Greg Minton	.08
113	Mike Phillips	.08
114	Tom Underwood	.08
115	Roy Smalley	.08
116	Joe Simpson	.08
117	Pete Falcone	.08
118	Kurt Bevacqua	.08
119	Tippy Martinez	.08
120	Larry Bowa	.20
123	Al Cowens	.08
124	Jerry Garvin	.08
125	Andre Dawson	2.00
126	*Charlie Leibrandt*	.40
127	Rudy Law	.08
128	Gary Allenson	.08
129	Art Howe	.08
130	Larry Gura	.08
131	*Keith Moreland*	.45
132	Tommy Boggs	.08
133	Jeff Cox	.08
134	Steve Mura	.08
135	Gorman Thomas	.10
136	Doug Capilla	.08
137	Hosken Powell	.08
138	Richard Dotson	.20
139	Oscar Gamble	.10
140	Bob Forsch	.10
141	Miguel Dilone	.08
144	Allen Ripley	.08
145	Mickey Rivers	.08
146	Bobby Castillo	.08
147	Dale Berra	.08
149	Joe Nolan	.08
150	Mark Fidrych	.10
151	Claudell Washington	.12
153	Tom Poquette	.08
154	Rick Langford	.08
155	Chris Chambliss	.08
156	Bob McClure	.08
157	John Wathan	.10
158	Fergie Jenkins	.45
159	Brian Doyle	.08
160	Garry Maddox	.10
161	Dan Graham	.08
162	Doug Corbett	.08
163	Billy Almon	.08

315 Kirk Gibson

164	*Lamarr Hoyt* (LaMarr)	.15
166	Floyd Bannister	.12
167	Terry Whitfield	.08
168	Don Robinson	.10
169	John Mayberry	.10
170	Ross Grimsley	.08
172	Gary Woods	.08
173	Bump Wills	.08
174	Doug Rau	.08
175	Dave Collins	.10
176	Mike Krukow	.10
177	Rick Peters	.08
178	Jim Essian	.08
179	Rudy May	.08
180	Pete Rose	3.50
181	Elias Sosa	.08
182	Bob Grich	.12
185	Dennis Leonard	.10
186	Wayne Nordhagen	.08
187	Mike Parrott	.08
188	Doug DeCinces	.12
189	Craig Swan	.08
190	Cesar Cedeno	.10
191	Rick Sutcliffe	.40
192	Braves FS (*Terry Harper*, Ed Miller, *Rafael Ramirez*)	.25
193	Pete Vuckovich	.10

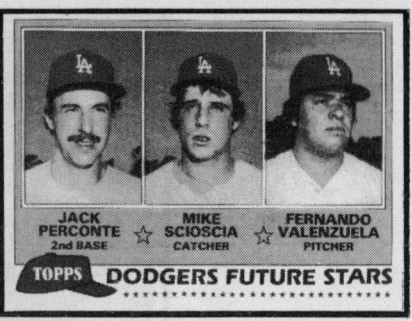

302 Dodgers Future Stars

194	*Rod Scurry*	.10	220	Tom Seaver	2.00
195	Rich Murray	.08	221	Bob Davis	.08
196	Duffy Dyer	.08	222	Jorge Orta	.08
197	Jim Kern	.08	223	Roy Lee Jackson	.08
198	Jerry Dybzinski	.08	224	Pat Zachry	.08
199	Chuck Rainey	.08	225	Ruppert Jones	.08
200	George Foster	.25	226	Manny Sanguillen	.08
201	Record Breaker (Johnny Bench)	.50	227	Fred Martinez	.08
			228	Tom Paciorek	.08
202	Record Breaker (Steve Carlton)	.40	229	Rollie Fingers	.75
			230	George Hendrick	.08
203	Record Breaker (Bill Gullickson)	.08	231	Joe Beckwith	.08
			232	Mickey Klutts	.08
204	Record Breaker (Ron LeFlore, Rodney Scott)	.10	233	Skip Lockwood	.08
			234	Lou Whitaker	.60
205	Record Breaker (Pete Rose)	.80	235	Scott Sanderson	.08
			237	Charlie Moore	.08
206	Record Breaker (Mike Schmidt)	.50	238	Willie Hernandez	.10
			239	Rick Miller	.08
207	Record Breaker (Ozzie Smith)	.20	240	Nolan Ryan	5.00
			241	Checklist 122-242	.08
208	Record Breaker (Willie Wilson)	.20	242	Chet Lemon	.10
			243	Sal Butera	.08
209	Dickie Thon	.10	244	Cardinals FS (*Tito Landrum,* Al Olmsted, Andy Rincon)	.15
210	Jim Palmer	1.50			
211	Derrel Thomas	.08			
212	Steve Nicosia	.08	245	Ed Figueroa	.08
213	*Al Holland*	.10	246	Ed Ott	.08
215	Larry Hisle	.10	247	Glenn Hubbard	.08
218	Paul Splittorff	.10	248	Joey McLaughlin	.08
219	Ken Landreaux	.08	249	Larry Cox	.08
			250	Ron Guidry	.50

490 Eddie Murray

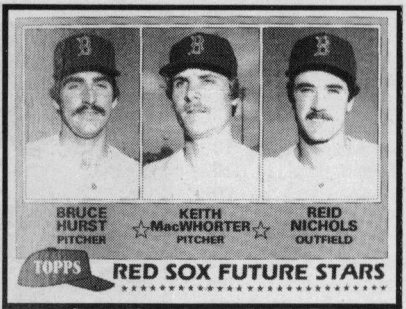

689 Red Sox Future Stars

441	Ken Reitz	.08
444	Garth Iorg	.08
446	Checklist 364-484	.25
450	Dave Kingman	.10
451	Indians FS (Chris Bando, Tom Brennan, Sandy Wihtol)	.12
455	Rick Burleson	.10
456	*Jeff Reardon*	2.00
457	Mike Lum	.08
458	Randy Jones	.10
460	Rich Gossage	.40
463	Milt May	.08
465	Bill Russell	.10
467	Dave Stieb	1.00
469	Jeff Leonard	.15
470	Manny Trillo	.10
475	Buddy Bell	.15
476	Jerry Koosman	.12
479	Expos FS (Bobby Pate, *Tim Raines,* Roberto Ramos)	11.00
480	Carlton Fisk	1.00
482	Jim Gantner	.10
485	Garry Templeton	.10
488	*Damaso Garcia*	.12
489	John Littlefield (photo is Mark Riggins)	.08
490	Eddie Murray	3.00
493	Dan Quisenberry	.40
494	*Bob Walk*	.50
495	Dusty Baker	.10
500	Jim Rice	1.00
504	Dale Murphy	2.50
510	Lee Mazzilli	.08
515	Robin Yount	1.00
517	Richie Zisk	.10
525	Mike Torrez	.08
528	Gary Matthews	.12
530	Steve Garvey	1.50
534	• *Dave Smith*	.40
540	Mike Schmidt	2.00
548	Dave Goltz	.08
550	Tommy John	.50
551	• Pirates FS (*Vance Law,* Tony Pena, Pascual Perez)	2.75
554	Bert Blyleven	.35
555	Cecil Cooper	.20

14 John Tudor

560	Joe Morgan	.75
562	Checklist 485-605	.25
563	Jim Kaat	.30
565	Burt Hooton	.10
570	Ken Singleton	.10
572	Jack Morris	.60
573	Phil Garner	.10
575	Tony Perez	.35
577	Blue Jays FS (Luis Leal, Brian Milner, *Ken Schrom*)	.20
578	*Bill Gullickson*	.20
580	Don Baylor	.15
582	Gaylord Perry	.70
585	Amos Otis	.10
590	Bruce Sutter	.25
593	Steve Kemp	.10
600	Johnny Bench	1.75
605	Don Sutton	.70
610	Darrell Porter	.10
615	Rick Dempsey	.10
616	Rick Wise	.10
620	Dennis Eckersley	.20
623	Sal Bando	.10
624	Bob Welch	.20
625	Bill Buckner	.15
627	Luis Tiant	.20
629	Tony Armas	.12

1981 Topps

660 Gary Carter

1981 TOPPS TRADED

Faced with its only competition in the baseball card market since 1963, Topps scrambled for an advantage over its new rivals in 1981. The company found a competitive edge in its Traded set. Unlike later years when Traded sets had a "T" designation following the card numbers and featured different color printing on the back, the 1981 Topps Traded series is a genuine extension of the 726-card regular issue. As a result, many collectors think of the extension set as the "high numbers" for 1981. Topps sold the issue in the form of a complete boxed set, and only to hobby dealers. The initial price of this 132-card edition was around nine dollars, which made the cost per card about seven cents. In comparison, cards in the major set that year cost only about two cents each.

		MINT
Complete set		**$36.00**
Commons		.10

727	Danny Ainge (FC)	$ .85
728	Doyle Alexander	.20
729	Gary Alexander	.10
730	Billy Almon	.10
731	Joaquin Andujar	.15
732	Bob Bailor	.10
735	Tony Bernazard	.10
737	Doug Bird	.10
738	Bert Blyleven	.50
740	Bobby Bonds	.20
741	Rick Bosetti	.10
742	Hubie Brooks	1.50
743	Rick Burleson	.15
744	Ray Burris	.10
745	Jeff Burroughs	.15
746	Enos Cabell	.10
748	Mark Clear	.10
749	Larry Cox	.10
750	Hector Cruz	.10
754	Brian Doyle	.10
755	Dick Drago	.10
756	Leon Durham	.25
757	Jim Dwyer	.10
758	Dave Edwards	.10
759	Jim Essian	.10
761	Rollie Fingers	1.00

816 Tim Raines

762	Carlton Fisk	4.00
763	Barry Foote	.10
764	Ken Forsch	.10
765	Kiko Garcia	.10
766	Cesar Geronimo	.10
768	Mickey Hatcher	.15
770	Marc Hill	.10
771	Butch Hobson	.10
772	Rick Honeycutt	.10

1981 Topps Traded

807 Joe Morgan

774	Mike Ivie	.10
776	Cliff Johnson	.10
777	Randy Jones	.15
780	Terry Kennedy	.20
781	Dave Kingman	.40
782	Bob Knepper	.10
784	Bob Lacey	.10
785	Dennis Lamp	.10
788	Carney Lansford	.25
789	Dave LaRoche	.10
791	Ron LeFlore	.15
793	Sixto Lezcano	.10
795	Mike Lum	.10
796	Greg Luzinski	.25
797	Fred Lynn	.50
800	Gary Matthews	.20
803	Rick Miller	.10
806	Jose Morales	.10
807	• Joe Morgan	2.00
809	Gene Nelson (FC)	.30
811	Bob Owchinko	.10
812	Gaylord Perry	1.25
814	Darrell Porter	.15
815	Mike Proly	.10
816	Tim Raines	8.00
818	Doug Rau	.10
819	Jeff Reardon	.75

820	Ken Reitz	.10
822	Rick Reuschel	.25
824	Dave Roberts	.10
826	Joe Rudi	.20
827	Kevin Saucier	.10
828	Tony Scott	.10
830	Ted Simmons	.40
835	Rusty Staub	.35
838	Bruce Sutter	.50
839	Don Sutton	1.25
840	Steve Swisher	.10
841	Frank Tanana	.20
842	Gene Tenace	.10
844	Dickie Thon	.10
845	Bill Travers	.10
847	John Urrea	.10
848	Mike Vail	.10
849	Ellis Valentine	.10
850	Fernando Valenzuela	5.00
851	Pete Vuckovich	.10
852	Mark Wagner	.10
853	Bob Walk	.10
854	Claudell Washington	.10
855	Dave Winfield	3.50
857	Richie Zisk	.15

762 Carlton Fisk

1982 DONRUSS

The Memphis company showed a number of improvements in its second full set of baseball cards. There were noticeable improvements in the quality of photography and reproduction, as well as statistical content. But because of a federal court ruling that Topps held the exclusive right to market baseball cards with confectionary products, the 1982 Donruss set was not distributed in gum packs. As a substitute, Donruss created a 63-piece Babe Ruth puzzle. Each wax pack contained three puzzle pieces. The new set was increased to 660 cards and contains the first series of paintings, called Diamond Kings, that portray one star from each team. These are shown in the lists that follow with the abbreviation "DK" in parentheses following the player name. Rookie cards of Kent Hrbek, Cal Ripken, Jr., and Steve Sax further enrich the set.

405 Cal Ripken, Jr.

		MINT
Complete set		$50.00
Commons		.06

1	Pete Rose (DK)	$1.50
2	Gary Carter (DK)	.50
3	Steve Garvey (DK)	.50
4	Vida Blue (DK)	.15
5	Alan Trammel (DK) (incorrect spelling)	1.50
5	Alan Trammell (DK) (correct spelling)	.40
6	Len Barker (DK)	.08
7	• Dwight Evans (DK)	.15
8	Rod Carew (DK)	.50
9	George Hendrick (DK)	.10
10	Phil Niekro (DK)	.35
11	Richie Zisk (DK)	.08
12	Dave Parker (DK)	.30
13	Nolan Ryan (DK)	2.00
14	Ivan DeJesus (DK)	.08
15	George Brett (DK)	.75
16	Tom Seaver (DK)	.50
17	Dave Kingman (DK)	.15
18	Dave Winfield (DK)	.50
19	Mike Norris (DK)	.10
20	Carlton Fisk (DK)	.25
21	Ozzie Smith (DK)	.25
22	Roy Smalley (DK)	.08
23	Buddy Bell (DK)	.10
24	Ken Singleton (DK)	.10
25	John Mayberry (DK)	.08
26	Gorman Thomas (DK)	.10
27	Earl Weaver	.10
28	Rollie Fingers	.20
29	Sparky Anderson	.10
30	Dennis Eckersley	.12
31	Dave Winfield	.50
32	Burt Hooton	.08
34	George Brett	1.25
36	Steve Rogers	.08
40	George Hendrick	.08
42	Steve Carlton	.50

1982 Donruss

410 Dave Stewart

54 Jorge Bell

113 Rickey Henderson

419 Nolan Ryan

340	Warren Cromartie	.06
341	Steve Comer	.06
342	Rick Burleson	.08
345	Mike Proly	.06
346	Ruppert Jones	.06
347	Omar Moreno	.06
349	*Rick Mahler* (FC)	.15
350	Alex Trevino	.06
351	Mike Krukow	.08
352	Shane Rawley (photo is Jim Anderson, shaking hands)	1.25
352	Shane Rawley (Shane Rawley, kneeling)	.15
353	Garth Iorg	.06
354	Pete Mackanin	.06
355	Paul Moskau	.06
356	Richard Dotson	.08
357	Steve Stone	.08
358	Larry Hisle	.08
359	Aurelio Lopez	.08
360	Oscar Gamble	.08
361	Tom Burgmeier	.06
362	Terry Forster	.08
363	Joe Charboneau	.08
364	Ken Brett	.08
365	Tony Armas	.10

366	Chris Speier	.06
367	Fred Lynn	.20
368	Buddy Bell	.12
369	Jim Essian	.06
371	Greg Gross	.06
372	• Bruce Sutter	.15
373	Joe Lefebvre	.06
374	Ray Knight	.10
375	Bruce Benedict	.06
376	Tim Foli	.06
377	Al Holland	.06
378	Ken Kravec	.06
380	Pete Falcone	.06
381	Ernie Whitt	.08
382	Brad Havens	.06
383	Terry Crowley	.06
384	Don Money	.06
385	Dan Schatzeder	.06
387	Yogi Berra	.15
388	Ken Landreaux	.06
389	Mike Hargrove	.06
390	Darryl Motley	.06
391	Dave McKay	.06
392	Stan Bahnsen	.06
393	Ken Forsch	.06
394	Mario Mendoza	.06
395	Jim Morrison	.06
396	Mike Ivie	.06
398	Darrell Evans	.15
399	Ron Reed	.08
400	Johnny Bench	.65
401	*Steve Bedrosian* (FC)	1.00
402	Bill Robinson	.06
403	Bill Buckner	.12
404	Ken Oberkfell	.06
405	*Cal Ripken, Jr.* (FC)	27.00
406	Jim Gantner	.08
407	Kirk Gibson (FC)	1.50
408	Tony Perez	.20
409	Tommy John	.20
410	*Dave Stewart* (FC)	8.25
411	Dan Spillner	.06
412	Willie Aikens	.06
413	Mike Heath	.06
416	*Mike Witt* (FC)	.75
417	Bobby Molinaro	.06
418	Steve Braun	.06
419	Nolan Ryan	4.25
420	Tug McGraw	.12

421	Dave Concepcion	.12
422	Juan Eichelberger (photo is Gary Lucas)	**1.25**
422	Juan Eichelberger (correct photo)	.15
423	Rick Rhoden	.10
424	Frank Robinson	.12
425	Eddie Miller	.06
426	Bill Caudill	.06
427	Doug Flynn	.06
428	Larry Anderson (Andersen) (FC)	.10
430	Jerry Garvin	.06
431	Glenn Adams	.06
432	Barry Bonnell	.06
434	John Stearns	.06
435	Mike Tyson	.06
436	Glenn Hubbard	.06
437	Eddie Solomon	.06
438	Jeff Leonard	.10
439	Randy Bass	.06
440	Mike LaCoss	.06
441	Gary Matthews	.10
442	Mark Littell	.06
443	Don Sutton	.30
444	John Harris	.06
445	• Vada Pinson	.08
446	Elias Sosa	.06
447	Charlie Hough	.10
448	Willie Wilson	.15
449	Fred Stanley	.06
450	Tom Veryzer	.06
452	Mark Clear	.06
453	Bill Russell	.08
454	Lou Whitaker	.45
456	Reggie Cleveland	.06
457	Sammy Stewart	.06
458	Pete Vuckovich	.08
459	John Wockenfuss	.06
461	Willie Randolph	.10
462	Fernando Valenzuela (FC)	.85
463	Ron Hassey	.06
464	Paul Splittorff	.06
465	Rob Picciolo	.06
466	Larry Parrish	.10
467	Johnny Grubb	.06
469	Silvio Martinez	.06
470	Kiko Garcia	.06
471	• Bob Boone	.10

624 Steve Sax

472	Luis Salazar	.08
473	Randy Niemann	.06
474	Tom Griffin	.06
475	Phil Niekro	.30
476	Hubie Brooks (FC)	.25
477	Dick Tidrow	.06
479	Damaso Garcia	.06
480	Mickey Hatcher	.08
481	Joe Price	.06
482	Ed Farmer	.06
483	Eddie Murray	.65
484	Ben Oglivie	.08
485	Kevin Saucier	.06
486	Bobby Murcer	.10
487	Bill Campbell	.06
488	Reggie Smith	.10
489	Wayne Garland	.06
490	Jim Wright	.06
491	• Billy Martin	.15
492	Jim Fanning	.06
493	Don Baylor	.12
494	Rick Honeycutt	.06
495	Carlton Fisk	.50
496	Denny Walling	.06
497	Bake McBride	.06
498	Darrell Porter	.08
500	Ron Oester	.06

1982 Donruss

140 Tim Wallach

501	*Ken Dayley* (FC)	.15
503	Milt May	.06
504	Doug Bird	.06
505	Bruce Bochte	.06
506	Neil Allen	.06
507	Joey McLaughlin	.06
508	Butch Wynegar	.06
509	Gary Roenicke	.06
510	Robin Yount	1.50
511	Dave Tobik	.06
512	*Rich Gedman* (FC)	.25
513	*Gene Nelson* (FC)	.10
514	Rick Monday	.10
515	Miguel Dilone	.06
516	Clint Hurdle	.06
518	Grant Jackson	.06
519	Andy Hassler	.06
521	Greg Pryor	.06
522	Tony Scott	.06
523	Steve Mura	.06
524	Johnnie LeMaster	.06
525	Dick Ruthven	.06
528	*Johnny Ray* (FC)	.75
529	*Pat Tabler* (FC)	.60
530	Tom Herr	.10
531	San Diego Chicken (with trademark symbol on front)	1.25

531	San Diego Chicken (w/o trademark symbol)	.50
532	Sal Butera	.06
535	Reggie Jackson	.65
536	Ed Romero	.06
537	Derrel Thomas	.06
540	*Bob Ojeda* (FC)	.40
541	Roy Lee Jackson	.06
542	Lynn Jones	.06
543	Gaylord Perry	.35
544	Phil Garner (photo is backward)	1.25
544	Phil Garner (correct photo)	.15
545	Garry Templeton	.10
546	Rafael Ramirez (FC)	.10
547	Jeff Reardon	.20
548	Ron Guidry	.25
549	*Tim Laudner* (FC)	.10
550	John Henry Johnson	.06
551	Chris Bando	.06
554	*Scott Fletcher* (FC)	.30
555	Jerry Royster	.06
556	Shooty Babbitt	.06
557	*Kent Hrbek* (FC)	3.00
558	Yankee Winners (Ron Guidry, Tommy John)	.15
559	Mark Bomback	.06
561	Buck Martinez	.06
562	*Mike Marshall* (FC)	.75
563	Rennie Stennett	.06
564	Steve Crawford	.06
565	Bob Babcock	.06
566	Johnny Podres	.08
568	Harold Baines (FC)	1.35
569	Dave LaRoche	.06
570	Lee May	.08
571	Gary Ward (FC)	.10
572	John Denny	.06
573	Roy Smalley	.06
574	*Bob Brenley* (FC)	.20
575	Bronx Bombers (Reggie Jackson, Dave Winfield)	.50
577	Butch Hobson	.06
578	Harvey Kuenn	.10
579	Cal Ripken, Sr.	.08
580	Juan Berenguer	.08
581	Benny Ayala	.06
582	Vance Law (FC)	.15
583	*Rich Leach* (FC)	.10

18 Dave Winfield (DK)

275 Brett Butler

1982 FLEER

After a triumphant debut into the baseball card world in 1981, Fleer's 1982 set of 660 cards paled in comparison. It featured many fuzzy photographs and was full of errors, only some of which were corrected. Some skeptics feel that the company purposely botched many cards just to sell more product. The hottest error card is number 576, which (due to a flipped negative) shows righty John Littlefield pitching left-handed, while Cal Ripken, Jr., is the set's biggest rookie-card draw. Due to a court ruling in favor of Topps, Fleer was prevented from issuing bubble gum in wax packs. The company distributed team logo stickers instead, which aren't considered collectibles by most hobbyists.

		MINT
Complete set		$55.00
Commons		.06

1	Dusty Baker	$ .10
2	Robert Castillo	.06
3	Ron Cey	.10
4	Terry Forster	.08
5	Steve Garvey	.50
6	Dave Goltz	.08
7	Pedro Guerrero (FC)	.75
8	Burt Hooton	.08
9	Steve Howe	.08
10	Jay Johnstone	.10
11	Ken Landreaux	.06
12	Davey Lopes	.10
13	*Mike Marshall* (FC)	.75
15	Rick Monday	.10
16	*Tom Niedenfuer* (FC)	.20
17	*Ted Power* (FC)	.20
18	Jerry Reuss	.10
19	Ron Roenicke	.06
20	Bill Russell	.08
21	*Steve Sax* (FC)	3.00
22	Mike Scioscia	.08
23	Reggie Smith	.10
24	*Dave Stewart* (FC)	3.25
25	Rick Sutcliffe	.15
26	Derrel Thomas	.06
27	Fernando Valenzuela	.60
28	Bob Welch	.15
31	Rick Cerone	.06
32	Ron Davis	.06
33	Bucky Dent	.10
34	Barry Foote	.06

176 Cal Ripken, Jr.

35	George Frazier	.06
36	Oscar Gamble	.08
37	Rich Gossage	.20
38	Ron Guidry	.25
39	Reggie Jackson	.60
40	Tommy John	.20
41	Rudy May	.06
42	Larry Milbourne	.06
43	Jerry Mumphrey	.06
44	Bobby Murcer	.10
45	*Gene Nelson*	.12
46	Graig Nettles	.15
47	Johnny Oates	.06
48	Lou Piniella	.15

92 Rickey Henderson

609 Jorge Bell

24 Dave Stewart

640 Pete & Re-Pete

646 Yankee Powerhouse

1982 Fleer

405 George Brett

260	Manny Trillo	.08
261	Del Unser	.06
262	George Vukovich	.06
263	Tom Brookens	.08
264	George Capuzzello	.06
265	Marty Castillo	.06
266	Al Cowens	.06
267	Kirk Gibson	.75
268	Richie Hebner	.06
271	Steve Kemp	.10
272	*Rick Leach* (FC)	.10
273	Aurelio Lopez	.06
274	Jack Morris	.35
275	Kevin Saucier	.06
276	Lance Parrish	.35
278	Dan Petry	.06
279	David Rozema	.06
280	Stan Papi	.06
281	Dan Schatzeder	.06
282	Champ Summers	.06
283	Alan Trammell	.40
284	Lou Whitaker	.40
285	Milt Wilcox	.06
286	John Wockenfuss	.06
287	Gary Allenson	.06
290	Mark Clear	.06
291	Steve Crawford	.06

292	Dennis Eckersley	.15
293	• Dwight Evans	.20
294	*Rich Gedman* (FC)	.20
295	Garry Hancock	.06
296	Glenn Hoffman	.06
297	Bruce Hurst (FC)	.35
298	Carney Lansford	.10
301	*Bob Ojeda* (FC)	.35
302	Tony Perez	.25
303	Chuck Rainey	.06
304	Jerry Remy	.06
305	Jim Rice	.40
306	Joe Rudi	.10
307	Bob Stanley	.06
308	Dave Stapleton	.08
309	Frank Tanana	.10
310	Mike Torrez	.10
311	John Tudor (FC)	.25
312	Carl Yastrzemski	1.00
313	Buddy Bell	.12
314	Steve Comer	.06
315	Danny Darwin	.06
317	John Grubb	.06
318	Rick Honeycutt	.06
319	Charlie Hough	.10
320	Ferguson Jenkins	.15
321	John Henry Johnson	.06
323	Jon Matlack	.08
324	Doc Medich	.06
325	Mario Mendoza	.06
326	Al Oliver	.15
327	Pat Putnam	.06
328	Mickey Rivers	.08
329	Leon Roberts	.06
330	Billy Sample	.06
331	Bill Stein	.06
332	Jim Sundberg	.08
333	Mark Wagner	.06
334	Bump Wills	.06
335	Bill Almon	.06
336	Harold Baines	.35
337	Ross Baumgarten	.06
338	Tony Bernazard	.06
339	Britt Burns	.06
340	Richard Dotson	.08
341	Jim Essian	.06
342	Ed Farmer	.06
343	Carlton Fisk	.50
344	Kevin Hickey	.06

345	Lamarr Hoyt (LaMarr)	.06
346	Lamar Johnson	.06
349	Dennis Lamp	.06
350	Ron LeFlore	.08
351	Chet Lemon	.08
352	Greg Luzinski	.15
353	Bob Molinaro	.06
355	Wayne Nordhagen	.06
356	Greg Pryor	.06
357	Mike Squires	.06
358	Steve Trout	.06
359	Alan Bannister	.06
360	Len Barker	.08
361	Bert Blyleven	.12
362	Joe Charboneau	.08
363	John Denny	.06
364	Bo Diaz	.08
367	Wayne Garland	.06
368	Mike Hargrove	.06
369	Toby Harrah	.08
370	Ron Hassey	.06
371	*Von Hayes* (FC)	1.25
373	Duane Kuiper	.06
374	Rick Manning	.06
375	Sid Monge	.06
376	Jorge Orta	.06
378	Dan Spillner	.06

603 Lee Smith

379	Mike Stanton	.06
380	Andre Thornton	.10
381	Tom Veryzer	.06
382	Rick Waits	.06
383	Doyle Alexander	.10
384	Vida Blue	.12
385	Fred Breining	.06
386	Enos Cabell	.06
387	Jack Clark	.25
388	Darrell Evans	.15
390	Larry Herndon	.08
391	Al Holland	.06
392	Gary Lavelle	.06
393	Johnnie LeMaster	.06
395	Milt May	.06
396	Greg Minton	.06
397	• Joe Morgan	.50
398	Joe Pettini	.06
399	Alan Ripley	.06
400	Billy Smith	.06
402	Ed Whitson	.06
404	Willie Aikens	.06
405	George Brett	1.35
406	Ken Brett	.08
407	Dave Chalk	.06
408	Rich Gale	.06
409	Cesar Geronimo	.06

371 Von Hayes

1982 Fleer

7 Pedro Guerrero

632 Steve and Carlton
(Steve Carlton, Carlton
Fisk)...................................... .25

633 3000th Game, May 25,
1981 (Carl Yastrzemski).... .35

634 Dynamic Duo (Johnny
Bench, Tom Seaver) .... .35

635 West Meets East
(Gary Carter,
Fernando Valenzuela) .... .30

636 NL SO King
(Fernando Valenzuela)...... .50

637 1981 HR King
(Mike Schmidt) .... .50

638 NL All Stars
(Gary Carter, Dave
Parker)............................... .25

640 Pete & Re-Pete
(Pete Rose, Pete
Rose Jr.) 2.75

641 Phillies' Finest (Steve
Carlton, Mike Schmidt,
Lonnie Smith) .... .50

642 Red Sox Reunion (Dwight
Evans, Fred Lynn) .... .15

643 1981 Most Hits, Most Runs
(Rickey Henderson)........... .35

644 Most Saves 1981 AL
(Rollie Fingers) .... .15

645 Most 1981 Wins
(Tom Seaver) .... .25

646 Yankee Powerhouse
(Reggie Jackson, Dave
Winfield) 1.50

1982 TOPPS

In 1982, Topps increased the number of cards to 792, where it remains today. This expansion eliminated double-printing and allowed the new set to be produced with an equal number of cards per press sheet (in six 132-card sheets). Collectors later found that the hobby was no longer flooded with certain cards. Despite these numbers, the 1982 set has only has a mediocre design, with indistinct blue-and-green printing on card backs. Two variations in the 1982 set are hard to locate: George Foster All-Star, number 342, is found with and without the facsimile autograph, while Pascual Perez, number 383, sometimes does not have the word "Pitcher" printed in the lower left corner.

	MINT
Complete set	**$125.00**
Commons	**.08**

1 1981 Highlight
(Steve Carlton) .... $ .50

2 1981 Highlight
(Ron Davis) .... .08

3 1981 Highlight
(Tim Raines)..................... .30

4 1981 Highlight
(Pete Rose) .... .70

5 1981 Highlight
(Nolan Ryan) 1.00

6 1981 Highlight
(Fernando Valenzuela)...... .30

9 Ron Guidry .... .35

10 Ron Guidry IA................... .15

14 Steve Howe .... .10

17 Darrell Evans.................... .25

19 Ernie Whitt....................... .10

20 Garry Maddox................... .10

21 Orioles FS (Bob Bonner,
Cal Ripken (FC),
Jeff Schneider) 36.00

1982 Topps

213 Dave Stewart

29	Dwayne Murphy	.10
30	Tom Seaver	.70
31	Tom Seaver IA	.30
39	Lou Whitaker	.40
40	Dave Parker	.35
41	Dave Parker IA	.15
47	Jeff Leonard	.15
50	Buddy Bell	.15
51	Cubs FS (*Jay Howell* (FC), Carlos Lezcano, Ty Waller)	.45
52	*Larry Andersen* (FC)	.10
55	Rick Burleson	.10
59	*Rich Gedman* (FC)	.35
60	Tony Armas	.12
63	Mario Soto	.10
65	Terry Kennedy	.10
66	Astros Ldrs (Art Howe, Nolan Ryan)	.25
70	Tim Raines	1.75
75	Tommy John	.35
80	Jim Palmer	.60
81	Jim Palmer IA	.30
82	Bob Welch	.35
83	Yankees FS (*Steve Balboni* (FC), Andy McGaffigan (FC), *Andre Robertson* (FC))	.50
90	Nolan Ryan	4.00
91	Carney Lansford	.10
93	Larry Hisle	.10
95	Ozzie Smith	1.00
96	Royals Ldrs (George Brett, Larry Gura)	.35
100	Mike Schmidt	2.50
101	Mike Schmidt IA	.70
105	Kirk Gibson	1.25
110	Carlton Fisk	.50
111	Carlton Fisk IA	.15
115	Gaylord Perry	.40
118	Expos FS (*Terry Francona*, Brad Mills, Bryn Smith (FC))	.45
125	• Danny Ainge	.20
126	Braves Ldrs (Rick Mahler, Claudell Washington)	.10
127	Lonnie Smith	.10
129	Checklist 1-132	.12
132	Lee May	.10
138	Tony Pena	.20
140	Ron LeFlore	.10
141	Indians FS (Chris Bando, Tom Brennan, *Von Hayes* (FC))	2.00
143	Mookie Wilson	.10
145	Bob Horner	.20
150	Ted Simmons	.20
156	A's Ldrs (Rickey Henderson, Steve McCatty)	.25
158	Brian Downing	.10
160	Luis Tiant	.15
161	Batting Ldrs (Carney Lansford, Bill Madlock)	.20
162	HR Ldrs (Tony Armas, Dwight Evans, Bobby Grich, Eddie Murray, Mike Schmidt)	.35
163	RBI Ldrs (Eddie Murray, Mike Schmidt)	.40
164	SB Ldrs (Rickey Henderson, Tim Raines)	.35
165	Victory Ldrs (Denny Martinez, Steve McCatty, Jack Morris, Tom Seaver, Pete Vuckovich)	.20
166	SO Ldrs (Len Barker, Fernando Valenzuela)	.20

610 Rickey Henderson

254 Jorge Bell

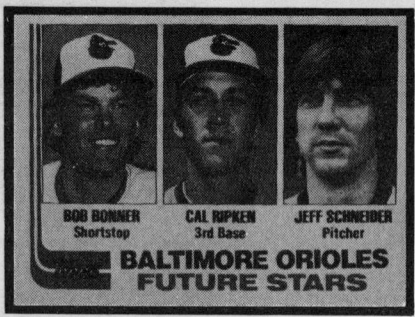

21 Orioles Future Stars

100 Mike Schmidt

203 Blue Jays Future Stars

452	*Lee Smith* (FC)	**1.35**
453	Art Howe	.08
454	Rick Langford	.08
455	Tom Burgmeier	.08
456	Cubs Ldrs (Bill Buckner, Randy Martz)	.15
457	Tim Stoddard	.08
458	Willie Montanez	.08
459	Bruce Berenyi	.08
460	Jack Clark	.30
461	Rich Dotson	.12
464	Juan Bonilla	.08
465	Lee Mazzilli	.10
466	Randy Lerch	.08
467	Mickey Hatcher	.10
468	Floyd Bannister	.12
470	John Mayberry	.10
471	Royals FS (*Atlee Hammaker,* Mike Jones, Darryl Motley)	.25
472	Oscar Gamble	.10
473	Mike Stanton	.08
474	Ken Oberkfell	.08
475	Alan Trammell	.50
476	Brian Kingman	.08
477	Steve Yeager	.08
480	Steve Carlton	.85
481	Steve Carlton IA	.40
482	Glenn Hubbard	.10
483	Gary Woods	.08
484	Ivan DeJesus	.08
485	Kent Tekulve	.10
486	Yankees Ldrs (Tommy John, Jerry Mumphrey)	.20
487	Bob McClure	.08
488	Ron Jackson	.08
489	Rick Dempsey	.10
490	Dennis Eckersley	.12
491	Checklist 397-528	.12
492	Joe Price	.08
493	Chet Lemon	.10
494	Hubie Brooks	.20
495	Dennis Leonard	.10
496	Johnny Grubb	.08
499	Paul Mirabella	.08
500	Rod Carew	**1.00**
501	Rod Carew IA	.40
502	Braves FS (*Steve Bedrosian* (FC), *Brett Butler* (FC), Larry Owen)	**2.50**
503	Julio Gonzalez	.08
504	Rick Peters	.08
505	Graig Nettles	.25
506	Graig Nettles IA	.12
507	Terry Harper	.08
508	*Jody Davis* (FC)	.40
509	Harry Spilman	.08
510	Fernando Valenzuela	**1.50**
511	Ruppert Jones	.08
512	Jerry Dybzinski	.08
513	Rick Rhoden	.10
514	Joe Ferguson	.08
515	Larry Bowa	.20
516	Larry Bowa IA	.12

517	Mark Brouhard	.08
518	Garth Iorg	.08
519	Glenn Adams	.08
520	Mike Flanagan	.10
521	Billy Almon	.08
524	Tom Hausman	.08
525	Ray Knight	.08
526	Expos Ldrs (Warren Cromartie, Bill Gullickson)	.10
527	John Henry Johnson	.08
528	Matt Alexander	.08
529	Allen Ripley	.08
530	Dickie Noles	.08
531	A's FS (Rich Bordi, Mark Budaska, Kelvin Moore)	.08
532	Toby Harrah	.10
533	Joaquin Andujar	.10
534	Dave McKay	.08
535	Lance Parrish	.50
536	Rafael Ramirez	.10
537	Doug Capilla	.08
538	Lou Piniella	.15
539	Vern Ruhle	.08
540	Andre Dawson	1.25
541	Barry Evans	.08
542	Ned Yost	.08
544	Larry Christenson	.08
545	Reggie Smith	.15
546	Reggie Smith IA	.10
547	Rod Carew AS	.35
548	Willie Randolph AS	.12
549	George Brett AS	.60
550	Bucky Dent AS	.12
551	Reggie Jackson AS	.50
552	Ken Singleton AS	.12
553	Dave Winfield AS	.40
554	Carlton Fisk AS	.20
555	Scott McGregor AS	.12
556	Jack Morris AS	.20
557	Rich Gossage AS	.20
558	John Tudor	.30
559	Indians Ldrs (Bert Blyleven, Mike Hargrove)	.15
560	Doug Corbett	.08
561	Cardinals FS (Glenn Brummer, Luis DeLeon, Gene Roof)	.08
562	Mike O'Berry	.08
563	Ross Baumgarten	.08

435 Robin Yount

564	Doug DeCinces	.15
565	Jackson Todd	.08
566	Mike Jorgensen	.08
567	Bob Babcock	.08
569	Willie Randolph	.15
570	Willie Randolph IA	.10
571	Glenn Abbott	.08
572	Juan Beniquez	.08
573	Rick Waits	.08
576	Giants Ldrs (Vida Blue, Milt May)	.15
577	Rick Monday	.10
578	Shooty Babitt	.08
579	*Rick Mahler* (FC)	.25
580	Bobby Bonds	.15
581	Ron Reed	.10
582	Luis Pujols	.08
583	Tippy Martinez	.08
584	Hosken Powell	.08
585	Rollie Fingers	.35
586	Rollie Fingers IA	.15
587	Tim Lollar	.08
588	Dale Berra	.08
590	Al Oliver	.20
591	Al Oliver IA	.10
592	Craig Swan	.08
593	Billy Smith	.08

653 Angels Future Stars

594	Renie Martin	.08	
595	Dave Collins	.10	
596	Damaso Garcia	.08	
597	Wayne Nordhagen	.08	
600	Dave Winfield	.65	
601	Sid Monge	.08	
602	Freddie Patek	.08	
603	Rich Hebner	.08	
604	Orlando Sanchez	.08	
605	Steve Rogers	.10	
606	Blue Jays Ldrs (John Mayberry, Dave Stieb)	.15	
607	Leon Durham	.10	
608	Jerry Royster	.08	
609	Rick Sutcliffe	.25	
610	Rickey Henderson	8.00	
611	Joe Niekro	.20	
613	Jim Gantner	.08	
614	Juan Eichelberger	.08	
615	• Bob Boone	.12	
616	Bob Boone IA	.10	
617	Scott McGregor	.10	
618	Tim Foli	.08	
619	Bill Campbell	.08	
620	Ken Griffey	.15	
621	Ken Griffey IA	.10	
622	Dennis Lamp	.08	
623	Mets FS (Ron Gardenhire, *Terry Leach* (FC), *Tim Leary* (FC))	.90	
624	Fergie Jenkins	.25	
625	Hal McRae	.15	

626	Randy Jones	.10	
627	Enos Cabell	.08	
628	Bill Travers	.08	
629	Johnny Wockenfuss	.08	
630	Joe Charboneau	.10	
631	Gene Tenace	.10	
634	Checklist 529-660	.12	
635	Ron Davis	.10	
636	Phillies Ldrs (Steve Carlton, Pete Rose)	.50	
637	Rick Camp	.08	
638	John Milner	.08	
639	Ken Kravec	.08	
640	Cesar Cedeno	.15	
641	Steve Mura	.08	
642	Mike Scioscia	.10	
643	Pete Vuckovich	.10	
644	John Castino	.08	
645	Frank White	.10	
646	Frank White IA	.10	
647	Warren Brusstar	.08	
648	Jose Morales	.08	
650	Carl Yastrzemski	1.50	
651	Carl Yastrzemski IA	.60	
652	Steve Nicosia	.08	
653	Angels FS (*Tom Brunansky* (FC), Luis Sanchez, Daryl Sconiers)	3.00	
656	Eddie Whitson	.08	
657	Tom Poquette	.08	
658	Tito Landrum	.08	

711 Mariners Future Stars

659 Fred Martinez .08	**690** Dave Kingman .20
660 Dave Concepcion .15	**691** Dan Schatzeder .08
661 Dave Concepcion IA .10	**692** Wayne Gross .08
662 Luis Salazar .08	**693** Cesar Geronimo .08
663 Hector Cruz .08	**694** Dave Wehrmeister .08
664 Dan Spillner .08	**695** Warren Cromartie .08
665 Jim Clancy .10	**696** Pirates Ldrs (Bill Madlock,
666 Tigers Ldrs (Steve Kemp,	Buddy Solomon) .15
Dan Petry) .15	**697** John Montefusco .10
667 Jeff Reardon .25	**699** Dick Tidrow .08
668 Dale Murphy 2.00	**700** George Foster .25
669 Larry Milbourne .08	**701** George Foster IA .12
670 Steve Kemp .12	**703** Brewers Ldrs (Cecil
671 Mike Davis .10	Cooper, Pete Vuckovich) .15
672 Bob Knepper .08	**704** Mickey Rivers .10
673 Keith Drumright .08	**705** Mickey Rivers IA .10
675 Cecil Cooper .10	**706** Barry Foote .08
676 Sal Butera .08	**708** Gene Richards .08
677 Alfredo Griffin .08	**709** Don Money .08
678 Tom Paciorek .08	**710** Jerry Reuss .10
679 Sammy Stewart .08	**711** Mariners FS (Dave Edler,
680 Gary Matthews .12	*Dave Henderson* (FC),
681 Dodgers FS (*Mike Marshall*	Reggie Walton) 3.00
(FC), Ron Roenicke,	**712** Denny Martinez .08
Steve Sax (FC)) 5.00	**713** Del Unser .08
683 Phil Garner .10	**714** Jerry Koosman .12
684 Harold Baines .75	**715** Willie Stargell .75
685 Bert Blyleven .20	**716** Willie Stargell IA .30
686 Gary Allenson .08	**717** Rick Miller .08
687 Greg Minton .08	**718** Charlie Hough .10
688 Leon Roberts .08	**720** Greg Luzinski .20
689 Lary Sorensen .08	**721** Greg Luzinski IA .12

141 Indians Future Stars

723	Junior Kennedy	.08
724	Dave Rosello	.08
725	Amos Otis	.10
726	Amos Otis IA	.10
727	Sixto Lezcano	.08
728	Aurelio Lopez	.08
729	Jim Spencer	.08
730	Gary Carter	.70
732	Mike Lum	.08
733	Larry McWilliams	.08
734	Mike Ivie	.08
735	Rudy May	.08
737	Reggie Cleveland	.08
739	Joey McLaughlin	.08
740	Dave Lopes	.12
741	Dave Lopes IA	.10
742	Dick Drago	.08
744	*Mike Witt*	.75
745	Bake McBride	.08
746	Andre Thornton	.10
747	John Lowenstein	.08
748	Marc Hill	.08
749	Bob Shirley	.08
750	Jim Rice	.75
751	Rick Honeycutt	.08
753	Tom Brookens	.08
754	• Joe Morgan	.50
755	Joe Morgan IA	.20
756	Reds Ldrs (Ken Griffey, Tom Seaver)	.30
757	Tom Underwood	.08
758	Claudell Washington	.10
759	Paul Splittorff	.08
760	Bill Buckner	.15
761	Dave Smith	.12
763	Tom Hume	.08
764	Steve Swisher	.08
765	Gorman Thomas	.10
766	Twins FS (Lenny Faedo, *Kent Hrbek* (FC), *Tim Laudner* (FC))	6.00
767	Roy Smalley	.08
769	Richie Zisk	.10
770	Rich Gossage	.35
771	Rich Gossage IA	.15
772	Bert Campaneris	.10
774	Jay Johnstone	.10
775	Bob Forsch	.10
776	Mark Belanger	.10
777	Tom Griffin	.08
778	Kevin Hickey	.08
780	Pete Rose	2.00
781	Pete Rose IA	1.00
783	*Greg Harris* (FC)	.15
785	Dan Driessen	.10
786	Red Sox Batting and Pitching Ldrs (Carney Lansford, Mike Torrez)	.12
787	Fred Stanley	.08
788	Woodie Fryman	.10
789	Checklist 661-792	.12
790	Larry Gura	.08
791	Bobby Brown	.08
792	Frank Tanana	.15

1982 TOPPS TRADED

Like it or not, Topps Traded cards returned in 1982. The company found enough enthusiasm to make the "extension" set into an annual affair. In addition, the Traded set deflected criticism from Topps' failure to include rookies and traded players in the principal set of the year, which was issued earlier than ever before. Topps added a "T" suffix to each card in the alphabetized set to distinguish it from the year's earlier issue (though the "T" has been omitted from the following lists). Once again, the Traded cards were available only from hobby dealers in boxed, complete sets. Noteworthy cards include the first solo Topps card of Cal Ripken, Jr., along with the first picture of Ozzie Smith in a Cardinals uniform.

		MINT
Complete set		$65.00
Commons		.10

98 Cal Ripken

1	Doyle Alexander	$ .20
2	Jesse Barfield	2.25
3	Ross Baumgarten	.10
4	Steve Bedrosian	.85
5	Mark Belanger	.15
6	Kurt Bevacqua	.10
8	Vida Blue	.25
9	Bob Boone	.20
10	Larry Bowa	.25
13	Tom Brunansky	1.75
14	Jeff Burroughs	.15
15	Enos Cabell	.10
16	Bill Campbell	.10
17	Bobby Castillo	.10
18	Bill Caudill	.10
19	Cesar Cedeno	.20
20	Dave Collins	.15
23	Chili Davis	1.50
24	Dick Davis	.10
26	Doug DeCinces	.20
27	Ivan DeJesus	.10
28	Bob Dernier	.20
29	Bo Diaz	.15
31	Jim Essian	.10
32	Ed Farmer	.10
33	Doug Flynn	.10
34	Tim Foli	.10
35	Dan Ford	.10
36	George Foster	.40
39	Ron Gardenhire	.10
40	Ken Griffey	.25
41	Greg Harris	.15
42	Von Hayes	1.75
43	Larry Herndon	.15
44	Kent Hrbek	6.00
45	Mike Ivie	.10
47	Reggie Jackson	5.00
48	Ron Jackson	.10

109 Ozzie Smith

47 Reggie Jackson

1983 DONRUSS

Donruss offered few innovations in its third year of baseball card production. Card backs retain the same format as the previous year, although a different yellow ink was used. Fronts again display a large photo along with a baseball bat graphic with the player name and position. A 63-piece Ty Cobb puzzle replaced the Babe Ruth puzzle of 1982, and the set was distributed in wax packs, three pieces per package. The final card of the numbered set shows the entire puzzle. For the first time Donruss sold complete boxed sets to dealers on a wholesale basis. Rookie cards of Wade Boggs, Tony Gwynn, and Ryne Sandberg are among the most popular cards in the set.

277 Ryne Sandberg

		MINT
Complete set		$110.00
Commons		.06

1	Fernando Valenzuela (DK)	$ .40
2	Rollie Fingers (DK)	.20
3	Reggie Jackson (DK)	.50
4	Jim Palmer (DK)	.40
5	Jack Morris (DK)	.25
6	George Foster (DK)	.20
7	Jim Sundberg (DK)	.08
8	Willie Stargell (DK)	.40
9	Dave Stieb (DK)	.10
10	Joe Niekro (DK)	.08
11	Rickey Henderson (DK)	1.65
12	Dale Murphy (DK)	.80
13	Toby Harrah (DK)	.08
14	Bill Buckner (DK)	.15
15	Willie Wilson (DK)	.15
16	Steve Carlton (DK)	.40
17	Ron Guidry (DK)	.25
18	Steve Rogers (DK)	.08
19	Kent Hrbek (DK)	.40
20	Keith Hernandez (DK)	.40
21	Floyd Bannister (DK)	.08
22	Johnny Bench (DK)	.40
23	Britt Burns (DK)	.08
24	Joe Morgan (DK)	.30
25	Carl Yastrzemski (DK)	.80
26	Terry Kennedy (DK)	.08
31	Ron Guidry	.25
32	Burt Hooton	.08
34	Vida Blue	.10
35	Rickey Henderson	4.00

39	Jerry Koosman	.10
40	Bruce Sutter	.15
41	Jose Cruz	.10
42	Pete Rose	1.00
43	Cesar Cedeno	.10
47	Dale Murphy	.85
49	Hubie Brooks	.10
50	Floyd Bannister	.08
53	*Gary Gaetti* (FC)	4.50
56	Mookie Wilson	.10
58	Bob Horner	.15
59	Tony Pena	.10
63	Garry Maddox	.10
64	Bob Forsch	.08
69	Charlie Hough	.10

1983 Donruss

586 Wade Boggs

598 Tony Gwynn

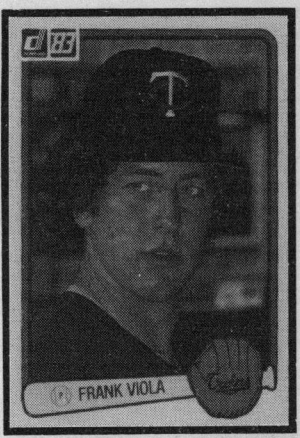

382 Frank Viola

35 Rickey Henderson

279 Cal Ripken

416	Mike Witt	.15
417	Steve Trout	.06
419	Denny Walling	.06
420	Gary Matthews	.10
421	Charlie Liebrandt (Leibrandt)	.08
422	Juan Eichelberger	.06
423	Matt Guante (FC)	.15
425	Jerry Royster	.06
426	Dickie Noles	.06
427	George Foster	.15
428	Mike Moore (FC)	1.25
429	Gary Ward	.08
432	Rance Mulliniks	.06
433	Mike Stanton	.06
434	Jesse Orosco	.10
435	Larry Bowa	.12
436	Biff Pocoroba	.06
437	Johnny Ray	.12
438	Joe Morgan	.35
439	Eric Show (FC)	.25
440	Larry Biittner	.06

168 Mike Schmidt

441	Greg Gross	.06
442	Gene Tenace	.08
443	Danny Heep	.06
446	Scott Sanderson	.06
447	Frank Tanana	.10
448	Cesar Geronimo	.06
449	Jimmy Sexton	.06
450	Mike Hargrove	.06
451	Doyle Alexander	.08
452	• Dwight Evans	.15
453	Terry Forster	.08
454	Tom Brookens	.08
457	Terry Crowley	.06
458	Ned Yost	.06
459	Kirk Gibson	.35
461	Oscar Gamble	.08
462	Dusty Baker	.08
463	Jack Perconte	.06
464	Frank White	.10
465	Mickey Klutts	.06
466	Warren Cromartie	.06
467	Larry Parrish	.10
468	Bobby Grich	.10
469	Dane Iorg	.06
470	Joe Niekro	.12
471	Ed Farmer	.06
472	Tim Flannery	.06

473	Dave Parker	.35
474	Jeff Leonard	.08
475	Al Hrabosky	.10
477	Leon Durham	.08
478	Jim Essian	.06
479	Roy Lee Jackson	.06
482	Tony Bernazard	.06
483	Scott McGregor	.08
484	Paul Molitor	.25
485	Mike Ivie	.06
486	Ken Griffey	.10
487	Dennis Eckersley	.10
488	Steve Garvey	.50
489	Mike Fischlin	.06
490	U.L. Washington	.06
491	Steve McCatty	.06
493	Don Baylor	.10
494	Bobby Johnson	.06
495	Mike Squires	.06
496	Bert Roberge	.06
497	Dick Ruthven	.06
498	Tito Landrum	.06
499	Sixto Lezcano	.06
500	Johnny Bench	.50
501	Larry Whisenton	.06
502	Manny Sarmiento	.06
504	Bill Campbell	.06

1983 Donruss

588 Dave Stewart

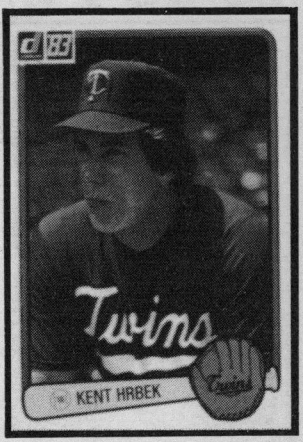

179 Kent Hrbek

557 Pascual Perez

1983 FLEER

After errors and variations plagued Fleer's first two offerings, the company rebounded in 1983 with a nearly perfect set of baseball cards. The 660-card edition is arranged by team, beginning with the 1982 World Champion St. Louis Cardinals, and then alphabetically by player within each team. For the first time since the 1971 Topps set, Fleer cards feature a black-and-white shot of each player on the back of his card. The biggest sellers in this edition include rookie cards of Wade Boggs, Tony Gwynn, and Ryne Sandberg. Because Fleer flooded the market with unsold cards at season's end, this set is still plentiful today.

		MINT
Complete set		**$110.00**
Commons (1-660)		**.06**

507 Ryne Sandberg

2	Doug Bair	$ .06
3	Steve Braun	.06
5	Bob Forsch	.08
6	David Green	.06
8	Keith Hernandez	.40
9	Tom Herr	.10
10	Dane Iorg	.06
11	Jim Kaat	.15
12	Jeff Lahti	.06
14	*Dave LaPoint* (FC)	.25
15	*Willie McGee* (FC)	4.00
16	Steve Mura	.06
18	Darrell Porter	.08
19	Mike Ramsey	.06
20	Gene Roof	.06
21	Lonnie Smith	.08
22	Ozzie Smith	.45
23	John Stuper	.06
24	Bruce Sutter	.15
25	Gene Tenace	.08
26	Jerry Augustine	.06
29	Mike Caldwell	.06
30	Cecil Cooper	.10
31	Jamie Easterly	.06
33	Rollie Fingers	.20
36	Roy Howell	.06
39	Doc Medich	.06
40	Paul Molitor	.20
41	Don Money	.06
44	Ed Romero	.06
45	Ted Simmons	.15
46	Jim Slaton	.06

47	Don Sutton	.30
48	Gorman Thomas	.10
50	Ned Yost	.06
51	Robin Yount	.50
54	Al Bumbry	.06
56	*Storm Davis* (FC)	.50
57	Rich Dauer	.06
59	Jim Dwyer	.06
60	Mike Flanagan	.08
67	Eddie Murray	.65
68	Joe Nolan	.06
69	Jim Palmer	.50
70	Cal Ripken Jr.	5.00
73	Ken Singleton	.10
75	Tim Stoddard	.06

76	Don Aase	.06
77	Don Baylor	.15
79	• Bob Boone	.10
81	Rod Carew	.50
82	Bobby Clark	.06
85	Doug DeCinces	.10
86	Brian Downing	.10
88	Tim Foli	.06
89	Ken Forsch	.06
90	Dave Goltz	.08
91	Bobby Grich	.10
93	Reggie Jackson	.50
94	Ron Jackson	.06
95	Tommy John	.20
96	Bruce Kison	.06
97	Fred Lynn	.20
98	Ed Ott	.06
101	Rob Wilfong	.06
102	Mike Witt	.10
103	Geoff Zahn	.06
104	Willie Aikens	.06
106	Vida Blue	.10
107	*Bud Black* (FC)	.25
108	George Brett	.75
109	Bill Castro	.06
111	Dave Frost	.06
113	Larry Gura	.06

179 Wade Boggs

360 Tony Gwynn

118	Lee May	.08
119	Hal McRae	.10
120	Amos Otis	.08
121	Greg Pryor	.06
122	Dan Quisenberry	.15
123	*Don Slaught* (FC)	.20
126	John Wathan	.08
127	Frank White	.10
128	Willie Wilson	.15
129	Steve Bedrosian (FC)	.35
132	Brett Butler (FC)	.25
133	Rick Camp	.06
134	Chris Chambliss	.08
135	Ken Dayley (FC)	.10
136	Gene Garber	.06
138	Bob Horner	.20
139	Glenn Hubbard	.08
140	Rufino Linares	.06
141	Rick Mahler	.08
142	Dale Murphy	.90
143	Phil Niekro	.30
144	Pascual Perez	.08
149	Bob Walk	.06
151	Bob Watson	.08
155	Steve Carlton	.50
159	Bob Dernier	.10
160	Bo Diaz	.08

332 Howard Johnson

163	Mike Krukow	.08
164	Garry Maddox	.10
165	Gary Matthews	.10
166	Tug McGraw	.12
171	Pete Rose	1.00
173	Mike Schmidt	.85
175	Ozzie Virgil (FC)	.10
177	Gary Allenson	.06
178	Luis Aponte	.06
179	*Wade Boggs* (FC)	22.00
181	Mark Clear	.06
182	Dennis Eckersley	.20
183	• Dwight Evans	.15
184	Rich Gedman	.06
186	Bruce Hearst	.10
187	Carney Lansford	.08
190	Bob Ojeda	.08
191	Tony Perez	.20
193	Jerry Remy	.06
194	Jim Rice	.40
195	Bob Stanley	.06
197	Mike Torrez	.08
198	John Tudor	.10
200	Carl Yastrzemski	1.00
201	Dusty Baker	.10
202	Joe Beckwith	.06
203	*Greg Brock* (FC)	.25

204	Ron Cey	.10
205	Terry Forster	.08
206	Steve Garvey	.40
207	Pedro Guerrero	.25
208	Burt Hooton	.08
209	Steve Howe	.08
211	Mike Marshall	.15
212	*Candy Maldonado* (FC)	1.00
213	Rick Monday	.10
215	Jorge Orta	.06
216	Jerry Reuss	.10
219	Bill Russell	.08
220	Steve Sax	.35
222	Dave Stewart	1.25
223	Derrel Thomas	.06
224	Fernando Valenzuela	.25
225	Bob Welch	.10
226	Ricky Wright	.06
227	Steve Yeager	.06
228	Bill Almon	.06
229	Harold Baines	.15
232	Britt Burns	.06
233	Richard Dotson	.10
235	Carlton Fisk	.30
236	Jerry Hairston	.06
238	LaMarr Hoyt	.06
239	Steve Kemp	.10

519 Rickey Henderson

241	*Ron Kittle* (FC)	.85
242	Jerry Koosman	.10
243	Dennis Lamp	.06
245	Vance Law	.06
246	Ron LeFlore	.10
247	Greg Luzinski	.10
250	Mike Squires	.06
251	Steve Trout	.06
252	Jim Barr	.06
253	Dave Bergman	.06
255	Bob Brenly (FC)	.08
256	Jack Clark	.25
257	Chili Davis (FC)	.35
258	Darrell Evans	.10
259	Alan Fowlkes	.06
260	Rich Gale	.06
261	Atlee Hammaker (FC)	.10
262	Al Holland	.06
263	Duane Kuiper	.06
264	Bill Laskey	.06
265	Gary Lavalle	.06
267	Renie Martin	.06
268	Milt May	.06
269	Greg Minton	.06
270	Joe Morgan	.40
272	Reggie Smith	.10
273	Guy Sularz	.06
275	Max Venable	.06
277	Ray Burris	.06
278	Gary Carter	.35
280	Andre Dawson	.35
281	Terry Francona	.06
282	Doug Flynn	.06
283	Woody Fryman	.08
286	Charlie Lea	.06
287	Randy Lerch	.06
290	Al Oliver	.15
292	Tim Raines	.35
293	Jeff Reardon	.12
294	Steve Rogers	.08
297	Bryn Smith	.08
298	Chris Speier	.06
299	Tim Wallach	.20
300	Jerry White	.06
303	Dale Berra	.06
304	John Candelaria	.10
306	Mike Easler	.06
307	Rich Hebner	.06
308	Lee Lacy	.06

616 Kent Hrbek

309	Bill Madlock	.10
311	John Milner	.06
312	Omar Moreno	.06
314	Steve Nicosia	.06
315	Dave Parker	.35
316	Tony Pena	.10
317	Johnny Ray	.10
318	Rick Rhoden	.08
320	Enrique Romo	.06
322	Rod Scurry	.06
323	Jim Smith	.06
324	Willie Stargell	.40
326	Kent Tukulve	.08
327	Tom Brookens	.08
328	Enos Cabell	.08
329	Kirk Gibson	.40
330	Larry Herndon	.06
331	Mike Ivie	.06
332	*Howard Johnson*	12.00
334	Rick Leach	.06
335	Chet Lemon	.08
336	Jack Morris	.35
337	Lance Parrish	.35
339	Dan Petry	.08
340	Dave Rozema	.06
341	Dave Rucker	.06
342	Elias Sosa	.06

1983 Fleer

222 Dave Stewart

386	John Mayberry	.08
387	Lee Mazzilli	.08
388	Mike Morgan (FC)	.20
390	Bobby Murcer	.10
391	Graig Nettles	.15
392	Lou Piniella	.10
393	Willie Randolph	.10
394	Shane Rawley	.06
395	Dave Righetti	.25
396	Andre Robertson	.06
397	Roy Smalley	.06
398	Dave Winfield	.50
399	Butch Wynegar	.06
400	Chris Bando	.06
401	Alan Bannister	.06
403	Tom Brennan	.06
404	*Carmelo Castillo* (FC)	.10
405	Miguel Dilone	.06
406	Jerry Dybzinski	.06
409	Mike Hargrove	.06
410	Toby Harrah	.08
412	Von Hayes	.15
413	Rick Manning	.06
414	Bake McBride	.06
415	Larry Milbourne	.06
417	Jack Perconte	.06
419	Dan Spillner	.06
420	Rick Sutcliffe	.12
421	Andre Thornton	.10
423	Eddie Whitson	.06
424	Jesse Barfield (FC)	.60
425	Barry Bonnell	.06
426	Jim Clancy	.08
427	Damaso Garcia	.06
429	Alfredo Griffin	.08
430	Garth Iorg	.06
432	Luis Leal	.06
433	Buck Martinez	.06
435	Lloyd Moseby	.12
439	*Gene Petralli* (FC)	.15
441	Dave Stieb	.12
442	Willie Upshaw	.08
443	Ernie Whitt	.08
444	Al Woods	.06
445	Alan Ashby	.06
446	Jose Cruz	.10
447	Kiko Garcia	.06
448	Phil Garner	.08
449	Danny Heep	.06

344	Alan Trammell	.40
348	Lou Whitaker	.45
349	Milt Wilcox	.06
350	*Glenn Wilson* (FC)	.45
353	Juan Bonilla	.06
354	Floyd Chiffer	.06
355	Luis DeLeon	.06
356	*Dave Dravecky* (FC)	.75
357	Dave Edwards	.06
359	Tim Flannery	.06
360	*Tony Gwynn* (FC)	18.00
361	Ruppert Jones	.06
362	Terry Kennedy	.08
365	Tim Lollar	.06
371	Luis Salazar	.06
372	*Eric Show* (FC)	.25
373	Garry Templeton	.10
374	Chris Welsh	.06
375	Alan Wiggins	.06
376	Rick Cerone	.06
377	Dave Collins	.08
380	Oscar Gamble	.08
381	Goose Gossage	.20
382	Ken Griffey	.15
383	Ron Guidry	.25
384	Dave LaRoche	.06
385	Rudy May	.06

451	Bob Knepper	.06
452	Alan Knicely	.06
453	Ray Knight	.10
455	Mike LaCoss	.06
456	Randy Moffitt	.06
457	Joe Niekro	.10
462	Vern Ruhle	.06
463	Nolan Ryan	3.00
464	Joe Sambito	.06
465	Tony Scott	.06
466	Dave Smith	.08
467	Harry Spilman	.06
468	Dickie Thon	.06
469	Denny Walling	.06
471	Floyd Bannister	.10
472	Jim Beattie	.06
473	Bruce Bochte	.06
475	Bill Caudill	.06
477	Al Cowens	.06
478	Julio Cruz	.06
481	• Dave Henderson (FC)	.30
482	*Mike Moore* (FC)	1.25
483	Gaylord Perry	.30
484	Dave Revering	.06
485	Joe Simpson	.06
486	Mike Stanton	.06
487	Rick Sweet	.06
488	*Ed Vande Berg* (FC)	.10
489	Richie Zisk	.08
490	Doug Bird	.06
491	Larry Bowa	.12
492	Bill Buckner	.12
493	Bill Campbell	.06
494	Jody Davis	.08
495	Leon Durham	.08
497	Willie Hernandez	.08
498	• Ferguson Jenkins	.15
499	• Jay Johnstone	.08
502	Jerry Morales	.06
504	Dickie Noles	.06
505	Mike Proly	.06
506	Allen Ripley	.06
507	*Ryne Sandberg* (FC)	31.00
508	Lee Smith	.15
509	Pat Tabler (FC)	.15
510	Dick Tidrow	.06
511	Bump Wills	.06
512	Gary Woods	.06
513	Tony Armas	.10

171 Pete Rose

515	Jeff Burroughs	.08
517	Wayne Gross	.06
518	Mike Heath	.06
519	Rickey Henderson	4.00
521	Matt Keough	.06
522	Brian Kingman	.06
523	Rick Langford	.06
524	Davey Lopes	.06
525	Steve McCatty	.06
530	Mike Norris	.06
532	Joe Rudi	.10
533	Jimmy Sexton	.06
534	Fred Stanley	.06
536	Neil Allen	.06
538	Bob Bailor	.06
539	Hubie Brooks	.12
540	Carlos Diaz	.06
541	Pete Falcone	.06
542	George Foster	.15
546	Randy Jones	.08
548	Dave Kingman	.15
549	Ed Lynch	.06
550	Jesse Orosco (FC)	.15
551	Rick Ownbey	.06
552	*Charlie Puleo* (FC)	.10
554	• Mike Scott	.15
555	Rusty Staub	.10

1983 Fleer

424 Jesse Barfield

336 Jack Morris

1983 TOPPS

Topps reached back 20 years for the design of this 726-card set. Like the 1963 set which it resembles, the 1983 edition features a large color photograph of the player with a small round portrait in a lower corner. This design works best when the portrait is contrasted with an action shot. Super Veterans constitute one of the most appealing subsets of the decade. They use a then-and-now theme that displays a contemporary 1983 pose along with a vintage shot from early in the player's career. Rod Carew, Reggie Jackson, Pete Rose, and Carl Yastrzemski highlight this series. In terms of cost, the value given for the complete set is somewhat misleading since a single card, the Ryne Sandberg rookie card (83), by itself accounts for about a third of the price of the entire set. Due to the popularity of the fall Traded sets, Topps omitted all rookie cards from this standard edition.

		MINT
Complete set		$150.00
Commons		.08

83 Ryne Sandberg

1	Record Breaker (Tony Armas)	$ .12
2	Record Breaker (Rickey Henderson)	.75
4	Record Breaker (Lance Parrish)	.20
8	Steve Balboni	.08
10	Gorman Thomas	.10
13	Larry Herndon	.08
15	Ron Cey	.10
17	Kent Tekulve	.08
18	Super Vet (Kent Tekulve)	.10
19	Oscar Gamble	.10
20	Carlton Fisk	.75
21	Orioles Ldrs (Eddie Murray, Jim Palmer)	.45
24	Steve Mura	.08
25	Hal McRae	.20
29	Randy Jones	.10
30	Jim Rice	.75
35	Rollie Fingers	.30
36	Super Vet (Rollie Fingers)	.25
37	Darrell Johnson	.08
40	Fernando Valenzuela	.50
43	Bob Dernier	.08
44	Don Robinson	.10
45	John Mayberry	.10
46	Richard Dotson	.12
47	Dave McKay	.08
49	*Willie McGee* (FC)	7.00
50	Bob Horner	.20
51	Cubs Ldrs (Leon Durham, Fergie Jenkins)	.15
53	Mike Witt	.30
55	Mookie Wilson	.12
58	Al Holland	.08
60	Johnny Bench	.65
61	Super Vet (Johnny Bench)	.35
62	Bob McClure	.08

498 Wade Boggs

63	Rick Monday	.10
64	Bill Stein	.08
65	Jack Morris	.35
67	Sal Butera	.08
68	*Eric Show*	.25
69	Lee Lacy	.08
70	Steve Carlton	.65
71	Super Vet (Steve Carlton)	.35
72	Tom Paciorek	.08
73	Allen Ripley	.08
75	Amos Otis	.10
76	Rick Mahler	.10
77	Hosken Powell	.08
78	Bill Caudill	.08
79	Mick Kelleher	.08
80	George Foster	.20
81	Yankees Ldrs (Jerry Mumphrey, Dave Righetti)	.15
82	Bruce Hurst	.15
83	*Ryne Sandberg* (FC)	51.00
84	Milt May	.08
85	Ken Singleton	.10
87	Joe Rudi	.10
88	Jim Gantner	.08
90	Jerry Reuss	.10
95	Alan Trammell	.50

96	Dick Howser	.08
98	Vance Law	.08
100	Pete Rose	2.00
101	Super Vet (Pete Rose)	.80
103	Darrell Porter	.08
104	Bob Walk	.08
105	Don Baylor	.15
109	Luis Leal	.08
110	Ken Griffey	.15
111	Expos Ldrs (Al Oliver, Steve Rogers)	.15
112	Bob Shirley	.08
114	Jim Slaton	.08
115	Chili Davis	.12
116	Dave Schmidt	.08
120	Len Barker	.08
121	Mickey Hatcher	.10
122	Jimmy Smith	.08
124	Marc Hill	.08
125	Leon Durham	.08
126	Joe Torre	.10
127	Preston Hanna	.08
128	Mike Ramsey	.08
129	Checklist 1-132	.12
130	Dave Stieb	.20
132	Todd Cruz	.08
133	Jim Barr	.08

482 Tony Gwynn

134	Hubie Brooks	.15
135	• Dwight Evans	.25
136	Willie Aikens	.08
137	Woodie Fryman	.08
138	Rick Dempsey	.08
140	Willie Randolph	.10
141	Indians Ldrs (Toby Harrah, Rick Sutcliffe)	.15
143	Joe Pettini	.08
144	Mark Wagner	.08
145	Don Sutton	.45
146	Super Vet (Don Sutton)	.25
147	Rick Leach	.08
150	Bruce Sutter	.20
151	Super Vet (Bruce Sutter)	.15
152	Jay Johnstone	.10
153	Jerry Koosman	.10
155	Dan Quisenberry	.20
156	Billy Martin	.15
157	Steve Bedrosian	.25
158	Rob Wilfong	.10
159	Mike Stanton	.08
160	Dave Kingman	.15
161	Super Vet (Dave Kingman)	.10
162	Mark Clear	.08
163	Cal Ripken	8.00
164	Dave Palmer	.08
165	Dan Driessen	.08
166	John Pacella	.08
167	Mark Brouhard	.08
170	Steve Howe	.10
171	Giants Ldrs (Bill Laskey, Joe Morgan)	.15
172	Vern Ruhle	.08
173	Jim Morrison	.08
174	Jerry Ujdur	.08
175	Bo Diaz	.08
176	Dave Righetti	.35
177	Harold Baines	.25
178	Luis Tiant	.15
179	Super Vet (Luis Tiant)	.10
180	Rickey Henderson	7.50
181	Terry Felton	.08
182	Mike Fischlin	.08
183	*Ed Vande Berg*	.10
184	Bob Clark	.08
185	Tim Lollar	.08
186	Whitey Herzog	.10

586 Frank Viola

187	Terry Leach	.08
189	Dan Schatzeder	.08
190	Cecil Cooper	.15
193	Harry Spilman	.08
195	Bob Stoddard	.08
196	Bill Fahey	.08
197	*Jim Eisenreich* (FC)	.15
200	Rod Carew	.75
201	Super Vet (Rod Carew)	.35
202	Blue Jays Ldrs (Damaso Garcia, Dave Stieb)	.15
203	Mike Morgan	.15
204	Junior Kennedy	.08
205	Dave Parker	.45
206	Ken Oberkfell	.08
207	Rick Camp	.08
208	Dan Meyer	.08
209	*Mike Moore* (FC)	2.00
210	Jack Clark	.30
211	John Denny	.08
212	John Stearns	.08
214	Jerry White	.08
215	Mario Soto	.08
216	Tony LaRussa	.10
220	Dusty Baker	.10
221	Joe Niekro	.10
222	Damaso Garcia	.08
224	Mickey Rivers	.10

180 Rickey Henderson

49 Willie McGee

288	*Joe Cowley* (FC)	.10
289	Jerry Dybzinski	.08
290	Jeff Reardon	.20
291	Pirates Ldrs (John Candelaria, Bill Madlock)	.15
292	Craig Swan	.08
293	Glenn Gulliver	.08
294	Dave Engle	.08
295	Jerry Remy	.08
296	Greg Harris	.08
297	Ned Yost	.08
298	Floyd Chiffer	.08
299	George Wright	.08
300	Mike Schmidt	2.50
301	Super Vet (Mike Schmidt)	.65
302	Ernie Whitt	.10
303	Miguel Dilone	.08
304	Dave Rucker	.08
305	Larry Bowa	.15
306	Tom Lasorda	.10
307	Lou Piniella	.15
308	Jesus Vega	.08
309	Jeff Leonard	.10
310	Greg Luzinski	.15
312	Brian Kingman	.08
314	Ken Dayley (FC)	.15
315	Rick Burleson	.08
316	Paul Splittorff	.08
317	Gary Rajsich	.08
318	John Tudor	.15
319	Lenn Sakata	.08
320	Steve Rogers	.10
321	Brewers Ldrs (Pete Vuckovich, Robin Yount)	.15
322	Dave Van Gorder	.08
323	Luis DeLeon	.08
324	Mike Marshall	.25
325	Von Hayes	.25
326	Garth Iorg	.08
327	Bobby Castillo	.08
328	Craig Reynolds	.08
329	Randy Niemann	.08
330	Buddy Bell	.15
331	Mike Krukow	.10
332	*Glenn Wilson* (FC)	.25
333	Dave LaRoche	.08
334	Super Vet (Dave LaRoche)	.08
335	Steve Henderson	.08

680 Andre Dawson

336	Rene Lachemann	.08
337	Tito Landrum	.08
338	Bob Owchinko	.08
340	Larry Gura	.08
341	Doug DeCinces	.10
342	Atlee Hammaker	.08
343	Bob Bailor	.08
344	Roger LaFrancois	.08
346	Joe Pittman	.08
347	Sammy Stewart	.08
348	Alan Bannister	.08
349	Checklist 265-396	.12
350	Robin Yount	1.50
351	Reds Ldrs (Cesar Cedeno, Mario Soto)	.12
352	Mike Scioscia	.10
353	Steve Comer	.08
354	Randy Johnson	.08
355	Jim Bibby	.08
356	Gary Woods	.08
357	*Len Matuszek* (FC)	.08
358	Jerry Garvin	.08
359	Dave Collins	.08
360	Nolan Ryan	4.00
361	Super Vet (Nolan Ryan)	.75
362	Bill Almon	.08
363	*John Stuper* (FC)	.08
364	Brett Butler	.20

532 Dave Stewart

501 Super Vet

1983 Topps

300 Mike Schmidt

350 Robin Yount

178 Luis Tiant

1983 TOPPS TRADED

Don't let the price of the complete set of the 1983 Topps Traded issue fool you. Much of the estimated value is found in one card: the first-card issue of New York Mets superstar Darryl Strawberry, number 108. Other newcomers featured in this late-season series include Greg Brock, Bill Doran, Julio Franco, Mel Hall, Ron Kittle, and John Shelby. Steve Garvey, now dressed as a Padre, heads the class of veteran players in new uniforms. Because these cards were sold only through hobby dealers, many of whom were skeptical about the set's selling power, fewer sets than usual were distributed to the public.

		MINT
Complete set		$100.00
Commons		.10

108 Darryl Strawberry

1	Neil Allen	$ .10
2	Bill Almon	.10
3	Joe Altobelli	.10
4	Tony Armas	.20
5	Doug Bair	.10
6	Steve Baker	.10
7	Floyd Bannister	.20
8	Don Baylor	.30
9	Tony Bernazard	.10
10	Larry Biittner	.10
11	Dann Bilardello	.10
12	Doug Bird	.10
14	Greg Brock (FC)	.40
16	Tom Burgmeier	.10
17	Randy Bush (FC)	.25
18	Bert Campaneris	.20
19	Ron Cey	.25
20	Chris Codiroli (FC)	.15
21	Dave Collins	.15
22	Terry Crowley	.10
23	Julio Cruz	.10
24	Mike Davis	.15
25	Frank DiPino	.10
26	Bill Doran (FC)	2.50
27	Jerry Dybzinski	.10
28	Jamie Easterly	.10
29	Juan Eichelberger	.10
30	Jim Essian	.10
31	Pete Falcone	.10
33	Terry Forster	.10
34	Julio Franco (FC)	6.00
35	Rich Gale	.10
36	Kiko Garcia	.10
37	Steve Garvey	2.00
39	Mel Hall (FC)	1.00
40	Von Hayes	.50
41	Danny Heep	.10
42	Steve Henderson	.10
43	Keith Hernandez	1.00
44	Leo Hernandez	.10
45	Willie Hernandez	.25

46	Al Holland	.10
47	Frank Howard	.15
48	Bobby Johnson	.10
53	Steve Kemp	.15
55	Ron Kittle (FC)	.60
58	Mike Krukow	.15
60	Carney Lansford	.25
66	• Billy Martin	.20
67	Lee Mazzilli	.15
69	Craig McMurtry (FC)	.25
77	• Joe Morgan	2.00
81	Pete O'Brien (FC)	1.25
83	Alejandro Pena (FC)	.60
84	Pascual Perez	.20
85	Tony Perez	.60
87	Tony Phillips (FC)	.20
90	Jamie Quirk	.10
91	Doug Rader	.15
94	Gary Redus (FC)	.40
95	Steve Renko	.10
96	Leon Roberts	.10
97	Aurelio Rodriguez	.15
100	Mike Scott	.50
101	Tom Seaver	4.00
102	John Shelby (FC)	.20
103	Bob Shirley	.10
104	Joe Simpson	.10

34 Julio Franco

105	Doug Sisk (FC)	.15
106	Mike Smithson (FC)	.20
107	Elias Sosa	.10
108	Darryl Strawberry (FC)	82.00
109	Tom Tellman	.10
110	Gene Tenace	.10
111	Gorman Thomas	.15
112	Dick Tidrow	.10
113	Dave Tobik	.10
114	Wayne Tolleson (FC)	.15
115	Mike Torrez	.15
116	Manny Trillo	.15
117	Steve Trout	.10
118	Lee Tunnell (FC)	.15
119	Mike Vail	.10
120	Ellis Valentine	.10
121	Tom Veryzer	.10
122	George Vukovich	.10
123	Rick Waits	.10
124	Greg Walker (FC)	.45
125	Chris Welsh	.10
126	Len Whitehouse	.10
127	Eddie Whitson	.15
128	Jim Wohlford	.10
129	Matt Young (FC)	.20
130	Joel Youngblood	.10
131	Pat Zachry	.10
132	Checklist 1-132	.10

26 Bill Doran

1984 DONRUSS

The combination of a limited print run and the presence of several flashy rookies make the 1984 Donruss set the most expensive regular-season issue of the decade—by far. For starters, nearly one fifth of the current estimated value can be traced to the incredible demand for the first-year card for Don Mattingly. Darryl Strawberry is another very popular rookie. Ironically, neither Mattingly nor Strawberry was included in Rated Rookies, the 20-card subset which highlights outstanding prospects. Two unnumbered cards for Living Legends were distributed only in wax packs: Johnny Bench and Carl Yastrzemski are featured on one; Rollie Fingers and Gaylord Perry on the other.

		MINT
Complete set		**$360.00**
Commons		**.10**

1	Robin Yount (DK)	$ .80
2	Dave Concepcion (DK)	.30
3	Dwayne Murphy (DK)	.25
4	John Castino (DK)	.20
5	Leon Durham (DK)	.25
6	Rusty Staub (DK)	.30
7	Jack Clark (DK)	.40
8	Dave Dravecky (DK)	.25
9	Al Oliver (DK)	.35
10	Dave Righetti (DK)	.40

68 Darryl Strawberry

248 Don Mattingly

11	Hal McRae (DK)	.30
12	Ray Knight (DK)	.25
13	Bruce Sutter (DK)	.35
14	Bob Horner (DK)	.40
15	Lance Parrish (DK)	.60
16	Matt Young (DK)	.25
17	Fred Lynn (DK)	.35
18	Ron Kittle (DK)	.35
19	Jim Clancy (DK)	.25
20	Bill Madlock (DK)	.30
21	Larry Parrish (DK)	.30
22	Eddie Murray (DK)	1.25
23	Mike Schimdt (DK)	1.25
24	Pedro Guerrero (DK)	.50

25	Andre Thornton (DK)	.30
26	Wade Boggs (DK)	4.00
29	Mike Stenhouse (RR) (number 29 on back)	8.00
29	Mike Stenhouse (RR) (no number on back)	.15
30	*Ron Darling* (RR) (FC) (number 30 on back)	12.00
30	*Ron Darling* (RR) (FC) (no number on back)	6.00
31	*Dion James* (RR) (FC)	.40
32	*Tony Fernandez* (RR) (FC)	8.00
34	*Kevin McReynolds* (RR) (FC)	12.00
35	*Dick Schofield* (RR) (FC)	.40
37	*Tim Teufel* (RR) (FC)	.40
39	*Greg Gagne* (RR) (FC)	.50
41	*Joe Carter* (RR) (FC)	20.00
44	*Sid Fernandez* (RR) (FC)	6.00
47	Eddie Murray	2.00
48	Robin Yount	2.50
49	Lance Parrish	.50
50	Jim Rice	.95
51	Dave Winfield	1.00
52	Fernando Valenzuela	.75
53	George Brett	4.00
54	Rickey Henderson	15.00
55	Gary Carter	.75
56	Buddy Bell	.20
57	Reggie Jackson	2.00
58	Harold Baines	.25
59	Ozzie Smith	1.00
60	Nolan Ryan	11.00
61	Pete Rose	3.00
62	Ron Oester	.10
63	Steve Garvey	1.00
65	Jack Clark	.35
66	Dale Murphy	2.00
67	Leon Durham	.10
68	*Darryl Strawberry* (FC)	41.00
69	Richie Zisk	.10
70	Kent Hrbek	.65
71	Dave Stieb	.25
72	Ken Schrom	.10
73	George Bell	2.00
74	John Moses	.15
81	Tom Foley	.10
83	*Andy Van Slyke* (FC)	8.00

311 Ryne Sandberg

84	Bob Lillis	.10
85	Rick Adams	.10
89	Ed Romero	.10
90	John Grubb	.10
93	Candy Maldonado	.20
94	Andre Thornton	.20
96	*Don Hill* (FC)	.20
97	Andre Dawson	1.50
98	Frank Tanana	.15
100	Larry Gura	.10
103	Dave Righetti	.40
104	Steve Sax	.40
105	Dan Petry	.10
106	Cal Ripken	3.50
107	Paul Molitor	.35
108	Fred Lynn	.35
109	Neil Allen	.10
110	Joe Niekro	.20
111	Steve Carlton	1.00
113	Bill Madlock	.20
114	Chili Davis	.25
115	Jim Gantner	.10
116	Tom Seaver	3.00
117	Bill Buckner	.20
120	John Castino	.10
121	Dave Concepcion	.15
122	Greg Luzinski	.15

1984 Donruss

41 Joe Carter

123	Mike Boddicker (FC)	.20
124	Pete Ladd	.10
127	Ed Jurak	.10
129	Bert Blyleven	.35
134	*Tom Henke* (FC)	1.50
136	Mike Scott	.30
137	Bo Diaz	.10
139	Sid Monge	.10
140	Rich Gale	.10
141	Brett Butler	.15
145	Pat Putnam	.10
146	*Jim Acker* (FC)	.15
148	Todd Cruz	.10
149	Tom Tellmann	.10
151	Wade Boggs	13.00
152	Don Baylor	.20
153	Bob Welch	.20
154	Alan Bannister	.10
155	Willie Aikens	.10
157	Bryan Little	.10
158	• Bob Boone	.15
162	Luis DeLeon	.10
163	Willie Hernandez	.15
166	Lee Mazzilli	.12
168	Bob Forsch	.12
169	Mike Flanagan	.15
171	Chet Lemon	.12

172	Jerry Remy	.10
173	Ron Guidry	.35
174	Pedro Guerrero	.50
175	Willie Wilson	.25
176	Carney Lansford	.20
177	Al Oliver	.30
179	Bobby Grich	.20
180	Richard Dotson	.20
182	Jose Cruz	.15
183	Mike Schmidt	12.00
184	*Gary Redus* (FC)	.30
185	Garry Templeton	.15
186	Tony Pena	.15
187	Greg Minton	.10
188	Phil Niekro	.50
189	Ferguson Jenkins	.35
190	Mookie Wilson	.15
193	Jesse Barfield	.40
194	Pete Filson	.10
196	Rick Sweet	.10
197	Jesse Orosco	.15
198	*Steve Lake* (FC)	.10
201	Mark Davis (FC)	.25
208	*Juan Agosto* (FC)	.20
209	Bobby Ramos	.10
210	Al Bumbry	.12
212	Howard Bailey	.10

183 Mike Schmidt

213	Bruce Hurst	.25
215	Pat Zachry	.10
216	Julio Franco	.25
218	Dave Beard	.10
219	Steve Rogers	.15
221	*Mike Smithson* (FC)	.20
222	Frank White	.20
224	Chris Bando	.10
225	Roy Smalley	.10
226	Dusty Baker	.20
227	Lou Whitaker	.65
229	Ben Oglivie	.10
230	Doug DeCinces	.15
231	Lonnie Smith	.12
232	Ray Knight	.15
233	Gary Matthews	.20
234	Juan Bonilla	.10
237	Mike Caldwell	.10
238	Keith Hernandez	.80
239	Larry Bowa	.25
242	Tom Brunansky	.35
243	Dan Driessen	.12

54 Rickey Henderson

244	Ron Kittle (FC)	.30
246	Bob Gibson	.10
247	Marty Castillo	.10
248	*Don Mattingly* (FC)	**81.00**
249	Jeff Newman	.10
250	*Alejandro Pena* (FC)	.40
251	Toby Harrah	.12
256	Odell Jones	.10
257	Rudy Law	.10
262	Jeff Jones	.10
263	*Gerald Perry* (FC)	**1.00**
264	Gene Tenace	.12
266	Dickie Noles	.10
268	Jim Gott	.15
269	Ron Davis	.10
271	Ned Yost	.10
272	Dave Rozema	.10
274	Lou Piniella	.10
275	Jose Morales	.10
277	Butch Davis	.10
278	*Tony Phillips* (FC)	.25
279	Jeff Reardon	.25
280	Ken Forsch	.10
281	*Pete O'Brien* (FC)	**1.00**
282	Tom Paciorek	.10
284	Tim Lollar	.10
285	Greg Gross	.10

286	Alex Trevino	.10
287	Gene Garber	.10
288	Dave Parker	.50
289	Lee Smith	.35
291	*John Shelby* (FC)	.25
293	Alan Trammell	.60
294	Tony Armas	.20
296	Greg Brock	.15
297	Hal McRae	.20
298	Mike Davis	.12
299	Tim Raines	.80
300	Bucky Dent	.15
301	Tommy John	.40
302	Carlton Fisk	1.00
303	Darrell Porter	.12
304	Dickie Thon	.10
305	Garry Maddox	.12
306	Cesar Cedeno	.20
307	Gary Lucas	.10
308	Johnny Ray	.20
311	Ryne Sandberg	21.00
312	George Foster	.30
313	*Spike Owen* (FC)	.30
314	Gary Gaetti	.90
315	Willie Upshaw	.12
316	Al Williams	.10
317	Jorge Orta	.10

83 Andy Van Slyke

44 Sid Fernandez

53 George Brett

1984 Donruss

Living Legends

1984 FLEER

One of the finest Fleer sets ever offered was the 660-card edition of 1984. The design is simple and clean, with large, unobstructed photos and no glaring errors or variations. Along with the traditional action shots and portraits, some of the zaniest cards of the decade surfaced in 1984. For example, Jay Johnstone posed wearing an umbrella hat (495), while Glenn Hubbard is shown with a boa constrictor draped around his shoulders (182). Card 638 commemorates George Brett's illegal bat coated with pine tar. As usual, the Fleer cards are arranged by team, with players listed alphabetically within each team.

		MINT
Complete set		**$190.00**
Commons		.08

1	Mike Boddicker (FC)	$ .35
2	Al Bumbry	.10
5	Storm Davis	.15
6	Rick Dempsey	.10
8	Mike Flanagan	.12
11	Dennis Martinez	.10
13	Scott McGregor	.10
14	Eddie Murray	.85
16	Jim Palmer	1.00
17	Cal Ripken Jr.	4.00
20	*John Shelby* (FC)	.25

504 Ryne Sandberg

131 Don Mattingly

21	Ken Singleton	.12
25	Steve Carlton	.75
29	Bo Diaz	.10
32	*Kevin Gross* (FC)	.25
33	Von Hayes	.15
34	Willie Hernandez	.10
36	*Charles Hudson* (FC)	.15
39	Garry Maddox	.10
40	Gary Matthews	.12
42	Tug McGraw	.12
43	Joe Morgan	.40
44	Tony Perez	.20
45	Ron Reed	.08
46	Pete Rose	1.00
47	*Juan Samuel* (FC)	3.50

1984 Fleer

392 Wade Boggs

48	Mike Schmidt	6.00
49	Ozzie Virgil	.08
50	*Juan Agosto* (FC)	.15
51	Harold Baines	.25
52	Floyd Bannister	.12
54	Britt Burns	.08
55	Julio Cruz	.08
56	Richard Dotson	.10
58	Carlton Fisk	.35
59	Scott Fletcher (FC)	.15
64	Ron Kittle	.15
65	Jerry Koosman	.12
66	Dennis Lamp	.08
67	Rudy Law	.08
68	Vance Law	.10
69	Greg Luzinski	.12
72	Dick Tidrow	.08
73	*Greg Walker* (FC)	.25
74	Glenn Abbott	.08
78	Tom Brookens	.08
79	Enos Cabell	.08
80	Kirk Gibson	.40
81	John Grubb	.08
82	Larry Herndon	.10
84	Rick Leach	.08
85	Chet Lemon	.10
87	Jack Morris	.30

88	Lance Parrish	.35
89	Dan Petry	.10
91	Alan Trammell	.40
92	Lou Whitaker	.40
93	Milt Wilcox	.08
94	Glenn Wilson	.10
96	Dusty Baker	.10
98	Greg Brock	.12
100	Pedro Guerrero	.35
102	Burt Hooton	.10
103	Steve Howe	.12
105	Mike Marshall	.15
106	Rick Monday	.10
107	Jose Morales	.08
109	*Alejandro Pena* (FC)	.30
110	Jerry Reuss	.12
111	Bill Russell	.10
112	Steve Sax	.20
115	Fernando Valenzuela	.40
116	Bob Welch	.15
118	Pat Zachry	.08
119	Don Baylor	.15
121	Rick Cerone	.08
122	*Ray Fontenot* (FC)	.10
124	Oscar Gamble	.10
125	Goose Gossage	.25
126	Ken Griffey	.20

447 Rickey Henderson

127	Ron Guidry	.30
128	Jay Howell (FC)	.15
129	Steve Kemp	.10
131	*Don Mattingly* (FC)	45.00
135	Graig Nettles	.20
136	Lou Piniella	.15
137	Willie Randolph	.12
139	Dave Righetti	.25
143	Dave Winfield	.40
145	*Jim Acker* (FC)	.12
146	Doyle Alexander	.12
147	Jesse Barfield	.25
148	Jorge Bell	1.50
150	Jim Clancy	.10
151	Dave Collins	.10
152	*Tony Fernandez* (FC)	6.00
155	Jim Gott (FC)	.10
156	Alfredo Griffin	.10
160	Luis Leal	.08
164	Lloyd Moseby	.12
166	Jorge Orta	.08
167	Dave Stieb	.15

301 Tony Gwynn

168	Willie Upshaw	.10
169	Ernie Whitt	.10
170	Len Barker	.10
171	Steve Bedrosian	.12
173	Brett Butler	.10
174	Rick Camp	.08
175	Chris Chambliss	.10
178	Terry Forster	.10
179	Gene Garber	.08
181	Bob Horner	.20
182	Glenn Hubbard	.10
184	Craig McMurtry (FC)	.12
185	Donnie Moore (FC)	.10
186	Dale Murphy	1.00
187	Phil Niekro	.30
188	Pascual Perez	.10
191	Jerry Royster	.08
192	Claudell Washington	.10
193	Bob Watson	.10
197	*Tom Candiotti* (FC)	.50
198	Cecil Cooper	.15
199	Rollie Fingers	.25
200	Jim Gantner	.10
201	Bob Gibson	.08
202	Moose Haas	.08
207	Paul Molitor	.20
208	Don Money	.08

212	Ed Romero	.08
213	Ted Simmons	.15
214	Jim Slaton	.08
215	Don Sutton	.30
218	Ned Yost	.08
219	Robin Yount	.50
221	Kevin Bass (FC)	.20
222	Jose Cruz	.12
223	*Bill Dawley* (FC)	.10
225	*Bill Doran* (FC)	1.00
226	Phil Garner	.10
229	Ray Knight	.12
231	Mike LaCoss	.08
232	Mike Madden	.08
237	Craig Reynolds	.08
238	Vern Ruhle	.08
239	Nolan Ryan	5.00
240	Mike Scott	.20
241	Tony Scott	.08
242	Dave Smith	.10
243	Dickie Thon	.10
244	Denny Walling	.08
245	Dale Berra	.08
246	Jim Bibby	.08
247	John Candelaria	.12
248	*Jose DeLeon* (FC)	.50
249	Mike Easler	.10

17 Cal Ripken, Jr.

353	Greg Pryor	.08
354	Dan Quisenberry	.15
355	Steve Renko	.08
356	Leon Roberts	.08
357	Pat Sheridan (FC)	.15
358	Joe Simpson	.08
359	Don Slaught	.08
362	John Wathan	.10
363	Frank White	.12
364	Willie Wilson	.15
365	Jim Barr	.08
366	Dave Bergman	.08
367	Fred Breining	.08
368	Bob Brenly	.08
369	Jack Clark	.25
370	Chili Davis	.15
371	Mark Davis (FC)	.12
372	Darrell Evans	.15
373	Atlee Hammaker	.08
374	Mike Krukow	.10
375	Duane Kuiper	.08
376	Bill Laskey	.08
377	Gary Lavelle	.08
379	Jeff Leonard	.12
380	Randy Lerch	.08
381	Renie Martin	.08
384	Tom O'Malley	.08
385	Max Venable	.08

640 Retiring Superstars

344 George Brett

389	Luis Aponte	.08
390	Tony Armas	.12
391	Doug Bird	.08
392	Wade Boggs	8.00
393	Dennis Boyd (FC)	.35
394	Mike Brown	.08
395	Mark Clear	.08
396	Dennis Eckersley	.15
397	• Dwight Evans	.20
398	Rich Gedman	.10
399	Glenn Hoffman	.08
400	Bruce Hurst	.15
404	Jeff Newman	.08
405	Reid Nichols	.08
406	Bob Ojeda	.10
407	Jerry Remy	.08
408	Jim Rice	.40
411	John Tudor	.10
412	Carl Yastrzemski	.85
413	Buddy Bell	.12
417	Bucky Dent	.12
418	Dave Hostetler	.08
419	Charlie Hough	.12
421	Odell Jones	.08
422	Jon Matlack	.10
423	Pete O'Brien (FC)	1.00
424	Larry Parrish	.12
425	Mickey Rivers	.10

225 Bill Doran

461	Mike Warren	.08
462	Johnny Bench	.85
465	Cesar Cedeno	.12
466	Dave Concepcion	.15
467	Dan Driessen	.10
468	*Nick Esasky* (FC)	.75
469	Rich Gale	.08
470	Ben Hayes	.08
478	Ted Power	.10
479	Joe Price	.08
481	*Gary Redus* (FC)	.25
483	Mario Soto	.10
486	Larry Bowa	.15
488	Bill Buckner	.15
490	Ron Cey	.12
491	Jody Davis	.10
492	Leon Durham	.08
493	Mel Hall (FC)	.20
494	Ferguson Jenkins	.20
495	• Jay Johnstone	.10
496	*Craig Lefferts* (FC)	.25
497	*Carmelo Martinez* (FC)	.25
501	Mike Proly	.08
503	Dick Ruthven	.08
504	Ryne Sandberg	13.00
505	Lee Smith	.15
506	Steve Trout	.08
507	Gary Woods	.08

426	Billy Sample	.08
427	Dave Schmidt	.08
428	*Mike Smithson* (FC)	.15
429	Bill Stein	.08
430	Dave Stewart	.15
431	Jim Sundberg	.10
432	Frank Tanana	.12
433	Dave Tobik	.08
434	Wayne Tolleson (FC)	.10
436	Bill Almon	.08
437	*Keith Atherton* (FC)	.20
438	Dave Beard	.08
440	Jeff Burroughs	.10
442	*Tim Conroy* (FC)	.12
443	Mike Davis	.10
444	Wayne Gross	.08
446	Mike Heath	.08
447	Rickey Henderson	7.50
448	*Don Hill* (FC)	.10
450	Bill Krueger	.08
451	Rick Langford	.08
452	Carney Lansford	.12
453	Davey Lopes	.10
455	Dan Meyer	.08
456	Dwayne Murphy	.08
457	Mike Norris	.08
459	*Tony Phillips* (FC)	.15

14 Eddie Murray

565 Gary Gaetti

509	• Bob Boone	.10
511	Rod Carew	1.00
512	Bobby Clark	.08
513	John Curtis	.08
514	Doug DeCinces	.12
515	Brian Downing	.12
516	Tim Foli	.08
517	Ken Forsch	.08
518	Bobby Grich	.12
520	Reggie Jackson	.60
521	Ron Jackson	.08
522	Tommy John	.25
523	Bruce Kison	.08
525	Fred Lynn	.25
526	*Gary Pettis* (FC)	.25
527	Luis Sanchez	.08
530	Rob Wilfong	.08
531	Mike Witt	.15
532	Geoff Zahn	.08
533	Bud Anderson	.08
534	Chris Bando	.08
536	Bert Blyleven	.20
540	Jim Essian	.08
542	Julio Franco (FC)	2.75
544	Toby Harrah	.10
545	Ron Hassey	.08
546	*Neal Heaton* (FC)	.15
550	Dan Spillner	.08

339 Andy Van Slyke

551	Rick Sutcliffe	.15
552	Pat Tabler	.10
553	Gorman Thomas	.10
554	Andre Thornton	.12
556	Darrell Brown	.08
557	Tom Brunansky	.20
558	*Randy Bush* (FC)	.15
560	John Castino	.08
561	Ron Davis	.08
562	Dave Engle	.08
564	Pete Filson	.08
565	Gary Gaetti	.60
567	Kent Hrbek	.40
568	Rusty Kuntz	.08
572	Ken Schrom	.08
573	Ray Smith	.08
574	*Tim Teufel* (FC)	.25
575	Frank Viola	.80
576	Gary Ward	.10
580	Bob Bailor	.08
582	Hubie Brooks	.15
583	Carlos Diaz	.08
584	George Foster	.20
585	Brian Giles	.08
586	Danny Heep	.08
587	Keith Hernandez	.35
588	Ron Hodges	.08

1984 Fleer

542 Julio Franco

1984 FLEER UPDATE

After Topps enjoyed free rein over the fall card market for three years with its Traded set, Fleer decided to try for a piece of the action. It duplicated the marketing formula used by Topps in precise detail by designing its own 132-card Update set. Fleer used the same front and back design as the standard 1984 set but added the letter "U" to each card number (it has been omitted from the following list, however). The company published 131 player cards and a checklist, though the checklist seems unnecessary since the cards were sold only as complete boxed sets through hobby dealers. Because Fleer's ability to compete with the Topps Traded set seemed questionable during the first year, some hobby dealers were hesitant to stock the Fleer Update sets. This accounts for the relative scarcity of these cards.

		MINT
Complete set		**$565.00**
Commons		**.15**
3	Mark Bailey (FC)	$ .20
5	Dusty Baker	.30
6	Steve Balboni (FC)	.40
8	Marty Barrett (FC)	2.00
15	Phil Bradley (FC)	4.00

43 Dwight Gooden

93 Kirby Puckett

18	Bill Buckner	.50
19	Ray Burris	.15
21	Brett Butler	.30
22	Enos Cabell	.15
24	Bill Caudill	.15
27	Roger Clemens (FC)	180.00
28	Jaime Cocanower	.15
29	Ron Darling (FC)	10.00
30	Alvin Davis (FC)	15.00

1984 Fleer Update

27 Roger Clemens

33	Mike Easler	.20
34	Dennis Eckersley	3.00
36	Darrell Evans	.65
37	Mike Fitzgerald (FC)	.20
38	Tim Foli	.15
39	John Franco (FC)	11.00
41	Rich Gale	.15
43	Dwight Gooden (FC)	100.00
44	• Goose Gossage	1.00
46	Mark Gubicza (FC)	8.00
48	Toby Harrah	.15
49	Ron Hassey	.15
51	Willie Hernandez	.40
52	Ed Hodge	.15
53	Ricky Horton (FC)	.65
54	Art Howe	.15
55	Dane Iorg	.15
56	Brook Jacoby (FC)	4.00
57	Dion James	.35
58	Mike Jeffcoat (FC)	.15
61	Jimmy Key (FC)	6.00
62	Dave Kingman	.75
63	Brad Komminsk (FC)	.15
64	Jerry Koosman	.50
66	Rusty Kuntz	.15
68	Dennis Lamp	.15
69	Tito Landrum	.15

70	Mark Langston (FC)	27.00
71	Rick Leach	.15
72	Craig Lefferts (FC)	.25
74	Jerry Martin	.15
75	Carmelo Martinez	.25
76	Mike Mason (FC)	.20
77	Gary Matthews	.30
80	Joe Morgan	5.00
81	Darryl Motley	.15
82	Graig Nettles	1.00
83	Phil Niekro	2.50
84	Ken Oberkfell	.15
85	Al Oliver	.75
86	Jorge Orta	.15
87	Amos Otis	.30
89	Dave Parker	3.00
90	Jack Perconte	.25
91	Tony Perez	2.00
92	Gerald Perry (FC)	1.50
93	Kirby Puckett (FC)	180.00
94	Shane Rawley	.35
95	Floyd Rayford	.20
96	Ron Reed	.25
97	R.J. Reynolds (FC)	.90
98	Gene Richards	.20
99	Jose Rijo (FC)	10.00
100	Jeff Robinson (FC)	1.00
101	Ron Romanick (FC)	.15
102	Pete Rose	20.00
103	Bret Saberhagen	27.00
104	Scott Sanderson	.25
105	Dick Schofield (FC)	.40
106	Tom Seaver	15.00
108	Mike Smithson	.20
109	Lary Sorensen	.15
111	Jeff Stone (FC)	.20
113	Jim Sundberg	.20
114	Rick Sutcliffe	.75
116	Derrel Thomas	.15
117	Gorman Thomas	.20
119	Manny Trillo	.20
120	John Tudor	.60
122	Mike Vail	.15
123	Tom Waddell (FC)	.15
124	Gary Ward	.15
125	Terry Whitfield	.15
127	Frank Williams (FC)	.35
128	Glenn Wilson	.35
131	Mike Young (FC)	.50

1984 TOPPS

Despite retaining the general format of the 1983 design, the 1984 Topps set was not an immediate hit with collectors. All the single-player cards show a large action photo with a smaller portrait on the front. The first six cards of this 792-card edition highlight events of the previous season, such as Steve Carlton winning his 300th game and becoming the all-time strikeout king; Dave Righetti, Bob Forsch, and Mike Warren pitching no-hitters; and Rickey Henderson stealing 100 bases three seasons in a row. Recognition was also given to Johnny Bench, Gaylord Perry, and Carl Yastrzemski on their retirement. For the second year in a row, no team rookie or Future Stars cards were included.

230 Rickey Henderson

		MINT
Complete set		**$125.00**
Commons		**.08**

1	1983 Highlight (Steve Carlton)	$.30
2	1983 Highlight (Rickey Henderson)	.80
3	1983 Highlight (Dan Quisenberry)	.10
4	1983 Highlight (Steve Carlton, Gaylord Perry, Nolan Ryan)	.30
5	1983 Highlight (Bob Forsch, Dave Righetti, Mike Warren)	.30
6	1983 Highlight (Johnny Bench, Gaylord Perry, Carl Yastrzemski)	.40
7	Gary Lucas	.08
8	*Don Mattingly* (FC)	**31.00**
9	Jim Gott	.08
10	Robin Yount	1.00
11	Twins Ldrs (Kent Hrbek, Ken Schrom)	.08
12	Billy Sample	.08
14	Tom Brookens	.08
15	Burt Hooton	.08
16	Omar Moreno	.08
18	Dale Berra	.08
19	*Ray Fontenot* (FC)	.10
20	Greg Luzinski	.12
21	Joe Altobelli	.08
22	Bryan Clark	.08
23	Keith Moreland	.08
24	John Martin	.08
25	Glenn Hubbard	.10
27	Daryl Sconiers	.08
28	Frank Viola	1.00
29	Danny Heep	.08
30	Wade Boggs	7.00
32	Bobby Ramos	.08
33	Tom Burgmeier	.08
35	Don Sutton	.30
36	Denny Walling	.08
37	Rangers Ldrs (Buddy Bell, Rick Honeycutt)	.12
38	Luis DeLeon	.08
39	Garth Iorg	.08

1984 Topps

251 Tony Gwynn

40	Dusty Baker	.08
41	Tony Bernazard	.08
42	Johnny Grubb	.08
43	Ron Reed	.08
45	Jerry Mumphrey	.08
47	Rudy Law	.08
48	Julio Franco (FC)	**2.00**
49	John Stuper	.08
50	Chris Chambliss	.08
52	Paul Splittorff	.08
53	Juan Beniquez	.08
54	Jesse Orosco	.10
55	Dave Concepcion	.10
56	Gary Allenson	.08
57	Dan Schatzeder	.08
59	Sammy Stewart	.08
60	Paul Molitor	.20
61	*Chris Codiroli*	.10
62	Dave Hostetler	.08
63	Ed Vande Berg	.08
64	Mike Scioscia	.08
65	Kirk Gibson	.40
66	Astros Ldrs (Jose Cruz, Nolan Ryan)	.25
67	Gary Ward	.08
68	Luis Salazar	.08
70	Gary Matthews	.12

71	Leo Hernandez	.08
72	Mike Squires	.08
73	Jody Davis	.08
74	Jerry Martin	.08
75	Bob Forsch	.08
76	Alfredo Griffin	.08
77	Brett Butler	.10
78	Mike Torrez	.10
79	Rob Wilfong	.08
80	Steve Rogers	.10
81	Billy Martin	.12
83	Richie Zisk	.10
85	Atlee Hammaker	.08
86	*John Shelby* (FC)	.20
88	Rob Picciolo	.08
89	*Mike Smithson* (FC)	.15
90	Pedro Guerrero	.40
91	Dan Spillner	.08
92	Lloyd Moseby	.12
93	Bob Knepper	.10
94	Mario Ramirez	.08
95	Aurelio Lopez	.08
96	Royals Ldrs (Larry Gura, Hal McRae)	.10
97	LaMarr Hoyt	.08
98	Steve Nicosia	.08
99	*Craig Lefferts* (FC)	.20
100	Reggie Jackson	.60

8 Don Mattingly

101	Porfirio Altamirano	.08
102	Ken Oberkfell	.08
105	Tony Armas	.08
106	Tim Stoddard	.08
107	Ned Yost	.08
108	Randy Moffitt	.08
109	Brad Wellman	.08
110	Ron Guidry	.25
111	Bill Virdon	.08
112	Tom Niedenfuer	.08
113	Kelly Paris	.08
114	Checklist 1-132	.12
115	Andre Thornton	.10
116	George Bjorkman	.08
117	Tom Veryzer	.08
118	Charlie Hough	.08
120	Keith Hernandez	.40
121	*Pat Sheridan* (FC)	.15
122	Cecilio Guante (FC)	.10
123	Butch Wynegar	.08
124	Damaso Garcia	.08
125	Britt Burns	.08
126	Braves Ldrs (Craig McMurtry, Dale Murphy)	.25
127	Mike Madden	.08
128	Rick Manning	.08
130	Ozzie Smith	.20
131	Batting Ldrs (Wade Boggs, Bill Madlock)	.50
132	HR Ldrs (Jim Rice, Mike Schmidt)	.50
133	RBI Ldrs (Cecil Cooper, Dale Murphy, Jim Rice)	.40
134	SB Ldrs (Rickey Henderson, Tim Raines)	.45
135	Victory Ldrs (John Denny, LaMarr Hoyt)	.10
136	SO Ldrs (Steve Carlton, Jack Morris)	.25
137	ERA Ldrs (Atlee Hammaker, Rick Honeycutt)	.10
138	Leading Firemen (Al Holland, Dan Quisenberry)	.12
139	Bert Campaneris	.12
140	Storm Davis	.12
141	Pat Corrales	.08
143	Jose Morales	.08
145	Gary Lavelle	.08

182 Darryl Strawberry

147	Dan Petry	.08
148	Joe Lefebvre	.08
149	Jon Matlack	.10
150	Dale Murphy	1.00
151	Steve Trout	.08
152	Glenn Brummer	.08
153	Dick Tidrow	.08
154	Dave Henderson	.12
155	Frank White	.12
156	Athletics Ldrs (Tim Conroy, Rickey Henderson)	.25
157	Gary Gaetti	.75
158	John Curtis	.08
160	Mario Soto	.10
161	*Junior Ortiz* (FC)	.10
162	Bob Ojeda	.10
164	Scott Sanderson	.08
165	Ken Singleton	.12
166	Jamie Nelson	.08
168	Juan Bonilla	.08
169	Larry Parrish	.12
170	Jerry Reuss	.10
171	Frank Robinson	.12
172	Frank DiPino	.08
173	*Marvell Wynne* (FC)	.20
174	Juan Berenguer	.08
175	Graig Nettles	.20

596 Ryne Sandberg

256	Dave Geisel	.08
257	Julio Cruz	.08
258	Luis Sanchez	.08
259	Sparky Anderson	.12
260	Scott McGregor	.10
262	*Tom Candiotti* (FC)	.65
264	Doug Frobel	.08
265	*Donnie Hill* (FC)	.12
267	*Carmelo Martinez* (FC)	.25
268	Jack O'Connor	.08
269	Aurelio Rodriguez	.08
270	*Jeff Russell* (FC)	.25
271	Moose Haas	.08
272	Rick Dempsey	.08
273	Charlie Puleo	.08
274	Rick Monday	.10
275	Len Matuszek	.08
276	Angels Ldrs (Rod Carew, Geoff Zahn)	.20
277	Eddie Whitson	.08
278	Jorge Bell	1.00
279	Ivan DeJesus	.10
280	Floyd Bannister	.10
281	Larry Milbourne	.08
283	Larry Biittner	.08
284	Howard Bailey	.08
285	Darrell Porter	.08

300 Pete Rose

288	Jim Beattie	.08
289	Randy Johnson	.08
290	Dave Dravecky	.10
295	Mike Flanagan	.12
300	Pete Rose	2.00
306	Dodgers Ldrs (Pedro Guerrero, Bob Welch)	.15
309	*Tony Phillips*	.12
310	Willie McGee	.35
311	Jerry Koosman	.12
315	Bob Grich	.10
324	*Alejandro Pena*	.30
329	Pat Tabler (FC)	.08
330	John Candelaria	.15
331	Bucky Dent	.12
332	*Kevin Gross* (FC)	.25
335	Don Baylor	.08
340	Hal McRae	.15
345	Kent Hrbek	.40
350	George Foster	.20
352	Dave Stewart	1.00
357	Ron Cey	.10
359	*Jim Acker* (FC)	.10
360	Willie Randolph	.10
364	Scott Fletcher (FC)	.15
365	Steve Bedrosian	.10
366	Padres Ldrs (Dave Dravecky, Terry Kennedy)	.12

470 Nolan Ryan

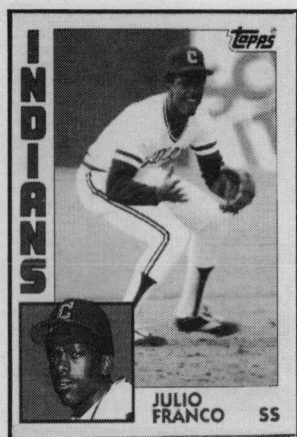

48 Julio Franco

490 Cal Ripken

485	Rick Rhoden	.10
486	Yankees Ldrs (Don Baylor, Ron Guidry)	.15
488	Jesse Barfield	.20
490	Cal Ripken	2.00
494	Chili Davis	.12
495	Rollie Fingers	.25
498	Rich Gedman	.10
499	Mike Witt	.10
500	George Brett	1.00
504	Mickey Rivers	.10
505	Pete Vuckovich	.10
508	Mel Hall	.15
510	Alan Trammell	.40
512	Oscar Gamble	.10
515	Gorman Thomas	.10
516	Expos Ldrs (Charlie Lea, Al Oliver)	.12
517	John Moses	.10
518	*Greg Walker*	.45
520	Bob Boone	.10
525	Willie Wilson	.15
529	*Keith Atherton* (FC)	.15
532	Eric Show	.10
534	*Pete O'Brien*	.75
537	Johnny Ray	.10
538	Kevin Bass	.15
540	George Hendrick	.10
543	*Craig McMurtry*	.12
545	Bill Buckner	.15
546	Indians Ldrs (Mike Hargrove, Lary Sorensen)	.10
547	Mike Moore	.15
549	*Walt Terrell*	.50
550	Jim Rice	.45
554	Ted Power (FC)	.10
555	Greg Brock	.10
558	Mike Davis	.10
559	Mike Scott	.20
560	Carlton Fisk	.35
561	Whitey Herzog	.10
563	Glenn Wilson	.10
565	Leon Durham	.08
570	Dan Quisenberry	.12
573	Dave Kingman	.15
574	Brian Downing	.12
575	Jim Clancy	.10
576	Giants Ldrs (Atlee Hammaker, Jeff Leonard)	.10

500 George Brett

580	Lonnie Smith	.10
581	*Jose DeLeon* (FC)	.65
586	Joe Niekro	.10
587	Von Hayes	.15
589	Mike Easler	.08
590	Dave Stieb	.15
591	Tony LaRussa	.10
595	Jeff Reardon	.15
596	Ryne Sandberg	9.00
599	*Doug Sisk*	.10
600	Rod Carew	.50
601	John Tudor	.10
606	Blue Jays Ldrs (Lloyd Moseby, Dave Stieb)	.15
610	Steve Sax	.25
611	Chet Lemon	.10
614	Len Barker	.10
615	Garry Templeton	.10
620	Al Oliver	.20
621	Frank Howard	.10
625	Larry Gura	.10
627	Dave LaPoint	.08
630	Ted Simmons	.15
631	Denny Martinez	.08
633	Mike Krukow	.10
634	Mike Marshall	.15
635	Dave Righetti	.25

1984 Topps

10 Robin Yount

391 Dale Murphy AS

1984 TOPPS TRADED

During its fourth year, the Topps Traded set reached a new high in popularity. Although the issue was still distributed only through hobby dealers in complete sets, the players are illustrious: Dwight Gooden's debut with Topps came in this series, along with cards for future Hall-of-Famers Joe Morgan, Pete Rose, and Tom Seaver. However, by the time the set was released in late September, Rose was no longer an Expo, which made his card outdated. Topps continued the practice of adding a "T" suffix to each card number so collectors could easily distinguish between Traded cards and the regular cards issued earlier in the season (though it has been omitted from the following lists).

		MINT
Complete set		**$115.00**
Commons		**.10**

5	Dusty Baker	$.20
6	Steve Balboni	.20
13	Yogi Berra	.20
15	Phil Bradley (FC)	1.25
17	Bill Buckner	.25
20	Brett Butler	.20
27	Ron Darling (FC)	4.00
28	Alvin Davis (FC)	7.50
30	Jeff Dedmon (FC)	.15
33	Mike Easler	.15
34	Dennis Eckersley	1.00
36	Darrell Evans	.25
37	Mike Fitzgerald (FC)	.15
41	Barbaro Garbey	.15
42	Dwight Gooden (FC)	45.00
43	Rich Gossage	.40
45	Mark Gubicza (FC)	3.25
47	Mel Hall	.20
48	Toby Harrah	.15
51	Willie Hernandez	.30
52	Ricky Horton (FC)	.40
55	Brook Jacoby (FC)	2.00
56	Mike Jeffcoat (FC)	.15
57	Dave Johnson	.15
59	Ruppert Jones	.10
61	Bob Kearney	.10
62	Jimmy Key (FC)	3.00
63	Dave Kingman	.45

42 Dwight Gooden

64	Jerry Koosman	.25
65	Wayne Krenchicki	.10
66	Rusty Kuntz	.10
67	Rene Lachemann	.10
68	Frank LaCorte	.10
69	Dennis Lamp	.10
70	Mark Langston (FC)	11.00
71	Rick Leach	.10
72	Craig Lefferts	.15
75	Carmelo Martinez	.25
76	Mike Mason (FC)	.15

70 Mark Langston

104 Bret Saberhagen

1985 DONRUSS

For the second straight year, a limited print run made Donruss the hottest collectible of 1985. By mid-spring, wax packs were virtually impossible to find on store shelves, and factory-collated sets were ransomed off by lucky dealers. And all this popularity came in spite of two major errors. Card number 424, meant to picture Tom Seaver, wound up with a photo of Floyd Bannister by mistake. The goof was enormous, since Bannister is shown pitching left-handed, while Seaver throws with his right hand. In addition, Terry Pendleton's card front originally gave his name as "Jeff." In both cases the corrections were available only in wax packs. Don Mattingly's card and rookie appearances by Eric Davis and Kirby Puckett highlight the set.

		MINT
Complete set		**$190.00**
Commons		**.08**

438 Kirby Puckett

1	Ryne Sandberg (DK)	$2.00
7	Don Mattingly (DK)	6.00
14	Cal Ripken, Jr. (DK)	.60
15	Jim Rice (DK)	.50
18	Alvin Davis (DK) (FC)	.60
23	Juan Samuel (DK) (FC)	.40
25	Tony Gwynn (DK)	.50
27	*Danny Tartabull* (RR) (FC)	5.00
36	*Larry Sheets* (RR) (FC)	.50
38	*Calvin Schiraldi* (RR) (FC)	.30
39	*Shawon Dunston* (RR) (FC)	7.00
41	*Billy Hatcher* (RR) (FC)	.85
45	*Jim Traber* (RR) (FC)	.30
47	Eddie Murray	.60
48	Robin Yount	.90
49	Lance Parrish	.30
50	Jim Rice	.50
51	Dave Winfield	.50
52	Fernando Valenzuela	.35
53	George Brett	.75
55	Gary Carter	.40
57	Reggie Jackson	.60
60	Nolan Ryan	4.00
61	Mike Schmidt	3.00
62	Dave Parker	.50
63	Tony Gwynn	2.00
66	Dale Murphy	.80
67	Ryne Sandberg	5.00
68	Keith Hernandez	.40
69	*Alvin Davis* (FC)	4.25
70	Kent Hrbek	.30
74	Jack Perconte	.10
75	Jesse Orosco	.10
76	Jody Davis	.10
77	Bob Horner	.15
79	Joel Youngblood	.08
81	Ron Oester	.08
82	Ozzie Virgil	.08
83	*Ricky Horton* (FC)	.25
84	Bill Doran	.12
85	Rod Carew	.75

86	LaMarr Hoyt	.08
87	Tim Wallach	.15
88	Mike Flanagan	.12
90	Chet Lemon	.10
91	Bob Stanley	.08
92	Willie Randolph	.12
93	Bill Russell	.10
94	Julio Franco	.15
95	Dan Quisenberry	.12
96	Bill Caudill	.08
98	Danny Darwin	.08
100	Bud Black	.08
101	Tony Phillips	.10
103	Jay Howell	.10
104	Burt Hooton	.10
105	Milt Wilcox	.08
106	Rich Dauer	.06
107	Don Sutton	.35
108	Mike Witt	.10
109	Bruce Sutter	.15
110	Enos Cabell	.08
112	Dave Dravecky	.08
113	Marvell Wynne	.08
115	Chuck Porter	.08
116	John Gibbons	.08
118	Darnell Coles	.08
119	Dennis Lamp	.08

325 Eric Davis

295 Don Mattingly

120	Ron Davis	.08
121	Nick Esasky	.10
122	Vance Law	.10
124	Bill Schroeder	.08
126	Bobby Meacham	.08
127	Marty Barrett (FC)	.35
128	*R.J. Reynolds* (FC)	.30
130	Jorge Orta	.08
133	Fred Lynn	.25
136	Kevin Bass	.10
137	Garry Maddox	.10
138	Dave LaPoint	.08
139	Kevin McReynolds	1.00
142	Rod Scurry	.08
143	Greg Minton	.08
144	Tim Stoddard	.08
146	George Bell	.65
154	Brook Jacoby	.15
156	Tim Conroy	.08
157	*Joe Hesketh* (FC)	.08
158	Brian Downing	.15
160	Marc Hill	.08
161	Phil Garner	.10
162	Jerry Davis	.08
164	*John Franco* (FC)	2.50
165	Len Barker	.10
168	Tito Landrum	.08

312 Darryl Strawberry

169	Cal Ripken	.60
170	Cecil Cooper	.15
171	Alan Trammell	.40
172	Wade Boggs	6.00
173	Don Baylor	.15
174	Pedro Guerrero	.30
175	Frank White	.12
176	Rickey Henderson	4.00
177	Charlie Lea	.08
178	Pete O'Brien	.20
179	Doug DeCinces	.12
180	Ron Kittle	.12
182	Joe Niekro	.12
183	Juan Samuel (FC)	.60
184	Mario Soto	.10
185	Goose Gossage	.25
186	Johnny Ray	.15
187	Bob Brenly	.08
189	Leon Durham	.08
190	*Dwight Gooden* (FC)	15.00
191	Barry Bonnell	.08
192	Tim Teufel	.12
193	Dave Stieb	.15
195	Jesse Barfield	.25
196	Al Cowens	.08
197	Hubie Brooks	.12
198	Steve Trout	.08

200	Bill Madlock	.15
201	*Jeff Robinson* (FC)	.35
202	Eric Show	.10
203	Dave Concepcion	.15
205	Neil Allen	.08
208	Carlton Fisk	.40
209	Bryn Smith	.08
211	Dion James	.10
213	Mike Easler	.08
214	Ron Guidry	.30
216	Brett Butler	.12
217	Larry Gura	.08
218	Ray Burris	.08
219	Steve Rogers	.10
220	Frank Tanana	.12
221	Ned Yost	.08
222	*Bret Saberhagen*	10.00
223	Mike Davis	.10
224	Bert Blyleven	.15
225	Steve Kemp	.10
226	Jerry Reuss	.10
227	Darrell Evans	.15
230	• Bob Boone	.10
231	Lonnie Smith	.10
233	Jerry Koosman	.12
234	Graig Nettles	.20
235	John Tudor	.12

39 Shawon Dunston

236 John Rabb .08
239 Gary Matthews .12
240 *Jim Presley* (FC) .80
241 Dave Collins .10
242 Gary Gaetti .30
244 Rudy Law .08
246 Tom Tellman .08
247 Howard Johnson 2.00
249 Tony Armas .12
251 *Mike Jeffcoat* (FC) .10
252 Dane Iorg .08
254 Pete Rose 1.25
255 Don Aase .08
257 Britt Burns .08
258 Mike Scott .20
260 Dave Rucker .08
262 *Jay Tibbs* (FC) .20
264 Don Robinson .10
265 Gary Lavelle .08
267 Matt Young .10
268 Ernie Whitt .10
270 *Ken Dixon* (FC) .10
271 Peter Ladd .08
273 *Roger Clemens* (FC) 27.00
274 Rick Cerone .08
275 Dave Anderson .08
277 Greg Pryor .08
278 Mike Warren .08
280 Bobby Grich .12
281 *Mike Mason* (FC) .12
282 Ron Reed .08
283 Alan Ashby .08
285 Joe Lefebvre .08
286 Ted Power .08
288 Lee Tunnell .08
289 Rich Bordi .08
292 Rollie Fingers .25
293 Lou Whitaker .40
294 • Dwight Evans .15
295 Don Mattingly 17.00
296 Mike Marshall .15
297 Willie Wilson .12
298 Mike Heath .08
299 Tim Raines .50
300 Larry Parrish .12
301 Geoff Zahn .08
302 Rich Dotson .10
304 Jose Cruz .12
305 Steve Carlton .50

176 Rickey Henderson

306 Gary Redus .08
307 Steve Garvey .50
308 Jose DeLeon .15
309 Randy Lerch .08
311 Lee Smith .15
312 Darryl Strawberry 7.50
313 Jim Beattie .08
314 John Butcher .08
316 Mike Smithson .08
317 Luis Leal .08
318 Ken Phelps (FC) .25
319 Wally Backman .10
320 Ron Cey .12
323 *Frank Williams* (FC) .20
324 Tim Lollar .08
325 *Eric Davis* (FC) 21.00
326 Von Hayes .15
327 Andy Van Slyke .40
328 Craig Reynolds .08
329 Dick Schofield .10
330 Scott Fletcher .10
331 Jeff Reardon .15
332 Rick Dempsey .10
333 Ben Oglivie .10
334 Dan Petry .10
336 Dave Righetti .25
338 Mel Hall .10

1985 Donruss

616 Joe Carter

342	Gary Ward	.10
343	Dave Stewart	.15
344	*Mark Gubicza* (FC)	2.00
345	Carney Lansford	.12
346	Jerry Willard	.08
347	Ken Griffey	.08
348	*Franklin Stubbs* (FC)	.50
349	Aurelio Lopez	.08
350	Al Bumbry	.10
351	Charlie Moore	.08
352	Luis Sanchez	.08
353	Darrell Porter	.10
357	Cecilio Guante	.08
358	Jeff Leonard	.10
359	Paul Molitor	.20
361	Larry Bowa	.12
362	Bob Kearney	.08
363	Garth Iorg	.08
364	Tom Brunansky	.15
365	Brad Gulden	.08
366	Greg Walker	.12
367	Mike Young	.10
368	Rick Waits	.08
369	Doug Bair	.08
371	Bob Ojeda	.10
372	Bob Welch	.15
373	Neal Heaton	.08

374	Danny Jackson (photo is Steve Farr)	.85
375	Donnie Hill	.08
377	Bruce Kison	.08
380	Vern Ruhle	.08
381	Tim Corcoran	.08
383	Bobby Brown	.08
385	Rick Mahler	.08
387	Bill Laskey	.08
388	Thad Bosley	.08
390	Tony Fernandez	.50
393	Bob Gibson	.08
394	Marty Castillo	.08
397	Bob Bailor	.08
401	Razor Shines	.08
402	Rob Wilfong	.08
403	Tom Henke	.10
404	Al Jones	.08
406	Luis DeLeon	.08
407	Greg Gross	.08
408	Tom Hume	.08
409	Rick Camp	.08
410	Milt May	.08
411	*Henry Cotto* (FC)	.20
414	Ted Simmons	.15
415	Jack Morris	.35
416	Bill Buckner	.15
418	Steve Sax	.25
421	Andre Dawson	.30
422	Charlie Hough	.10
423	Tommy John	.25
424	Tom Seaver (photo is Floyd Bannister, throwing left)	1.00
424	Tom Seaver (correct photo, throwing right)	15.00
426	Terry Puhl	.08
427	Al Holland	.08
428	Eddie Milner	.08
429	Terry Kennedy	.08
430	John Candelaria	.12
431	Manny Trillo	.10
433	Rick Sutcliffe	.15
434	Ron Darling	.60
435	Spike Owen	.10
436	Frank Viola	.25
437	Lloyd Moseby	.12
438	*Kirby Puckett* (FC)	27.00
439	Jim Clancy	.10

440	Mike Moore	.15
441	Doug Sisk	.08
442	Dennis Eckersley	.20
443	Gerald Perry	.15
444	Dale Berra	.08
445	Dusty Baker	.10
446	Ed Whitson	.08
447	Cesar Cedeno	.12
448	*Rick Schu* (FC)	.20
449	Joaquin Andujar	.10
450	*Mark Bailey* (FC)	.12
451	*Ron Romanick* (FC)	.12
452	Julio Cruz	.08
453	Miguel Dilone	.08
454	Storm Davis	.12
456	Barbaro Garbey	.08
457	Rich Gedman	.08
458	Phil Niekro	.30
460	Pat Tabler	.08
461	Darryl Motley	.08
464	Billy Sample	.08
465	Mickey Rivers	.10
466	John Wathan	.10
468	Andre Thornton	.12
469	Rex Hudler	.10
470	*Sid Bream* (FC)	.50
471	Kirk Gibson	.40
472	John Shelby	.10

247 Howard Johnson

473	Moose Haas	.08
474	Doug Corbett	.08
475	Willie McGee	.35
476	Bob Knepper	.08
477	Kevin Gross	.12
479	Kent Tekulve	.10
480	Chili Davis	.15
481	Bobby Clark	.08
482	Mookie Wilson	.12
484	Ed Nunez	.08
486	Ken Schrom	.08
487	Jeff Russell	.12
488	Tom Paciorek	.08
492	*Jose Rijo* (FC)	2.00
493	Bruce Hurst	.15
495	Mike Fischlin	.08
496	Don Slaught	.08
498	Gary Lucas	.08
499	Gary Pettis	.10
500	Marvis Foley	.08
501	Mike Squires	.08
502	*Jim Pankovitz* (FC)	.08
505	Bruce Bochy	.08
508	Lee Lacy	.08
510	Bob Dernier	.08
515	Ed Romero	.08
516	Rusty Kuntz	.08

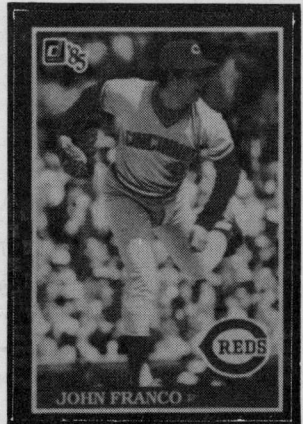

164 John Franco

1985 Donruss

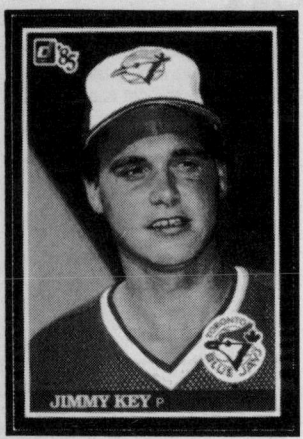

559 Jimmy Key

517	Rick Miller	.08
518	Dennis Rasmussen	.15
519	Steve Yeager	.08
520	Chris Bando	.08
521	U.L. Washington	.08
522	Curt Young (FC)	.40
525	Odell Jones	.08
526	Juan Agosto	.08
528	Andy Hawkins	.12
529	Sixto Lezcano	.08
534	Jeff Pendleton (FC) (first name incorrect)	.85
534	Terry Pendleton (FC) (correct name)	3.00
535	Vic Rodriguez	.08
538	Mark Clear	.08
539	Mike Pagliarulo (FC)	1.00
545	Jim Slaton	.08
546	Greg Luzinski	.12
547	Mark Salas (FC)	.15
548	Dave Smith	.10
552	Rick Rhoden	.10
553	Mark Davis	.15
554	Jeff Dedmon (FC)	.15
557	Mark Langston (FC)	7.00
559	Jimmy Key (FC)	1.75
560	Rick Lysander	.08
561	Doyle Alexander	.12
562	Mike Stanton	.08
563	Sid Fernandez	.50
565	Alex Trevino	.08
566	Brian Harper	.08
567	Dan Gladden (FC)	.40
568	Luis Salazar	.08
569	Tom Foley	.08
571	Danny Cox	.12
572	Joe Sambito	.08
575	Randy St. Claire (FC)	.15
581	Orel Hershiser (FC)	11.00
584	• Joe Morgan	.30
586	Dave Schmidt	.08
588	Hal McRae	.12
592	Ken Howell (FC)	.20
596	Tom Nieto (FC)	.12
597	Walt Terrell	.10
598	Al Oliver	.15
599	Shane Rawley	.08
601	Mark Grant (FC)	.15
603	George Foster	.15
604	Davey Lopes	.10
609	Glenn Wilson	.10
610	Rafael Santana (FC)	.20
614	Al Nipper (FC) (photo is Mike Brown)	.20
616	Joe Carter	3.25
617	Ray Knight	.12
624	Jeff Stone (FC)	.15
628	Steve Bedrosian	.12
630	Mike Krukow	.10
631	Phil Bradley (FC)	.95
634	Tom Browning (FC)	2.50
637	Dan Pasqua (FC)	.75
640	Mike Jones (last line of highlights starts "spent some...")	1.25
640	Mike Jones (last line of highlights starts "Was 11-7...")	.10
641	Pete Rose	1.25
648	John Russell (FC)	.20
649	Ron Robinson (FC)	.25
651	Two for the Title (Don Mattingly, Dave Winfield) (player names in yellow)	4.00
651	Two for the Title (player names in white)	7.00
653	Steve Farr (FC)	.35

1985 FLEER

Other than its distinctive numbering system, the 1985 Fleer set of 660 cards has little that is noteworthy when compared to similar offerings from Donruss and Topps. Following Fleer tradition, the set is arranged by team, ranking the clubs by their 1984 results. Thus, the World Champion Detroit Tigers appear first, followed by the San Diego Padres, and then the rest of the teams in order, based on their winning percentages. Players are listed alphabetically within each team. A large, unobstructed color photo highlights the front of all single-player cards, while card backs, despite a small black-and-white portrait, are plain and boring. Rookies are grouped as Major League Prospects, two players to a card. Glenn Davis, Shawon Dunston, and Danny Tartabull top this group.

		MINT
Complete set		$165.00
Commons		.06

1	Doug Bair	$ .06
6	Darrell Evans	.12
8	Kirk Gibson	.40
9	John Grubb	.06
11	Larry Herndon	.06
12	Howard Johnson	2.00
15	Chet Lemon	.08
16	Aurelio Lopez	.06
17	Sid Monge	.06
18	Jack Morris	.35
19	Lance Parrish	.30
20	Dan Petry	.08
23	Alan Trammell	.35
24	Lou Whitaker	.35
25	Milt Wilcox	.06
27	*Greg Booker* (FC)	.15
28	Bobby Brown	.06
29	Luis DeLeon	.06
32	Steve Garvey	.40
33	Goose Gossage	.20
34	Tony Gwynn	2.00
35	Greg Harris	.06
36	Andy Hawkins	.08
37	Terry Kennedy	.08
38	Craig Lefferts	.08
41	Kevin McReynolds	1.00
42	Graig Nettles	.15
44	Eric Show	.08
45	Garry Templeton	.08

155 Roger Clemens

47	Ed Whitson	.06
50	Larry Bowa	.12
52	Ron Cey	.10
53	*Henry Cotto* (FC)	.15
54	Jody Davis	.08
56	Leon Durham	.06
57	Dennis Eckersley	.12
60	Dave Lopes	.08
61	Gary Matthews	.10
63	Rick Reuschel	.10
65	Ryne Sandberg	.50
67	Lee Smith	.10
69	Rick Sutcliffe	.12

1985 Fleer

533 Eric Davis

82 Dwight Gooden

652 Major League Prospect

161	Bruce Hurst	.15
165	Al Nipper (FC)	.15
166	Bob Ojeda	.10
167	Jerry Remy	.06
168	Jim Rice	.35
169	Bob Stanley	.06
170	Mike Boddicker	.15
171	Al Bumbry	.08
172	Todd Cruz	.06
173	Rich Dauer	.06
174	Storm Davis	.10
176	Jim Dwyer	.06
179	Wayne Gross	.06
184	Eddie Murray	.50
185	Joe Nolan	.06
187	Cal Ripken, Jr.	1.00
195	Mike Young	.08
198	Bud Black	.06
199	George Brett	.50
201	*Mark Gubicza*	2.00
202	Larry Gura	.06
204	Dane Iorg	.06
205	Danny Jackson (FC)	.90
207	Hal McRae	.12
209	Jorge Orta	.06
212	*Bret Saberhagen*	8.00
216	John Wathan	.08
217	Frank White	.10
218	Willie Wilson	.10
219	Neil Allen	.06
222	Danny Cox (FC)	.25
223	Bob Forsch	.08
224	David Green	.06
226	Tom Herr	.10
227	*Ricky Horton*	.20
228	Art Howe	.06
231	Jeff Lahti	.06
233	Dave LaPoint	.08
234	Willie McGee	.30
235	*Tom Nieto* (FC)	.10
236	*Terry Pendleton* (FC)	1.00
237	Darrell Porter	.08
238	Dave Rucker	.06
239	Lonnie Smith	.08
240	Ozzie Smith	.15
241	Bruce Sutter	.12
242	Andy Van Slyke	.35
245	Bill Campbell	.06
246	Steve Carlton	.50
249	John Denny	.06
250	Bo Diaz	.08
251	Greg Gross	.06
252	Kevin Gross	.08
253	Von Hayes	.15
259	Garry Maddox	.10
261	Tug McGraw	.12
262	Al Oliver	.12
263	Shane Rawley	.06
264	Juan Samuel	.30
265	Mike Schmidt	2.00
266	*Jeff Stone*	.12
268	Glenn Wilson	.08
271	Tom Brunansky	.12
272	Randy Bush	.08
273	John Butcher	.06
277	Pete Filson	.06

649 Major League Prospect

278	Gary Gaetti	.25	
280	Ed Hodge	.06	
281	Kent Hrbek	.35	
283	Tim Laudner	.06	
285	Dave Meier	.06	
286	*Kirby Puckett*	22.00	
288	Ken Schrom	.06	
290	Tim Teufel	.08	
291	Frank Viola	.50	
293	Don Aase	.06	
295	• Bob Boone	.08	
296	Mike Brown	.06	
297	Rod Carew	.85	
300	Brian Downing	.10	
301	Ken Forsch	.08	
302	Bobby Grich	.10	
303	Reggie Jackson	.60	
304	Tommy John	.20	
306	Bruce Kison	.06	
307	Fred Lynn	.20	
311	Dick Schofield	.10	
313	Jim Slaton	.06	
316	Mike Witt	.12	
317	Geoff Zahn	.06	
318	Len Barker	.08	
319	Steve Bedrosian	.12	
321	Rick Camp	.06	
323	*Jeff Dedmon* (FC)	.12	
324	Terry Forster	.08	
325	Gene Garber	.06	
326	*Albert Hall* (FC)	.15	
327	Terry Harper	.06	
328	Bob Horner	.15	
333	Craig McMurtry	.06	
335	Dale Murphy	.60	
337	Pascual Perez	.10	
338	Gerald Perry	.20	
341	Alex Trevino	.06	
343	Alan Ashby	.06	
344	*Mark Bailey*	.10	
345	Kevin Bass	.10	
346	Enos Cabell	.06	
347	Jose Cruz	.10	
348	Bill Dawley	.06	
350	Bill Doran	.12	
351	Phil Garner	.08	
353	Mike LaCoss	.06	
355	Joe Niekro	.10	
356	Terry Puhl	.06	
358	Vern Ruhle	.06	
359	Nolan Ryan	4.00	
360	Joe Sambito	.06	
361	• Mike Scott	.15	
362	Dave Smith	.08	
364	Dickie Thon	.06	
367	Bob Bailor	.06	
368	Greg Brock	.08	
369	Carlos Diaz	.06	
370	Pedro Guerrero	.25	
371	*Orel Hershiser* (FC)	11.00	
373	Burt Hooton	.08	
374	*Ken Howell* (FC)	.15	
376	Candy Maldonado	.12	
377	Mike Marshall	.15	

380	Jerry Reuss	.08
381	*R.J. Reynolds*	.25
383	Bill Russell	.08
384	Steve Sax	.25
386	*Franklin Stubbs* (FC)	.40
387	Fernando Valenzuela	.35
388	Bob Welch	.15
390	Steve Yeager	.06
391	Pat Zachry	.06
393	Gary Carter	.35
394	Andre Dawson	.50
395	Miguel Dilone	.06
396	Dan Driessen	.08
397	Doug Flynn	.06
398	Terry Francona	.06
399	Bill Gullickson	.06
403	Gary Lucas	.06
404	David Palmer	.06
405	Tim Raines	.35
406	Mike Ramsey	.06
407	Jeff Reardon	.12
408	Steve Rogers	.08
410	Bryn Smith	.08
411	Mike Stenhouse	.06
412	Tim Wallach	.12
413	Jim Wohlford	.06
414	Bill Almon	.06
415	Keith Atherton	.06

492 Mark Langston

93 Darryl Strawberry

416	Bruce Bochte	.06
417	Tom Burgmeier	.06
418	Ray Burris	.06
420	Chris Codiroli	.06
421	Tim Conroy	.06
422	Mike Davis	.08
423	Jim Essian	.06
424	Mike Heath	.06
425	Rickey Henderson	4.25
427	Dave Kingman	.15
428	Bill Krueger	.06
429	Carney Lansford	.10
430	Steve McCatty	.06
431	• Joe Morgan	.35
432	Dwayne Murphy	.08
433	Tony Phillips	.08
436	*Curt Young* (FC)	.35
437	Luis Aponte	.06
438	Chris Bando	.06
439	Tony Bernazard	.06
440	Bert Blyleven	.15
441	Brett Butler	.10
442	Ernie Camacho	.06
443	Joe Carter (FC)	4.25
445	Jamie Easterly	.06
446	*Steve Farr* (FC)	.30
447	Mike Fischlin	.06

425 Rickey Henderson

443 Joe Carter

514	Scott Fletcher	.08
515	Jerry Hairston	.06
517	LaMarr Hoyt	.08
518	Ron Kittle	.10
519	Rudy Law	.06
520	Vance Law	.08
521	Greg Luzinski	.10
522	Gene Nelson	.06
523	Tom Paciorek	.06
526	Tom Seaver	.50
527	Roy Smalley	.06
528	Dan Spillner	.06
529	Mike Squires	.06
530	Greg Walker	.12
531	Cesar Cedeno	.10
532	Dave Concepcion	.12
533	*Eric Davis* (FC)	19.00
534	Nick Esasky	.15
535	Tom Foley	.06
536	*John Franco*	2.00
537	Brad Gulden	.06
542	Ron Oester	.06
543	Bob Owchinko	.06
544	Dave Parker	.25
545	Frank Pastore	.06
546	Tony Perez	.15
547	Ted Power	.06
548	Joe Price	.06
549	Gary Redus	.08
550	Pete Rose	1.00
551	Jeff Russell (FC)	.15
552	Mario Soto	.08
553	*Jay Tibbs* (FC)	.15
554	Duane Walker	.06
555	Alan Bannister	.06
556	Buddy Bell	.12
557	Danny Darwin	.06
558	Charlie Hough	.10
559	Bobby Jones	.06
560	Odell Jones	.06
561	*Jeff Kunkel* (FC)	.10
562	*Mike Mason*	.10
563	Pete O'Brien	.12
564	Larry Parrish	.10
565	Mickey Rivers	.08
566	Billy Sample	.06
569	Dave Stewart	.35
570	Frank Tanana	.10
572	Gary Ward	.08

359 Nolan Ryan

574	George Wright	.06
575	Ned Yost	.06
576	Mark Brouhard	.06
580	Cecil Cooper	.15
581	Rollie Fingers	.20
584	Dion James	.20
588	Paul Molitor	.15
590	Ben Oglivie	.08
591	Chuck Porter	.06
592	*Randy Ready* (FC)	.20
593	Ed Romero	.06
594	Bill Schroeder (FC)	.10
596	Ted Simmons	.12
597	Jim Sundberg	.08
598	Don Sutton	.30
600	Rick Waits	.06
601	Robin Yount	.75
602	Dusty Baker	.06
603	Bob Brenly	.06
604	Jack Clark	.20
605	Chili Davis	.15
606	Mark Davis	.10
607	*Dan Gladden* (FC)	.50
609	Mike Krukow	.08
611	Bob Lacy	.06
615	Jeff Leonard	.10
616	Randy Lerch	.06

1985 Fleer

536 John Franco

236 Terry Pendleton

1985 FLEER UPDATE

The realization among hobbyists of the scarcity of the 1984 Fleer Updates generated a massive demand for this 1985 edition. But this 132-card set, issued near the close of the 1985 baseball season, lacked the big names found in the year's earlier edition. That, plus the relative abundance of sets, meant that prices for the boxed update sets have remained low, in stark contrast to the 1984 set. Except for the "U" prefix of the card number on the back (omitted from the following list), there is nothing to distinguish the Updates from the regular 1985 Fleer cards. Many unknown rookies appear in the 1985 Fleer Update because Fleer, unlike Topps, agreed with the Major League Players Association to print cards for all of its members.

		MINT
Complete set		**$21.00**
Commons		**.10**

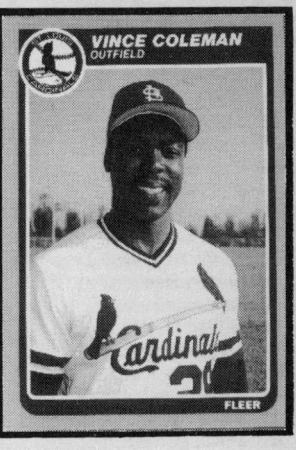

28 Vince Coleman

1	Don Aase	$.15
3	Dusty Baker	.15
4	Dale Berra	.10
5	Karl Best	.15
6	Tim Birtsas (FC)	.20
7	Vida Blue	.20
8	Rich Bordi	.10
9	Daryl Boston (FC)	.20
10	Hubie Brooks	.20
11	Chris Brown (FC)	.25
12	Tom Browning (FC)	1.25
14	Tim Burke (FC)	.45
15	Ray Burris	.10
16	Jeff Burroughs	.15
17	Ivan Calderon (FC)	2.00
18	Jeff Calhoun	.20
19	Bill Campbell	.10
20	Don Carman (FC)	.35
21	Gary Carter	.85
24	Rick Cerone	.10
25	Jack Clark	.35
26	Pat Clements (FC)	.20
27	Stewart Cliburn (FC)	.15
28	Vince Coleman (FC)	12.00
29	Dave Collins	.15
30	Fritz Connally	.15
31	Henry Cotto (FC)	.20

32	Danny Darwin	.15
33	Darren Daulton (FC)	.20
34	Jerry Davis	.15
35	Brian Dayett	.15
36	Ken Dixon	.10
38	Mariano Duncan (FC)	.20
39	Bob Fallon	.15
40	Brian Fisher (FC)	.25
43	Greg Gagne (FC)	.35
44	Oscar Gamble	.15

1985 Fleer Update

51 Rickey Henderson

1985 TOPPS

For the first time in its history, Topps added amateur players to its annual edition of baseball cards. The 792-card set features 16 cards showing members of the 1984 U.S. Olympic baseball team. Each player (as well as head coach Rod Dedeaux) appears in his Olympic uniform on what would come to be known as "pre-rookie" cards. Mark McGwire and Cory Snyder are the top names in this group. Another specialty subset presents a dozen "#1 Draft Pick" cards. As for the rest of the set, notable regular rookies include Roger Clemens, Alvin Davis, Eric Davis, Dwight Gooden, Mark Gubicza, Orel Hershiser, Mark Langston, Kirby Puckett, and Bret Saberhagen.

		MINT
Complete set		**$110.00**
Commons		**.06**

401 Mark McGwire

1	Record Breaker (Carlton Fisk)	$ .15
2	Record Breaker (Steve Garvey)	.20
3	Record Breaker (Dwight Gooden)	1.00
4	Record Breaker (Cliff Johnson)	.08
5	Record Breaker (Joe Morgan)	.15
6	Record Breaker (Pete Rose)	.60
7	Record Breaker (Nolan Ryan)	.30
8	Record Breaker (Juan Samuel) (FC)	.20
9	Record Breaker (Bruce Sutter)	.12
10	Record Breaker (Don Sutton)	.20
15	Jerry Koosman	.10
17	Mike Scott	.15
23	*Bret Saberhagen*	5.00
24	Jesse Barfield	.25
25	Steve Bedrosian	.12
30	Cal Ripken	.50
35	Graig Nettles	.15
40	Phil Niekro	.25
48	Tony Fernandez (FC)	1.25
50	John Candelaria	.10
54	Cesar Cedeno	.10
55	Frank Tanana	.10
65	Bill Buckner	.10
67	*Rafael Santana* (FC)	.15
68	Von Hayes	.10
69	*Jim Winn* (FC)	.10
70	Don Baylor	.15
72	Rick Sutcliffe	.12
80	Keith Hernandez	.30
85	Mike Marshall	.15
90	Rich Gossage	.20
93	*Don Schulze* (FC)	.10
95	Jose Cruz	.12
96	Johnny Ray	.10
100	George Brett	.50
105	Ron Kittle	.10

1985 Topps

760 Nolan Ryan

627 Eric Davis

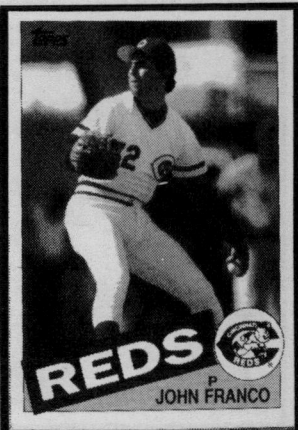

417 John Franco

181 Roger Clemens

414	Gary Ward	.08
415	Ron Darling	.50
416	Wayne Gross	.06
417	*John Franco* (FC)	1.50
418	Ken Landreaux	.08
419	Mike Caldwell	.08
420	Andre Dawson	.30
421	Dave Rucker	.08
422	Carney Lansford	.10
423	Barry Bonnell	.08
424	*Al Nipper* (FC)	.12
425	Mike Hargrove	.06
426	Vern Ruhle	.06
429	Rick Cerone	.06
430	Ron Davis	.06
431	U.L. Washington	.06
432	Thad Bosley	.06
433	Jim Morrison	.06
434	Gene Richards	.06
435	Dan Petry	.06
436	Willie Aikens	.08
437	Al Jones	.06
438	Joe Torre	.08
439	Junior Ortiz	.06
440	Fernando Valenzuela	.30
441	Duane Walker	.06
442	Ken Forsch	.06
443	George Wright	.06

625 Mark Langston

23 Bret Saberhagen

444	Tony Phillips	.10
445	Tippy Martinez	.06
446	Jim Sundberg	.08
447	Jeff Lahti	.06
448	Derrel Thomas	.06
449	*Phil Bradley*	.50
450	Steve Garvey	.45
451	Bruce Hurst	.12
454	Glenn Wilson	.08
455	Bob Knepper	.08
456	Tim Foli	.06
457	Cecilio Guante	.06
458	Randy Johnson	.06
459	Charlie Leibrandt	.06
460	Ryne Sandberg	.65
461	Marty Castillo	.06
462	Gary Lavelle	.06
463	Dave Collins	.08
464	*Mike Mason* (FC)	.08
465	Bob Grich	.10
466	Tony LaRussa	.10
467	Ed Lynch	.06
468	Wayne Krenchicki	.06
469	Sammy Stewart	.06
470	Steve Sax	.25
471	Pete Ladd	.06
472	Jim Essian	.06

48 Tony Fernandez

473	Tim Wallach	.12
474	Kurt Kepshire	.06
475	Andre Thornton	.10
476	*Jeff Stone* (FC)	.12
477	Bob Ojeda	.10
478	Kurt Bevacqua	.06
479	Mike Madden	.06
480	Lou Whitaker	.25
481	Dale Murray	.08
483	Mike Smithson	.06
484	Larry Bowa	.10
485	Matt Young	.06
487	*Frank Williams*	.15
488	Joel Skinner (FC)	.08
489	Bryan Clark	.06
490	Jason Thompson	.06
491	Rick Camp	.06
492	Dave Johnson	.08
493	*Orel Hershiser* (FC)	7.00
494	Rich Dauer	.06
495	Mario Soto	.08
496	Donnie Scott	.06
497	Gary Pettis	.15
498	Ed Romero	.06
499	Danny Cox (FC)	.20
500	Mike Schmidt	1.00
501	Dan Schatzeder	.06
502	Rick Miller	.06
503	Tim Conroy	.06
504	Jerry Willard	.06
505	Jim Beattie	.06
506	*Franklin Stubbs* (FC)	.25
507	Ray Fontenot	.06
508	John Shelby	.08
509	Milt May	.06
510	Kent Hrbek	.25
511	Lee Smith	.15
512	Tom Brookens	.06
515	Dave Concepcion	.12
516	Roy Lee Jackson	.06
517	Jerry Martin	.06
518	Chris Chambliss	.08
519	Doug Rader	.06
520	LaMarr Hoyt	.06
521	Rick Dempsey	.08
522	Paul Molitor	.15
523	Candy Maldonado	.10
524	Rob Wilfong	.06
525	Darrell Porter	.08
526	Dave Palmer	.06
528	Bill Krueger	.06
529	Rich Gedman	.10
530	Dave Dravecky	.15
531	Joe Lefebvre	.06
532	Frank DiPino	.06
533	Tony Bernazard	.06
534	Brian Dayett (FC)	.06
535	Pat Putnam	.06
536	*Kirby Puckett* (FC)	**16.00**
537	Don Robinson	.10
538	Keith Moreland	.08
539	Aurelio Lopez	.06
540	Claudell Washington	.10
541	Mark Davis	.08
542	Don Slaught	.06
543	Mike Squires	.06
544	Bruce Kison	.06
545	Lloyd Moseby	.10
546	Brent Gaff	.06
547	Pete Rose	.60
548	Larry Parrish	.08
549	Mike Scioscia	.08
550	Scott McGregor	.08
551	Andy Van Slyke	.40
552	Chris Codiroli	.06
555	Bob Stanley	.06

556	Sixto Lezcano	.06
557	Len Barker	.06
558	Carmelo Martinez	.06
559	Jay Howell	.08
560	Bill Madlock	.12
561	Darryl Motley	.06
562	Houston Jimenez	.06
563	Dick Ruthven	.06
564	Alan Ashby	.06
565	Kirk Gibson	.35
566	Ed Vande Berg	.06
567	Joel Youngblood	.06
568	Cliff Johnson	.06
569	Ken Oberkfell	.06
570	Darryl Strawberry	4.00
571	Charlie Hough	.08
572	Tom Paciorek	.06
573	*Jay Tibbs* (FC)	.15
574	Joe Altobelli	.06
575	Pedro Guerrero	.25
576	Jaime Cocanower	.06
577	Chris Speier	.06
578	Terry Francona	.06
579	*Ron Romanick*	.10
580	• Dwight Evans	.15
581	Mark Wagner	.06
582	Ken Phelps (FC)	.20
583	Bobby Brown	.06
584	Kevin Gross	.10
585	Butch Wynegar	.06
586	Bill Scherrer	.06
587	Doug Frobel	.06
588	Bobby Castillo	.06
589	Bob Dernier	.06
590	Ray Knight	.10
591	Larry Herndon	.06
592	*Jeff Robinson*	.30
593	Rick Leach	.06
594	Curt Wilkerson (FC)	.08
595	Larry Gura	.06
596	Jerry Hairston	.06
598	Jose Oquendo	.08
599	Storm Davis	.12
600	Pete Rose	1.00
601	Tom Lasorda	.12
602	*Jeff Dedmon*	.10
603	Rick Manning	.06
604	Daryl Sconiers	.06
605	Ozzie Smith	.15

115 Rickey Henderson

606	Rich Gale	.06
607	Bill Almon	.06
608	Craig Lefferts	.08
609	Broderick Perkins	.06
610	Jack Morris	.35
611	Ozzie Virgil	.06
612	Mike Armstrong	.06
613	Terry Puhl	.06
614	Al Williams	.06
615	Marvell Wynne	.06
616	Scott Sanderson	.06
617	Willie Wilson	.10
618	Pete Falcone	.06
619	Jeff Leonard	.10
620	*Dwight Gooden*	10.00
621	Marvis Foley	.06
622	Luis Leal	.06
623	Greg Walker	.10
624	Benny Ayala	.06
625	*Mark Langston*	3.75
626	German Rivera	.06
627	*Eric Davis* (FC)	16.00
628	Rene Lachemann	.06
629	Dick Schofield	.12
630	Tim Raines	.35
638	*Mike Pagliarulo* (FC)	.75
649	Sid Fernandez (FC)	.90

1985 Topps

127 Mark Gubicza

771	Geoff Zahn	.06
772	Johnnie LeMaster	.06
773	Hal McRae	.10
774	Dennis Lamp	.06
775	Mookie Wilson	.10
776	Jerry Royster	.06
777	Ned Yost	.06
778	Mike Davis	.08
779	Nick Esasky	.10
780	Mike Flanagan	.10
781	Jim Gantner	.08
782	Tom Niedenfuer	.08
783	Mike Jorgensen	.06
784	Checklist 661-792	.06
785	Tony Armas	.08
786	Enos Cabell	.06
787	Jim Wohlford	.06
788	Steve Comer	.06
789	Luis Salazar	.06
790	Ron Guidry	.25
791	Ivan DeJesus	.06
792	Darrell Evans	.10

1985 TOPPS TRADED

Collectors began evaluating the Traded sets more on the basis of the specific players included rather than on considerations of scarcity. In 1985, the pickings were slim indeed; the lack of appealing names caused a drastic drop in demand. As for first-card originals, Vince Coleman of the Cardinals and Milwaukee Brewers pitcher Ted Higuera head the list, while Rickey Henderson and Howard Johnson are tops among veteran players. Meanwhile, the hobby debate about the legitimacy of the Traded set continued. Card purists maintained that the 132-card set wasn't a real collectible because it wasn't sold through retail chains and candy stores like standard baseball cards.

		MINT
Complete set		**$23.00**
Commons		**.10**

1	Don Aase	$ .10
2	Bill Almon	.10
3	Benny Ayala	.10
4	Dusty Baker	.15
5	George Bamberger	.10
6	Dale Berra	.10
8	Daryl Boston (FC)	.20
9	Hubie Brooks	.25
10	Chris Brown (FC)	.25
11	Tom Browning (FC)	1.25
12	Al Bumbry	.10
13	Ray Burris	.10
14	Jeff Burroughs	.15
15	Bill Campbell	.10
16	Don Carman (FC)	.35
17	Gary Carter	.75
18	Bobby Castillo	.10
19	Bill Caudill	.10
20	Rick Cerone	.10
22	Jack Clark	.35
23	Pat Clements (FC)	.20
24	Vince Coleman (FC)	10.00
25	Dave Collins	.15
26	Danny Darwin	.15
27	Jim Davenport	.10
30	Ivan DeJesus	.10
31	Ken Dixon	.10
32	Mariano Duncan (FC)	.20
34	Mike Fitzgerald	.10
35	Ray Fontenot	.10
36	Greg Gagne (FC)	.35

1985 Topps Traded

24 Vince Coleman

88	Al Oliver	.30
89	Joe Orsulak (FC)	.20
92	Jim Presley (FC)	.75
93	Rick Reuschel	.25
100	Paul Runge (FC)	.15
101	Mark Salas (FC)	.15
102	Luis Salazar	.10
104	Rick Schu (FC)	.20
106	Larry Sheets (FC)	.50
108	Roy Smalley	.15
109	Lonnie Smith	.15
110	Nate Snell	.20
112	Mike Stenhouse	.15
114	Jim Sundberg	.15
115	• Bruce Sutter	.25
116	Don Sutton	.65
117	Kent Tekulve	.15
119	Walt Terrell	.15
120	Mickey Tettleton (FC)	**1.25**
122	Rich Thompson	.15
124	John Tudor	.25
125	Jose Uribe (FC)	.25
126	Bobby Valentine	.10
127	Dave Von Ohlen	.10
128	U.L. Washington	.10
129	• Earl Weaver	.15
131	Herm Winningham (FC)	.20

37	Oscar Gamble	.15
38	Scott Garrelts	.60
39	Bob Gibson	.10
40	Jim Gott	.10
42	Alfredo Griffin	.15
43	Ozzie Guillen (FC)	**1.00**
46	Toby Harrah	.15
48	Ron Hassey	.10
49	Rickey Henderson	**4.00**
51	George Hendrick	.15
52	Joe Hesketh (FC)	.20
53	Teddy Higuera (FC)	**2.50**
54	Donnie Hill	.10
56	Burt Hooton	.15
57	Jay Howell	.15
58	Ken Howell (FC)	.15
59	LaMarr Hoyt	.10
60	Tim Hulett (FC)	.15
62	Steve Jeltz (FC)	.10
64	Howard Johnson	**2.00**
66	Steve Kemp	.10
71	Dave LaPoint	.20
73	Vance Law	.15
77	Fred Lynn	.30
78	• Billy Martin	.20
81	Gene Mauch	.15
82	Oddibe McDowell	.60
83	Roger McDowell (FC)	**1.00**

49 Rickey Henderson

1986 DONRUSS

The 660-card Donruss set for 1986 kept the Memphis company popular among collectors. This simply designed set offers a unique blend of single-player cards and unusual subsets. Specialty cards include a pair honoring record-breaker Pete Rose, a card of brothers Joe and Phil Niekro, and a shot of the base-stealing tandem of Vince Coleman and Willie McGee. The Rated Rookie cards, however, remain the favorite subset in the issue (they are not to be confused with the similar but separate 1986 Donruss Rookies set). Jose Canseco, Kal Daniels, Andres Galarraga, Fred McGriff, Cory Snyder, Danny Tartabull, and Todd Worrell star in the 20-card run. Note that Canseco's card alone makes up close to half the set's total value.

39 Jose Canseco

		MINT
Complete set		**$210.00**
Commons		**.06**
1	Kirk Gibson (DK)	$ .30
4	George Bell (DK)	.30
11	Bret Saberhagen (DK)	.25
18	Orel Hershiser (DK)	1.00
19	Johnny Ray (DK)	.12
20	Gary Ward (DK)	.10
25	Andre Dawson (DK)	.30
26	Dwight Gooden (DK)	1.00
27	*Kal Daniels* (RR) (FC)	4.00
28	*Fred McGriff* (RR) (FC)	21.00
29	*Cory Snyder* (RR) (FC)	2.00
30	*Jose Guzman* (RR) (FC)	.30
31	*Ty Gainey* (RR) (FC)	.10
33	*Andres Galarraga (RR) (FC)*	4.50
35	*Mark McLemore* (RR) (FC)	.20
37	*Paul O'Neill* (RR) (FC)	3.00
38	*Danny Tartabull* (RR)	.85
39	*Jose Canseco* (RR) (FC)	91.00
40	*Juan Nieves* (RR) (FC)	.40
41	*Lance McCullers* (RR) (FC)	.35
42	*Rick Surhoff* (RR) (FC)	.08
43	*Todd Worrell* (RR) (FC)	1.00
44	*Bob Kipper* (RR) (FC)	.20
45	*John Habyan* (RR) (FC)	.15
46	*Mike Woodard* (RR) (FC)	.10
47	Mike Boddicker	.15
48	Robin Yount	1.00
49	Lou Whitaker	.30
50	"Oil Can" Boyd	.08
51	Rickey Henderson	2.00
52	Mike Marshall	.15
53	George Brett	.50
54	Dave Kingman	.15
55	Hubie Brooks	.12
56	*Oddibe McDowell* (FC)	.25
57	Doug DeCinces	.10
58	Britt Burns	.06
59	Ozzie Smith	.15
60	Jose Cruz	.12
61	Mike Schmidt	2.00

1986 Donruss

28 Fred McGriff

512 Cecil Fielder

122	Dan Spillner	.06
123	Mike Young	.06
124	Paul Molitor	.15
125	Kirk Gibson	.35
126	Ken Griffey	.12
127	Tony Armas	.08
128	*Mariano Duncan* (FC)	.20
129	Pat Tabler	.08
130	Frank White	.10
131	Carney Lansford	.10
132	Vance Law	.08
133	Dick Schofield	.06
134	Wayne Tolleson	.06
135	Greg Walker	.10
136	Denny Walling	.06
137	Ozzie Virgil	.06
138	Ricky Horton	.08
139	LaMarr Hoyt	.06
140	Wayne Krenchicki	.06
142	Cecilio Guante	.06
143	Mike Krukow	.08
144	Lee Smith	.10
145	Edwin Nunez	.06
146	Dave Stieb	.12
149	Danny Darwin	.06
150	Chris Pittaro	.06
151	Bill Buckner	.12
152	Mike Pagliarulo	.20
153	Bill Russell	.08
154	Brook Jacoby	.15
155	Pat Sheridan	.06
156	*Mike Gallego* (FC)	.15
159	Toby Harrah	.08
160	Richard Dotson	.10
161	Bob Knepper	.08
162	Dave Dravecky	.08
164	Eric Davis	3.50
165	Gerald Perry	.10
166	Rick Rhoden	.10
167	Keith Moreland	.08
168	Jack Clark	.20
169	Storm Davis	.15
170	Cecil Cooper	.12
171	Alan Trammell	.35
172	Roger Clemens	6.00
173	Don Mattingly	7.00
174	Pedro Guerrero	.20
175	Willie Wilson	.10
177	Tim Raines	.40

172 Roger Clemens

179	Mike Witt	.10
180	Harold Baines	.15
181	*Vince Coleman* (FC)	5.25
182	*Jeff Heathcock* (FC)	.10
183	Steve Carlton	.45
184	Mario Soto	.08
185	Goose Gossage	.20
186	Johnny Ray	.12
187	Dan Gladden	.08
188	Bob Horner	.15
189	Rick Sutcliffe	.12
190	Keith Hernandez	.35
191	Phil Bradley	.20
192	Tom Brunansky	.15
193	Jesse Barfield	.20
194	Frank Viola	.25
195	Willie Upshaw	.08
196	Jim Beattie	.06
197	Darryl Strawberry	4.50
198	Ron Cey	.10
199	Steve Bedrosian	.12
200	Steve Kemp	.08
201	Manny Trillo	.08
202	Garry Templeton	.08
203	Dave Parker	.25
205	Terry Pendleton	.15
206	Terry Puhl	.06

1986 Donruss

181 Vince Coleman

207	Bobby Grich	.10
208	*Ozzie Guillen* (FC)	1.50
209	Jeff Reardon	.12
210	Cal Ripken, Jr	1.00
211	Bill Schroeder	.06
212	Dan Petry	.08
213	Jim Rice	.40
214	Dave Righetti	.20
215	Fernando Valenzuela	.35
216	Julio Franco	.12
217	Darryl Motley	.06
218	Dave Collins	.08
219	Tim Wallach	.12
222	Steve Balboni	.08
223	Jay Howell	.10
224	Joe Carter	.65
225	Ed Whitson	.08
226	Orel Hershiser	1.25
229	Rollie Fingers	.20
230	• Bob Boone	.10
234	Eric Show	.08
235	Jose DeLeon	.12
236	*Jose Uribe* (FC)	.25
237	Moose Haas	.06
239	Dennis Eckersley	.15
240	Mike Moore	.10
242	Tim Teufel	.06

243	Dave Concepcion	.12
244	Floyd Bannister	.10
245	Fred Lynn	.20
247	Walt Terrell	.06
248	Dave Winfield	.45
249	• Dwight Evans	.12
250	*Dennis Powell* (FC)	.08
251	Andre Thornton	.10
254	David Palmer ("P" on front)	1.00
257	Julio Cruz	.06
258	Nolan Ryan	2.00
265	Mark Davis	.10
266	Bob Dernier	.06
267	Matt Young	.06
268	Jim Clancy	.08
271	Bob Gibson	.06
273	Rich Gedman	.06
275	Ken Howell	.06
276	Mel Hall	.08
279	*Herman Winningham* (FC)	.12
280	Rod Carew	.75
281	Don Slaught	.06
286	Nick Esasky	.15
289	Jody Davis	.06
290	Darrell Porter	.10
292	Ted Simmons	.12
295	Dale Berra	.06
296	Greg Brock	.08
297	Charlie Leibrandt	.06
299	Bryn Smith	.08
300	Burt Hooton	.08
301	*Stu Cliburn* (FC)	.08
302	Luis Salazar	.06
304	Frank DiPino	.06
305	Von Hayes	.10
306	Gary Redus (1983 2B is 20)	1.00
310	Rick Cerone	.06
311	Shawon Dunston	.25
312	Howard Johnson	.25
313	Jim Presley	.10
314	Gary Gaetti	.20
315	Luis Leal	.06
317	Bill Caudill	.06
318	Dave Henderson	.15
319	Rafael Santana	.06
320	Leon Durham	.08
321	Bruce Sutter	.15

482 Lenny Dykstra

197 Darryl Strawberry

1986 Donruss

37 Paul O'Neill

67 Ryne Sandberg

514	Tippy Martinez	.06
515	*Billy Robidoux* (FC)	.10
517	Bruce Hurst	.12
518	Rich Bordi	.06
519	Steve Yeager	.06
521	Hal McRae	.10
522	Jose Rijo	.10
523	*Mitch Webster* (FC)	.20
524	*Jack Howell* (FC)	.35
526	Ron Kittle	.10
527	Phil Garner	.08
529	Kevin Gross	.08
530	Bo Diaz	.08
532	Rick Reuschel	.10
540	Steve Sax	.25
541	Dan Quisenberry	.10
543	*Floyd Youmans* (FC)	.35
544	*Steve Buechele* (FC)	.25
546	Joe DeSa	.06
548	Kevin Bass	.10
549	Tom Foley	.06
551	Bruce Bochy	.06
553	*Chris Brown* (FC)	.15
556	Danny Heep	.06
557	Darnell Coles	.08
558	Greg Gagne	.08
559	Ernie Whitt	.08
561	Jimmy Key	.15
562	Billy Swift (FC)	.15
563	Ron Darling	.15
565	Zane Smith (FC)	.20
566	Sid Bream	.10
567	Joel Youngblood ("IF" on front)	1.00
567	Joel Youngblood ("P" on front)	.08
570	Rick Schu	.06
573	Al Holland	.06
576	Mike Flanagan	.10
577	Tim Leary (FC)	.35
580	Phil Niekro	.30
583	Mark Gubicza	.12
584	*Stan Javier* (FC)	.15
586	Jeff Russell	.10
588	Steve Farr	.08
589	*Steve Ontiveros* (FC)	.10
593	Larry Herndon	.08
596	*Pat Perry* (FC)	.12
597	Ray Knight	.10

371 Wade Boggs

598	*Steve Lombardozzi* (FC)	.20
600	*Pat Clements* (FC)	.12
601	Joe Niekro	.10
603	*Dwayne Henry* (FC)	.10
604	Mookie Wilson	.10
609	Tom Seaver (green stripes around name)	.40
609	Tom Seaver (yellow stripes around name)	2.00
610	Neil Allen	.06
611	Don Sutton	.30
612	*Fred Toliver* (FC)	.15
617	Bill Madlock	.12
619	Dave Stewart	.12
625	Sid Fernandez	.12
629	*Roger McDowell* (FC)	.65
634	*Mike Felder* (FC)	.15
636	Bob Ojeda	.08
644	Ty-Breaking Hit (Pete Rose)	.50
645	• Knuckle Brothers (Joe Niekro, Phil Niekro)	.15
648	Cesar Cedeno	.10
649	Bert Blyleven	.15
651	Fleet Feet (Vince Coleman (FC), Willie McGee)	.35
653	King of Kings (Pete Rose)	.75

1986 DONRUSS ROOKIES

Donruss followed the leaders in 1986 by creating "The Rookies," a separate set issued in the fall to compete with Topps and Fleer. Unlike the other companies, however, Donruss ignored cards of traded players. This streamlined concept resulted in just 55 cards of the leading rookies of 1986 (along with a rather useless unnumbered checklist). To distinguish the two Donruss sets, border colors switched from the blue of the regular issue to green, and "The Rookies" logo is found on the lower left portion of the front of each card. High-powered newcomers include Jose Canseco, Will Clark, Bo Jackson, Kevin Mitchell, and Ruben Sierra. The value of the set tripled in its first year.

	MINT
Complete set	**$57.00**
Commons	**.15**

1	Wally Joyner (FC)	**$4.00**
2	Tracy Jones (FC)	.50
3	Allan Anderson (FC)	.40
4	Ed Correa (FC)	.25
5	Reggie Williams	.20
6	Charlie Kerfeld	.20

32 Will Clark

38 Bo Jackson

7	Andres Galarraga	.80
8	Bob Tewksbury	.20
9	Al Newman	.15
10	Andres Thomas (FC)	.40
11	Barry Bonds (FC)	**7.00**
12	Juan Nieves	.20
13	Mark Eichhorn (FC)	.25
14	Dan Plesac (FC)	.40
15	Cory Snyder	.75
16	Kelly Gruber	**3.25**
17	Kevin Mitchell (FC)	**9.00**

19	Mitch Williams	.40	36	Scott Bankhead (FC)	.20
20	John Cerutti (FC)	.25	37	Dale Sveum (FC)	.25
21	Todd Worrell	.50	38	Bo Jackson (FC)	12.00
22	Jose Canseco	11.00	39	Rob Thompson (FC)	.50
23	Pete Incaviglia (FC)	.90	40	Eric Plunk	.25
24	Jose Guzman	.25	41	Bill Bathe	.20
25	Scott Bailes (FC)	.25	42	John Kruk (FC)	.40
26	Greg Mathews (FC)	.25	43	Andy Allanson	.20
27	Eric King (FC)	.20	44	Mark Portugal	.20
28	Paul Assenmacher	.20	45	Danny Tartabull	1.00
29	Jeff Sellers	.25	46	Bob Kipper	.15
30	Bobby Bonilla (FC)	6.00	47	Gene Walter	.20
31	Doug Drabek (FC)	.30	48	Rey Quinones	.15
32	Will Clark (FC)	13.00	49	Bobby Witt (FC)	1.25
34	Jim Deshaies (FC)	.25	50	Bill Mooneyham	.15
35	Mike Lavalliere (LaValliere) (FC)	.30	51	John Cangelosi (FC)	.20
			52	Ruben Sierra (FC)	8.00

1986 FLEER

Striking photographs and a simple card design make the 1986 Fleer set a winner. Maximum space on each of the 660 cards is devoted to photos, which are surrounded by a dark blue border. Fleer was the only company to provide complete major and minor league stats for all players on card backs, which are otherwise bleak and no longer contain the black-and-white photo of past years. Popular with collectors is a run of 10 Major League Prospect cards, on which two potential rookie sensations, usually teammates, share a card front. Notables in this subset include Jose Canseco, Kal Daniels, and Cory Snyder. The card that pairs Canseco with Eric Plunk is the most expensive in the set.

		MINT			
Complete set		**$130.00**	19	Bret Saberhagen	1.50
Commons		**.06**	23	John Wathan	.08
			24	Frank White	.10
			25	Willie Wilson	.12
4	Bud Black	$ .06	27	Steve Braun	.06
5	George Brett	.50	30	Jack Clark	.20
7	Steve Farr	.08	31	*Vince Coleman*	5.00
8	Mark Gubicza	.12	32	Danny Cox	.10
9	Dane Iorg	.06	35	Bob Forsch	.08
10	Danny Jackson	.20	37	Tom Herr	.10
14	Hal McRae	.10	40	Jeff Lahti	.06
17	Jorge Orta	.06	42	Willie McGee	.15
			43	Tom Nieto	.06

649 Major League Prospect

44	Terry Pendleton	.15		
46	Ozzie Smith	.15		
47	John Tudor	.10		
48	Andy Van Slyke	.15		
49	*Todd Worrell* (FC)	.90		
50	Jim Acker	.06		
52	Jesse Barfield	.20		
53	George Bell	.30		
56	Jim Clancy	.06		
60	Tom Henke	.12		
61	Garth Iorg	.06		
63	Jimmy Key	.15		
64	Dennis Lamp	.06		
67	Lloyd Moseby	.10		
69	Al Oliver	.10		
70	Dave Stieb	.12		
72	Willie Upshaw	.08		
73	Ernie Whitt	.08		
74	*Rick Aguilera* (FC)	.25		
76	Gary Carter	.25		
77	Ron Darling	.15		
'78	*Len Dykstra* (FC)	4.00		
79	Sid Fernandez	.12		
80	George Foster	.15		
81	Dwight Gooden	3.00		
83	Danny Heep	.06		
84	Keith Hernandez	.30		
85	Howard Johnson	.15		
86	Ray Knight	.08		
87	Terry Leach	.08		
89	*Roger McDowell* (FC)	.50		
94	Doug Sisk	.06		
95	Rusty Staub	.10		
96	Darryl Strawberry	4.00
97	Mookie Wilson	.10
98	Neil Allen	.06
99	Don Baylor	.12
100	Dale Berra	.06
104	*Brian Fisher*	.25
105	Ken Griffey	.10
106	Ron Guidry	.20
108	Rickey Henderson	.50
109	Don Mattingly	5.00
112	Phil Niekro	.25
113	Mike Pagliarulo	.20
114	Dan Pasqua	.20
115	Willie Randolph	.10
116	Dave Righetti	.20
121	Dave Winfield	.35
124	Bob Bailor	.06
125	Greg Brock	.08
126	Enos Cabell	.06
128	Carlos Diaz	.06
129	*Mariano Duncan*	.15
130	Pedro Guerrero	.25
131	Orel Hershiser	1.25
135	Bill Madlock	.12
136	Candy Maldonado	.10
137	Mike Marshall	.15
143	Steve Sax	.25
145	Fernando Valenzuela	.30
146	Bob Welch	.12
149	• Bob Boone	.08
150	John Candelaria	.10
151	Rod Carew	.40
152	*Stewart Cliburn* (FC)	.12

345 Roger Clemens

31 Vince Coleman

646 Major League Prospect

232	Jack Morris	.25	278	Fred Lynn	.20
234	Lance Parrish	.20	282	Eddie Murray	.40
235	Dan Petry	.08	283	Floyd Rayford	.06
236	Alex Sanchez	.06	284	Cal Ripken Jr.	.75
237	Bill Scherrer	.06	286	Larry Sheets	.15
239	Frank Tanana	.10	287	John Shelby	.06
241	Alan Trammell	.25	288	Nate Snell	.06
242	Lou Whitaker	.30	291	Mike Young	.06
243	Milt Wilcox	.06	292	Alan Ashby	.06
244	Hubie Brooks	.10	293	Mark Bailey	.06
245	*Tim Burke* (FC)	.45	294	Kevin Bass	.10
246	Andre Dawson	.35	296	Jose Cruz	.15
249	Bill Gullickson	.06	297	Glenn Davis	2.00
250	Joe Hesketh	.06	300	Bill Doran	.10
251	Bill Laskey	.06	301	Phil Garner	.08
252	Vance Law	.08	303	*Charlie Kerfeld* (FC)	.15
256	Tim Raines	.35	304	Bob Knepper	.08
257	Jeff Reardon	.15	305	Ron Mathis	.06
258	Bert Roberge	.06	306	Jerry Mumphrey	.06
259	Dan Schatzeder	.06	307	Jim Pankovits	.06
260	Bryn Smith	.08	309	Craig Reynolds	.06
262	Scot Thompson	.06	310	Nolan Ryan	2.50
263	Tim Wallach	.12	311	Mike Scott	.15
264	U.L. Washington	.06	312	Dave Smith	.08
265	*Mitch Webster* (FC)	.25	313	Dickie Thon	.08
266	*Herm Winningham*	.15	316	Al Bumbry	.06
267	*Floyd Youmans* (FC)	.20	321	Steve Garvey	.30
268	Don Aase	.06	322	Goose Gossage	.20
270	Rich Dauer	.06	323	Tony Gwynn	.90
271	Storm Davis	.10	324	Andy Hawkins	.06
274	Jim Dwyer	.06	330	*Lance McCullers* (FC)	.25
276	Wayne Gross	.06	331	Kevin McReynolds	.30
277	Lee Lacy	.06	332	Graig Nettles	.15

653 Major League Prospect

334	Eric Show	.08	383	Rick Sutcliffe	.12
339	Tony Armas	.08	384	Steve Trout	.06
340	Marty Barrett	.10	386	Bert Blyleven	.15
341	Wade Boggs	2.75	387	Tom Brunansky	.15
343	Bill Buckner	.10	393	Pete Filson	.06
344	Mark Clear	.06	394	Gary Gaetti	.20
345	Roger Clemens	5.00	395	Greg Gagne	.10
346	Steve Crawford	.06	396	Mickey Hatcher	.06
347	Mike Easler	.08	397	Kent Hrbek	.25
348	• Dwight Evans	.12	398	Tim Laudner	.06
349	Rich Gedman	.08	399	Rick Lysander	.06
350	Jackie Gutierrez	.06	400	Dave Meier	.06
352	Bruce Hurst	.15	401	Kirby Puckett	4.50
354	Tim Lollar	.06	403	Ken Schrom	.06
355	Steve Lyons	.08	404	Roy Smalley	.06
356	Al Nipper	.06	405	Mike Smithson	.06
357	Bob Ojeda	.08	406	Mike Stenhouse	.06
358	Jim Rice	.30	407	Tim Teufel	.06
361	Thad Bosley	.06	408	Frank Viola	.35
363	Ron Cey	.10	409	Ron Washington	.06
364	Jody Davis	.06	410	Keith Atherton	.06
365	Bob Dernier	.06	411	Dusty Baker	.08
366	Shawon Dunston	.75	412	*Tim Birtsas*	.10
367	Leon Durham	.08	413	Bruce Bochte	.06
368	Dennis Eckersley	.20	414	Chris Codiroli	.08
369	Ray Fontenot	.06	415	Dave Collins	.08
371	Bill Hatcher	.10	416	Mike Davis	.08
372	Dave Lopes	.10	417	Alfredo Griffin	.08
373	Gary Matthews	.10	419	Steve Henderson	.06
377	Dick Ruthven	.06	420	Donnie Hill	.06
378	Ryne Sandberg	3.00	421	Jay Howell	.10
380	Lee Smith	.10	422	Tommy John	.20
382	Chris Speier	.06	423	Dave Kingman	.15

644 Major League Prospect

424	Bill Krueger	.06
425	Rick Langford	.06
426	Carney Lansford	.10
427	Steve McCatty	.06
428	Dwayne Murphy	.06
429	Steve Ontiveros (FC)	.10
430	Tony Phillips	.08
431	Jose Rijo	.10
432	Mickey Tettleton	.85
434	Larry Andersen	.06
435	Steve Carlton	.30
436	Don Carman	.25
437	Tim Corcoran	.06
438	Darren Daulton	.15
439	John Denny	.08
440	Tom Foley	.06
441	Greg Gross	.06
442	Kevin Gross	.06
443	Von Hayes	.12
444	Charles Hudson	.06
445	Garry Maddox	.08
446	Shane Rawley	.06
447	Dave Rucker	.06
448	John Russell	.06
449	Juan Samuel	.12
450	Mike Schmidt	.50
451	Rick Schu	.06
452	Dave Shipanoff	.06
453	• Dave Stewart	.15
454	Jeff Stone	.06
455	Kent Tekulve	.08
456	Ozzie Virgil	.06
457	Glenn Wilson	.08
458	Jim Beattie	.06
459	Karl Best	.06
460	Barry Bonnell	.06
461	Phil Bradley	.20
462	Ivan Calderon	1.25
463	Al Cowens	.06
464	Alvin Davis	.30
465	Dave Henderson	.10
466	Bob Kearney	.06
467	Mark Langston	.40
468	Bob Long	.06
469	Mike Moore	.12
470	Edwin Nunez	.06
471	Spike Owen	.06
472	Jack Perconte	.06
473	Jim Presley	.12
474	Donnie Scott	.06
475	Bill Swift (FC)	.10
476	Danny Tartabull	.45
477	Gorman Thomas	.10
478	Roy Thomas	.06
479	Ed Vande Berg	.06
480	Frank Wills	.06
481	Matt Young	.06
482	Ray Burris	.06
483	Jaime Cocanower	.06
484	Cecil Cooper	.10
485	Danny Darwin	.06
486	Rollie Fingers	.20
487	Jim Gantner	.06
488	Bob Gibson	.06

489	Moose Haas	.06
490	*Teddy Higuera*	1.00
491	Paul Householder	.06
492	Pete Ladd	.06
493	Rick Manning	.06
494	Bob McClure	.06
495	Paul Molitor	.15
496	Charlie Moore	.06
497	Ben Oglivie	.08
498	Randy Ready	.06
499	*Earnie Riles*	.20
500	Ed Romero	.06
503	Ted Simmons	.15
505	Rick Waits	.06
506	Robin Yount	.30
507	Len Barker	.08
508	Steve Bedrosian	.12
510	Rick Camp	.06
513	Jeff Dedmon	.08
514	Terry Forster	.08
515	Gene Garber	.08
516	Terry Harper	.06
517	Bob Horner	.15
521	Rick Mahler	.08
522	Dale Murphy	.50
524	Pascual Perez	.10
525	Gerald Perry	.08

96 Darryl Strawberry

81 Dwight Gooden

527	*Steve Shields* (FC)	.10
528	Zane Smith	.10
529	Bruce Sutter	.12
530	*Milt Thompson* (FC)	.30
533	Vida Blue	.10
534	Bob Brenly	.08
535	*Chris Brown*	.15
536	Chili Davis	.10
537	Mark Davis	.15
538	Rob Deer	.10
541	Dan Gladden	.08
542	Jim Gott	.08
543	David Green	.06
548	Jeff Leonard	.10
549	Greg Minton	.06
550	Alex Trevino	.06
552	*Jose Uribe*	.20
558	*Steve Buechele* (FC)	.30
559	*Jose Guzman* (FC)	.20
560	Toby Harrah	.08
563	Burt Hooton	.08
564	Charlie Hough	.08
566	*Oddibe McDowell*	.20
568	Pete O'Brien	.10
569	Larry Parrish	.10
572	Don Slaught	.08
574	Duane Walker	.06

1986 Fleer

378 Ryne Sandberg

1986 FLEER UPDATE

What a difference a year makes! With the inclusion of popular players such as Jose Canseco, Wally Joyner, Kevin Mitchell, and Ruben Sierra, the 1986 Fleer Update set became an immediate hit. In contrast to Topps, the Fleer "extension" set contains a higher percentage of rookies in its 131 cards (and complete set checklist). Although the company skipped Bo Jackson, it scooped Topps by including the phenomenal Ruben Sierra of the Rangers. The Fleer Update cards differ from the standard 1986 cards only by a "U" prefix on the card numbers (omitted from the following lists). To satisfy collectors of rookie cards, hobby dealers broke up sets and sold popular cards in lots of 50 or 100.

		MINT
Complete set		**$41.00**
Commons		**.08**

20 Jose Canseco

1	Mike Aldrete (FC)	$ .35
2	Andy Allanson (FC)	.20
3	Neil Allen	.10
4	Joaquin Andujar	.10
5	Paul Assenmacher (FC)	.15
6	Scott Bailes (FC)	.25
7	Jay Baller (FC)	.15
8	Scott Bankhead (FC)	.20
9	Bill Bathe	.10
10	Don Baylor	.15
11	Billy Beane	.15
12	Steve Bedrosian	.15
14	Barry Bonds (FC)	7.00
15	Bobby Bonilla (FC)	6.00
16	Rich Bordi	.08
18	Tom Candiotti	.10
19	John Cangelosi (FC)	.10
20	Jose Canseco	12.00
21	Chuck Cary (FC)	.10
22	Juan Castillo (FC)	.10
23	Rick Cerone	.10
24	John Cerutti (FC)	.25
25	Will Clark (FC)	12.00
26	Mark Clear	.08
27	Darnell Coles (FC)	.20
28	Dave Collins	.10
30	Ed Correa (FC)	.20

31	Joe Cowley	.10
33	Rob Deer	.15
34	John Denny	.15
35	Jim DeShaies (Deshaies) (FC)	.25
36	Doug Drabek (FC)	.35
37	Mike Easler	.10
38	Mark Eichhorn (FC)	.20
41	Scott Fletcher	.15
42	Terry Forster	.10

1986 Fleer Update

105 Ruben Sierra

1986 TOPPS

At 792 cards, Topps continued as the largest set of baseball cards on the market. This design was one of Topps' boldest of the decade, with the team name in large letters at the top of each card. Because of the large size of the edition, there was room for a number of specialty subsets. Topps remained the only company to devote a card to each team manager (with a team checklist on the back). Twenty-two All-Star cards are also included, along with a seven-card subset of all-time hit king Pete Rose. On the negative side, Topps included few rookies in the set, opting to save them for the fall Traded set.

	MINT
Complete set	**$48.00**
Commons	**.05**

1	Pete Rose	$1.00
2	Rose Special 1963-1966	.35
3	Rose Special 1967-1970	.35
4	Rose Special 1971-1974	.35
5	Rose Special 1975-1978	.35
6	Rose Special 1979-1982	.35
7	Rose Special 1983-1985	.35
8	Dwayne Murphy	.07
10	Tony Gwynn	.50
11	Bob Ojeda	.07
12	*Jose Uribe* (FC)	.20
14	Julio Cruz	.05
15	Eddie Whitson	.05
16	Rick Schu (FC)	.07
17	Mike Stenhouse	.05
18	Brent Gaff	.05
19	Rich Hebner	.07
20	Lou Whitaker	.25
21	George Bamberger	.05
22	Duane Walker	.05
23	*Manny Lee* (FC)	.15
24	Len Barker	.07
25	Willie Wilson	.12
26	Frank DiPino	.05
27	Ray Knight	.07
28	Eric Davis	3.00
29	Tony Phillips	.10
30	Eddie Murray	.40
31	Jamie Easterly	.05
32	Steve Yeager	.05
33	Jeff Lahti	.05
34	Ken Phelps (FC)	.07
35	Jeff Reardon	.12
36	Tigers Ldrs (Lance Parrish)	.12
37	Mark Thurmond	.05
40	Ken Griffey	.10
41	Brad Wellman	.05
44	*Lance McCullers* (FC)	.25
45	Damaso Garcia	.05
46	Billy Hatcher (FC)	.20
47	Juan Berenguer	.05
50	Dan Quisenberry	.07
51	Not Issued	
52	Chris Welsh	.05
53	*Len Dykstra* (FC)	2.50
54	John Franco	.12
55	Fred Lynn	.15

386 Cecil Fielder

1986 Topps

661 Roger Clemens

389 Glenn Davis

120	Steve Carlton	.30
121	Nelson Simmons	.05
123	Greg Walker	.10
124	Luis Sanchez	.05
125	Dave Lopes	.07
126	Mets Ldrs (Mookie Wilson)	.07
127	*Jack Howell* (FC)	.25
128	John Wathan	.07
129	Jeff Dedmon (FC)	.05
130	Alan Trammell	.30
132	Razor Shines	.05
133	Andy McGaffigan	.05
134	Carney Lansford	.10
135	Joe Niekro	.10
136	Mike Hargrove	.05
137	Charlie Moore	.05
138	Mark Davis	.10
139	Daryl Boston	.07
140	John Candelaria	.10
143	Dave Van Gorder	.05
144	Doug Sisk	.05
145	Pedro Guerrero	.20
146	Jack Perconte	.05
147	Larry Sheets	.15
148	Mike Heath	.05
149	Brett Butler	.07
150	Joaquin Andujar	.07
151	Dave Stapleton	.05
152	Mike Morgan	.05
155	Bob Grich	.10
156	White Sox Ldrs (Richard Dotson)	.07
157	Ron Hassey	.05
158	Derrel Thomas	.05
159	Orel Hershiser	1.50
160	Chet Lemon	.07
162	Greg Gagne	.07
163	Pete Ladd	.05
164	Steve Balboni	.07
165	Mike Davis	.07
166	Dickie Thon	.07
167	Zane Smith (FC)	.10
168	Jeff Burroughs	.07
169	George Wright	.06
170	Gary Carter	.25
172	Jerry Reed	.05
175	Steve Sax	.25
176	Jay Tibbs	.05
177	Joel Youngblood	.05

329 Kirby Puckett

178	Ivan DeJesus	.05
179	*Stu Cliburn* (FC)	.10
180	Don Mattingly	3.00
181	Al Nipper	.05
183	Larry Andersen	.05
184	Tim Laudner	.05
185	Rollie Fingers	.25
186	Astros Ldrs (Jose Cruz)	.07
187	Scott Fletcher	.07
188	Bob Dernier	.05
190	George Hendrick	.07
191	Wally Backman	.07
192	Milt Wilcox	.05
193	Daryl Sconiers	.05
195	Dave Concepcion	.12
196	Doyle Alexander	.07
197	Enos Cabell	.05
199	Dick Howser	.05
200	Mike Schmidt	.90
201	Record Breaker (Vince Coleman) (FC)	.30
202	Record Breaker (Dwight Gooden)	.40
203	Record Breaker (Keith Hernandez)	.20
204	Record Breaker (Phil Niekro)	.15

250 Dwight Gooden

205	Record Breaker (Tony Perez)	.10
206	Record Breaker (Pete Rose)	.50
207	Record Breaker (Fernando Valenzuela)	.20
208	Ramon Romero	.05
209	Randy Ready	.05
210	Calvin Schiraldi (FC)	.10
212	Chris Speier	.07
213	Bob Shirley	.07
214	Randy Bush	.07
215	Frank White	.10
216	A's Ldrs (Dwayne Murphy)	.07
217	Bill Scherrer	.05
219	Dennis Lamp	.05
220	Bob Horner	.15
221	Dave Henderson	.10
223	Atlee Hammaker	.05
224	Cesar Cedeno	.10
225	Ron Darling	.15
228	Tom Lawless	.05
229	Bill Gullickson	.05
230	Terry Kennedy	.07
231	Jim Frey	.05
232	Rick Rhoden	.10
233	Steve Lyons (FC)	.07

234	Doug Corbett	.05
235	Butch Wynegar	.05
237	Ted Simmons	.10
238	Larry Parrish	.10
240	Tommy John	.20
241	Tony Fernandez	.20
242	Rich Thompson	.05
243	Johnny Grubb	.05
244	Craig Lefferts	.05
245	Jim Sundberg	.07
246	Phillies Ldrs (Steve Carlton)	.15
247	Terry Harper	.05
248	Spike Owen	.05
249	Rob Deer (FC)	.40
250	Dwight Gooden	2.00
251	Rich Dauer	.05
252	Bobby Castillo	.05
254	*Ozzie Guillen*	1.15
255	Tony Armas	.07
256	Kurt Kepshire	.05
257	Doug DeCinces	.10
258	*Tim Burke* (FC)	.45
259	Dan Pasqua	.20
260	Tony Pena	.10
261	Bobby Valentine	.05
264	*Darren Daulton* (FC)	.15
265	Ron Davis	.05
266	Keith Moreland	.07
267	Paul Molitor	.15
268	Mike Scott	.15
269	Dane Iorg	.05
270	Jack Morris	.25
271	Dave Collins	.07
272	Tim Tolman	.05
273	Jerry Willard	.05
274	Ron Gardenhire	.05
275	Charlie Hough	.10
276	Yankees Ldrs (Willie Randolph)	.07
277	Jaime Cocanower	.05
278	Sixto Lezcano	.05
279	Al Pardo	.05
280	Tim Raines	.30
281	Steve Mura	.05
282	Jerry Mumphrey	.05
285	Buddy Bell	.10
286	Luis DeLeon	.05
287	*John Christensen* (FC)	.10

288	Don Aase	.05
289	Johnnie LeMaster	.05
290	Carlton Fisk	.35
291	Tom Lasorda	.07
292	Chuck Porter	.05
293	Chris Chambliss	.07
294	Danny Cox	.10
295	Kirk Gibson	.30
296	Geno Petralli (FC)	.07
297	Tim Lollar	.05
298	Craig Reynolds	.05
299	Bryn Smith	.05
300	George Brett	.50
301	Dennis Rasmussen	.12
302	Greg Gross	.05
304	*Mike Gallego* (FC)	.15
305	Phil Bradley	.15
306	Padres Ldrs (Terry Kennedy)	.07
307	Dave Sax	.05
308	Ray Fontenot	.05
311	Dick Schofield	.05
312	Tom Filer	.05
313	Joe DeSa	.05
314	Frank Pastore	.05
315	Mookie Wilson	.10
316	Sammy Khalifa	.05

690 Ryne Sandberg

317	Ed Romero	.05
320	Jim Rice	.30
321	Earl Weaver	.07
322	Bob Forsch	.07
323	Jerry Davis	.05
324	Dan Schatzeder	.05
325	Juan Beniquez	.05
326	Kent Tekulve	.07
327	Mike Pagliarulo	.20
328	Pete O'Brien	.12
329	Kirby Puckett	3.00
330	Rick Sutcliffe	.12
331	Alan Ashby	.05
332	Darryl Motley	.05
333	Tom Henke (FC)	.20
334	Ken Oberkfell	.05
335	Don Sutton	.25
336	Indians Ldrs (Andre Thornton)	.07
337	Darnell Coles	.07
338	Jorge Bell	.25
339	Bruce Berenyi	.05
340	Cal Ripken	.40
343	Carlos Diaz	.05
344	Jim Wohlford	.05
346	Bryan Little	.05
347	*Teddy Higuera*	1.00

100 Nolan Ryan

1986 Topps

80 Darryl Strawberry

500 Rickey Henderson

254 Ozzie Guillen

382 Ivan Calderon

615	Johnny Ray	.10
620	Bruce Sutter	.15
628	*Kirk McKaskill* (FC)	.35
629	*Mitch Webster* (FC)	.25
630	Fernando Valenzuela	.30
636	Cubs Ldrs (Lee Smith)	.07
640	Jose Cruz	.10
644	Mark Gubicza	.12
647	Mel Hall	.07
648	Steve Bedrosian	.12
650	Dave Stieb	.12
651	Billy Martin	.12
652	Tom Browning	.25
660	Steve Garvey	.30
661	Roger Clemens	4.00
666	Rangers Ldrs (Charlie Hough)	.07
669	Ron Cey	.10
680	George Foster	.15
683	Andy Van Slyke	.12
685	Tim Wallach	.10
689	Dave Stewart	.12
690	Ryne Sandberg	1.50
696	Dodgers Ldrs (Bill Russell)	.07
700	Reggie Jackson	.35
701	Keith Hernandez AS	.15
702	Tom Herr AS	.07

703	Tim Wallach AS	.07
704	Ozzie Smith AS	.10
705	Dale Murphy AS	.30
706	Pedro Guerrero AS	.12
707	Willie McGee AS	.12
708	Gary Carter AS	.20
709	Dwight Gooden AS	.40
710	John Tudor AS	.07
711	Jeff Reardon AS	.07
712	Don Mattingly AS	.80
714	George Brett AS	.30
715	Cal Ripken AS	.25
716	Rickey Henderson AS	.25
717	Dave Winfield AS	.20
718	Jorge Bell AS	.20
719	Carlton Fisk AS	.15
720	Bret Saberhagen AS	.15
721	Ron Guidry AS	.10
722	Dan Quisenberry AS	.07
726	Orioles Ldrs (Rick Dempsey)	.07
728	Mike Marshall	.12
730	Ozzie Smith	.15
732	*Floyd Youmans* (FC)	.15
734	Marty Barrett	.10
735	Dave Dravecky	.07
736	Glenn Wilson	.07
737	Pete Vuckovich	.07
740	Lance Parrish	.20

175 Steve Sax

741	Pete Rose	.40
742	Frank Viola	.15
745	Willie Upshaw	.05
747	Rick Cerone	.05
748	Steve Henderson	.05
749	Ed Jurak	.05
750	Gorman Thomas	.05
751	Howard Johnson	.15
752	Mike Krukow	.07
754	*Pat Clements*	.10
755	Harold Baines	.15
756	Pirates Ldrs (Rick Rhoden)	.07
757	Darrell Porter	.07
760	Andre Dawson	.30
761	Don Slaught	.05
762	Eric Show	.07
763	Terry Puhl	.05
764	Kevin Gross	.05
765	Don Baylor	.12
766	Rick Langford	.05
767	Jody Davis	.07
768	Vern Ruhle	.05
769	• *Harold Reynolds* (FC)	.75
770	Vida Blue	.10
771	John McNamara	.05
772	Brian Downing	.07
773	Greg Pryor	.05
774	Terry Leach	.05
775	Al Oliver	.10
779	Rick Reuschel	.10
780	Robin Yount	.50
781	Joe Nolan	.05
782	Ken Landreaux	.05
783	Ricky Horton	.07
784	Alan Bannister	.05
785	Bob Stanley	.05
786	Twins Ldrs (Mickey Hatcher)	.07
787	Vance Law	.07
790	Phil Niekro	.25
792	Charles Hudson	.05

1986 TOPPS TRADED

After an off year for the regular set in 1986, the Topps Traded set for 1986 delivered the types of big names that rookie-card fans love. Like Fleer and Donruss, Topps provided cards of top rookie stars. Included in the set are Barry Bonds, Bobby Bonilla, Jose Canseco, Will Clark, Bo Jackson, and Kevin Mitchell, while Ruben Sierra was conspicuous by his absence. Collectors buying the set today should find it still in the specially designed box created by Topps. As usual, the complete 132-card sets were distributed only through hobby dealers. For easy handling, the cards are numbered in alphabetical order.

	MINT
Complete set	**$35.00**
Commons	.08

1	Andy Allanson (FC)	$ .20
3	Joaquin Andujar	.10
4	Paul Assenmacher (FC)	.20
5	Scott Bailes (FC)	.20
6	Don Baylor	.15
7	Steve Bedrosian	.15
10	Mike Bielecki (FC)	.35
11	Barry Bonds (FC)	5.00
12	Bobby Bonilla (FC)	4.00
16	Rick Burleson	.10
19	John Cangelosi (FC)	.20
20	Jose Canseco (FC)	11.00
23	John Cerutti (FC)	.25

1986 Topps Traded

24 Will Clark

24	Will Clark (FC)	11.00
26	Darnell Coles	.15
27	Dave Collins	.10
30	Joel Davis (FC)	.10
31	Rob Deer	.15
33	Mike Easler	.10
34	Mark Eichhorn (FC)	.20
36	Scott Fletcher	.15
37	Terry Forster	.10
40	Andres Galarraga (FC)	1.00
41	Ken Griffey	.20
43	Jose Guzman (FC)	.35
45	Billy Hatcher	.20
48	Pete Incaviglia (FC)	.50
50	Bo Jackson (FC)	10.00
51	Wally Joyner (FC)	3.00
52	Charlie Kerfeld (FC)	.15
53	Eric King (FC)	.20
54	Bob Kipper (FC)	.10
55	Wayne Krenchicki	.08
56	John Kruk (FC)	.50
57	Mike LaCoss	.08
59	Mike Laga	.08
60	Hal Lanier	.08
61	Dave LaPoint	.12
62	Rudy Law	.08
63	Rick Leach	.08
67	Steve Lyons	.10
68	Mickey Mahler	.08
69	Candy Maldonado	.15
70	Roger Mason (FC)	.10
71	Bob McClure	.08
72	Andy McGaffigan	.08
73	Gene Michael	.08
74	Kevin Mitchell (FC)	5.00
77	Phil Niekro	.40
78	Randy Niemann	.08
79	Juan Nieves (FC)	.25
80	Otis Nixon (FC)	.10
81	Bob Ojeda	.12
82	Jose Oquendo	.12
83	Tom Paciorek	.10
85	Frank Pastore	.08
86	Lou Piniella	.15
87	Dan Plesac (FC)	.40
88	Darrell Porter	.10
89	Rey Quinones (FC)	.10
90	Gary Redus	.08
91	Bip Roberts	.10
92	Billy Jo Robidoux (FC)	.15
93	Jeff Robinson	.10
94	Gary Roenicke	.08
95	Ed Romero	.08
98	Billy Sample	.08
99	Dave Schmidt	.08
100	Ken Schrom	.08
101	Tom Seaver	.65
102	Ted Simmons	.20
104	Kurt Stillwell (FC)	.30
105	Franklin Stubbs	.20
106	Dale Sveum (FC)	.25
107	Chuck Tanner	.08
108	Danny Tartabull (FC)	1.00
109	Tim Teufel	.15
110	Bob Tewksbury (FC)	.15
111	Andres Thomas (FC)	.15
112	Milt Thompson	.12
113	Robby Thompson (FC)	.40
117	Manny Trillo	.10
120	Bob Walk	.15
121	Gene Walter (FC)	.10
122	Claudell Washington	.15
123	Bill Wegman (FC)	.20
125	Mitch Williams (FC)	.65
126	Bobby Witt (FC)	1.00
127	Todd Worrell (FC)	.60

1987 DONRUSS

While Topps and Fleer issued relatively conservative cards in 1987, Donruss broke loose with a wacky design. Look closely at the borders of the 1987 cards and you'll discover that each photo covers a wide gold band of tiny baseballs. But the black border surrounding the photos is problematic: As with the 1971 Topps set, scuffing occurs easily and fewer mint cards remain. Top cards in the 1987 set include specially marked Rated Rookie cards for Bo Jackson, Mark McGwire, Benito Santiago, and Greg Swindell. Donruss showed a willingness to scatter other rookies throughout the set, providing lots of buried treasure for rookie-card fanatics.

361 Barry Bonds

		MINT
Complete set		**$90.00**
Commons		**.05**

1	Wally Joyner (DK)	$1.00
2	Roger Clemens (DK)	.70
3	Dale Murphy (DK)	.40
4	Darryl Strawberry (DK)	.40
5	Ozzie Smith (DK)	.12
6	Jose Canseco (DK)	1.50
7	Charlie Hough (DK)	.07
8	Brook Jacoby (DK)	.10
9	Fred Lynn (DK)	.12
10	Rick Rhoden (DK)	.10
11	Chris Brown (DK)	.10
12	Von Hayes (DK)	.10
13	Jack Morris (DK)	.20
14	Kevin McReynolds (DK) ("Donruss Diamond Kings" in white band on back)	1.25
15	George Brett (DK)	.40
16	Ted Higuera (DK)	.20
17	Hubie Brooks (DK)	.10
18	Mike Scott (DK)	.12
19	Kirby Puckett (DK)	.25
20	Dave Winfield (DK)	.25
21	Lloyd Moseby (DK)	.10
22	Eric Davis (DK) ("Donruss Diamond Kings" in white band on back)	3.00
22	Eric Davis (DK) ("Donruss Diamond Kings" in yellow band on back)	1.00
23	Jim Presley (DK)	.12
24	Keith Moreland (DK)	.07
25	Greg Walker (DK) ("Donruss Diamond Kings" in white band on back)	1.25
26	Steve Sax (DK)	.12
28	B.J. Surhoff (RR) (FC)	.60
29	Randy Myers (RR) (FC)	.85
30	Ken Gerhart (RR) (FC)	.15
31	Benito Santiago (RR) (FC)	3.00
32	Greg Swindell (RR) (FC)	1.25
33	Mike Birkbeck (RR) (FC)	.20
34	Terry Steinbach (RR) (FC)	1.00
35	Bo Jackson (RR)	11.00
36	Greg Maddux (RR) (FC)	2.00

1987 Donruss

46 Mark McGwire

66 Will Clark

91	Lance Parrish	.20
92	Jim Rice	.30
93	Ron Guidry	.15
94	Fernando Valenzuela	.25
95	*Andy Allanson*	.15
96	Willie Wilson	.10
97	Jose Canseco	10.00
98	Jeff Reardon	.10
99	*Bobby Witt*	1.25
100	Checklist 28-133	.05
101	Jose Guzman	.07
102	Steve Balboni	.07
104	Brook Jacoby	.10
105	Dave Winfield	.30
106	Orel Hershiser	.40
107	Lou Whitaker	.25
108	Fred Lynn	.15
109	Bill Wegman	.07
111	Jack Clark	.15
113	Von Hayes	.10
115	Tony Pena	.08
117	Paul Molitor	.15
118	Darryl Strawberry	1.00
119	Shawon Dunston	.20
120	Jim Presley	.07
121	Jesse Barfield	.20
122	Gary Gaetti	.15
123	*Kurt Stillwell*	.60
125	Mike Boddicker	.07
126	Robin Yount	.35
127	Alan Trammell	.25
128	Dave Righetti	.15
129	• Dwight Evans	.12
130	Mike Scioscia	.07
131	Julio Franco	.10
132	Bret Saberhagen	.15
133	Mike Davis	.07
135	*Wally Joyner*	2.00
138	Nolan Ryan	1.25
139	Mike Schmidt	.50
140	Tommy Herr	.10
141	Garry Templeton	.07
142	Kal Daniels	1.00
144	Johnny Ray	.10
145	*Rob Thompson*	.30
147	Danny Tartabull	.25
148	Ernie Whitt	.07
149	Kirby Puckett	1.25
152	Frank Tanana	.07

22 Eric Davis

154	Willie Randolph	.10
155	Bill Madlock (name in brown band)	.12
155	Bill Madlock (name in red band)	.07
156	Joe Carter (name in brown band)	.70
156	Joe Carter (name in red band)	.30
157	Danny Jackson	.15
158	Carney Lansford	.10
161	Oddibe McDowell	.10
162	*John Cangelosi*	.12
163	Mike Scott	.15
164	Eric Show	.07
165	Juan Samuel	.15
166	Nick Esasky	.10
167	Zane Smith	.07
169	Keith Moreland	.07
170	John Tudor	.10
172	Jim Gantner	.07
173	Jack Morris	.20
174	Bruce Hurst	.10
175	Dennis Rasmussen	.10
176	Mike Marshall	.12
177	Dan Quisenberry	.10
178	Eric Plunk (FC)	.10

1987 Donruss

43 Rafael Palmeiro

302	*Bill Mooneyham*	.10
303	Andres Galarraga	.25
304	Scott Fletcher	.07
305	Jack Howell	.07
306	*Russ Morman* (FC)	.10
307	Todd Worrell	.20
308	Dave Smith	.07
315	*Jamie Moyer* (FC)	.12
316	Wally Backman	.07
317	Ken Phelps	.07
321	*Mark Eichhorn*	.15
322	*Lee Guetterman*	.15
323	Sid Fernandez	.12
327	Candy Maldonado	.07
328	*John Kruk*	.40
330	Milt Thompson	.07
331	*Mike LaValliere*	.35
334	*Ron Karkovice* (FC)	.10
335	Mitch Webster	.07
337	*Glenn Braggs* (FC)	.30
339	Don Baylor	.12
340	Brian Fisher	.07
341	*Reggie Williams*	.10
344	Curt Young	.07
346	*Ruben Sierra*	7.00
347	*Mitch Williams*	.50
351	Ron Kittle	.10
353	Chet Lemon	.07

31 Benito Santiago

35 Bo Jackson

361	*Barry Bonds*	8.00
362	Vida Blue	.10
363	Cecil Cooper	.10
364	Bob Ojeda	.07
365	Dennis Eckersley	.15
367	Willie Upshaw	.07
368	*Allan Anderson* (FC)	.25
369	Bill Gullickson	.07
370	*Bobby Thigpen* (FC)	.45
373	Dan Petry	.07
375	Tom Seaver	.40
381	Kirk McCaskill	.07
383	Rich Dotson	.07
388	Dave Parker	.20
389	Bob Horner	.12
391	Jeff Leonard	.07
397	*Bryan Clutterbuck* (FC)	.10
398	Darrell Evans	.12
401	*Phil Lombardi* (FC)	.10
407	*Chuck Finley* (FC)	.15
408	Toby Harrah	.07
410	Kevin Bass	.10
413	*Tracy Jones*	.25
417	Andy Van Slyke	.12
419	Ben Oglivie	.07
422	*Bob Tewksbury*	.12

1987 Donruss

558 Bobby Bonilla

424	*Mike Kingery* (FC)	.15
425	Dave Kingman	.15
426	Al Newman	.07
427	Gary Ward	.07
429	Harold Baines	.15
432	Don Carman	.07
435	Rick Rhoden	.10
436	Jose Uribe	.07
439	Jesse Orosco	.10
442	*John Cerutti*	.20
444	Kelly Gruber	.10
446	*Ed Hearn*	.10
450	*Mike Aldrete*	.15
451	Kevin McReynolds	.15
452	*Rob Murphy* (FC)	.20
453	Kent Tekulve	.07
454	Curt Ford (FC)	.07
455	Davey Lopes	.07
456	Bobby Grich	.10
457	Jose DeLeon	.10
458	Andre Dawson	.20
459	Mike Flanagan	.07
460	*Joey Meyer* (FC)	.20
461	*Chuck Cary* (FC)	.10
462	Bill Buckner	.10
464	*Jeff Hamilton* (FC)	.20
465	Phil Niekro	.20
466	Mark Gubicza	.12
468	*Bob Sebra* (FC)	.10
469	Larry Parrish	.10
470	Charlie Hough	.07
471	Hal McRae	.10
472	*Dave Leiper* (FC)	.10
473	Mel Hall	.07
474	Dan Pasqua	.10
475	Bob Welch	.10
477	Jim Traber	.07
478	*Chris Bosio* (FC)	.30
479	Mark McLemore	.07
481	Billy Hatcher	.07
483	Rich Gossage	.15
487	Mookie Wilson	.10
488	*Dave Martinez* (FC)	.25
489	• Harold Reynolds	.10
492	*Barry Larkin* (FC)	3.25
495	*Jim Adduci* (FC)	.07
498	Tony Armas	.07
502	*David Cone* (FC)	2.50
503	Jay Howell	.07
505	*Ray Chadwick* (FC)	.10
506	*Mike Loynd* (FC)	.15
511	Gene Walter	.07
512	*Terry McGriff* (FC)	.12
513	Ken Griffey	.12

97 Jose Canseco

515 *Terry Mulholland* (FC) .... .12
518 Manny Lee (FC) .... .07
520 Scott McGregor .... .07
522 Willie Hernandez .... .07
523 Marty Barrett...................... .10
525 *Jose Gonzalez* (FC) .... .15
526 Cory Snyder .... .70
529 *Wilfredo Tejeda* (FC) .... .10
531 *Dale Mohorcic* (FC) .... .20
535 *Mike Maddux* (FC)............. .15
537 Ted Simmons .... .12
538 *Rafael Belliard* (FC)........... .12
540 Bob Forsch .... .07
542 Dale Sveum...................... .20
544 *Jeff Sellers*...................... .20
546 Alex Trevino .... .05
547 *Randy Kutcher* (FC) .... .10
548 Joaquin Andujar .... .07
549 *Casey Candaele* (FC)........ .15
550 Jeff Russell...................... .10
551 John Candelaria .... .10
553 Danny Cox........................ .07
555 *Bruce Ruffin* (FC) .... .20
556 Buddy Bell .... .10
557 *Jimmy Jones* (FC) .... .20
558 *Bobby Bonilla* 1.75
559 Jeff Robinson .... .07
561 *Glenallen Hill* (FC) 1.15
562 Lee Mazzilli...................... .07
565 *Mike Sharperson* (FC) .... .15
566 *Mark Portugal*.................. .10
567 Rick Leach...................... .10
568 Mark Langston.................. .12
570 Manny Trillo...................... .07
573 *Kelly Downs* (FC) .... .30
574 *Randy Asadoor* (FC) .... .10
575 *Dave Magadan* (FC)........ 2.25
576 *Marvin Freeman* (FC) .... .12
579 Gus Polidor (FC) .... .07
585 *Mike Greenwell* (FC) 7.50
586 Ray Knight........................ .07
587 *Ralph Bryant* (FC) .... .12
591 *Jeff Musselman* (FC) .... .20
592 *Mike Stanley* (FC)............. .20
593 Darrell Porter .... .07
594 *Drew Hall* (FC).................. .20
595 *Rob Nelson* (FC) .... .10
597 *Scott Nielsen* (FC) .... .10
598 *Brian Holton* (FC) .... .20

135 Wally Joyner

599 *Kevin Mitchell* 6.00
602 *Barry Jones* (FC) .... .10
608 Don Robinson.................... .07
609 Mike Krukow...................... .07
610 *Dave Valle* (FC)................ .12
611 Len Dykstra .... .85
613 Mike Trujillo (FC) .... .05
617 Steve Carlton.................... .25
620 Rick Aguilera .... .05
621 Fred McGriff 3.00
622 Dave Henderson .... .10
623 *Dave Clark* (FC) .... .20
627 *Kevin Brown* (FC) .... .07
632 *Ray Hayward* (FC).............. .12
635 *Kevin Elster* (FC) .... .40
638 *Rey Quinones*.................. .15
641 Calvin Schiraldi................. .07
642 *Stan Jefferson* (FC) .... .20
646 Howard Johnsn .... .10
648 Dave Stewart.................... .12
651 *Bob Brower* (FC) .... .15
652 Rob Woodward.................. .07
654 *Tim Pyznarski* (FC)............. .10
655 *Luis Aquino* (FC) .... .10
656 *Mickey Brantley* (FC)......... .10
657 Doyle Alexander .... .07
659 Jim Acker.......................... .05

1987 DONRUSS ROOKIES

For the second year in a row, Donruss issued "The Rookies," a 56-card set highlighting players overlooked in the earlier 660-card issue. Donruss hedged its bets by including Bo Jackson and Mark McGwire in this edition, issued in the fall, even though McGwire had been in the larger 1987 set, and Jackson was a member of The Rookies in 1986. Other appealing names in the set include Ellis Burks, Mike Greenwell, Kevin Seitzer, and Matt Williams. The 55 player cards and one checklist card came in a specially designed box. Although the card numbers hold no special prefixes, Donruss altered these cards slightly in comparison to the regular set by changing the border color from black to green and by stamping "The Rookies" logo on each card front.

45 Matt Williams

		MINT
Complete set		**$25.00**
Commons		**.10**

1	Mark McGwire	$3.50
4	Mike Greenwell	2.50
5	Ellis Burks (FC)	4.00
6	DeWayne Buice (FC)	.15
8	Devon White	.50
10	Lester Lancaster (FC)	.15
11	Ken Williams (FC)	.15
12	Matt Nokes (FC)	.50
13	Jeff Robinson (FC)	.40
14	Bo Jackson	4.00
15	Kevin Seitzer (FC)	1.00
16	Billy Ripken (FC)	.25
17	B.J. Surhoff	.20
21	Les Straker (FC)	.20
23	Gene Larkin (FC)	.25
25	Luis Polonia (FC)	.35
26	Terry Steinbach	.25
28	Mike Stanley	.20
30	Todd Benzinger (FC)	.35
31	Fred McGriff	2.25
32	Mike Henneman (FC)	.30
34	Dave Magadan	.25
35	David Cone	1.25
36	Mike Jackson (FC)	.20
37	John Mitchell (FC)	.20
38	Mike Dunne (FC)	.15
39	John Smiley (FC)	.40
40	Joe Magrane (FC)	1.00
42	Shane Mack (FC)	.25
44	Benito Santiago	.90
45	Matt Williams (FC)	7.00
46	Dave Meads (FC)	.20
47	Rafael Palmeiro	1.50
48	Bill Long (FC)	.20
51	Paul Noce (FC)	.15
52	Greg Maddux	.65
55	Chuck Jackson (FC)	.20

1987 FLEER

Fleer produced an attractive and innovative set of baseball cards in 1987. Each of the 660 cards in the annual set features a light blue border fading to white down the sides as it approaches a solid blue bottom. Photos extend into the top border, creating a novel three-dimensional look. The only obstruction on the card fronts are team logos in the lower corners (which seem redundant, since the same logos usually appear on the player's cap or uniform). Fleer produced its last Pete Rose card, number 213, labeling him a player-manager. The card of Will Clark, number 269, has turned out to be the most valuable rookie card in the bunch.

		MINT
Complete set		**$135.00**
Commons		**.06**

1	Rick Aguilera	$ .30
3	Wally Backman	.08
4	Gary Carter	.25
5	Ron Darling	.15
6	Len Dykstra	.75
7	*Kevin Elster* (FC)	.50
8	Sid Fernandez	.12
9	Dwight Gooden	1.00
10	*Ed Hearn* (FC)	.10
11	Danny Heep	.06

549 Kirby Puckett

369 Bo Jackson

12	Keith Hernandez	.25
13	Howard Johnson	.65
14	Ray Knight	.08
15	Lee Mazzilli	.08
16	Roger McDowell	.12
17	*Kevin Mitchell*	9.00
19	Bob Ojeda	.08
20	Jesse Orosco	.08
23	Darryl Strawberry	1.50
24	Tim Teufel	.06
25	Mookie Wilson	.10
26	Tony Armas	.08
27	Marty Barrett	.10

269 Will Clark

62	Dave Lopes	.08
67	Nolan Ryan	2.00
68	Mike Scott	.15
69	Dave Smith	.08
70	Dickie Thon	.08
73	• Bob Boone	.08
75	John Candelaria	.10
78	Brian Downing	.08
79	*Chuck Finley* (FC)	.15
80	Terry Forster	.08
81	Bobby Grich	.10
83	Jack Howell (FC)	.10
84	Reggie Jackson	.35
86	Wally Joyner	2.00
87	Gary Lucas	.06
88	Kirk McCaskill	.08
91	Vern Ruhle	.06
93	Don Sutton	.20
94	Rob Wilfong	.06
95	Mike Witt	.10
96	*Doug Drabek*	3.00
97	Mike Easler	.08
99	Brian Fisher	.08
100	Ron Guidry	.15
101	Rickey Henderson	1.50
102	Tommy John	.20
103	Ron Kittle	.10
104	Don Mattingly	3.00

28	Don Baylor	.12
29	Wade Boggs	2.00
30	Oil Can Boyd	.08
31	Bill Buckner	.10
32	Roger Clemens	3.00
34	• Dwight Evans	.12
35	Rich Gedman	.08
36	Dave Henderson	.10
37	Bruce Hurst	.10
40	Spike Owen	.06
41	Jim Rice	.30
42	Ed Romero	.06
43	Joe Sambito	.06
44	Calvin Schiraldi	.08
45	Tom Seaver	.40
46	*Jeff Sellers* (FC)	.20
48	Sammy Stewart	.06
51	Kevin Bass	.10
52	Jeff Calhoun	.06
53	Jose Cruz	.12
54	Danny Darwin	.06
55	Glenn Davis	.30
56	*Jim Deshaies*	.25
57	Bill Doran	.10
58	Phil Garner	.06
59	Billy Hatcher	.08
60	Charlie Kerfeld	.06

389 Jose Canseco

106	Joe Niekro	.10
108	Dan Pasqua	.10
109	Willie Randolph	.10
111	Dave Righetti	.15
112	Gary Roenicke	.06
116	Tim Stoddard	.06
117	*Bob Tewksbury*	.12
118	Wayne Tolleson	.06
120	Dave Winfield	.30
121	Steve Buechele	.08
122	*Ed Correa*	.15
123	Scott Fletcher	.08
124	Jose Guzman	.08
125	Toby Harrah	.08
127	Charlie Hough	.08
128	*Pete Incaviglia*	.60
130	Oddibe McDowell	.10
131	*Dale Mohorcic* (FC)	.20
132	Pete O'Brien	.10
133	Tom Paciorek	.06
134	Larry Parrish	.08
135	Geno Petralli	.06
136	Darrell Porter	.08
137	Jeff Russell	.10
138	*Ruben Sierra*	12.00
139	Don Slaught	.06
140	Gary Ward	.08
142	*Mitch Williams*	.65
143	*Bobby Witt*	2.00
144	Dave Bergman	.06
147	*Chuck Cary*	.10
148	Darnell Coles	.08
149	Dave Collins	.08
150	Darrell Evans	.12
151	Kirk Gibson	.25
152	John Grubb	.06
155	*Eric King*	.25
156	Chet Lemon	.08
157	Dwight Lowry	.06
158	Jack Morris	.20
159	Randy O'Neal	.06
160	Lance Parrish	.20
161	Dan Petry	.08
164	Frank Tanana	.08
165	Walt Terrell	.08
167	Alan Trammell	.25
168	Lou Whitaker	.25
169	Luis Aguayo	.06
170	Steve Bedrosian	.12

138 Ruben Sierra

171	Don Carman	.10
173	Greg Gross	.06
174	Kevin Gross	.08
175	Von Hayes	.15
178	Steve Jeltz	.06
179	*Mike Maddux* (FC)	.15
181	Gary Redus	.06
183	*Bruce Ruffin* (FC)	.20
185	Juan Samuel	.12
187	Mike Schmidt	1.00
188	Rick Schu	.06
190	Kent Tekulve	.08
191	Milt Thompson	.08
192	Glenn Wilson	.08
193	Buddy Bell	.10
194	Tom Browning	.10
195	Sal Butera	.06
196	Dave Concepcion	.12
197	Kal Daniels	.80
198	Eric Davis	1.50
199	John Denny	.06
200	Bo Diaz	.08
201	Nick Esasky	.15
202	John Franco	.12
204	*Barry Larkin* (FC)	8.00
205	Eddie Milner	.06
206	*Rob Murphy* (FC)	.20

605 Bobby Bonilla

208	Dave Parker	.20
209	Tony Perez	.15
213	Pete Rose	.60
214	Mario Soto	.08
215	*Kurt Stillwell*	.50
218	*Carl Willis* (FC)	.10
219	Jesse Barfield	.15
220	George Bell	.25
221	Bill Caudill	.06
222	*John Cerutti*	.20
223	Jim Clancy	.08
224	*Mark Eichhorn*	.15
225	Tony Fernandez	.12
227	Kelly Gruber	.08
228	Tom Henke	.08
229	Garth Iorg	.06
232	Jimmy Key	.12
233	Dennis Lamp	.06
235	Buck Martinez	.06
236	Lloyd Moseby	.10
238	Dave Stieb	.12
240	Ernie Whitt	.08
241	*Andy Allanson*	.15
242	*Scott Bailes*	.20
243	Chris Bando	.06
245	John Butcher	.06
246	Brett Butler	.08

249	Joe Carter	.20
251	Julio Franco	.10
252	Mel Hall	.08
253	Brook Jacoby	.10
254	Phil Niekro	.20
255	Otis Nixon	.06
260	Cory Snyder	.45
261	Pat Tabler	.08
263	*Rich Yett* (FC)	.12
264	*Mike Aldrete*	.15
266	Vida Blue	.10
268	Chris Brown	.08
269	*Will Clark*	27.00
270	Chili Davis	.08
271	Mark Davis	.12
272	*Kelly Downs* (FC)	.30
273	Scott Garrelts	.06
274	Dan Gladden	.06
275	Mike Krukow	.08
277	Mike LaCoss	.06
278	Jeff Leonard	.08
281	Bob Melvin (FC)	.08
282	Greg Minton	.06
283	Jeff Robinson	.08
284	Harry Spilman	.06
285	*Rob Thompson*	.35
286	Jose Uribe	.08
287	Frank Williams	.06
289	Jack Clark	.15
290	Vince Coleman	.25
291	Tim Conroy	.06
292	Danny Cox	.08
295	Bob Forsch	.08
296	Tom Herr	.10
297	Ricky Horton	.08
298	Clint Hurdle	.06
301	Tito Landrum	.06
302	*Mike LaValliere*	.25
303	*Greg Mathews* (FC)	.20
304	Willie McGee	.12
305	Jose Oquendo	.10
306	Terry Pendleton	.10
308	Ozzie Smith	.15
309	Ray Soff	.06
310	John Tudor	.10
311	Andy Van Slyke	.12
312	Todd Worrell	.20
314	Hubie Brooks	.10
315	Tim Burke	.12

316	Andre Dawson	.25
318	Tom Foley	.06
319	Andres Galarraga	.40
320	Joe Hesketh	.06
323	Vance Law	.08
327	*Al Newman*	.08
328	Tim Raines	.35
329	Jeff Reardon	.10
330	*Luis Rivera* (FC)	.10
331	*Bob Sebra* (FC)	.10
332	Bryn Smith	.10
333	Jay Tibbs	.06
334	Tim Wallach	.12
335	Mitch Webster	.08
336	Jim Wohlford	.06
337	Floyd Youmans	.06
338	*Chris Bosio* (FC)	.25
339	*Glenn Braggs* (FC)	.40
340	Rick Cerone	.06
341	Mark Clear	.06
342	*Bryan Clutterbuck* (FC)	.10
343	Cecil Cooper	.12
344	Rob Deer	.10
345	Jim Gantner	.08
346	Ted Higuera	.20
348	Tim Leary (FC)	.30
350	Paul Molitor	.20
352	Juan Nieves	.10
353	Ben Oglivie	08
354	*Dan Plesac*	.35
358	*Dale Sveum*	.20
360	Bill Wegman (FC)	.10
361	Robin Yount	.35
362	Steve Balboni	.08
363	*Scott Bankhead*	.30
365	Bud Black	.08
366	George Brett	.60
367	Steve Farr	.08
368	Mark Gubicza	.12
369	*Bo Jackson*	20.00
370	Danny Jackson	.15
371	*Mike Kingery*	.15
372	Rudy Law	.06
375	Hal McRae	.10
376	Jorge Orta	.06
377	Jamie Quirk	.06
379	Bret Saberhagen	.35
380	Angel Salazar	.06
381	Lonnie Smith	.10

32 Roger Clemens

382	Jim Sundberg	.08
383	Frank White	.10
384	Willie Wilson	.12
387	Dusty Baker	.08
389	Jose Canseco	13.00
391	Mike Davis	.08
392	Alfredo Griffin	.08
393	Moose Haas	.06
395	Jay Howell	.10
396	Dave Kingman	.15
397	Carney Lansford	.12
398	*David Leiper* (FC)	.12
399	*Bill Mooneyham*	.10
400	Dwayne Murphy	.08
402	Tony Phillips	.10
403	Eric Plunk	.08
404	Jose Rijo	.10
405	*Terry Steinbach* (FC)	1.00
406	Dave Stewart	.12
407	Mickey Tettleton	.10
410	Curt Young	.08
414	Steve Garvey	.25
415	Goose Gossage	.15
416	Tony Gwynn	.35
418	LaMarr Hoyt	.06
420	*John Kruk*	.45
421	Dave LaPoint	.08

96 Doug Drabek

422	Craig Lefferts	.06
425	Kevin McReynolds	.15
426	Graig Nettles	.12
429	Benito Santiago	.85
430	Eric Show	.08
433	Gene Walter	.06
434	Ed Whitson	.08
437	Greg Brock	.08
438	Enos Cabell	.06
440	Pedro Guerrero	.15
441	Orel Hershiser	.40
443	Ken Howell	.08
445	Bill Madlock	.12
446	Mike Marshall	.10
451	Jerry Reuss	.08
452	Bill Russell	.08
453	Steve Sax	.15
457	Fernando Valenzuela	.25
459	Bob Welch	.15
460	*Reggie Williams*	.08
465	Rich Bordi	.06
466	Storm Davis	.15
473	Lee Lacy	.06
474	Fred Lynn	.15
476	Eddie Murray	.35
478	Cal Ripken Jr.	.50
481	Nate Snell	.06

482	Jim Traber (FC)	.10
483	Mike Young	.06
484	Neil Allen	.06
485	Harold Baines	.15
487	Daryl Boston	.06
488	Ivan Calderon	.08
489	*John Cangelosi*	.12
490	Steve Carlton	.25
492	Julio Cruz	.06
493	Bill Dawley	.06
494	Jose DeLeon	.15
496	Carlton Fisk	.25
497	Ozzie Guillen	.10
507	*Bobby Thigpen* (FC)	3.00
508	Greg Walker	.10
509	Jim Acker	.06
511	*Paul Assenmacher*	.15
515	Gene Garber	.06
516	Ken Griffey	.15
518	Bob Horner	.12
520	Rick Mahler	.06
522	Dale Murphy	.40
524	Ed Olwine	.06
527	Billy Sample	.06
528	Ted Simmons	.12
529	Zane Smith	.15
530	Bruce Sutter	.12
531	*Andres Thomas*	.20
532	Ozzie Virgil	.06
533	• *Allan Anderson* (FC)	.25
535	Billy Beane	.06
536	Bert Blyleven	.12
537	Tom Brunansky	.10
538	Randy Bush	.06
540	Gary Gaetti	.15
541	Greg Gagne	.06
543	Neal Heaton	.06
544	Kent Hrbek	.15
549	Kirby Puckett	2.50
550	Jeff Reed	.06
551	Mark Salas	.06
554	Frank Viola	.20
556	Ron Cey	.10
557	Jody Davis	.08
558	Ron Davis	.06
561	Shawon Dunston	.15
563	Dennis Eckersley	.15
566	Guy Hoffman	.08
570	*Jamie Moyer* (FC)	.15

507 Bobby Thigpen

1987 FLEER UPDATE

Following a custom that began in 1984, Fleer continued with its Update series in 1987. A checklist and 131 player cards are included, numbered U-1 through U-132, and arranged alphabetically (the letter "U" has been omitted from the following list). The cards retain the format of the regular 1987 issue and were available solely through hobby dealers in a specially designed collector's box. Fleer made up for past sins by finally adding Mark McGwire to this year's edition. Additional newcomers who make the set appealing are Mike Greenwell, Kevin Mitchell, Kevin Seitzer, and Matt Williams. A total of 44 cards are included in this edition that are not in the 1987 Topps Traded set.

	MINT
Complete set	**$24.00**
Commons	.06

1	Scott Bankhead	$ .15
2	Eric Bell (FC)	.15
5	Mike Birkbeck (FC)	.20
6	Randy Bockus (FC)	.10
7	Rod Booker (FC)	.10
8	Thad Bosley	.10
9	Greg Brock	.10
10	Bob Brower (FC)	.15
11	Chris Brown	.10
12	Jerry Browne	.10
13	Ralph Bryant	.10
14	DeWayne Buice (FC)	.20
15	Ellis Burks (FC)	3.50
16	Casey Candaele (FC)	.15
17	Steve Carlton	.30
19	Chuck Crim (FC)	.15
20	Mark Davidson (FC)	.20
21	Mark Davis	.10
22	Storm Davis	.10
24	Andre Dawson	.50
26	Rick Dempsey	.10
27	Ken Dowell (FC)	.10
28	Dave Dravecky	.10
29	Mike Dunne (FC)	.20
30	Dennis Eckersley	.35
31	Cecil Fielder	2.50
32	Brian Fisher	.10
33	Willie Fraser	.10

129 Matt Williams

34	Ken Gerhart (FC)	.15
35	Jim Gott	.06
36	Dan Gladden	.15
37	Mike Greenwell (FC)	2.50
41	Mickey Hatcher	.15
42	Mike Heath	.08
44	Mike Henneman (FC)	.30
45	Guy Hoffman	.15
47	Chuck Jackson (FC)	.20
48	Mike Jackson (FC)	.20
49	Reggie Jackson	.50

50	Chris James	.35
51	Dion James	.15
52	Stan Javier	.15
53	Stan Jefferson (FC)	.20
54	Jimmy Jones	.10
55	Tracy Jones	.20
57	Mike Kingery	.15
58	Ray Knight	.10
59	Gene Larkin (FC)	.30
60	Mike LaValliere	.10
61	Jack Lazorko	.05
62	Terry Leach	.08
63	Rick Leach	.10
65	Jim Lindeman (FC)	.10
66	Bill Long (FC)	.15
67	Mike Loynd (FC)	.15
68	Greg Maddux (FC)	1.25
69	Bill Madlock	.20
70	Dave Magadan	.25
71	Joe Magrane (FC)	1.00
72	Fred Manrique (FC)	.15
74	Lloyd McClendon (FC)	.15
75	Fred McGriff (FC)	2.75
76	Mark McGwire (FC)	3.00
78	Kevin McReynolds	.30
79	Dave Meads (FC)	.15
80	Greg Minton	.06
81	John Mitchell (FC)	.10
82	Kevin Mitchell	2.00
83	John Morris	.06
84	Jeff Musselman (FC)	.25
85	Randy Myers (FC)	.65
87	Joe Niekro	.10
88	Tom Nieto	.06
89	Reid Nichols	.08
90	Matt Nokes (FC)	.75
91	Dickie Noles	.08
92	Edwin Nunez	.08
93	Jose Nunez (FC)	.25
94	Paul O'Neill	.10
95	Jim Paciorek	.15
96	Lance Parrish	.20
97	Bill Pecota (FC)	.15
98	Tony Pena	.15
99	Luis Polonia (FC)	.25
100	Randy Ready	.15
101	Jeff Reardon	.15
102	Gary Redus	.08
103	Rick Rhoden	.10

15 Ellis Burks

104	Wally Ritchie (FC)	.15
105	Jeff Robinson (FC)	.35
106	Mark Salas	.06
107	Dave Schmidt	.08
108	Kevin Seitzer	1.50
109	John Shelby	.08
110	John Smiley (FC)	.35
111	Lary Sorensen	.08
112	Chris Speier	.10
114	Jim Sundberg	.08
115	B.J. Surhoff (FC)	.35
116	Greg Swindell	.50
117	Danny Tartabull	.35
118	Dorn Taylor (FC)	.10
119	Lee Tunnell	.06
120	Ed Vande Berg	.08
121	Andy Van Slyke	.15
122	Gary Ward	.06
123	Devon White	.50
124	Alan Wiggins	.08
125	Bill Wilkinson (FC)	.15
126	Jim Winn	.06
127	Frank Williams	.06
128	Ken Williams (FC)	.20
129	Matt Williams (FC)	7.00
130	Herm Winningham	.06
131	Matt Young	.06

1987 TOPPS

Topps provided collectors with a blast from the past in its 1987 set. Cards use a simulated wood-grain finish for a border, much like the 1962 Topps or 1955 Bowman sets. Aside from the use of the team logo, a generous photo space is largely unobstructed. For the first time since 1972, player positions did not appear on the card fronts. Although it was first seen in the U.S. Olympic baseball team subset in 1985, Mark McGwire's 1987 Topps card became the hottest "rookie" in this set. Barry Bonds, Will Clark, Mike Greenwell, and Ruben Sierra round out the popular first-timers spotlighted in 1987.

420 Will Clark

		MINT
Complete set		**$45.00**
Commons		**.05**

1	Record Breaker (Roger Clemens)	$ .35
2	Record Breaker (Jim Deshaies)	.07
3	Record Breaker (Dwight Evans)	.07
4	Record Breaker (Dave Lopes)	.07
5	Record Breaker (Dave Righetti)	.07
6	Record Breaker (Ruben Sierra)	.25
7	Record Breaker (Todd Worrell)	.07
8	Terry Pendleton	.07
9	Jay Tibbs	.05
10	Cecil Cooper	.10
11	Indian Ldrs (Jack Aker, Chris Bando, Phil Niekro)	.07
12	*Jeff Sellers* (FC)	.15
13	Nick Esasky	.10
14	Dave Stewart	.20
15	Claudell Washington	.07
17	Pete O'Brien	.10
18	Dick Howser	.05
20	Gary Carter	.20
21	Mark Davis	.10
22	Doug DeCinces	.07
23	Lee Smith	.10
24	Tony Walker	.05
25	Bert Blyleven	.12
26	Greg Brock	.07
28	Rick Dempsey	.07
29	Jimmy Key	.10
30	Tim Raines	.25
31	Braves Ldrs (Glenn Hubbard, Rafael Ramirez)	.07
32	Tim Leary	.07
33	Andy Van Slyke	.12
34	Jose Rijo	.07
35	Sid Bream	.07
36	*Eric King*	.25
37	Marvell Wynne	.05
38	Dennis Leonard	.07
39	Marty Barrett	.07
40	Dave Righetti	.12
41	Bo Diaz	.07

170 Bo Jackson

320 Barry Bonds

178 Cecil Fielder

184 Bobby Bonilla

155	Eddie Whitson	.07
156	Mariners Ldrs (Bob Kearney, Phil Regan, Matt Young)	.07
158	Tim Teufel	.05
159	Ed Olwine	.05
160	Julio Franco	.10
161	Steve Ontiveros	.05
162	*Mike LaValliere*	.25
165	Jeff Reardon	.10
166	• Bob Boone	.07
167	*Jim Deshaies*	.25
168	Lou Piniella	.07
169	Ron Washington	.05
170	Future Stars (Bo Jackson)	4.00
171	*Chuck Cary* (FC)	.10
172	Ron Oester	.05
173	Alex Trevino	.05
174	Henry Cotto	.07
176	Steve Buechele	.05
177	Keith Moreland	.07
178	Cecil Fielder	2.00
180	Chris Brown	.05
181	Cardinals Ldrs (Mike LaValliere, Ozzie Smith, Ray Soff)	.07
182	Lee Lacy	.05
183	Andy Hawkins	.07
184	*Bobby Bonilla*	2.00
185	Roger McDowell	.10
186	Bruce Benedict	.05
187	Mark Huismann	.05
188	Tony Phillips	.07
189	Joe Hesketh	.05
190	Jim Sundberg	.07
191	Charles Hudson	.05
192	Cory Snyder (FC)	.50
193	Roger Craig	.07
194	Kirk McCaskill	.07
195	Mike Pagliarulo	.10
198	Lee Mazzilli	.05
199	Mariano Duncan	.05
200	Pete Rose	.60
201	*John Cangelosi*	.12
203	*Mike Kingery* (FC)	.15
204	Sammy Stewart	.05
205	Graig Nettles	.10
206	Twins Ldrs (Tim Laudner, Frank Viola)	.07

634 Rafael Palmeiro

207	George Frazier	.05
208	John Shelby	.07
209	Rick Schu	.05
210	Lloyd Moseby	.10
211	John Morris (FC)	.05
212	Mike Fitzgerald	.05
213	*Randy Myers* (FC)	.50
214	Omar Moreno	.05
215	Mark Langston	.15
216	Future Stars (*B.J. Surhoff* (FC))	.50
217	Chris Codiroli	.05
218	Sparky Anderson	.07
219	Cecilio Guante	.05
220	Joe Carter	.20
221	Vern Ruhle	.05
222	Denny Walling	.05
223	Charlie Leibrandt	.05
224	Wayne Tolleson	.05
225	Mike Smithson	.05
226	Max Venable	.05
227	*Jamie Moyer* (FC)	.15
229	*Mike Birkbeck* (FC)	.15
230	Don Baylor	.10
231	Giants Ldrs (Bob Brenly, Mike Krukow)	.07
232	*Reggie Williams*	.10
233	*Russ Morman* (FC)	.10
234	Pat Sheridan	.05

319 Greg Swindell

412 Eric Davis

340 Roger Clemens

476 Danny Tartabull

371	*Mark Eichhorn*	.15
375	Ron Guidry	.12
380	Rich Gossage	.15
385	Orel Hershiser	.30
393	Pete Rose	.40
400	George Brett	.35
404	Doug Sisk	.05
405	Brook Jacoby	.10
406	Yankees Ldrs (Rickey Henderson, Don Mattingly)	.15
409	Milt Thompson	.10
410	Fernando Valenzuela	.25
411	Darnell Coles	.05
412	Eric Davis	.90
413	Moose Haas	.05
414	Joe Orsulak	.05
415	*Bobby Witt*	.30
416	Tom Nieto	.05
417	Pat Perry (FC)	.07
418	Dick Williams	.05
419	*Mark Portugal* (FC)	.10
420	*Will Clark*	5.00
421	Jose DeLeon	.07
422	Jack Howell	.07
423	Jaime Cocanower	.05
424	Chris Speier	.05
425	Tom Seaver	.35

427	Ed Nunez	.05
428	Bruce Bochy	.05
429	*Tim Pyznarski* (FC)	.10
430	Mike Schmidt	.40
431	Dodgers Ldrs (Tom Niedenfuer, Ron Perranoski, Alex Trevino)	.07
432	Jim Slaton	.05
433	*Ed Hearn* (FC)	.10
434	Mike Fischlin	.05
435	Bruce Sutter	.15
436	*Andy Allanson*	.15
437	Ted Power	.05
438	*Kelly Downs* (FC)	.30
439	Karl Best	.05
440	Willie McGee	.10
441	*Dave Leiper* (FC)	.10
442	Mitch Webster	.05
443	John Felske	.05
444	Jeff Russell	.07
445	Dave Lopes	.07
446	*Chuck Finley* (FC)	.25
447	Bill Almon	.05
448	*Chris Bosio* (FC)	.25
449	*Pat Dodson* (FC)	.10
450	Kirby Puckett	.30
451	Joe Sambito	.05

130 Dwight Gooden

452	Dave Henderson	.10
453	*Scott Terry* (FC)	.12
454	Luis Salazar	.05
455	Mike Boddicker	.07
456	A's Ldrs (Carney Lansford, Tony LaRussa, Mickey Tettleton, Dave Von Ohlen)	.07
458	Kelly Gruber (FC)	1.00
459	Dennis Eckersley	.10
460	Darryl Strawberry	.35
463	Tom Candiotti	.07
464	Butch Wynegar	.05
465	Todd Worrell	.30
466	Kal Daniels (FC)	1.00
469	*Mike Diaz* (FC)	.15
470	Dave Dravecky	.12
472	Bill Doran	.07
476	Danny Tartabull	.90
479	*Bob Sebra* (FC)	.10
480	Jim Rice	.25
481	Phillies Ldrs (Von Hayes, Juan Samuel, Glenn Wilson)	.07

61 Bobby Thigpen

484	Jim Traber (FC)	.15
485	Tony Fernandez	.10
490	Dale Murphy	.40
491	*Ron Karkovice* (FC)	.10
494	*Barry Jones* (FC)	.12
495	Gorman Thomas	.10
497	*Dale Mohorcic* (FC)	.15
499	*Bruce Ruffin* (FC)	.20
500	Don Mattingly	1.25
506	Orioles Ldrs (Rich Bordi, Rick Dempsey, Earl Weaver)	.07
508	Scott Bankhead	.15
512	*Dave Magadan* (FC)	.50
516	Ted Simmons	.10
520	Jack Clark	.15
521	Rick Reuschel	.10
525	Phil Bradley	.10
530	Tony Gwynn	.35
531	Astros Ldrs (Yogi Berra, Hal Lanier, Denis Menke, Gene Tenace)	.07
536	*Terry Mulholland* (FC)	.10
541	*Rafael Belliard* (FC)	.10
547	Rob Deer	.10
548	Bill Mooneyham (FC)	.10

550	*Pete Incaviglia*	.40
553	*Mike Maddux* (FC)	.15
555	Dennis Rasmussen	.10
556	Angels Ldrs (Bob Boone, Marcel Lachemann, Mike Witt)	.07
557	*John Cerutti*	.15
559	Lance McCullers	.07
560	Glenn Davis	.25
561	*Rey Quinones*	.15
562	*Bryan Clutterbuck* (FC)	.10
567	*Greg Mathews* (FC)	.20
568	Earl Weaver	.07
569	Wade Rowdon (FC)	.07
570	Sid Fernandez	.10
581	Cubs Ldrs (Ron Cey, Steve Trout)	.07
585	*Scott Bailes*	.15
587	Eric Plunk (FC)	.10
590	Vince Coleman	.25
595	Keith Hernandez AS	.12
596	Steve Sax AS	.07
597	Mike Schmidt AS	.20
598	Ozzie Smith AS	.07
599	Tony Gwynn AS	.20
600	Dave Parker AS	.10

1987 Topps

458 Kelly Gruber

1987 TOPPS TRADED

One of the least expensive Topps Traded sets of the past decade, this 132-card issue features more than a few notable first-card appearances. David Cone, Joe Magrane, Fred McGriff, Benny Santiago, Kevin Seitzer, and Matt Williams lead the parade of newcomers. One surprising new face in the Traded set is that of veteran outfielder Kevin McReynolds. The Mets outfielder refused to sign baseball card contracts for several years before finally relenting in 1987. Managers Larry Bowa, Tom Trebelhorn, and Cal Ripken, Sr., are also included. These extras had been overlooked by other card companies.

		MINT
Complete set		**$16.00**
Commons		**.06**

1	Bill Almon	$ .06
2	Scott Bankhead	.08
3	Eric Bell (FC)	.15
5	Juan Berenguer	.06
7	Thad Bosley	.06
8	Larry Bowa	.10
9	Greg Brock	.10
10	Bob Brower (FC)	.15
11	Jerry Browne (FC)	.30
12	Ralph Bryant (FC)	.10
13	DeWayne Buice (FC)	.15
14	Ellis Burks (FC)	2.50
15	Ivan Calderon	.12
17	Casey Candaele (FC)	.10
18	John Cangelosi	.06
19	Steve Carlton	.30
20	Juan Castillo (FC)	.06
21	Rick Cerone	.06
22	Ron Cey	.10
24	Dave Cone (FC)	1.75
25	Chuck Crim (FC)	.15
26	Storm Davis	.06
27	Andre Dawson	.50
28	Rick Dempsey	.10
29	Doug Drabek	.50
30	Mike Dunne	.20
31	Dennis Eckersley	.25
33	Brian Fisher	.10

129 Matt Williams

34	Terry Francona	.06
35	Willie Fraser (FC)	.15
37	Ken Gerhart (FC)	.15
39	Jim Gott	.06
46	Mike Henneman (FC)	.20
49	Brian Holton (FC)	.15
51	Danny Jackson (FC)	.40
52	Reggie Jackson	.50
53	Chris James (FC)	.40
54	Dion James	.40
55	Stan Jefferson (FC)	.20

81 Kevin Mitchell

94	Lance Parrish	.20
95	Tony Pena	.10
96	Luis Polonia (FC)	.30
98	Jeff Reardon	.12
99	Gary Redus	.08
101	Rick Rhoden	.10
103	Wally Ritchie (FC)	.10
104	Jeff Robinson (FC)	.40
109	Benny Santiago (FC)	1.25
110	Dave Schmidt	.08
111	Kevin Seitzer (FC)	.75
113	Steve Shields (FC)	.08
114	John Smiley (FC)	.40
116	Mike Stanley (FC)	.20
117	Terry Steinbach (FC)	.75
118	Les Straker (FC)	.20
119	Jim Sundberg	.08
120	Danny Tartabull	.35
121	Tom Trebelhorn	.08
122	Dave Valle (FC)	.15
124	Andy Van Slyke	.20
125	Gary Ward	.08
126	Alan Wiggins	.08
127	Bill Wilkinson (FC)	.15
128	Frank Williams	.08
129	Matt Williams (FC)	4.00
131	Matt Young	.10

56	Joe Johnson (FC)	.08
57	Terry Kennedy	.08
58	Mike Kingery	.08
59	Ray Knight	.10
60	Gene Larkin (FC)	.25
61	Mike LaValliere	.10
65	Jim Lindeman (FC)	.10
67	Bill Long (FC)	.20
68	Barry Lyons (FC)	.15
69	Shane Mack	.20
70	Greg Maddux (FC)	.65
71	Bill Madlock	.15
72	Joe Magrane (FC)	1.25
73	Dave Martinez (FC)	.25
74	Fred McGriff (FC)	2.50
75	Mark McLemore (FC)	.10
76	Kevin McReynolds (FC)	.65
77	Dave Meads (FC)	.15
80	John Mitchell (FC)	.15
81	Kevin Mitchell	1.75
83	Jeff Musselman (FC)	.25
85	Graig Nettles	.10
88	Tom Niedenfuer	.08
89	Joe Niekro	.10
91	Matt Nokes (FC)	.45
93	Pat Pacillo	.15

117 Terry Steinbach

1988 DONRUSS

Known for gutsy speculation on unknowns while playing down prospective retirees, the 1988 Donruss set includes beginners such as Roberto Alomar, Mark Grace, and Gregg Jefferies. The 660-card set of standard-sized cards features the usual bizarre Donruss design, with off-beat borders of red, black, and blue; Diamond Kings artwork; and a series of Rated Rookies. New was a 26-card separately numbered Bonus Card series with stars such as Cal Ripken, Jr., and Darryl Strawberry, but these cards came only in random wax packs. High-numbered cards—600 and up—were scarce early in 1988, causing a permanent price hike. Superstars commanding top dollar here include Wade Boggs, Don Mattingly, and Mark McGwire.

	MINT
Complete set	**$30.00**
Commons	**.05**

1	Mark McGwire (DK)	$ .75
2	Tim Raines (DK)	.25
3	Benito Santiago (DK)	.30
4	Alan Trammell (DK)	.25
5	Danny Tartabull (DK)	.20
6	Ron Darling (DK)	.12
7	Paul Molitor (DK)	.12
8	Devon White (DK)	.20
9	Andre Dawson (DK)	.20
10	Julio Franco (DK)	.10
11	Scott Fletcher (DK)	.07
12	Tony Fernandez (DK)	.12
13	Shane Rawley (DK)	.07
14	Kal Daniels (DK)	.20
15	Jack Clark (DK)	.15
16	• Dwight Evans (DK)	.12
17	• Tommy John (DK)	.15
18	Andy Van Slyke (DK)	.15
19	Gary Gaetti (DK)	.12
20	Mark Langston (DK)	.10
21	Will Clark (DK)	.85
22	Glenn Hubbard (DK)	.07
23	Billy Hatcher (DK)	.07
24	Bob Welch (DK)	.10
25	Ivan Calderon (DK)	.10
26	Cal Ripken, Jr. (DK)	.35
27	Checklist 1-27	.10
28	*Mackey Sasser* (RR) (FC)	.20
29	*Jeff Treadway* (RR) (FC)	.40
30	*Mike Campbell* (RR) (FC)	.25

34 Roberto Alomar

31	*Lance Johnson* (RR) (FC)	.40
32	*Nelson Liriano* (RR) (FC)	.25
33	Shawn Abner (RR) (FC)	.20
34	*Roberto Alomar (RR) (FC)*	3.00
35	*Shawn Hillegas* (RR) (FC)	.25
36	Joey Meyer (RR)	.15
37	Kevin Elster (RR)	.30
38	*Jose Lind* (RR) (FC)	.30
39	*Kirt Manwaring* (RR) (FC)	.35
40	*Mark Grace* (RR) (FC)	4.00
41	*Jody Reed* (RR) (FC)	.50
42	*John Farrell* (RR) (FC)	.25

1988 Donruss

657 Gregg Jefferies

40 Mark Grace

118	Sid Fernandez	.10
120	Mike Morgan	.05
121	Mark Eichhorn	.07
122	Jeff Reardon	.10
123	John Franco	.10
124	Richard Dotson	.07
126	Juan Nieves	.07
127	Jack Morris	.20
128	Rick Rhoden	.07
129	Rich Gedman	.07
131	Brook Jacoby	.10
132	Danny Jackson	.10
137	Ozzie Guillen	.15
139	*Mike Jackson*	.20
140	*Joe Magrane*	.50
141	Jimmy Jones	.07
144	*Felix Fermin* (FC)	.15
145	Kelly Downs	.10
146	Shawon Dunston	.10
148	Dave Stieb	.10
149	Frank Viola	.15
150	Terry Kennedy	.07
152	*Matt Nokes*	.50
153	Wade Boggs	.75
156	Julio Franco	.10
157	Charlie Leibrandt	.07
158	Terry Steinbach	.10
160	Jack Lazorko	.07
161	Mitch Williams	.07
162	Greg Walker	.07
164	Tony Gwynn	.35
165	Bruce Ruffin	.07
170	Tony Pena	.07
171	Cal Ripken	.35
172	B.J. Surhoff	.10
173	Lou Whitaker	.25
174	Ellis Burks	2.00
175	Ron Guidry	.15
176	Steve Sax	.15
177	Danny Tartabull	.20
178	Carney Lansford	.10
182	Ivan Calderon	.07
183	Jack Clark	.15
184	Glenn Davis	.15
186	Bo Diaz	.07
188	Sid Bream	.07
190	Dion James	.07
191	Leon Durham	.05
192	Jesse Orosco	.07

654 Ron Gant

193	Alvin Davis	.12
194	Gary Gaetti	.15
195	Fred McGriff	.50
198	Rey Quinones	.07
199	Gary Carter	.25
200	Checklist 134-239	.10
201	Keith Moreland	.07
202	Ken Griffey	.10
203	*Tommy Gregg* (FC)	.30
204	Will Clark	1.25
205	John Kruk	.15
206	Buddy Bell	.07
207	Von Hayes	.07
208	Tommy Herr	.07
211	Harold Baines	.12
212	Vance Law	.07
213	Ken Gerhart	.07
215	Chet Lemon	.07
216	Dwight Evans	.12
217	Don Mattingly	1.00
218	Franklin Stubbs	.07
219	Pat Tabler	.07
220	Bo Jackson	1.00
222	Tim Wallach	.10
223	Ruben Sierra	.65
225	Frank White	.07
226	Alfredo Griffin	.07

217 Don Mattingly

280 Kevin Seitzer

1 Mark McGwire

51 Roger Clemens

223 Ruben Sierra

528	*Greg Cadaret* (FC)	.20
534	*Eric Nolte* (FC)	.10
535	Kent Tekulve	.07
536	*Pat Pacillo* (FC)	.15
538	*Tom Prince* (FC)	.15
539	Greg Maddux	.15
541	*Pete Stanicek* (FC)	.25
545	*Jay Buhner* (FC)	.30
546	*Mike Devereaux* (FC)	.30
548	Jose Rijo	.10
552	Dave LaPoint	.07
553	John Tudor	.10
554	*Rocky Childress* (FC)	.10
555	*Wally Ritchie* (FC)	.15
558	Jeff Robinson	.07
560	Ted Simmons	.10
561	*Lester Lancaster*	.15
562	*Keith Miller* (FC)	.25
563	Harold Reynolds	.10
564	*Gene Larkin* (FC)	.20
567	Duane Ward	.07
568	*Bill Wilkinson* (FC)	.15
569	Howard Johnson	.15
571	*Pete Smith* (FC)	.20
575	Dennis Rasmussen	.10
577	*Tom Pagnozzi* (FC)	.15
582	*Rene Gonzales* (FC)	.15
584	Doyle Alexander	.07
587	Tim Belcher (FC)	.35
588	*Doug Jones* (FC)	.50
589	*Melido Perez* (FC)	.30
591	Pascual Perez	.07
594	*John Davis* (FC)	.20
595	Storm Davis	.12
598	Alejandro Pena	.07
600	Checklist 558-660	.10
601	*Jose Mesa* (FC)	.20
602	*Don August* (FC)	.25
603	Terry Leach	.07
604	*Tom Newell* (FC)	.20
605	*Randall Byers* (FC)	.20
608	John Candelaria	.10
609	*Mike Brumley* (FC)	.20
610	Mickey Brantley	.07
611	*Jose Nunez* (FC)	.25
613	Rick Reuschel	.10
614	Lee Mazzilli	.10
615	*Scott Lusader* (FC)	.20
617	Kevin McReynolds	.15

330 Mike Schmidt

619	*Barry Lyons* (FC)	.15
620	Randy Myers	.10
624	*Greg Myers* (FC)	.20
625	Ripken Baseball Family (Billy Ripken, Cal Ripken, Jr., Cal Ripken, Sr.)	.20
627	Andres Thomas	.08
628	*Matt Williams*	3.00
629	*Dave Hengel* (FC)	.20
634	*Wes Gardner* (FC)	.25
635	*Roberto Kelly* (FC)	1.50
636	Mike Flanagan	.12
637	*Jay Bell* (FC)	.20
639	*Damon Berryhill* (FC)	.40
640	*David Wells* (FC)	.25
643	*Keith Hughes* (FC)	.20
644	*Tom Glavine* (FC)	.50
649	Garry Templeton	.10
651	Roger McDowell	.10
652	Mookie Wilson	.15
653	David Cone	.60
654	*Ron Gant* (FC)	2.00
656	George Bell	.25
657	*Gregg Jefferies* (FC)	4.00
658	*Todd Stottlemyre* (FC)	.40
659	*Geronimo Berroa* (FC)	.40
660	Jerry Royster	.10

1988 DONRUSS ROOKIES

Donruss marked its third year of producing "The Rookies" in 1988. Once again, a specially designed box held the set of 55 player cards and an unnumbered checklist. These rookie cards differ in design from the regular set only in border color and "The Rookies" logo in the lower-right portion of each card. But due to a lackluster crop of rookies, this set has just three who are in high demand: Roberto Alomar, Mark Grace, and Chris Sabo. Collectors have overlooked this edition in favor of the larger and more affordable fall issues from Fleer, Score, and Topps.

		MINT
Complete set		$14.00
Commons		.10

1 Mark Grace

1	Mark Grace	$5.00
3	Todd Frohwirth (FC)	.20
5	Shawn Abner	.20
6	Jose Cecena (FC)	.25
7	Dave Gallagher (FC)	.20
8	Mark Parent (FC)	.25
11	Jay Buhner	.25
12	Pat Borders (FC)	.30
13	Doug Jennings (FC)	.25
14	Brady Anderson (FC)	.30
15	Pete Stanicek	.20
16	Roberto Kelly	.75
17	Jeff Treadway	.20
18	Walt Weiss (FC)	1.00
19	Paul Gibson (FC)	.20
21	Melido Perez	.20
22	Steve Peters (FC)	.20
23	Craig Worthington (FC)	.30
27	Al Leiter	.20
28	Tim Belcher	.25
29	Johnny Paredes (FC)	.20
30	Chris Sabo (FC)	2.75
31	Damon Berryhill	.25
32	Randy Milligan (FC)	.50
33	Gary Thurman	.20
34	Kevin Elster	.20
35	Roberto Alomar	1.25
36	Edgar Martinez	.75
37	Todd Stottlemyre	.20
38	Joey Meyer	.15
41	Jose Bautista (FC)	.20
42	Sil Campusano (FC)	.15
43	John Dopson (FC)	.20
44	Jody Reed	.35
45	Darrin Jackson (FC)	.20
46	Mike Capel (FC)	.20
47	Ron Gant	1.00
50	Cris Carpenter (FC)	.35
51	Mackey Sasser	.25
53	Bryan Harvey (FC)	.30
55	Mike Macfarlane	.25

1988 FLEER

This 660-card set features backs that carry a wealth of information. Full career statistics and graphs showing performance in various ballparks are complemented by "At Their Best" individualized highlights. Card fronts are white, with a border of busy blue and red diagonals, while player photos feature blended backgrounds. Star combo cards join players by team or position, with Major League Prospects pairing off rookies, Mark Grace among them. Photos featuring surfboards or players with two gloves pleased some purchasers but offended others. As always, however, the greatest complaints concerned spotty distribution.

378 Edgar Martinez

		MINT
Complete set		**$48.00**
Commons		**.06**

2	Don Baylor	S .10
4	Bert Blyleven	.12
5	Tom Brunansky	.15
6	Randy Bush	.08
7	Steve Carlton	.25
8	*Mark Davidson* (FC)	.12
10	Gary Gaetti	.10
11	Greg Gagne	.08
13	Kent Hrbek	.15
14	*Gene Larkin*	.20
18	Joe Niekro	.08
19	Kirby Puckett	.60
20	Jeff Reardon	.12
21	Dan Schatzader (incorrect spelling)	.40
21	Dan Schatzeder (correct spelling)	.10
24	*Les Straker* (FC)	.15
25	Frank Viola	.25
26	Jack Clark	.15
27	Vince Coleman	.30
28	Danny Cox	.08
33	Bob Forsch	.08
35	Tom Herr	.08
37	*Lance Johnson* (FC)	.35
40	*Joe Magrane*	.45
42	Willie McGee	.12
45	Tony Pena	.08
47	Ozzie Smith	.20
48	John Tudor	.10
50	Todd Worrell	.10
54	Darrell Evans	.10
55	Kirk Gibson	.20
57	*Mike Henneman*	.25
58	Willie Hernandez	.08
60	Eric King	.08
61	Chet Lemon	.08
62	*Scott Lusader* (FC)	.15
63	Bill Madlock	.10
64	Jack Morris	.20
66	*Matt Nokes*	.40
68	Jeff Robinson (born 12/13/60 on back)	.70
68	*Jeff Robinson* (born 12/14/61 on back)	.20

429 Rafael Palmeiro

214 Don Mattingly

166	Ted Higuera	.10
169	Paul Molitor	.12
170	Juan Nieves	.08
171	Dan Plesac	.10
174	*Steve Stanicek* (FC)	.15
175	B.J. Surhoff	.15
176	Dale Sveum	.08
178	Robin Yount	.35
179	Hubie Brooks	.10
180	Tim Burke	.08
184	Andres Galarraga	.15
187	Vance Law	.08
193	Tim Raines	.25
195	Bob Sebra	.08
196	Bryn Smith	.08
198	Tim Wallach	.10
199	Mitch Webster	.08
202	*Brad Arnsberg* (FC)	.20
203	Rick Cerone	.06
205	Henry Cotto	.08
206	Mike Easler	.08
207	Ron Guidry	.15
209	Rickey Henderson	.60
211	Tommy John	.15
212	*Roberto Kelly* (FC)	1.75
213	Ron Kittle	.08
214	Don Mattingly	1.50
216	Mike Pagliarulo	.10
217	Dan Pasqua	.10
219	Rick Rhoden	.08
220	Dave Righetti	.15
226	Dave Winfield	.30
227	Buddy Bell	.08
228	Tom Browning	.10
230	Kal Daniels	.25
231	Eric Davis	.40
233	Nick Esasky	.12
234	John Franco	.10
237	Tracy Jones	.12
238	*Bill Landrum* (FC)	.20
239	Barry Larkin	.90
241	Rob Murphy	.08
243	Dave Parker	.20
248	Kurt Stillwell	.10
249	*Jeff Treadway* (FC)	.35
252	Bud Black	.08
253	Thad Bosley	.06
254	George Brett	.40
255	John Davis (FC)	.20

101 Matt Williams

256	Steve Farr	.08
257	Gene Garber	.08
259	Mark Gubicza	.12
260	Bo Jackson	3.25
261	Danny Jackson	.12
262	*Ross Jones* (FC)	.12
264	*Bill Pecota*	.15
265	*Melido Perez* (FC)	.40
268	Bret Saberhagen	.25
270	Kevin Seitzer	.30
271	Danny Tartabull	.20
272	*Gary Thurman* (FC)	.20
273	Frank White	.08
274	Willie Wilson	.10
276	Jose Canseco	3.00
277	Mike Davis	.08
278	Storm Davis	.12
279	Dennis Eckersley	.12
280	Alfredo Griffin	.08
282	Jay Howell	.08
283	Reggie Jackson	.50
284	Dennis Lamp	.08
285	Carney Lansford	.10
286	Mark McGwire	2.75
288	Gene Nelson	.06
290	Tony Phillips	.08
291	Eric Plunk	.08

137 Gregg Jefferies

292	Luis Polonia	.50
294	Terry Steinbach	.12
295	Dave Stewart	.20
296	Curt Young	.08
298	Steve Bedrosian	.12
300	Don Carman	.08
301	Todd Frohwirth (FC)	.20
304	Von Hayes	.12
305	Keith Hughes (FC)	.20
306	Mike Jackson	.15
307	Chris James	.20
310	Lance Parrish	.17
312	Wally Ritchie	.15
313	Bruce Ruffin	.08
314	Juan Samuel	.12
315	Mike Schmidt	.65
318	Kent Tekulve	.08
319	Milt Thompson	.08
320	Glenn Wilson	.08
322	Barry Bonds	1.10
323	Bobby Bonilla	.90
324	Sid Bream	.08
327	Doug Drabek	.25
328	Mike Dunne	.25
329	Brian Fisher	.08
334	Jose Lind (FC)	.50
335	Junior Ortiz	.06

336	Vicente Palacios (FC)	.25
337	Bob Patterson (FC)	.12
338	Al Pedrique (FC)	.20
339	R.J. Reynolds	.06
340	John Smiley	.65
341	Andy Van Slyke	.17
344	Todd Benzinger (FC)	.30
345	Wade Boggs	1.00
346	Tom Bolton (FC)	.35
348	Ellis Burks	3.00
349	Roger Clemens	1.00
351	• Dwight Evans	.15
352	Wes Gardner (FC)	.25
354	Mike Greenwell	2.00
355	Sam Horn (FC)	.30
356	Bruce Hurst	.10
357	John Marzano (FC)	.20
358	Al Nipper	.06
360	Jody Reed (FC)	.75
361	Jim Rice	.20
366	Jeff Sellers	.08
367	Bob Stanley	.06
369	Phil Bradley	.10
370	Scott Bradley	.06
372	Mike Campbell (FC)	.25
373	Alvin Davis	.12
375	Dave Hengel (FC)	.20
377	Mark Langston	.17
378	Edgar Martinez (FC)	1.35
379	Mike Moore	.10
380	Mike Morgan	.06
381	John Moses	.06
382	Donnell Nixon (FC)	.20
385	Jim Presley	.08
387	Jerry Reed	.06
388	Harold Reynolds	.10
390	Bill Wilkinson (FC)	.15
391	Harold Baines	.12
393	Daryl Boston	.06
394	Ivan Calderon	.30
395	Jose DeLeon	.10
397	Carlton Fisk	.25
398	Ozzie Guillen	.08
399	Ron Hassey	.06
402	Dave LaPoint	.06
403	Bill Lindsey (FC)	.12
404	Bill Long (FC)	.20
405	Steve Lyons	.06
406	Fred Manrique	.15

407	*Jack McDowell* (FC)	**1.35**
409	Ray Searage	.06
410	Bobby Thigpen	.25
411	Greg Walker	.08
412	*Kenny Williams*	.20
413	Jim Winn	.06
414	Jody Davis	.06
415	Andre Dawson	.30
419	Shawon Dunston	.25
420	Leon Durham	.06
421	*Les Lancaster* (FC)	.15
422	Ed Lynch	.06
423	Greg Maddux	.60
425	Keith Moreland (bunting, photo is Jody Davis)	**3.50**
425	Keith Moreland (standing, correct photo)	.10
426	Jamie Moyer	.06
428	*Paul Noce* (FC)	.10
429	Rafael Palmeiro (FC)	**1.50**
430	Wade Rowdon (FC)	.06
431	Ryne Sandberg	.80
433	Lee Smith	.10
435	Rick Sutcliffe	.10
436	Manny Trillo	.06
439	Alan Ashby	.06
440	Kevin Bass	.08
441	*Ken Caminiti* (FC)	.35
442	*Rocky Childress* (FC)	.12
443	Jose Cruz	.10
445	Glenn Davis	.25
447	Bill Doran	.08
449	Billy Hatcher	.08
451	Bob Knepper	.06
452	*Rob Mallicoat* (FC)	.10
453	*Dave Meads*	.15
455	Nolan Ryan	**1.10**
456	Mike Scott	.15
457	Dave Smith	.08
459	*Robbie Wine* (FC)	.10
460	*Gerald Young* (FC)	.20
461	Bob Brower	.08
462	Jerry Browne (photo is Bob Brower)	**3.50**
462	Jerry Browne (correct photo)	.10
465	*Cecil Espy* (FC)	.20
468	Greg Harris	.06
470	Pete Incaviglia	.15

78 Will Clark

471	*Paul Kilgus* (FC)	.20
472	Mike Loynd	.06
475	Pete O'Brien	.10
478	Jeff Russell	.10
479	Ruben Sierra	**1.25**
482	Mitch Williams	.10
483	Bobby Witt	.20
484	Tony Armas	.06
485	• Bob Boone	.25
486	Bill Buckner	.10
487	*DeWayne Buice*	.15
489	Chuck Finley	.08
490	Willie Fraser	.06
491	Jack Howell	.08
493	Wally Joyner	.40
501	Gus Polidor	.06
502	Johnny Ray	.10
503	Mark Ryal (FC)	.06
505	Don Sutton	.20
506	Devon White	.20
507	Mike Witt	.08
509	Tim Belcher (FC)	.40
510	Ralph Bryant	.06
511	*Tim Crews* (FC)	.15
512	*Mike Devereaux* (FC)	.35
514	Pedro Guerrero	.15
515	Jeff Hamilton (FC)	.12

641 Major League Prospects

518	Orel Hershiser	.25	570	Cal Ripken Jr. ..... .45
519	*Shawn Hillegas* (FC)	.15	573	*Pete Stanicek* (FC) ..... .25
521	Tim Leary	.08	574	*Mark Williamson* (FC) ..... .15
522	Mike Marshall	.12	575	Mike Young ..... .06
523	Steve Sax	.15	576	Shawn Abner (FC) ..... .20
526	John Shelby	.06	578	Chris Brown ..... .06
528	Fernando Valenzuela	.12	579	*Keith Comstock* (FC) ..... .10
529	Bob Welch	.10	580	*Joey Cora* (FC) ..... .12
530	Matt Young	.06	581	Mark Davis ..... .10
531	Jim Acker	.06	583	Goose Gossage ..... .15
533	*Jeff Blauser* (FC)	.25	584	Mark Grant ..... .06
534	*Joe Boever* (FC)	.15	585	Tony Gwynn ..... .35
536	*Kevin Coffman* (FC)	.10	587	Stan Jefferson ..... .06
538	*Ron Gant* (FC)	3.00	589	John Kruk ..... .10
539	*Tom Glavine* (FC)	.50	590	*Shane Mack* (FC) ..... .20
540	Ken Griffey	.08	593	*Eric Nolte* (FC) ..... .15
543	Dion James	.08	594	Randy Ready ..... .06
544	Dale Murphy	.40	595	Luis Salazar ..... .06
547	Gerald Perry	.08	596	Benito Santiago ..... .45
549	Ted Simmons	.10	597	Eric Show ..... .08
550	Zane Smith	.06	598	Garry Templeton ..... .08
552	Ozzie Virgil	.06	599	Ed Whitson ..... .08
553	Don Aase	.06	600	Scott Bailes ..... .06
554	*Jeff Ballard* (FC)	.35	601	Chris Bando ..... .06
555	Eric Bell	.06	602	*Jay Bell* (FC) ..... .35
557	Ken Dixon	.06	603	Brett Butler ..... .08
558	Jim Dwyer	.06	604	Tom Candiotti ..... .06
560	*Rene Gonzales* (FC)	.15	605	Joe Carter ..... .25
564	Ray Knight	.08	606	Carmen Castillo ..... .06
565	Lee Lacy	.06	607	*Brian Dorsett* (FC) ..... .15
566	Fred Lynn	.15	608	*John Farrell* (FC) ..... .25
567	Eddie Murray	.35	609	Julio Franco ..... .15
569	*Bill Ripken* (FC)	.25	610	Mel Hall ..... .06

407 Jack McDowell

1988 FLEER UPDATE

This 132-card fall "extension" set, the fifth such release from Fleer, failed to compete successfully with the Olympian-filled Topps Traded set. Cards for Roberto Alomar, Mark Grace, and Chris Sabo are the most precious. And there is one unusual pairing in the set: Card U-113, supposedly of Tommy Gregg, actually depicts Pirates teammate Randy Milligan (Milligan also got his own card, number U-115). Unlike the alphabetical system used by Topps, Fleer Updates are arranged by team. (The "U" that appears on the actual cards has been omitted from the following lists.)

		MINT
Complete set		**$14.00**
Commons		**.06**

77 Mark Grace

1	Jose Bautista (FC)	$ .15
4	Craig Worthington (FC)	.30
5	Mike Boddicker	.10
8	Lee Smith	.10
10	John Trautwein (FC)	.15
11	Sherman Corbett (FC)	.15
12	Chili Davis	.10
14	Bryan Harvey (FC)	.35
16	Dave Gallagher (FC)	.15
19	Melido Perez	.15
20	Jose Segura (FC)	.15
21	Andy Allanson	.10
23	Domingo Ramos	.12
26	Paul Gibson (FC)	.15
27	Don Heinkel (FC)	.15
30	Luis Salazar	.10
31	Mike McFarlane (Macfarlane) (FC)	.20
32	Jeff Montgomery	.12
34	Israel Sanchez (FC)	.15
35	Kurt Stillwell	.10
37	Don August (FC)	.20
38	Darryl Hamilton (FC)	.20
39	Jeff Leonard	.12
40	Joey Meyer	.15
41	Andy Allanson	.10
43	Tom Herr	.10
46	John Candelaria	.10
47	Jack Clark	.15
48	Richard Dotson	.12
49	Al Leiter (FC)	.20
52	Todd Burns (FC)	.20
53	Dave Henderson	.20
54	Doug Jennings (FC)	.15
55	Dave Parker	.12
56	Walt Weiss	.60
57	Bob Welch	.10
59	Mario Diaz	.12
60	Mike Jackson	.12
61	Bill Swift	.12
62	Jose Cecena (FC)	.15

64	Jim Steels	.15	96	Jesse Orosco	.08
65	Pat Borders (FC)	.35	98	Tracy Woodson	.15
66	Sil Campusano (FC)	.20	99	John Dopson (FC)	.20
68	Todd Stottlemyre (FC)	.50	100	Brian Holman (FC)	.50
69	David Wells	.20	102	Jeff Parrett (FC)	.10
70	Jose Alvarez (FC)	.15	103	Nelson Santovenia (FC)	.20
72	Cesar Jiminez		104	Kevin Elster	.12
	(German) (FC)	.15	105	Jeff Innis (FC)	.15
74	John Smoltz (FC)	1.00	106	Mackey Sasser (FC)	.25
75	Damon Berryhill	.20	107	Phil Bradley	.15
76	Goose Gossage	.15	108	Danny Clay (FC)	.15
77	Mark Grace	4.00	110	Ricky Jordan (FC)	1.00
80	Jeff Pico (FC)	.20	112	Jim Gott	.08
81	Gary Varsho (FC)	.15	113	Tommy Gregg (photo is	
82	Tim Birtsas	.10		Randy Milligan) (FC)	.20
83	Rob Dibble (FC)	1.00	115	Randy Milligan (FC)	.60
84	Danny Jackson	.10	116	Luis Alicea (FC)	.15
85	Paul O'Neill	.15	117	Tom Brunansky	.15
86	Jose Rijo	.15	118	John Costello (FC)	.15
87	Chris Sabo (FC)	2.00	121	Scott Terry (FC)	.08
88	John Fishel (FC)	.15	122	Roberto Alomar (FC)	2.25
89	Craig Biggio (FC)	1.50	125	Mark Parent (FC)	.15
92	Louie Meadows (FC)	.15	128	Brett Butler	.12
93	Kirk Gibson	.20	129	Donell Nixon	.12
94	Alfredo Griffin	.12	131	Roger Samuels	.15

1988 SCORE

Score's 660-card 1988 set was applauded for information-filled backs and color photo insets. Fronts feature a simple bold border in one of six colors. Player names and positions are prominently centered at the bottom with the Score logo at the lower right. The cards were sold in poly-bags that could not be tampered with and resealed (unlike the wax packs from Donruss, Fleer, and Topps). Initially, many cards from the poly-bags were damaged, but they were replaced by the company. Subsets include Rookie Prospects, 1987 Highlights, and a five-card salute to Reggie Jackson. (Rookie Prospects are identified on the following list with the abbreviation RP.)

		MINT			
Complete set		**$25.00**	3	Tim Raines	.20
Commons		**.04**	4	Andre Dawson	.15
			5	Mark McGwire	1.00
1	Don Mattingly	$1.50	6	Kevin Seitzer	.30
2	Wade Boggs	1.00	7	Wally Joyner	.35

645 Gregg Jefferies

8	Jesse Barfield	.10
9	Pedro Guerrero	.12
10	Eric Davis	.60
11	George Brett	.30
12	Ozzie Smith	.15
13	Rickey Henderson	.50
14	Jim Rice	.15
15	*Matt Nokes*	.25
16	Mike Schmidt	.50
17	Dave Parker	.12
18	Eddie Murray	.25
19	Andres Galarraga	.15
20	Tony Fernandez	.15
21	Kevin McReynolds	.15
22	B.J. Surhoff	.10
23	Pat Tabler	.06
24	Kirby Puckett	.30
25	Benny Santiago	.35
26	Ryne Sandberg	.40
27	Kelly Downs	.08
28	Jose Cruz	.06
29	Pete O'Brien	.06
30	Mark Langston	.15
31	Lee Smith	.08
32	Juan Samuel	.10
33	Kevin Bass	.06
35	Steve Sax	.12

36	John Kruk	.12
37	Alan Trammell	.15
38	Chris Bosio	.06
39	Brook Jacoby	.08
40	Willie McGee	.10
41	Dave Magadan	.10
42	Fred Lynn	.10
43	Kent Hrbek	.12
44	Brian Downing	.06
45	Jose Canseco	1.75
46	Jim Presley	.06
47	Mike Stanley	.06
48	Tony Pena	.06
49	David Cone	.60
50	Rick Sutcliffe	.08
51	Doug Drabek	.15
52	Bill Doran	.06
53	Mike Scioscia	.06
54	Candy Maldonado	.06
55	Dave Winfield	.25
56	Lou Whitaker	.20
57	Tom Henke	.06
58	Ken Gerhart	.06
59	Glenn Braggs	.08
60	Julio Franco	.08
61	Charlie Leibrandt	.06
62	Gary Gaetti	.10

118 Matt Williams

63	• Bob Boone	.08
64	*Luis Polonia*	.25
65	• Dwight Evans	.10
66	Phil Bradley	.08
67	Mike Boddicker	.15
68	Vince Coleman	.15
69	Howard Johnson	.15
70	Tim Wallach	.08
71	Keith Moreland	.06
72	Barry Larkin	.30
73	Alan Ashby	.04
74	Rick Rhoden	.06
75	Darrell Evans	.08
76	Dave Stieb	.08
77	Dan Plesac	.08
78	Will Clark	1.25
79	Frank White	.08
80	Joe Carter	.18
81	Mike Witt	.06
82	Terry Steinbach	.15
83	Alvin Davis	.10
84	Tom Herr	.06
85	Vance Law	.06
86	Kal Daniels	.15
88	Alfredo Griffin	.06
89	Bret Saberhagen	.35
90	Bert Blyleven	.10
91	Jeff Reardon	.08
92	Cory Snyder	.15
93	Greg Walker	.06
94	*Joe Magrane*	.25
95	Rob Deer	.06
96	Ray Knight	.06
97	Casey Candaele	.04
98	John Cerutti	.06
99	Buddy Bell	.08
100	Jack Clark	.12
101	Eric Bell	.06
102	Willie Wilson	.08
103	Dave Schmidt	.04
104	Dennis Eckersley	.10
105	Don Sutton	.12
106	Danny Tartabull	.15
107	Fred McGriff	.90
108	*Les Straker*	.15
109	Lloyd Moseby	.06
110	Roger Clemens	.50
112	*Ken Williams*	.10
113	Ruben Sierra	.50

45 Jose Canseco

114	Stan Jefferson	.06
115	Milt Thompson	.08
116	Bobby Bonilla	.35
118	Matt Williams	2.25
119	Chet Lemon	.06
120	Dale Sveum	.06
123	Terry Kennedy	.06
124	Jack Howell	.06
125	Curt Young	.06
126	Dale Valle (first name incorrect)	.25
126	Dave Valle (first name correct)	.12
127	Curt Wilkerson	.04
128	Tim Teufel	.04
130	Brian Fisher	.06
131	Lance Parrish	.12
132	Tom Browning	.08
133	Larry Anderson (incorrect spelling)	.25
133	Larry Andersen (correct spelling)	.10
134	Bob Brenley (incorrect spelling)	.25
134	Bob Brenly (correct spelling)	.10
135	Mike Marshall	.10

175 Mike Greenwell

2 Wade Boggs

647 Ronnie Gant

180 Bo Jackson

280	Ted Higuera	.08
283	*Mark Wasinger*	.10
285	Ted Simmons	.08
287	*John Smiley*	.30
290	Dan Quisenberry	.06
293	John Candelaria	.06
297	Terry Franconia (incorrect spelling)	.25
297	Terry Francona (correct spelling)	.08
299	Andres Thomas	.06
301	*Alfredo Pedrique*	.12
302	Jim Lindeman	.06
303	Wally Backman	.06
304	Paul O'Neill	.15
305	Hubie Brooks	.08
307	Bobby Thigpen	.15
308	George Hendrick	.06
310	Ron Guidry	.12
312	*Jose Nunez*	.12
315	Scott McGregor	.06
322	Jose Guzman	.06
325	Gary Carter	.15
326	Tracy Jones	.10
329	*Paul Noce*	.10
331	Goose Gossage	.12
335	Mike Scott	.10

336	Randy Myers	.15
338	Eric Show	.06
339	Mitch Williams	.10
340	Paul Molitor	.10
344	Bob Knepper	.04
345	Mitch Webster	.06
350	Dwight Gooden	.40
351	Dave Righetti	.12
360	Darryl Strawberry	.35
376	*DeWayne Buice*	.15
377	*Bill Pecota*	.15
385	Tony Gwynn	.25
400	Keith Hernandez	.15
414	*Shane Mack*	.15
419	John Christansen (incorrect spelling)	.25
419	John Christensen (correct spelling)	.08
432	*Mike Dunne*	.20
436	*Donnell Nixon*	.15
442	*Gerald Young*	.12
450	Dale Murphy	.25
460	Glenn Davis	.12
470	Orel Hershiser	.20
472	*Ellis Burks*	1.50
481	Kevin Mitchell	.60
485	Pete Incaviglia	.12

186 Rafael Palmeiro

495	Jesse Orosco	.06
496	*Robby Wine Jr.*	.10
497	*Jeff Montgomery*	.18
500	Reggie Jackson (1968-75, Oakland Athletics)	.20
501	Reggie Jackson (1976, Baltimore Orioles)	.20
502	Reggie Jackson (1977-81, New York Yankees)	.20
503	Reggie Jackson (1982-86, California Angels)	.20
504	Reggie Jackson (1987, Oakland Athletics)	.20
505	Billy Hatcher	.06
507	Willie Hernandez	.06
508	Jose DeLeon	.08
510	Bob Welch	.08
513	Juan Nieves	.06
515	Von Hayes	.12
516	Mark Gubicza	.10
519	Rick Reuschel	.08
520	*Mike Henneman*	.20
522	Jay Howell	.06
524	Manny Trillo	.06
525	Kirk Gibson	.15
526	*Wally Ritchie*	.12
527	Al Nipper	.04
529	Shawon Dunston	.15
530	Jim Clancy	.06
535	John Franco	.08
536	*Paul Kilgus*	.20
537	Darrell Porter	.06
538	Walt Terrell	.06
539	*Bill Long*	.15
540	George Bell	.20
541	Jeff Sellers	.06
542	*Joe Boever*	.12
543	Steve Howe	.06
545	Jack Morris	.15
546	*Todd Benzinger*	.20
549	*Jeff Robinson*	.12
550	Cal Ripken Jr.	.25
552	Kirk McCaskill	.06
554	Darnell Coles	.06
555	Phil Niekro	.15
556	Mike Aldrete	.06
559	Rob Murphy	.06
560	Dennis Rasmussen	.08
562	*Jeff Blauser*	.20

481 Kevin Mitchell

564	Dave Dravecky	.06
567	*Tommy Hinzo*	.12
568	*Eric Nolte*	.12
570	*Mark Davidson*	.12
571	*Jim Walewander*	.12
573	Jamie Moyer	.06
575	Nolan Ryan	.55
578	*Jay Aldrich*	.10
579	Claudell Washington	.06
580	Jeff Leonard	.06
583	*Jeff DeWilis*	.15
584	*John Marzano*	.20
585	Bill Gullickson	.06
586	Andy Allanson	.08
589	Dave LaPoint	.06
590	Harold Baines	.10
591	Bill Buckner	.08
592	Carlton Fisk	.25
594	*Doug Jones*	.25
597	*Jose Lind*	.25
598	*Ross Jones*	.12
599	Gary Matthews	.06
600	Fernando Valenzuela	.12
601	Dennis Martinez	.06
602	*Les Lancaster*	.15
603	Ozzie Guillen	.06
605	Chili Davis	.06

26 Ryne Sandberg

575 Nolan Ryan

1988 SCORE ROOKIE & TRADED

This modest 110-card offering from Score became the sleeper hit of the year in the hobby world. Although Score's debut set of 660 cards earlier in the year was an immediate success, the cards were taken for granted due to an abundant supply. Hobbyists slow to pick up the regular issue found a smaller supply of the fall extension sets. As with other companies, Score maintained the same card design and marketing formula for the Rookie & Traded set. However, Score grouped all the first-time players in the last half of the set (66 to 110), making things easier for rookie-card specialists. Prominent rookies include Roberto Alomar, Mark Grace, and Chris Sabo. This set is three times more valuable than the company's regular set for 1988.

	MINT
Complete set	**$75.00**
Commons	.15

1	Jack Clark	$ .20
2	Danny Jackson	.20
4	Kurt Stillwell	.25
5	Tom Brunansky	.20
6	Dennis Lamp	.10
7	Jose DeLeon	.10
8	Tom Herr	.10
10	Kirk Gibson	.30
14	Goose Gossage	.15
15	Bob Welch	.10
18	Dan Quisenberry	.10
20	Lee Smith	.10
22	Pat Tabler	.15
23	Larry McWilliams	.15
24	Ricky Horton	.15
25	Graig Nettles	.10
26	Dan Petry	.10
27	Jose Rijo	.15
28	Chili Davis	.15
29	Dickie Thon	.10
30	Mackey Sasser (FC)	.40
31	Mickey Tettleton	.15
32	Rick Dempsey	.15
33	Ron Hassey	.15
34	Phil Bradley	.10

80 Mark Grace

35	Jay Howell	.15
37	Alfredo Griffin	.15
38	Gary Pettis	.15
44	Ron Kittle	.15
45	Bob Dernier	.15
46	Steve Balboni	.15
47	Steve Shields	.15

1988 Score Rookie & Traded

105 Roberto Alomar

84	Pete Smith (FC)	.30
85	Jack McDowell (FC)	3.00
86	Rob Dibble (FC)	2.50
87	Brian Harvey (FC)	.85
88	John Dopson (FC)	.35
89	Dave Gallagher (FC)	.35
90	Todd Stottlemyre (FC)	1.75
91	Mike Schooler (FC)	1.00
92	Don Gordon (FC)	.10
93	Sil Campusano (FC)	.40
94	Jeff Pico (FC)	.25
95	Jay Buhner (FC)	2.25
96	Nelson Santovenia (FC)	.30
97	Al Leiter (FC)	.30
98	Luis Alicea (FC)	.20
99	Pat Borders (FC)	.80
100	Chris Sabo (FC)	8.00
101	Tim Belcher (FC)	1.00
102	Walt Weiss (FC)	2.00
103	Craig Biggio (FC)	4.00
104	Don August (FC)	.25
105	Roberto Alomar (FC)	10.00
106	Todd Burns (FC)	.45
107	John Costello (FC)	.20
108	Melido Perez (FC)	.90
109	Darrin Jackson (FC)	.10
110	Orestes Destrade (FC)	.50

49	Dave Henderson	.30
50	Dave Parker	.25
54	Rafael Santana	.15
55	Don Baylor	.15
58	Glenn Hubbard	.15
59	Mike Smithson	.15
60	Richard Dotson	.15
62	Mike Jackson	.15
64	Jesse Orosco	.15
65	Larry Parrish	.15
66	Jeff Bittiger (FC)	.15
67	Ray Hayward (FC)	.15
68	Ricky Jordan (FC)	1.50
69	Tommy Gregg (FC)	.30
70	Brady Anderson (FC)	.50
72	Darryl Hamilton (FC)	.50
73	Cecil Espy (FC)	.25
74	Greg Briley (FC)	1.25
75	Joey Meyer (FC)	.20
76	Mike Macfarlane (FC)	.35
77	Oswald Peraza (FC)	.20
78	Jack Armstrong (FC)	1.75
79	Don Heinkel (FC)	.20
80	Mark Grace (FC)	27.00
81	Steve Curry (FC)	.20
82	Damon Berryhill (FC)	.75
83	Steve Ellsworth (FC)	.20

95 Jay Buhner

1988 TOPPS

The design of the 1988 Topps cards was simple—often compared to a magazine cover—but effective. Sharply focused action photos have soft backgrounds, with bold team names across the top that are partially obscured by the players' heads. Diagonal stripes in the lower right-hand corner display the player name, and gray card backs show complete major league stats. Subsets in this 792-card issue include seven Record Breakers (with McGwire and Mattingly, among others), five Future Stars, 26 team leaders with vintage photos, 22 All-Stars, and 10 All-Star rookies honored with special trophy designations (such as second-year player Matt Nokes).

	MINT
Complete set	$27.00
Commons	.04

778 Keith Comstock

1	'87 Record Breakers (Vince Coleman)	$ .20
2	'87 Record Breakers (Don Mattingly)	.60
3	'87 Record Breakers (Mark McGwire)	.60
4	'87 Record Breakers (Eddie Murray) (record headline on front)	.65
4	'87 Record Breakers (Eddie Murray) (no headline)	.40
5	'87 Record Breakers (Joe Niekro, Phil Niekro)	.10
6	'87 Record Breakers (Nolan Ryan)	.25
7	'87 Record Breakers (Benito Santiago)	.15
8	Kevin Elster (FC)	.10
10	Ryne Sandberg	.35
18	*Al Leiter* (FC) (photo is Steve George; no "NY" on jersey)	.40
18	*Al Leiter* (FC) (correct photo; "NY" on jersey)	.15
19	*Mark Davidson* (FC)	.12
21	Red Sox Ldrs (Wade Boggs, Spike Owen)	.15
22	Greg Swindell	.12
25	Andres Galarraga	.12
28	*Jose Nunez* (FC)	.20
30	Sid Fernandez	.08
35	Harold Baines	.10
39	Gerald Perry	.08
40	Orel Hershiser	.20
42	*Bill Landrum* (FC)	.17
45	Kent Hrbek	.12
49	Dave Clark (FC)	.10
50	Hubie Brooks	.10
51	Orioles Ldrs (Eddie Murray, Cal Ripken)	.12
55	Phil Bradley	.10
57	*Tim Crews* (FC)	.15
58	Dave Magadan	.15
60	Rickey Henderson	.35

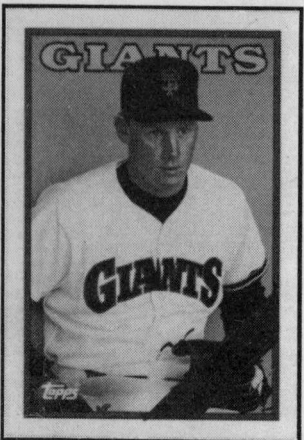

372 Matt Williams

269 Ellis Burks

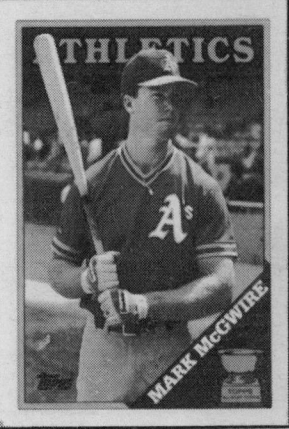

580 Mark McGwire

618 Cecil Fielder

200 Wade Boggs

250 Nolan Ryan

70 Roger Clemens

275 Kevin Seitzer

666	Mario Soto	.06
667	Luis Quinones	.04
668	Walt Terrell	.06
669	Phillies Ldrs (Lance Parrish, Mike Ryan)	.06
670	Dan Plesac	.08
671	Tim Laudner	.04
672	John Davis (FC)	.15
673	Tony Phillips	.08
674	Mike Fitzgerald	.04
675	Jim Rice	.10
676	Ken Dixon	.04
677	Eddie Milner	.04
678	Jim Acker	.04
679	Darrell Miller	.04
680	Charlie Hough	.08
681	Bobby Bonilla	.12
682	Jimmy Key	.08
683	Julio Franco	.10
684	Hal Lanier	.04
685	Ron Darling	.10
686	Terry Francona	.04
687	Mickey Brantley	.04
688	Jim Winn	.04
689	Tom Pagnozzi	.12
690	Jay Howell	.08
691	Dan Pasqua	.08

692	Mike Birkbeck	.06
693	Benny Santiago	.40
694	Eric Nolte (FC)	.12
695	Shawon Dunston	.15
696	Duane Ward	.06
697	Steve Lombardozzi	.08
698	Brad Havens	.04
699	Padres Ldrs (Tony Gwynn, Benny Santiago)	.12
700	George Brett	.30
701	Sammy Stewart	.04
702	Mike Gallego	.04
703	Bob Brenly	.04
704	Dennis Boyd	.06
705	Juan Samuel	.10
706	Rick Mahler	.06
707	Fred Lynn	.10
708	Gus Polidor (FC)	.06
709	George Frazier	.04
710	Darryl Strawberry	.35
711	Bill Gullickson	.06
712	John Moses	.04
713	Willie Hernandez	.06
714	Jim Fregosi	.06
715	Todd Worrell	.08
716	Lenn Sakata	.04
717	Jay Baller (FC)	.06
718	Mike Felder	.04
719	Denny Walling	.04
720	Tim Raines	.20
721	Pete O'Brien	.10
722	Manny Lee	.04
723	Bob Kipper	.04
724	Danny Tartabull	.15
725	Mike Boddicker	.06
726	Alfredo Griffin	.06
727	Greg Booker	.04
728	Andy Allanson	.04
729	Blue Jays Ldrs (George Bell, Fred McGriff)	.10
730	John Franco	.10
731	Rick Schu	.04
732	Dave Palmer	.04
733	Spike Owen	.04
734	Craig Lefferts	.06
735	Kevin McReynolds	.17
736	Matt Young	.04
737	Butch Wynegar	.04
738	Scott Bankhead	.06

739	Daryl Boston	.04
740	Rick Sutcliffe	.08
741	Mike Easler	.04
742	Mark Clear	.04
743	Larry Herndon	.04
744	Whitey Herzog	.06
745	Bill Doran	.08
746	*Gene Larkin*	.15
747	Bobby Witt	.15
748	Reid Nichols	.06
749	Mark Eichhorn	.06
750	Bo Jackson	1.05
751	Jim Morrison	.04
752	Mark Grant	.06
753	Danny Heep	.04
754	Mike LaCoss	.04
755	Ozzie Virgil	.04
756	Mike Maddux	.04
757	*John Marzano*	.20
758	Eddie Williams (FC)	.20
759	A's Ldrs (Jose Canseco, Mark McGwire)	.45
760	Mike Scott	.10
761	Tony Armas	.06
762	Scott Bradley	.04
767	*Jose Lind* (FC)	.25
768	Dickie Noles	.04
769	Cecil Cooper	.08
770	Lou Whitaker	.20
771	Ruben Sierra	.35
772	Sal Butera	.04
774	Gene Mauch	.06
775	Dave Stieb	.08
776	Checklist 661-792	.06
777	Lonnie Smith	.06
778	*Keith Comstock* (FC) (team name in white)	3.50
778	*Keith Comstock* (FC) (team name in blue)	.12
779	*Tom Glavine* (FC)	.25
780	Fernando Valenzuela	.10
781	*Keith Hughes* (FC)	.12
782	*Jeff Ballard* (FC)	.18
785	Alvin Davis	.10
786	Joe Price	.04
789	Indians Ldrs (Joe Carter, Cory Snyder)	.08
790	Dave Righetti	.12
791	Ted Simmons	.08
792	John Tudor	.08

1988 TOPPS TRADED

Topps pumped up its standard 132-card Traded issue with the addition of a 20-card subset featuring the 1988 U.S. Olympic Baseball Team. The Olympians won the gold medal, and the cards feature big-name rookies who enjoy above-average acclaim, wearing colorful Team USA uniforms. Jim Abbott, Tino Martinez, and Robin Ventura highlight this group. The 1988 edition could be a quality investment as more Olympians achieve fame in the big leagues. Other notables in the set include Mark Grace and Chris Sabo. This set continues the Topps custom of being sold only through hobby dealers in complete, boxed sets.

	MINT
Complete set	**$30.00**
Commons	.06

1	Jim Abbott (FC) (USA)	**$4.00**
3	Luis Alicea (FC)	.15
4	Roberto Alomar (FC)	2.25
5	Brady Anderson (FC)	.20

1988 Topps Traded

66 Tino Martinez

6	Jack Armstrong (FC)	.75
7	Don August	.15
9	Brett Barberie (FC) (USA)	.35
10	Jose Bautista (FC)	.10
12	Tim Belcher	.20
14	Andy Benes (FC) (USA)	2.50
15	Damon Berryhill (FC)	.25
17	Pat Borders (FC)	.30
19	Jeff Branson (FC) (USA)	.20
21	Jay Buhner (FC)	.50
23	Jim Campanis (FC) (USA)	.20
24	Sil Campusano (FC)	.25
26	Jose Cecena (FC)	.15
28	Jack Clark	.15
29	Kevin Coffman (FC)	.10
30	Pat Combs (FC) (USA)	.70
34	• Jose DeLeon	.10
35	Richard Dotson	.10
36	Cecil Espy (FC)	.15
38	Mike Fiore (FC) (USA)	.20
39	Ron Gant (FC)	1.50
40	Kirk Gibson	.15
41	Rich Gossage	.15
42	Mark Grace (FC)	4.00
44	Ty Griffin (FC) (USA)	.75
45	Bryan Harvey (FC)	.30

48	Dave Henderson	.15
49	Tom Herr	.10
50	Bob Horner	.10
52	Jay Howell	.10
54	Jeff Innis (FC)	.15
55	Danny Jackson	.15
56	Darrin Jackson (FC)	.10
57	Roberto Kelly (FC)	.75
58	Ron Kittle	.15
62	Mike Macfarlane (FC)	.20
63	Scotti Madison (FC)	.15
64	Kirt Manwaring (FC)	.20
66	Tino Martinez (FC) (USA)	3.50
67	Billy Masse (FC) (USA)	.20
68	Jack McDowell (FC)	.80
71	Mickey Morandini (FC) (USA)	.50
74	Charles Nagy (FC) (USA)	.80
80	Mark Parent (FC)	.20
81	Dave Parker	.15
82	Dan Pasqua	.10
83	Melido Perez (FC)	.30
84	Steve Peters (FC)	.15
87	Jeff Pico (FC)	.15
88	Jim Poole (FC) (USA)	.12
94	Luis Rivera (FC)	.08
95	Doug Robbins (FC) (USA)	.12
96	• Frank Robinson	.15
98	Chris Sabo (FC)	2.50
102	Nelson Santovenia (FC)	.20
103	Mackey Sasser (FC)	.25
105	Mike Schooler (FC)	.35
106	Scott Servais (FC) (USA)	.12
107	Dave Silvestri (FC) (USA)	.12
109	Joe Slusarski (FC) (USA)	.40
110	Lee Smith	.10
111	• Pete Smith (FC)	.15
113	Ed Sprague (FC) (USA)	.60
114	Steve Stanicek (FC)	.15
115	Kurt Stillwell	.10
116	Todd Stottlemyre (FC)	.50
119	Scott Terry (FC)	.10
122	Jeff Treadway (FC)	.25
124	Robin Ventura (FC) (USA)	3.00
126	Walt Weiss (FC)	1.00
127	Bob Welch	.10
128	David Wells (FC)	.20
130	Ted Wood (FC) (USA)	.30

1989 DONRUSS

Once again a Diamond King from each team appears at the beginning of this 660-card, standard-dimension set. These painted portraits display striking background colors and designs. All cards use fading neon colors for the tops and bottoms, with black borders along the sides. Except for the Diamond Kings, player names appear in a simple print style, with the upper right-hand corner reserved for more elaborate team logos or the Rated Rookie subset identification. The white backs, while criticized for having few stats, are packed with full names, team records, specifics of a player's acquisition, and detailed career highlights.

	MINT
Complete set	**$25.00**
Commons	.04

1	Mike Greenwell (DK)	$ .30
2	Bobby Bonilla (DK)	.12
3	Pete Incaviglia (DK)	.12
4	Chris Sabo (DK)	.10
5	Robin Yount (DK)	.15
6	Tony Gwynn (DK)	.12
7	Carlton Fisk (DK)	.15
8	Cory Snyder (DK)	.15
9	David Cone (DK)	.10
10	Kevin Seitzer (DK)	.25
11	Rick Reuschel (DK)	.10
12	Johnny Ray (DK)	.10
14	Andres Galarraga (DK)	.15
15	Kirk Gibson (DK)	.10
16	Fred McGriff (DK)	.15
17	Mark Grace (DK)	.30
18	Jeff Robinson (DK)	.12
19	Vince Coleman (DK)	.20
20	Dave Henderson (DK)	.10
22	Gerald Perry (DK)	.10
23	Frank Viola (DK)	.10
24	Steve Bedrosian (DK)	.10
25	Glenn Davis (DK)	.12
26	Don Mattingly (DK)	.25
28	Sandy Alomar Jr. (RR) (FC)	2.00
29	Steve Searcy (RR) (FC)	.15
30	Cameron Drew (RR) (FC)	.10
31	Gary Sheffield (RR) (FC)	2.00
32	Erik Hanson (RR) (FC)	.75
33	Ken Griffey Jr. (RR) (FC)	7.50

26 Don Mattingly

34	Greg Harris (RR) (FC)	.15
35	Gregg Jefferies (RR)	1.00
36	Luis Medina (RR) (FC)	.20
37	Carlos Quintana (RR)	.35
38	Felix Jose (RR) (FC)	.75
39	Cris Carpenter (RR) (FC)	.20
40	Ron Jones (RR) (FC)	.15
41	Dave West (RR) (FC)	.15
42	• Randy Johnson (RR) (FC)	.25
43	Mike Harkey (RR) (FC)	.25
44	Pete Harnisch (RR) (FC)	.15
45	Tom Gordon (RR) (FC)	.50

1989 Donruss

33 Ken Griffey Jr.

46	*Gregg Olson* (RR) (FC)	.55
47	*Alex Sanchez* (RR) (FC)	.12
48	Ruben Sierra	.25
49	Rafael Palmeiro	.20
50	Ron Gant	.25
51	Cal Ripken, Jr.	.20
52	Wally Joyner	.15
53	Gary Carter	.15
54	Andy Van Slyke	.12
55	Robin Yount	.25
56	Pete Incaviglia	.10
58	Melido Perez	.06
61	Danny Tartabull	.12
63	Ozzie Smith	.12
64	Gary Gaetti	.12
65	Mark Davis	.08
66	Lee Smith	.08
67	Dennis Eckersley	.10
68	Wade Boggs	.55
69	Mike Scott	.10
70	Fred McGriff	.50
73	Mel Hall	.06
74	Don Mattingly	1.10
76	Juan Samuel	.10
78	Dave Righetti	.12
80	Eric Davis	.30
82	Todd Worrell	.08

83	Joe Carter	.12
84	Steve Sax	.12
86	John Kruk	.10
90	Frank Tanana	.06
91	Jose Canseco	1.30
92	Barry Bonds	.25
95	Mark McGwire	.50
96	Eddie Murray	.25
97	Tim Raines	.25
99	Kevin McReynolds	.12
101	Carlton Fisk	.20
104	Dale Murphy	.30
105	Ryne Sandberg	.25
110	Mike Marshall	.10
112	Tom Brunansky	.10
115	*Keith Brown* (FC)	.08
116	Matt Nokes	.15
117	Keith Hernandez	.20
118	Bob Forsch	.06
119	Bert Blyleven	.10
122	Jim Rice	.15
124	Danny Jackson	.12
128	Tony Gwynn	.25
130	Andres Galarraga	.15
132	Kirk Gibson	.15
136	Kirk McCaskill	.06
144	Bret Saberhagen	.15
147	Darryl Strawberry	.35
148	Harold Baines	.12
149	George Bell	.20
150	Dave Parker	.12
151	Bobby Bonilla	.20
152	Mookie Wilson	.06
154	Nolan Ryan	.50
155	Jeff Reardon	.08
156	Tim Wallach	.08
158	Rich Gossage	.10
159	Dave Winfield	.18
160	Von Hayes	.10
161	Willie McGee	.10
163	Tony Pena	.06
167	Andre Dawson	.18
168	Joe Boever (FC)	.08
170	• Bob Boone	.08
171	Ron Darling	.10
172	Bob Walk	.06
173	Rob Deer	.08
175	Ted Higuera	.08
176	Ozzie Guillen	.12

179	Mark Gubicza	.10
180	Alan Trammell	.15
181	Vince Coleman	.15
182	Kirby Puckett	.45
186	Mike Greenwell	.35
187	Billy Hatcher	.06
188	Jimmy Key	.08
189	Nick Esasky	.12
191	Cory Snyder	.15
193	Mike Schmidt	.40
195	John Tudor	.10
197	Orel Hershiser	.15
198	Kal Daniels	.12
199	Kent Hrbek	.15
201	• Joe Magrane	.08
203	Tim Belcher	.10
204	George Brett	.30
205	Benito Santiago	.15
206	Tony Fernandez	.10
207	Gerald Young	.10
208	Bo Jackson	.75
210	Storm Davis	.10
211	Doug Drabek	.06
213	Devon White	.10
214	Dave Stewart	.10
218	Bob Ojeda	.06
219	*Steve Rosenberg* (FC)	.10
220	Hubie Brooks	.08
221	B.J. Surhoff	.08
223	Rick Sutcliffe	.08
225	Mitch Williams	.10
227	Mark Langston	.12
232	Greg Swindell	.10
233	John Franco	.10
234	Jack Morris	.15
235	Howard Johnson	.15
236	Glenn Davis	.15
237	Frank Viola	.15
238	Kevin Seitzer	.15
240	• Dwight Evans	.10
245	Rickey Henderson	.35
246	Roberto Alomar	.30
249	Will Clark	.80
250	Fernando Valenzuela	.10
252	Sid Bream	.06
253	Steve Lyons	.06
255	Mark Grace	1.50
257	Barry Larkin	.20
258	Mike Krukow	.06

28 Sandy Alomar Jr.

259	Billy Ripken	.06
263	Pete Smith	.08
265	Roger McDowell	.10
266	Bobby Thigpen	.08
268	Terry Steinbach	.08
270	Dwight Gooden	.25
272	Dave Smith	.08
275	Damon Berryhill	.12
276	Vance Law	.06
277	Rich Dotson	.06
278	Lance Parrish	.12
280	Roger Clemens	.50
281	Greg Mathews	.06
283	Paul Kilgus	.20
284	Jose Guzman	.08
287	Joe Orsulak	.06
289	Kevin Elster	.08
290	Jose Lind	.10
291	Paul Molitor	.12
292	Cecil Espy	.08
294	Dan Pasqua	.08
298	Lou Whitaker	.20
303	Ellis Burks	.50
305	Jody Reed	.10
306	Bill Doran	.08
307	David Wells	.10
310	Julio Franco	.10

1989 Donruss

31 Gary Sheffield

311	Jack Clark	.12
312	Chris James	.08
315	Al Leiter	.15
317	*Chris Sabo*	.75
318	Greg Gagne	.06
320	John Farrell	.10
322	Kurt Stillwell	.06
323	Shawn Abner	.10
325	Kevin Bass	.06
326	Pat Tabler	.06
329	John Smiley	.10
331	Johnny Ray	.08
332	Bob Welch	.08
333	Larry Sheets	.06
334	Jeff Parrett	.06
336	Randy Myers	.10
339	Joey Meyer	.06
344	Dan Petry	.06
345	Alvin Davis	.12
349	Dave Stieb	.08
351	Jeff Treadway	.10
355	Gene Larkin	.10
356	Steve Farr	.06
358	Todd Benzinger	.12
360	Paul O'Neill	.10
366	*Nelson Santovenia* (FC)	.12
367	Kelly Downs	.08
369	Phil Bradley	.10
372	Mike Witt	.08
373	Greg Maddux	.10
375	Jose Rijo	.08
381	Tom Glavine	.10
382	Dan Plesac	.08
384	*Dave Gallagher*	.12
386	Luis Polonia	.12
388	David Cone	.20
392	*John Dopson*	.12
395	Willie Randolph	.06
397	Scott Terry	.06
401	Mickey Tettleton	.08
403	Jeff Russell	.08
405	*Jose Alvarez* (FC)	.15
406	Rick Schu	.06
407	*Sherman Corbett* (FC)	.15
408	Dave Magadan	.10
412	Chris Bosio	.06
413	Jerry Reuss	.08
416	*Mike Macfarlane*	.10
418	Pedro Guerrero	.15
419	• Alan Anderson	.06
420	*Mark Parent*	.10
423	Bruce Hurst	.08
425	Jesse Barfield	.06
426	*Rob Dibble* (FC)	.40
428	Ron Kittle	.10
433	Roberto Kelly	.15
437	Jose DeLeon	.12
438	Doug Jones	.10
443	*John Fishel* (FC)	.20
445	*Paul Gibson*	.15
446	Walt Weiss	.25
448	Mike Moore	.10
449	Chili Davis	.08
451	*Jose Bautista*	.10
458	Bruce Sutter	.08
461	Bobby Witt	.08
464	• *Ramon Martinez* (FC)	1.50
466	Luis Alicea	.20
470	Jeff Robinson	.12
471	Sid Fernandez	.08
474	*Israel Sanchez* (FC)	.08
479	Greg Cadaret	.10
480	*Randy Kramer* (FC)	.10
481	*Dave Eiland* (FC)	.12
483	Garry Templeton	.06
485	Kevin Mitchell	.35

488	Dave LaPoint	.06
491	Doug Dascenzo (FC)	.12
492	Willie Upshaw	.06
493	Jack Armstrong (FC)	.25
494	Kirt Manwaring	.10
497	Mike Campbell	.08
498	Gary Thurman	.10
499	Zane Smith	.06
505	Doug Jennings	.12
511	Brian Holman (FC)	.17
513	Jeff Pico (FC)	.09
517	Jeff Sellers	.06
518	John Costello (FC)	.20
519	Brady Anderson	.20
522	Drew Hall	.08
523	Mark Lemke (FC)	.10
524	Oswald Peraza (FC)	.09
525	Bryan Harvey	.15
527	Tom Prince	.06
533	Darrell Evans	.08
536	Ken Hill (FC)	.15
538	Shane Mack	.06
542	Ken Caminiti	.10
544	Norm Charlton (FC)	.18
545	Hal Morris (FC)	1.00
547	Hensley Meulens (FC)	.75
552	Tim Leary	.06
555	Tim Jones (FC)	.07
558	Jose DeJesus (FC)	.12
559	Dennis Rasmussen	.08
560	Pat Borders	.12
561	Craig Biggio (FC)	.40
562	Luis de los Santos (FC)	.10
563	Fred Lynn	.10
564	Todd Burns (FC)	.12
569	Craig Worthington	.15
570	Johnny Paredes	.20
574	Tracy Jones	.10
575	Juan Nieves	.06
576	Andres Thomas	.06
577	Rolando Roomes (FC)	.10
579	Chad Kreuter (FC)	.08
581	Jay Buhner	.10
582	Ricky Horton	.06
584	Sil Campusano	.20
585	Dave Clark	.06
586	Van Snider (FC)	.09
589	William Brennan (FC)	.09
590	German Gonzalez (FC)	.08

464 Ramon Martinez

591	Ernie Whitt	.08
592	Jeff Blauser	.08
594	Matt Williams	.35
597	Scott Medvin (FC)	.11
598	Hipolito Pena (FC)	.15
599	Jerald Clark (FC)	.25
603	Mike Devereaux	.15
604	Alex Madrid (FC)	.09
606	Lance Johnson	.15
607	Terry Clark (FC)	.09
609	Scott Jordan (FC)	.11
610	Jay Howell	.06
611	Francisco Melendez (FC)	.10
613	Kevin Brown	.10
614	Dave Valle	.06
616	Andy Nezelek (FC)	.10
617	Chuck Crim	.06
618	Jack Savage (FC)	.10
619	Adam Peterson (FC)	.10
620	Todd Stottlemyre	.10
621	Lance Blankenship (FC)	.11
622	Miguel Garcia (FC)	.08
624	Ricky Jordan (FC)	.25
629	Scott Sanderson	.05
634	Dante Bichette (FC)	.25
635	Curt Schilling (FC)	.15

Erik Hanson P

32 Erik Hanson

636	*Scott May* (FC)	.08
637	*Mike Schooler* (FC)	.20
639	*Tom Lampkin* (FC)	.09
640	*Brian Meyer* (FC)	.15
642	*John Smoltz* (FC)	.30
643	40/40 Club (Jose Canseco)	.45
645	Edgar Martinez (FC)	.30
646	*Dennis Cook* (FC)	.20
648	59 and Counting (Orel Hershiser)	.10
649	*Rod Nichols* (FC)	.10
650	Jody Davis	.06
651	*Bob Milacki* (FC)	.18
652	Mike Jackson	.06
653	*Derek Lilliquist* (FC)	.11
655	Mike Diaz	.06
657	Jerry Reed	.04
658	*Kevin Blankenship* (FC)	.11
660	*Eric Hetzel* (FC)	.10

1989 DONRUSS ROOKIES

Rookie fever raged on in 1989, as shown by the popularity of the 1989 Donruss set, "The Rookies." The concept was originated by Donruss in 1986, and the company continued in 1989 to feature 55 players and a checklist card in a boxed, complete set. Ironically, more than a third of the 55 "rookies" actually had made prior appearances in Donruss sets, some more than a year before. This hobby-wise company, however, gave leading newcomers encore appearances in this season-ending set. The cards are just like the standard 660-card set from earlier in the year except for "The Rookies" logo in the upper right corner.

		MINT
Complete set		**$21.00**
Commons		**.10**
1	Gary Sheffield	$1.25
2	Gregg Jefferies	1.00
3	Ken Griffey, Jr.	7.50
4	Tom Gordon	.75
5	Billy Spiers (FC)	.35

6	Deion Sanders (FC)	.95
8	Steve Carter (FC)	.20
9	Francisco Oliveras (FC)	.15
10	Steve Wilson	.10
11	Bob Geren (FC)	.15
12	Tony Castillo	.12
13	Kenny Rogers (FC)	.17
14	Carlos Martinez (FC)	.17
16	Jim Abbott	1.10
18	Mark Carreon	.11

20	Luis Medina	.11
21	Sandy Alomar, Jr.	1.00
22	Bob Milacki	.15
23	Joe Girardi	.20
25	Craig Worthington	.15
26	Jerome Walton	1.75
27	Gary Wayne (FC)	.11
29	Dante Bichette	.10
30	Alexis Infante (FC)	.11
32	Dwight Smith	.50
34	Eric Yelding (FC)	.20
35	Gregg Olson	.70
37	Ken Patterson	.15
38	Rick Wrona (FC)	.15
41	Jeff Brantley (FC)	.20
42	Ron Jones	.20
44	Kevin Brown	.20
45	Ramon Martinez	1.75
46	Greg Harris	.20
47	Steve Finley	.35
49	Erik Hanson	.75
52	Clay Parker	.10
53	Omar Visquel (FC)	.10

3 Ken Griffey, Jr.

| 54 | Derek Lilliquist | .10 |
| 55 | Junior Felix (FC) | .50 |

1989 FLEER

Some of Fleer's best photos in the standard-sized 1989 set were not well cropped. The gray pin-striped borders are broad and cut diagonally by poorly edited photos. Bats are often missing, or, even worse, arms are sliced off (as on Chris Sabo, number 170). This tends to disrupt the dynamic concept. Furthermore, print within the pin-striped background is cluttered and hard to read. Gray card backs include "Did You Know" trivia quizzes and charts marking player progress before and after the All-Star break. Informal group cards, star tribute cards, and duo rookie cards are rounded out by a dozen All-Stars with bios on backs.

		MINT
Complete set		$35.00
Commons		.05
1	Don Baylor	$ .10
2	*Lance Blankenship* (FC)	.25
3	*Todd Burns*	.30
5	Jose Canseco	.80

6	Storm Davis	.10
7	Dennis Eckersley	.12
10	Dave Henderson	.10
14	*Doug Jennings*	.20
15	*Felix Jose* (FC)	.90
17	Mark McGwire	.75
19	Dave Parker	.12
20	Eric Plunk	.07
22	Terry Steinbach	.10

548 Ken Griffey Jr.

138	Fred Lynn	.10
139	Jack Morris	.15
140	Matt Nokes	.20
143	Jeff M. Robinson	.12
145	Steve Searcy (FC)	.15
148	Alan Trammell	.17
151	Lou Whitaker	.20
153	Tom Browning	.10
154	Keith Brown (FC)	.10
155	Norm Charlton (FC)	.30
157	Kal Daniels	.15
158	Eric Davis	.40
160	Rob Dibble	.55
161	Nick Esasky	.10
162	John Franco	.10
163	Danny Jackson	.15
164	Barry Larkin	.25
166	Paul O'Neill	.12
168	Jose Rijo	.10
170	Chris Sabo	1.10
171	Candy Sierra (FC)	.15
172	Van Snider (FC)	.12
173	Jeff Treadway	.15
177	Don August	.10
187	Darryl Hamilton	.18
188	Ted Higuera	.12
193	Paul Molitor	.15
195	Dan Plesac	.10
196	Gary Sheffield (FC)	2.00
197	B.J. Surhoff	.10
198	Dale Sveum	.07
200	Robin Yount	.25
202	Barry Bonds	.30
203	Bobby Bonilla	.25
206	Doug Drabek	.07
207	Mike Dunne	.07
214	Jose Lind	.10
217	Tom Prince (FC)	.10
221	John Smiley	.12
222	Andy Van Slyke	.15
225	Jesse Barfield	.10
226	George Bell	.20
227	Pat Borders	.30
228	John Cerutti	.07
230	Mark Eichhorn	.07
231	Tony Fernandez	.12
233	Mike Flanagan	.10
234	Kelly Gruber	.15
235	Tom Henke	.10

67 Ramon Martinez

236	Jimmy Key	.10
240	Fred McGriff	.50
241	Lloyd Moseby	.10
244	Dave Stieb	.10
245	Todd Stottlemyre	.25
246	Duane Ward	.07
247	David Wells	.12
250	Neil Allen (Home: Sarasota, FL)	1.50
252	Jack Clark	.15
254	Rickey Henderson	.40
255	Tommy John	.12
256	Roberto Kelly	.20
257	Al Leiter	.15
258	Don Mattingly	.75
260	Hal Morris (FC)	3.00
261	Scott Nielsen (FC)	.10
262	Mike Pagliarulo	.10
263	Hipolito Pena (FC)	.20
267	Dave Righetti	.12
272	Claudell Washington	.07
274	Dave Winfield	.20
277	George Brett	.30
278	Bill Buckner	.10
279	Nick Capra (FC)	.20
280	Jose DeJesus (FC)	.18

170 Chris Sabo

283	Mark Gubicza	.10
284	*Tom Gordon* (FC)	.75
285	Bo Jackson	.90
286	Charlie Leibrandt	.07
287	*Mike Macfarlane*	.12
289	Bill Pecota	.07
291	Bret Saberhagen	.15
292	Kevin Seitzer	.15
293	Kurt Stillwell	.07
294	Pat Tabler	.07
295	Danny Tartabull	.15
296	Gary Thurman	.12
298	Willie Wilson	.10
299	Roberto Alomar	.80
300	*Sandy Alomar Jr.* (FC)	1.75
302	Mike Brumley (FC)	.07
303	Mark Davis	.10
305	Tony Gwynn	.30
306	*Greg Harris* (FC)	.18
309	John Kruk	.12
312	Lance McCullers	.07
314	Dennis Rasmussen	.10
316	Benito Santiago	.20
318	Todd Simmons	.20
324	Brett Butler	.07
325	Will Clark	1.00
326	Kelly Downs	.10
327	Dave Dravecky	.07
330	*Charlie Hayes* (FC)	.20
333	Candy Maldonado	.07
334	Kirt Manwaring	.10
336	Kevin Mitchell	.45
338	*Tony Perezchica* (FC)	.15
340	Rick Reuschel	.10
346	Matt Williams	.45
347	*Trevor Wilson* (FC)	.25
351	Kevin Bass	.07
353	*Craig Biggio*	.60
355	Glenn Davis	.20
358	*John Fishel*	.20
359	Billy Hatcher	.10
361	*Louie Meadows*	.15
367	Mike Scott	.12
368	Nolan Ryan	.65
370	Gerald Young	.12
371	Hubie Brooks	.10
373	*John Dopson*	.15
376	Andres Galarraga	.15
379	*Brian Holman*	.30
381	*Randy Johnson* (FC)	.35
383	Tracy Jones	.10
384	Dave Martinez	.07
385	Dennis Martinez	.07
388	*Johnny Paredes* (FC)	.20
389	Jeff Parrett	.10
391	Tim Raines	.20
393	*Nelson Santovenia*	.15
394	Bryn Smith	.07
395	Tim Wallach	.10
397	*Rod Allen*	.10
400	Joe Carter	.17
402	Dave Clark	.10
403	John Farrell	.10
404	Julio Franco	.10
408	Brook Jacoby	.10
409	Doug Jones	.20
410	*Jeff Kaiser* (FC)	.12
411	*Luis Medina* (FC)	.17
412	Cory Snyder	.15
413	Greg Swindell	.15
414	*Ron Tingley* (FC)	.15
418	Damon Berryhill	.10
420	*Doug Dascenzo* (FC)	.15
422	Andre Dawson	.20
424	Shawon Dunston	.15

425 "Goose" Gossage .... .12
426 Mark Grace 1.50
427 *Mike Harkey* (FC) .... .40
429 Les Lancaster .... .07
430 Vance Law .... .07
431 Greg Maddux .... .12
434 Rafael Palmeiro .... .18
436 *Jeff Pico* .... .10
437 Ryne Sandberg .... .40
439 Rick Sutcliffe .... .10
441 *Gary Varsho* .... .12
443 *Luis Alicea* .... .20
444 Tom Brunansky .... .12
445 Vince Coleman .... .15
446 *John Costello* .... .20
449 Jose DeLeon .... .10
451 Pedro Guerrero .... .12
452 Bob Horner .... .10
453 *Tim Jones* (FC) .... .10
455 • Joe Magrane .... .10
457 Willie McGee .... .12
461 Terry Pendleton .... .10
462 *Steve Peters* (FC) .... .10
463 Ozzie Smith .... .15
464 Scott Terry .... .08
466 Todd Worrell .... .10
468 *Dante Bichette* (FC) .... .35
469 • Bob Boone .... .07
470 *Terry Clark* (FC) .... .10
472 *Mike Cook* (FC) .... .10
473 *Sherman Corbett* .... .15
474 Chili Davis .... .07
479 *Bryan Harvey* .... .25
481 Wally Joyner .... .25
483 Kirk McCaskill .... .07
486 Dan Petry .... .07
489 Devon White .... .10
490 Mike Witt .... .07
491 Harold Baines .... .12
492 Ivan Calderon .... .07
495 Carlton Fisk .... .20
496 *Dave Gallagher* .... .12
497 Ozzie Guillen .... .15
498 Shawn Hillegas .... .07
499 Lance Johnson .... .07
503 Fred Manrique .... .07
504 Jack McDowell .... .15
505 *Donn Pall* .... .12
507 Dan Pasqua .... .10

549 Erik Hanson

508 *Ken Patterson* .... .12
509 Melido Perez .... .10
512 Bobby Thigpen .... .15
516 *Jose Cecena* .... .10
517 Cecil Espy .... .07
518 Scott Fletcher .... .07
523 Pete Incaviglia .... .12
525 Paul Kilgus .... .15
526 *Chad Kreuter* (FC) .... .10
528 Oddibe McDowell .... .07
532 Ruben Sierra .... .50
536 Mitch Williams .... .15
537 Bobby Witt .... .10
538 Steve Balboni .... .07
542 Jay Buhner (FC) .... .20
543 Mike Campbell .... .10
544 Darnell Coles .... .07
546 Alvin Davis .... .15
547 Mario Diaz .... .20
548 *Ken Griffey Jr.* (FC) 10.00
549 *Erik Hanson* (FC) 1.00
551 Mark Langston .... .12
552 Edgar Martinez .... .20
553 *Bill McGuire* (FC) .... .10
555 Jim Presley .... .07
558 Harold Reynolds .... .12

1989 Fleer

299 Roberto Alomar

642 Major League Prospects
(*Jerald Clark. Brad
Pounders*) (FC)................... .50

643 Major League Prospects
(*Mike Capel.
Drew Hall*) (FC) .... .25

644 Major League Prospects
(*Joe Girardi. Rolando
Roomes*) (FC)..................... .20

645 Major League Prospects
(*Marty Brown. Lenny
Harris*) (FC) .... .40

646 Major League Prospects
(*Luis de los Santos.
Jim Campbell*) (FC) .... .25

647 Major League Prospects
(*Miguel Garcia. Randy
Kramer*) (FC) .... .25

648 Major League Prospects
(*Torey Lovullo. Robert
Palacios*) (FC) .... .20

649 Major League Prospects
(*Jim Corsi.
Bob Milacki*) (FC)............... .25

650 Major League Prospects
(*Grady Hall. Mike
Rochford*) (FC) .... .25

651 Major League Prospects
(*Vance Lovelace. Terry
Taylor*) (FC) .... .25

652 Major League Prospects
(*Dennis Cook,
Ken Hill*) (FC) .... .35

653 Major League Prospects
(*Scott Service,
Shane Turner*) .... .20

1989 FLEER UPDATE

Tradition dictated the production and distribution of another Update set for 1989. Thanks to the fact that some hot rookie names were included, the 132-card 1989 Fleer Update set zoomed in value immediately after its fall release. Rookie card fanatics embraced popular cards of Jim Abbott, Joey Belle, Dwight Smith, Greg Vaughn, Robin Ventura, Jerome Walton, and Todd Zeile. The later decline of Walton and Smith caused the set's value to drop somewhat, however. Fleer also included a special card commemorating Mike Schmidt's retirement. Unfortunately, the Updates retain the gaudy design of their 1989 Fleer counterparts. Once again cards are arranged by team and then alphabetically by player within each team. A "U" prefix was added to the card number to distinguish this set from the 660-card set issued earlier in the year (though the letter "U" has been omitted from the following list).

	MINT
Complete set	**$18.00**
Commons	.07
1 Phil Bradley	$ .15
2 Mike Devereaux	.15
3 Steve Finley......................	.25

6 Bob Milacki	.12
7 Randy Milligan...................	.17
8 John Dopson	.20
9 Nick Esasky	.25
11 Jim Abbott (FC)	1.00
12 Bert Blyleven	.25
13 Jeff Manto (FC)	.25
15 Lance Parrish	.20

41 Greg Vaughn

16	Lee Stevens (FC)	.50
17	Claudell Washington	.15
18	Mark Davis	.20
19	Eric King	.12
21	Matt Merullo (FC)	.12
22	Steve Rosenberg	.12
23	Robin Ventura	1.50
25	Joey Belle (FC)	1.75
29	Pete O'Brien	.15
31	Tracy Jones	.15
32	Mike Schwabe (FC)	.10
35	Kevin Appier	.50
36	• Bob Boone	.15
37	Luis de los Santos	.20
38	Jim Eisenreich	.12
39	Jamie Navarro (FC)	.30
40	Bill Spiers (FC)	.25
41	Greg Vaughn (FC)	3.00
42	Randy Veres (FC)	.12
46	Jesse Barfield	.15
47	Alvaro Espinoza	.15
48	Bob Geren (FC)	.12
50	Andy Hawkins	.15
51	Hensley Meulens	1.00
52	Steve Sax	.20
53	Deion Sanders (FC)	.75
54	Rickey Henderson	.50
55	Mike Moore	.20
57	Greg Briley	.40
58	Gene Harris (FC)	.18
59	Randy Johnson	.15
60	Jeffrey Leonard	.20
62	Omar Vizquel (FC)	.15
63	Kevin Brown	.15
64	Julio Franco	.12
66	Rafael Palmeiro	.20
67	Nolan Ryan	1.85
68	Francisco Cabrera (FC)	.35
69	Junior Felix (FC)	1.00
70	Al Leiter	.12
71	Alex Sanchez	.20
72	Geronimo Berroa	.07
73	Derek Lilliquist	.15
74	Lonnie Smith	.15
75	Jeff Treadway	.12
77	Lloyd McClendon	.10
78	Scott Sanderson	.07
79	Dwight Smith	.35
80	Jerome Walton	1.25
81	Mitch Williams	.25
82	Steve Wilson	.15
83	Todd Benzinger	.15
84	Ken Griffey	.20
86	Rolando Roomes	.20
87	Scott Scudder (FC)	.30
91	Mike Morgan	.15
92	Eddie Murray	.20
93	Willie Randolph	.15
96	Kevin Gross	.07
97	Mark Langston	.15
98	Spike Owen	.07
101	Barry Lyons	.15
102	Juan Samuel	.25
103	Wally Whitehurst	.20
104	Dennis Cook	.10
105	Lenny Dykstra	.15
106	Charlie Hayes	.15
107	Tommy Herr	.07
109	John Kruk	.15
110	Roger McDowell	.15
111	Terry Mulholland	.15
112	Jeff Parrett	.15
114	Jeff King	.20
115	Randy Kramer	.07
116	Bill Landrum	.20
117	Cris Carpenter	.15

119	Ken Hill	.10	125	Mark Parent	.15
120	Dan Quisenberry	.15	126	Bip Roberts	.15
121	Milt Thompson	.20	127	Jeff Brantley (FC)	.25
122	Todd Zeile (FC)	1.50	129	Mike LaCoss	.07
123	Jack Clark	.15	130	Greg Litton (FC)	.20
124	Bruce Hurst	.20	131	Mike Schmidt	2.00

1989 SCORE

Card backs had been neglected for years, but Score's second set of 660 cards maintained its reputation for presenting baseball's most appealing card backs. The company continued to adorn the reverse sides of its cards with color photos, stats, and interesting bios. Unfortunately, the company insisted on including action photos on the front of most cards. Several shots are dark or blurred, others show their subjects' faces blocked by helmets, still others catch players with their backs turned to the camera. Score also began to get repetitive in photo selection: Most non-pitchers are shown in their batting stances, while pitchers are seen in their windups. Several valuable cards are found in a specially designated Rookie subset.

	MINT
Complete set	**$25.00**
Commons	.03

1	Jose Canseco	$.85
2	Andre Dawson	.15
3	Mark McGwire	.50
4	Benny Santiago	.12
5	Rick Reuschel	.08
6	Fred McGriff	.27
7	Kal Daniels	.10
8	Gary Gaetti	.15
9	Ellis Burks	.35
10	Darryl Strawberry	.35
11	Julio Franco	.10
12	Lloyd Moseby	.06
13	*Jeff Pico*	.10
15	Cal Ripken Jr.	.20
17	Mel Hall	.06
18	Bill Ripken	.06
19	Brook Jacoby	.08
20	Kirby Puckett	.30
23	Matt Nokes	.15
25	Jack Clark	.12

635 Ramon Martinez

28	Willie Wilson	.08
29	Curt Young	.06
30	Dale Murphy	.20
31	Barry Larkin	.20
32	Dave Stewart	.12

104 Chris Sabo

71	Mitch Webster	.06
72	Rob Deer	.06
75	George Brett	.40
76	Brian Downing	.06
78	Scott Fletcher	.06
79	Phil Bradley	.08
80	Ozzie Smith	.15
81	Larry Sheets	.06
83	Darnell Coles	.06
84	Len Dykstra	.15
85	Jim Rice	.10
86	Jeff Treadway	.10
87	Jose Lind	.08
88	Willie McGee	.10
90	Tony Gwynn	.35
92	Milt Thompson	.06
93	Kevin McReynolds	.15
94	Eddie Murray	.25
95	Lance Parrish	.15
96	Ron Kittle	.06
97	Gerald Young	.10
98	Ernie Whitt	.06
100	Don Mattingly	.50
101	Gerald Perry	.08
102	Vance Law	.06
104	*Chris Sabo*	.75
105	Danny Tartabull	.15
108	Dave Parker	.10
109	Eric Davis	.25
110	Alan Trammell	.15
112	Frank Tanana	.06
114	Dennis Martinez	.06
115	Jose DeLeon	.08
117	Doug Drabek	.06
119	Greg Maddux (FC)	.10
120	Cecil Fielder (photo on back reversed)	.50
124	Kelly Downs	.08
125	Greg Gross (first name incorrect on back)	.20
126	Fred Lynn	.10
127	Barry Bonds	.20
128	Harold Baines	.10
130	Kevin Elster	.08
132	Teddy Higuera	.08
135	Ray Knight (photo reversed)	.25
136	Howard Johnson	.12
137	Terry Pendleton	.08

35	Ryne Sandberg	.35
36	Tony Pena	.06
37	Greg Walker	.06
38	Von Hayes	.08
39	Kevin Mitchell	.30
40	Tim Raines	.15
41	Keith Hernandez	.20
42	Keith Moreland	.06
43	Ruben Sierra	.25
44	Chet Lemon	.06
45	Willie Randolph	.06
47	Candy Maldonado	.06
50	Dave Winfield	.25
51	Alvin Davis	.10
52	Cory Snyder	.15
53	Hubie Brooks	.08
54	Chili Davis	.06
55	Kevin Seitzer	.25
57	Tony Fernandez	.10
61	Billy Hatcher	.06
63	Marty Barrett	.06
64	Nick Esasky	.08
65	Wally Joyner	.20
66	Mike Greenwell	.25
68	Bob Horner	.08
69	Steve Sax	.15
70	Rickey Henderson	.40

142	*Rich Renteria* (FC)	.10
143	Jose Guzman	.08
144	Andres Galarraga	.15
148	John Kruk	.10
149	Mike Schmidt	.50
150	Lee Smith	.08
151	Robin Yount	.25
154	B.J. Surhoff	.08
155	Vince Coleman	.15
158	Lance McCullers	.06
160	Jesse Barfield	.08
161	Mark Langston	.10
162	Kurt Stillwell	.06
164	Glenn Davis	.15
165	Walt Weiss	.15
166	Dave Concepcion	.08
167	Alfredo Griffin	.06
168	*Don Heinkel*	.06
170	Shane Rawley	.06
171	Darrell Evans	.08
174	Andy Van Slyke	.15
175	Wade Boggs	.35

630 Sandy Alomar

179	Carney Lansford	.06
180	Ron Darling	.10
181	Kirk McCaskill	.06
184	Tom Brunansky	.10
185	*Bryan Harvey*	.20
189	Mike Pagliarulo	.08
193	• Dwight Evans	.10
195	Bobby Bonilla	.20
197	Dave Stieb	.08
198	*Pat Borders*	.20
199	Rafael Palmeiro	.15
200	Doc Gooden	.30
201	Pete Incaviglia	.08
202	Chris James	.08
205	Don Baylor	.08
207	Pete Smith	.08
210	Kirk Gibson	.10
211	Claudell Washington	.06
213	Joe Carter	.10
214	Bill Buckner	.08
215	Bert Blyleven	.15
216	Brett Butler	.06
217	Lee Mazzilli	.06
220	Tim Wallach	.08
221	David Cone	.15
223	Rich Gossage	.10
225	Dave Righetti	.10

230	Lou Whitaker	.15
231	*Luis Alicea*	.15
232	Roberto Alomar	.45
233	• Bob Boone	.06
235	Shawon Dunston	.08
236	Pete Stanicek	.08
237	*Craig Biggio*	.50
238	Dennis Boyd	.06
240	Gary Carter	.15
245	Dave Smith	.06
247	Joe Orsulak	.06
248	Storm Davis	.10
250	Jack Morris	.15
251	Bret Saberhagen	.15
254	Eric Show	.06
255	Juan Samuel	.10
260	Steve Bedrosian	.08
261	Jack Howell	.06
265	Todd Worrell	.10
266	John Farrell	.08
268	Sid Fernandez	.08
270	Shane Mack	.06
271	Paul Kilgus	.10
276	Dennis Eckersley	.10
277	Graig Nettles	.10
280	Gene Larkin	.08
281	Roger McDowell	.08

625 Gary Sheffield

282	Greg Swindell	.10
285	Mike Dunne	.08
286	Greg Mathews	.06
287	Kent Tekulve	.06
289	Jack McDowell	.15
290	Frank Viola	.15
291	Mark Gubicza	.10
293	Mike Henneman	.08
295	Charlie Hough	.06
298	Mike Witt	.06
299	Pascual Perez	.06
300	Nolan Ryan	.65
301	Mitch Williams	.08
302	Mookie Wilson	.06
303	Mackey Sasser	.06
304	John Cerutti	.06
305	Jeff Reardon	.08
306	Randy Myers	.08
308	Bob Welch	.08
309	Jeff Robinson	.10
310	Harold Reynolds	.06
312	Dave Magadan	.08
319	*Mike Macfarlane*	.20
320	Dan Plesac	.08
323	Devon White	.10
325	Bruce Hurst	.06
330	Bo Jackson	.60
331	Ivan Calderon	.06

336	Damon Berryhill	.15
338	Dan Pasqua	.08
342	Ron Guidry	.15
345	Rich Gedman	.06
346	*Nelson Santovenia*	.12
347	George Bell	.20
350	Roger Clemens	.50
352	Jay Bell (FC)	.06
353	Steve Balboni	.06
356	Jesse Orosco	.06
360	Darrin Jackson (FC)	.08
362	Mark Grace	1.00
365	Terry Steinbach	.08
370	Orel Hershiser	.20
371	Todd Benzinger	.10
372	Ron Gant	.25
374	Joey Meyer	.08
377	Jeff Parrett (FC)	.08
378	Jay Howell	.06
380	Luis Polonia	.06
382	Kent Hrbek	.15
384	Dave LaPoint	.06
386	Melido Perez	.08
387	Doug Jones	.10
389	Alejandro Pena	.06
390	Frank White	.06
391	Pat Tabler	.06
394	Allan Anderson (FC)	.06
397	Scott Terry (FC)	.08
399	Bobby Thigpen	.08
400	Don Sutton	.15
401	Cecil Espy	.06
407	Rick Sutcliffe	.08
409	John Smiley	.10
410	Juan Nieves	.06
411	Shawn Abner	.08
412	Wes Gardner (FC)	.06
418	Tim Belcher	.08
419	Don August	.08
425	Bruce Sutter	.08
433	Ozzie Guillen	.06
437	Fernando Valenzuela	.15
442	• Tom Glavine	.10
449	Carlton Fisk	.15
450	Will Clark	.50
453	Todd Stottlemyre	.15
455	*Dave Gallagher*	.10
457	Fred Manrique	.06
459	*Doug Jennings* (FC)	.12

629 Felix Jose

600 Gregg Jefferies

1989 SCORE ROOKIE & TRADED

After hobbyists overwhelmed Score with their ceaseless demands for its initial Rookie & Traded set in 1988, the company was prepared for collectors in 1989. Greater availability and fewer hot rookie names kept the second-year set of 110 cards from booming in price immediately. However, it seemed just as popular as the regular Score set. The company even scooped its competition by becoming the only card manufacturer with a photo of Los Angeles Dodgers rookie hurler John Wetteland. Following the lead of rival companies, Score sold its extension offering only through hobby dealers in boxed, complete sets.

106 Joey Belle

		MINT
Complete set		**$16.00**
Commons		**.06**

1	Rafael Palmeiro	$ .12
2	Nolan Ryan	1.50
3	Jack Clark	.12
5	Mike Moore	.20
6	Pete O'Brien	.15
7	Jeffrey Leonard	.20
9	Tom Herr	.10
10	Claudell Washington	.15
11	Mike Pagliarulo	.12
14	Andy Hawkins	.15
15	Todd Benzinger	.15
16	Mookie Wilson	.15
17	Bert Blyleven	.25
18	Jeff Treadway	.12
19	Bruce Hurst	.20
20	Steve Sax	.15
21	Juan Samuel	.20
22	Jesse Barfield	.15
23	Carmelo Castillo	.12
24	Terry Leach	.08
25	Mark Langston	.20
26	Eric King	.12
27	Steve Balboni	.15
28	Lenny Dykstra	.15
29	Keith Moreland	.10
31	Eddie Murray	.15
32	Mitch Williams	.15
33	Jeff Parrett	.12
34	Wally Backman	.12
35	Julio Franco	.12
36	Lance Parrish	.20
37	Nick Esasky	.15
38	Luis Polonia	.12
39	Kevin Gross	.08
41	Willie Randolph	.15
43	Tracy Jones	.12
44	Phil Bradley	.15
45	Milt Thompson	.20
46	Chris James	.12
47	Scott Fletcher	.07
48	Kal Daniels	.12

49	Steve Bedrosian	.15
50	Rickey Henderson	.50
51	Dion James	.15
52	Tim Leary	.12
53	Roger McDowell	.15
54	Mel Hall	.12
56	Zane Smith	.10
57	Danny Heep	.07
58	Bob McClure	.10
59	Brian Holton	.07
62	Harold Baines	.20
64	Jody Davis	.10
65	Darrell Evans	.15
67	Frank Viola	.15
69	Greg Cadaret	.07
70	John Kruk	.15
72	Oddibe McDowell	.07
73	Tom Brookens	.07
74	• Bob Boone	.15
75	Walt Terrell	.15
77	Randy Johnson	.15
78	Felix Fermin	.06
79	Rick Mahler	.10
80	Rich Dotson	.15
81	Cris Carpenter	.25
82	Billy Spiers (FC)	.30
83	Junior Felix (FC)	1.00
84	Joe Girardi (FC)	.35
85	Jerome Walton	1.25
86	Greg Litton (FC)	.35
87	Greg Harris	.20
88	Jim Abbott	.85
89	Kevin Brown	.20
90	John Wetteland (FC)	.20
91	Gary Wayne (FC)	.25
92	Rich Monteleone (FC)	.15
93	Bob Geren (FC)	.35
94	Clay Parker	.15
95	Steve Finley	.30
96	Gregg Olson	.75
97	Ken Patterson	.15
98	Ken Hill	.25
99	Scott Scudder (FC)	.30
100	Ken Griffey, Jr.	6.75
101	Jeff Brantley (FC)	.20
102	Donn Pall	.15
103	Carlos Martinez (FC)	.20
104	Joe Oliver (FC)	.35
105	Omar Vizquel (FC)	.30
106	Joey Belle (FC)	1.75
107	Kenny Rogers (FC)	.20
108	Mark Carreon	.15
109	Rolando Roomes	.12
110	Pete Harnisch	.25

1989 TOPPS

Although Topps maintained the same card size, the company offered several design alterations for 1989. While retaining simple white front borders and crisp, well-cropped photos, bold lettering on the borders sometimes turned overwhelmingly neon (shades of 1972 Topps). Player positions do not appear on card fronts, and player names are dwarfed by team designations. But Topps saved the day by including several appealing subsets. A group of 10 cards, called #1 Draft Picks, consists of promising rookies (mostly former Olympians) in their college uniforms. Jim Abbott, Steve Avery, and Robin Ventura are big names in this category. Top rookies like Sandy Alomar, Jr., Gregg Jefferies, and Gary Sheffield are spotlighted with specially marked Future Star cards.

	MINT		
Complete set	$25.00	2	Record Breaker (Wade Boggs) ... $ .35
Commons	.03	3	Record Breaker (Gary Carter) ... .10

5 Record Breaker
   (Orel Hershiser) .... .10
6 Record Breaker
   (Doug Jones) .... .06
8 *Dave Eiland* (FC) .... .10
10 Andre Dawson .... .15
11 Bruce Sutter .... .10
15 Robby Thompson .... .06
17 Brian Downing .... .06
18 Rick Rhoden .... .06
20 Steve Bedrosian .... .08
22 Tim Crews .... .06
27 *Orestes Destrade* (FC) ..... .20
30 Doc Gooden .... .40
33 B.J. Surhoff .... .08
34 Ken Williams .... .06
35 John Tudor .... .08
36 Mitch Webster .... .06
40 Steve Sax .... .15
45 Kal Daniels .... .10
49 *Craig Biggio* (FC) .... .50
50 George Bell .... .25
53 Ruben Sierra .... .35
55 Julio Franco .... .06
59 Mark Davis .... .07
60 Tom Brunansky .... .10
65 Rick Reuschel .... .06
70 Mark McGwire .... .50
73 Pascual Perez .... .06
75 Tom Henke .... .06
76 *Terry Blocker* (FC) .... .10
77 Doyle Alexander .... .06
80 Cory Snyder .... .15
83 Jeff Blauser (FC) .... .15
84 *Bill Bene*
   (#1 Draft Pick) (FC) .... .30
85 Kevin McReynolds .... .15
88 *Darryl Hamilton* (FC) .... .15
90 Vince Coleman .... .12
95 Gerald Young .... .10
97 Greg Mathews .... .06
98 Larry Sheets .... .06
99 *Sherman Corbett* (FC) .... .12
100 Mike Schmidt .... .35
105 Ron Darling .... .10
106 Willie Upshaw .... .06
107 Jose DeLeon .... .10
109 *Hipolito Pena* (FC) .... .10
110 Paul Molitor .... .15

225 Ramon Martinez

112 Jim Presley .... .06
115 Jody Davis .... .06
120 Frank Viola .... .15
122 Lance Johnson (FC) .... .12
124 Jim Traber .... .06
126 Sid Bream .... .06
127 Walt Terrell .... .06
129 *Terry Clark* (FC) .... .10
130 Gerald Perry .... .06
135 Jose Rijo .... .08
141 Indians Ldrs
   (Brook Jacoby) .... .06
144 Jay Bell .... .06
145 Dave Stewart .... .08
148 Bill Pecota .... .06
149 *Doug Dascenzo* (FC) .... .15
150 Fernando Valenzuela .... .15
155 Marty Barrett .... .06
156 *Dave Gallagher* (FC) .... .20
157 Tom Glavine .... .12
160 Jeffrey Leonard .... .06
161 *Gregg Olson*
   (#1 Draft Pick) (FC) .... .70
163 Bob Forsch .... .06
165 Mike Dunne .... .06
166 *Doug Jennings* (FC) .... .12
167 FS (*Steve Searcy*) (FC) ..... .15

1989 Topps

343 Gary Sheffield

303 Felix Fermin........................ .06
305 Dave Smith.......................... .06
309 Mario Diaz (FC) .... .20
310 Rafael Palmeiro .... .25
315 Greg Swindell .... .10
316 Walt Weiss .... .20
317 *Jack Armstrong* .... .25
318 Gene Larkin .... .08
320 Lou Whitaker .... .15
321 Red Sox Ldrs (Jody Reed) .. .06
322 John Smiley .... .10
323 Gary Thurman .... .10
324 *Bob Milacki* (FC) .... .25
326 Dennis Boyd .... .06
327 *Mark Lemke* (FC) .... .20
330 Eric Davis .... .35
332 Tony Armas .... .06
333 Bob Ojeda .... .06
335 Dave Righetti .... .10
336 Steve Balboni .... .06
340 Kirk Gibson......................... .15
343 FS (*Gary Sheffield*) (FC) ... **1.50**
349 *Ron Jones* (FC) .... .30
350 Andy Van Slyke .... .15
351 Giants Ldrs (Bob Melvin)... .06
354 Larry Parrish .... .06
355 Mark Langston .... .12
356 Kevin Elster .... .08
358 *Ricky Jordan* (FC) .... .45
359 Tommy John .... .10
360 Ryne Sandberg .... .35
361 Kelly Downs......................... .08
364 Rob Deer .... .06
365 Mike Henneman .... .06
367 *Johnny Paredes* (FC) .... .15
368 Brian Holton........................ .06
369 Ken Caminiti .... .06
370 Dennis Eckersley................ .10
373 Tracy Jones .... .08
374 John Wathan .... .06
375 Terry Pendleton .... .08
380 Rickey Henderson .... .35
382 *John Smoltz* (FC) .... .50
383 Howard Johnson .... .10
385 Von Hayes .... .08
386 Andres Galarraga AS .... .08
387 Ryne Sandberg AS............. .15
388 Bobby Bonilla AS................ .10
389 Ozzie Smith AS .... .10

648 Sandy Alomar

390 Darryl Strawberry AS......... .15
391 Andre Dawson AS .... .12
392 Andy Van Slyke AS .... .12
393 Gary Carter AS .... .10
394 Orel Hershiser AS............. .12
395 Danny Jackson AS .... .08
396 Kirk Gibson AS .... .08
397 Don Mattingly AS............... .60
398 Julio Franco AS .... .10
399 Wade Boggs AS .... .35
400 Alan Trammell AS .... .08
401 Jose Canseco AS............... .30
402 Mike Greenwell AS............ .12
403 Kirby Puckett AS .... .15
404 Bob Boone AS.................... .06
405 Roger Clemens AS............. .15
406 Frank Viola AS .... .08
407 Dave Winfield AS .... .15
408 Greg Walker .... .06
410 Jack Clark .... .15
411 Mitch Williams .... .08
415 Rich Gossage .... .10
416 Fred Lynn .... .10
420 Joe Carter.......................... .15
421 Kirk McCaskill .... .06
422 Bo Diaz.............................. .06

233 Gregg Jefferies

465 Mark Grace

1989 Topps

784 Steve Avery

1989 TOPPS TRADED

Topps stuck with its custom by releasing a ninth annual 132-card Traded set in 1989. The company maintained the same format for the set (which copied the 792-card Topps set from the same year), and packaged the cards in a specially designed box. However, for the first time, the company experimented with selling complete sets in selected retail outlets such as toy stores. This added a new phase to the continuing debate over whether collectors would have to consider Traded cards as official "rookie" cards. Hot cards in the set include Tom Gordon, Ken Griffey, Jr., and Jerome Walton, all of whom are pictured on Topps cards for the first time.

2 Jim Abbott

		MINT
Complete set		**$15.00**
Commons		**.05**

2	Jim Abbott	$.75
3	Kent Anderson (FC)	.12
6	Steve Balboni	.10
7	Jesse Barfield	.12
8	Steve Bedrosian	.20
9	Todd Benzinger	.15
11	Bert Blyleven	.20
12	• Bob Boone	.15
13	Phil Bradley	.12
14	Jeff Brantley (FC)	.30
15	Kevin Brown	.20
16	Jerry Browne	.15
17	Chuck Cary	.10
20	Jack Clark	.20
23	Mike Devereaux	.20
26	John Dopson	.10
28	Jim Eisenreich	.15
30	Alvaro Espinoza	.12
31	Darrell Evans	.10
32	Junior Felix (FC)	.65
34	Julio Franco	.20
37	Bob Geren (FC)	.20
38	Tom Gordon (FC)	.60
39	Tommy Gregg	.15
40	Ken Griffey	.15
41	Ken Griffey, Jr. (FC)	6.75
43	Lee Guetterman	.10
45	Erik Hanson	.75
46	Gene Harris (FC)	.35
48	Rickey Henderson	.50
49	Tom Herr	.10
50	Ken Hill	.20
51	Brian Holman	.30
55	Bruce Hurst	.15
56	Chris James	.10
57	Randy Johnson	.30
61	Eric King	.12

62	Ron Kittle	.10
63	John Kruk	.12
66	Mark Langston	.35
70	Jim Lefebvre	.10
71	Al Leiter	.15
72	Jeffrey Leonard	.15
73	Derek Lilliquist	.20
75	Tom McCarthy (FC)	.15
76	Lloyd McClendon	.10
79	Roger McDowell	.15
81	Randy Milligan	.30
82	Mike Moore	.20
83	Keith Moreland	.10
87	Eddie Murray	.25
88	Pete O'Brien	.15
89	Gregg Olson	.75
90	Steve Ontiveros	.10
91	Jesse Orosco	.10
92	Spike Owen	.10
93	Rafael Palmeiro	.20
94	Clay Parker	.25
95	Jeff Parrett	.10
96	Lance Parrish	.20
100	Willie Randolph	.15
103	Bip Roberts	.15
104	Kenny Rogers (FC)	.20
106	Nolan Ryan	1.50
108	Juan Samuel	.15
109	Alex Sanchez	.25
110	Deion Sanders (FC)	.65
111	Steve Sax	.20
113	Dwight Smith	.45
114	Lonnie Smith	.15
115	Billy Spiers (FC)	.30
118	Milt Thompson	.20
120	Jeff Torborg	.10
121	Jeff Treadway	.15
122	Omar Vizquel (FC)	.20
123	Jerome Walton (FC)	1.25
124	Gary Ward	.10
125	Claudell Washington	.12
127	Eddie Williams	.15
130	Mitch Williams	.20
131	Steve Wilson	.20

1989 UPPER DECK

The biggest hobby event of 1989 in the baseball card world was the arrival of a brand new card company: Upper Deck, a card manufacturer from Anaheim, California, managed to penetrate the market split up among Donruss, Fleer, Score and Topps. The Upper Deck cards feature large, crisp color images on both sides and are printed on glossy stock of a heavy weight. The company sold them in foil packs containing 15 cards for 89 cents per pack, but within weeks the price shot up to $1.50 a pack. Upper Deck announced that no more than 60,000 to 70,000 foil pack cases were produced in 1989. The set, originally thought to number 700, grew to 800 when the company issued a second series in July, though factory-collated sets contain all 800 cards. Each card includes a small hologram on the back that is said to be counterfeit-proof. (Star Rookies are identified below with the abbreviation SR.)

	MINT
Complete set (1-700)	$58.00
Commons (1-700)	.08
Complete set (1-800)	90.00
Commons (701-800)	.10

1	*Ken Griffey Jr.* (SR)	$45.00
2	*Luis Medina* (SR)	.25
3	*Tony Chance* (SR)	.15
5	*Sandy Alomar Jr.* (SR)	5.00
6	*Rolando Roomes* (SR)	.25
7	*David West* (SR)	.25

8 *Cris Carpenter* (SR) .... .35
9 *Gregg Jefferies* (SR) 2.75
10 *Doug Dascenzo* (SR) .... .30
11 *Ron Jones* (SR) .... .25
12 *Luis de los Santos* (SR)..... .20
13 *Gary Sheffield* (SR) (SS
   designation on front
   is inverted) 5.00
13 *Gary Sheffield* (SR)
   (SS position correct) 4.00
14 *Mike Harkey* (SR) .... .65
15 *Lance Blankenship* (SR).... .25
16 *William Brennan* (SR) .... .12
17 *John Smoltz* (SR) 1.00
18 *Ramon Martinez* (SR)...... 8.00
19 *Mark Lemke* (SR) .... .20
20 *Juan Bell* (SR) .... .20
21 *Rey Palacios* (SR) .... .15
22 *Felix Jose* (SR) 2.75
23 *Van Snider* (SR) .... .20
24 *Dante Bichette* (SR) .... .55
25 *Randy Johnson* (SR) .... .50
26 *Carlos Quintana* (SR) .... .95
28 *Mike Schooler*.................... .50
30 *Jerald Clark* .... .70
32 *Dan Firova*........................ .20
35 *Ricky Jordan*..................... .80
37 Bret Saberhagen .... .20
39 Dave Dravecky .... .15
41 Jeff Musselman .... .10
45 *Sil Campusano*.................. .25
47 *Paul Gibson*...................... .20
53 Steve Sax .... .20
54 Pete O'Brien .... .12
56 Rick Rhoden .... .10
57 John Dopson .... .25
59 Dave Righetti..................... .15
68 Mike Devereaux .... .15
70 Mike Marshall .... .12
72 Brian Holton (photo is
   Shawn Hillegas) 2.00
73 Jose Guzman .... .10
85 Allan Anderson.................. .12
87 Jesse Orosco .... .10
88 Felix Fermin....................... .10
92 Cecil Espy .... .10
95 Mitch Williams .... .12
96 Tracy Jones....................... .10
101 Bill Doran........................... .10

Nolan Ryan

774 Nolan Ryan

102 Tim Wallach....................... .12
103 • Joe Magrane .... .12
105 Alvin Davis........................ .12
107 Shawon Dunston .... .17
109 Nelson Liriano ...... .10
110 Devon White...................... .15
112 Buddy Bell......................... .10
115 Andres Galarraga............... .15
116 Mike Scioscia .... .10
118 Ernie Whitt........................ .10
119 • Bob Boone .... .10
120 Ryne Sandberg .... .65
122 Hubie Brooks..................... .10
123 Mike Moore .... .10
125 Bob Horner........................ .10
126 Chili Davis......................... .10
128 Chet Lemon....................... .10
130 Orel Hershiser .... .20
131 Terry Pendleton .... .10
132 Jeff Blauser .... .10
138 Jack Howell .... .10
139 Tony Fernandez .... .12
140 Mark Grace 2.00
141 Ken Caminiti .... .15
145 Nolan Ryan..................... 2.50
149 Jesse Barfield.................... .10
150 Matt Nokes .... .25

22 Felix Jose

Hensley Meulens

746 Hensley Meulens

5 Sandy Alomar Jr.

453	Ed Whitson	.10
455	Damon Berryhill	.12
461	Jeff Russell	.10
464	*Sherman Corbett*	.20
467	Cal Ripken, Jr.	.35
468	John Farrell	.10
471	Roberto Alomar	1.25
472	Jeff Robinson	.12
477	*Johnny Paredes*	.20
481	Johnny Ray	.10
484	Pete Incaviglia	.12
485	Brian Downing	.10
489	Jay Bell	.15
491	*Jeff Pico*	.15
492	*Mark Parent*	.15
498	Pascual Perez	.10
500	Kirt Manwaring	.12
504	Glenn Braggs	.10
509	*Jeff Bittiger*	.15
510	Kevin Seitzer	.20
511	Steve Bedrosian	.12
512	Todd Worrell	.12
513	Chris James	.10
516	John Smiley	.12
521	Lee Smith	.10
525	Paul Molitor	.15
526	Mark Langston	.15
530	Jack McDowell	.40
537	Andy Van Slyke	.15
540	Doug Jones	.15
542	Mike Boddicker	.12
543	Greg Brock	.10
546	*Mike Macfarlane*	.20
547	*Rich Renteria*	.15
553	Mickey Tettleton	.12
555	Mike Witt	.10
557	Bobby Witt	.10
559	Randy Milligan	.30
560	*Jose Cecena*	.12
561	Mackey Sasser	.10
562	Carney Lansford	.12
565	Dwight Gooden	.45
569	Mike Pagliarulo	.10
572	Fred McGriff	.40
573	Wally Joyner	.25
574	*Jose Bautista*	.15
575	Kelly Gruber	.20
578	Bobby Bonilla	.30
580	Gene Larkin	.12

392	Curt Young	.10
393	Jeff Treadway	.12
394	Darrell Evans	.12
397	Frank Viola	.15
398	Jeff Parrett	.12
399	*Terry Blocker*	.15
401	*Louie Meadows*	.20
402	Tim Raines	.25
406	Mike Schmidt	1.25
407	John Franco	.12
408	*Brady Anderson*	.30
410	Eric Davis	.40
412	Pete Smith	.10
413	Jim Rice	.15
414	Bruce Sutter	.10
416	Ruben Sierra	.50
424	Ted Higuera	.12
431	Gerald Perry	.10
432	Mike Greenwell	.40
434	Ellis Burks	.50
437	Charlie Hough	.10
440	Barry Bonds	.20
442	Rob Deer	.10
443	Glenn Davis	.15
451	Lou Whitaker	.15
452	Goose Gossage	.12

Chris Sabo

180 Chris Sabo

1989 Upper Deck

754 Todd Zeile

709	Mickey Hatcher	.10
710	Lance McCullers	.10
711	Ron Kittle	.10
712	Bert Blyleven	.20
713	Rick Dempsey	.10
714	Ken Williams	.10
715	Steve Rosenberg (FC)	.15
716	Joe Skalski (FC)	.20
717	Spike Owen	.10
718	Todd Burns (FC)	.25
719	Kevin Gross	.10
720	Tommy Herr	.10
721	Rob Ducey (FC)	.15
722	Gary Green (FC)	.15
723	Gregg Olson (FC)	2.00
724	Greg W. Harris (FC)	.20
725	Craig Worthington (FC)	.30
726	Tom Howard (FC)	.35
727	Dale Mohorcic	.10
728	Rich Yett	.10
731	Lonnie Smith	.15
732	Wally Backman	.10
733	Trevor Wilson (FC)	.30
734	Jose Alvarez (FC)	.15
735	Bob Milacki (FC)	.25
736	Tom Gordon (FC)	1.75

737	Wally Whitehurst (FC)	.30
738	Mike Aldrete	.10
739	Keith Miller (FC)	.12
740	Randy Milligan	.20
741	Jeff Parrett	.12
742	Steve Finley (FC)	.40
743	Junior Felix (FC)	1.50
744	Pete Harnisch (FC)	.35
745	Bill Spiers (FC)	.50
746	Hensley Meulens (FC)	3.00
747	Juan Bell	.20
748	Steve Sax	.25
749	Phil Bradley	.15
751	Tommy Gregg (FC)	.15
752	Kevin Brown (FC)	.35
753	Derek Lilliquist (FC)	.20
754	Todd Zeile (FC)	3.50
755	Jim Abbott (FC)	4.00
756	Ozzie Canseco (FC)	1.00
757	Nick Esasky	.20
758	Mike Moore	.25
759	Rob Murphy	.10
760	Rick Mahler	.10
761	Fred Lynn	.15
762	Kevin Blankenship (FC)	.15
763	Eddie Murray	.30
764	Steve Searcy (FC)	.20
765	Jerome Walton (FC)	3.00
766	Erik Hanson (FC)	2.50
767	• Bob Boone	.15
768	Edgar Martinez (FC)	1.25
769	Jose DeJesus (FC)	.15
770	Greg Briley (FC)	.75
771	Steve Peters (FC)	.20
772	Rafael Palmeiro	.25
773	Jack Clark	.20
774	Nolan Ryan	5.00
775	Lance Parrish	.20
776	Joe Girardi (FC)	.30
777	Willie Randolph	.20
778	Mitch Williams	.30
779	Dennis Cook (FC)	.25
780	Dwight Smith (FC)	1.00
781	Lenny Harris (FC)	.45
782	Torey Lovullo (FC)	.12
783	Norm Charlton (FC)	.40
784	Chris Brown	.10
785	Todd Benzinger	.15
786	Shane Rawley	.10

1990 DONRUSS

The nicest part about the 1990 Donruss set is its clean design. While other manufacturers cluttered cards with team logos and other ornamentation, Donruss chose to use large rectangular photos, unblemished by frills. Orange card backs are easy to read, thanks to the placement of player stats in a white box. Following tradition, the 1990 set begins with 26 Diamond Kings (with paintings by Dick Perez), followed by a like number of Rated Rookies. This year's Rookies subset should be an investment winner in future years thanks to the popularity of Eric Anthony, Steve Avery, Juan Gonzalez, Ben McDonald, Greg Vaughn, and Todd Zeile. Donruss closed the set with a commemorative card of late commissioner Bart Giamatti. Flipped negatives, inverted pairs of card backs, and statistical glitches have created numerous error/variation challenges for advanced collectors.

	MINT
Complete set	**$29.00**
Commons	**.05**

716 Bart Giamatti

1990 Donruss

36 Marquis Grissom

96	Cal Ripken	.15
97	Andres Galarraga	.15
98	Kevin Mitchell	.25
99	Howard Johnson	.10
101	Melido Perez	.07
103	Paul Molitor	.10
105	Ryne Sandberg	.28
106	Bryn Smith	.06
108	Jim Abbott	.25
109	Alvin Davis	.10
110	Lee Smith	.06
111	Roberto Alomar	.12
112	Rick Reuschel	.08
113	Kelly Gruber	.10
114	Joe Carter	.10
115	Jose Rijo	.06
118	Glenn Davis	.10
119	Jeff Reardon	.06
121	John Smoltz	.10
122	Dwight Evans	.08
123	Eric Yelding	.08
124	John Franco	.06
125	Jose Canseco	.50
126	Barry Bonds	.15
128	Jack Clark	.08
135	Ozzie Guillen	.09
136	Chili Davis	.05
140	Robby Thompson	.07
141	Craig Worthington	.10
142	Julio Franco	.10
143	Brian Holman	.07
144	George Brett	.15
145	Tom Glavine	.10
146	Robin Yount	.18
147	Gary Carter	.08
148	Ron Kittle	.07
149	Tony Fernandez	.07
150	Dave Stewart	.10
151	Gary Gaetti	.07
152	Kevin Elster	.05
157	Rick Sutcliffe	.06
158	Greg Maddux	.10
160	John Kruk	.06
162	John Dopson	.06
163	Joe Magrane	.06
166	Nolan Ryan	.45
168	Dale Murphy	.10
169	Mickey Tettleton	.08
171	Dwight Gooden	.18

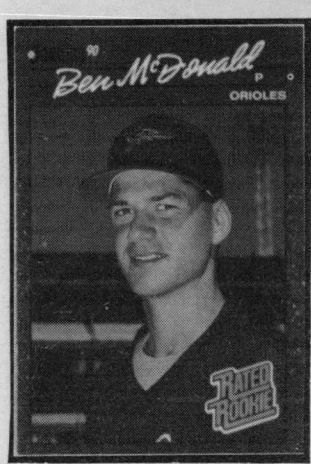

32 Ben McDonald

174	Ruben Sierra	.15
175	Dan Plesac	.08
178	Matt Nokes	.05
180	Frank Tanana	.05
181	Tony Pena	.07
184	Roger Clemens	.25
185	Mark McGwire	.30
188	Fred McGriff	.15
190	Don Mattingly	.50
192	Roberto Kelly	.10
196	Eric Plunk	.05
197	Orel Hershiser	.12
201	Ozzie Smith	.10
202	Pete O'Brien	.06
203	Jay Howell	.06
204	Mark Gubicza	.08
206	George Bell	.10
207	Mike Scott	.08
210	Dennis Eckersley	.10
213	Lance Parrish	.07
214	Mike Moore	.06
215	*Steve Finley*	.10
216	Tim Raines	.10
217	Scott Garrelts	.07
218	Kevin McReynolds	.09
219	Dave Gallagher	.06

659 Nolan Ryan

268	Terry Steinbach	.07
269	Kirby Puckett	.25
270	Gregg Jefferies	.25
272	Cory Snyder	.07
275	Mitch Williams	.08
278	Von Hayes	.10
279	Vince Coleman	.10
280	Mike Boddicker	.07
283	*Kenny Rogers*	.10
284	Jeff Russell	.06
285	*Jerome Walton*	.35
287	Joe Orsulak	.05
289	Ron Darling	.08
290	Bobby Bonilla	.15
294	Ivan Calderon	.07
295	Steve Bedrosian	.06
296	Mike Henneman	.07
297	Tom Gordon	.15
298	Lou Whitaker	.08
299	Terry Pendleton	.06
302	Mark Davis	.07
303	Nick Esasky	.06
304	Rickey Henderson	.35
305	Rick Cerone	.05
306	Craig Biggio	.15
308	Tom Browning	.08
310	Greg Swindell	.08
311	Dave Righetti	.07
312	Mike Maddux	.05
313	• Lenny Dykstra	.10
316	Mike Scioscia	.07
317	Ron Oester	.05
318	*Gary Wayne*	.10
319	Todd Worrell	.06
320	Doug Jones	.07
322	Danny Tartabull	.08
326	Bob Boone	.10
328	Dave Parker	.10
330	Mike Schooler	.06
331	Bert Blyleven	.08
332	Bob Welch	.08
334	Tim Burke	.06
336	Randy Myers	.08
338	Mark Langston	.10
339	Ted Higuera	.07
342	Pascual Perez	.05
343	Kevin Brown	.08
344	Chuck Finley	.10
345	Erik Hanson	.17

220	Tim Wallach	.08
222	Lonnie Smith	.06
223	Andre Dawson	.12
224	Nelson Santovenia	.06
225	Rafael Palmeiro	.12
226	Devon White	.07
227	Harold Reynolds	.07
228	Ellis Burks	.12
230	Will Clark	.40
231	Jimmy Key	.07
233	Eric Davis	.25
234	Johnny Ray	.06
235	Darryl Strawberry	.25
242	Chris Sabo	.15
243	Dave Henderson	.08
244	Andy Van Slyke	.08
245	Alvaro Espinosa	.08
247	Gene Harris	.08
249	Brett Butler	.07
250	Willie Randolph	.07
251	Roger McDowell	.07
257	Todd Benzinger	.06
259	Phil Bradley	.08
260	Cecil Espy	.05
262	Frank White	.07
265	David Cone	.10
266	Bobby Thigpen	.10

348	Matt Williams	.20
349	Tom Henke	.07
353	Frank Viola	.12
363	Clay Parker	.06
365	Ken Griffey, Jr.	2.25
368	Kirk Gibson	.08
373	Mike Bielecki	.06
374	*Tom Magrann* (FC)	.12
377	Gregg Olson	.15
379	Randy Johnson	.10
380	Jeff Montgomery	.06
382	*Bill Spiers*	.10
383	Dave Magadan	.07
384	*Greg Hibbard* (FC)	.35
387	Dave West	.07
388	Keith Hernandez	.06
390	*Joey Belle* (FC)	.75
391	Rick Aguilera	.08
393	*Dwight Smith*	.15
394	*Steve Wilson*	.12
395	*Bob Geren*	.20
399	Tom Brunansky	.07
402	Harold Baines	.07
404	Joe Girardi	.08
405	*Sergio Valdez* (FC)	.12
408	*Jeff Innis* (FC)	.10
411	Charlie Hough	.06
414	*Trevor Wilson* (FC)	.10
415	*Kevin Ritz* (FC)	.12
426	Norm Charlton	.06
427	• *Deion Sanders*	.25
432	Kal Daniels	.08
434	Lenny Harris (FC)	.10
435	*Scott Scudder* (FC)	.15
438	*Steve Olin* (FC)	.10
448	Jay Buhner	.08
449	*Lee Stevens* (FC)	.20
453	*Greg Litton* (FC)	.10
454	Mark Carreon	.06
457	*Tony Fossas* (FC)	.12
461	Jack Daugherty	.12
462	*Rich Monteleone* (FC)	.10
463	Greg Briley (FC)	.15
465	Benito Santiago	.12
466	*Jeff Brantley*	.12
469	Ken Griffey	.05
473	*Kevin Tapani* (FC)	.30
474	Bill Buckner	.05
475	Ron Gant	.06

711 John Olerud

476	Kevin Romine (FC)	.05
479	Storm Davis	.06
480	Jeff King (FC)	.15
481	*Kevin Mmahat* (FC)	.20
483	*Omar Vizquel*	.10
487	Ron Jones	.06
489	Sammy Sosa (FC)	.65
490	*Kent Anderson* (FC)	.10
499	Pete Smith	.06
501	Gary Sheffield	.25
502	*Terry Bross* (FC)	.15
503	Jerry Kutzler (FC)	.12
504	Lloyd Moseby	.06
508	*Mike Stanton* (FC)	.12
510	*Tim Drummond* (FC)	.12
512	*Rick Wrona*	.12
514	Hal Morris	.30
517	Carlos Quintana	.10
519	Randy Milligan	.10
522	Mike Harkey	.10
527	*Rick Reed* (FC)	.12
529	Dean Palmer (FC)	.35
530	*Jeff Peterek* (FC)	.12
531	*Carlos Martinez*	.20
535	*Doug Strange* (FC)	.12
536	Jose DeLeon	.07
538	Joey Cora (FC)	.10

1990 Donruss

390 Joey Belle

695	Eric Davis AS	.10	**706**	Greg Myers	.06
697	Mark McGwire AS	.10	**707**	Will Clark AS	.15
698	*Steve Cummings* (FC)	.10	**708**	Benito Santiago AS	.10
699	*George Canale* (FC)	.10	**710**	Ozzie Smith AS	.10
701	Julio Franco AS	.10	**711**	*John Olerud* (FC)	**2.00**
702	*Dave Johnson* (FC)	.10	**712**	Wade Boggs AS	.10
703	Dave Stewart AS	.10	**713**	*Gary Eave* (FC)	.10
704	*Dave Justice* (FC)	**2.25**	**715**	Kevin Mitchell AS	.10
705	Tony Gwynn AS	.12	**716**	Bart Giamatti	.60

1990 DONRUSS ROOKIES

Although Donruss was one of the leading card makers of 1990 with its attractive standard set, the company lost steam with "The Rookies," its 56-card extension set. Because of a limited concept, fewer cards, and high cost relative to its competition, collectors were able to restrain their enthusiasm for the set. In fact, "The Rookies" paled in comparison with the larger fall sets from Fleer, Score, Topps, and Upper Deck. Each of these companies produced more cards in their season-ending subsets than Donruss, and each included traded players within its run. In a way, Donruss became a victim of the success of its earlier edition, since so many noted newcomers were featured in the Rated Rookies subset that was part of the standard Donruss edition. The only hot cards in this Rookies set are those of Dave Justice, Ben McDonald, and John Olerud. Special logos on the card fronts and bright green borders identify the Donruss Rookies, in contrast to the red borders used on the earlier set.

		MINT
Complete set		**$12.00**
Commons		**.07**

1	Sandy Alomar	$ .30	**12**	Bill Sampen	.25
2	John Olerud	1.50	**13**	Brian Bohanon	.10
3	Pat Combs	.15	**14**	Dave Justice	2.25
4	Brian Dubois	.07	**15**	Robin Ventura	.25
5	Felix Jose	.15	**16**	Greg Vaughn	.55
6	Delino DeShields	.50	**17**	Wayne Edwards	.15
7	Mike Stanton	.10	**18**	Shawn Boskie	.25
8	Mike Munoz	.10	**19**	Carlos Baerga	.40
9	Craig Grebeck	.15	**20**	Mark Gardner	.15
10	Joe Kraemer	.10	**21**	Kevin Appier	.25
11	Jeff Huson	.07	**22**	Mike Harkey	.15
			23	Tim Layana	.15
			24	Glenallen Hill	.10
			25	Jerry Kutzler	.07
			26	Mike Blowers	.12
			27	Scott Ruskin	.15

2 John Olerud

1990 FLEER

A modest card design and, at 660 cards, a set smaller in number than some of its competition prevented the 1990 Fleer set from becoming a popular collectible. Card fronts with small photos and large white borders seem unimaginative, while backs, using red-and-blue ink (along with annoying pink-and-white stripes), are hard to read. The company's newest innovation was also its most successful: A "Players of the Decade" subset highlights memorable stars from the 1980s. While Fleer's 1990 set includes many rookies, a number of important names wind up sharing cards. In an outdated practice from previous years, Fleer created a subset for rookie stars using photos of two players. Surprisingly, several of these cards pair rookies of different teams and unrelated positions.

		MINT
Complete set		$23.00
Commons		.05

2	Todd Burns	$ .06
3	Jose Canseco	.75
5	Storm Davis	.07
6	Dennis Eckersley	.15

9	Dave Henderson	.10
10	Rickey Henderson	.35
12	Stan Javier	.06
13	Felix Jose	.25
14	Carney Lansford	.09
15	Mark McGwire	.50
16	Mike Moore	.10
18	Dave Parker	.12
20	Terry Steinbach	.10
21	Dave Stewart	.15
22	Walt Weiss	.10
23	Bob Welch	.10
27	Mike Bielecki	.08
29	Andre Dawson	.15
30	Shawon Dunston	.10
31	Joe Girardi	.20
32	Mark Grace	.25
33	Mike Harkey	.12
35	Les Lancaster	.06
37	Greg Maddux	.10
40	Ryne Sandberg	.25
42	Dwight Smith	.10
43	Rick Sutcliffe	.08
44	*Jerome Walton*	.20
47	*Dean Wilkins* (FC)	.10
48	Mitch Williams	.15
50	Steve Bedrosian	.07
51	*Mike Benjamin* (FC)	.20
52	*Jeff Brantley*	.10
53	Brett Butler	.07
54	Will Clark	.60
56	Scott Garrelts	.07
61	*Greg Litton*	.10
62	Candy Maldonado	.08
63	Kirt Manwaring	.06
64	*Randy McCament* (FC)	.10
65	Kevin Mitchell	.15
68	Rick Reuschel	.09
73	Robby Thompson	.07
75	Matt Williams	.20
76	George Bell	.10
77	Pat Borders	.07
79	*Junior Felix*	.15
80	Tony Fernandez	.09
82	*Mauro Gozzo* (FC)	.10
83	Kelly Gruber	.12
84	Tom Henke	.07
85	Jimmy Key	.06
89	Fred McGriff	.15

110 Bo Jackson

90	Lloyd Moseby	.07
92	Alex Sanchez	.06
93	Dave Stieb	.09
94	Todd Stottlemyre	.10
99	Mookie Wilson	.07
100	*Kevin Appier* (FC)	.15
102	Bob Boone	.08
103	George Brett	.15
104	Jose DeJesus	.06
108	Tom Gordon	.15
109	Mark Gubicza	.09
110	Bo Jackson	.50
113	*Rick Luecken* (FC)	.10
115	Jeff Montgomery	.06
116	Bret Saberhagen	.10
117	Kevin Seitzer	.09
118	Kurt Stillwell	.08
122	Frank White	.07
123	Willie Wilson	.06
124	*Matt Winters* (FC)	.15
125	Jim Abbott	.15
127	Dante Bichette	.09
128	Bert Blyleven	.09
129	Chili Davis	.06
130	Brian Downing	.06
131	*Mike Fetters* (FC)	.10

1990 Fleer

485 Joey Belle

277	Mike Greenwell	.25
279	Eric Hetzel	.08
283	Carlos Quintana	.10
284	Jody Reed	.06
287	Lee Smith	.07
290	Harold Baines	.09
291	Kevin Brown	.08
293	*Scott Coolbaugh* (FC)	.25
294	*Jack Daugherty* (FC)	.12
295	Cecil Espy	.06
296	Julio Franco	.10
297	*Juan Gonzalez* (FC)	2.50
303	Chad Krueter	.06
308	Rafael Palmeiro	.12
311	*Kenny Rogers* (FC)	.08
312	Jeff Russell	.06
313	• Nolan Ryan	.60
314	Ruben Sierra	.15
316	Chris Bosio	.06
317	Glenn Braggs	.07
320	Rob Deer	.06
323	*Tony Fossas* (FC)	.10
326	Ted Higuera	.08
329	*Tim McIntosh* (FC)	.18

534 Greg Hibbard

330	Paul Molitor	.08
331	*Jaime Navarro*	.20
333	*Jeff Peterek* (FC)	.10
334	Dan Plesac	.07
336	Gary Sheffield	.25
337	*Bill Spiers*	.08
339	*Greg Vaughn*	.55
340	Robin Yount	.25
342	Tim Burke	.06
345	Andres Galarraga	.15
347	*Marquis Grissom* (FC)	.40
350	*Jeff Huson* (FC)	.10
352	Mark Langston	.07
358	Pascual Perez	.06
359	Tim Raines	.10
360	Nelson Santovenia	.08
361	Bryn Smith	.06
363	*Larry Walker* (FC)	.30
364	Tim Wallach	.07
365	Rick Aguilera	.10
366	Allan Anderson	.06
372	*Mike Dyer* (FC)	.15
373	Gary Gaetti	.07
378	Kent Hrbek	.10
383	Kirby Puckett	.30
385	Jeff Reardon	.07
387	*Gary Wayne* (FC)	.08
388	Dave West	.25
389	Tim Belcher	.10
393	Kirk Gibson	.08
399	Orel Hershiser	.12
400	Jay Howell	.06
401	Mike Marshall	.06
402	• Ramon Martinez	.35
404	Eddie Murray	.10
407	Mike Scioscia	.07
409	Fernando Valenzuela	.10
410	*Jose Vizcaino* (FC)	.15
411	*John Wetteland* (FC)	.10
412	• Jack Armstrong	.18
413	Todd Benzinger	.07
415	Tom Browning	.07
416	Norm Charlton	.06
417	Eric Davis	.25
418	Rob Dibble	.15
419	John Franco	.07
421	*Chris Hammond* (FC)	.30
422	Danny Jackson	.06
423	Barry Larkin	.15
426	*Joe Oliver* (FC)	.10
427	Paul O'Neill	.07

586 David Justice

430	Jose Rijo	.07
433	Chris Sabo	.20
434	*Scott Scudder*	.20
437	Jesse Barfield	.07
438	*Mike Blowers* (FC)	.20
441	Alvaro Espinosa	.25
442	*Bob Geren*	.25
444	Mel Hall	.06
445	Andy Hawkins	.06
446	Roberto Kelly	.15
447	Don Mattingly	.50
449	Hensley Muelens	.20
451	Clay Parker	.10
453	Dave Righetti	.07
454	• *Deion Sanders*	.25
455	Steve Sax	.12
458	Dave Winfield	.15
461	Barry Bonds	.15
462	Bobby Bonilla	.15
463	Sid Bream	.06
465	Doug Drabek	.06
467	Billy Hatcher	.07
468	Neal Heaton	.07
469	Jeff King	.20
472	Bill Landrum	.06
474	Jose Lind	.06

476	Gary Redus	.06
477	*Rick Reed* (FC)	.10
480	John Smiley	.07
481	Andy Van Slyke	.09
485	*Joey Belle*	.65
486	Bud Black	.06
487	Jerry Browne	.06
488	Tom Candiotti	.07
489	Joe Carter	.10
493	Brook Jacoby	.07
495	Doug Jones	.07
498	Pete O'Brien	.07
499	*Steve Olin* (FC)	.10
502	Cory Snyder	.06
503	Greg Swindell	.10
505	Scott Bankhead	.06
507	Greg Briley	.10
508	Jay Buhner	.10
512	Alvin Davis	.12
513	• Ken Griffey, Jr.	2.25
514	Erik Hanson	.20
515	Gene Harris	.10
516	Brian Holman	.07
518	Randy Johnson	.15
519	Jeffrey Leonard	.06
520	Edgar Martinez	.10
524	Harold Reynolds	.07
525	Mike Schooler	.07
528	*Omar Vizquel*	.10
529	Ivan Calderon	.06
530	Carlton Fisk	.12
532	Dave Gallagher	.06
533	Ozzie Guillen	.10
534	*Greg Hibbard* (FC)	.35
536	Lance Johnson	.07
538	Ron Kittle	.07
540	Carlos Martinez	.10
541	*Tom McCarthy* (FC)	.10
542	*Matt Merullo*	.25
544	Dan Pasqua	.06
546	Melido Perez	.07
548	*Sammy Sosa* (FC)	.60
549	Bobby Thigpen	.07
550	Robin Ventura	1.00
553	*Pat Combs* (FC)	.15
554	Dennis Cook	.20
556	• Lenny Dykstra	.10
559	Von Hayes	.09
560	Tom Herr	.06

513 Ken Griffey, Jr.

1990 FLEER UPDATE

Although this set is Fleer's tenth anniversary edition, there is nothing remarkable about it. The Update cards use exactly the same design used by the larger Fleer set issued earlier in the year. Unfortunately, Fleer (and most other companies) continued the practice of distributing its extension sets only through hobby dealers. Limiting the means available to collectors to obtain them results in all extension sets becoming more expensive. One customer benefit Fleer provided in 1990 was to shrink-wrap individual sets in an effort to deter tampering. This positive move could make it harder for dealers to break open sets and offer individual cards for sale. Notable single cards include a three-image card honoring Nolan Ryan's 300 career victories and 6 no-hitters, along with cards of newcomers Alex Fernandez, Kevin Maas, John Olerud, and Frank Thomas. Fleer continued as the only major manufacturer to group and number players by team.

		MINT
Complete set		**$14.00**
Commons		**.07**

113 Kevin Maas

1	Steve Avery	$ .40
2	Francisco Cabrera	.10
4	Jimmy Kremers	.12
5	Greg Olson	.20
7	Shawn Boskie	.25
8	Joe Kraemer	.10
10	Hector Villanueva	.20
12	Mariano Duncan	.07
13	Billy Hatcher	.15
14	Tim Layana	.20
15	Hal Morris	.35
16	Javier Ortiz	.15
17	Dave Rohde	.12
18	Eric Yelding	.20
20	Kal Daniels	.10
21	Dave Hansen	.20
22	Mike Hartley	.20
24	Jose Offerman	.70
27	Delino DeShields	1.00
28	Steve Frey	.20
29	Mark Gardner	.25
30	Chris Nabholz	.25
31	Bill Sampen	.15
34	Chuck Carr	.15
35	John Franco	.10
36	Todd Hundley	.20
37	Julio Machado	.12
39	Darren Reed	.15
40	Kelvin Torve	.09
41	Darrel Akerfelds	.10

24 Jose Offerman

1 Steve Avery

1990 SCORE

Score was the surprise hit of the hobby world in 1990. After a mediocre showing in 1989, the 704 cards in the 1990 set surpassed the $40 mark before the All-Star break. Rumors of a short printing drove prices up throughout the summer, but when Score flooded the stores (non-hobby outlets) before Christmas, prices plunged. Still, one of the hottest cards in the set remains number 697, a black-and-white reproduction of Bo Jackson's football/baseball Nike poster. It shows him posing in football shoulder pads and toting a bat across his shoulders. Special subsets include cards of top draft picks from each team, and a 13-card Dream Team with tinted photographs of top stars in a tobacco-card format. Card backs in the Dream Team group include one-paragraph profiles by famous sportswriters.

		MINT
Complete set		$25.00
Commons		.05

1	Don Mattingly	$1.00
2	Cal Ripken, Jr.	.25
3	Dwight Evans	.08
4	Barry Bonds	.20
5	Kevin McReynolds	.08
6	Ozzie Guillen	.10
9	Alan Trammell	.09
10	Cory Snyder	.09
12	Roberto Alomar	.15
13	Pedro Guerrero	.10
16	Ricky Jordan	.10
20	Jack Clark	.09
23	Lenny Harris (FC)	.12
24	Phil Bradley	.09
25	Andres Galarraga	.15
31	Mike Boddicker	.09
36	Von Hayes	.10
37	Lee Smith	.08
40	Mike Scott	.08
46	Dave Magadan	.07
50	Orel Hershiser	.12
51	Bip Roberts (FC)	.10
52	Jerry Browne	.08
54	Fernando Valenzuela	.10
55	Matt Nokes	.07
56	Brook Jacoby	.09
60	Bob Boone	.08
63	Gregg Olson	.20
65	Todd Benzinger	.07

672 Chuck Knoblauch

66	Dale Murphy	.12
69	Cecil Espy	.07
70	Chris Sabo	.17
72	Tom Brunansky	.08
75	Lou Whitaker	.09
76	Ken Caminiti	.08
78	Tommy Gregg	.08
80	Eddie Murray	.12
81	Joe Boever	.08
89	Tony Fernandez	.09
90	Ryne Sandberg	.35

97	Gary Sheffield	.25
100	Roberto Kelly	.12
101	Alvaro Espinoza (FC)	.15
110	Walt Weiss	.15
115	Dave Gallagher	.07
120	Wally Joyner	.15
121	Mark Gubicza	.08
122	Tony Pena	.07
124	Howard Johnson	.15
125	Steve Sax	.20
126	Tim Belcher	.10
127	Tim Burke	.08
130	Doug Jones	.08
131	Fred Lynn	.07
135	Dave Parker	.10
137	Dennis Boyd	.07
138	Candy Maldonado	.08
140	George Brett	.15
145	Gary Gaetti	.12
146	Kirt Manwaring	.08
149	Mike Schooler	.09
150	Mark Grace	.35
154	Jim Deshaies	.08
155	Barry Larkin	.15
157	Tom Henke	.08
159	Bob Welch	.10
160	Juli Franco	.10
162	Terry Steinbach	.10
165	Tom Browning	.10
167	Harold Reynolds	.10
169	Shawon Dunston	.10
170	Bobby Bonilla	.20
175	Pete O'Brien	.08
176	Lloyd McClendon (back lists uniform number 1)	2.00
176	Lloyd McClendon (correct card—uniform number 10)	.25
180	Bert Blyleven	.10
182	Bill Doran	.07
184	Mike Henneman	.07
185	Eric Davis	.25
187	*Steve Davis* (FC)	.10
190	Mike Moore	.10
192	Tim Wallach	.10
193	Keith Hernandez	.07
194	Dave Righetti	.08
195	Bret Saberhagen	.15
198	Juan Samuel	.07
199	Kevin Seitzer	.15

675 Maurice Vaughn

200	Darryl Strawberry	.30
201	Dave Stieb	.10
203	Jack Morris	.07
205	Alvin Davis	.15
208	Terry Pendleton	.09
210	Kevin Brown (FC)	.10
214	Kevin Hickey (FC)	.06
222	Jesse Barfield	.09
225	Pete Smith	.09
229	*Jerome Walton*	.20
230	Greg Swindell	.15
233	Ken Hill	.08
234	Craig Worthington	.15
236	Brett Butler	.09
240	Dwight Smith	.25
244	Danny Tartabull	.12
245	Wade Boggs	.35
250	Nolan Ryan	.55
255	Tony Gwynn	.20
258	*Junior Felix*	.20
259	Mark Davis	.08
260	Vince Coleman	.15
262	Mitch Williams	.10
264	*Omar Vizquel*	.15
265	Andre Dawson	.20
269	Tom Candiotti	.08

681 Greg Blosser

270	Bruce Hurst	.09
271	Fred McGriff	.15
272	Glenn Davis	.15
273	John Franco	.10
275	Craig Biggio	.15
277	• Rob Dibble	.15
279	Kevin Bass	.07
280	Bo Jackson	.75
285	Ozzie Smith	.10
286	George Bell	.10
288	Pat Borders	.10
289	Danny Jackson	.06
290	Carlton Fisk	.12
296	Carney Lansford	.10
298	Claudell Washington	.07
299	Hubie Brooks	.07
300	Will Clark	.65
301	*Kenny Rogers*	.20
302	Darrell Evans	.07
303	Greg Briley	.10
305	Teddy Higuera	.08
306	Dan Pasqua	.07
307	Dave Winfield	.20
309	Jose DeLeon	.08
310	Roger Clemens	.25
311	Melido Perez	.10

312	Devon White	.10
313	Doc Gooden	.25
314	*Carlos Martinez*	.20
315	Dennis Eckersley	.10
316	Clay Parker	.08
319	Joe Carter	.12
320	Robin Yount	.20
321	Felix Jose	.20
322	Mickey Tettleton	.08
324	Edgar Martinez	.08
325	Dave Henderson	.09
326	Chili Davis	.08
330	Jim Abbott	.30
331	John Dopson	.10
333	Jeff Robinson	.08
335	Bobby Thigpen	.09
338	Ken Griffey, Sr. (lists uniform number 25)	**2.25**
338	Ken Griffey, Sr. (correct card—uniform number 30)	.15
340	Ellis Burks	.25
343	Kevin Mitchell	.25
345	Mike Greenwell	.25
351	Randy Myers	.10
355	Pete Harnisch	.08
360	Rickey Henderson	.50
363	Mark Carreon	.10
364	Ron Jones	.10
365	Jeff Montgomery	.08
369	*Greg Hibbard* (FC)	.35
370	John Smoltz	.12
371	*Jeff Brantley*	.10
372	Frank White	.08
374	Willie McGee	.09
375	Jose Canseco	.60
381	Kent Hrbek	.12
384	Mike Marshall	.07
385	Mark McGwire	.60
388	*John Wetteland*	.35
395	Willie Randolph	.07
398	Mike Scioscia	.08
399	Lonnie Smith	.08
400	Kirby Puckett	.45
401	Mark Langston	.12
403	Greg Maddux	.15
405	Rafael Palmeiro	.10
406	Chad Kreuter	.10
407	Jimmy Key	.09
409	Tim Raines	.15

596 Tino Martinez

606 Kevin Maas

568	Roy Smith (FC)	.15
569	Jaime Navarro (FC)	.10
570	Lance Johnson (FC)	.20
571	Mike Dyer (FC)	.12
572	Kevin Ritz (FC)	.10
573	Dave West	.10
574	Gary Mielke (FC)	.10
575	Scott Lusader (FC)	.07
576	Joe Oliver	.10
577	Sandy Alomar Jr.	.40
578	Andy Benes (FC)	.20
579	Tim Jones	.05
580	Randy McCament (FC)	.10
581	Curt Schilling (FC)	.15
582	John Orton (FC)	.10
583	Milt Cuyler (FC) (back reads "pitched in 989 games")	1.50
583	Milt Cuyler (FC) (back reads "pitched in 98 games")	.40
584	Eric Anthony (FC)	.50
585	Greg Vaughn (FC)	.55
586	• Deion Sanders (FC)	.30
587	Jose DeJesus (FC)	.15
588	Chip Hale (FC)	.10
589	John Olerud (FC)	1.75
590	Steve Olin (FC)	.10
591	Marquis Grissom (FC)	.40
592	Moises Alou (FC)	.30
593	Mark Lemke (FC)	.08
594	Dean Palmer (FC)	.40
595	Robin Ventura (FC)	.30
596	Tino Martinez (FC)	.60
597	Mike Huff (FC)	.20
598	Scott Hemond (FC)	.20
599	Wally Whitehurst (FC)	.10
600	Todd Zeile (FC)	.60
601	Glenallen Hill (FC)	.15
602	Hal Morris (FC)	.50
603	Juan Bell (FC)	.10
604	Bobby Rose (FC)	.20
605	Matt Merullo (FC)	.10
606	Kevin Maas (FC)	2.25
607	Randy Nosek (FC)	.10
608	Billy Bates (FC)	.10
609	Mike Stanton (FC)	.10
610	Goose Gozzo (FC)	.10
611	Charles Nagy (FC)	.20
612	Scott Coolbaugh (FC)	.20
613	• Jose Vizcaino (FC)	.15
614	Greg Smith (FC)	.15
615	Jeff Huson (FC)	.10
616	Mickey Weston (FC)	.10
617	John Pawlowski (FC)	.20
618	Joe Skalski (FC)	.20
619	Bernie Williams (FC)	.35
620	Shawn Holman (FC)	.10
621	Gary Eave (FC)	.15
622	Darrin Fletcher (FC)	.20
623	Pat Combs (FC)	.10
624	Mike Blowers (FC)	.20
625	Kevin Appier (FC)	.20
626	Pat Austin (FC)	.10
627	Kelly Mann (FC)	.10
628	Matt Kinzer (FC)	.10
629	Scott Hammond (FC)	.35
630	Dean Wilkins (FC)	.10
631	Larry Walker (FC)	.30
632	Blaine Beatty (FC)	.12
633	Tom Barrett (FC).	.10
634	Stan Belinda (FC)	.15
635	Tex Smith (FC)	.10
636	Hensley Meulens (FC)	.25
637	Juan Gonzalez (FC)	2.50
638	Lenny Webster (FC)	.12

689	Barry Larkin (Dream Team) .... .15	696	Nolan Ryan (5000 K) .... .50
690	Kirby Puckett (Dream Team) .... .15	697	Bo Jackson (NIKE poster photo)......... 5.00
691	Ryne Sandberg (Dream Team) .... .25	698	Rickey Henderson (ALCS MVP)..................... .25
692	Mike Scott (Dream Team) .... .20	699	Will Clark (NLCS MVP) ..... .35
693	Terry Steinbach (Dream Team) .... .20	700	World Series Games 1 and 2.................. .35
694	Bobby Thigpen (Dream Team) .... .20	701	Lights Out: Candlestick........................ .15
695	Mitch Williams (Dream Team) .... .20	702	World Series Game 3 .... .35
		703	World Series Game 4 .... .35
		704	Wade Boggs (200 hits)...... .20

1990 SCORE ROOKIE & TRADED

Score's popularity continued with its 110-card Rookie & Traded set. Unlike other companies, Score divided its updated set into two parts. Cards numbered 1 through 66 portray traded players in their new uniforms, while numbers 67 to 110 depict rookies and newcomers. This second group, though no more difficult to find than the first, is generally more valuable. Top names among rookies include Steve Avery, Bernard Gilkey, Ray Lankford, and Frank Thomas. Surprisingly, the most talked about cards feature two of the least-known players. Card number 97 features D.J. Dozier, a football star attempting to start a second career with the Mets. And card number 100 shows Blue Jays prospect Eric Lindros, another two-sport man, who will also pop up in current cards for hockey players. The cards of Thomas and Lindros will help drive the value of this update set, Score's third, which is available mainly from hobby dealers.

	MINT		
Complete set	**$18.00**	15	John Franco .... .12
Commons	**.07**	16	Randy Myers .... .12
		17	Jeff Reardon .... .10
		18	Sandy Alomar, Jr .... .25
1	Dave Winfield .... .15	19	Joe Carter........................ .12
2	Kevin Bass .... .07	23	Pete O'Brien .... .07
7	Tony Pena .... .07	24	Dennis Boyd .... .09
8	Candy Maldonado .... .07	25	Lloyd Moseby .... .07
9	Cecil Fielder .... .35	27	Tim Leary .... .07
11	Mark Langston................... .12	28	Gerald Perry .... .07
12	Dave Parker .... .12	31	Dale Murphy .... .10

84 Ray Lankford

32	Alejandro Pena	.07
34	Hubie Brooks	.07
35	Gary Carter	.10
37	Wally Backman	.07
41	Jeff Huson	.10
42	Billy Hatcher	.15
46	Luis Polonia	.07
48	Lee Smith	.12
49	Tom Brunansky	.10
51	Willie Randolph	.07
57	Keith Hernandez	.10
67	Francisco Cabrera	.15
68	*Gary DiSarcina*	.10
69	Greg Olson	.15
70	Beau Allred	.20
71	Oscar Azocar	.20
72	Kent Mercker	.20
73	John Burkett	.20
74	Carlos Baerga	.40
75	Dave Hollins	.20
76	Todd Hundley	.25
77	Rick Parker	.12
78	Steve Cummings	.15
79	Bill Sampen	.30
80	Jerry Kutzler	.12
81	Derek Bell	.20
82	Kevin Tapani	.35

83	Jim Leyritz	.25
84	Ray Lankford	.90
85	Wayne Edwards	.25
86	Frank Thomas	2.00
87	Tim Naehring	.25
88	Willie Blair	.12
89	Alan Mills	.20
90	Scott Radinsky	.20
91	Howard Farmer	.20
92	Julio Machado	.15
93	Rafael Valdez	.25
94	Shawn Boskie	.25
95	David Segui	.30
96	Chris Hoiles	.30
97	D.J. Dozier	.75
98	Hector Villanueva	.30
99	Eric Gunderson	.15
100	Eric Lindros	3.75
101	Dave Otto	.12
102	Dana Kiecker	.20
103	Tim Drummond	.15
104	Mickey Pina	.15
105	Craig Grebeck	.15
106	Bernard Gilkey	.40
107	Tim Layana	.20
108	Scott Chiamparino	.30
109	Steve Avery	.45
110	Terry Shumpert	.20

106 Bernard Gilkey

1990 TOPPS

Topps unveiled an eye-popping card design for one of its wildest-looking sets in nearly two decades. Not since 1972 had the usually conservative company dabbled with such a gaudy array of multi-colored borders. Surprisingly, the two-tone, partially speckled borders are contrasted with traditional plain backs of yellow-and-black ink on gray card stock. One of the most popular features of the 1990 set is the return of #1 Draft Pick cards, which show pre-rookies in collegiate uniforms. An All-Star subset also resurfaced. In a new twist, future Hall-of-Famer Nolan Ryan is honored on the first five cards of the set. Due to what seemed like a higher-than-normal public distribution of cards and the abundance of prepackaged factory sets in retail stores, Topps prices have risen at a slower rate than most other 1990 sets.

		MINT
Complete set		$27.00
Commons		.05

336 Ken Griffey, Jr.

1	Nolan Ryan	$ .65
2	Nolan Ryan (The Mets Years)	.25
3	Nolan Ryan (The Angels Years)	.25
4	Nolan Ryan (The Astros Years)	.25
5	Nolan Ryan (The Rangers)	.25
6	1989 Record Breaker (Vince Coleman)	.10
7	1989 Record Breaker (Rickey Henderson)	.20
8	1989 Record Breaker (Cal Ripken)	.15
10	Barry Larkin	.15
12	Joe Girardi (FC)	.15
14	*Mike Fetters* (FC)	.20
15	Teddy Higuera	.08
16	*Kent Anderson*	.10
17	Kelly Downs	.05
18	Carlos Quintana	.09
20	Mark Gubicza	.10
23	Randy Velarde	.07
25	Willie Randolph	.08
30	David Cone	.10
32	John Farrell	.05
33	Greg Walker	.05
34	*Tony Fossas* (FC)	.07
35	Benito Santiago	.12
40	Jay Howell	.06
41	Matt Williams	.25
42	Jeff Robinson	.07
43	Dante Bichette	.07
44	*Roger Salkeld* (#1 Draft Pick) (FC)	.50
45	Dave Parker	.08
46	•Rob Dibble	.12
50	Glenn Davis	.10
57	*Greg Vaughn* (FC)	1.25

60	George Brett	.25
61	*Deion Sanders*	.35
62	Ramon Martinez	.50
65	Devon White	.07
66	*Greg Litton* (FC)	.25
68	Dave Henderson	.06
70	Mike Greenwell	.30
71	Allan Anderson	.05
72	*Jeff Huson* (FC)	.25
73	Bob Milacki	.05
74	*Jeff Jackson* (#1 Draft Pick) (FC)	.25
75	Doug Jones	.07
79	Ron Kittle	.07
80	Jeff Russell	.05
83	Hensley Meulens	.75
85	Juan Samuel	.08
87	*Rick Luecken* (FC)	.15
89	*Clint Zavaras* (FC)	.15
90	Jack Clark	.07
91	*Steve Frey* (FC)	.20
95	Todd Worrell	.06
97	*Curt Schilling* (FC)	.10
98	Jose Gonzalez (FC)	.07
99	*Rich Monteleone* (FC)	.15
100	Will Clark	.60
103	Marvin Freeman	.07
105	Randy Myers	.07
107	Fred Lynn	.06
109	Roberto Kelly	.20
111	Ed Whited	.20
114	Mike Bielecki	.05
115	Tony Pena	.06
117	*Mike Sharperson* (FC)	.08
118	Erik Hanson	.15
119	Billy Hatcher	.05
120	John Franco	.07
121	Robin Ventura	.40
125	Kent Hrbek	.15
127	Mike Devereaux	.06
129	Ron Jones	.10
130	Bert Blyleven	.06
131	Matt Nokes	.06
132	Lance Blankenship (FC)	.10
134	*Earl Cunningham* (#1 Draft Pick) (FC)	.65
135	Dave Magadan	.07
136	Kevin Brown	.05
137	*Marty Pevey* (FC)	.12

134 Earl Cunningham

140	Andre Dawson	.15
141	*John Hart* (FC)	.15
142	*Jeff Wetherby* (FC)	.20
145	Terry Steinbach	.09
146	*Rob Richie* (FC)	.20
147	Chuck Finley	.05
148	Edgar Martinez (FC)	.15
150	Kirk Gibson	.09
153	Randy Milligan	.06
155	Ellis Burks	.25
157	Craig Biggio	.15
160	Dave Righetti	.06
161	Harold Reynolds	.06
162	*Todd Zeile* (FC)	1.00
163	Phil Bradley	.06
164	*Jeff Juden* (#1 Draft Pick) (FC)	.35
165	Walt Weiss	.08
167	*Kevin Appier* (FC)	.20
170	George Bell	.12
172	Tom Lampkin (FC)	.07
173	Tim Belcher	.12
175	Mike Moore	.07
177	Mike Henneman	.07
178	Chris James	.05
180	Rock Raines	.10

1990 Topps

62 Ramon Martinez

334	Johnny Ray	.05
335	Andy Hawkins	.05
336	Ken Griffey Jr.	2.00
340	Fernando Valenzuela	.08
343	Frank Tanana	.05
344	George Canale (FC)	.25
345	Harold Baines	.07
347	Junior Felix	.25
348	Gary Wayne (FC)	.15
349	Steve Finley (FC)	.15
350	Bret Saberhagen	.10
352	Bryn Smith	.05
353	• Sandy Alomar	.35
354	Stan Belinda (FC)	.20
357	Dave West	.12
360	Paul Molitor	.08
361	Randy McCament (FC)	.12
364	Rolando Roomes (FC)	.12
365	Ozzie Guillen	.10
370	Tim Wallach	.07
371	Jimmy Key	.08
373	Alvin Davis	.12
374	Steve Cummings (FC)	.15
375	Dwight Evans	.09
377	Mickey Weston (FC)	.15
380	Dave Winfield	.15
384	Pat Combs	.25
385	Fred McGriff AS	.15
386	Julio Franco AS	.12
387	Wade Boggs AS	.15
388	Cal Ripken AS	.15
389	Robin Yount AS	.15
390	Ruben Sierra AS	.15
391	Kirby Puckett AS	.15
392	Carlton Fisk AS	.12
393	Bret Saberhagen AS	.10
394	Jeff Ballard AS	.08
395	Jeff Russell AS	.08
396	A. Bartlett Giamatti	.15
397	Will Clark AS	.15
398	Ryne Sandberg AS	.15
399	Howard Johnson AS	.15
400	Ozzie Smith AS	.10
401	Kevin Mitchell AS	.15
402	Eric Davis AS	.15
403	Tony Gwynn AS	.15
404	Craig Biggio AS	.08
405	Mike Scott AS	.08
406	Joe Magrane AS	.08

224 Delino DeShields

407	Mark Davis AS	.08
408	Trevor Wilson	.07
409	Tom Brunansky	.07
410	Joe Boever	.06
413	Brian DuBois (FC)	.15
414	Frank Thomas (#1 Draft Pick) (FC)	2.00
416	Dave Johnson (FC)	.15
417	Jim Gantner	.06
418	Tom Browning	.08
419	Beau Allred (FC)	.20
420	Carlton Fisk	.10
425	Bill Landrum	.06
428	Steve Davis (FC)	.12
430	Pete Incaviglia	.06
431	Randy Johnson	.12
433	Steve Olin (FC)	.12
334	Mark Carreon (FC)	.10
435	Kevin Seitzer	.10
438	Greg Myers (FC)	.10
439	Jeff Parrett	.06
440	Alan Trammell	.09
442	Jerry Browne	.07
443	Cris Carpenter	.05
444	Kyle Abbott (#1 Draft Pick) (FC)	.30

331 Juan Gonzalez

446	Dan Pasqua	.06
450	Rickey Henderson	.35
451	Mark Lemke (FC)	.10
454	Jeff King (FC)	.15
455	Jeffrey Leonard	.06
456	Chris Gwynn (FC)	.09
457	Gregg Jefferies	.35
460	Mike Scott	.09
461	*Carlos Martinez* (FC)	.15
464	*Jerome Walton*	.25
465	Kevin Gross	.05
469	John Kruk	.05
470	Frank Viola	.15
472	Jose Uribe	.05
475	Bob Welch	.08
479	Frank White	.06
480	Sid Fernandez	.08
482	*Steve Carter* (FC)	.12
486	Jeff Treadway	.05
490	Dan Plesac	.07
491	*Dave Cochrane* (FC)	.12
493	*Jason Grimsley* (FC)	.15
495	Lee Smith	.06
500	Kevin Mitchell	.25
505	Kelly Gruber	.10
506	Tom Glavine	.10

510	Doc Gooden	.25
511	Clay Parker	.06
515	• Len Dykstra	.12
516	Tim Leary	.05
517	Roberto Alomar	.15
520	Mitch Williams	.09
521	Craig Worthington	.15
525	Wally Joyner	.15
528	*Kevin Wickander* (FC)	.12
529	Greg Harris	.05
530	Mark Langston	.10
531	Ken Caminiti	.06
533	Tim Jones (FC)	.05
535	John Smoltz	.10
536	*Bob Geren*	.10
538	*Billy Spiers*	.12
539	Neal Heaton	.06
540	Danny Tartabull	.08
544	Dennis Boyd	.05
545	Kevin McReynolds	.09
547	Jack Howell	.05
550	Julio Franco	.10
552	*Mike Smith* (FC)	.15
553	*Scott Scudder* (FC)	.15
554	Jay Buhner	.08
555	Jack Morris	.07
557	*Jeff Innis*	.12
560	Steve Sax	.12
562	Chad Kreuter	.09
563	Alex Sanchez	.09
564	*Tyler Houston* (#1 Draft Pick) (FC)	.20
567	Ron Gant	.07
568	John Smiley	.06
569	Ivan Calderon	.06
570	Cal Ripken	.15
571	Brett Butler	.06
572	Greg Harris	.09
575	Lance Parrish	.07
576	*Mike Dyer* (FC)	.15
577	Charlie Hayes (FC)	.10
578	Joe Magrane	.07
580	Joe Carter	.15
581	Ken Griffey. Sr.	.05
584	*Phil Stephenson* (FC)	.09
585	Kal Daniels	.10
587	Lance Johnson	.10
589	Mike Aldrete	.05
590	Ozzie Smith	.12

591	Todd Stottlemyre	.08
594	*Luis Sojo* (FC)	.20
595	Greg Swindell	.10
596	Jose DeJesus (FC)	.10
597	Chris Bosio	.07
598	Brady Anderson	.05
600	Darryl Strawberry	.35
601	Luis Rivera	.05
602	Scott Garrelts	.07
605	Mike Scioscia	.06
606	Storm Davis	.07
608	*Eric Anthony* (FC)	.50
610	Pedro Guerrero	.10
612	Dave Gallagher	.05
614	Nelson Santovenia	.08
615	Rob Deer	.07
616	Brian Holman	.10
617	Geronimo Berroa	.05
618	Eddie Whitson	.05
619	Rob Ducey	.08
620	*Tony Castillo* (FC)	.20
621	Melido Perez	.08
622	Sid Bream	.05

162 Todd Zeile

625	Roger McDowell	.07
627	Jose Rijo	.07
628	Candy Maldonado	.08
629	Eric Hetzel (FC)	.10
630	Gary Gaetti	.12
631	*John Wetteland* (FC)	.12
632	Scott Lusader	.05
633	Dennis Cook (FC)	.10
634	Luis Polonia	.06
635	Brian Downing	.05
638	Jeff Montgomery	.07
640	Rick Sutcliffe	.06
641	*Doug Strange* (FC)	.12
642	• Jack Armstrong	.12
643	Alfredo Griffin	.05
645	Jose Oquendo	.06
649	*Dan Murphy* (FC)	.12
650	Mike Witt	.06
651	Rafael Santana	.06
652	Mike Boddicker	.09
654	Paul Coleman (#1 Draft Pick) (FC)	.30
656	Mackey Sasser	.05
657	Terry Mulholland	.07
660	Vince Coleman	.10
666	Brian Fisher	.05

668	*Joe Oliver* (FC)	.12
670	Dennis Eckersley	.10
671	Bob Boone	.09
674	Spike Owen	.05
675	Jim Abbott	.35
676	Randy Kutcher (FC)	.07
678	Kirt Manwaring	.09
680	Howard Johnson	.15
681	Mike Schooler	.08
683	*Kenny Rogers*	.10
684	*Julio Machado* (FC)	.12
685	Tony Fernandez	.09
686	Carmelo Martinez	.08
688	Milt Thompson	.05
690	Mark McGwire	.30
692	Sammy Sosa	.50
694	*Mike Stanton* (FC)	.15
695	Tom Henke	.07
698	*Omar Vizquel*	.10
700	Kirby Puckett	.25
701	*Bernie Williams* (FC)	.25
702	Tony Phillips	.05
703	*Jeff Brantley*	.12
704	*Chip Hale* (FC)	.15
705	Claudell Washington	.07
710	Von Hayes	.09

711	Rick Aguilera	.08	
712	Todd Benzinger	.07	
713	*Tim Drummond* (FC)	.15	
714	*Marquis Grissom* (FC)	.50	
715	Greg Maddux	.10	
718	Gary Sheffield	.35	
719	*Wally Whitehurst* (FC)	.15	
720	Andres Galarraga	.15	
723	Jeff Robinson	.05	
724	Juan Bell (FC)	.10	
725	Terry Pendleton	.07	
730	Tony Gwynn	.20	
733	John Dopson	.08	
734	Kevin Elster	.06	
735	Charlie Hough	.06	
737	Chris Sabo	.15	
738	*Gene Harris*	.10	
740	Jesse Barfield	.08	
741	Steve Wilson	.10	
743	Tom Candiotti	.07	
744	*Kelly Mann* (FC)	.25	
746	Dave Smith	.06	
750	Dale Murphy	.10	
752	Tom Gordon	.50	
755	Rafael Palmeiro	.10	
757	*Larry Walker* (FC)	.35	
760	Wade Boggs	.35	
761	Mike Jackson	.05	
762	Doug Dascenzo	.07	
764	Tim Teufel	.05	
765	Chili Davis	.07	
766	*Brian Meyer* (FC)	.07	
769	*Greg Hibbard* (FC)	.15	
770	Cory Snyder	.09	
771	Pete Smith	.07	
774	*Ben McDonald* (FC)	1.65	
775	Andy Van Slyke	.09	
779	Lloyd Moseby	.07	
780	Orel Hershiser	.20	
785	Jim Rice	.07	
790	Gary Carter	.07	
792	Gerald Perry	.06	

1990 TOPPS TRADED

Topps wasn't the first company to issue an updated set, but its yearly fall issue continues as one of the most popular. Card fronts duplicate the gaudy, multi-colored borders found in the 792-card set issued earlier in the year. The company scooped the competition with its annual practice of creating manager cards. World Championship manager Lou Piniella made his first appearance in a Reds uniform, and yet another card was issued for Hall-of-Famer Red Schoendienst (because of his brief interim service as a Cardinals manager). Again, rookie newcomers remain the most popular traded-set entries with collectors. In terms of value, cards of Dave Justice, Kevin Maas, Ben McDonald, and John Olerud are tops with hobbyists. The Traded sets were issued in specially-designed boxes, available mainly through hobby dealers. Gray-backed cards were circulated in test-issue wax packs.

	MINT			
Complete set	**$15.00**	1	Darrel Akerfelds	$ .06
Commons	**.06**	2	Sandy Alomar	.35
		3	Brad Arnsberg	.10
		4	Steve Avery	.35

6	Carlos Baerga	.40
7	Kevin Bass	.06
8	Willie Blair	.15
9	Mike Blowers	.20
10	Shawn Boskie	.25
16	John Burkett	.25
17	Casey Candaele	.08
19	Gary Carter	.10
20	Joe Carter	.15
22	Scott Coolbaugh	.20
26	Edgar Diaz	.08
27	Wayne Edwards	.15
29	Scott Erickson	.15
31	Cecil Fielder	.35
32	John Franco	.10
33	Travis Fryman	1.25
35	Darryl Hamilton	.08
36	Mike Harkey	.30
38	Billy Hatcher	.10
41	Dave Hollins	.08
43	Steve Howard	.10
44	Todd Hundley	.15
45	Jeff Huson	.12
48	Dave Justice	2.75
49	Jeff Kaiser	.15
50	Dana Kiecker	.20
51	Joe Klink	.15
52	Brent Knackert	.10
54	Mark Langston	.10
55	Tim Layana	.15
61	Jim Leyritz	.25
63	Kevin Maas	2.25
65	Candy Maldonado	.10
69	John Marzano	.08
70	Ben McDonald	1.30
71	Jack McDowell	.12
73	Orlando Mercado	.06
74	Stump Merrill	.06
75	Alan Mills	.20
76	Hal Morris	.35
77	Lloyd Moseby	.08
78	Randy Myers	.10
79	Tim Naehring	.30
81	Matt Nokes	.06
82	Pete O'Brien	.06
83	John Olerud	2.50
84	Greg Olson	.20
85	Junior Ortiz	.06
86	Dave Parker	.12

48 Dave Justice

87	Rick Parker	.12
88	Bob Patterson	.06
89	Alejandro Pena	.08
90	Tony Pena	.10
91	Pascual Perez	.08
92	Gerald Perry	.06
94	Gary Pettis	.06
95	Tony Phillips	.08
96	Lou Piniella	.10
97	Luis Polonia	.06
98	Jim Presley	.12
99	Scott Radinsky	.20
100	Willie Randolph	.08
101	Jeff Reardon	.12
102	Greg Riddoch	.06
103	Jeff Robinson	.06
104	Ron Robinson	.08
105	Kevin Romine	.06
106	Scott Ruskin	.20
107	John Russell	.06
108	Bill Sampen	.20
109	Juan Samuel	.12
110	Scott Sanderson	.08
112	Dave Schmidt	.06
113	Red Schoendienst	.20
114	Terry Shumpert	.20

115	Matt Sinatro	.06	**123**	Wayne Tolleson	.06
116	Don Slaught	.06	**124**	John Tudor	.06
117	Bryn Smith	.06	**125**	Randy Veres	.12
118	Lee Smith	.15	**126**	Hector Villanueva	.25
119	Paul Sorrento	.12	**127**	Mitch Webster	.06
120	Franklin Stubbs	.10	**128**	Ernie Whitt	.06
121	Russ Swan	.08	**130**	Dave Winfield	.12
122	Bob Tewksbury	.08	**131**	Matt Young	.06

1990 UPPER DECK

After the impressive debut of the 1989 set, only a few changes were made to the 1990 Upper Decks. The color photos are larger due to the elimination of some ornamentation, and the Upper Deck logo was moved from the lower left corner to the upper right. But apart from the presence of the team logo, this design is closer than any other to the simple beauty of the stunning 1953 Bowman Color edition. Although the initial printing contained a few notable errors, they were quickly corrected. For example, Ben McDonald's card first appeared with an Orioles rather than a Rookies logo; Mickey Weston was incorrectly identified as "Jamie," both on his card and on the Orioles checklist; and incorrect photos were used for both Scott Garrelts and Jim Gott. As in 1989, team checklist cards display star portraits by artist Vernon Wells, who also created cards honoring Mike Schmidt's retirement and Nolan Ryan's 5,000th strikeout. The final 100 cards of the 1990 set were issued in a popular mid-season, high-number series, 701-800. This final series came both in foil packs and in a factory-collated complete "set." In the following list, Star Rookies are identified with the abbreviation SR.

		MINT
Complete set (1-700)		**$50.00**
Commons (1-700)		**.07**
Complete set (1-800)		**80.00**
Commons (701-800)		**.10**

2	*Randy Nosek* (FC)	$ .15
3	*Tom Drees* (SR) (FC)	.15
9	*Marquis Grissom* (SR) (FC)	.85
11	Rick Aguilera	.14
13	*Deion Sanders* (SR) (FC)	.65
15	David West	.15
17	*Sammy Sosa* (SR) (FC)	1.25
20	Mike Schmidt (special card)	1.50

21	Robin Ventura (SR) (FC)	.85
22	Brian Meyer (FC)	.20
23	*Blaine Beatty* (FC)	.25
25	*Greg Vaughn* (SR) (FC)	1.15
26	*Xavier Hernandez* (FC)	.15
27	*Jason Grimsley* (FC)	.25
28	*Eric Anthony* (SR) (FC)	.85
31	Hal Morris (FC)	.85
33	*Kelly Mann* (SR) (FC)	.15
34	Nolan Ryan (special card)	1.75
35	*Scott Service* (FC)	.15
37	*Tino Martinez* (SR) (FC)	1.25
38	Chili Davis	.10
42	*Scott Coolbaugh* (SR) (FC)	.40
43	*Jose Cano* (FC)	.15

44	*Jose Vizcaino* (FC)	.20
45	*Bob Hamelin* (SR) (FC)	.35
46	*Jose Offerman* (SR) (FC)	.75
47	Kevin Blankenship	.10
49	*Tommy Greene* (SR) (FC)	.90
50	Will Clark (special card)	.50
52	*Chris Hammond* (SR) (FC)	.15
54	*Ben McDonald* (Orioles logo) (FC)	**28.00**
54	*Ben McDonald* (SR) (FC)	**4.00**
55	Andy Benes (FC)	.45
56	*John Olerud* (SR) (FC)	**4.25**
59	*George Canale* (FC)	.25
60	Orioles Checklist (reads "Jamie Weston")	**3.00**
60	Orioles Checklist (correct card—reads "Mickey Weston")	.15
61	*Mike Stanton* (FC)	.15
63	*Kent Mercker* (SR) (FC)	.40
64	*Francisco Cabrera* (FC)	.30
65	Steve Avery (SR) (FC)	.95
66	Jose Canseco	.90
67	*Matt Merullo* (FC)	.15
70	*Kevin Maas* (SR) (FC)	**5.00**
71	Dennis Cook	.10
72	*Juan Gonzalez* (SR) (FC)	**3.50**
74	*Dean Palmer* (SR) (FC)	.75
75	Bo Jackson (special card)	.50
76	*Rob Richie* (SR) (FC)	.20
77	*Bobby Rose* (FC)	.20
78	*Brian DuBois* (SR) (FC)	.15
87	*Kevin Tapani* (SR) (FC)	.50
89	Jim Gott (photo is Rick Reed)	**6.00**
89	Jim Gott (correct photo)	.25
90	Lance Johnson (FC)	.10
93	*Julio Machado* (SR) (FC)	.15
94	Ron Jones	.10
98	*Kevin Ritz* (SR) (FC)	.15
102	*Kevin Appier* (FC)	.35
103	Julio Franco	.10
104	Craig Biggio	.15
105	Bo Jackson	.70
106	*Junior Felix*	.40
107	Mike Harkey (FC)	.35
108	Fred McGriff	.20
111	Kelly Gruber	.12
113	Dwight Evans	.10

Ramon Martinez

675 Ramon Martinez

114	Dwight Gooden	.25
115	*Kevin Batiste* (FC)	.20
116	Eric Davis	.25
117	Kevin Mitchell	.25
122	Ken Caminiti	.10
123	Kevin Brown	.10
124	George Brett	.15
125	Mike Scott	.10
126	Cory Snyder	.10
127	George Bell	.15
128	Mark Grace	.45
129	Devon White	.10
130	Tony Fernandez	.10
135	Mark Carreon (FC)	.15
156	Ken Griffey Jr.	**4.25**
157	Gary Sheffield	.50
162	*Jeff McKnight* (FC)	.20
163	*Alvaro Espinosa* (FC)	.15
164	*Scott Scudder* (FC)	.20
166	Gregg Jefferies	.50
167	Barry Larkin	.15
170	Rolando Roomes	.15
171	Mark McGwire	.45
172	Steve Sax	.15
174	Mitch Williams	.15
177	Tim Raines	.15

1990 Upper Deck

Hal Morris

31 Hal Morris

37 Tino Martinez

1990 Upper Deck

711 Dave Justice

741	*Hector Villanueva* (FC)	.35	767	*Mike Blowers* (FC) .20
742	Mike Fetters	.15	769	Pascual Perez .10
743	Mark Gardner	.25	770	Gary Pettis .10
744	Matt Nokes	.10	771	Fred Lynn .10
745	Dave Winfield	.15	772	*Mel Rojas* (FC) .20
746	*Delino DeShields* (FC)	1.25	773	*David Segui* (FC) .45
747	*Dann Howitt* (FC)	.20	774	Gary Carter .15
748	Tony Pena	.15	775	Rafael Valdez .20
749	Oil Can Boyd	.10	776	Glenallen Hill .15
750	*Mike Benjamin* (FC)	.25	777	Keith Hernandez .12
751	*Alex Cole* (FC)	1.00	778	Billy Hatcher .10
752	Eric Gunderson	.10	780	Candy Maldonado .10
753	Howard Farmer	.10	783	Mark Langston .12
754	Joe Carter	.20	784	Paul Sorrento (FC) .20
755	*Ray Lankford* (FC)	1.50	785	*Dave Hollins* (FC) .30
756	Sandy Alomar Jr.	.60	786	Cecil Fielder .75
757	Alex Sanchez	.10	787	Matt Young .10
758	Nick Esasky	.10	791	Hubie Brooks .10
759	Stan Belinda	.20	792	Craig Lefferts .10
760	Jim Presley	.20	793	Kevin Bass .10
761	*Gary DiSarcina* (FC)	.20	794	Bryn Smith .12
762	*Wayne Edwards* (FC)	.20	795	Juan Samuel .12
763	Pat Combs	.15	796	Sam Horn .10
764	*Mickey Pina* (FC)	.25	797	Randy Myers .15
765	*Wilson Alvarez* (FC)	.25	799	Bill Gullickson .10
766	Dave Parker	.15	800	Checklist 701-800 .10

1991 DONRUSS

For the first time in its history, Donruss decided to issue its regular set in two individual series. Blue borders distinguish the first-series cards, which number 1 through 386; the second-series cards, issued in February, run from 387 through 770 and have green borders. These late-series cards have current photos so Darryl Strawberry, for example, is shown wearing the cap of his new team, the Dodgers. In factory-collated complete sets, Donruss included sample cards from the Leaf set that the company had issued in late summer. However, dealers removed the specially marked Leaf "preview" cards from the Donruss sets, sold them for $5 to $10 each, and then discounted the standard set from $5 to $15. Donruss Elite or mini cards were also added at random in wax packs as surprise bonuses, but they are not considered part of the regular set.

	MINT			
		1	Dave Stieb (DK)	.08
Complete set	**$27.00**	2	Craig Biggio (DK)	.06
Commons	**.04**	3	Cecil Fielder (DK)	.15
		4	Barry Bonds (DK)	.12

59 Alex Fernandez

77 Ken Griffey, Jr.

1991 Donruss

430 Mo Vaughn

767 Scott Erickson

1991 Donruss

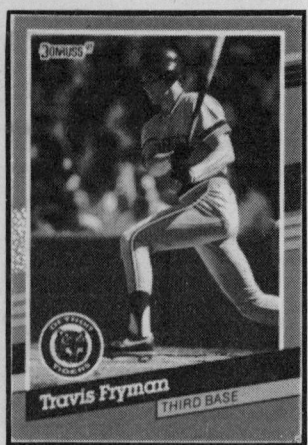

768 Travis Fryman

43 Ray Lankford

1991 DONRUSS ROOKIES

A cash-crop of successful newcomers points to a bright future for the 1991 Donruss Rookies. The set caught on quickly because it became available in mid-September of 1991, before the comparable extension sets were distributed by Fleer, Score, and Topps. Cards of Jeff Bagwell, Ivan Rodriguez, and Todd Van Poppel also boosted its popularity. In appearance, the cards closely resemble their standard-set counterparts except that these have a red border with a neon-green back. Available through hobby dealers, each set comes shrink wrapped in a collector's box, complete with a miniature puzzle of Hall-of-Famer Willie Stargell. One unusual card, number 50, shows Reds Rookie Chris Jones in a vestlike jersey reminiscent of the 1950s. It was worn during a nostalgia promotion game against the Phillies.

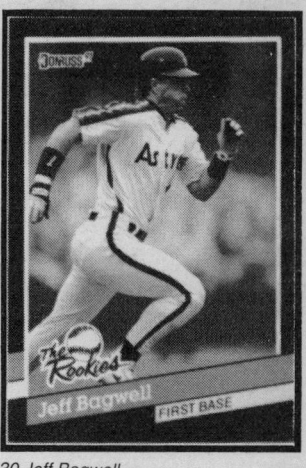

30 Jeff Bagwell

		MINT
Complete set		**$13.00**
Commons		.08

1	Pat Kelly (FC)	.75
2	Rich DeLucia	.15
3	Wes Chamberlain	.50
4	Scott Leius (FC)	.15
5	Darryl Kile (FC)	.15
7	Todd Van Poppel (FC)	1.75
8	Ray Lankford	.35
9	Brian Hunter (FC)	.65
11	Ced Landrum (FC)	.25
12	Dave Burba (FC)	.12
13	Ramon Garcia (FC)	.12
14	Ed Sprague (FC)	.15
15	Warren Newson (FC)	.35
16	Paul Faries (FC)	.12
17	Luis Gonzalez	.50
18	Charles Nagy	.15
20	Frank Castillo (FC)	.12
21	Pedro Munoz	.25
22	Orlando Merced (FC)	.35
24	Kirk Dressendorfer (FC)	.35
25	Heathcliffe Slocumb (FC)	.12
26	Doug Simons (FC)	.12
27	Mike Timlin (FC)	.25
28	Jeff Fassero (FC)	.12
29	Mark Leiter (FC)	.20
30	Jeff Bagwell (FC)	2.50
31	Brian McRae	.45
32	Mark Whiten	.25
33	Ivan Rodriguez (FC)	2.50
34	Wade Taylor (FC)	.25
35	Darren Lewis (FC)	.25
36	Mo Vaughn	.45
37	Mike Remlinger (FC)	.12
38	Rick Wilkins (FC)	.25
39	Chuck Knoblauch	.25
42	Mark Lewis	.15
44	Chris Haney (FC)	.25

1991 FLEER

Although Fleer's 720-card set was the smallest among the big five in 1991, the company pioneered two upgrades. First and most impressive was the color portrait on each card back. Second, instead of leaving white space on the back of the card when stats didn't fill the space, Fleer added text to create a more finished and consistent look. But the company abandoned its past practice of pairing two popular rookies on a single card, and the set has been criticized by collectors because it uses outdated photos of relocated players wearing their old team uniforms. One of the most popular novelty cards is number 710, aptly called Second Generation Stars, which pictures Ken Griffey, Jr., and Barry Bonds.

502 Andujar Cedeno

		MINT
Complete Set		$24.00
Commons		.05

117 Alex Fernandez

40	Bob Kipper	.07
41	Bill Landrum	.07
51	Zane Smith	.07
52	*Randy Tomlin* (FC)	.25
53	Andy Van Slyke	.10
59	Tom Browning	.10
60	Norm Charlton	.08
61	Eric Davis	.20
62	Rob Dibble	.15
68	Barry Larkin	.10
69	*Tim Layana*	.20
70	*Terry Lee* (FC)	.15
72	Hal Morris	.15
73	Randy Myers	.08
76	Paul O'Neill	.10
79	Jose Rijo	.10
80	Chris Sabo	.12
81	Scott Scudder	.07
85	Mike Boddicker	.08
86	Wade Boggs	.20
88	Tom Brunansky	.08
89	Ellis Burks	.15
90	Roger Clemens	.25
91	Scott Cooper (FC)	.15
93	Dwight Evans	.08
95	*Jeff Gray* (FC)	.15
96	Mike Greenwell	.12
98	*Daryl Irvine* (FC)	.20
105	*Tim Naehring*	.30
106	Tony Pena	.07
107	*Phil Plantier* (FC)	.65
108	Carlos Quintana	.08
109	Jeff Reardon	.08
115	Ivan Calderon	.08
117	*Alex Fernandez*	.50
118	Carlton Fisk	.12
120	*Craig Grebeck*	.12
121	Ozzie Guillen	.07
123	Lance Johnson	.08
128	Carlos Martinez	.08
129	Jack McDowell	.08
131	Dan Pasqua	.07
135	*Scott Radinsky*	.12
136	Sammy Sosa	.15
137	Bobby Thigpen	.10
138	Frank Thomas	1.35
139	Robin Ventura	.12
141	*Chuck Carr*	.20
143	David Cone	.08
145	Kevin Elster	.07
147	John Franco	.08
148	Dwight Gooden	.25
150	*Todd Hundley*	.20
151	Gregg Jefferies	.15
152	Howard Johnson	.15
153	Dave Madagan	.08
154	Kevin McReynolds	.08
159	*Darren Reed*	.20
161	Darryl Strawberry	.25
164	Julio Valera	.20
165	Frank Viola	.15
168	*Derek Bell* (FC)	.45
169	George Bell	.15
173	Junior Felix	.08
174	Tony Fernandez	.08
175	Kelly Gruber	.10
176	Tom Henke	.08
177	Glenallen Hill	.15
178	Jimmy Key	.06
180	Fred McGriff	.15
181	Rance Mulliniks	.05
183	John Olerud	.50
184	Luis Sojo	.08
185	Dave Stieb	.10
186	Todd Stottlemyre	.08

1991 Fleer

336 Travis Fryman

360	Carlos Baerga	.20
361	Kevin Bearse	.15
364	Tom Candiotti	.07
365	Alex Cole	.20
368	Keith Hernandez	.08
372	Doug Jones	.07
379	Greg Swindell	.10
381	Mike Walker (FC)	.20
382	Colby Ward (FC)	.20
383	Turner Ward (FC)	.25
385	Kevin Wickander (FC)	.15
391	Wes Chamberlain (FC)	.35
394	Jose DeJesus	.08
395	Len Dykstra	.10
398	Von Hayes	.08
399	David Hollins	.15
401	Ricky Jordan	.06
404	Chuck Malone (FC)	.12
405	Roger McDowell	.08
406	Chuck McElroy	.15
407	Mickey Morandini (FC)	.15
409	Dale Murphy	.12
416	Shawn Boskie	.15
419	Andre Dawson	.20
420	Shawon Dunston	.12
422	Mark Grace	.20
423	Mike Harkey	.08
426	Greg Maddux	.06
427	Derrick May	.25
431	Ryne Sandberg	.25
432	Dwight Smith	.08
434	Rick Sutcliffe	.06
436	Hector Villanueva	.15
437	Jerome Walton	.08
446	Jay Buhner	.10
447	Dave Burba (FC)	.15
449	Alvin Davis	.08
450	Ken Griffey, Jr.	.75
451	Erik Hanson	.15
453	Brian Holman	.06
455	Randy Johnson	.07
457	Edgar Martinez	.07
458	Tino Martinez	.35
460	Harold Reynolds	.07
461	Mike Schooler	.06
468	Juan Bell (FC)	.25
470	Steve Finley	.08
472	Leo Gomez (FC)	.45
476	Chris Hoiles	.20

138 Frank Thomas

481	Ben McDonald	.15
484	Randy Milligan	.06
485	John Mitchell (FC)	.15
486	Gregg Olson	.08
489	Bill Ripken	.08
490	Cal Ripken, Jr.	15
491	Curt Schilling	.06
492	David Segui	.35
493	Anthony Telford (FC)	.20
494	Mickey Tettleton	.06
498	Eric Anthony	.10
499	Craig Biggio	.08
500	Ken Caminiti	.06
502	Andujar Cedeno (FC)	.75
505	Glenn Davis	.12
506	Jim Deshaies	.05
507	Luis Gonzalez (FC)	.35
514	Karl Rhodes (FC)	.20
515	Mike Scott	.06
516	Mike Simms (FC)	.20
523	Roberto Alomar	.08
524	Andy Benes	.15
525	Joe Carter	.15
526	Jack Clark	.06
528	Paul Faries (FC)	.20
529	Tony Gwynn	.20

507 Luis Gonzalez

1991 FLEER UPDATE

The 1991 Fleer Update won little applause from the hobby community. Why? Due to the company's unimpressive card choices earlier in the year, the updated subset was filled with names common to other 1991 issues. For example, Fleer was one of the last companies to offer cards of rookies Jeff Bagwell and Chuck Knoblauch. On the other hand, the company atoned for one of its worst mistakes of the summer—omitting Tommy Greene, Philadelphia's no-hit hurler. Fleer did manage to include cards of major stars like Darryl Strawberry on their current teams, but this was a feat accomplished months earlier by rival companies. As usual, each Fleer card resembles the larger 1991 set and is numbered U-1 through U-132 (though the "U" has been omitted from the following list). The set was issued in a specially designed collector's box and was originally distributed only in complete-set form through hobby dealers. But don't expect any quick price climbs from this 132-card offering, one of Fleer's most forgettable post-season products in years.

1991 Fleer Update

37 Chuck Knoblauch

1991 SCORE

With large doses of rookie cards and innovative subsets, Score's 900-card set for 1991 outdistances its competitors in both size and value. Specialty cards in the set include caricatures of All-Stars, artistic poses for the "Dream Team," and a subset of black-and-white poses called The Franchise that honors a top player from every team. Among the creative photos found in the set is an extreme close-up of Bob Welch's hand, showing the proper grip for launching a forkball. There is also a Cooperstown series of seven players that is found only in factory-collated sets. (Rookie Prospects are identified on the following list with the abbreviation "RP.")

892 Ken Griffey, Jr.

		MINT
Complete set		$40.00
Commons		.05
1	Jose Canseco	.35
2	Ken Griffey Jr.	1.00
3	Ryne Sandberg	.20
4	Nolan Ryan	.35
5	Bo Jackson	.35
6	Bret Saberhagen	.08
7	Will Clark	.25
8	Ellis Burks	.10
9	Joe Carter	.08
10	Rickey Henderson	.25
11	Ozzie Guillen	.08
12	Wade Boggs	.15
17	Ron Dibble	.10
21	Mark Langston	.10
23	Don Mattingly	.25
24	Dave Righetti	.08
25	Roberto Alomar	.08
30	Dave Stieb	.10
32	Steve Sax	.12
35	Tim Raines	.12
40	Alan Trammell	.10
49	Paul Molitor	.10
55	Dave Justice	.75
56	Greg Olson	.08
60	Kevin Tapani	.08
61	Dave Hollins	.08
65	Jim Leyritz	.08
67	*Lee Stevens*	.12
72	Oscar Azocar	.10
74	Carlos Baerga	.15
75	Charles Nagy	.15
78	*Tom Edens*	.10
80	Steve Avery	.20
83	Dave Winfield	.10
84	Bill Spiers	.08
95	Cal Ripken, Jr.	.15
100	Chuck Finley	.10
105	Jim Abbott	.10
110	Greg Swindell	.09
114	Jack Morris	.10
119	Roberto Kelly	.12
120	George Brett	.15
125	Jay Buhner	.12
130	Mike Greenwell	.15

1991 Score

840 Frank Thomas

137	Eric Davis	.15
140	Pedro Guerrero	.08
145	Bruce Hurst	.08
146	Eric Anthony	.10
149	Carlos Quintana	.08
150	Dave Stewart	.08
168	Cecil Fielder	.25
170	Rick Aguilera	.07
171	Walt Weiss	.08
175	Mark Grace	.12
185	Howard Johnson	.15
186	Ken Caminiti	.08
189	Matt Williams	.12
190	Dave Magadan	.08
195	George Bell	.15
196	Hubie Brooks	.10
197	Tom Gordon	.10
200	Kirby Puckett	.20
201	Shawon Dunston	.12
206	Tom Glavine	.15
208	John Smoltz	.10
215	Gary Carter	.08
216	Rafael Palmeiro	.15
220	Mitch Williams	.09
221	Jose DeLeon	.08

225	Dwight Evans	.08
227	Paul O'Neill	.12
229	Tom Browning	.08
230	Terry Pendleton	.08
232	Mike Boddicker	.08
234	Marquis Grissom	.12
235	Bert Blyleven	.08
240	Todd Zeile	.25
241	Larry Walker	.10
250	Lenny Dykstra	.07
256	Sammy Sosa	.10
264	Edgar Martinez	.08
265	Carlton Fisk	.15
266	Chuck Finley	.10
268	Kevin Appier	.10
280	Bobby Thigpen	.10
291	Harold Baines	.12
292	Kent Hrbek	.10
297	Lou Whitaker	.12
300	Ramon Martinez	.20
310	Eddie Murray	.15
311	Bob Welch	.07
315	Bobby Bonilla	.12
320	Robin Ventura	.10
324	Mark McGwire	.12
325	Gary Gaetti	.10
330	Barry Bonds	.25
331	*Brian McRae* (FC)	.75
332	*Pedro Munoz* (FC)	.45
333	*Daryl Irvine* (FC)	.20
335	*Thomas Howard* (FC)	.15
336	*Jeff Schultz* (FC)	.12
337	Jeff Manto (FC)	.15
338	Beau Allred	.12
339	*Mike Bordick* (FC)	.15
340	*Todd Hundley*	.15
341	*Jim Vatcher* (FC)	.15
343	Jose Offerman (FC)	.30
344	*Pete Coachin* (FC)	.20
345	Mike Benjamin (FC)	.10
346	Ozzie Canseco	.10
347	Tim McIntosh (FC)	.15
348	*Phil Plantier* (FC)	.50
349	*Terry Shumpert* (FC)	.20
350	*Darren Lewis* (FC)	.45
351	*David Walsh* (FC)	.15
352	*Scott Chiamparino*	.15
353	*Julio Valera*	.10
356	*Tim Naehring*	.35

358	*Mark Whiten* (FC)	.40
359	*Terry Wells* (FC)	.20
361	*Mel Stottlemyre, Jr.* (FC)	.15
363	Paul Abbott	.15
364	*Steve Howard* (FC)	.15
365	*Karl Rhodes* (FC)	.25
367	*Joe Grahe* (FC)	.15
368	*Darren Reed* (FC)	.20
370	Scott Leuis (FC)	.12
373	*Rosario Rodriguez* (FC)	.12
375	*Mike Bell* (FC)	.15
379	Derrick May (FC)	.30
380	*Jeromy Burnitz* (1st Round Pick) (FC)	.50
382	*Alex Fernandez* (FC)	.65
389	*Todd Van Poppel* (1st Round Pick) (FC)	2.50
390	*Rondell White* (1st Round Pick) (FC)	.40
391	*Marc Newfield* (FC)	.75
392	Julio Franco (All-Star Cartoon)	.10
393	Wade Boggs AS	.20
394	Ozzie Guillen AS	.10
395	Cecil Fielder AS	.20
396	Ken Griffey, Jr. AS	.35
397	Rickey Henderson AS	.25
398	Jose Canseco AS	.25
399	Roger Clemens AS	.15
400	Sandy Alomar. Jr. AS	.12
401	Bobby Thigpen AS	.12
402	Bobby Bonilla (Master Blaster)	.10
403	Eric Davis (Master Blaster)	.10
404	Fred McGriff (Master Blaster)	.10
405	Glenn Davis (Master Blaster)	.10
406	Kevin Mitchell (Master Blaster)	.10
407	Rob Dibble (K-Man)	.15
408	Ramon Martinez (K-Man)	.15
409	David Cone (K-Man)	.10
410	Bobby Witt (K-Man)	.10
411	Mark Langston (K-Man)	.10
412	Bo Jackson (Rifleman)	.30
413	Shawon Dunston (Rifleman)	.10

570 Travis Fryman

416	Benito Santiago (Rifleman)	.10
417	Nolan Ryan (Highlight)	.35
418	Bobby Thigpen (Highlight)	.12
419	Ramon Martinez (Highlight)	.15
420	Bo Jackson (Highlight)	.20
421	Carlton Fisk (Highlight)	.12
432	Tony Fernandez	.08
436	*Steve Frey*	.08
441	Jose Canseco (Dream Team)	3.25
445	Andre Dawson	.15
448	Ron Gant	.12
450	Vince Coleman	.12
451	Kevin Mitchell	.15
460	Frank Viola	.12
462	Chris Sabo	.10
465	John Smiley	.10
470	Wally Joyner	.15
472	Doug Drabek	.08
473	Gary Sheffield	.10
475	Andy Van Slyke	.10
480	Fred McGriff	.15
484	Dave Parker	.10
485	Dennis Eckersley	.12

1991 Score

812 Scott Erickson

691 Darryl Strawberry
(Master Blaster) .... .15
692 Bo Jackson
(Master Blaster) .... .25
693 Cecil Fielder
(Master Blaster) .... .15
694 Sandy Alomar, Jr.
(Rifleman) .... .10
696 Eric Davis (Rifleman) .... .10
697 Ken Griffey, Jr. (Rifleman) ... .20
698 Andy Van Slyke
(Rifleman) .... .10
699 Langston/Witt (No-Hit
Club) .... .10
700 Randy Johnson
(No-Hit Club) .... .10
701 Nolan Ryan
(No-Hit Club) .... .25
702 Dave Stewart
(No-Hit Club) .... .10
703 Fernando Valenzuela
(No-Hit Club) .... .10
708 *Brian Barnes* (RP) (FC) ..... .15
709 *Bernard Gilkey* (RP) .... .35
710 *Steve Decker* (RP) (FC) .... .45
711 *Paul Faries* (RP) (FC) .... .10
713 *Wes Chamberlain*
(RP) (FC) .... .25
717 *Geronimo Pena* (RP) (FC) ... .12
719 *Mark Leonard* (RP) (FC) ..... .25
721 *Mike Gardiner* (RP) (FC) .... .15
722 *Jeff Conine* (RP) (FC) .... .70
725 *Leo Gomez* (RP) (FC) .... .50
727 *Mark Leiter* (RP) (FC) .... .12
728 *Rich DeLucia* (RP) (FC) ..... .15
731 *Ray Lankford* (RP) .... .45
732 *Turner Ward* (RP) (FC) ...... .25
733 *Gerald Alexander*
(RP) (FC) .... .15
734 *Scott Anderson* (RP) (FC) ... .15
735 *Tony Perezchica*
(RP) (FC) .... .12
736 *Jimmy Kremers* (RP) (FC) ... .12
737 American Flag .... .20
741 *Rico Brogna* (RP) (FC) ...... .20
744 Eric Gunderson (RP) .... .08
745 *Troy Afenir* (RP) (FC) .... .15
748 *Omar Oliveras* (RP) .... .15
750 *Maurice Vaughn* (RP) .... .45

391 Marc Newfield

751 *Matt Stark* (RP) (FC) .... .20
753 *Andujar Cedeno* (RP) (FC) .25
754 Kelvin Torve (RP) (FC) ...... .10
756 *Phil Clark* (RP) (FC) .... .20
758 *Mike Perez* (RP) .... .12
761 *Ray Young* (RP) .... .15
763 *Rodney McCray* (RP) .... .12
764 *Sean Berry* (RP) (FC) .... .12
765 *Brent Mayne* (RP) (FC) ..... .15
766 *Mike Simms* (RP) (FC) ...... .15
767 *Glenn Sutko* (RP) (FC) ...... .12
769 1990 Highlight
(George Brett) .... .12
770 1990 Highlight
(Cecil Fielder) .... .12
773 Bo Breaker (Bo Jackson) .. .20
782 *Randy Tomlin* .... .15
784 Felix Jose .... .20
793 Sandy Alomar, Jr. .... .12
795 Barry Larkin
(Reds' October)
(1990 World Series) .... .10
798 Tino Martinez .... .25
800 Kirk Gibson .... .10
803 Chili Davis .... .08
805 Juan Gonzalez .... .35

1991 Score

722 Jeff Conine

1991 SCORE ROOKIE & TRADED

The primary outward difference between this late-season update edition and the regular set issued earlier in the year is in the borders: On the Rookies and Traded set they have a metallic-maroon color. Although Score's enormous 900-card two-series set provides more than its fair share of newcomers making rookie-card appearances, this 110-card addition has an abundance of fresh faces as well. Specifically, cards numbered 81-110 depict rookies; the remainder show traded players. As usual, cards are available primarily from hobby-related sources in boxed, complete-set form, instead of being sold through department stores and other standard outlets. While this R & T offering was more widely available than in previous years, expect a gradual carryover effect in popularity (and price appreciation) from the principal set.

	MINT
Complete set	$13.00
Commons	.07

93 Chuck Knoblauch

1	Bo Jackson	.35
2	Mike Flanagan	.07
3	Pete Incaviglia	.09
4	Jack Clark	.12
5	Hubie Brooks	.07
6	Ivan Calderon	.09
7	Glenn Davis	.10
10	Tim Raines	.15
11	Joe Carter	.20
12	Sid Bream	.09
13	George Bell	.20
14	Steve Bedrosian	.09
16	Darryl Strawberry	.25
18	Kirk Gibson	.10
19	Willie McGee	.12
20	Junior Felix	.07
21	Steve Farr	.07
23	Brett Butler	.09
25	Mickey Tettleton	.09
26	Gary Carter	.09
27	Mitch Williams	.10
28	Candy Maldonado	.07
29	Otis Nixon	.08
31	Tom Candiotti	.07
34	Deion Sanders	.10
35	Willie Randolph	.07
36	Pete Harnisch	.08
37	Dante Bichette	.08
39	Gary Gaetti	.08
40	John Cerutti	.07
41	Rick Cerone	.07
42	Mike Pagliarulo	.07
44	Roberto Alomar	.09
45	Mike Boddicker	.08

46	Bud Black	.07	83	David Howard (FC)	.10
47	Rob Deer	.07	84	Heath Slocumb (FC)	.12
48	Devon White	.09	85	Mike Timlin (FC)	.15
49	Luis Sojo	.08	86	Darryl Kile (FC)	.20
50	Terry Pendleton	.10	87	Pete Schourek (FC)	.15
52	Mike Huff	.07	88	Bruce Walton (FC)	.12
53	Dave Righetti	.12	89	Al Osuna (FC)	.25
55	Ernest Riles	.07	90	Gary Scott (FC)	.15
56	Bill Gullickson	.07	91	Doug Simons (FC)	.12
57	Vince Coleman	.12	92	Chris Jones (FC)	.10
58	Fred McGriff	.20	93	Chuck Knoblauch (FC)	.50
59	Franklin Stubbs	.08	94	Dana Allison (FC)	.12
61	Cory Snyder	.07	95	Erik Pappas (FC)	.12
62	• Dwight Evans	.08	96	Jeff Bagwell (FC)	.25
63	Gerald Perry	.07	97	Kirk Dressendorfer (FC)	.12
66	Tony Fernandez	.09	98	Freddie Benavides (FC)	.12
67	Tim Teufel	.07	99	Luis Gonzalez (FC)	.25
68	Mitch Webster	.07	100	Wade Taylor (FC)	.15
70	Chili Davis	.12	101	Ed Sprague (FC)	.15
73	Juan Berenguer	.07	102	Bob Scanlan (FC)	.15
74	Jack Morris	.12	103	Rick Wilkins (FC)	.15
75	Barry Jones	.07	104	Chris Donnels (FC)	.20
76	Rafael Belliard	.07	105	Joe Slusarski (FC)	.12
77	Steve Buechele	.10	106	Mark Lewis (FC)	.20
78	Scott Sanderson	.07	107	Pat Kelly (FC)	.20
80	Curt Schilling	.08	108	John Briscoe (FC)	.12
81	Brian Drahman (FC)	.12	109	Luis Lopez (FC)	.15
82	Ivan Rodriguez (FC)	.25	110	Jeff Johnson (FC)	.12

1991 TOPPS

To celebrate 40 seasons of card making, Topps organized a season-long promotion to tout its 1991 set and highlighted each card with a baseball logo overwritten with "Topps 40 Years of Baseball." The Brooklyn-based company also gave away previously published Topps cards by inserting them in assorted wax packs. Because of the anniversary connection, Topps went to considerable trouble to correct a number of statistical errors in an early printing, some of which approach the $.50 to $1.50 range. The 792-card set provided Topps debuts for 118 players, and the company continues to be the only one willing to print individual cards of team managers. Due to the easy availability of this set, however, gains in value will come slowly.

	MINT
Complete set	$25.00
Commons	.05

1	Nolan Ryan	.35
2	Record Breaker (George Brett)	.08

329 Dave Justice

3	Record Breaker (Carlton Fisk)	.08
4	Record Breaker (Kevin Mass)	.08
5	Record Breaker (Cal Ripken)	.08
6	Record Breaker (Nolan Ryan)	.15
7	Record Breaker (Ryne Sandberg)	.08
9	Darrin Fletcher (FC)	.10
10	Gregg Olson	.10
11	Roberto Kelly	.08
15	Von Hayes	.08
25	Tim Belcher	.08
30	Gregg Jefferies	.15
31	Colby Ward (FC)	.12
32	Mike Simms (FC)	.15
35	Greg Maddux	.08
39	Jim Neidlinger (FC)	.15
40	Kevin Mitchell	.20
42	Chris Hoiles (FC)	.15
45	Chris Sabo	.10
50	Bob Welch	.12
52	Francisco Oliveras (FC)	.10
58	Mel Stottlemyre	.08
60	Frank Viola	.12
65	Bruce Hurst	.08
68	Gary Sheffield	.12
70	Ellis Burks	.15
73	Craig Worthington	.07
74	Shane Andrews (#1 Draft Pick) (FC)	.35
75	Jack Morris	.12
79	Frank Thomas	.60
80	Fernando Valenzuela	.08
82	Tom Glavine	.15
85	Jesse Barfield	.08
90	Danny Tartabull	.08
91	Greg Colbrunn (FS) (FC)	.15
93	Ivan Calderon	.08
95	Paul Molitor	.10
100	Don Mattingly	.45
103	Tim Costo (#1 Draft Pick)	.50
105	Kevin McReynolds	.08
110	Tom Henke	.08
113	Carl Everett (#1 Draft Pick) (FC)	.40
114	Lance Dickson (FC)	.45

115	Hubie Brooks	.08
118	Tom Edens (FC)	.10
120	Joe Carter	.15
122	Paul O'Neill	.15
126	Bernard Gilkey (FC)	.35
128	Travis Fryman	.60
130	Ozzie Smith	.08
133	Greg Briley	.08
134	Kevin Elster	.08
135	Jerome Walton	.08
140	Fred McGriff	.10
144	Dave Henderson	.12
145	Lou Whitaker	.08
147	Carlos Baerga	.20
149	Al Osuna (FC)	.15
150	Cal Ripken	.12
155	Dwight Evans	.08
157	John Smoltz	.08
160	Vince Coleman	.08
162	Ozzie Canseco (FC)	.15
165	Sandy Alomar	.15
166	Harold Baines	.08
167	Randy Tomlin	.20
168	Randy Tomlin (FC)	.15
170	Carlton Fisk	.10
171	Tony LaRussa	.25

790 Ken Griffey, Jr.

335	Mitch Williams	.07
336	Matt Nokes	.07
337	Keith Comstock (Cubs)	1.50
337	Keith Comstock (Mariners)	.10
339	Larry Walker	.10
340	Ramon Martinez	.15
342	*Mickey Morandini*	.15
345	Len Dykstra	.12
347	Greg Vaughn	.15
348	Todd Stottlelmyre	.08
350	Glenn Davis	.10
351	Joe Torre	.15
352	Frank White	.10
355	Chili Davis	.08
360	Rock Raines	.20
361	Scott Garrelts	.07
362	*Hector Villanueva*	.15
365	Mike Schooler	.08
366	Checklist	.15
367	*David Walsh* (FC)	.15
368	Felix Jose	.10
370	Kelly Gruber	.12
375	Tony Pena	.08
376	Mike Harkey	.08
380	Willie McGee	.15
381	Jim Leyland	.08
385	Mickey Tettleton	.07
386	Cecil Fielder AS	.10
387	Julio Franco AS	.12
388	Kelly Gruber AS	.08
389	Alan Trammell AS	.10
390	Jose Canseco AS	.25
391	Rickey Henderson AS	.25
392	Ken Griffey, Jr. AS	.30
393	Carlton Fisk AS	.20
394	Bob Welch AS	.10
395	Chuck Finley AS	.08
396	Bob Thigpen AS	.08
397	Eddie Murray AS	.15
398	Ryne Sandberg AS	.15
399	Matt Williams AS	.10
400	Barry Larkin AS	.10
401	Barry Bonds AS	.12
402	Darryl Strawberry AS	.15
403	Bobby Bonilla AS	.10
404	Mike Scioscia AS	.08
405	Doug Drabek AS	.08
406	Frank Viola AS	.10
407	John Franco AS	.08

278 Alex Fernandez

410	Dave Righetti	.10
414	Sammy Sosa	.08
420	Bob Thigpen	.10
421	Alex Cole (FC)	.20
425	Andy Van Slyke	.10
426	*Joe Grahe* (FC)	.15
428	*John Barfield* (FC)	.10
430	Gary Gaetti	.08
432	Delino DeShields	.15
434	Julio Machado (FC)	.10
435	Kevin Maas	.45
440	George Bell	.15
441	Zane Smith	.07
445	Greg Swindell	.08
446	*Craig Grebeck* (FC)	.15
447	John Burkett	.12
450	Wade Boggs	.15
454	Kevin Appier	.08
455	Walt Weiss	.07
457	*Todd Hundley*	.12
460	Dave Stieb	.08
461	Robin Ventura	.08
466	Charles Nagy (FC)	.10
470	Howard Johnson	.12
471	*Mike Lieberthal* (#1 Draft Pick) (FC)	.40

474 Phil Plantier

616	Todd Zeile	.15
620	Ozzie Guillen	.08
624	Tom Candiotti	.07
625	Terry Steinbach	.07
627	*Tim Layana*	.15
630	Dave Winfield	.12
631	Mike Morgan	.06
632	Lloyd Moseby	.08
633	Kevin Tapani	.12
636	*Geronimo Pena* (FC)	.25
639	• Frank Robinson	.10
640	Andre Dawson	.10
642	Hal Morris	.15
645	Juan Samuel	.08
646	*Andujar Cedeno* (FC)	.50
648	Lee Stevens (FC)	.15
649	*Bill Sampen*	.15
650	Jack Clark	.10
651	Alan Mills	.12
653	*Anthony Teleford* (FC)	.20
654	Paul Sorrento (FC)	.15
655	Erik Hanson	.10
658	*Scott Aldred* (FC)	.15
659	*Oscar Azocar* (FC)	.25
660	Lee Smith	.10
662	Rob Dibble	.12
663	Greg Brock	.05
666	Danny Darwin	.07
669	Lou Piniella	.08
670	Rickey Henderson	.35
672	Shane Mack	.07
673	*Greg Olson*	.15
675	Tom Brunansky	.08
676	*Scott Chiamparino* (FC)	.20
677	Bill Ripken	.08
680	David Cone	.08
681	*Jeff Schaefer* (FC)	.08
682	*Ray Lankford* (FC)	.75
684	Milt Cuyler (FC)	.15
685	Doug Drabek	.08
688	Rosario Rodriguez	.15
690	Orel Hershiser	.10
691	Mike Blowers	.10
692	*Efrain Valdez* (FC)	.15
695	Kevin Seitzer	.08
700	Jose Canseco	.40
702	*Tim Naehring*	.25
710	Kent Hrbek	.08
720	Cecil Fielder	.20

682 Ray Lankford

721	*Mark Lee* (FC)	.15
724	*David Segui* (FC)	.25
725	Ron Gant	.12
730	Barry Larkin	.12
731	*Jeff Gray* (FC)	.15
735	Ron Darling	.06
739	*Russ Swan*	.10
740	Ryne Sandberg	.20
750	Bobby Bonilla	.12
751	*Wayne Edwards*	.10
752	Kevin Bass	.05
753	*Paul Marak* (FC)	.15
755	Mark Langston	.15
760	Benny Santiago	.08
763	*Dana Kiecker*	.10
765	Shawon Dunston	.08
767	*Dan Wilson* (#1 Draft Pick)	.30
769	*Tim Sherrill* (FC)	.15
772	Kent Mercker (FC)	.10
775	Julio Franco	.10
776	Brent Mayne (FC)	.15
780	Randy Myers	.08
786	Eric Plunk	.05
790	Ken Griffey, Jr.	.90
791	Mike Benjamin (FC)	.15
792	Mike Greenwell	.10

1991 TOPPS TRADED

Topps had boasted for months that its 1990 Traded set would include cards for members of the U.S. Olympic baseball team. But the company backed out at the last minute with the claim that using cards of underclassmen would endanger their amateur standing. This 1991 edition, however, is loaded with Olympians (identified on the following lists with USA after their names). It has recaptured much of the appeal of the 1988 Traded set, when phenoms like Mark McGwire and Jim Abbott were pictured in their Team USA finery. Another feature of the 1991 Topps Traded set is the addition of newly hired baseball managers: Jim Essian of the Chicago Cubs, Montreal's Tom Runnels, Cleveland's Mike Hargrove, Philadelphia's Jim Fregosi, Kansas City's Hal McRae, and Baltimore's Johnny Oates make exclusive appearances. This issue is likely to repeat the experience of the 1988 Topps Traded set, which enjoyed large price gains as the many featured Olympians began to achieve recognition in the majors.

		MINT
Complete Set		19.00
Commons		.07

1	Juan Agosto	.07
4	Jeff Bagwell (FC)	.25
7	Derek Bell (FC)	.25
8	George Bell	.25
9	Rafael Belliard	.07
10	Dante Bichette	.08
12	Mike Boddicker	.09
13	Sid Bream	.08
14	Hubie Brooks	.07
15	Brett Butler	.10
16	Ivan Calderon	.09
18	Tom Candiotti	.09
19	Gary Carter	.09
20	Joe Carter	.12
22	Jack Clark	.12
23	Vince Coleman	.12
24	Scott Coolbaugh	.08
25	Danny Cox	.07
26	Danny Darwin	.07
27	Chili Davis	.10
28	Glenn Davis	.09
29	Steve Decker (FC)	.25
30	Rob Deer	.07

77 Fred McGriff

31	Rich DeLucia (FC)	.15
32	John Dettmer (USA) (FC)	.20
33	Brian Downing	.07
34	Darren Dreifort (USA) (FC)	.12
35	Kirk Dressendorfer (FC)	.12

69 Chuck Knoblauch

1991 UPPER DECK

While Upper Deck's main set displayed few obvious changes, collectors pursued the 800 cards for another reason: Throughout the season, individual packs chosen at random contained specially produced, limited-edition cards signed by Nolan Ryan and Hank Aaron (the latter only in the high-number series, 701-800). Another pack premium was a card of basketball star Michael Jordan wearing a White Sox uniform. Two of the more unusual cards in the regular set feature minor stars with famous companions: Ozzie Canseco's photo includes his brother, Jose, while Ken Griffey shares his card with his superstar son. Investment started at a moderate level in 1991 sets because of an abundance of 1990 complete sets flooding department stores and other retail, non-hobby markets. Several abbreviations are used in the following list to identify subsets: SR for Star Rookies, TC for Team Checklist, and TP for Top Player.

	MINT
Complete set (1-700)	$45.00
Commons (1-700)	.06
Commons (701-800)	.07
Complete set (1-800)	55.00
Autographed Aaron card	600.00
Autographed Ryan card	500.00
Michael Jordan insert	25.00

53 Todd Van Poppel

1 Star Rookie checklist .... .08
2 *Phil Plantier* (SR) (FC).... 1.00
3 *D.J. Dozier* (SR) (FC) .... .35
4 Dave Hansen (SR) (FC) .... .20
5 *Maurice Vaughn* (SR) (FC) 1.25
6 *Leo Gomez* (SR) (FC) .... .75
7 *Scott Aldred* (SR) (FC) .... .25
8 *Scott Chiamparino* (SR) (FC)........................ .25
9 *Lance Dickson* (SR) (FC) .. .35
10 *Sean Berry* (SR) (FC)......... .20
11 Bernie Williams (SR) (FC) ... .25
12 *Brian Barnes* (SR) (FC) ..... .20
13 *Narciso Elvira* (SR) (FC).... .20
15 *Greg Colbrunn* (SR) (FC) .. .25
16 *Bernard Gilkey* (SR) (FC).. .65
17 *Mark Lewis* (SR) (FC)......... .50
18 *Mickey Morandini* (SR) (FC) .... .20
19 Charles Nagy (SR) (FC) ..... .25
20 *Geronimo Pena* (SR) (FC)... .35
21 *Henry Rodriguez* (SR) (FC) .... .75
22 Scott Cooper (SR) (FC)..... .20
23 *Andujar Cedeno* (SR) (FC) 1.10

246 Frank Thomas

645 Alex Fernandez

133	Paul O'Neill	.09
134	Mark Grace	.15
135	Chris Sabo	.12
136	Ramon Martinez	.20
141	Craig Worthington	.08
143	Tim Raines	.15
144	Sandy Alomar Jr.	.15
145	John Olerud	.50
146	*Ozzie Canseco*	.15
148	Harold Reynolds	.10
149	Tom Henke	.10
152	Bobby Bonilla	.25
153	Terry Steinbach	.08
154	Barry Bonds	.25
155	Jose Canseco	.50
156	Gregg Jefferies	.15
157	Matt Williams	.20
158	Craig Biggio	.09
160	Ricky Jordan	.09
161	Stan Belinda	.10
162	Ozzie Smith	.15
163	Tom Brunansky	.10
164	Todd Zeile	.35
165	Mike Greenwell	.12
166	Kal Daniels	.10
167	Kent Hrbek	.12

171	*Hector Villaneuva*	.30
172	Dennis Eckersley	.15
173	Mitch Williams	.10
174	Mark McGwire	.20
175	Fernando Valenzuela	.10
176	Gary Carter	.10
177	Dave Magadan	.10
178	Robby Thompson	.08
180	Ken Caminiti	.08
183	Jay Bell	.08
188	Shane Mack	.08
192	Walt Weiss	.08
194	Carney Lansford	.08
197	Eric Yelding	.08
199	John Kruk	.08
206	Mike Pagliarulo	.06
212	Brian Harper	.07
215	Tim Burke	.07
216	Doug Jones	.08
217	Hubie Brooks	.08
218	Tom Candiotti	.08
222	*Alan Mills* (FC)	.18
223	Alan Trammell	.15
224	Dwight Gooden	.25
225	*Travis Fryman* (FC)	1.25
226	Joe Carter	.20
227	Julio Franco	.12
232	Carlos Quintana	.10
233	Gary Gaetti	.08
234	Mark Langston	.15
236	Greg Swindell	.10
237	Eddie Murray	.20
238	Jeff Manto (FC)	.15
243	*Jim Leyritz*	.25
244	Cecil Fielder	.25
245	Darryl Strawberry	.35
246	Frank Thomas (FC)	2.50
247	Kevin Mitchell	.20
248	Lance Johnson	.08
255	Tony Gwynn	.20
256	Andy Van Slyke	.10
257	Todd Stottlemyre	.08
261	Bobby Thigpen	.08
262	*Jimmy Kremers* (FC)	.15
263	Robin Ventura	.20
264	John Smoltz	.10
265	Sammy Sosa	.20
266	Gary Sheffield	.12
267	Lenny Dykstra	.10

225 Travis Fryman

1991 Upper Deck

5 Maurice Vaughn

2 Phil Plantier

1991 Upper Deck

567 Luis Gonzalez

24 Eric Karros

1991 UPPER DECK FINAL EDITION

The Upper Deck Company gave in to temptation after two years and decided to produce a season-ending set to compete with its rivals. However, their 100-card Final Edition shows more creativity than the usual traded or update sets by including several notable minor leaguers. Together with *Baseball America,* Upper Deck salutes 10 American League and 10 National League Prospects to begin the set. Boston's Frankie Rodriguez and Cincinnati's Reggie Sanders are cited as examples of "Most Exciting Players." Other players are recognized in "Diamond Skills" categories such as "best throwing arm," "best power," and so on, while the last 20 cards honor the 1991 All-Stars. Technically, the Final Edition isn't considered an extension of the 800-card set because these cards were not available in foil packs. The cards are also numbered separately from the principal set 1F through 100F (the letter "F" has been omitted from the following list), and began selling at a suggested retail price of $10.99.

		MINT
Complete set		25.00
Commons		.08
2	Pedro Martinez (FC)	**3.00**
3	Lance Dickson	.10
4	Royce Clayton	.12
5	Scott Bryant (FC)	.20
6	Dan Wilson (FC)	.25
7	Dmitri Young (FC)	.20
8	Ryan Klesko (FC)	**1.00**
9	Tom Goodwin	.10
10	Rondell White (FC)	.50
11	Reggie Sanders	.15
12	Todd Van Poppel	.25
13	Arthur Rhodes (FC)	.15
14	Eddie Zosky	.10
15	Gerald Williams (FC)	.25
16	Robert Eenhoorn (FC)	.25
17	Jim Thome (FC)	.20
18	Marc Newfield (FC)	.35
19	Kerwin Moore (FC)	.15
20	Jeff McNeely (FC)	.15
21	Frankie Rodriguez	**1.00**
22	Andy Mota (FC)	.15
23	Chris Haney (FC)	.20
24	Kenny Lofton (FC)	.25

2 Pedro Martinez

25	Dave Nilsson (FC)	.25
26	Derek Bell (FC)	.25
27	Frank Castillo (FC)	.15
28	Candy Maldonado	.08

10 Rondell White

18 Marc Newfield